Date Due

DEC 22 1988			

BRODART, INC.   Cat. No. 23 233   Printed in U.S.A.

THE BURNS MANTLE BEST PLAYS
OF 1948-49

EDITED BY

BURNS MANTLE

THE BEST PLAYS OF 1899-1909
(*With Garrison P. Sherwood*)
THE BEST PLAYS OF 1909-19
(*With Garrison P. Sherwood*)
THE BEST PLAYS OF 1919-20
THE BEST PLAYS OF 1920-21
THE BEST PLAYS OF 1921-22
THE BEST PLAYS OF 1922-23
THE BEST PLAYS OF 1923-24
THE BEST PLAYS OF 1924-25
THE BEST PLAYS OF 1925-26
THE BEST PLAYS OF 1926-27
THE BEST PLAYS OF 1927-28
THE BEST PLAYS OF 1928-29
THE BEST PLAYS OF 1929-30
THE BEST PLAYS OF 1930-31
THE BEST PLAYS OF 1931-32
THE BEST PLAYS OF 1932-33
THE BEST PLAYS OF 1933-34
THE BEST PLAYS OF 1934-35
THE BEST PLAYS OF 1935-36
THE BEST PLAYS OF 1936-37
THE BEST PLAYS OF 1937-38
THE BEST PLAYS OF 1938-39
THE BEST PLAYS OF 1939-40
THE BEST PLAYS OF 1940-41
THE BEST PLAYS OF 1941-42
THE BEST PLAYS OF 1942-43
THE BEST PLAYS OF 1943-44
THE BEST PLAYS OF 1944-45
THE BEST PLAYS OF 1945-46
THE BEST PLAYS OF 1946-47
CONTEMPORARY AMERICAN
PLAYWRIGHTS (1938)

EDITED BY

JOHN CHAPMAN

THE BURNS MANTLE
BEST PLAYS OF 1947-48
THE BURNS MANTLE
BEST PLAYS OF 1948-49

THE BURNS MANTLE BEST PLAYS OF 1948-49

AND THE
YEAR BOOK OF THE DRAMA
IN AMERICA

EDITED BY
JOHN CHAPMAN

With Illustrations

DODD, MEAD AND COMPANY
NEW YORK - - - 1949

"Death of a Salesman," copyright, 1949, by Arthur Miller
Published by the Viking Press, New York
"Anne of the Thousand Days," copyright, 1948, by Maxwell Anderson
Published by William Sloane Associates, New York
"The Madwoman of Chaillot," copyright, 1947, by Maurice Valency,
under the title of "La Folle de Chaillot," by Jean Giraudoux.
English version by Maurice Valency
Published by Random House, New York, and Random House of Canada, Toronto
"Detective Story," copyright, 1949, by Sidney Kingsley and Madge Evans
Published, 1949, by Random House, New York
"Edward, My Son," copyright, 1948, by Robert Morley and Noel Langley
Published in the United States by Random House, New York
Published in England by Samuel French, Ltd., London
"Life with Mother," copyright, 1938, by Howard Lindsay, Russel Crouse and
Katherine B. Day
Published by Alfred A. Knopf, Inc., New York
"Light Up the Sky," copyright, 1948, as an unpublished work, by Moss Hart
Copyright, 1949, by Moss Hart
Published by Random House, New York, and Random House of Canada, Toronto
"The Silver Whistle," copyright, 1949, by Robert Edward McEnroe
Copyright, 1948, as a dramatic composition under the title of
"Oliver Erwenter," by Robert Edward McEnroe
Published by Dramatists Play Service, Inc., New York
"Two Blind Mice," copyright, 1949, by Samuel Spewack
Dramatic Composition, copyright, 1948, by Samuel Spewack
Published by Dramatists Play Service, Inc., New York
"Goodbye, My Fancy," copyright, 1947, by Fay Kanin,
under title of "Most Likely to Succeed"
Copyright, 1949, by Fay Kanin and Michael Kanin
Published by Samuel French, New York

COPYRIGHT, 1949,
BY DODD, MEAD AND COMPANY, INC.

CAUTION: Professionals and amateurs are hereby warned that the above-mentioned plays, being fully protected under the copyright laws of the United States of America, the British Empire, including the Dominion of Canada, and all other countries of the Copyright Union, are subject to a royalty. All rights, including professional, amateur, motion picture, recitation, public reading, radio broadcasting, and the rights of translation into foreign languages, are strictly reserved. In their present form these plays are dedicated to the reading public only. All inquiries regarding them should be addressed to their publishers or authors.

PRINTED IN THE UNITED STATES OF AMERICA

INTRODUCTION

IT was, as you will discover in the chapter on the season in New York, an exciting year in the commercial theatre. There were triumphs as well as disasters; there were new heroes and heroines in both the writing and acting professions; the play-going public set a new record for persistence and patience in catching its favorite shows, ordering tickets by mail far in advance and giving producers fabulous sums ranging up to half a million dollars.

It was not at all difficult to find ten plays worthy of being included in these digests, and these plays have a wide range of style and method. Of particular interest is Mr. Miller's "Death of a Salesman," for, although it seems on the stage to be a completely natural and uncommonly human work, it is essentially a sharp departure from our familiar naturalistic school of playmaking.

Of interest, too, is "The Madwoman of Chaillot," for its extraordinary mixture of hard-headed irony and Alice in Wonderland whimsey. To be noted and studied is the fine, high style of Maxwell Anderson's "Anne of the Thousand Days." To be brief about it, I think you will find all of these digests extraordinarily readable, for the authors have made dramas and comedies which read well as well as play well. (And for all its "wells" I'm going to let that sentence stand.)

Our season was blessed with some fine work by the members of Equity, including some players from Hollywood. Lee J. Cobb and Mildred Dunnock in "Salesman"; Rex Harrison and Joyce Redman in "Anne"; Martita Hunt and Estelle Winwood in "Madwoman"; Ralph Bellamy and James Westerfield in "Detective Story"; Robert Morley and Leueen MacGrath in "Edward, My Son"; Dorothy and Howard Lindsay in "Life with Mother"; Sam Levene in "Light Up the Sky"; Jose Ferrer in "The Silver Whistle"; Mabel Paige, Laura Pierpont and Melvyn Douglas in "Two Blind Mice," and Madeleine Carroll in "Goodbye, My Fancy"—these were some of the ones who made playgoing a pleasure. And there were many, many others, such as Charles Boyer in "Red Gloves," Lee Tracy in "The Traitor" and the dozens and dozens more who gave their best wherever they happened to be—in a hit or a flop.

We had a number of fine musicals, ranging from the ebullient and unpretentious "Lend an Ear" to such stylish offerings as "Kiss Me, Kate" and "South Pacific." Musical stars such as Bobby Clark, Ray Bolger, Mary Martin, Alfred Drake and Patricia Morison entertained throngs of patrons, and Ezio Pinza, from the Metropolitan Opera, was the new music-show sensation.

This volume continues the work begun by the late and beloved Burns Mantle, keeping straight the record of the New York theatre from 1899 down to the most recent season. In it is an innovation—a section devoted to the seasons of Boston and Philadelphia, contributed by Elliot Norton and Arthur B. Waters. In addition to being self-contained and important theatrical centers, these cities have a decided influence on the artistic quality of the attractions in New York. These are the major centers for try-outs, and it is in them—thanks to their audiences—that many plays and musicals really are made. Philadelphia and Boston are important in and to themselves, obviously; but they also have a direct bearing on the New York season, just as Chicago, Los Angeles and San Francisco often do; so I think you will find the record of their seasons an interesting one.

My gratitude for support in preparing this volume is extended to all those who make playgoing an unmatchable pleasure. In particular it is offered to Lydia Sears Mantle, for entrusting the voluminous records begun by her husband; to Clara Sears Taylor, for having kept this material in such splendid order for so many years, and to the lady who goes to the theatre with me—my wife, Georgia—for going to the theatre with me and maintaining the statistical history of the season.

J. C.

Westport, Connecticut, July, 1949

CONTENTS

	PAGE
INTRODUCTION	v
THE SEASON IN NEW YORK	3
THE SEASON IN BOSTON	18
THE SEASON IN PHILADELPHIA	33
THE SEASON IN CHICAGO	37
THE SEASON IN SAN FRANCISCO	41
THE SEASON IN SOUTHERN CALIFORNIA	45
DEATH OF A SALESMAN, BY ARTHUR MILLER	53
ANNE OF THE THOUSAND DAYS, BY MAXWELL ANDERSON	88
THE MADWOMAN OF CHAILLOT, BY JEAN GIRAUDOUX	118
DETECTIVE STORY, BY SIDNEY KINGSLEY	147
EDWARD, MY SON, BY ROBERT MORLEY AND NOEL LANGLEY	179
LIFE WITH MOTHER, BY HOWARD LINDSAY AND RUSSEL CROUSE	207
LIGHT UP THE SKY, BY MOSS HART	238
THE SILVER WHISTLE, BY ROBERT E. MCENROE	266
TWO BLIND MICE, BY SAMUEL SPEWACK	301
GOODBYE, MY FANCY, BY FAY KANIN	333
THE PLAYS AND THEIR AUTHORS	368
PLAYS PRODUCED IN NEW YORK	375
OFF BROADWAY	425
STATISTICAL SUMMARY	431
LONG RUNS ON BROADWAY	432
NEW YORK DRAMA CRITICS' CIRCLE AWARD	434

CONTENTS

	PAGE
PULITZER PRIZE WINNERS	435
PREVIOUS VOLUMES OF BEST PLAYS	437
WHERE AND WHEN THEY WERE BORN	454
NECROLOGY	463
THE DECADES' TOLL	469
INDEX OF AUTHORS	471
INDEX OF PLAYS AND CASTS	476
INDEX OF PRODUCERS, DIRECTORS AND DESIGNERS	483

ILLUSTRATIONS

Following page 86

DEATH OF A SALESMAN
ANNE OF THE THOUSAND DAYS
THE MADWOMAN OF CHAILLOT
DETECTIVE STORY
EDWARD, MY SON
LIFE WITH MOTHER
LIGHT UP THE SKY
THE SILVER WHISTLE
TWO BLIND MICE
GOODBYE, MY FANCY

THE BURNS MANTLE BEST PLAYS
OF 1948-49

THE BURNS MANTLE BEST PLAYS OF 1948-49

THE SEASON IN NEW YORK

THERE are precisely as many ways of estimating the pleasures and values of a theatrical season as there are people who have witnessed it, for, in the words of George S. Kaufman, one man's Mede is another man's Persian. No two views of a year of the Broadway stage could be alike, any more than your fingerprints could resemble mine. Nevertheless, each time the first of June comes to signalize the end of one year and the beginning of a new one in the New York theatre, a number of summaries are compiled, including this one.

These estimates are in one of two categories—financial or artistic. This year the former is discouraging and the latter is cheerful. There were fewer productions than we saw the year before and the money lost verged on the appalling, but among these productions were enough good plays and musicals to make 1948-49 the best of recent seasons. The playgoer had a wide range of choice, for among the admirable offerings were human tragedy, historical pageantry, farce, parlor comedy, melodrama, fantasy and the usual excellencies in the musical field.

The financial record of the Broadway season was compiled by *Variety*, and it showed the same hopes and discouragements, successes and disasters, as a horse race. There were, said *Variety*, fifteen box office hits. Their total cost of production was $1,940,-000 and as of June 1 they had earned back $2,176,000. "Edward, My Son" cost $70,000 and by the time it closed had earned a profit of $130,000; Tallulah Bankhead's athletic revival of "Private Lives" was a $25,000 investment and it brought back five times that amount; "As the Girls Go" had cost $340,000, but its earnings were so phenomenal that by June 1 it had brought back $330,000 and was nowhere near the end of its run.

Such figures as these keep capitalists investing in the theatre. Even in these times of high costs, the stage offers profits which are unmatched in more sedate forms of business. But *Variety* submitted other statistics which were horrific. It counted forty-seven failures, and these unhappy enterprises lost a total of $4,535,000. Two musicals, "Magdalena" and "Heaven on Earth," lost $650,000 for their investors. After enthusiastic notices and good audiences for the greater part of the season, "Life with Mother" wound up $40,000 in the red, and it will take most of this new season on the road to put it in the black.

Since the theatre is an art, a discussion of money matters in connection with it may seem sordid and irrelevant to lovers of art in its pure form. To the idealist it is unimportant that "Mister Roberts," which had an opening-night deficit of $100,000, has returned to its happy angels $550,000, with the end not in sight. The stage can and does flourish in attics, basements, colleges, churches, clubs and community playhouses. Art, says the idealist, is not bound to the professional theatre.

Yet, as a reporter and historian rather than as an idealist, I am inclined to maintain that art is bound to the professional theatre, because it is the commercial stage which will give it its fairest hearing. The commercial stage has found and developed our playwrights, actors, directors and set designers, and the so-called tributary theatre has been content to take the leavings—to wait for the release of stock and amateur rights of Broadway hits. The health of the commercial stage is important to the theatre as an art form, and during the 1948-49 season it was of primary concern to everybody from dramatists and actors to audiences. Serious efforts were being made by all elements and unions to bring down costs; and as this was being written there was hope of real results.

In these results lies the future of the New York theatre. The cheaper a ticket, the more people can see a play; when more people can attend, there will be more plays; when there are more plays there must be more playwrights; when there are more plays and playwrights there will be more investors to finance them— and among the dramatists thus encouraged will be the artists of the years to come. As Joe E. Lewis says, money isn't everything but it is handy to have around to soothe the nerves, and *Variety's* financial summary of the season should be interesting even to idealists.

The artistic pleasures and values of 1948-49 were quite notably on the profit side. Four times since 1936 the New York Drama Critics' Circle was so discouraged that, when it came to picking the best play of the season, it voted "no award." Four times since 1918 the judges entrusted with the Pulitzer drama prize also voted "no award." In the season covered by this volume, both the critics and the Pulitzers chose Arthur Miller's "Death of a Salesman"—and this was no act of desperation. The drama was forceful enough practically to demand these encomiums, but it was not the only one which could have qualified. Maxwell Anderson's "Anne of the Thousand Days" was perhaps the best of his many historical ventures, and it would give distinction to any season. Sidney Kingsley returned to the footlights with an excellently made documentary melodrama, "Detective Story," and neither the Pulitzers nor the Critics could have been ashamed of voting for this one.

Under the Pulitzer will the play prize must be confined to an American and to Americana, and the critics ape this practice. Therefore, the best prize a distinguished foreign play can hope for is a citation from the critics—a sort of consolation prize, I feel—that it is the best foreign play of the year. In 1948-49 there were two dramas which qualified as admirable imports. "Edward, My Son," by Robert Morley and Noel Langley, was an effectively contrived vehicle for Mr. Morley's interesting qualities as an actor. "The Madwoman of Chaillot," by the late Jean Giraudoux, as adapted by Maurice Valency, was the first French comedy of style and pith to reach these shores in many seasons. The critics gave their benevolent nod to "The Madwoman"—but if it had not arrived they could have blessed "Edward" with their scroll with no loss of face.

The season began on June 4 with a musical version of "Sleepy Hollow," the Washington Irving fable, that was more inspired in its inception than it was in execution. It should have made an engaging evening, but it was rather slow and sleepy and short-lived. The season then went into its summer snooze and had a fitful start early in September when Morey Amsterdam, a radio and night club comedian, attempted to revive vaudeville with a series of acts titled "Hilarities." Vaudeville remained dead. The touring "Show Boat" company came back for a short visit, and the drama as a form of art had its beginning with the presentation of "Sundown Beach."

Great expectations were held for "Sundown Beach." The advance report was that it was a seriously wrought play, to be rendered by a new group of young hopefuls called the Actors Studio. Since the progress of the theatre depends on old hopefuls hoping for young hopefuls to come and fill their shoes, the Actors Studio group was assured of a welcome. The players, who had worked together for many months on many plays, were directed by Elia Kazan, whose record for theatrical sagacity is enviable. Yet

"Sundown Beach" was a confused and diffuse slice-of-life montage about what goes on in a hospital for combat-fatigued war fliers. There was a cast of twenty-eight, and the author, Bessie Breuer, tried to write a big scene for almost every one of them. The result was less a play than it was a laboratory exercise for twenty-eight eager and variously talented young actors.

In mid-September a small revue titled "Small Wonder" and a big musical, "Heaven on Earth," made their bids for popularity. The former was unpretentious, good-looking and engaging, but it was handicapped by having to charge too high prices. For the amount of money they had to spend, patrons felt that they should have more chorus girls and more scenery, and, although it had a comfortable run, "Small Wonder" wound up as a red-ink statistic in *Variety*. "Heaven on Earth," on the other hand, had been designed as a big wonder—Central Park for a setting and a large cast. It was a fantasy about a hansom cab driver, a poor but beautiful girl and a boy who lived in a park tree because he also was poor. Its intentions were delightful but its achievements were not.

The closing evenings of September brought the season's first success, "Edward, My Son," the season's second costliest and first loveliest failure, "Magdalena," a Marc Connelly comedy titled "A Story for Strangers" which failed its purpose, and another comedy, "Grandma's Diary," which was a strong contender for the title of Worst Play of the Season.

"Grandma's Diary," by Albert Wineman Barker, was a woefully unfunny piece about a woman radio writer who got her inspiration from her grandmother's diary. It was atrociously acted by a dispirited company. Mr. Connelly spun a thin fable in "A Story for Strangers" about a talking horse which caused a whole town to reform. The play's whimsical philosophy was handicapped by a flashback technique and by slow-moving scenery. It had charm, but not enough charm.

"Edward, My Son" offered the second American appearance of Robert Morley, English actor who came here eleven years previously and was mightily impressive in the title role of "Oscar Wilde." The new play, by Mr. Morley and Noel Langley, was unerringly contrived to fit the former's highly individual qualities as an actor. With "Edward" a good season had really begun.

Another late September offering was "Town House," which had a fine production by Max Gordon and direction by George S. Kaufman. It was another slice-of-life job, based on some fictional essays by John Cheever, relating the adventures and relationships of a number of dissimilar people forced by poverty to live together in an outdated mansion. It was neither witty nor wacky enough to survive.

"Magdalena" offered the first healthy controversy of the season. Some critics, including this one, were enthusiastic, and others were offended; and so it went with audiences, too. "Magdalena" was a musical fable about religion, love and capitalism on the Magdalena River in Colombia and its score was by the noted South American, Heitor Villa-Lobos. The production, by California's Homer Curran and Edwin Lester, was flamboyant and lavish beyond anything seen since the days of Ziegfeld and Carroll. This lavishness was pleasing to some of us who were wearying of the scenic austerities imposed by modern economy, but it apparently was offensive and old-hat to others. Villa-Lobos' score was so intense, so full and so unorthodox as to be a remarkable work—but it had little Hit Parade appeal.

The final September offering, "Time for Elizabeth," was remarkable more for its authorship than for its good qualities, which were modest. It was a gentle family comedy about a man who had retired to Florida. It was as mild as mush—yet its authors were Groucho Marx and Norman Krasna, two very sharp movie and stage characters.

October got under way when Tallulah Bankhead, dauntless, indefatigable and incorrigible, came to town with her touring revival of Noel Coward's "Private Lives." In its first production, with Mr. Coward and Gertrude Lawrence acting the principal roles, the comedy earned such descriptives as brittle and sophisticated. In its revival it was a romp and a circus which prompted me to bestow on Miss Bankhead the title of Best Supporting Actress of the Season—in support of herself, of course. She was ably and courteously abetted in this achievement by Donald Cook, playing the Coward role. Mr. Cook miraculously managed to maintain his own identity and that of the character he was acting in spite of Miss Bankhead's overpowering onslaughts. "Private Lives" was a great success.

Tennessee Williams, who had become the theatre's Number One active playwright with "The Glass Menagerie" and "A Streetcar Named Desire," was represented by another drama of the frustrations of a female titled "Summer and Smoke." This one had been produced by Margo Jones at her theatre-in-the-round in Dallas in 1947, and New York scouts who caught it were so enthusiastic that Miss Jones ventured a New York production. Physically it was one of the finest offerings of the season, having a poetically lovely setting by Jo Mielziner—but artistically it left room for debate. I thought it was muddled, wordy and juvenile.

An early October musical offering was "Love Life," with book and lyrics by Alan Jay Lerner and score by Kurt Weill. This was a well-made, intelligent production, purporting to relate the love life of a young American couple from early Colonial days to the present. Always the same couple, mind you, and always young, as they progressed from the simplicities of early times to the complexities of today and found it increasingly difficult to remain in love. The show ran out the season.

Another October musical was a great success, even though its first-night reviews were not entirely ecstatic. This was "Where's Charley?"—a song-and-dance version of "Charley's Aunt." Blessed with the presence of Ray Bolger, who sang, acted and danced with the utmost energy and charm, "Where's Charley?" became an immense favorite with the public. I had found it dullish as to book and undistinguished as to score, and not quite up to Mr. Bolger's copious gifts as an entertainer. Happily, the public was much more enthusiastic—and one reason was, I think, that here was a show children would enjoy. Aside from circuses and ice revues, there are not many entertainments which young fry will appreciate and which at the same time will keep their parents contented—and there is a vast, vast market for such.

As I wrote at the opening of Ruth Gordon's "The Leading Lady," there is an extra risk in fabricating a play about stage people, for this exposes audiences to a double dose of actors. When actors act ordinary people with reasonable conviction, they are effective; but when actors act actors, they may be too, too much. Miss Gordon, who had written a fine autobiographical comedy in "Years Ago," was unable to make "The Leading Lady" a success. It was a story about two married stars, with Miss Gordon playing one of them, and it elicited no great interest.

The Shuberts, Lee and J. J., have had immeasurable profits from romantic operettas such as "The Student Prince" and "Blossom Time," and there is no particular reason for thinking that this type of entertainment is outmoded. For some time the brothers felt that a musical version of a fine old heart-throbber, Edward Sheldon's "Romance," would be a natural and perhaps another touring perennial. After considerable preparation they offered "My Romance," with a properly schmaltzy score by Sigmund Romberg. The public was not receptive.

After another long period of preparation, Howard Lindsay and Russel Crouse offered "Life with Mother" as a sequel to the historically successful "Life with Father." With their producer, Oscar Serlin, they knew that making a sequel to so great and so familiar a hit was tempting fate. They knew that comparisons would be inevitable and, human nature being what it is, possibly unfavorable. Yet they went ahead, and Mr. Lindsay and his wife, Dorothy Stickney, resumed their characters of Father and Mother Day.

The comedy got off to an ideal start, with public interest at a high pitch and with reviewers unanimously enthusiastic. One felt that it should run at least a couple of years—and it was the surprise of the season when the management announced that it would close June 4, 1949. Various reasons for the comparative shortness of the run have been advanced. One is that people did not read the title carefully and thought "Life with Father" was still playing. Another is that sequels never are successful—which is not true. My own belief is that the management got too greedy and played too safe by booking so many charity benefit parties early in the run. So many performances were sold out to benevolent organizations during the first two months that ordinary playgoers with ordinary cash in their wallets got tired of being rebuffed at the box office. One can always go to a movie, or stay home and watch television.

"Life with Mother" was a splendid comedy. It deserved a better fate and, perhaps, a more venturesome management.

The financial hazards of the theatre have become so great as to threaten the existence of its art, and any effort to lessen them is vastly important. There was, in October, a little play titled "Minnie and Mr. Williams," a Welsh play written some years ago by Richard Hughes, under the title of "A Comedy of Good and Evil." It was a fantasy about a Welsh minister and his wife who befriend a female emissary of the devil, and are so truly good and kind that the young lady from hell is practically converted to Christianity. "Minnie and Mr. Williams" was the slightest of plays, unequipped for a rough-and-tumble Broadway struggle. One might say it should never have come to Broadway in the first place—but where else could it go? It wanted to go somewhere and it deserved to go somewhere, for it was kindly and gently funny and it would have afforded much pleasure to many people had it been able to find a haven. In a less harsh theatrical economy, "Minnie" could have found its modest corner somewhere—and could have bestowed its pleasures upon more people than the few who managed to see it during less than a week's run.

In 1941 Dorothy Heyward wrote a play about a Negro zealot, Denmark Vesey, who plotted to deliver Charleston from the whites early in the Nineteenth Century. It was not until November of 1948 that the Theatre Guild got around to producing this drama by the distinguished co-author of "Porgy." The Guild gave the play a fine setting and good Negro actors, including Juano Hernandez and Canada Lee, but Mrs. Heyward's writing failed to provide the excitement necessary for a success. This was not to be one of the Theatre Guild's good years.

The evening of Armistice Day, 1948, should have been historic as well as commemorative in the eyes of playgoers, for it marked the return of a fabled writing team. George S. Kaufman and Edna Ferber, of "Royal Family" fame, had collaborated upon a drama titled "Bravo!" It was given another fine production by Max Gordon—and it was another disappointment. Here again was a play about stage people—in this case two refugees living in reduced circumstances in New York. Once the man had been Hungary's most popular playwright, and the woman—then his mistress—its most dazzling star. In New York their life was not so good, but even so they felt—and so did Mr. Kaufman and Miss Ferber—that this is a good country. The trouble was that the play was not as good.

Michael Todd is not a believer in fancy musicals; he simply strives to purvey what he calls meat and potatoes, without any side trimmings. All he wants is Bobby Clark and some pretty girls—and that is exactly what he had when he opened "As the Girls Go" in November. Mr. Clark, being the greatest living American clown, carried the show, and the girls were indeed very pretty. At this writing Mr. Todd is on his way to another fortune, the amazing Mr. Clark is in the best of health and the artistic qualities of the musical comedy business are right where they were.

November also turned up a pair of Best Plays and another Worst Play candidate—the latter having been titled "For Heaven's Sake, Mother!" One of the good plays was "Goodbye, My Fancy," by a newcomer named Fay Kanin. Mrs. Kanin, a screenwriter, had written a comedy about a famous woman coming back to her Alma Mater for a reunion, and her husband, Michael Kanin, had had the sagacity to employ Hollywood's Madeleine Carroll for the leading role. The combination of play and player was irresistible. Miss Carroll displayed charm and intelligent comedy style, and Mrs. Kanin wrote a play with a well-stated opinion or two about educational problems.

Another Best Play for November was Moss Hart's "Light Up the Sky," a noisy and well-directed farce about show business. Here was another play in which actors were playing the parts of actors, but this time they were being funny about themselves and were therefore not particularly objectionable.

A rather over-wrought and cluttered drama about a girls' school, "The Young and Fair," failed to have anywhere near the dramatic impact of Lillian Hellman's early success, "The Children's Hour." The new play, by N. Richard Nash, was distinguished chiefly by one short, melodramatic scene played by Julie Harris, a newcomer to the commercial stage. Miss Harris indulged in a mental crackup so quickly and so effectively as to mark her a promising young actress. Later in the season she got another part in another play, but the play was so bad she was lost in it.

There is no way of telling whether a play will be a hit in New York except to wait until it opens in New York and see what happens. The Theatre Guild had produced, during the previous Summer at its Westport, Connecticut, Playhouse a comedy by an unknown writer, Richard McEnroe, titled "The Silver Whistle." It set nobody in Westport afire, but it seemed to warrant being monkeyed with further, and in the Fall it was put into Boston, Detroit and elsewhere for further trials. Still nobody was ablaze, and when time came for the New York opening there was no enthusiasm among the commercial handicappers.

"The Silver Whistle" revealed itself as a very charming fantasy about a tramp who brightens life in an old people's home. It was the Guild's only New York hit of the season—one hit out of five tries. Its success was due not only to Mr. McEnroe's kindly whimseys but also to an extraordinarily graceful and vibrant performance by Jose Ferrer. Mr. Ferrer, who is ambitious, tireless, enthusiastic and intelligent, will take on any role at any time and is rapidly becoming Broadway's First Actor.

Much more publicity than it was worth was given to Jean-Paul Sartre's "Red Gloves," which was produced early in December. Monsieur Sartre had been represented a couple of seasons before by "The Respectful Prostitute," a melodramatic cartoon which was quite a hit. "Red Gloves" purported in advance to be loaded with politics and philosophy, and when Sartre, in Paris, disavowed responsibility for the American production, newspapers made much of it.

But the play was badly made and even silly now and then, and except for one role it was not very well acted. The exceptional player was Charles Boyer, one of the great screen lovers, who instantly persuaded cynical New Yorkers that he was a round actor of solid quality. Considering his material, Mr. Boyer gave one of the best performances of the season, and his success, on top of Madeleine Carroll's, gave playgoers a new respect for movie actors.

As has been stated, there is no way of telling in advance whether a play will be a hit—or a failure. The advance reports from Philadelphia and elsewhere were that Maxwell Anderson, an old standby and a good craftsman, had really come a cropper with "Anne of the Thousand Days." There were reports—and practically all of them were true—of script trouble, casting trouble, scene trouble and customer trouble. Less experienced and less courageous workers than Anderson, the Playwrights' Company, Leland Hayward, H. C. Potter and Jo Mielziner might have thrown up the sponge in Philadelphia. But they did not quit and they did not quit working, and when "Anne of the Thousand Days" arrived at the Shubert Theatre it was a distinguished drama—the best, I think, of all of Mr. Anderson's investigations of the loves of kings and queens.

About eight years ago one Charles Gaynor wrote a revue and it was produced briefly and modestly in Pittsburgh. Came the war. After fighting the war, Mr. Gaynor dug up his show and persuaded William Eythe and a young group of Hollywood companions to produce it in Los Angeles in the Summer of 1948. It was a hit, so it was brought to New York under the title of "Lend an Ear," and it became a hit here, too. Mr. Gaynor had written it all—songs and sketches. One of the skits, a burlesque of an operetta of the 1920s titled "The Gladiola Girl," was the season's high spot for humor.

The next two plays to arrive were nicely done, but neither found public favor. Leo G. Carroll gave one of his meticulous performances as a priest who reluctantly took into his home an unattractive 18-year-old orphan girl—and from there on the story was the one about the Ugly Duckling and a Prince Charming. This historian felt that Mr. Carroll's comedy, "Jenny Kissed Me," was quite suitable for stock and amateur performances, being pleasant and harmless. Of considerably higher caliber was John van Druten's "Make Way for Lucia," based on E. F. Benson's "Lucia" novels. Here was a literate and gently witty parlor comedy about the rivalry between two women for the social domination of an English village, and it was played with style by Isabel Jeans, Catherine Willard and Cyril Ritchard.

I admired the craftsmanship which had gone into the writing, staging and acting—but the customers did not and the play was another failure for the Theatre Guild.

The post-Christmas week brought the customary rush of productions to playhouses, and they offered grounds for rejoicing and regret. On the regrettable side were a too-mild comedy for Ernest Truex, "Oh, Mr. Meadowbrook!" and a brave and elaborate production of a Benjamin Britten-Ronald Duncan opera, "The Rape of Lucretia." The opera, offered at the Ziegfeld with alternate casts, was visually stunning and ultramodern in its staging, but I felt that it did not measure up to Britten's "Peter Grimes," which usually is in the Metropolitan Opera's repertoire. However, the fine new investiture of "Lucretia" made most Metropolitan productions seem even dingier than they are. A third after-Christmas mistake was made by Jack Buchanan, the fashionable Briton, in appearing in a Sacha Guitry comedy, "Don't Listen, Ladies." It was extremely old-style French sex comedy and quite unfunny.

The hat-tossing began when only three of the newspaper reviewers, including this one, found that "The Madwoman of Chaillot" was an offering of distinction. Written by the late Jean Giraudoux and adapted from the French by Maurice Valency, "The Madwoman" was a comedy of intelligence and imagination, with splendid settings by the late Christian Berard and remarkably engaging performances by Martita Hunt, Estelle Winwood and many others in a large company. "The Madwoman" began slowly at the Belasco, but gradually the public began to find it, and by the season's end, it was secure. The Critics' Circle voted it the best foreign play.

More hat-tossing was earned by "Kiss Me, Kate," a musical based by Samuel and Bella Spewack on Shakespeare's "The Taming of the Shrew," with score and lyrics by Cole Porter. It was a triumph for Porter, who had been plagued by broken bones and had not had a success in several seasons. It was generally agreed that his songs for "Kiss Me, Kate," which were exuberant and melodious, were among the best he had ever done. Mr. Porter's opening was so stylish it was attended by Mrs. William K. Vanderbilt, who usually confines her first-nighting to the opera.

Ruth Gordon, having tried and failed with a play of her own earlier in the season, now essayed one by her husband, Garson Kanin, which fared no better. Titled "The Smile of the World" and involving the sentiments and ideals of a Supreme Court justice and his wife, it was a Washington, D. C., version of "Candida." It did not exhibit the brilliance of Shaw—or of Kanin, for that matter. Another early January offering which managed to run into the Summer was a revue, "Along Fifth Avenue," featuring the comicalities of Nancy Walker. This one was neither completely good nor completely bad, but it did not have the sparkle of "Lend an Ear."

Mid-January brought an English "psychological" thriller, "The Shop at Sly Corner," with the always-psychological Boris Karloff as the villain. In 1941 this play, by Edward Percy, was tried out with Henry Hull under the title of "Play with Fire," but it never got as far as Broadway. In its second attempt it did not tarry, and it should be evident by now that American audiences have not the patience and the leisure to savor the quiet horrors of the English melodrama.

The greatest productional fuss over the least amount of drama was made in connection with "Leaf and Bough," an errant radio serial about a simple farm family and a bad town family. Another of Margo Jones' Dallas discoveries, it was directed within considerably less than an inch of its life by Rouben Mamoulian and it had a notable setting by Carl Kent. It was a short-lived error.

Next, something quite memorable happened—the appearance of the season's most remarkable theatrical figure. His name is Anthony Brady Farrell; place of business: Albany, N. Y.; age: late forties. A well-heeled manufacturer and an heir of the traction magnate, Anthony F. Brady, Mr. Farrell had become show-smitten in the Spring of 1948 and had produced a revue, "Hold It," which was a failure.

Undaunted, Mr. Farrell announced that he would put the show on again in the Fall, and would keep his company on the payroll all Summer. He did keep a number of the company on the payroll. Next he bought the Warners' film palace, the Broadway, renamed it the Mark Hellinger, refurbished it at great expense. By now he decided not to repeat "Hold It," but to offer a new revue. Assembling songs and sketches, carloads of scenery and such entertainers as Paul and Grace Hartman and Bert Wheeler, he gave New York "All for Love."

The reviews were completely unfavorable, but Mr. Farrell remained brave. He felt he had a good show and that the public would find it in time, and he was prepared to wait forever, if necessary, at losses ranging upward of $12,000 a week. Unhappily, the public outwaited him, and he closed "All for Love" in the late Spring of 1949. He intimated, too, that he was through with show business, although he would keep his theatre as a sound investment. *Variety* estimated that the production loss on the revue was half a million dollars; add another million and a half or so far the theatre and it makes the dogged Mr. Farrell the season's most remarkable figure.

"Forward the Heart," a gentle romance about a blind, white war veteran and a Negro girl, was simple and honest but not much of a play—not nearly so much of a play as was the next one, Mae West's "Diamond Lil." It had been twenty years since the first production of this remarkable piece of hokum by its remarkable star, and in the revival they both seemed better and funnier than ever.

Miss West had a big hit on her hands. But, two weeks after her premiere, as she was preparing to leave her hotel apartment with me to appear on a television broadcast, she slipped on a door sill and broke her ankle. The reopening of "Diamond Lil" was announced several times and postponed several times. It finally was laid over until September, 1949.

A Boston repertory production of "Richard III," with Richard Whorf in the title role, was brought to Broadway for a limited engagement. Mr. Whorf and company acted it with a great deal of clatter and zest. Next, the Theatre Guild came another cropper by offering the French actor, Jean Pierre Aumont, in his own comedy, "My Name Is Aquilon" (which had tried out under the title of "Figure of a Girl"). Even though Philip Barry had revised it, it remained another frail and desperately Gallic sex comedy.

By the time Arthur Miller's "Death of a Salesman" opened on February 10, 1949, everybody knew that this one was going to be "it." The grapevine from the tryout had incited the public into storming the box office and flooding the mails with checks long before the premiere, and this time the public was not mistaken. The night of the opening the *Herald Tribune's* Howard Barnes called "Salesman" "a great play of our day" and the *Times'* Brooks Atkinson, a very careful man with words, lavished upon it such descriptives as superb, rich and memorable. I called it "a very fine work in the American theatre." In it all the elements of the stage—script, staging, setting and acting—were in perfect balance and perfect combination.

"They Knew What They Wanted," by the late Sidney Howard, once won the Pulitzer prize—but it seemed to have lost its punch when John Golden revived it, a 25-year-old relic, in mid-February. Paul Muni offered one of his vastly detailed and overmannered performances in the role of the Napa Valley vintner, but not even Muni's fame and Golden's vigor could save "They Knew What They Wanted" for long.

Another film star, John Garfield, returned to the stage in Clifford Odets' "The Big Knife," a drama about the wicked machinations of the moguls of Hollywood. Mr. Odets' play faired fairly well, but it seemed cluttered and muddled. Another hopeless comedy, "Anybody Home," made its bid for the Worst Play championship on February 25, 1949.

Right after a Worst Play came a Best Play—Samuel Spewack's farce about Government bureaucracy, "Two Blind Mice." Mr. Spewack, who knows his Washington, confected an amiable and satirical piece about two old ladies clinging to their Office of Medicinal Herbs even though they had been abolished by Congress some years before. With his share in "Kiss Me, Kate," Mr. Spewack now had two concurrent successes.

Another farce, "At War with the Army," was brought down from the Yale drama laboratories early in March and engaged in a brave struggle. Written by James B. Allardice, a pupil of Prof. Marc Connelly, and staged by Ezra Stone in the best George Abbott or helter-skelter manner, the comedy was at times hilarious, but thinnish. Its existence was a prolonged skirmish with the sinister forces of theatrical economy.

The first post-Easter hit was Sidney Kingsley's "Detective Story," a sound and rugged melodrama set in a police stationhouse. Mr. Kingsley's fine reportorial eye and ear had not been so well employed for some time, and a first-rate cast headed by Ralph Bellamy did extremely well.

Those who expected a treatise on political liberalism in Dalton Trumbo's "The Biggest Thief in Town" were, so to speak, disappointed. Mr. Trumbo, a screenwriter who had acquired some fame in Hollywood philosophical circles, had merely brought forth a rather clumsy and slightly tasteless farce about an undertaker.

The season's mystery was the failure of another melodrama, "The Traitor," by Herman Wouk. This one seemed to have everything. Most of the notices were heavily in its favor. It had been staged by Jed Harris, one of the ablest of directors. Its company included Lee Tracy and Walter Hampden. It was up-to-the-minute, involving spies, the atom bomb and scientific detection with a Geiger counter. The customers who saw it were highly enthusiastic—but somehow they failed to persuade their friends to go and Mr. Harris finally abandoned hopes of an upswing. It was quite a season for the public making hits out of shows the critics were lukewarm about and being lukewarm about some that the critics liked.

A brief visitor was "The Ivy Green," a biographical work about Charles Dickens. Either Dickens was a dull fellow or Mervyn Nelson was a dull dramatist—or both.

In most precincts, the arrival of "South Pacific" on April 7 was regarded as the most stirring phenomenon since Halley's comet. The authors were Richard Rodgers, Oscar Hammerstein 2d and Joshua Logan. The plot was from James A. Michener's best-seller, "Tales of the South Pacific." The stars were Mary Martin, Broadway's darling, and Ezio Pinza, the Metropolitan Opera's finest singing actor. By the opening the public had put up more than $300,000 in mail orders; by June advance sales were well over $500,000 and the ticket racks were bare down to October.

It was, indeed, a fine musical—but in the opinion of this observer it was not the real work of art that Rodgers and Hammerstein created in "Carousel" or in "Oklahoma!" "South Pacific" was voted the best musical of the season by the critics, but there also was strong voting for Mr. Porter's "Kiss Me, Kate."

George Batson some seasons ago had a ramshackle success with a ramshackle play titled "Ramshackle Inn," a farcical melodrama for ZaSu Pitts. Now, late in the 1949 period, he essayed a comedy about faded Southern womanhood titled "Magnolia Alley." It, too, was ramshackle, but it was not a success.

Late in April Peggy Wood, an admirable comedienne, returned to the stage in "The Happiest Years." Unfortunately, the play was not admirable or worth her time and trouble, casting Miss Wood as a nosey and objectionable campus mother. George Abbott missed the boat with a farce about a doting mother and her three hoodlum sons, "Mrs. Gibbons' Boys."

Another able star, Fay Bainter, returned to the stage in "Gayden," a rather unpleasant drama about a mother and her perverted son. It wasn't worth anybody's time and trouble, and all it will be remembered for is an exceptionally lovely setting by Willis Knighton.

The season closed on schedule—and conclusively. There already had been a Best Play, "Death of a Salesman," but there was some doubt as to which of several offerings was best qualified for the Worst Play prize. Jack Kirkland removed the doubt by writing and producing "Mr. Adam," based on a novel by Pat Frank. There may have been other candidates which were equally inept, but certainly none as tasteless.

THE SEASON IN BOSTON

By Elliot Norton
Drama Critic of the *Boston Post*

LOOKING back over the Boston season of '48-49, one gets something of the same feeling which Lot's wife must have had in the fraction of a second before she was turned to salt. Some pleasant things were done in our theatres during the year, and a few fine things, but the number of disappointments, failures and disasters was more than ordinarily high. In retrospect, the picture is not pleasant.

The number of productions made available in the seven commercial theatres—the Shubert, Plymouth, Colonial, Wilbur, Majestic, Copley and Boston Opera House—was as large as it usually is. Between June 1, 1948, fifty-two "regular" dramatic attractions played in those houses. In addition, the Boston Summer Theatre, which must be included in the record because it operates downtown on a professional level, offered 10 plays in as many weeks and the Boston Repertory Association, occupying the Copley Theatre for twelve and a half weeks, presented seven. The overall figure is 70 plays, or shows, for the 12 months.

One half of the Summer Theatre's shows prospered. Of those offered by the Boston Repertory group, two were successful for one week each, a third, the "Richard III" revival by Richard Whorf, managed to get by for two weeks. Not more than 10 of 52 plays and musicals done in the downtown playhouses could be counted as financial or popular hits.

In scanning the record of the "tryouts," the recorder is appalled at the rate of failure.

Now and then plays in tryout for Broadway are done here successfully only to fall later under the axes of the New York reviewers. Others—the horrible example was "Our Town"—are rejected in Boston and acclaimed in New York. This year, our audiences attended in great numbers the "Red Gloves" of Jean-Paul Sartre, "The Big Knife" of Clifford Odets and "They Knew What They Wanted," in John Golden's revival with Paul Muni. None of these triumphed in New York.

However, most of the other new productions which were successful here won a following in Manhattan, and the flops died in Boston, too, except for those mentioned. And what a sad legion they were!

Thirty-three productions, or three of every five presented here in the commercial theatres during the regular season, were "tryouts," plays or musical shows offered to Bostonians in tentative form, prior to Broadway. Richard Whorf's "Richard III," although it was presented here in a repertory company production, may rightly be considered as a tryout, too, which brings the total to 34.

Only six of the 34 went on to real unqualified success on Broadway, and it took many weeks of additional performances in such other centers as Pittsburgh, Chicago and Detroit before one of them, "The Silver Whistle" became a winner. Similarly, "As the Girls Go," had to be ripped to pieces here and in New Haven by Producer Michael Todd before it won fame.

The other four winners which began their careers in Boston were "South Pacific," most successful of them all; "Love Life," the musical "vaudeville" by Alan Jay Lerner and Kurt Weill; Charles Gaynor's bright little revue, "Lend an Ear," which some of us had seen in the Summer theatre at nearby Cohasset in 1941, with the same William Eythe in the same roles; and Moss Hart's comical "Light Up the Sky," a good play about a mythical play being tried out in Boston.

Two other Boston tryouts, the revues "Small Wonder" and "Along Fifth Avenue," did fairly well here and fairly well in the other world of New York. Whether they can be classed as "moderate successes" or not is a matter for the historians of Broadway to decide.

Also in the dubious category, it seems from this distance, would be "The Big Knife," and the farce comedy "At War with the Army." The army play did fairly well here and managed to continue from week to week during the latter part of the New York season, though the trade said its producers were losing money regularly for art's sake.

Even more depressing than the tremendous casualty list among the tryouts, it seems to some of us, was the failure in Boston of four substantial plays which had been well favored in New York the previous season. When imperfect plays, or plays which have not yet been fully perfected, fail to win enthusiastic support from our playgoers, it is easy enough to see why. But '48-49 was the season in which Boston rejected, or accepted only half-heartedly, four fine productions which had been proved long since in New

York and elsewhere: "Command Decision," with Paul Kelly and most of the New York cast; the "Medea" of Robinson Jeffers, with Judith Anderson giving a performance of tremendous skill; "The Winslow Boy," acted by the players who made it a success in London and New York, and "The Heiress," without Wendy Hiller, but with Basil Rathbone still in command as Dr. Austin Sloper.

Various reasons were offered by various authorities for the failure of these shows. General business conditions, the increased unemployment in some of the cities near here which would ordinarily feed the Boston theatres and even television were named to explain why "Medea," for instance, despite the universally acclaimed acting of Judith Anderson, played to smaller houses here than in any comparable city in the country. The fact would seem to be that all serious dramas except "Red Gloves," "The Big Knife" and "They Knew What They Wanted"—each of which had a major movie star among its personnel acting as a special lure —were rejected by Bostonians during the season. This is the most depressing fact in the record.

When the official theatrical year began, on June 1, 1948, two plays were available. Bert Lahr was beginning a second week in "Burlesque," which was good fun because of him, but less convincing than it had been in New York because Jean Parker had been replaced in the principal girl's role. "Oklahoma!" had just opened its fourth engagement in Boston since that night in 1943 when it was first offered at the Colonial Theatre as "Away We Go." Booked for four weeks, the national company stayed six, from May 31 to July 10, despite hot weather.

The Boston Summer Theatre, which has been operated by various managers during the last five years and is now in the hands of two comic strip cartoonists, Lee Falk ("Mandrake the Magician") and Al Capp ("L'il Abner") began its season in modern, air-cooled New England Mutual Hall, on Monday evening, June 21. The opening attraction was William Gaxton in a truncated version of "Seven Keys to Baldpate," which the star played with a great deal of nervous energy and charm, charm, charm. They loved him.

On successive weeks, the managing cartoonists presented Jackie Cooper in "John Loves Mary"; Kay Francis in "The Last of Mrs. Cheyney"; "Othello," with Canada Lee fumbling uneasily through the title part; Lillian Gish in Noel Coward's "The Marquise"; Ilka Chase in "Design for Living"; Ruth Chatterton in "The Little Foxes"; Brian Aherne in the Restoration comedy,

"The Beaux' Stratagem"; Sylvia Sidney in "Kind Lady" and, of course, Edward Everett Horton in "Springtime for Henry"—what else?

The Lee "Othello" was most disappointing, leading to the perhaps premature conclusion that this work is out of Mr. Lee's range. Claire Luce (the other one) had a try at Desdemona in the same production and hers was not one of the year's best performances, either. On the other hand, the Iago of Wesley Addy was impressively clever.

Ruth Chatterton's version of Regina Giddens was impressive, too. Never having seen Tallulah Bankhead's icily brilliant performance, Miss Chatterton devised this one herself. Her Regina is no less diabolical, but she reveals her full nature much more slowly and slyly.

The first of the Boston season's long parade of tryouts emerged from the Summer circuit in July. From nearby Marblehead, where it had actually brought a first-night audience of normally cool New Englanders to their feet cheering, Bessie Breuer's drama, "Sundown Beach" was hastily booked into the Shubert Theatre on July 26 for two weeks.

An author of some distinction who had not previously written a play, Miss Breuer had spent time in Florida near a war department camp for aviators who were being treated for nervous and mental disorders. What she saw and heard so impressed her that she tried to write a novel about it, then decided this was the stuff of which strong dramas are made.

A first draft of her play got into the hands of Director Elia Kazan, who sent her home to make some changes, then staged the second draft privately in New York in his Actors' Studio, where he and Cheryl Crawford and others were giving young and older actors an opportunity to learn more about their work.

Professional people, among them well-known playwrights and producers, were invited to watch "Sundown Beach" at the Actors' Studio, because its sponsors wanted their players to work before an audience. The professional people were not only pleased, they were also impressed, so much so that presently "Sundown Beach" was booked into the Summer theatres at Westport, Conn., and Marblehead, Mass., with such audience response that the Boston booking followed.

Every Boston reviewer liked "Sundown Beach" for the immensity of its compassion and for the vivid performances of its young actors. Though business at the Shubert Theatre was not good, the heat was blamed. Then into New York went "Sundown Beach," to be cut to ribbons by every reviewer who saw it.

Here, nobody knows yet why it failed so completely, and the special mystery lies in the universal condemnation of the acting. Here it seemed spontaneous. Over there, it was cursed for being stilted. Something which hasn't yet been explained must have happened to those actors in the six weeks between the opening in Marblehead and the catastrophe on Broadway.

Another new production, the first of the season's musicals, got into the Shubert Theatre on Aug. 23. It was "Heaven on Earth," which had something or other to do with Central Park. Despite the charm of Peter Lind Hayes and other participants and the sudden, though silent, importation of John Murray Anderson to help Eddie Dowling with the directing, "Heaven on Earth" seemed less than paradisiacal to Bostonians, and its subsequent failure in New York was mourned yet not unexpected. They can't fool us all the time!

One week later, the Majestic Theatre opened to present a revue called "Small Wonder," whose largest wonder was the miming of Tom Ewell, a real droll. "Small Wonder" fell flat on its first act at the premiere, but Mr. Ewell and the others picked it up in the second.

Because every producer is eager to see his new work properly tried out in the Fall so that, if successful, it may have a long season where long seasons count most, Boston's theatres are invariably busiest in September, October and November. In 1948, they were crowded as usual during that period.

Max Gordon, a veteran hit-maker, arrived on Labor Day with "Town House," a play made from *New Yorker* magazine stories. Despite the direction of George S. Kaufman and some able antics by comedienne Mary Wickes, "Town House" didn't bring the house down here.

Only four days after the "Town House" premiere, the attractive Wilbur Theatre was turned over to one of those unfortunate little dramas which are apparently unavoidable in any season. It was called "Grandma's Diary" by the management. It was called quite a few other things by first-nighters in our town.

Our season's first good musical was "Love Life," which picked things up where "Diary" had let them down. This gay and tuneful "vaudeville," as it was called, enlisted wonderful people on both sides of the stage to tell effectively and entertainingly the story of American marriage over a period of 150 years. Nanette Fabray and Ray Middleton spoke the lines of Alan Jay Lerner and sang the tunes of Kurt Weill, under the direction of Elia

Kazan and the production sponsorship of Cheryl Crawford. Good people involved in a fine show. A hit in Boston; a big hit on Broadway. The season was under way.

From Cambridge at this time, interrupting the flow of attractions from New York, came members of the Summer Theatre company, most of them Harvard students and some of them talented. They hired Sara Allgood and Whitford Kane to enact with them, at the Majestic Theatre, Sean O'Casey's "Juno and the Paycock," Mr. Kane taking the role of the Paycock. Of course, Miss Allgood was fine, but the overall production was not exciting, nor was it popular. One week was enough.

Frank Fay returned to Boston in September. Four years earlier, he had opened Mary Coyle Chase's "Harvey" (known first as "The Pooka") at our Copley Theatre. Having made a run of it in New York, he was back for a run here. He got it. "Harvey" stayed 12 weeks at the Colonial Theatre, and although that is not a Boston record, it was the longest engagement of the '48-49 season. Runner-up among the long runners, incidentally, was "Finian's Rainbow," which stayed 9 weeks at the Shubert Theatre, beginning Oct. 18.

"Command Decision" started at the Wilbur Theatre the night of "Harvey's" homecoming. Played beautifully by Paul Kelly and the others, it stimulated all who went to see it at the Wilbur Theatre, including the reviewers, but it lost money during each of its three weeks.

Entering also on the night of Sept. 20, was a revival of "The Trial of Mary Dugan," at the Majestic. Jay Jostyn of radio's "Mr. District Attorney" program was starred in this one. Though they had New York in mind, this one went to the warehouse, instead, after only one of a scheduled two weeks. Something about the acting, people said.

Boston has always liked "Show Boat," the Kern and Hammerstein musical. With Carol Bruce serving it in the role created by the late Helen Morgan it was played here with some success at the Opera House, opening the night after "Command Decision." It seemed to me the Boat is beginning to list pretty badly and is not nearly so seaworthy as she once was; but the melodies linger on, of course.

"The Silver Whistle," a first work by Robert McEnroe, was opened here by the Theatre Guild, with Jose Ferrer as star. The fact that it jeered at the helpless old people in an institution for the aged made it seem a dubious work to some of us, despite Mr. Ferrer. The Guild and Mr. McEnroe went to work on it, later, and on the testimony of Lawrence Langner, took pains to answer some of the Boston objections, with what success everyone now knows.

Ruth Gordon's play "The Leading Lady," which had been trying out in Chicago, was booked into Boston suddenly on Saturday, Oct. 2. Handsomely mounted, employing its greatly gifted author as star and utilizing other excellent actors, it managed to create something of the atmosphere of theatrical life in an earlier era but its story was not credible. An expensive production, it did pathetically poor business at the Copley Theatre, and went on from here after two weeks to collapse in New York.

The second of the Theatre Guild's entries, called here "Charleston, 1822" and later known as "Set My People Free" did little to brighten the season. Though Dorothy Heyward had written a good deal of warmth into this chronicle of a slave rebellion, it lacked force and coherence.

One of the curious works of the season was "My Romance." It opened here on Oct. 6, 1948, for the third time in less than a year! In its first visit, it had seemed a rather pleasant musical play based on the old tear-jerker "Romance" of Edward Sheldon. Here for the second time, its story had become less coherent, its staging more dubious. For its third visit it had acquired a new score by Sigmund Romberg and by now it had reached a state of dramatic chaos which defied all the efforts of Anne Jeffreys, who sang beautifully and looked the same, but was not able to rescue it.

The week of Oct. 11 brought three new shows on three successive evenings: Moss Hart's "Light Up the Sky," at the Plymouth Theatre; the fantasy "Minnie and Mr. Williams," with Josephine Hull and Eddie Dowling, at the Wilbur; and Michael Todd's musical, "As the Girls Go." at the big Boston Opera House.

Mr. Hart's comedy was of special concern here, for was it not a play about a play in tryout in Boston, and did its action not transpire in the Ritz Carlton Hotel? Of course. Moreover, did it not seem to be concerned with real people of the theatre, among them a lady star, all disguised only thinly? Yes. Did its story not turn on the reading of reviews by Boston reviewers, who were not even thinly disguised, but named and "quoted"? Yes. And didn't all this make it something of a family party? Natch.

Despite the fact that it had some aspects of a private joke, "Light Up the Sky" did pretty well in the beginning and a less astute dramatist and director than Mr. Hart might have failed to discern that its "message" wasn't going down too well with playgoers who were interested only in its comic aspects. Like the author who is the hero of his play-within-a-play, Mr. Hart went into his room in the same Ritz Carlton which he had written about and emerged 10 days later with a new second and third act, both geared to gaiety. In Philadelphia, he rewrote the final 10 minutes of the last act for the second time.

"As the Girls Go" was really in trouble at its premiere. Bobby Clark, who is always wonderful, wasn't funny at all on that first night. The book of the show was a very dull volume indeed; the singers couldn't sing, and neither the songs nor the dances were good. Mr. Todd did a tremendous job of reconstruction in three weeks here and an extra one in New Haven. Credit to Mr. Todd!

The failure of "Minnie and Mr. Williams" was regrettable. There was charm in the fantasy of its Welsh story, but not much else.

After "Finian's Rainbow" got off to a fine start, with Mimi Kelly (daughter of Paul) in the role Ella Logan had created for Broadway, Max Gordon came back to Boston with another new play, from the typewriters of George S. Kaufman and Edna Ferber, a formidable and previously successful team. Though it was full of compassion and presented an aspect of our times which seemed to me most important and sufficiently dramatic, nobody else was impressed by it, either here or in New York.

"The Winslow Boy" was well played, but for whatever reason, only moderately well received by the public in Boston. It came here on the first evening of November.

Later in the same week, there began at the Copley Theatre an ambitious undertaking which was eventually and unfortunately to come to grief. The Boston Repertory Association was an acting company organized and managed by Gerald Savory, who had written one play, and Michael Linenthal, manager of the Woodstock, N. Y., Summer theatre, and a resident of Cambridge, Mass.

During a year of organizing, they had solicited a fund originally meant to be $50,000, but which dwindled eventually to a smaller amount. They would give Boston a season of five plays, each to be enacted for two weeks, all to be out of the drama's top drawer, or at least from an upper one. Having got the Copley Theatre from the Messrs. Shubert for an extremely reasonable rent, they persuaded the stage hands to accept reasonable wages and hours, then opened their season on Friday evening, Nov. 5, with good actors in "The Road to Rome," by Robert E. Sherwood.

Within a few days, they discovered that business was not good. After two and one half weeks of "The Road to Rome," they brought in "Heartbreak House" with Mady Christians and Philip Bourneuf added to their resident company. This they cut short at the end of a week and then, while soliciting additional funds, changed their basic policy from repertory to stock. After hasty single weeks of "George and Margaret" and "Payment Deferred," both of which did poorly, they got "Heartbreak House" back for an additional eight performances, then offered "The Skin of Our Teeth," their best production, with Polly Rowles as an antic Sabina, and a fairly good version of "Knickerbocker Holiday," by Maxwell Anderson and Kurt Weill. To wind up a season which lost a good deal of money, they imported Richard Whorf in a production of "Richard III," which was colorful enough but which seemed, at the opening, to be acted with less authentic force than "Richard" requires. This one was taken to New York by other producers; it stayed there for three lean weeks.

The failure of the Boston Repertory company, regretted by everyone, was apparently due to insufficient planning, insufficient funds and failure to recognize that Boston has only a small audience interested in repertory. In a 400-seat playhouse, with a comparatively small overhead, this troupe might have been a big success.

There were, of course, other openings in November. That was the month when Ernest Truex came to town in a dull little comedy called "Japhet," by Ronald Telfer and Pauline Jameson. It failed here and went on to do the same in New York under a new title, "Oh, Mr. Meadowbrook."

"Red Gloves," from Jean-Paul Sartre's "Les Mains Sales," created a good deal of stir and general interest in Boston, whatever its defects, and not only his fans but also his critics were happy to discover that Charles Boyer is more than a mere matinee idol; he proved himself a good actor.

"Allegro" returned to Boston in November. A tryout of the season before, it had met with a controversial reception here originally. Those of us who had liked it in the beginning found it just as enjoyable the second time; those opposed were even more indignant.

Charles Gaynor's "Lend an Ear," which created nothing but good will, came to Boston on December first, getting the month off to a nice start. A week later, there was less joy in Boston over "Jenny Kissed Me," despite the presence in it of Leo G. Carroll. Another December failure here was John van Druten's "Make

Way for Lucia." Everybody knew that Mr. van Druten was attempting in this dramatization of the Benson stories to achieve something like a modern high comedy; and almost everybody wished he had been able to do it. But the actors, except Cyril Ritchard, weren't up to it. Besides, he hadn't given them enough witty lines.

"Make Way for Lucia" made way for Blackstone, the magician, whose comedy is high neither in aim nor in fact, but who manages to please a good many of the customers.

Another new musical of December brought us Nancy Walker and Jackie Gleason. "Along Fifth Avenue" was not very tuneful nor very funny at the local premiere. It would seem to have improved more than somewhat, as Damon Runyon might have said, in the interim between the Boston and New York openings. Oh, that interim!

Our Christmas gift was not worth the unwrapping. In "The Shop at Sly Corner" Boris Karloff was only proving again that a melodrama can be effective in Britain and deadly here.

"Leaf and Bough," here for a first showing two nights later, was the work of a new and young dramatist, Joseph Hayes. The great hunt of the theatre being for new and young dramatists, much kindly attention was bestowed on Mr. Hayes. Though we liked his play better here than they did in New York, it was a great deal less than perfect.

Less than overwhelming, too, though the audiences didn't seem to think so, was a revival at the Opera House of "The Desert Song," brought all the way from the desert of Southern California by Robert Lewis and Howard Young. Its elderly story and tunes seems saccharine enough now to warrant a new spelling of the title; let them add an s and make it "The Dessert Song."

The Theatre Guild, midway in an unfortunate season, brought in a play by the French actor Jean Pierre Aumont by way of giving the new year an uncertain start. "Figure of a Girl," as it was called here (the title was changed for New York) had some charm, but not very much conviction, some wit but not enough, despite the fact that Philip Barry had worked to adapt it. A fair success the year before in Paris, where it had run for five months, some of its Gallic flavor and plot had had to be eliminated or altered for the U. S. A., and with the sultry stuff out, there wasn't much left.

Bert Lahr came to brighten Boston at this point in "Make Mine Manhattan," which was not the greatest show we had ever seen, but pleasant. On the same evening, Jan. 10, which brought us "Figure of a Girl" and "Make Mine Manhattan," we were also introduced to Sylvia Sidney and John Loder in "O Mistress Mine." Since the Lunts had never found time to present that comedy here, it was anticipated with much pleasure. Mr. Loder did well in Mr. Lunt's shoes; for Miss Sidney, Lynn Fontanne's are the wrong size.

For farce, Boston first saw "At War with the Army" in January. Reaction to this army comedy out of the Yale School of the Drama were mixed, ranging from the favorable to the indignant. Its producers played it here for two weeks, took it to Philadelphia for two, then brought it back again for another fortnight. In its second appearance, it had two new actors, including one principal, and had lost some of the smut which had previously marred it. Yale can have it.

Our January ended on an evening of some theatrical excitement. Not in many seasons do you get John Garfield and Paul Muni opening against one another. Mr. Garfield, of course, sparked Clifford Odets' "The Big Knife" while Mr. Muni was trying the part of the fruit grower in a revival of Sidney Howard's "They Knew What They Wanted." As has already been recorded, both plays were very well patronized in Boston, but there was some confusion about the quality of "The Big Knife" and a general feeling that Mr. Muni had not yet managed to act his part with conviction, though Paula Stone was acting skillfully the role of the girl Amy.

February was disappointing in that it should have brought back "Brigadoon," if the booking office hadn't changed its mind and sent that musical to the wrong coast. Since it produced "Inside U. S. A.," with Jack Haley and Beatrice Lillie, we had some consolation, however; and there was still another visit from "Oklahoma!" beginning on the last day of the month.

For a week at the Colonial, in the Yiddish language, there was the favorite star of his group, Maurice Schwartz, in "Herschel, the Jester."

For the commercial audience, beginning also on the last day of the month, there was "The Emerald Staircase," a curious drama about an undertaker who stole a corpse. Packed originally with social significance by Author Dalton Trumbo, this one arrived here in a tangle of farce, melodrama, message and meringue. They purged it of everything but the farce before it left, but it was still doubtful and the New York reviewers later removed the doubts. Thomas Mitchell and Walter Abel, both good actors, were unfortunately involved.

About this time of the year, the season was getting thin and the plays even thinner. One called "The Ivy Green," for instance, opened at the Plymouth Theatre on Monday evening, March 14. A night club entertainer, Mervyn Nelson, had written it about Charles Dickens. Despite the acting aid of Judith Evelyn as Mrs. Dickens, and despite some strenuous revisions here, it was a failure in Boston.

The very next evening, by way of bringing the theatre back to life, "South Pacific" had its first showing at the Shubert Theatre, and the whole city tried to get in. For an engagement lasting three weeks less one day, all seats were sold in advance and the clamor to get in reached a crescendo that brought the ticket speculators into business. Box-office price of best seats was $5.40, including tax. The speculators got $20 a pair and some customers offered up to $50 at the end of the engagement.

This Rodgers-Hammerstein-Logan musical play was wonderful at the first performance, and was altered here in only minor ways. A new song was written during the engagement for Ezio Pinza, but after a brief test was discarded. It would have been done in the scene where now the basso sings a reprise of "Some Enchanted Evening."

While "South Pacific" was still wowing the city, other attractions came in, but the showmen's hopes that general business would now be fine, were not fulfilled.

For one evening at the Opera House, Menasha Skulnik presented in Yiddish, for his special audience, a comedy called "What a Guy." For everyone who wanted a good play, the Colonial Theatre brought in Basil Rathbone in "The Heiress," but not many people wanted to go. I missed Wendy Hiller in it, but playgoers who hadn't seen her in New York were delighted by the performance of Beatrice Straight. Everyone was happy about Mr. Rathbone's Dr. Sloper, but the engagement was not successful.

We were still getting tryouts at the end of March. Jessie Royce Landis and Jackie Cooper entered the Plymouth in George Batson's melodrama of the South, "Magnolia Alley," on March 28. It was not as bad as Mr. Batson's previous "Ramshackle Inn," but bad enough.

Judith Anderson came in with "Medea" in April. Audiences at the Shubert Theatre were enthusiastic, but not numerous, which is hard to report, for certainly this was one of the great performances of the year.

A new surge of tryouts in April produced nothing successful. "The Happiest Years," a comedy by actors Tom Coley and William Roerick, proved slight and slightly ridiculous and not the right thing for Peggy Wood. A farce by Will Glickman and Joseph Stein entitled "Mrs. Gibbons' Boys" made one Boston reviewer whose name I withhold, laugh quite a lot, but few shared his joy. For a final tryout there was "Gayden," a melodrama of the quiet sort by new playwrights Robert and Mignon McLaughlin, who didn't quite manage to make it effective, despite the good acting of Fay Bainter.

The last opening of the regular downtown season was a return engagement of Garson Kanin's comedy "Born Yesterday," presented by a touring company, with Lew Eckels as the junkman, Harry Brock, and Joan Morgan as his lady, and everybody acting competently. Being watched because of its low scale of prices, with best seats at $1.80, "Born Yesterday" began what was planned as a long engagement at the Colonial Theatre, on Monday, May 9, 1949. The fact that two other companies had played it here previously was a handicap, but Producer Max Gordon's hopes were high.

To complete this chronicle, it is necessary to report some of the activities of the "little theatre" groups and also the ballet and opera companies.

The little theatres here crop up now and then, and disappear just as regularly. Some are poorly run by visionaries; some are handicapped by terribly poor acting; all suffer from the comparison of their work with that of the professionals.

Most successful and longest lived of these troupes is the Tributary Theatre of Boston, which has just completed its eighth season, playing twice weekly, Fridays and Saturdays, at New England Mutual Hall, under the direction of Eliot Duvey and with Saturday matinee performances for children.

A true repertory company, though handicapped by lack of rehearsal facilities and very uneven acting, they gave 17 regular productions during the 1948-49 season, including Boston premieres of Saroyan's "Jim Dandy" and the "Salome" of Oscar Wilde, which had long been banned here; and Rodney Ackland's dramatization of "Crime and Punishment." Of Shakespeare's plays they offered "Julius Caesar," "A Midsummer Night's Dream," "The Merchant of Venice" and "Cymbeline." They produced also Bernard Shaw's "Arms and the Man," O'Neill's "Anna Christie"; "The School for Scandal"; Ibsen's "Ghosts"; a new adaptation of "The Trojan Women"; Ben Jonson's "Volpone";

Dekker's "The Shoemakers' Holiday" and Synge's "The Playboy of the Western World."

Another small group, the Actors' Theatre, offered four productions downtown, each for two performances. Their productions included "Rise Above It," a new musical by Jack Gold and Phyllis Stone; the first Boston performances (somewhat cut by the censor) of "No Exit," by Jean-Paul Sartre; "Rocket to the Moon," by Clifford Odets, and "The Wanhope Building," by John Finch.

Interesting for its potentialities is the Boston Catholic Theatre, which began to operate this past season, under the patronage of Archbishop Richard J. Cushing, with occasional performances at New England Mutual Hall. There are more than 1,000,000 Catholics in the area known to the church as the Boston Archdiocese, and if the new theatrical project is successful, the general belief is that the professional theatre will benefit.

Performances this season were given by a number of parish or college companies. Later, perhaps next year, it is expected that the best actors of all the Catholic companies will be joined in one.

Plays presented thus far would seem to indicate that the theatre aims at dramatic entertainment rather than teaching. Three of them were purely religious in theme: "The Hound of Heaven," by a local playwright, Robert O'Donnell; "Career Angel," by the Rev. Gerard Murray; and "Song of Bernadette," by Walter and Jean Kerr. Some of the others, however, were Sheridan's "The Rivals," a Gilbert and Sullivan offering, "The Pirates of Penzance," and "Joan of Lorraine."

The ballet season in Boston was brief this year. The Ballet Russe De Monte Carlo, featuring Mia Slavenska, appeared for 10 days starting Thursday, April 28, 1949.

In the *Christian Science Monitor,* Margaret Lloyd referred to their season as "ten days that failed to shake the world," and suggested that some Bostonians who applauded mightily during the 10 days were enthusing over the second rate for lack of familiarity with the first rate.

Boston got its opera during 1948-49 from three sources. The local New England Opera Theatre, presided over by Boris Goldovsky and dedicated to opera in English, gave performances on Sunday afternoons in October, November, January and February, at the Opera House, of "Boheme," "The Turk in Italy," "Carmen," and "Idomeneo." Pretty nearly everybody was pleased; some were ecstatic.

For 10 days beginning Friday evening, Jan. 28, the San Carlo

Opera Company performed at the Boston Opera House under Producer Fortune Gallo, presenting 10 evening performances and three matinees of the standard French and Italian repertories. The highbrows were not excited. Middle and lower brows were content.

The visit of the Metropolitan Opera Company began on March 23 with the usual blaze of social brilliance, heightened as the evening wore on, perhaps, by the sale of light wine and champagne (domestic) in the second floor waiting room.

Included in the personnel were most of the principal Metropolitan stars, except, of course, the favorite Ezio Pinza, who had gone Broadway. Novelties in the repertory included "Salome," which everybody seemed to admire very much, and "Peter Grimes" which found a good deal less favor. High spot of the season was "Otello," over which all the music critics enthused, a very rare thing in this vicinity.

THE SEASON IN PHILADELPHIA
By Arthur B. Waters
Dramatic Editor and Critic of the *Gazette-Democrat*

IT is, of course, a familiar and popular cliché that the theatrical business ("game" if you prefer the word!) is filled with paradoxes. Certainly the Philadelphia legitimate theatrical season of 1948-49, just completed, bears out the theory in emphatically triumphant fashion. From first to last it was as paradoxical as a G. K. Chesterton essay.

Viewed artistically, 1948-49 brought us the world premiere of one of the few really great plays of the past quarter-century, and trotted out a number of other far-above-average productions, both straight and musical, as well. It (the season) also compelled long-suffering local playgoers to sit through some of the most awful tripe that has been viewed hereabouts in many a blue moon.

Financially, 1948-49 was just as unpredictable. It was noteworthy for some of the biggest gross receipts this city has ever known, it had generally first-rate attendance—especially up to the half-way mark—and then, without warning, it folded up in the middle of March for the earliest Spring closing this writer can remember in thirty years of show-covering.

For the statistical fan, 1948-49 discloses some interesting figures, most of them disheartening. There were forty-eight legitimate attractions in the city's four regular playhouses (this doesn't include "Miss Liberty" which was to open a three weeks' engagement at the Forrest on June 13 after the regular season had been in mothballs for over a month!) and that number (48) was a dozen or more under the records of the past two seasons and considerably less than half the number of bookings Philadelphia could expect back in the boom days of the late Twenties. A high-water mark then, as I recall, was 130-odd legitimate attractions in one season.

These 48 bookings of 1948-49 played a total of 105 weeks. The Locust, Walnut and Shubert, oddly enough, were lighted and active twenty-five weeks each while the Forrest—the flag-house of the Shubert's local fleet—was occupied 30 weeks.

There were twenty-one tryouts, excluding three revivals which used Philadelphia as a testing ground before daring Broadway. Of these twenty-one tryouts, seven were what *Variety* calls "world preems." A mere mention of the names of the seven serves to further emphasize the paradoxical angle. Five were instantaneous hits and went from here to win Broadway laurels. Paced by the phenomenal "Death of a Salesman" (already referred to but not named), the happy quintet also included "Kiss Me, Kate," "Anne of the Thousand Days," "Detective Story" and "Where's Charley?" The two painful and better-forgotten shows that tried out their fledgling wings here were "That's the Ticket," a musical that existed for less than two weeks at the Shubert, and "For Heaven's Sake, Mother," which staggered through a dismal fortnight at the Walnut.

New shows which had local tryout engagements after making their first bows elsewhere included such interesting offerings as "Life with Mother," "Light Up the Sky," "At War with the Army," "Two Blind Mice" and, possibly, "Set My People Free"; but in the same category—on the wrong side of the ledger—were "Make Way for Lucia," "Along Fifth Avenue" (which was under an extra handicap here due to the illness of the late Willie Howard, then the star), "Oh, Mr. Meadowbrook," "Smile of the World," "Shop at Sly Corner," "Leaf and Bough," "Figure of a Girl," "Biggest Thief in Town" and "Ivy Green."

Oddly enough, there were only six shows with Broadway reputations but new to this city that visited here during the season. They were "The Heiress," "For Love or Money," "Command Decision," "Allegro," "O Mistress Mine" and "Present Laughter." To this unprecedentedly small list might be added "The Play's the Thing" and "Man and Superman," which had been seen here in the past but not in their new revival togs. As a matter of fact, 1948-49 was also distinguished by the number of its revivals on local stages. In addition to the pair just mentioned, there were "Private Lives," "Diamond Lil" and "They Knew What They Wanted," all Broadway-bound, as well as "Escape Me Never," "Desert Song," and "The Cat and the Canary."

Returning theatrical visitors were also quite common and included the always-welcome "Brigadoon" and "Finian's Rainbow," "Born Yesterday," "High Button Shoes," "Make Mine Manhattan," "Oklahoma!", "Harvey," "Medea" and "Inside U. S. A." Properly listed as "special bookings" would be Blackstone, the magician, and engagements of Maurice Schwartz and Menasha Skulnik, Jewish stars, and a Jewish company in "Anna Lucasta."

The Locust Street Theatre, which for a couple of seasons had

THE SEASON IN PHILADELPHIA

the distressing record of housing more flops than any other local theatre, has had a much happier fate this year. Here it was that the memorable "Death of a Salesman" played two capacity weeks and here too were seen "Private Lives," "Light Up the Sky," "Born Yesterday" and "Detective Story," all of which fared very well. "At War with the Army," which was well received by local critics and playgoers, would probably have been graced by equally good attendance had it not been for the all-out transit strike. The biggest surprise and disappointment at the Locust was the complete failure of "The Play's the Thing" revival. Poor business here resulted in the immediate cancellation of its extensive tour.

The Shubert started out with two capacity weeks of "Brigadoon" (which still has enough vitality to stand a third local engagement of a month or six weeks), then skidded badly with "That's the Ticket," floundered through a fortnight of "Command Decision" by use of cut-rate tickets, and then had seventeen fine weeks divided between "Allegro," "Kiss Me, Kate" (which was solid capacity for most of its four weeks), "High Button Shoes," "Desert Song" and "Oklahoma!" Less fortunate was "Inside U. S. A.," which essayed a two weeks' return in March.

The Walnut—last season's lucky house with such hits as "Mister Roberts" and "A Streetcar Named Desire" to its credit—started out 1948-49 handsomely with "The Heiress," "Life with Mother" and "Man and Superman" in a row, but then encountered a flock of disappointments including "For Heaven's Sake, Mother," "Make Way for Lucia," "Oh, Mr. Meadowbrook," "Smile of the World," "Figure of a Girl," and "Biggest Thief in Town." The returning "Harvey" didn't do too well either, partly because of Joe E. Brown's illness here. Blackstone was his usual box-office magnet.

As for the Forrest, it had both sweet and bitter. "Where's Charley?" gave the house a sturdy start with three highly profitable weeks and the returning "Finian's Rainbow" also did well in two. However, "Set My People Free," although accredited an artistic success for the Guild, attracted few customers and, sad to relate, "Anne of the Thousand Days," although receiving "rave" notices from the local critics, did not fare at all well at the box office. In this respect it was one of the few deserving plays of the year that failed to win the concrete support it deserved. "Along Fifth Avenue" limped through three weeks, handicapped as mentioned by the tragic illness of Howard; Mae West's "Diamond Lil" was a flourishing holiday offering, "Leaf and Bough" laid a solid (and deserved) "egg." The "They Knew What They Wanted" revival was very much enjoyed here by the reviewers and the patrons, "Make Mine Manhattan" was a little disappointing on its return, "Two Blind Mice" drew on Melvyn Douglas' popularity, "Medea" got by nicely on return, "The Cat and the Canary" never got started, and "Present Laughter," with Edward Everett Horton in the role previously played by Noel Coward and Clifton Webb, wound the season up with dismal business despite fine notices and apparently friendly word-of-mouth.

Perhaps the paradoxical nature of the 1948-49 season and the extremity of its contrasts may be shown that while it was a comparatively simple matter to pick a "Ten Best" list ("Death of a Salesman," "Detective Story," "Kiss Me, Kate," "Anne of the Thousand Days," "The Heiress," "Light Up the Sky," "Life with Mother," "Command Decision," "Man and Superman" and "They Knew What They Wanted" naturally came to mind) it would have been next to impossible to choose a supplementary or "second ten" list. There just weren't another ten worthwhile offerings (except return engagements) on the charts.

THE SEASON IN CHICAGO

By Claudia Cassidy
Drama Critic of the *Chicago Tribune*

CHICAGO'S 1948-49 season broke to a fast start, tired in the middle, and fairly crawled down the stretch. It was a season when distinguished Chicago companies of "Mister Roberts" and "A Streetcar Named Desire" deserved and achieved the longest runs, when censorship reared its ugly head, and when Beatrice Lillie not only broke a tooth trying to escape a fire in her hotel suite, but got so haplessly snarled in a zipper that Mme. Lapis de Lazuli missed a rendezvous with the Messrs. Chopin, Liszt and Tschaikowsky on a memorable night "Inside U. S. A."

It was a season when the prized Harris Theatre was 12 weeks dark for lack of a booking; when its twin, the Selwyn, turned in desperation to the movies and had held "The Red Shoes" for 23 weeks at season's end, and when the little Civic, birthplace of "The Glass Menagerie," went over to television. It was a time when producers began to worry a little about Chicago, which was only fair, considering how long Chicago has worried about producers. Seeking the lodestar of our favor the hard way, they made serious inquiry, "What *does* Chicago want?", when all Chicago ever wanted is its share of the playgoer's dream: more good shows before they moult, and something better than the 16th row on the side.

A cockeyed optimist, Mary Martin or other vintage, could prove his point that in quality this season was better than last season. It still did not add up to a theatre season unless you are content to think of playgoing as an occasional pastime except when you go to New York on a binge of shows. For one rather bleak example, the three nights Miss Lillie was hospitalized by her misadventure in a smoke-filled room the only show in town was "Mister Roberts," and it had been around nine months or so.

Of our 37 shows this season (40 last season) the 18 plays stacked up far better than the 19 musicals—and that musical count is more imposing as a statistic than otherwise, for it includes a bedraggled season of Gilbert and Sullivan repertoire in which "Trial by Jury" was so uniquely cut as to have neither trial nor jury, and which enlivened each production with a pas de deux danced by Ballet Theatre's Nana Gollner and John Kriza.

Thirteen of the plays were new, and it was not an unlucky number. Not when it held Judith Anderson in "Medea," Paul Kelly in "Command Decision," and Basil Rathbone in "The Heiress" to augment the stunning impact of Uta Hagen's performance in "Streetcar" and a "Mister Roberts" so superbly spliced it survived not only the opening night breakdown of the Erlanger's brand new $125,000 air conditioning system, but the late season breakup of the cast when Richard Carlson and Murray Hamilton stepped out in favor of John Forsythe (who resembled a junior Henry Fonda in the title role) and Jackie Cooper.

"Mister Roberts" ran into a touch of censorship before it opened. By some quaint quirk of the police mind it was considered more decorous to say Ensign Pulver had "made life worth living" for certain young ladies than to cling to the text's "rendered pregnant." When next heard from, the censors had denied "The Respectful Prostitute" access to the Studebaker Theatre. This stirred such commotion in and out of the newspapers that Meg Mundy came to appear in a protest performance at the University of Chicago, and the play eventually was permitted to open at the Harris, with "Hope Is the Thing with Feathers" as its companion piece.

Both productions seemed to have been thrown together on the train—Nina Foch had the Mundy role—and the very critics who had fought the censorship wrote sharply disparaging reviews. I mention this because it was rather comically hailed in some quarters by people who apparently had thought you wouldn't mind censorship if it hit a play you didn't like.

The double bill never caught on at the box office, and it closed in three weeks in one of those octopus clouds of undercover controversy that only a deep-sea diver could hope to clear. The management insisted that both plays had been hounded by censorship, damaged by deletion, and finally closed on order. Both the police and Mayor Kennelly flatly denied the charges and suggested they might be a press agent's way to drum up some business. The management's moan that nobody bothered "Mr. Adam" was not to be denied. As far as I could tell, no one bothered that one, least of all customers.

Otherwise, not much happened in the play line. "The Winslow Boy" flourished briefly, "The Silver Whistle" was so bad here that Joshua Logan must have worked a miracle to make it a

New York hit, and I wish he could have done the same for Ruth Gordon's "The Leading Lady," which seemed to me considerably more deserving. F. Hugh Herbert made the paternal error of thinking Diana Herbert could replace June Lockhart in "For Love or Money," and Edward Everett Horton was a week's aberration in "Present Laughter." Frank Fay restored our faith in "Harvey," though not to the extent of explaining that Pulitzer prize. "Man and Superman" had skidded down the performance scale, and we had a Canadian troupe in "The Drunkard," fresh from Moose Jaw and Saskatoon.

To say that eight of our musicals were "new" is to send your eyebrows flying, for they included "Finian's Rainbow," "Brigadoon" and "Allegro," not to forget four hours the first night of "Funzapoppin" in which Olsen and Johnson dispensed refrigerators, sun lamps, heating pads—in fact, almost everything but entertainment—in a Chicago Stadium cut to a mere 18,500 capacity by nipping off one end for the stage.

Despite Bert Lahr, "Make Mine Manhattan" never caught on. "Raze the Roof" was a shoddy little horror with Jerry Lester, its "special songs and material" gravely attributed to one Snag Werris. "Angel in the Wings" either had cut its payroll past the bone, or had shown singularly bad judgment in replacements. "Annie Get Your Gun" shot itself full of holes by attempting to come back with Joan Edwards toting Mary Martin's gun, an error hastily remedied by rushing in Billie Worth, the understudy. "Inside U. S. A." had scarcely struck town when Valerie Bettis quit the cast (Olga Lunick, a mermaidish dancer, replaced her), but had you been at the Shubert opening night when Miss Lillie made her first Chicago entrance in 13 seasons your deafened ears would have told you this town was never trapped in that ancient enigma of choice—the Lady or the Tiger.

For the record, 249 weeks of playgoing in nine theatres in 1948-49, as compared to 265 in 1947-48, also in nine theatres, though not quite the same nine. The 1948-49 listing, compiled as of June 4:

Shubert: 51 weeks—"Show Boat," four weeks' holdover, 17 in all; "Annie Get Your Gun," 12 weeks' return engagement; "Brigadoon," 17; "Finian's Rainbow," 15; "Inside U. S. A," 3 to date.

Great Northern: 47 weeks—"High Button Shoes," 30 weeks' holdover, 32 in all; "Man and Superman," 3; "Raze the Roof," 6; "Make Mine Manhattan," 2; "Allegro," 6.

Erlanger: 42 weeks—"Oklahoma!", 3 weeks' return engagement; "Mister Roberts," 39 to date.

Harris: 41 weeks—"John Loves Mary," 15 weeks' holdover, 31 in all; "A Streetcar Named Desire," 23; "The Respectful Prostitute" and "Hope Is the Thing with Feathers," 3.

Blackstone: 28 weeks—"Angel in the Wings," 3; "The Silver Whistle," 3; "Medea," 8; "Harvey," 5 weeks' return engagement; "The Desert Song," 3; "Mr. Adam," 5; "Present Laughter," 1.

Selwyn: 18 weeks—"On Approval," 1; "For Love or Money," 4; "The Leading Lady," 2; "The Winslow Boy," 3; "The Heiress," 8.

Studebaker: 16 weeks—"Blossom Time," 2 weeks' holdover, 3 in all; "Command Decision," 7; Dante the magician in "Foolies of 1949," 5; "The Drunkard," 2.

Civic Opera House: 3 weeks—Breden-Savoy Gilbert and Sullivan company in repertoire of "The Mikado," "The Pirates of Penzance," "Pinafore," "Patience" and "Trial by Jury."

Chicago Stadium: 3 weeks—Olsen and Johnson in "Funzapoppin."

THE SEASON IN SAN FRANCISCO

By Fred Johnson
Drama Editor of the San Francisco *Call-Bulletin*

THE statistician of a theatrical town of somewhat lowered standing faces his chore with a little more of hope than of pride. Even this hopefulness—of more if not better things to come—is currently reduced by the temerity of managers in venturing too frequently with their wares to this far outpost, once the mecca of touring companies nearing a hundred within the year. The score for this past twelve months has been an even dozen.

Most of these were late-season and most welcome arrivals, following a depressed state of mind among theatregoers through a period of doldrums, little encouraged by a quartet of West Coast productions. These met with a fate which has become far too common. For too common as well have been the merits of these offerings from Los Angeles and Hollywood, which came even more numerously in the lush war years of a fast dollar at the box office.

Rather than tryouts in the city of their production origin, they were lured by the tradition of San Francisco as "a good show town," unmindful that GOOD SHOW demanded its capital letters in a legend so familiar since the Gold Rush days, whose centennial this year is being celebrated in California.

Something in contrast has long been in the mind of Gilbert Miller, who was arriving in San Francisco as this was written, with hope extended for the support by the American National Theatre and Academy in founding a permanent and professional theatre of civic sponsorship.

This project had been under survey by researchers and zealots of the San Francisco Theatre Association for three years, lacking only a sound organizational and financial backing.

Miller has had a sentimental eye on the city's theatrical scene ever since the 1920s, when his father, Henry, made it his Summer tryout point for Broadway-bound productions.

Naturally, no fair prospect could be envisioned for him by the city's two legitimate theatres' owners, one of whom had just broken bread with the San Francisco Critics Council. The aisle observers were impressed—and a little surprised—by the showman's report on the slim pickings of his firm, even from touring shows understood to be safely in the hit category.

This was taken to be a reasonable explanation of the managements' inability to refurbish their adjoining theatres, the Curran and Geary, now the sole housing for touring attractions. The Tivoli, a former home of Tetrazzini operas and musical comedy, has of late been devoted to a one-hour vaudeville show with screen program accompaniment.

The better to dispose of hapless Coast-production ventures and get on to pleasanter affairs: There was the impertinence called "April Fool," by Norman Krasna and Groucho Marx, starring Otto Kruger. First undergoing critical disesteem and then rewriting in the course of its forced three weeks' stay, its Broadway finish in one third that time became more generally known. (The play came to Broadway under the title of "Time for Elizabeth." —Ed.)

A shorter local existence was given "One Fine Day," Hugh White's domestic comedy, starring Charlie Ruggles and Mary Boland. And even more disdain was met by "Mr. Adam," Jack Kirkland's adaptation of the Pat Frank novel about atom-bomb sterilization. With a cast headed by Hollywood's Frank Albertson and Elisabeth Fraser, its subsequent fate in the final week of Broadway's season is recorded elsewhere in this volume.

What may have been a record musical flop was the mysterious Manhattan Light Opera Company's "The Blue Danube," based on Johann Strauss music, with book and lyrics by Ambrose Barker and Ralph Paonessa. Devised mainly as a vehicle for soprano Milizia Korjus, with comedy by vaudeville's Shaw and Lee, its starvation period was one week.

George White was more successful in launching here, in his show business re-entry, a "Varieties" exhibit headed by Lou Holtz, Composer Joe Howard and Buck and Bubbles, scoring three weeks' fair business. And at the same starting point, but to greater acclaim, Paul Small resumed his vaudeville ventures with "Ed Wynn's Laugh Carnival," starring, of course, "The Perfect Fool." Accompanying him were Phil Baker, Sid Silvers, Allan Jones and Pat Rooney, Sr. The entertainment did well for a full month.

In the city of their "Amphitryon 38" premiere, Alfred Lunt and Lynn Fontanne made another pre-Broadway offering of their new S. N. Behrman play, "I Know My Love," adapted from Marcel Achard's "Aupres de Ma Blonde." Playing as always to capacity audiences, the Lunts were seen here for the first time in roles spanning a good many years. Their versatility impressed to the same extent that their vehicle puzzled in the turning back of their years in the manner of movie flashbacks.

At Los Angeles, midway in their Spring tour, Behrman had appeared with a change in the retrogression after the curtain's rise on the stars as octogenarians in 1939. Rather than making a steady course backward, the periods were switched abruptly to 1888 and then forward to a final scene in 1920, in the interest of more forceful climax.

Both Behrman and the Theatre Guild's Lawrence Langner were observers of San Francisco's reaction to the zigzagging process. Not that it seemed to matter—while the Lunts were on stage.

The San Francisco-Los Angeles Civic Light Opera Association's production of "Magdalena" played to capacity houses for four weeks and was voted by the Critics Council the best musical of the year to be seen locally, a salute in disagreement generally with the New York commentators. Its Villa-Lobos music and its dancing were specially commended, despite the melodies' minor appeal to the popular taste.

The Light Opera's 1948 and ninth season included "Naughty Marietta," with Susanna Foster; "Annie Get Your Gun," starring Mary Martin, and "Sweethearts," with Bobby Clark. Opening the current season in April was Edwin Lester's elaborate revival of "The Great Waltz," starring Walter Slezak, Dorothy Sarnoff, Melva Niles and Charles Fredericks. It was to be followed by "Brigadoon," a new company in "Kiss Me, Kate" and "High Button Shoes," with Eddie Foy—the first season in which more than one Broadway musical success had been programmed.

"Carousel" and "Allegro" were musicals rewarded with a month's run each. And Olsen and Johnson made their first San Francisco appearance in "Hellzapoppin," playing to capacity in a first engagement, but to dwindling profits in the second. Tallulah Bankhead in "Private Lives" scored the season's longest run with five weeks; Maurice Evans, a San Francisco favorite, starred for three in "Man and Superman," the same tenure awarded Basil Rathbone in "The Heiress," and Frank Fay brought "Harvey" to the city of his birth for the first time as the season closed, according to Broadway reckoning.

"The Winslow Boy" had played to disappointing business, while that of "Lady Windermere's Fan," in a return engagement, was only fair. Judith Anderson's patronage in "Medea" built from the first three performances, extending to three weeks, a period which could have been doubled. "Born Yesterday," with Jean Parker and Lon Chaney, held on well for a month and Ethel Waters registered neatly in her one-woman show.

The year's special attraction was a Hollywood Masquers Club revival of "What Price Glory," with such stars as Gregory Peck, John Wayne, Maureen O'Hara, Pat O'Brien and Ward Bond, many of whom appeared in minor roles. The Opera House engagement was a benefit for the Military Order of the Purple Heart.

The San Francisco Municipal Theatre, sponsored by the Board of Education, gained in importance with its productions of "Androcles and the Lion," "All My Sons" and "The Druid Circle." Theatre Arts Colony, an older project, continued active.

The University of California's Department of Dramatic Art carried on with increased importance, but still without an adequate theatre. Ingenuity is a phase of its productions on a postage stamp platform in Wheeler Hall on the Berkeley campus. The season, ended with performances of "The Double Dealer," had included "All My Sons," Gilbert Murray's adaptation of Menander's "The Arbitration," Ibsen's "Little Eyolf," "The Hasty Heart," "King Oedipus" in the W. B. Yeats version, "Arms and the Man" and "The Sultan of Sulu."

Stanford University's Department of Speech and Drama, with its two modern theatres operating under the name of Stanford Players, continued its guest star productions with "The Rivals," featuring Aline MacMahon, Clarence Derwent and Whitford Kane. A presentation of Daudet's "L'Arlésienne," a French masterpiece known in this country only by its musical score, was acted by Derwent, Miss MacMahon, Theodore Marcuse and a student cast.

Another special production, with Hollywood's Jane Darwell featured, was "Build No Fence Around Me," a new play by Alexander Greendale," a Stanford student on a writing fellowship. The season closed with Jaromir Weinberger's romantic folk opera, "Shvanda, the Bagpiper," its four campus performances followed by one in San Francisco's Memorial Opera House. This was a repetition of last year's experiment when "Peter Grimes" was given a metropolitan showing.

The regular subscription season included "Othello," Van Brough's "The Relapse," "The Return of Peter Grimm" and "Shvanda." The studio theatre, operated by graduate students, presented "Of Mice and Men," "Antigone," "The Hairy Ape" and "The Petrified Forest."

THE SEASON IN SOUTHERN CALIFORNIA
By Edwin Schallert
Drama Editor of the *Los Angeles Times*

THE theatre in Southern California fought a valiant battle against the recession which hit the show business generally during the 1948-49 season. It is surprising how much progress may be recorded for the year which ended June 1st. In musical productions Los Angeles gained. Summer theatres were unusually active in 1948, though prospects seemed less bright for 1949. A new manifestation was Winter resort theatres in tributary areas like Arizona and Nevada. Southern California creativeness in the theatre was more manifest. Community and little playhouses were especially enterprising. Circle Players took over the Coronet Theatre. Eugenie Leontovich and Rita Glover, converting an industrial establishment into a unique playhouse, set a new standard with their project called The Stage.

Pasadena Playhouse gave noteworthy presentations with professional stars like Jane Cowl and Lenore Ulric, as well as attempting the mammoth undertaking of bringing Percy Mackaye's tetralogy, "The Mystery of Hamlet, King of Denmark," to the public. The New York Theatre Guild intensified its sponsorship of road attractions and Coast productions.

It could hardly be called a year of big money-making because audience reception was erratic, but ambition ran rampant in new promotions and efforts.

Good musical shows were soundly profitable. Edwin Lester of the Los Angeles Civil Light Opera Association anticipated a greater gross revenue for his 1949 productions than in 1948, which topped any previous year. He made this prediction just about the time the later season opened, on the strength of an advance sale that exceeded $400,000.

"Lend an Ear," as presented by William Eythe at Las Palmas Theatre, ran seven months, with a replacement company during the later weeks. It afterward made New York history for the season. "Annie Get Your Gun," with Mary Martin, which opened the 1948 Civic Light Opera series, was a persistent sell-out. "Magdalena," notwithstanding it suffered plenty of criticism for its book, was a major attraction. "The Naughty Marietta" with Susanna Foster, Wilbur Evans and Edward Everett Horton, was lavish and successful. "Sweethearts," with Bobby Clark starred and featuring Marjorie Gateson, June Knight and others, scored less of a hit.

"Carousel" and "Allegro" as Theatre Guild offerings were popular champions. Stephen Douglass, Iva Withers, Margot Moser, Jane McGowan, Mario De Laval and Eric Mattson were in the "Carousel" cast; Roberta Jonay, James Jewell, William Chimp, Annamary Dickey, Muriel O'Malley and others were in "Allegro." Their well-attended engagements were limited.

The Greek Theatre in its Summer open-air setting succeeded in giving musical shows a new gloss, as does the Civic Light Opera Association. High examples were "Anything Goes" with Gertrude Niesen, Johnnie Johnston, Buster West, Gloria Lind, Arthur Gould-Porter and Dorothy Dare, and the final "Student Prince," with Jane Powell, borrowed from the Metro-Goldwyn-Mayer studio, Felix Knight, Alan Mowbray, Paul Keast, Isabel Randolph and Lynne Lyons. The closing performance became one of those legendary sentimental triumphs, with Miss Powell singing her heart out to the audience.

"Lend an Ear" set such a pace for musical revues that it was bound to have successors. These were all promised as the equal of or better than the pioneer. None lived up to that expectation. "Tongue in Cheek," as presented by Ross Hunter and Jacque Mapes, which ran about six or seven weeks; "Music Sends Me" at the Highland Playhouse; "Out of Order," which came in for two weeks from San Francisco, following "Lend an Ear" and preceding "Tongue in Cheek" at Las Palmas, were among the entrants. "Tongue in Cheek" had merit, and "Music Sends Me" enjoyed a fair run.

Most promising was the Eugenie Leontovich presentation of "Marie Antoinette in Pennsylvania," a musical play by Eugene Berton and James Snodgrass, at The Stage, where it was still being played at the close of the 1948-49 season. It told a naive story of the arrival of a carnival performer in a Shaker community, who was mistaken for the fugitive French monarch.

While the impression made by the show was in many respects delightful, work was being done on the book to make it more logical and acceptable during the engagement. Miss Leontovich was apparently an inspiration to her company, for the work of such principals as Theodora Lynch, Queenie Smith, Olin Howlin, Shirley O. Mills, Mitchell Brother, Nelson Barclift and others engraved their names in the permanent record of theatrical activities.

Light opera revivals included the Rodgers and Hammerstein production of "Show Boat," which toured in with Billy House, Pamela Caveness, Norwood Smith, Sammy White, Terry Saunders, William C. Smith and Ruth Gates; "The Desert Song" with Edward Roecker, Gale Sherwood and Jack Good, which visited Pasadena; "The Blue Danube" with Miliza Korjus, Fortunio Bonanova and Paul Keast (music by Johann Strauss), which fared badly; "Oklahoma!" which closed a run early in the season. "The Merry Widow" starring Anne Jeffreys, with Roger Dann, Frances McCann and Raymond Walburn; "The Vagabond King," with Dorothy Sandlin and Lawrence Brooks, Lionel Stander and Ian Keith; "Music in the Air" with Polyna Stoska, Charles Fredricks and Jan Clayton were given during the Summer of 1948 at the Greek Theatre. "The Great Waltz," much revised, with Walter Slezak, Dorothy Sarnoff, Melva Niles, Charles Fredricks, Sig Arno, Eric Brotherson, Mitzi Gerber, Ralph Morgan, Leon Belasco, Fred Essler and George Zorich brilliantly inaugurated the 1949 Los Angeles Civic Light Opera season.

In addition to all this a San Gabriel Valley Festival was instituted at the Mission Playhouse, traditional home of John S. McGroarty's "The Mission Play," with repertoire including "The Merry Widow," "The Naughty Marietta," "New Moon," "The Desert Song" and "Good News." Full destiny of this venture was still to be determined at time of writing. With all this music show and light opera activity, Los Angeles should be designated as a new Vienna.

In the dramatic sphere, highly professional, the new vied with the established in attractions. Alfred Lunt and Lynn Fontanne brought "I Know My Love," by S. N. Behrman, from "Aupres de Ma Blonde" by Marcel Achard, to Southern California as part of their tryout campaign. It is one of their most ingenious strategies to prove how fabulously young they both can look on the stage. It goes into a reverse that rivals "Death of a Salesman," "Lady in the Dark," "The Wisdom Tooth" or "Merrily We Roll Along." It needed doctoring in the midsection when the couple are in their maturity, but was not uninteresting at the outset because of their very aged characterizations, nor at the close of the play when they both bloomed youthfully. Considerable of the Behrman writing as witnessed in Los Angeles was on the dull side. Geoffrey Kerr, Anne Sargent, Betty Caulfield, Lilian

Kemble-Cooper, Katherine Bard, Noel Leslie and others were in the company.

Great in memory, even though it was early in the theatrical pageant, is "Medea," by Robinson Jeffers and with Judith Anderson. She proved herself a superwoman of the stage in this dynamic adaptation of a Euripidean tragedy. Guthrie McClintic came west to supervise Miss Anderson's return to her role, while Hilda Vaughn, Frederick Worlock, Henry Brandon and Mary Servoss were included in the surrounding cast.

Another star triumph was won later in the season by Maurice Evans in the differently exacting "Man and Superman," by George Bernard Shaw. The star was aided by Frances Rowe as Ann Whitfield, Josephine Brown, Malcolm Keen, Chester Stratton, Nan McFarland, Victor Sutherland and others. He played a short but effective engagement at the Biltmore.

Better productions, brought more or less intact from New York, were "The Winslow Boy" with Alan Webb, Valerie White and Frank Allenby, fine acting distinguishing the Terence Rattigan play throughout, and "The Heiress" by Ruth and Augustus Goetz, with Basil Rathbone, Beatrice Straight and Patricia Collinge. Due for presentation just after the close of the season was "Harvey," with Frank Fay. Los Angeles saw "Private Lives" with Tallulah Bankhead and Donald Cook prior to its New York staging, and was impressed with the fact that Miss Bankhead had a field day in the show. The Noel Coward comedy was pretty faded apart from that.

Theatre Guild sponsored "I Know My Love," "The Winslow Boy," "The Heiress," and "Private Lives," in addition to the musicals, "Carousel" and "Allegro," practically all with good box-office results. Disappointment attended the Coast endeavors of Russell Lewis and Howard Young, in conjunction with the Guild, in staging such plays as "April Fool" with Otto Kruger and Katherine Alexander and "Happy Birthday" with Miriam Hopkins starred. "April Fool," by Norman Krasna and Groucho Marx, failed later as "Time for Elizabeth" in New York. "Happy Birthday," by Anita Loos, doubtless missed Helen Hayes, though Miss Hopkins is well known for her skill as an actress. The play seemed hopelessly weak. Enid Markey, Philip Faversham and Margaret Irving were in the Coast cast.

As might be anticipated, "Born Yesterday" qualified as a hit with Jean Parker and Lon Chaney starred. "Burlesque," with Bert Lahr and Rochelle Hudson, did rather poorly. "One Fine Day," by Hugh White, with Charles Ruggles and Mary Boland, practically died abornin'. The stars did their utmost for the impossibly old-hat play.

"All My Sons" wound up a successful engagement early in the season at Las Palmas Theatre. Eugenie Leontovich inaugurated her stagings with "And So to Bed," in which she herself appeared as Mrs. Pepys. Donald Porter as the peripatetic Samuel, Alan Napier as Charles II, Theodore Lynch as the monarch's inamorata and Eric Sinclair were included in the excellent cast, and the presentation in the small theatre ran about three months.

"Rain," starring June Havoc, with William Schallert as the Rev. Davidson, was the Circle Theatre's best central-staging effort, yielding a 12 weeks' run. Patricia Englund, from the British "Oklahoma!" company, replaced Miss Havoc in the final two weeks. The organization made a preliminary entry into the Coronet Theatre with "The Adding Machine," featuring Joe Mantell and Naomi Stevens, and after regularly leasing this showhouse tried a much-excised "Caligula" by Albert Camus, with James Anderson, brother of Mary Anderson, as the title character. It came off poorly. The organization was preparing a revised version of "Anna Lucasta" for staging with Lois Andrews in the title role, and Shaw's "Major Barbara" with Diana Douglas and Ron Randell, as the season closed. Under its sponsorship Helen Craig, John Beal and Colin Keith-Johnston did noteworthy duty by "Antigone," the Jean Anouilh play.

"Eurydice," early in the season at the Coronet, also exampled the work of Anouilh, though less satisfactorily. Its cast included Viveca Lindfors, Christian Kelleen and John Beal, who were directed by Mel Ferrer, the vitalizing force in La Jolla's Summer theatre. Melville Cooper brightened this rather tedious, though not entirely uninteresting, play.

Francis Lederer, last seen as an apostle of Ibsen in "The Doll's House," evidenced his adherence to the Norwegian dramatist again during the season in a revival of "Ghosts" at El Patio Theatre, with Isobel Elsom, George Zucco, Leonid Kinskey and Elisabeth Fraser in the company. "The Survivors," by Irwin Shaw and Peter Viertel, with Albert Dekker, Jeff Corey, Peter Brocco, Leo Penn, Houseley Stevenson, Olive Deering, James Anderson, Ellen Corby. Dekker, Penn and Stevenson were credited with especially good performances.

"Café Crown" had an enjoyable Los Angeles production with Hugo Haas and Ludwig Donath heading the unusually capable cast. "Separate Rooms" had a lengthy run with Ann Corio featured for a short time. Circle Players, with John Crawford, a young actor, featured, proved "A Doctor in Spite of Himself" could be a romp in central staging.

Jane Cowl, who is to become a cinema personality because of several picture deals in rapid succession, twice figured in the Southern California stage scene, first at La Jolla in "The First Mrs. Fraser," in which she appeared while still hospitalized due to a traffic accident, and then in Maxwell Anderson's "Elizabeth the Queen" staged at the Pasadena Playhouse. Blevins Davis brought the latter to the public as an American National Theatre Association enterprise. The opening was not too auspicious, though Miss Cowl's appearance evoked enthusiasm throughout the short engagement. "The Bunner Sisters," De Witt Bodeen adaptation of an Edith Wharton novel, with Lenore Ulric and Sally O'Neil cast as unhappy sisters trying to eke out a living, had less appeal. Both were striking experiments with professional stars.

"The Mystery of Hamlet, King of Denmark," Percy Mackaye's tetralogy, remained a mystery to even the comparatively small audiences which it drew. The Mackaye place in American letters was established many years ago, though he has not been represented in later times on the American stage. His sequence of plays includes "The Ghost of Elsinore," "The Fool in Eden Garden," "Odin Versus Christus" and "The Serpent in the Orchard." The final play weaves into the first act of Shakespeare's "Hamlet," which comes somewhat like the dawn after a troubled nightmarish experience. Here at least, the poetry seemed clear and understandable. Literary values appeared to come and go in the undramatical continuity, which concerned various manifestations of the perfidy of Claudius prior to Shakespeare's "Hamlet," activities of ghosts around Elsinore, and apparent sociological parallels drawn out of the past.

Probably Mackaye's writing reads better than it acts. The performers were not too successful in interpreting what he had to say, though the task which confronted them must have been baffling. Onslow Stevens as Claudius, Charlotte Fletcher as Gertrude, Frank Sundstrom as King Hamlet, father of the Prince of Denmark, George Phelps as Yorick, Robert Ben Ali as Polonius and John Baer as the young prince, did the most to convey the text, not all being uniformly successful. Pasadena Playhouse merits unlimited credit for its courage in attempting what few other institutions would assume to undertake.

The Playhouse dedicated its Summer festival (1948) to the so-called Gold Coast plays, like "Lady of Lyons," "The Honeymoon," "The Marble Heart," "London Assurance," "Damon and Pythias," "Fanchon, the Cricket," "Fashion" and "Camille," which date back to the last century. During the regular season, apart from productions already mentioned, the repertoire included "Dark of the Moon," "The Winslow Boy," "I Remember Mama," "The Shop at Sly Corner," "Command Decision," "Antigone," "Dream Girl," "The Constant Wife," "The Road to Rome," "An Inspector Calls," Zoe Akins' new "Castle on the Sand," which missed of full approval; "The Glass Menagerie," "Life with Father," "Three Men on a Horse" and "Gentleman from Athens." Tested just as the beginning of the season, besides the Akins play, was "This Young World," by Judith Kandel, directed by Arthur Lubin, and played by juveniles. The play was, at least, interesting in reflecting strained and turbulent conditions of today as they seem to affect a group of youngsters. Darryl Hickman was among those appearing.

Sociological issues—that is, those in Germany—were dealt with in "The Glass Pool," by Henrietta Buckmaster and Peter John Stephens, with Whit Bissell, William Challee, Jark Dennis, George Zucco, Lisa Golm, Luis Van Rooten and Alan Hale, Jr., presented at the Coronet.

An account of Summer theatres might go on indefinitely. They operated in 1948 in La Jolla, Laguna Beach, Santa Barbara, Newport Beach, Tustin and elsewhere, drawing a large complement of Hollywood actors. A high point was believed to have been reached in the staging of "The Glass Menagerie" at La Jolla with Ann Harding, Richard Basehart, Betsy Blair and John Ireland. Sylvia Sidney did an unusual interpretation in "Kind Lady" to begin the season, and Jennifer Jones climaxed it in "Serena Blandish" with Constance Collier importantly assigned.

Ann Lee and Richard Charlton, with their Sombrero Theatre in Phoenix during the Winter and a showhouse in Santa Fe, N. M., during the Summer, are attracting Hollywood personalities inland. They had William Bendix and Audrey Totter in "Born Yesterday" to open their Phoenix season. Tucson and Las Vegas (Nev.) resort theatres both boasted film names.

"The Drunkard" in its 16th year at the Theatre Mart, Puppets and live revue in their eighth year at the Turnabout, and Ken Murray's "Blackouts" in its seventh season remained features of the 1948-49 period. The Pilgrimage Play celebrated its 21st anniversary, and similarly long-lived is the "Ramona" pageant play given every Spring. Earl Carroll's "Vanities" pursued its way with Pinky Lee as comedy star. The death of the famous musical showman in an airplane accident was recorded. George White's "Scandals" in revival was about the last event at Florentine Gardens, which ceased as a theatre restaurant.

The Century Theatre and an elaborate new theatre project in Beverly Hills seem to have important film colony backing. Little Theatres and showcases like the Call Board, Actors Lab, Bliss-Hayden, Geller, Jewel Box and others, keep the wheels humming. Of plays produced, "All You Need Is One Good Break," by Arnold Manoff, in which John Berry appeared, will probably reach New York. "You Twinkle Only Once," by Aben Kandel, which featured Nancy Kelly, Robert Armstrong, Alan Nixon and others at Laguna in 1948, showed some promise, and a number of shows in smaller theatres may develop Broadway values with proper polishing.

Space does not permit the coverage of each and every activity. It has reached a point where lurking endeavors have become a veritable epidemic, even though comparatively few reach the better realization. However, Southern California is today satisfied that it is the crucible for a multitude of theatrical aspirations.

Noteworthy was "What Price Glory?" staged as a Purple Heart benefit by John Ford, film director, on a fleeting California tour with Ward Bond as Captain Flagg, Pat O'Brien as Sergeant Quirt, Maureen O'Hara as Charmaine, and Gregory Peck, John Wayne, Charles Kemper, William Lundigan, Wallace Ford and other Hollywood "names" in supporting roles. Henry Hull tried out "George Worthing, American" by Jules Eckert Goodman as a play with some appeal. GIs appeared in "Now Is the Winter" by John O'Dea after testing the play at the Actors Lab. "Love in Upper Sandusky" by Edward Emerson and Charles Williams, with Lyle Talbot and Louise Arthur, had some merit as a farce-comedy. And the list still rambles on.

DEATH OF A SALESMAN *
A Play in Two Acts
By Arthur Miller

ARTHUR MILLER is by no means the first dramatist who believes that tragedy—tragedy in its complete and classic sense, and not merely something with an unhappy ending—can be written about the modern common man as well as about such rather special characters as Lear, Hamlet, Oedipus and Joan of Arc. But Mr. Miller is one of the dramatists who has demonstrated his belief by writing a tragedy concerning a very common common man—a salesman who lives in Brooklyn.

Mr. Miller is somewhat impatient with the widespread impression that a tragedy is merely a play with an unhappy ending. To him, it is what leads up to the ending that makes a tragedy. In the *New York Times* he wrote, after his "Death of a Salesman" had opened, "The tragic feeling is evoked in us when we are in the presence of a character who is ready to lay down his life, if need be, to secure one thing—his sense of personal dignity." To him, also, tragedy implies more optimism on the part of an author than it does pessimism—more, even, than comedy implies. "For," wrote Mr. Miller, "if it is true to say that in essence the tragic hero is intent upon claiming his whole due as a personality, and if this struggle must be total and without reservation, then it automatically demonstrates the indestructible will of man to achieve his humanity. . . . In tragedies, and in them alone, lies the belief—optimistic if you will—in the perfectibility of man."

Mr. Miller's Brooklyn salesman, Willy Loman, who seeks in the play to secure his sense of personal dignity, is, along with the other characters in the play, described as fictional by the author. "However," writes the author to this editor, "it is obvious that I write out of life as I know it, rather than construct plays out of a theatrical imagination, as it were. The remem-

---

* Copyright, 1949, by Arthur Miller.
Published by the Viking Press, New York.
Published in Canada by the Macmillan Company of Canada.
Author's agent, MCA Management, 444 Madison Avenue, New York City 22.

bered thing about 'Salesman' is really the basic situation in which these people find themselves—a situation which I have seen repeated throughout my life. If Willy Loman could be taken apart, I suppose five or six salesmen I have met would be found in him. The play is really a recollection of a destiny that has oppressed me since youth."

The setting is the Salesman's house. Once it was part of a neighborhood of houses, but now it is surrounded by the towering, angular shapes of apartment buildings. An air of the dream clings to the place—a dream rising out of reality. The kitchen, at center, seems real enough, for there are a table, chairs and a refrigerator—but no other fixtures are seen. At the back of the kitchen is a draped entrance leading to the living room. To the right, up a couple of steps, is the ground-floor bedroom occupied by Willy Loman and his wife; it has only a brass bedstead and a straight chair, and a shelf over the bed holding a silver athletic trophy. Behind and above the kitchen, on the second floor, is the boys' bedroom, with two beds.

The setting is wholly for, in some places, partly transparent. The roof-line of the house is one-dimensional, like a line drawing; under or over it one can see the oppressive apartment buildings. In front of the house is an apron extending into the orchestra which serves two purposes. It is, at some moments, the back yard of Willy's home, and at others the various locales of Willy's imaginings. Whenever the action is in the present, the actors respect the imaginary "fourth wall" of the theatre and come in and out of the house through its door; but in the scenes of the past this fourth wall vanishes and characters may enter or leave a room by stepping "through" the wall into the back yard or wherever they may be going.

A melody is heard, played upon a flute, "telling of grass and green trees and the horizon." (The music for the play was composed by Alex North.) Willy Loman, the salesman, comes home, unlocking the front door and going into the kitchen. He is past sixty, quietly dressed, carrying two large sample cases; and he is quite obviously exhausted. He lugs the cases into the living room, and in the bedroom Linda, his wife, stirs from her sleep, listens, gets out of bed and puts on a robe.

Linda, who once was jovial, has developed an iron repression of her feelings as to Willy's behavior; for she more than loves him. She admires him, as though his mercurial nature, his temper, his massive dreams and little cruelties, have served her only as sharp reminders of the turbulent longings within him.

DEATH OF A SALESMAN 55

Linda is surprised that Willy has so suddenly come home at night like this. Something must have happened, and she calls from the bedroom, "You didn't smash the car, did you?"

Willy calls back, a little irritated, that nothing happened. He is just tired to death. He comes into the bedroom and sits on the bed beside her, a little numb. The music of the flute fades away as Willy sighs, "I just couldn't make it, Linda."

Very carefully and delicately his wife asks him where he has been all day. He does look terrible.

"I got as far as a little above Yonkers. I suddenly couldn't drive any more. The car kept going off onto the shoulder. . . ."

Linda tries to be helpful and cheerful. Maybe it was the Studebaker's fault, and the steering has gone wrong again.

"No, it's me," says Willy. "Suddenly I realize I'm goin' sixty miles an hour and I don't remember the last five minutes." So Willy has turned around and crawled back to Brooklyn at ten miles per hour, and it took him four hours. Linda insists that he must take a rest, but he points out that he just came back from Florida. Linda points out, "But you didn't rest your mind."

WILLY (*with wonder*)—I was driving along, you understand? And I was fine. I was even observing the scenery. You can imagine, me looking at scenery, on the road every week of my life. But it's so beautiful up there, Linda, the trees are so thick, and the sun is warm. I opened the windshield and just let the warm air bathe over me. And then all of a sudden I'm goin' off the road! I'm tellin' ya, I absolutely forgot I was driving. If I'd've gone the other way over the white line I might've killed somebody. So I went on again—and five minutes later I'm dreamin' again, and I nearly— (*He presses two fingers against his eyes.*) I have such thoughts, I have such strange thoughts.

LINDA—Willy, dear. Talk to them again. There's no reason why you can't work in New York.

WILLY—They don't need me in New York. I'm the New England man. I'm vital in New England.

LINDA—But you're sixty years old. They can't expect you to keep traveling every week.

WILLY—I'll have to send a wire to Portland. I'm supposed to see Brown and Morrison tomorrow morning at ten o'clock to show the line. Goddammit, I could sell them! (*He starts putting on his jacket.*)

LINDA (*taking the jacket from him*)—Why don't you go down

to the place tomorrow and tell Howard you've simply got to work in New York? You're too accommodating, dear.

WILLY—If old man Wagner was alive, I'd a been in charge of New York now! That man was a prince, he was a masterful man. But that boy of his, that Howard, he don't appreciate. When I went north the first time, the Wagner Company didn't know where New England was!

LINDA—Why don't you tell those things to Howard, dear?

WILLY (*encouraged*)—I will, I definitely will. Is there any cheese?

LINDA—I'll make you a sandwich.

WILLY—No, go to sleep. I'll take some milk. I'll be up right away. The boys in?

LINDA—They're sleeping. Happy took Biff on a date tonight.

WILLY (*interested*)—That so?

LINDA—It was so nice to see them shaving together, one behind the other, in the bathroom. And going out together. You notice? The whole house smells of shaving lotion.

WILLY—Figure it out. Work a lifetime to pay off a house. You finally own it, and there's nobody to live in it.

LINDA—Well, dear, life is a casting off. It's always that way.

WILLY—No, no, some people—some people accomplish something. Did Biff say anything after I went this morning?

LINDA—You shouldn't have criticized him, Willy, especially after he just got off the train. You mustn't lose your temper with him.

WILLY—When the hell did I lose my temper? I simply asked him if he was making any money. Is that a criticism?

LINDA—But, dear, how could he make any money?

WILLY (*worried and angered*)—There's such an undercurrent in him. He became a moody man. Did he apologize when I left this morning?

LINDA—He was crestfallen, Willy. You know how he admires you. I think if he finds himself, then you'll both be happier and not fight any more.

Querulously, Willy asks how Biff could be finding himself on a farm; in the beginning, when the boy was young, it was good for him to tramp around and take different jobs—but it's more than ten years now and Biff has yet to make $35 a week.

"The trouble is he's lazy, goddammit!"

Linda quiets her husband and suggests that he go into the kitchen and get something to eat, but Willy is still upset about his elder son. He takes back what he said about Biff being lazy, and reassures himself that the boy is a hard worker and has such personal attractiveness. He resolves to see him in the morning and have a nice talk and get him a job selling. "He could be big in no time. My God! Remember how they used to follow him around in high school? . . ."

Willy loses himself in reminiscence and Linda tries to snap him out of it by reminding him of food. She has bought him a new type of whipped American cheese. Willy snaps out of his reminiscent mood long enough to inquire testily why she got American when she knows he likes Swiss. He feels stifled, with the house boxed in, no air, no grass any more, and the elm trees gone, just on account of apartment buildings. Population is getting out of control and ruining the country.

His voice has risen, and the boys, Biff and Happy, are awakened in their upstairs bedroom. The lights come up on their room as Linda urges Willy into the kitchen to get himself a snack. She tries to buck him up. He's got too much on the ball to be worrying about anything—and if it's warm on Sunday they will all drive into the country with the windshield open, and take a lunch along.

"The windshields don't open on the new cars," Willy points out.

"But you opened it today."

Willy becomes amazed and frightened, as the flute music begins in the distance. He remembers how, that when he was driving in Yonkers he thought he was driving the Chevvy, and they had the Chevvy in 1928. "Remember those days? The way Biff used to simonize that car?"

Willy leaves Linda and goes to the kitchen. The boys are fully awake now and listening, and Happy asks Biff, "Jesus, maybe he smashed up the car again!"

The scene in the kitchen dims out, with Willy muttering something, and the boys' bedroom becomes more apparent. Happy tells Biff he's getting worried about his father's driving. He sees perfectly well, says Happy, but doesn't keep his mind on it. Biff, not too sympathetic, would like to roll over and go to sleep again.

Happy asks, anxiously, "You're not still sour on Dad, are you, Biff?"

"He's all right, I guess."

Below, their father is talking about the Chevvy and the eighty thousand miles it racked up, and what a simonizing job it had. In the bedroom, Happy is frankly glad to have his big brother back again, in the same old room where they used to talk everything over—including girls. With a deep, masculine laugh he comments, "About five hundred women would like to know what was said in this room." They talk about women, and Biff remembers how bashful Happy used to be. But Biff hasn't quite fallen into his brother's spirit; he is uneasy, and he begins to move restlessly around the room.

"Why does Dad mock me all the time?" he asks, suddenly.

Happy reassures Biff that their father isn't mocking; he just wants Biff to make good. But there is something about Dad which has been worrying the younger brother for a long time— his talking to himself. It's getting more and more noticeable. And most of the time he seems to be talking to Biff, worrying about whether he has a future.

BIFF—I tell ya, Hap, I don't know what the future is. I don't know—what I'm supposed to want.

HAPPY—What do you mean?

BIFF—Well, I spent six or seven years after high school trying to work myself up. Shipping clerk, salesman, business of one kind or another. And it's a measly manner of existence. To get on that subway on the hot mornings in Summer. To devote your whole life to keeping stock, or making phone calls, or selling or buying. To suffer fifty weeks of the year for the sake of a two-week vacation, when all you really desire is to be outdoors, with your shirt off. And always to have to get ahead of the next fella. And still—that's how you build a future.

HAPPY—Well, you really enjoy it on a farm? Are you content out there?

BIFF (*with rising agitation*)—Hap, I've had twenty or thirty different kinds of jobs since I left home before the war, and it always turns out the same. I just realized it lately. In Nebraska when I herded cattle, and the Dakotas, and Arizona, and now in Texas. It's why I came home now, I guess, because I realized it. This farm I work on, it's Spring there now, see? And they've got about fifteen new colts. There's nothing more inspiring or— beautiful than the sight of a mare and a new colt. And it's cool there now, see? Texas is cool now, and it's Spring. And whenever Spring comes to where I am, I suddenly get the feeling, my God, I'm not gettin' anywhere! What the hell am I doing, playing around with horses, twenty-eight dollars a week! I'm thirty-four years old, I oughta be makin' my future. That's when I come running home. And now, I get here, and I don't know what to do with myself. (*After a pause.*) I've always made a point of not wasting my life, and every time I come back here I know that all I've done is to waste my life.

HAPPY—You're a poet, you know that, Biff? You're a—you're an idealist!

BIFF—No, I'm mixed up very bad. Maybe I oughta get married. Maybe I oughta get stuck into something. Maybe that's my trouble. I'm like a boy. I'm not married, I'm not in business, I just—I'm like a boy. Are you content, Hap? You're a success, aren't you? Are you content?

HAPPY—Hell, no!

BIFF—Why? You're making money, aren't you?

HAPPY (*moving about with energy, expressiveness*)—All I can do now is wait for the merchandise manager to die. And suppose I get to be merchandise manager? He's a good friend of mine, and he just built a terrific estate on Long Island. And he lived there about two months and sold it, and now he's building another one. He can't enjoy it once it's finished. And I know that's just what I would do. I don't know what the hell I'm workin' for. Sometimes I sit in my apartment—all alone. And I think of the rent I'm paying. And it's crazy. But then, it's what I always wanted. My own apartment, a car, and plenty of women. And still, goddammit, I'm lonely.

BIFF (*with enthusiasm*)—Listen, why don't you come out West with me?

HAPPY—You and I, heh?

BIFF—Sure, maybe we could buy a ranch. Raise cattle, use our muscles. Men built like we are should be working out in the open.

HAPPY (*avidly*)—The Loman Brothers, heh?

It is a rosy dream they both share, and they enlarge upon it. "I gotta show some of those pompous, self-important executives over there that Hap Loman can make the grade," says the younger brother. And they could find a couple of women, steady, with character, like Mom. Happy is tired of just knocking them over and its not meaning anything. For instance, the girl Hap was with tonight is engaged to be married to a guy who's in line for the vice-presidency of the store. "I don't know what gets into me. Maybe I just have an overdeveloped sense of competition or something, but I went and ruined her and furthermore I can't get rid of her. And he's the third executive I've done that to.

Isn't that a crummy characteristic? And to top it all, I go to their weddings!"

Biff would like to go back to sleep now, but he has found a new idea. It's Bill Oliver. When Biff quit that time, Bill Oliver had said, "If you ever need anything, come to me." Maybe Bill Oliver would lend him ten thousand, or seven or eight, to buy the ranch—unless Bill still thinks that Biff stole that carton of basketballs. This is a happy idea, and upon it the boys prepare to snooze . . . but Willy has begun again in the kitchen. They hear him asking, "You gonna wash the engine, Biff?"

A look of pain crosses Biff's face as he hears his father talking about washing and polishing the Chevvy just as if it were happening right now. The boys' room fades from sight and Willy is seen dimly in the kitchen, searching in the refrigerator. Now the surrounding apartment houses seem to fade out and to be replaced everywhere with tree leaves.

As the lights rise on the kitchen, Willy is admonishing Biff to be careful with "those girls. Don't make any promises. . . . Because a girl, y'know, they always believe what you tell 'em." Willy pours a glass of milk and still is totally immersed in himself as he continues to lecture Biff. The boy is too young, and should watch his schooling first. As he talks, Willy gradually seems physically to be addressing a point through the kitchen wall, and his voice rises.

"Don't leave the hubcaps, boys. . . . Happy, use newspapers on the windows. . . . Show him how to do it, Biff! . . . Soon as you finish the car, I gotta surprise for you."

Offstage Biff is heard asking, "Whattaya got, Dad?" In a moment the brothers appear from the direction Willy was addressing. They are kids now; Hap carries rags and a pail of water, and Biff, in a sweater with a block "S" on it, has a football. Biff points back of him and asks, "How's that, Pop, professional?"

Willy admits it's a terrific job and tells the boys his surprise is in the back seat of the car. Hap runs to get it, and brings back a punching bag—with Gene Tunney's signature on it! The boys are enchanted. "It's the finest thing for timing," Willy counsels. Hap lies on his back, pedals his legs and proclaims, "I'm losing weight, you notice, Pop?"

Biff shows the new football he's got. The coach told him to practice his passing and—well, didn't exactly give Biff the ball. Biff just borrowed it from the locker room. Willy laughingly advises the boy to return it.

Eagerly the boys ask Dad where he has been this time, and he puts an arm around each of them as he confides, almost like a conspirator, "Some day I'll have my own business and I'll never have to leave home any more." As to where he went—well, he got on the road and went to Providence and met the Mayor, and then to Waterbury and sold a nice bill there, and then to Boston, and a couple of other towns in Mass., and on to Portland and Bangor—and then straight home.

It sounds wonderful to the boys. How they'd love to go with him some time! Their father promises that some day they will. They'll see all the towns, and they'll meet the finest people. "I can park my car in any street in New England and the cops protect it like their own," Willy boasts.

Biff begins prancing around and pretending to pass the football. "You nervous about the game?" his father asks. No, Biff isn't nervous—not if his father is going to be there. Happy says that now Biff has been made captain there's a crowd of girls behind him every time classes change. Biff, warmed, promises his father that this Saturday he will break through and make a special touchdown just for his Pop.

All this fine enthusiasm is markedly dampened by the appearance of one Bernard, an earnest, worried but loyal little hero-worshiper in knickers. Seeing him, Willy jovially inquires, "What're you lookin' so anemic about, Bernard?"

Bernard is looking anemic because Biff has gotta study. He's got Regents next week, and Mr. Birnbaum has said that if Biff doesn't get down to his math he will be flunked. This news is of as little concern to the father as it is to the son, and Willy angrily dismisses Bernard with, "What're you talking about? With scholarships to three universities they're gonna flunk him?" Athletic scholarships, obviously. Bernard goes away, worrying, and Willy analyzes the boy for his sons. Bernard may be liked, in school, but not well liked. "Bernard can get the best marks in school, y'understand, but when he gets out in the business world, y'understand, you are going to be five times ahead of him. That's why I thank Almighty God you're both built like Adonises. Because the man who makes an appearance in the business world, the man who creates personal interest, is the man who gets ahead. Be liked and you will never want. You take me, for instance. I never have to wait in line to see a buyer. 'Willy Loman is here!' That's all they have to know, and I go right through."

Linda comes into the yard, just as she used to, carrying a basket of washing and wearing a ribbon in her hair. She has youthful energy, and she gives her husband a youthful and energetic greeting. Did the Chevvy run all right? she wants to know. Greatest car ever built, he assures her. Willy orders the boys to snap to it and take their mother's basket of washing. "Hang them up on the line," says Linda. "And you better go down to your friends, Biff. The cellar is full of boys. They don't know what to do with themselves."

Ah, says Biff, when Pop comes home the boys can wait. Pop laughs appreciatively and suggests that Biff better go down and tell them what to do. Biff decides he will assign them to sweeping out the furnace room, and hollers out the assignment. An "Okay" is heard from the cellar. Biff detaches three of the crew down there to help hang out his mother's wash.

"The way they obey him!" marvels Linda. And now she wants to hear about her husband—did he sell anything? At first he boasts of having done five hundred gross in Providence and seven hundred in Boston, and his wife fishes a pencil and paper out of her apron pocket to compute the commission. "Two hundred—my God! Two hundred and twelve dollars!" He begins to hedge and she pins him down to real figures. It was only a hundred and eight gross in Providence—well, no, it came to about two hundred gross for the whole trip. Linda tots this up and announces, "It makes seventy dollars and some pennies. That's very good."

Willy wonders if it will help cover what they owe, but they owe plenty. Payment and repairs on the refrigerator, and quite a lot due on the washing machine, and a payment on the vacuum cleaner, and a carburetor for the Chevvy. It tots up to $120. "My God," Willy moans, "if business don't pick up I don't know what I'm gonna do!"

Willy is downcast. People don't seem to take to him—they seem to laugh at him. As he is telling his wife this, she goes through the wall back into the kitchen and begins to darn stockings, while Willy remains far toward us on the apron of the stage. "I talk too much," he continues—and to himself, "I joke too much."

LINDA—Why? You're—

WILLY—I'm fat. I'm very—foolish to look at, Linda. I didn't tell you, but Christmas time I happened to be calling on F. H. Stewarts, and a salesman I know, as I was going in to see the buyer I heard him say something about—walrus. And I—I cracked him right across the face. I won't take that. I simply will not take that. But they do laugh at me. I know that.

LINDA—Darling. . . .

WILLY—I gotta overcome it. I know I gotta overcome it. I'm not dressing to advantage, maybe.

LINDA—Willy, darling, you're the handsomest man in the world—

WILLY—Oh, no, Linda.

LINDA—To me you are. (*Slight pause.*) The handsomest. (*From the darkness is heard the laughter of a woman.* WILLY *doesn't turn to it, but it continues through* LINDA'S *lines.*)

LINDA—And the boys, Willy. Few men are idolized by their children the way you are. (*Music is heard as behind a scrim, to the left of the house,* THE WOMAN, *dimly seen, is dressing.*)

WILLY (*with great feeling*)—You're the best there is, Linda, you're a pal, you know that? On the road—on the road I want to grab you sometimes and just kiss the life outa you. (*The laughter is loud now, and he moves into a brightening area at the left, where* THE WOMAN *has come from behind the scrim and is standing, putting on her hat, looking into a "mirror" and laughing.*) 'Cause I get so lonely—especially when business is bad and there's nobody to talk to. I get the feeling that I'll never sell anything again, that I won't make a living for you, or a business, a business for the boys. (*He talks through* THE WOMAN'S *subsiding laughter;* THE WOMAN *primps at the "mirror."*) There's so much I want to make for—

THE WOMAN—Me? You didn't make me, Willy? I picked you.

WILLY (*pleased*)—You picked me?

THE WOMAN (*who is quite proper-looking, Willy's age*)—I did. I've been sitting at that desk watching all the salesmen go by, day in, day out. But you've got such a sense of humor, and we do have such a good time together, don't we?

WILLY—Sure, sure. (*He takes her in his arms.*) Why do you have to go now?

THE WOMAN—It's two o'clock. . . .

WILLY—No, come on in! (*He pulls her.*)

THE WOMAN—. . . my sisters'll be scandalized. When'll you be back?

WILLY—Oh, two weeks about. Will you come up again?

THE WOMAN—Sure thing. You do make me laugh. It's good for me. (*She squeezes his arm, kisses him.*) And I think you're a wonderful man.

WILLY—You picked me, heh?

THE WOMAN—Sure. Because you're so sweet. And such a kidder.

WILLY—Well, I'll see you next time I'm in Boston.

THE WOMAN—I'll put you right through to the buyers.

WILLY (*slapping her bottom*)—Right. Well, bottoms up!

THE WOMAN (*slaps him gently and laughs*)—You just kill me, Willy. (*He suddenly grabs her and kisses her roughly.*) You kill me. And thanks for the stockings. I love a lot of stockings. Well, good night.

WILLY—Good night. And keep your pores open!

THE WOMAN—Oh, Willy! (THE WOMAN *bursts out laughing, and* LINDA's *laughter blends in.* THE WOMAN *disappears into the dark. Now the area at the kitchen table brightens.* LINDA *is sitting where she was at the kitchen table, but now is mending a pair of her silk stockings.*)

LINDA—You are, Willy. The handsomest man. You've got no reason to feel that—

WILLY (*coming out of* THE WOMAN's *dimming area and going over to* LINDA)—I'll make it all up to you, Linda, I'll—

LINDA—There's nothing to make up, dear. You're doing fine, better than—

WILLY (*noticing her mending*)—What's that?

LINDA—Just mending my stockings. They're so expensive—

WILLY (*angrily, taking them from her*)—I won't have you mending stockings in this house! Now throw them out!

A very agitated Bernard runs onto the forestage looking for Biff. Biff has got to study! Linda chimes in: Biff had better give back that football—and he shouldn't be so rough with the girls, because all the mothers are getting afraid of him. Bernard points out that Biff is driving without a license . . . and he's going to flunk. . . .

The problems of Biff are piling in upon Willy . . . and now he is sitting alone in the kitchen again, staring. The leaves outside have disappeared and once again the apartment houses look down from behind and all around. Happy has come downstairs to try to calm his father down, and asks, "What brought you back tonight?"

Willy explains that he got an awful scare—nearly hit a kid in Yonkers. God! Why didn't he go to Alaska with his brother Ben that time, when Ben had begged him to go? A genius, was Ben—success incarnate. Started with the clothes on his back and ended up with diamond mines!

Happy assures Pop that he will take care of him for life. "On seventy goddam dollars a week?" snarls Willy. "And your women and your car and your apartment."

Charley, from next door, appears in the doorway in slippers, pajamas and robe. He is a large man, immovable and slow of speech. Uneasily he asks if everything is all right. He signals Happy to go back to bed and suggests a card game with Willy, pretending that he has been unable to sleep because of heartburn when in truth it is Willy's talking to himself which has wakened him.

These two are old friends and neighbors and they begin a game with cards which Charley has brought in the pocket of his robe. They make small talk for a while. Then Charley offers Willy a job and Willy, insulted, snaps that he's *got* a job. Willy broods about Biff's plan to go back to Texas, and Charley advises him to let the boy go—to forget about him. Willy is getting pretty angry when Uncle Ben, carrying a valise and an umbrella, comes onto the forestage. He is a stolid man in his sixties with an authoritative air and an aura of far places about him. As he comes on, Willy, at the card game, sighs, "I'm getting awfully tired, Ben."

"Did you call me Ben?" Charley asks.

Willy now is confused. He says for a second Charley reminded him of his brother Ben, and tells Charley something about the man. Only a couple of weeks ago they got a letter from Africa saying Ben had died. He was rich, yes—but he had seven sons and Willy wouldn't be getting any of the money.

Ben, from outside, cuts into the conversation; he is heard only by Willy, of course. He offers his brother the chance to come with him to Alaska, where opportunity is tremendous, and Willy has a puzzling time trying to talk to Ben and his card partner at the same time because they don't seem to be talking about the same things. No less puzzled is Charley, and when his neighbor makes several misplays at the game he gets angry, picks up his cards and goes across home.

Willy comes through the wall to clasp Ben's hand, and Linda joins them. After all these years Ben is back, and there is so much to know. "Where is Dad?" asks Willy. "Did you follow him?" Willy can't remember much about his Dad, because he was not yet four, and sitting under the wagon somewhere in Nebraska or South Dakota, the last time he saw his father. He remembers Ben walking away down some open road.

Ben laughs, "I was going to find Father in Alaska."

Willy eagerly asks, "Where is he?"

"At that age," Ben replies, "I had a very faulty view of geography, William. I discovered after a few days that I was heading due south, so instead of Alaska I ended up in Africa."

Ben seems to be in a hurry to get away—he has an appointment in Ketchikan Tuesday week—but Willy holds him until he can call Biff and Happy. The boys are wide-eyed as Ben begins to reminisce about the grandfather they have never seen. "Father was a very great and a very wild-hearted man," Ben begins. He'd toss the whole family into the wagon, starting in Boston, and drive right across the country, making flutes on the way and selling them. (*As* BEN *talks a high, rollicking tune is heard.*)

The confusion in Willy's mind increases. Ben is trying to get away for his appointment in Ketchikan, and now Charley, wearing plus-fours, comes into the yard with a warning that the boys had better stop stealing from that new building or the watchman will put the cops on them. Bernard skitters in, crying, "The watchman's chasing Biff!" All this amuses Ben greatly—but now he has to go. He'll stop by on his way back to Africa.

Willy longingly begs him to stay a few days, because he is somebody to talk to. "Dad left when I was such a baby and I never had a chance to talk to him and I still feel—kind of temporary about myself," he falters. He'd like to talk about his boys, for instance—they'd go into the jaws of hell for him, but is he teaching them the right kind of—? How should he teach them?

Giving great weight to each word, and with a certain vicious audacity, Ben proclaims, "William, when I walked into the jungle, I was seventeen. When I walked out I was twenty-one. And, by God, I was rich!" He disappears around the corner of the house.

Linda, aroused again, comes looking for Willy in the kitchen, finally locates him in the yard. She soothes, "It's very late, darling. Come back to bed, heh?" Willy is half thinking of Ben, half listening to her. No—he's going to take a walk, even if he is in his slippers. As he disappears around a corner of the house Biff comes downstairs, and when his mother comes back in he demands, "God Almighty, Mom, how long has he been doing this?" Happy comes down, too, saying, "I never heard him so loud, Mom."

To Biff Linda says, "It's when you come that he's always the worst. When you write you're coming, he's all smiles. . . . And then the closer you seem to come the more shaky he gets. . . . Why are you so hateful to each other?"

Biff denies that he's hateful. "I'm trying, Mom." He touches her hair affectionately and calls her his pal, but she will not be softened. Biff cannot love his mother unless he loves his father, too.

"Sure I can," says Biff.

"No, you just can't come to see me, because I love him." With a threat of tears, but gallantly, she continues, "He's the dearest man in the world to me, and I won't have anyone making him feel unwanted and low and blue. . . ."

"Stop making excuses for him! He always, always wiped the floor with you." In his anger Biff continues to rail against his father, and observes that Charley wouldn't be doing anything like this—spewing out the vomit from his mind in his own house.

LINDA—Then make Charley your father, Biff. You can't do that, can you? I don't say he's a great man. Willy Loman never made a lot of money. His name was never in the paper. He's not the finest character that ever lived. But he's a human being, and a terrible thing is happening to him. So attention must be paid. He's not to be allowed to fall into his grave like an old dog. Attention, attention must be finally paid to such a person. You called him crazy—

BIFF—I didn't mean—

LINDA—No, a lot of people think he's lost his—balance. But you don't have to be very smart to know what his trouble is. The man is exhausted.

HAPPY—Sure!

LINDA—A small man can be just as exhausted as a great man. He works for a company thirty-six years this March, opens up unheard-of territories to their trademark, and now in his old age they take his salary away.

HAPPY (*indignantly*)—I didn't know that, Mom.

LINDA—You never asked, my dear! Now that you get your spending money someplace else you don't trouble your mind with him.

HAPPY—But I gave you money last—

LINDA—Christmas time, fifty dollars! To fix the hot water it cost ninety-seven fifty! For five weeks he's been on straight commission, like a beginner, an unknown!

BIFF—Those ungrateful bastards!

LINDA—Are they any worse than his sons? When he brought them business, when he was young, they were glad to see him. But now his old friends, the old buyers that loved him so and always found some order to hand him in a pinch—they're all dead, retired. He used to be able to make six, seven calls a day in Boston. Now he takes his valises out of the car and puts them back and takes them out again and he's exhausted. Instead of walking he talks now. He drives seven hundred miles, and when he gets there no one knows him any more, no one welcomes him. And what goes through a man's mind, driving seven hundred miles home without having earned a cent? Why shouldn't he talk to himself? Why? When he has to go to Charley and borrow fifty dollars a week and pretend to me that it's his pay? How long can that go on? How long? You see what I'm sitting here and waiting for? And you tell me he has no character? The man who never worked a day but for your benefit? When does he get the medal for that? Is this his reward—to turn around at the age of sixty-three and find his sons, who he loved better than his life, one a philandering bum—

HAPPY—Mom!

LINDA—That's all you are, my baby! (*To* BIFF.) And you! What happened to the love you had for him? You were such pals! How you used to talk to him on the phone every night! How lonely he was till he could come home to you!

BIFF—All right, Mom. I'll live here in my room, and I'll get a job. I'll keep away from him, that's all.

LINDA—No, Biff. You can't stay here and fight all the time.

BIFF—He threw me out of this house, remember that.

LINDA—Why did he do that? I never knew why.

BIFF—Because I know he's a fake and he doesn't like anybody around who knows!

LINDA—Why a fake? In what way? What do you mean?

BIFF—Just don't lay it all at my feet. It's between me and him—that's all I have to say. I'll chip in from now on. He'll settle for half my pay check. He'll be all right. I'm going to bed. (*He starts for the stairs.*)

LINDA—He won't be all right.

BIFF (*turning on the stairs, furiously*)—I hate this city and I'll stay here. Now what do you want?

LINDA—He's dying, Biff.

Happy is shocked, and Biff is halted. Their mother confides that Willy has been trying to kill himself. That automobile smashup in February, and all the accidents last year—they weren't accidents. The insurance company has been investigating, and in one case and probably more it has found direct evidence that Willy deliberately drove the car into a smashup. And, last month . . .

She wipes her eyes. "I was looking for a fuse. The lights blew out, and I went down the cellar. And behind the fuse box— it happened to fall out—was a length of rubber pipe. There's a little attachment on the end of it. I knew right away. And sure enough, on the bottom of the water heater there's a new little nipple on the gas pipe."

Happy is angry. "That jerk!" he exclaims. Biff is practical. Why couldn't his mother have the nipple removed?

"I'm ashamed to. How can I mention it to him?" Every day she goes down and takes the pipe away, but when Willy comes home she puts it back again. She can't insult him. She is weeping now as she tells her sons, "He put his whole life into you and now you've turned your backs on him! Biff, his life is in your hands!"

Biff, deeply moved, kisses his mother and makes his decision. It's settled. He will stay. He doesn't fit in business, but he will try to make good. His younger brother cracks that the trouble with Biff in business was that he never tried to please people, and the two get into an angry argument, with Biff maintaining that the family doesn't belong in this nuthouse of a city.

Willy has returned from his walk and has been listening to the quarrel. He comes in and advises Biff to go back to the West and be a carpenter or a cowboy and enjoy himself. Linda calms her husband, and Willy suggests to Biff that he might paint the new ceiling he has put up in the living room.

"I'm leaving early tomorrow," says Biff.

Eagerly, Happy explains, "He's going to see Bill Oliver."

Willy has become interested, and somewhat stiffly Biff explains that he'd like to go into business, and Oliver always had said he'd stake him. This is great news for Willy, for Oliver is a sporting goods man and his son Biff knows more sporting goods than Spalding. "How much is he going to give you?" he asks eagerly.

Biff tries to hedge, and Willy figures it's another of his son's useless dreams—but Happy comes to the rescue. Thinking fast, Happy comes up with a great idea. Biff and Hap will form the Loman Line of sporting goods, and together put on exhibitions— each with his own team—of basketball, water polo . . .

Willy exclaims, "That is a one-million-dollar idea!" Happy continues his enthusiastic buildup and soon the wildly excited Willy has taken charge. He tells Biff just how he should dress tomorrow, and how he should talk big, and ask for fifteen thousand if he wants ten. Linda catches the enthusiasm and tries to chime in, but Willy says to her, roughly, "Will you let me talk?"

"Stop yelling at her!" Biff commands, furious again. The wind out of his sails, Willy goes off to bed. Linda and Happy urge the reluctant Biff to go in and buck him up some more, and the three of them join the salesman in the bedroom. "Take it easy, Pop," says Biff. Some of Willy's enthusiasm revives. "You got all kinds a greatness," he tells his son—and when he and Linda are alone he lies back, exhausted but happy. Linda sings him a lullaby, and he sinks into a pleasant state of hope and reminiscence. That game for the championship of the city at Ebbets Field. . . . Biff like a young god, and the crowd cheering him. "God Almighty, he'll be great yet. . . ."

The light on Willy and Linda is fading. Behind the kitchen wall the gas heater begins to glow. Biff, returning to the kitchen, stares toward the heater. In the bedroom, Linda pleads, "Willy, will you ask Howard to let you work in New York?"

"First thing in the morning. Everything'll be all right."

Biff reaches behind the heater, finds the tubing, and, looking horrified, takes it upstairs with him to his and Happy's room.

The curtain falls.

ACT II

The background music is bright and gay, so is the morning and so is Willy as he sits in the kitchen relishing a cup of coffee. It's the first time in months he has slept till ten on a Tuesday morning. "Boys left nice and early, heh?"

His wife replies that they were out of the house by eight, and she was so thrilled to see them go off together. Biff was very changed, too—hopeful, and couldn't wait to get down town to see Oliver.

It is a fine morning and Willy is full of plans. They'll have a little place in the country, and some vegetables and a couple of chickens . . . and when the boys get married he'll build them a little guest house where they can stay on visits. . . .

Linda brings out a suit jacket she has been mending for her husband and helps him into it—for he, too, has a date with a new destiny. He is going to see Howard and get taken off the road.

Linda suggests that he ask for a little advance, too, because they are short. The insurance premium, and the motor job on the car, and the repair of the refrigerator—about two hundred dollars will do. "But," she adds, "that will include the last payment on the mortgage. After this payment, Willy, the house belongs to us." He can hardly believe it has been twenty-five years.

Linda is urging him out, and at the last moment remembers something. "You're supposed to meet them for dinner." She explains that Biff had suggested that he and Happy blow their father to a big meal at Frank's chop house on 48th Street. Willy now is sailing. He will knock Howard for a loop, get the advance and come home with a New York job!

"Oh, that's the spirit, Willy!" She checks him over, making sure he has his handkerchief and his saccharin, and waves him out of the house.

There is a ring on the telephone. It is Biff, checking about the dinner date with his father. Linda is extraordinarily happy—not only because of Willy's recovery but also because the rubber pipe behind the heater is gone. Willy took it away himself. . . . She is dampened somewhat when Biff tells her he is the one who took it, but she recovers and pleads, "Be sweet to him tonight, dear. Be loving to him. Because he's only a little boat looking for a harbor. . . ."

While Linda still talks with Biff, the lights fade on her and Howard Wagner, an assured man of thirty-six, wheels on a small typewriter table holding a wire recorder. He is absorbed in threading the machine when Willy appears and says, "Like to have a talk with you, Howard."

Howard remains absorbed in the machine. He explains to Willy what it is. He just got it, for dictation, but last night he took it home to try it out. "Listen to what I picked up. The first one is my daughter." He switches on the recorder and a child is heard whistling.

Willy is polite about admiring the machine, but he still has something on his mind. "Like to ask a little favor if you . . ." he begins again. Howard shushes him and listens to a recording of his son reciting a geography lesson. Finally the record ends and Willy desperately maneuvers Howard into serious talk. "I'd rather not travel any more," he announces.

"Not travel? Well, what'll you do?"

"Remember Christmas time, when you had the party here? You said you'd try to think of some spot for me here in town."

"With us?"

"Well, sure."

"Oh, yeah, yeah. I remember. . . . Well, I couldn't think of anything for you, Willy."

Howard is the cold executive now, and Willy is the supplicant who soon becomes a cringing one. He doesn't want much. Sixty. Howard says he just doesn't have a spot. The desperate Willy is becoming angry. Even fifty will lay his table.

"Business is business," says Howard.

Willy angrily agrees that business is business, and tells the bored-looking Howard a long story about how he got into selling. When he was eighteen or nineteen he was going to join his father in Alaska when he met a salesman in the Parker House—a salesman who was eighty-four years old. And this man, at that age, could move into a town, put on his slippers and pick up the phone in his hotel room, and announce to the buyers that he was there. Without ever leaving his room he made his living. "And when I saw that," Willy continues, "I realized that selling was the greatest career a man could want.

"Do you know, when he died—and by the way he died the death of a salesman, in his green velvet slippers in the smoker of the New York, New Haven and Hartford, going into Boston—when he died, hundreds of salesmen and buyers were at his funeral. . . . Today it's all cut and dried, and there's no chance for bringing friendship to bear, or personality. You see what I mean? They don't know me any more."

Howard has been edging away. "That's just the thing, Willy," he comments.

Willy begs for forty a week, and his mental pressure is rising. He bangs the desk and reminds Howard of his father, for whom Willy worked before Howard was born. Howard keeps edging away, and, saying he has somebody to see, advises Willy to pull himself together. He assures, "I'll be back in a little while."

Willy suddenly realizes he has been yelling at his boss. He leans on the table and accidentally switches on the recorder. The voice of Howard's son doing his geography recitation begins again, and Willy, leaping away with fright, yells for Howard. His employer comes running back in and pulls the plug. Willy, pressing his hands to his eyes, mutters, "I'll go to Boston."

"You can't go to Boston for us. I don't want you to represent us. I've been meaning to tell you for a long time now."

"Howard, are you firing me?"

"I think you need a good long rest, Willy." And the old stuff about when he comes back they'll see if they can work something out.

"But I gotta earn money, Howard!"

"Why don't your sons give you a hand?"

Willy won't throw himself on his sons, not when they're working on a big deal. He begs again to be allowed to go to Boston, but Howard is keeping himself hard. He practically orders Willy out of the office. "Pull yourself together, kid, there's people outside."

Howard pushes his recorder table offstage and Willy, exhausted, stares into space . . . and in a moment Ben appears, with his valise and umbrella. "I've got to talk to you," says Willy. Ben looks at his watch and answers, "Haven't the time, William." But he does say that he does want a man to look after some timber land in Alaska, and Willy calls for Linda.

Linda, looking as she used to, greets Ben and is told that Willy has a proposition in Alaska. She says her husband is doing well enough here.

BEN (*to* LINDA)—Enough for what, my dear?

LINDA (*frightened of* BEN *and angry at him*)—Don't say those things to him! Enough to be happy right here, right now. (*To* WILLY, *while* BEN *laughs.*) Why must everybody conquer the world? You're well liked, and the boys love you, and someday— (*To* BEN.)—why, old man Wagner told him just the other day that if he keeps it up he'll be a member of the firm, didn't he, Willy?

WILLY—Sure, sure. I am building something with this firm, Ben, and if a man is building something he must be on the right track, mustn't he?

BEN—What are you building? Lay your hand on it. Where is it?

WILLY (*hesitantly*)—That's true, Linda, there's nothing.

LINDA—Why? (*To* BEN.) There's a man eighty-four years old—

WILLY—That's right, Ben, that's right. When I look at that man I say, what is there to worry about?

BEN—Bah!

WILLY—It's true, Ben. All he has to do is go into any city, pick up the phone, and he's making his living and you know why?

BEN (*picking up his valise*)—I've got to go.

WILLY (*holding* BEN *back*)—Look at this boy! (BIFF, *in his high school sweater, enters carrying suitcase.* HAPPY *carries* BIFF'S *shoulder guards, gold helmet, and football pants.*) Without a penny to his name, three great universities are begging for him, and from there the sky's the limit, because it's not what you do, Ben. It's who you know and the smile on your face! It's contacts, Ben, contacts! The whole wealth of Alaska passes over the lunch table at the Commodore Hotel, and that's the wonder, the wonder of this country, that a man can end with diamonds here on the basis of being liked! (*He turns to* BIFF.) And that's why when you get out on that field today it's important. Because thousands of people will be rooting for you and loving you. (*To* BEN, *who has again begun to leave.*) And, Ben! when he walks into a business office his name will sound out like a bell and all the doors will open to him! I've seen it, Ben, I've seen it a thousand times! You can't feel it with your hand like timber, but it's there!

BEN—Good-by, William.

WILLY—Ben, am I right? Don't you think I'm right? I value your advice.

BEN—There's a new continent at your doorstep, William. You could walk out rich. Rich! (*He is gone.*)

WILLY—We'll do it here, Ben! You hear me? We're gonna do it here!

The others in the salesman's mind return in an eventful kaleidoscope. The gay music of the boys is heard as Bernard runs in, gasping, "Oh, gee, I was afraid you left already!" Willy is at his home now and it is the day of the big game at Ebbets Field. Biff is limbering up, and the adoring Bernard begs to be allowed to carry Biff's helmet or shoulder guards or something and thus get into the clubhouse as a helper. Biff grandly permits it. Willy dashes into the house and comes back with a fistful of pennants for everybody. He gives his son a last-minute pep talk. "You're comin' home this afternoon captain of the All-Scholastic Championship Team of the City of New York."

"I got it, Pop. And remember, pal, when I take off my helmet that means I'm going to make a touchdown for you."

Charley intrudes, in his plus-fours again, pretending that he doesn't know what the commotion is about. He thought he'd like a game of casino. Willy laughs at him and pushes his crowd out toward the Chevvy. Charley affects not to know whether the game is going to be baseball or football, and when Willy boasts that his son is going to be another Red Grange Charley innocently asks who Red Grange is. "When," he demands of his friend, "are you going to grow up?"

Charley chuckles and walks away, and the music rises in a mocking frenzy. In a moment Charley's son, Bernard, now mature, is sitting in the reception room of his father's office. At his feet are an overnight bag and a pair of tennis racquets. Jenny, Charley's secretary, comes into the reception room and asks Bernard if he will go out in the hall. She is distressed. It's Mr. Loman, and he is out there, arguing—but there isn't anybody with him. She says, "I've got a lot of typing to do, and your father's waiting to sign it. Will you see him?"

Willy enters, shouting "Touchdown! Touch—"

At the sight of Jenny he halts his cheers and greets her. Then sees Bernard, who calls him Uncle Willy. They shake hands warmly. Bernard explains that he has dropped in to see his Pop before getting the train to Washington in a few minutes.

"What're you going to do in Washington?"

"Oh, just a case I've got down there, Willy."

The salesman is impressed. He sees the racquets. Bernard explains he is staying with a friend who has a court. Willy is even more impressed—must be fine people, with their own tennis court. Very nice people, Bernard agrees—and what is Biff doing?

"Well, he's been doing very big things in the West. But he decided to establish himself here. . . . Did I hear your wife had a boy?"

That's right, Bernard replies—their second. And what kind of a deal has Biff got?

"Well, Bill Oliver, very big sporting goods man, he wants Biff very badly. Called him in from the West."

Bernard asks, "You still with the old firm?"

Willy ignores the question and tries for a moment to keep up his front, but at last he becomes emotional, desperate and frank. Why was it, he asks Bernard, that Biff's life ended after that Ebbets Field game. From that time, at the age of seventeen, nothing good has happened to him. Bernard is willing to talk candidly, and confesses there is one question he's always wanted to ask Willy. "When he was supposed to graduate, and that math teacher flunked him—"

WILLY—Oh, that son-of-a-bitch ruined his life.
BERNARD—Yeah, but, Willy, all he had to do was go to Summer school and make up that subject.
WILLY—That's right, that's right.

BERNARD—Did you tell him not to go to Summer school?
WILLY—Me? I begged him to go. I ordered him to go!
BERNARD—Then why wouldn't he go?
WILLY—Why? Why! Bernard, that question has been trailing me like a ghost for the last fifteen years. He flunked the subject, and laid down and died like a hammer hit him!
BERNARD—Take it easy, kid.
WILLY—Let me talk to you—I got nobody to talk to. Bernard, Bernard, was it my fault? Y'see? It keeps going around in my mind, maybe I did something to him. I got nothing to give him.
BERNARD—Don't take it so hard.
WILLY—Why did he lay down? What is the story there? You were his friend!
BERNARD—Willy, I remember, it was June, and our grades came out. And he'd flunked math.
WILLY—That son-of-a-bitch!
BERNARD—No, it wasn't right then. Biff just got very angry, I remember, and he was ready to enroll in Summer school.
WILLY (*surprised*)—He was?
BERNARD—He wasn't beaten by it at all. But then, Willy, he disappeared from the block for almost a month. And I got the idea that he'd gone up to New England to see you. Did he have a talk with you then? (WILLY *stares in silence.*)
BERNARD—Willy?
WILLY (*with a strong edge of resentment in his voice*)—Yeah, he came to Boston. What about it?
BERNARD—Well, just that when he came back—I'll never forget this, it always mystifies me. Because I'd thought so well of Biff, even though he'd always taken advantage of me. I loved him, Willy, y'know? And he came back after that month and took his sneakers—remember those sneakers with "University of Virginia" printed on them? He was so proud of those, wore them every day. And he took them down in the cellar, and burned them up in the furnace. We had a fist fight. It lasted at least half an hour. Just the two of us, punching each other down the cellar, and crying right through it. I've often thought of how strange it was that I knew he'd given up his life. What happened in Boston, Willy?

Willy says angrily that nothing happened. Charley comes in in his vest, carrying a bottle of bourbon which he gives to his son. Bernard hurries away to catch his train, and Charley boasts that his son is off to argue a case before the Supreme Court—to Willy's great impressment. Charley hauls out his wallet and counts money on his desk. The bemused Willy marvels, "And you never told him what to do, did you?"

Charley offers Willy the fifty dollars he has counted out, and with difficulty Willy explains that he needs a hundred and ten to cover his insurance.

"Willy, what're you doing? What the hell is goin' on in your head?"

"Well, I'm simply . . ."

"I offered you a job. You can make fifty dollars a week. And I won't send you on the road."

"I've got a job."

Charley knows Willy has no job, and pleads with Willy to take this one. The salesman becomes angry. "I don't want your goddam job!"

Charley, baffled, asks, "When the hell are you going to grow up?"—and his friend offers to rap him on the nose. But Charley makes one more try. "How much do you need, Willy?" he asks, kindly.

Willy confesses that he has been fired and is strapped—but he just can't work for Charley. The latter, angered, pushes more money into Willy's hands. "Take care of yourself. And pay your insurance."

"Funny, y'know?" muses Willy. "After all the highways, and the trains, and the appointments, and the years, you end up worth more dead than alive."

Charley is sharp. "Willy, nobody's worth nothin' dead. . . . Did you hear what I said?"

Willy is dreaming, but he recovers to bid an affectionate good-by as Charley departs. Suddenly raucous music is heard, the lights fade on Loman—and come up on a waiter carrying a table, with Happy following him carrying two chairs. "Whenever you got a party, Mr. Loman," the waiter tells Happy, "you just tell me and I'll put you back here." Happy explains that this party is with his brother, who has come back from the West, and his father. It's a celebration. He thinks his brother has pulled off a big deal today.

While the waiter is setting the table and passing the time of day a furred, lavishly dressed girl enters and sits at the next table. With the expert technique of a field general Happy addresses the girl, says he is a champagne salesman and orders some champagne for her. Has she a friend? Because he is meeting his brother, a famous football player, and maybe—

Biff arrives. He is introduced to the girl but is more interested in knowing if Dad has arrived. Happy demonstrates his power over women by persuading the girl to go out and call up a friend for Biff. "That's why I can't get married," he says. "There's not a good woman in a thousand. New York is loaded with them, kid."

Biff doesn't care one way or another. He is strangely unnerved. Yes, he saw Oliver all right, he tells his brother, and now he wants Hap to help him tell Dad a couple of things. "I did a terrible thing today, Hap. It's been the strangest day I ever went through. I'm all numb, I swear."

Biff had waited for six hours to see Oliver—all day. Kept sending his name in. Finally, about five o'clock, Oliver comes out, and doesn't remember who Biff was or anything. "I felt like such an idiot, Hap."

Oliver just walked away and Biff had no time to tell about the Florida idea or anything. "He gave me one look and—I realized what a ridiculous lie my whole life has been! We've been talking in a dream for fifteen years. I was a shipping clerk."

Happy asks, "What'd you do?"

With great tension and wonder at himself Biff answers, "Well, he left, see. And the secretary went out. . . . I don't know what came over me, Hap. The next thing I know I'm in his office—paneled walls, everything. I can't explain it. I—Hap, I took his fountain pen. I ran out. I ran down all eleven flights. I ran and ran and ran."

Now Biff wants help from his brother—for he is gonna tell Pop exactly what happened. Pop has got to understand that he's not the man somebody lends that kind of money to. Pop thinks that Biff has been spiting him all these years and it has been eating him up—and it would be better if he knew the truth.

Hap thinks it would be better if they told Pop something nice —that Oliver is considering things, and he and Biff have a lunch date tomorrow, and then Oliver can think it over a couple more weeks, and gradually it will fade away and nobody will be the worse. "Dad," Hap reminds Biff, "is never so happy as when he's looking forward to something."

Willy arrives and Happy gives him a fine greeting. They sit down and Happy suggests a drink. "Let's get loaded," Biff agrees.

Willy thinks Biff looks worried and senses that his son has had some drinks already. "Everything go all right?" he inquires.

BIFF (*high, slightly alcoholic, above the earth*)—I'm going to tell you everything from first to last. It's been a strange day. (*Silence. He looks around, composes himself as best he can, but his breath keeps breaking the rhythm of his voice.*) I had to wait quite a while for him, and—

WILLY—Oliver?

BIFF—Yeah, Oliver. All day, as a matter of cold fact. And a lot of—instances—facts, Pop, facts about my life came back to me. Who was it, Pop? Who ever said I was a salesman with Oliver?

WILLY—Well, you were.

BIFF—No, Dad, I was a shipping clerk.

WILLY—But you were practically—

BIFF (*with determination*)—Dad, I don't know who said it first, but I was never a salesman for Bill Oliver.

WILLY—What're you talking about?

BIFF—Let's hold on to the facts tonight, Pop. We're not going to get anywhere bullin' around. I was a shipping clerk.

WILLY (*angrily*)—All right, now listen to me—

BIFF—Why don't you let me finish?

WILLY—I'm not interested in stories about the past or any crap of that kind because the woods are burning, boys, you understand? There's a big blaze going on all around. I was fired today.

BIFF (*shocked*)—How could you be?

WILLY—I was fired, and I'm looking for a little good news to tell your mother, because the woman has waited and the woman has suffered. The gist of it is that I haven't got a story left in my head, Biff. So don't give me a lecture about facts and aspects. I am not interested. Now what've you got to say to me? (STANLEY *enters with three drinks. They wait until he leaves.*)

WILLY—Did you see Oliver?

BIFF—Jesus, Dad!

WILLY—You mean you didn't go up there?

HAPPY—Sure he went up there.

BIFF—I did. I—saw him. How could they fire you?

WILLY (*on the edge of his chair*)—What kind of a welcome did he give you?

BIFF—He won't even let you work on commission?
BIFF—He won't even let you work on commission?
WILLY—I'm out! (*Driving.*) So tell me, he gave you a warm welcome?
HAPPY—Sure, Pop, sure!
BIFF (*driven*)—Well, it was kind of—
WILLY—I was wondering if he'd remember you. (*To* HAPPY.) Imagine, man doesn't see him for ten, twelve years and gives him that kind of a welcome!
HAPPY—Damn right!
BIFF (*trying to return to the offensive*)—Pop, look—

It just is no use. Willy, the salesman, keeps talking and questioning so enthusiastically, and is so sure that the big deal with Oliver is set, that his sweating and angry son has no chance to unburden himself. To Happy Biff exclaims, helplessly, "I can't talk to him!"

A single trumpet note jars the ear. The light of green leaves stains the Loman house once more, and the house holds the air of night and a dream. Young Bernard knocks frantically on the door, calling for Mrs. Loman. While Biff and his father are talking in the restaurant, Bernard raises Linda and wildly informs her that Biff has flunked math—and in the restaurant Willy is furiously saying, "If you hadn't flunked you'd've been set by now!"

Linda, in the house, is agitated by the news from young Bernard. She wonders where Biff is, and Bernard tells her he went to Grand Central and was going to see his father in Boston. In the restaurant, Biff desperately manages to tell his father what he has been trying to say—that he saw Oliver, and is washed up with him, and that he took the pen out of Oliver's office. He didn't exactly steal it, which is just what he has been trying to explain.

The light on the Loman house vanishes as Willy, looking at the pen, gasps a "My God, Biff!" Somewhere the voice of a hotel telephone operator is heard—the precise sing-song of an experienced operator. "Standish Arms, good evening," she says as she plugs in a line.

Willy, in the restaurant with his sons, shouts, "I'm not in my room!" Biff and Hap become frightened. "Ringing Mr. Loman for you!" chants the operator, and Willy cries, "I'm not there, stop it!" Biff gets on his knees before his father's chair and promises, "Dad, I'll make good. I'll make good."

Willy tries to get up but his son holds him down in his chair.

"No, you're no good, you're no good for anything," snarls Willy.

"Mr. Loman does not answer. Shall I page him?" Willy has no trouble hearing the operator, and, struggling to stand, he shouts, "No, no, no!"

Happy is afraid his father is going to become violent. In final desperation Biff tells his father some of the lie that Hap had suggested, about Oliver considering the proposition and a lunch date tomorrow. "But I can't go tomorrow," says the agonized Biff. "I took those balls years ago, now I walk out with his fountain pen. That clinches it, don't you see?"

A page boy now is paging Mr. Loman in that hotel which is so distant in time and space. . . . And somewhere else a Woman is laughing. At the restaurant, Willy is angry and threatening. Biff will go to that lunch tomorrow, or—

Biff again protests that he can't. "Are you spiting me?" demands his father. "You rotten little louse, are you spiting me?" He strikes Biff, and Happy separates them. The two chippies Happy has arranged for come in and Hap tells them to sit down . . . and somewhere The Woman still is laughing. The boys introduce their father to the girls and suggest a drink, but Willy is being pulled in another direction because The Woman now is urging, "Willy, are you going to answer the door!"

The salesman gets up, befuddled. "The washroom . . . the door . . . Where's the door?" Biff leads him off and shows him where "the place" is, and Happy says, brightly, "Well, girls, what's the program?"

Biff, near crying, is very far from Happy's happy mood; he has in his pocket the rubber hose he took from the water heater, and he puts it on the table. "You could help him—I can't," he accuses his brother. "Don't you understand what I am talking about? He's going to kill himself, don't you know that?" Now at the edge of a breakdown, Biff goes blindly out. "Come on, girls, we'll catch up with him," Happy suggests. He promises they will paint the town. The waiter, Stanley, calls indignantly after Happy as the trio departs.

The lights on this scene dim, and at the other side of the stage they reveal Willy and The Woman in a hotel room, and there is a knocking at the door. She is in a black slip and he is buttoning his shirt. The knocking has been going on for some time and it is getting on The Woman's nerves. Finally Willy agrees to open the door if she will go into the bathroom and stay hidden there. She has had enough liquor to hold her for a while.

Willy opens the door, and it's his young son Biff, carrying a suitcase and wanting to know why his father didn't answer sooner. Willy was in the bathroom and had the door closed, is the explanation.

The father is surprised to see his son. "Dad, I flunked math," the boy announces. He can't graduate. Bernard had tried to give him the answers for the exams, but Biff failed anyway by four points. If Pop would only talk to Birnbaum, and Birnbaum saw the kind of man Pop was, maybe he'd forget the four points.

Willy announces, "We'll drive right back," and Biff is overjoyed. Biff tells a story about Birnbaum and the two begin to laugh—and The Woman in the bathroom joins in. Willy tries to hurry his son out of the room, but he is too late; The Woman comes in to join the party.

Biff's father pretends that this is a tenant next door whose room is being painted, and he is allowing her to use his bath—but it is a flimsy dodge and it doesn't work. As the light dawns on Biff, Willy pushes The Woman out and gives her the stockings he has promised her—two boxes of size nines. After she has gone Willy lamely suggests that he and his son better get going, to be at the school first thing in the morning. But Biff remains motionless—and weeping. "I'll see Birnbaum first thing in the morning," says the father.

BIFF—Never mind.

WILLY (*getting down beside* BIFF)—Never mind! He's going to give you those points. I'll see to it.

BIFF—He wouldn't listen to you.

WILLY—He certainly will listen to me. You need those points for the U. of Virginia.

BIFF—I'm not going there.

WILLY—Heh? If I can't get him to change that mark you'll make it up in Summer school. You've got all Summer to—

BIFF (*his weeping breaking from him*)—Dad. . . .

WILLY (*infected by it*)—Oh, my boy. . . .

BIFF—Dad. . . .

WILLY—She's nothing to me, Biff. I was lonely. I was terribly lonely.

BIFF—You—you gave her Mama's stockings! (*His tears break through and he rises to go.*)

WILLY (*grabbing for* BIFF)—I gave you an order!

BIFF—Don't touch me, you—liar!

WILLY—Apologize for that!

BIFF—You fake! You phony little fake! You fake! (*Over-*

DEATH OF A SALESMAN 83

come, he turns quickly and weeping fully goes out with his suitcase. WILLY *is left on the floor on his knees.*)
WILLY—I gave you an order! Biff, come back here or I'll beat you! Come back here! I'll whip you! (STANLEY, *the waiter, comes quickly in from the right and stands in front of* WILLY, *for the scene is back in the restaurant.*)
WILLY (*shouts at* STANLEY)—I gave you an order. . . .
STANLEY—Hey, let's pick it up, pick it up, Mr. Loman. (*He helps* WILLY *to his feet.*) Your boys left with the chippies. They said they'll see you home. (*A second waiter watches some distance away.*)
WILLY—But we were supposed to have dinner together. (*Music is heard,* WILLY'S *theme.*)
STANLEY—Can you make it?
WILLY—I'll—sure, I can make it. (*Suddenly concerned about his clothes.*) Do I—I look all right?
STANLEY—Sure, you look all right. (*He flicks a speck off* WILLY'S *lapel.*)
WILLY—Here—here's a dollar.
STANLEY—Oh, your son paid me. It's all right.
WILLY—(*putting it in* STANLEY'S *hand*)—No, take it. You're a good boy.

Willy forces even more money on the waiter, and Stanley quietly slips it back into the salesman's jacket pocket. And now Willy would like to buy some seeds. "Is there a seed store in the neighborhood?" he inquires of Stanley. There might be some hardware stores on Sixth Avenue still open, and Loman hurries out in search of one.
The scene dims on the restaurant and comes up on the kitchen of the house, where Happy arrives carrying a large bunch of roses, followed by Biff. The boys look for their mother, and Happy freezes when he sees her in the living room. Linda moves ominously and quietly into the kitchen and her younger son recoils, fearfully. "Where's Pop? Is he sleeping?" he asks.
He offers the flowers and his mother knocks them to the floor. To Biff she cries, "Don't you care whether he lives or dies? . . . Get out of my sight! Get out of here!"
Linda is in a cold and implacable fury. Her sons have invited their father to dinner, and he has looked forward to it all day—and then they desert him to go off with a couple of their lousy, rotten whores. For once Happy has something on his side, but Linda won't believe him. She will not believe that the boys had

been with their father and that they'd had a swell time—and that all Happy and the women did was follow Biff around trying to cheer him up.

Their mother calls them a pair of animals and orders both of them out of the house. She knows what must have happened, for their father was so humiliated he nearly limped when he walked into the house. They hadn't even gone into the toilet in the restaurant to see if their father was all right! "You louse, you," she shrills at Biff as he is picking the flowers off the floor.

Biff doesn't want to go without seeing his father, but she will not permit it. Biff thinks he must be in bed . . . but from outside comes a kind of hammering noise. . . .

Biff and his mother go into the back-yard garden, and here is Willy tamping a hoe into its handle. He has the hoe, a flashlight and a handful of seed packages. With the light he reads the directions—so far apart for carrots, so far for carrots, so far for beets, and lettuce. At the proper distance he puts each package down as he reads the directions to himself.

Ben appears, and as if in answer to an unspoken question Willy says, " 'Cause she's suffered Ben, the woman has suffered. A man can't go out the way he came in, Ben, a man has got to add up to something. . . . Remember, it's a guaranteed twenty thousand dollar proposition. . . ."

"They might not honor the policy," says the practical Ben. But Willy is confident they'll honor it all right, because he has worked like a coolie to meet every premium on the nose. Linda and Biff are listening.

Willy sees the whole thing now, enthusiastically, as a fine project—like a diamond shining in the dark that he can pick up and touch in his hand. Not like an appointment. And the funeral will be massive, with all the old-timers coming from all over! That boy Biff will be thunderstruck, seeing how his father is known all over.

Ben disagrees. "He'll call you a coward. Yes, and a damned fool."

Willy is suddenly fearful, broken and desperate. Biff must not think that! "Oh, Ben," he pleads, "how do we get back to all the great times? Used to be so full of light, and comradeship, the sleigh-riding in Winter, and the ruddiness on his cheeks. And always some kind of good news coming up, always something nice coming up ahead. And never even let me carry the valises in the house, and simonizing, simonizing that little red car! Why, why can't I give him something and not have him hate me?"

Ben asks time to ponder the problem and moves off, out of sight. Biff comes up and tells his father, "There are people all around here. Don't you realize that?" He takes the hoe from Willy. "I'm saying good-by to you, Pop. I'm not coming back any more."

"You're not going to see Oliver tomorrow?" Willy's clinging to this notion is pitiful, and once again Biff explains that there is no appointment. Now, he suggests, let's just wrap it all up and tell Mom.

Willy, highly nervous, tries to pull away. He doesn't want to see his wife, but Biff finally manages to urge him in. The loving Linda queries ever so gently, "Did you plant, dear?" Willy does not answer. Biff offers his hand to his father in farewell, and it is refused. Biff shrugs and turns toward the stair to go up and get his things.

"May you rot in hell," exclaims Willy, "if you leave this house!"

"Exactly what is it that you want from me?"

"I want you to know, on the train, in the mountains, in the valleys, wherever you go, that you cut down your life for spite!"

Biff is past endurance. "All right, phony! Then let's lay it on the line," he cries—and whips the rubber tube out of his pocket and lays it on the table. Linda grabs for it but her son holds her off. Willy, caged, pretends he never saw the tube before.

Biff's rage is out of control. Now, for once, his father is going to hear the truth about his sons—his sons, who never told the truth for ten minutes in this house. Happy is not an assistant buyer—he's just one of two assistants to the assistants. And as for himself—the time Biff had no address for three months was because he was in jail in Kansas City for stealing a suit. As his mother begins to weep into her hands, Biff cries, "I stole myself out of every good job since high school. And I never got anywhere because you blew me so full of hot air that I could never stand taking orders from anybody!"

"Then hang yourself for spite," Willy shouts.

"No! Nobody's hanging himself," Biff answers. "Willy! I ran down eleven flights with a pen in my hand today. And suddenly I stopped, you hear me? And in the middle of that office building, do you hear this? I stopped in the middle of that building and I saw—the sky. I saw the things that I love in this world. The work and the food and time to sit and smoke. And I looked at the pen and said to myself, what the hell am I grabbing this for? Why am I trying to become what I don't want to be? What am I doing in an office, making a contemptuous, begging fool of myself, when all I want is out there, waiting for me the minute I say I know who I am! Why can't I say that, Willy?"

As best he can, Willy defends himself as his son continues to lash him and to cry, "Pop, I'm nothing!" Finally, Biff's fury ebbs and the young man breaks down, sobbing, holding on to Willy. Willy dumbly fumbles for his son's face and a look of astonishment comes over him. Biff breaks away and goes up to bed, promising he will go in the morning.

Willy is astonished, elevated. He marvels, "Isn't that—isn't that remarkable? Biff—he likes me!"

His wife soothes, "He loves you."

"Always did, Pop," Happy agrees.

Linda, sensing the racing of her husband's mind, urges him to bed—but Ben has appeared just outside the kitchen and is talking in seeming riddles: "Yes, outstanding, with twenty thousand behind him. . . . And it does take a great kind of a man to crack the jungle."

Happy, sensing what his mother does, chips in with chatter about his getting married and making good . . . but Willy is listening to Ben outside. "One must go in to fetch a diamond out. . . . Not like an appointment at all. . . ."

Heeding Linda's pleas to come to bed, Willy suggests that she go on. She looks tired, and he'll be there in two minutes. She goes to her bedroom, and Willy moves just outside the kitchen door. "Loves me," he is saying to himself, wonderingly. "Always loved me."

"It's dark there, but full of diamonds." Ben is offering rewards. Willy muses, "Can you imagine that magnificence with twenty thousand dollars in his pocket?"

Willy is in an elegiac mood. Now Biff and he are going to make good. . . . Suddenly he realizes that Ben has left, and his wife is calling for him to come up. He utters a gasp of fear as sounds, faces and voices seem to swarm in upon him, and the music rises to almost an unbearable scream. Willy rushes off around the house.

"Willy!" Linda is calling. There is no answer. Biff and Happy get out of their beds. There is the sound of a car starting and moving away at full speed. Linda gasps, "No!" Biff, rushing downstairs, calls, "Pop!"

As the car speeds off the music crashes down, then dies to the

Photo by Eileen Darby, Graphic House, New York.

"DEATH OF A SALESMAN"

Willy—I was fired, and I'm looking for a little good news to tell your mother, because the woman has waited and the woman has suffered.

(*Arthur Kennedy, Lee J. Cobb, Cameron Mitchell*)

Photo by John Swope, New York.

"ANNE OF THE THOUSAND DAYS"

Anne—Some day, somebody will translate from the French into English a book on good manners—and maybe the King of England will read it.

Henry—Read it, my dear—I'll write it!

(*Joyce Redman, Rex Harrison*)

Photo by Bob Golby, New York.

"THE MADWOMAN OF CHAILLOT"

The Ragpicker—Countess, little by little the pimps have taken over the world. They don't do anything, they don't make anything—they just stand there and take their cut.

(*Martita Hunt, John Carradine*)

Photo by John Swope, New York.

"DETECTIVE STORY"

Mary—You're a cruel and vengeful man. You're everything you always said you hated in your own father.

(*Ralph Bellamy, Meg Mundy*)

Photo by Eileen Darby, Graphic House, New York.

"EDWARD, MY SON"

Arnold—Who did we know who always took their holidays in the Isle of Wight?
Evelyn—Mr. Soames.
Parker—He still does.

(*Robert Morley, Ian Hunter, Peggy Ashcroft*)

Photo by Vandamm, New York.

"LIFE WITH MOTHER"

Vinnie—Oh, Mr. Miller, I was just speaking to Mr. Day about you. Clare, this is Mr. Miller.

(*Dorothy Stickney, Robert Emhardt, Howard Lindsay*)

Photo by Lucas & Monroe, Inc., New York.

"LIGHT UP THE SKY"

Irene—Well, my dears, suddenly I was dreaming that I was on the stage and the curtain was going up . . . and then I began to speak. I took the lines from all the other actors . . .

(*Jane Middleton, Barry Nelson, Virginia Field, Sam Levene*)

Photo by Vandamm, New York.

"THE SILVER WHISTLE"

Erwenter—Whiskey and the potion of Twingsti! We're in for a wild night!

(*Jose Ferrer, Burton Mallory, William Lynn*)

Photo by Lucas & Monroe, Inc., New York.

"TWO BLIND MICE"

Thurston—I'm afraid I'll have to burn them. Miss Norwood will take the only notes. Eighteen copies, Miss Norwood!

(*Jan Sterling, Melvyn Douglas*)

Photo by Vandamm, New York.

"GOODBYE, MY FANCY"

Agatha—Oh, I'm not going to plead with you any more. I'm going to make a deal with you. A business deal.
Merrill—What are you talking about?

(*Madeleine Carroll, Conrad Nagel*)

DEATH OF A SALESMAN

note of a single string. Biff and Happy gravely don their jackets, and Linda slowly walks out of her room—in mourning. In the kitchen Charley and Bernard are there. They all move toward the audience, through the wall, and the music has developed into a dead march. They come down to the apron and stare down at the grave.

After a while Charley and Biff and Happy try to get Linda to come away now—but she does not want to come away yet because she does not yet understand. First time they were free and clear in thirty-five years. . . . He only needed a little salary. . . .

Biff remembers some of the nice days they used to have, working around the house. Willy, says Charley in requiem, was a salesman. A salesman don't put a bolt to a nut or tell you the law or give you medicine. "He's a man way out there in the blue, riding on a smile and a shoeshine. And when they start not smiling back—that's an earthquake. . . ."

Happy's chin is up. He is not going to be licked. He'll beat this racket. "The Loman Brothers!" But Biff adds, as he bends to urge his mother to go once more, "I know who I am, kid."

For a moment they all withdraw, leaving Linda at the grave, and the flute begins to play again not far away.

"Forgive me, dear, I can't cry," Linda says with utmost tenderness. "I don't know what it is, but I can't cry. I don't understand it. Why did you ever do that? Help me, Willy, I can't cry. It seems to me that you're just on another trip. I keep expecting you. Willy, dear, I can't cry. Why did you do it? I search and search and I search, and I can't understand it, Willy. I made the last payment on the house today. Today, dear. And there'll be nobody home. (*A sob rises in her throat.*) We're free and clear. (*Sobbing more fully, released.*) We're free. (BIFF *comes slowly toward her.*) We're free. . . . We're free. . . ."

Biff lifts her to her feet and leads her off; the others follow. Only the flute music is heard as, over the darkening stage, the hard towers of the apartment buildings come into focus over the house.

THE CURTAIN FALLS

ANNE OF THE THOUSAND DAYS *
A Drama in Two Acts
By Maxwell Anderson

STARTING with "What Price Glory?" in 1924, Maxwell Anderson has been represented in these Best Plays volumes by fifteen dramas and comedies, and this is the sixteenth. A notable record for a notable playwright, edging over the fifteen appearances of George S. Kaufman and outnumbering Eugene O'Neill by seven. Once again Mr. Anderson has returned to his favorite combination—historic figures and a verse-and-prose style.

The success of "Anne of the Thousand Days" was a triumph of skill and perseverance on the part of the author, his fellow producers, the Playwrights' Company, and Jo Mielziner, the scenic artist. For, at the beginning of its tryout, "Anne" looked pretty hopeless. Witnesses found it cumbersome, and it needed an extraordinary amount of work—work which took time and increased the losses on the road. Mr. Anderson wrote this editor, "As to a possible article about script changes on 'Anne,' I can only say that such horror should not be revealed to the reading public. I've been through some trying times both with failures and successes, but this tops them all for both the duration and the intensity of the agony. . . . Anyway, the only way to get over one of them is to start another—which I have done, though I know damn well what it will get me into." (The new one is a musical, "Cry the Beloved Country," by Anderson and Kurt Weill.)

Most of the stage is in darkness as the prologue opens on Anne, in the year 1536. She is in prison, talking to herself:

If I were to die now—
but I must not die yet,
not yet.
It's been too brief. A few weeks and days.

* Copyright, 1948, by Maxwell Anderson.
Published by William Sloane Associates, New York.
Author's agent, Harold Freedman, c/o Brandt & Brandt, 101 Park Avenue, New York City.

ANNE OF THE THOUSAND DAYS

How many days, I wonder, since the first time
I gave myself, to that last day when he—
when he left me at the lists and I saw him no more?
Well, I can reckon it.
I have time enough. Those who sit in the Tower
don't lack for time.

He would never cipher.
He was shrewd and heavy—
and cunning with his tongue, and wary in intrigue,
but when it came to adding up an account
he filled it with errors and bit his tongue—
and swore—
till I slapped his hands like a child and took the pen
and made it straight.
"A king," I said, "a king, and cannot reckon."
I was his clever girl then, his Nan;
he'd kiss me then, and maul me, and take me down.
On the rushes. Anywhere.
Why do I think of it now? Would he kill me? Kill me?
Henry? The fool? That great fool kill me?

Anne continues her tragic musing, observing that if she were to die now, her Elizabeth, her firstling, all she has, must face the new world in the morning.

The light upon Anne fades and she vanishes; and on the other side of the stage illumination comes up on the richly costumed and always-hatted Henry VIII. (He wore a hat to hide his baldness—and Anne Boleyn devised the fashion of the long-flowing sleeve to conceal a sixth finger on one of her hands.)

Henry, too, is thinking aloud:

This is hard to do
when you come to put pen to paper.
You say to yourself,
She must die. And she must—
if things are to go as planned.
Yes, if they are to go at all.
If I am to rule
and keep my sanity and hold my England off the rocks.
It's a lee shore—and a low tide—and the wind's a gale—
and the Spanish rocks are bare and sharp.
Go back to it, Henry, go back to it.

Keep your mind
on this parchment you must sign.
Dip the pen in the ink; write your name.

You've condemned men, nobles and peasants.
She's struck down a few herself—
or driven you to it.
It's only that a woman you've held in your arms
and longed for when she was away,
and suffered with her—no, but she promised you an heir. Write
  it down—
Write Henry Rex, and it's done.

How, he wonders, has he ever come to this? What was he like, ten years ago, when she flashed her first anger at him?

The lights black out.

Scene II

It is Thomas Boleyn's house, and Cardinal Wolsey has come to warn Boleyn that the King is coming—not to see Mary, but to see Anne! Boleyn is disturbed, for the King wants his younger daughter after having had the elder one as a mistress for four years. What is he to say?

The Cardinal is a hard and forthright man. "Tell her in plain words that the King wants her."

But this is not so easy. Boleyn has encouraged Anne with the Earl of Northumberland, and they have a sort of engagement between them. He wants more time to think it out, and the Cardinal suggests that he think of some such delaying maneuver as taking the King to see his hounds while Wolsey himself tackles Anne and the Earl of Northumberland.

Two servants, Norris and Smeaton, announce the King; Henry, jovial, greets Thomas and inquires of Wolsey, "And how's the vicar of hell this chilly Spring morning?"

"I keep warm, Majesty."

"I'm sure you do. With your feet on the devil's fender. Meanwhile toasting your paddocks at God's altar."

"And running the King's errands," Wolsey adds drily. "It's a busy life."

Now, to Boleyn, Henry says, "May I smell this pretty posy of yours?" Boleyn pleads that Anne still needs a half hour at her mirror, and suggests they kill the time by going to look at a clump of red deer on the estate—but first Henry would have a word or two.

BOLEYN—Yes? My lord!

HENRY—There's always a temptation when a man's in my position, that he'll think of the nation as his own trough, and get all four feet in it and eat from one end to the other. I don't want to look like that to anybody.

BOLEYN—You don't, my sovereign.

HENRY—I'm a religious man, Boleyn. I want to do what's right in the eyes of God and the church. And myself—and my people—and you.

BOLEYN—That's a swath of folk to satisfy—if you include God.

HENRY—I include both God and the women—among them your daughters. What will your daughters say of me—the two of them together—talking at night? Um?

BOLEYN—What two women say together—talking at night of one man who has wanted them both—and taken both—no man will ever know that.—But I think—if you don't mind—

HENRY—I've asked you.

BOLEYN—I think you go a little rapid with Annie. You'll need to be gentle.

HENRY—But she'll have me—in the end?

BOLEYN—She's no fool, my lord.

HENRY (*after a pause*)—What I do is God's will.

BOLEYN—Now, if a man or a monarch could be sure of that.

HENRY—
  I've worked it out, in my mind.—
  I pray to God.
  I tell you this first, Boleyn.
  God answers prayer. That's known. Every morning I go
    on my knees
  and pray that what I do may be God's will.
  I pray him to direct me—that whatever thought
  comes to my mind—whatever motion
  floods in my heart—shall be God's will—and I
  only his instrument. Wherever I turn,
  whatever I do—whether to reach for food,
  or thread my way among the crossed paths of the law,
  or interpret the holy word,
  or judge men innocent—or guilty—
  every morning I pray him on my knees

nothing shall rise in my brain or heart but He
has wished it first.
And since He answers prayer,
and since he's given me such heavy power to act,
power for good and evil,
He must answer this. He does answer.
I find such peace in this,
that not one morning my whole life long
shall I fail these devotions.

BOLEYN—This is a noble thought, of course, but your Majesty realizes that it might be used as an excuse for—

HENRY—For what?

BOLEYN—For doing as you please.

Henry does not relish the sarcasm. The two servants, Norris and Smeaton, reappear, with a message that Boleyn's wife wants to see him in the house. Thomas excuses himself, and Henry seizes the opportunity to get the servants' advice, man to man. What's the best way to get a maiden? Not medically a maiden, perhaps, but young and wild—and uncaught.

Norris recommends writing her poems; he knows that Tom Wyatt does and it's unfailing. Smeaton's favorite maneuver is singing songs—and, if these fail, tell the object of pursuit that he can be potent only with her . . . that he has tried others with no success. "They can't resist that," he advises his monarch.

The Duke of Norfolk, coming upon the scene, joins the discussion. His advice is extremely simple: "If you want a woman, take her." Don't bother about consent—why should a woman have anything to say about it?

Henry is doubtful. It might have been so in the old days, but not now. Besides, he wants this woman to be in love with him. Norfolk ends the colloquy by suggesting that they all go look at the venison. Henry acquiesces, saying, "Next to the haunch of a virgin there's nothing like a haunch of venison."

The lights black out.

SCENE III

Percy, Earl of Northumberland, and Anne are having a tryst in the woods. She is laughing at him, but tenderly, and pretending to be angry with herself. During her two years at the court of Queen Claude she could have had the silkened flower of the aristocracy—galiant, captivating men. "And I fell in love with none of them. I came home and promptly fell in love with a—a thistle. A countryman from the north. With no graces at all. Can't dance. Can't sing. Can hardly speak English."

Percy defends himself. "Can put his arms around you," he points out. "Silks are for holiday. Honest homespun wears through the years."

Anne becomes serious. If they love enough to marry, they must keep nothing back. She asks him point-blank if he is a virgin. "I'm a man," he replies. "Are you a virgin?"

"No," Anne admits—but she was never in love before. "Tell me about the girls," she invites him.

"One thing you'd best learn now, my sweet. I'll be the man of the house when we have a house, and if any game's to be played I'll lead in that game and not follow. The game I like now is to put my arms about you and say nothing."

Their long embrace is interrupted by the appearance of Cardinal Wolsey. He is glad he has found them together, for he must speak to both—yet sorry to find them so intimate. For, he informs Percy, Percy's father and the King have arranged an alliance with the Talbots through one of the daughters of the Earl of Shrewsbury—with Percy, of course, doing the allying.

The young man stoutly declares he will do no such thing. Wolsey, ignoring him for a moment, turns to Anne. As for Anne —it has been arranged that she marry the Earl of Ormond in Ireland.

The lovers will accept no such arrangement. "We've pledged ourselves to each other, and our hearts go with that pledge!" Percy declares.

WOLSEY—No doubt. And this is the reward I get for my kindness to you. (*He turns away.*)

ANNE (*softly*)—My lord Cardinal, that we two are in love, and have been these two months, every servant in the house knows, for we've made no secret of it before them or anyone. That we are in love, that we mean to marry, has been no secret from the whole world all that time. Why you've come here now to tell us suddenly that we're to match elsewhere, we don't know. There must be some reason behind it. Tell us what it is.

WOLSEY—I have told you.

ANNE—Then you talk nonsense, and I won't listen!

PERCY—Nor I!

WOLSEY—I stand here as the king's minister, and you're aware of that. I knew a great lord to die for less than you have just said. His name was Buckingham.

PERCY (*more humbly*)—You know I have no wish to anger the King. But tell us what this means and why you say it to us.

WOLSEY (*thundering*)—Do you think the King and I come lightly to such decisions as this? Do you think we have not weighed every reason for and against before we issue a command? One thing I can tell you, you will obey or your estates are forfeit! If you continue disloyal it's doubtful how long you will live! Go now, I wish to speak to Anne alone.

PERCY—Anne—

ANNE—Yes, you must go.

PERCY—Kiss me, then.

WOLSEY—Do not touch her.

PERCY—All this talk of sudden death makes it very easy for you, my lord. But I shall kiss her if I like. (*And he does so.*)

ANNE—Only take care of yourself. I shall see you.

PERCY—Yes. (*He turns and goes stage right into darkness.* ANNE *stands silent and defiant, looking at* WOLSEY.)

WOLSEY—Look your knives through and through me, mistress. At my age it will do me no hurt—and at yours, though you hurt easily, you will cure quickly. Are you serious about this thorn-apple from the north?

ANNE—My lord—he's mine—and I'm his.

WOLSEY—But if there were another and worthier, well, you could change?

ANNE—No. I want no other. And if you do him harm—this my chosen husband—I am only a girl, but you will know you have an enemy!

Craftily, Wolsey tries to hint to Anne what really is in store for her. He pretends that he sees writing on her necklace, in Latin, and offers a translation: "Touch me not. I belong to the King."

Anne cannot quite believe that the King has looked at her, but finally she realizes that Wolsey is Henry's emissary when he says, "It is sometimes my pleasure to anticipate his desires."

Anne is spirited, and she is angry. "Perhaps," she suggests, "you would be wise to anticipate the answer he will receive from me if he comes." He has had Mary four years, and she is probably with child by him and of no further use to him. She is not going to go the way of her sister.

Anne's parents, Thomas and Elizabeth, come out of the shadows. "Do you also offer me up to this royal bull—you, my father? And you, my mother?"

They hush the girl—Henry is here, and might hear.

"Well—you've let him come—I haven't. Find some way out of it."

Boleyn protests it is not his doing—and how, anyway, was he to know that it would displease her.

"Do you know what it is to be in love?" she begs. "Do you remember? Remember what it is like to have your whole life follow one person out at the door—and not to live again, and not to want to live, until he returns?"

Yes, Elizabeth remembers—but she, too, is helpless.

Anne pleads with the Cardinal that the King could look elsewhere, since he already has had Mary. . . .

Henry comes upon the scene, saying, "I have greeted all here, I think, save only the lady Anne. Sweet Nan, will you give me a kiss?" Dutifully she gives it—but on his hand.

That was not the kind of kiss he meant, the monarch says. Anne pleads that she has been drinking medicine for a cold and her breath is bad—but Henry catches her at her lie by suddenly stooping and kissing her. Then he orders the others to depart, and they bow out, backward.

Henry begs Anne to look on him, not as a monarch who commands, but as a doubting, hoping, tremulous man who wants to be loved for himself. Then why did he send Wolsey as an ambassador? she parries.

"I was afraid that you wouldn't care for me."

"Then perhaps you will understand the very cruel thing that has happened to me: I have fallen in love—and not with you."

The King is shocked at first, but then remembers that he has heard something. He guesses correctly that it is Northumberland, and for a moment considers a familiar solution of letting Anne marry her man and then taking her as a mistress. It can be done, he declares cynically, for all husbands can be placated. "But I don't want you that way! I want you to myself!"

ANNE—What can I do?
HENRY—
　Give up this young wattle-and-daub—
　give him up, I tell you,
　and this kingdom shall turn around you, bishops and peers—

and whatever you've wanted, for anyone,
a knighthood,
an estate, a great income rolling in forever,
titles and places, you shall dispose of them
just as you please!
ANNE—
And be thrown out in the end
like a dirty rag.—I haven't seen Mary disposing
of revenues.
HENRY—
She asked for nothing. Look, Anne,
I'm here desperate. I can't bargain with you.
Ask for what you want.
ANNE—
To be free. To be free
to marry where I love.
(HENRY *pauses*.)
HENRY—No.
ANNE—
I too can say no!
I've seen you too close
and known you too long. I've heard what your courtiers say
and then I've seen what you are. You're spoiled and vengeful,
and malicious and bloody. The poetry they praise
so much is sour, and the music you write's worse.
You dance like a hobbledehoy; you make love
as you eat—with a good deal of noise and no subtlety.
It was my doubtful pleasure once to sleep in Mary's room—
or to lie awake when you thought me asleep, and observe
the royal porpoise at play—
HENRY—This is not safe.
ANNE—
Yes, I've been told it's not safe for any of us
to say no to our squire Harry. This put-on, kindly
hail-fellow-well-met of yours. My father's house
will be pulled down—and Northumberland's too, they tell me.
Well, pull them down. You are what I said.
HENRY—
I had no wish to come here. I came
because I must, and couldn't help myself.
Well—I'm well out of it. Let it end here tonight.

ANNE OF THE THOUSAND DAYS

I thank you for your anger,
and for raising anger in me. There's no better way
to make an end.—Wolsey! Where's the fat saddlebags?
(*He turns.*)
ANNE—You will not—touch—Northumberland?
HENRY—
I'll try not.
Vengeful as I am, I'll try not.
(*He calls.*) Wolsey! (*He turns and goes into darkness.*)
Where's the vicar of hell?

The lights go out.

SCENE IV

As the lights come up there is a sound of music, and Anne's mother and Norfolk are talking of this new plan of the King's—to set up the courtyard as if for a little play. Servants bring on a table and two chairs. Elizabeth informs Norfolk that the King has brought his singers and musicians, and the performance is to be only for the Boleyn family.

Yet there is Nan to think about. She may not appear tonight. "It's been two years since she quarreled with the King, and much has happened. She's not the same girl. I have no influence over her, nor has her father." All she does is sit in her room.

"But since Northumberland's dead—what does she wait for?" Norfolk asks. Elizabeth does not know. All she knows is that Northumberland had been married off to that Shrewsbury horror, and when the letter came telling of his death Anne took to her room. "I think that marriage killed Northumberland. And it came near to killing Anne."

Mary brings information that Anne is curious about her new dress—her first one in two years—and there is some hope that she may come down.

Mary remarks that the Boleyn family seems to have a strange fascination for the King; she has even heard that there was talk of him and her mother when they were young.

Elizabeth admits they danced together a good deal—he had the face of an angel in those days, and he wanted to be a good king. Mary recalls that when he first came to her he was still naive.

"You may yet be the mother of a king of England," Elizabeth offers hopefully.

"Small chance of that. And small reward in it."

"My dear," says the mother gently, "it's as much as a woman ever has."

Anne has come down in her new dress, but she isn't talking. "You will live, Anne," says her mother. "You won't die. If women died as easily as men there would be no women in this world. And since you will live, you will fill your life with something."

The King is inside, ready.

Scene V

Three choir boys, Wolsey, Norfolk and Henry come into the court. "I am not here tonight as your king," Henry addresses the group. "Something was said at one time—I forget by whom—about my bad poetry and bad music. It rankled deep—but then I saw that there was only one answer—to write great poetry and great music. And since I have a cause for anguish in my life, many songs came to me. . . ." At his command the boys sing:

> Alas, alas,
> What shall I do
> For love, for love,
> Alas, what shall I do—
> Since now so kind I do you find—
> To keep you me unto?
> To keep you me unto?
>
> Oh my heart,
> Oh my heart,
> My heart it is so sore,
> Since I must needs from my love depart,
> And know no cause therefore—
> And know no cause therefore!

And now, Henry announces, the musicians will play a saraband of his writing. "Will you dance with me?" he asks Anne.

She complies, and as they dance they talk.

"Why are you still sullen toward me?"

"Northumberland is dead."

"Not by my order."

"You sent him to marry elsewhere—and it killed him."

"I couldn't let him marry you. I tried—but I couldn't."

"When I look in your face I see his murderer."

Henry pleads that he has had a humbling experience—learning that one cannot choose where he will love. He has tried to love elsewhere, but now has been drawn back here bringing the best he has—his music, his poetry and his love for her.

Anne points out that even if she loved him, he is not free; he is married to Catherine—and even if he is a king who makes his own rules, he still is not free.

Henry desperately argues that it isn't really a marriage. He was hounded into it for political reasons. They can't have sons—all their sons are born dead and there is no male heir to the crown. More than anything, he wants a son—but he must remain Catherine's husband because of the Church and England's friendship with Spain. This marriage is important to churchcraft and statecraft—but it should not be to Anne.

ANNE—
  Important or not, you can't break it. It's stronger
  than you are—and so you offer me nothing.
HENRY—
  It's not nothing, Nan. It's my whole life. I know
  because I tried to erase you and fill my life with
  other things. It won't work. I can think of nothing
  but you.
  It's not only this pain, this stitch in the side,
  this poetry I can't keep from writing, this music
  that I hear when I think of you and must write down.
  —I'm a man, too, Nan. I want you—and only you.
  —I find myself—when I'm talking to an ambassador,
  perhaps—I find myself thinking of you. And what
  am I thinking?—Of you and me playing at dog and
  bitch. Of you and me playing at horse and mare. Of
  you and me every way there is. I want to fill
  you up—night after night. I want to fill you
  with sons.
ANNE—Bastards? For they would be bastards, you know.
HENRY—
  If you say one more word I shall strike you. One
  word more.
ANNE—
  But it's quite obvious that if you and I had
  children they would be bastards.
(HENRY *strikes her hard. She falls to the floor.* WOLSEY, BOLEYN, ELIZABETH *and* MARY *enter.*)

WOLSEY—Your Majesty! (ANNE *slowly gets to her feet.*)

ANNE—You have not yet understood what I mean, I think. What I am trying to tell you is that you not only offer me nothing—you offer yourself nothing. You say you want a son, an heir to the throne. You need such an heir, and the kingdom needs him. But an heir must be legitimate—not base-born—and while you are married to Catherine you can have only bastards. Fill me with as many sons as you like, you would still have no heir, and I would have—nothing.

HENRY—Would you marry me if I were free?

ANNE—You can't get free of Catherine. You know that. And I know it.

HENRY—But if I were free. Free to marry you, and would have you crowned queen of England, would you marry me?

ANNE (*long pause*)—Yes, if you'll make me queen of England, I will marry you.

Wolsey is up immediately with objections. "Try to divorce Catherine and you'll have the whole world against you," he warns Henry. And, he points out, any son of Henry's, legitimate or not, could be made his heir.

Yes, taunts Anne, he could have mistress after mistress and son after son—but she will not be a mistress! "If you will marry and make me queen of England I will give you boys in plenty, but I will take nothing less."

Wolsey, alarmed, begs the King to give up the idea. Henry has made up his mind. "I shall make this girl queen," he announces.

"She hates you," Wolsey points out. To Anne Henry declares:

"If it breaks the earth in two like an apple
and flings the halves into the void
I shall make you queen."

The lights black out.

SCENE VI

Once again as the lights rise there is music, and Norris, one of the attendants, is teaching a group the steps of a dance. The others are Smeaton, Jane Seymour, Madge Shelton and the Boleyn family. Soon they are joined by Norfolk, Sir Thomas More and, in a moment, Anne, who dances a while with Norris.

And next, she announces, Smeaton is going to teach them a new card game Henry has invented, called King's Ransom.

They have a bantering time of it, with Henry joining in when he, too, arrives. It used to be a dull court but now there are dancing and games, he exults. He kisses Anne passionately and she reproves him with, "Some day, somebody will translate from French into English a book on good manners—and maybe the King of England will read it."

He laughs, replying, "Read it—my dear, I'll write it!"

Anne further rebukes him by saying there is more to a court than dances and games. Poets, musicians and philosophers should be encouraged. If, for instance, Sir Thomas More is honored here for his Utopia, then he is honored through England. Cardinal Wolsey and Thomas Cromwell arrive, and some of the others drift away. Wolsey has something on his mind—something for Henry's private ear. Henry becomes angry. He has no private ear—not from Nan, and he resents Wolsey's recent habit of slighting his wife and overlooking her presence and counsel. "Speak now—and before her," he commands.

So be it, shrugs Wolsey. "The Pope will not annul your marriage to Catherine."

A messenger has returned from Rome, with this news and with the further information that the Emperor Charles has invaded Italy, captured the Vatican and made the Pope prisoner. Charles being Catherine's nephew, he has ordered Pope Clement to forbid the annulment.

Henry is desperate. "There must be a divorce this year. Nan is with child—and her child must be heir to the throne."

Wolsey can do nothing more; he has tried everything—money, influence and temporal power. And this is the end of it. Henry and Anne must live as they are and wait. "Children don't wait," she points out.

Wolsey and Cromwell take leave and a furious quarrel begins.

ANNE—How do I know what you've agreed with Wolsey? In all your pacts with kings and princes of the whole earth, I've never known you to tell the truth—never!

HENRY—But I've told it to you!

ANNE—I thought you had. I've tried to take the place you wanted me to take—and do what must be done—because I had promised, and you had promised. But what I feared has come about.

HENRY—God in Heaven damn this spotted bitch! To be called

a liar by my own bitch! Damn you!

ANNE—I've heard you lie to too many. You've never yet told truth when a lie would serve! And we had a bargain, remember. I said, "If you will make me queen I will marry you." But our marriage was at night and in secret; the church does not hold it valid; I am not the queen, and my child will not inherit the throne! Was this planned? It's like many plans I've known you to make!

HENRY—I'll strangle you yet! I'll make an end of you!

ANNE—No doubt.

HENRY—You've lied at times! And to me! What's all this sudden passion about lying?

ANNE—I could have said, "I love you, I love you, I love you!" I didn't say it. Because I don't.—And whether you love me I don't know. You've been unfaithful to me often enough—and I've known where and with whom!

HENRY—If I have you've spoiled it for me, with your damned mocking face watching me through the walls! You spoil everything for me! Faithful—what kind of faith do you want of me? To be impotent in every bed but yours? Well, that's happened, too! They've laughed at me in their beds—more than one. Laughed at their king—and he impotent—with all but you! It's as if you were a disease within me—so that I'm in a fever when you're with me and a fever when you're absent—and it grows worse with the years that should burn it out! What more can I give, in faith or anything I have?

ANNE—What you promise! What you gave your pledged word to do!

HENRY—Anne—I have tried. Not always the right way, perhaps, but my best.

ANNE—You see—if I have a child before this divorce is granted —well, you are still as you are, untouched, but I'm not.

HENRY—I know, Anne, and it's unfair. But it's not what I meant. I meant it all quite honestly—quite as I said. I like what you've done with the court. I want you for my queen. I've lied to all the others, but not to you.—Why must she anger me? Why am I tied to this alabaster face and this pinched-up mouth and these slanted eyes?

Cromwell, a foxy-looking man, comes boldly in and introduces himself as the Cardinal's secretary. He hints that Henry may have his divorce. It needs only the will to do it—the Cardinal's will. But the Cardinal isn't thinking of Henry, he's thinking of

ANNE OF THE THOUSAND DAYS

how to get himself made Pope. Cromwell goes on: He has read the laws of England, and one of them makes it treason to acknowledge any higher authority than the will of the King. The church in England must grant the divorce, if Henry wishes it, and to claim that the Pope governs such a matter is traitorous. He suggests, "Say this to Cardinal Wolsey. He will turn white to the edge of his cape. . . . To bring about all these things you wish, the King has only to appoint a new primate who will legalize his divorce and new marriage."

Henry protests that he has always been a defender of the faith and the church, and it is his greatest strength with his people. Cromwell boldly argues that Henry is only half a king and that England is only half free if a foreign prelate can call him to account. He should get what he wants. At one stroke he can obtain his divorce . . . and make himself the wealthiest monarch in Europe, for the monasteries of England are richer than the gold mines of the new world. Wolsey himself is rich.

Cromwell's arguments are diabolically clever, and Henry has begun a struggle with his conscience. Brusquely he dismisses this strange schemer—then adds, "But I shall be able to find you if I need you?"

"The cardinal seems to have stolen an immense amount of money," Anne hints when the two are again alone. Henry knows it—for some times they went halves. Henry studied stealing under a master—his father, Henry VII. No other king ever died so rich—and he stole from the church, too, but not enough to turn the church against him.

Henry thinks things through, aloud. Yes, he could make Anne his queen and himself wealthy. But he'd have to make the church his enemy. Suppose he made himself head of the church —then many who are his friends now would oppose him, and he would have to kill them for treason. The ones who have integrity of mind will be the first to die. Parliament and the nation can be bludgeoned into silence—but a lot of blood will run. "Yes, I can make my Nan queen—but we must consider the price. In how much we dare be hated. Are we willing to pay it?"

"I am," she announces.

So, though many must die, Anne Boleyn will be Queen of England. . . .

"If only you could love me a little—no, with your whole heart —then it wouldn't matter what happened—"

"Sometimes," Anne starts to reply. "—No. If you were ever honest—if you were ever true—"

"Yes?"
"But you never are."
The lights black out.

Scene VII

Outside York Palace a few voices can be heard cheering and crying "Long live Queen Anne!" Inside, in a sun-splashed room, Norfolk and Cromwell are listening. They hear one voice cry, "Long live Queen Catherine!"

Norfolk observes that the shouting for Anne was somewhat sparse during the royal wedding and coronation. Cromwell should have paid the crowds a bit to be really spontaneous. Cromwell retorts that they were paid—fifteen hundred apprentices got a groat apiece. And even if they had got a half-crown each, they wouldn't cheer Anne the way they'd like to be cheering Catherine.

The cheering outside begins again, and Henry and Anne enter the room. Anne thinks the applause is rather flimsy, but Norfolk lies and says Londoners are like that when they are deeply moved —they just stand and weep instead of cheer. Anne sees through him and calls him an unprincipled old sinner.

York Palace is all Anne's. No one else shall live here, Henry tells her. There won't even be an apartment for him unless she asks him. . . .

In a corner they descry Wolsey, working at a desk. York Palace once was his—and now he is totting up an inventory for the new owner. Cynically he comments, "Let us admit that I stole the palace in the first place and that now you take it from me."

Henry had thought the Cardinal had already left—but no, he has remained to see some friends . . . friends who also want to see Henry. They are Sir Thomas More, Bishop Fisher, and John Houghton, prior of the Charter House. Henry agrees to see them, and when they arrive he gives them a hearty welcome.

More—It's good of you to see us, Your Majesty.

Henry—Make it plural, More. Our majesties are both seeing you.

More—It's about that we wish to speak, my lord. Bishop Fisher!

Fisher—I have known you from a child, King Henry. I was present when you took your first three steps. You know I would not willingly say any word unpleasing to you. I have not opposed your divorce. I have not opposed your new marriage or the coronation of Queen Anne. Such things are sometimes necessary in the conduct of a state.—But you also ask that every religious in England swear fealty to you as spiritual head of the church. And I cannot accept your guidance in spiritual matters.

HENRY—But if I were not head of your church there could have been no divorce and no marriage to Anne. Anne could not have been crowned. Her child could not succeed me.

FISHER—I know that. And still I cannot accept you as my spiritual guide.

HENRY—Do you accept the church of Rome?

FISHER—Yes.

HENRY—Is the Pope moved by spiritual considerations?

FISHER—Your Majesty, I accept the spiritual authority of the church. I cannot accept your usurpation of that authority.

HENRY—Then—though I'm very sorry to lose my friend— I'm afraid you are guilty of treason and will die for it.

FISHER—If it were only I, my king, it wouldn't matter. But there are thousands of my order and of similar orders who cannot take this oath. Must they all die?

HENRY—
If they wish to die, they may. If they insist, they will.—
And I'll tell you why!
I had no mind to cut adrift from Rome
when this thing started. But I was driven to it—by Rome—
and now the cable's cut, and we're adrift.
I see no anchor but the king,
and it happens I'm the king!
John Houghton, why are you here?

HOUGHTON—I could sign everything that's asked, Your Majesty, except the act that constitutes the king head of the church I serve.

HENRY—You will sign it or die.

HOUGHTON—Then all my Charter House dies with me.

Henry pleads for them to see that he has no alternative. Sir Thomas adjures him, saying that he may use his power unjustly or illegally, but he must never go beyond what the people will support. How can Henry hope that the people will go with him now?

The King is confident they will, because they want to be free of Rome.

The visitors ask if they may go. "Gentlemen," Henry urges them, "think again. You move away from this world of your own will." They go, and Henry bids them farewell. Wolsey departs on the arm of Cromwell. He seems old and crippled now and senses that he too will die, saying, "Some men die for their principles, I observe, others because it's the next thing to do."

To Anne Henry begins:

> "I think there's never been
> in all this world
> a king who gave so much to find his way
> to the heart of her he loved. . . ."

But does she love him? He feels that she's never his. He wrote a poem and some music about her last night, asking that question . . . and now here he stands, planning murder, robbery and lies—without a star. He sings her his song:

> "Waking at night, I go to my window,
>   Scanning the stars in a portion of sky,
> Fixing on one that hangs yonder—and over
>   The street of the house where you lie.
>   If you sleep, do you dream?
>   If you dream, is it of me?
>   The clock strikes; I hear your voice in the chimes,
> Repeating your words when I ask if you love me:
>   'Always, never, sometimes.'"

ANNE—I love you.
HENRY—Nan!
ANNE—I love you. Now I know. I love you.
HENRY—I think you mean this.
ANNE—
  I've said it, and it's true.
  These men who were to die, Henry—
  Sir Thomas More
  and all the others—they must live.
HENRY—
  That was all done for you, sweet.
  They shall not die. We'll lift the sentences.
ANNE—
  It doesn't matter about the divorce—or the marriage—
  or having this palace. Let them swear or not swear

as they like. Let Catherine keep her throne, and Mary
inherit. You love me, and I love you,
and I can say it.
HENRY—
Why can you say it?
ANNE—
Because of the things you are—
when we speak, and are close together. . . .
I've been afraid to say it, afraid to be it,
but now—
Let it come, whatever it brings. I'm deep in love.
With one I hated.
Who took me anyway. Took me from my first love.
With you.
HENRY—
I thought you'd never say it.
Oh, if it's true, and you'll lie in my arms and love me,
Then it's a new age. Gold
or some choicer metal—or no metal at all,
but exaltation, darling. Wildfire in the air,
wildfire in the blood!
Have you room in your heart for much loving?
ANNE—
All you have.
(*Embrace.*)

The curtain falls.

ACT II

For a moment Anne and Henry are as they were in the beginning—each dimly lighted on his side of the stage.

"He knew I'd love him when once he'd made me his. And so it was. After that night I loved him more and more and hated him less and less—and I was lost."

Henry now is pondering what he will seem to be in history, after he has done what he is about to do. He guesses that the books will say, "He loved her and he killed her." And all of his stolen love-letters, in which he played the fool like a country boy to his milkmaid, will be printed. He remembers there was a heart drawn at the bottom, and in the heart, "A. B.," and with it "Henry Rex seeks A. B., no other." He draws Anne's initials with a finger in the air.

Anne resumes:

> "From the day he first made me his,
> to the last day I made him mine,
> yes,
> let me set it down in numbers,
> I who can count and reckon, and have the time.
> Of all the days I was his and did not love him—
> this; and this; and this many.
> Of all the days I was his—
> and he had ceased to love me—
> this many; and this. In days—
> it comes to a thousand days—
> out of the years.
> Strangely, just a thousand.
> And of that thousand—
> one—
> when we were both in love. Only one
> when our loves met, and overlapped and were both
> mine and his.
> When I no longer hated him, he began to hate me.
> Except for that one day.
> One day, out of the years."

The lights black out.

Scene II

It is a nursery. Outside a crier is proclaiming that Her Majesty is lying in child bed, and all's well. Inside, Elizabeth and Norfolk are admiring the baby in its crib. When Henry arrives he goes straight to his Nan—not to the crib. He seems to be a normally excited father. "I won't stay long. I just wanted to look at you two—my queen—and my prince—my son. I shall call him Edward. . . ."

Gently Anne brings his dreams to earth. "My lord, we have a little daughter—and her name's to be Elizabeth."

For a moment Henry seems crushed, and demands why had no one told him. "They're all afraid of you," says Norfolk.

Anne is penitent. "I'm sorry, Henry. As if it were my fault."

Henry rises to a height of gallantry. It's nobody's fault, and there must be girls as well as boys in the world. And this one has a sweet face. "We'll let this beauty grow a foot or two, and then we'll have our son . . . and so nothing's lost."

This has been an effort. Now, as Henry prepares to go about some desk work, Anne begs him to kiss his new daughter. He bends over the cradle—but does not kiss the child. Harshly he commands Norfolk, "Come, Duke . . . sharpen pens for me and talk high treason."

The lights black out.

Scene III

It is the West Chapel, and somewhere outside Jane Seymour is heard calling that by order of the King no one is to enter before sundown. Inside, Henry is coaching three choir boys to sing the song tenderly and softly to the lady who is approaching. And, as Jane appears, he exclaims, tenderly, "Jane!"

The boys are to sing for her—a lyric, a little poem, some music he wrote last night as he lay thinking of her. . . .

It is the same song—"Always, never, sometimes," that Anne once had heard. Anne herself comes in in time to hear it—and sees Jane Seymour. She runs out, saying, "This song is not for me."

The lights black out.

Scene IV

It is a tranquil, touching scene beside the cradle of the infant Elizabeth. Anne is winding yarn, Madge Shelton and Henry Norris are in the room, and Smeaton is singing a song to the baby. Norris suggests that he and Anne dance to the song, and they do so as the child falls asleep.

Henry, entering the room with Cromwell, orders all but Anne out. Two gentlemen of his court, he storms, named Edward and Thomas Seymour, came to him an hour or two ago demanding where they could find their sister. "Where is Jane Seymour?"

"In Northumberland. And a very good place for her." Anne is calm in her announcement that she has thus banished Jane from her court.

Henry demands that Jane be brought back, and Anne refuses. "If you want her near you, why, find a suite for her in your own palace. This York place is mine."

Henry appeals to Norfolk to reason with the Queen, and Norfolk warns her that she is on slippery ground. More and more the common folk are crying down her name, and she has no defenders. The people are for having the old queen back.

Cromwell confirms this. Soon it may be that the Commons will revolt and the divorce and Anne's marriage will be invalidated. The King is safe, but the dogs are at his and Anne's throats—and her child shall never rule. And so, Henry points out, the Queen should be a little less absolute about what she will and will not have.

Anne is unmoved. "Jane Seymour will not couch here." When Henry insists, Anne becomes coldly resolved. If Henry needs Jane so much, all right—but he must finish what he began with her and left undone at their marriage. Houghton and More and Fisher, for whom she once asked mercy, must die—and those who refuse to sign the Act of Succession must die, too, for Elizabeth must succeed him.

Still Henry balks, and his wife threatens. "Don't trust your lady here, within reach of my hands! . . . I'll spoil her with my hands!" Fiercely she insists that their child must be royal, and if not—let Jane keep her distance.

Henry argues that it was Anne herself who canceled the order for the deaths that were needed to make her child royal. Since that time the revolt has spread, and now it would cost twice as many lives to set up their own church and legalize what's been done. Could Anne sign those death warrants—the infinite death warrants? Cries Anne:

"Oh, King of England, King of England,
you blind king!
I'd sign ten thousand to die
rather than disinherit my blood!"

Henry recoils at the prospect of unlimited, pitiless murder, but Anne presses on. "You will demand it, Henry. . . . Let there be no mistaking, no leniency, no mercy! High or low they will sign . . . and so I shall be queen of this island, and Elizabeth shall be queen."

Anne is magnificent in her fierce and ruthless fight for her child—and Henry realizes it. He notes that she is beautiful when she is angry, as she once was long before, and an idea is impelled by his quixotic nature. "If we had a son . . ."

For Elizabeth, no, he will not commit these murders. But if they had a male heir—

Anne warns that she can get angrier yet. "I know where your heart is! It's not with me!"

Henry asks, "What has the heart to do with the begetting of kings?" He confesses he is not young, not true, aging and venomous. It is Anne's misfortune that she loves him and he no longer loves her—yet at this moment he wants her. If she gives him a prince, things may change. . . .

Anne will not budge. "Not unless you kill them . . . not until Elizabeth is your heir."

Henry has met more than his match. He orders Cromwell, "Put them to death, then. Go out and do it!" And to Anne, "See, now I rob and murder at your order."

Anne is not to be fooled. "You do what you wish to do and call it my deed. I hate you. I hate your desire. And mine."

Henry takes her in his arms and urges, "Things could change. . . . Give me a son!"

The lights black out.

Scene V

King Henry is in his closet when Cromwell brings him the ill news—the Queen has borne a son, dead. Cromwell is dismissed, and Henry, alone, utters a long poem of anguish.

> "Oh, my God, help me! What do you want of me?
> Was this girl not to your mind? Not ever?
> Or am I
> not to your mind?"

There is a load every man must lug behind him, he continues, heavy, invisible—a package of dead things he drags along, never opened save to put in some new horror of the mind, some horror of his own doing. He turns his eyes outward, to the future, and asks:

> "Have you done so much better,
> you out there in the future,
> you whom I see with the thousand eyes, looking back
> on my secret ways?
> If you have, then you're young and unlucky—
> it's still to come.
> Or else you're old and unlucky—
> it never was."

He still is pondering his own fate, his own misdoings, his loss of love for Anne, his own blame, as
The lights black out.

Scene VI

In the nursery Smeaton is singing to the baby again and Madge and Norris are playing cards, and Anne is there, when Norfolk and Cromwell appear. Norfolk asks for a private word with Anne, his niece, and the others withdraw.

"Why are we so secret, Uncle?"

"My dear, do you think you could bring yourself to live quietly somewhere—out of the kingdom—such a place as Antwerp—and not claim your rights here further?"

Anne cannot understand why he asks, and he states more bluntly that if she made it easy to annul her marriage, why, then he could be kind.

"What would it mean for Elizabeth?"

"She'd go to Antwerp with you."

Anne sees the future. She'd be a discarded mistress with a disinherited child. "No!" Again she is becoming magnificent.

Norfolk warns that Cromwell has a warrant for her arrest; there will be a trial, and Norfolk must sit as her judge. She demands to know on what ground, and summons Cromwell to produce the warrant.

It is for adultery. Adultery with Norris and Smeaton and three others.

"All men know this is untrue," Anne proclaims, and again she refuses to leave the kingdom. Bailiffs seize her and Norris and Smeaton and take them to the Tower.

The lights black out.

Scene VII

Norfolk is presiding at the trial; Norris is on the witness stand, Cromwell is prosecutor.

Norris vehemently defends his own innocence and proclaims his belief in the virtue of Queen Anne. Whoever has slandered her has lied.

Cromwell coldly proclaims, "Your guilt is open and known, sir." And he orders in the next witness, Mark Smeaton. In vain Norris pleads, as he is led away, for Norfolk not to lend his conscience to this unjust procedure. The one witness the prosecution has found is a loose-mouthed woman of sinister reputation, and all the men accused deny their guilt, Norris proclaims —but Norfolk is not swayed.

Smeaton is led in—a shuddering wreck—and is sworn. Yes, he gasps desperately, he did have carnal relations with Queen Anne. Cromwell adjures the court clerk to make sure this confession is written.

From her prisoner's seat Anne begs her uncle for permission to question Smeaton. "You know this is not a trial, Uncle Norfolk! It's like an evil dream, with no witnesses, no defense for the accused, no sifting of evidence, no wafting of air from outside, and yet I'm being tried here for my life—and five men are being tried!"

Norfolk allows her questions and Anne begins, "Mark, look at me! I know well you've been tortured, but you know it's not true. . . . Why do you say it?"

"It is true," Mark insists in a low voice.

Anne guesses why Mark has said so—they have promised him his life. She pleads, "Isn't it better, if we're to die, that we die with the truth on our lips?"

Smeaton has become desperate, hysterical, and he screams again that he's guilty. "Let me go free!"

Cromwell orders Mark to be taken out, but Henry, who has been hiding on the stairs and listening, halts the removal and takes over the questioning like an expert cross-examiner. Mark is hazy on the details of his adulteries, and sometimes Henry catches him in a lie. He demands if Mark has been promised his life by Cromwell and Mark gasps a "Yes."

Henry is like some towering, unearthly judge. Mark is to die anyway, he promises—and now that he knows it, what really did happen between him and the Queen? Since he is to die in any case, he may as well speak the truth.

"Nothing," says Mark. "She was kind and pleasant and just. I wouldn't hurt her. But they've broken me with ropes and irons—and wooden wedges. . . ." He faints, and is carried away as Henry demands of Cromwell, "Do you convict on such testimony?"

Cromwell stands by his guns. There is no lack of testimony. Five men have sworn.

Henry muses that it could be true. Anne had told him when they first met she was no virgin. He was a fool to come here.

"Why did you come?" she asks.

He cries, "Because I wanted to know! . . . And no man ever knows! . . . Fool that I am! That all men are!"

Even so, Anne has been glad that this fool of fools has come. Now he knows about her and can go, and she asks no pity.

"I have no wish to harm you," Henry says, brokenly. "Did you say truly you were glad of me here?"

"I won't say it again. But I did say it. And it was true."

Then, he urges, let's do all this gently, for old times' sake. He has to prove he can father a king, and they will never have one, for God has spoken on this subject. "Sign the nullification," he pleads.

She continues to refuse, but in turn makes a plea. He is not old, and it could be he'd change. One day, when he said he loved her and she said she loved him, he had promised he would change, and be such a king as men had hoped he'd be. But if he hardens in his mind toward her—then the great king he might have been will have died in vain.

Henry replies, "I do want to begin again. And I can't with you. You brought me into blood—that bloody business of the death of More and all the pitiful folk. . . . Your hand was to that. It's bloodstained."

"And yours?" she queries. How about what he stole from the monasteries, and the men executed? Will he resume with Rome? When he will do this she will take his word again, but she knows he won't. All he wants is some other Jane Seymour, and when he has had her he will want someone else. "Meanwhile, to get her, you'll murder if you must."

HENRY (*angry*)—Why, then you've decided.—And so have I. (*He starts away.*)

ANNE (*flashing out*)—Before you go, perhaps you should hear one thing—I lied to you. I loved you, but I lied to you! I was untrue! Untrue with many!

HENRY—This is a lie.

ANNE—Is it? Take it to your grave! Believe it! I was untrue!

HENRY—Why, then, it's settled. You asked for it. You shall have it.

ANNE—Quite correct. Only what I take to my grave you take to yours! With many! Not with one! Many!

HENRY (*to* NORFOLK)—She's guilty! Proceed with this mummery. (*He turns to go.*)

CROMWELL—May we have your signature, my lord?

HENRY—Lend me your pen. (*He takes the clerk's pen from his hand, pulls a paper from his pocket, and sits to write. The lights dim on all those present save* HENRY *and* ANNE.) She lies, she lies. She was not unfaithful to me. And yet—if she

were— If she lies, let her die for lying! Let her die. (*He writes.*)
Oh, God, Oh, God,
sometimes I seem to sit in a motionless dream,
and watch while I do a horrible thing
and know that I do it,
and all the clocks in all the world stand still—waiting.
What is she thinking in this halted interval
while no mote falls through the shaft of sunlight
and no man takes a breath?

ANNE—
I've never thought what it was like to die.
To become meat that rots. Then food for shrubs,
and the long roots of vines.
The grape could reach me.
I may make him drunk before many years.
Someone told me the story
of the homely daughter of Sir Thomas More
climbing at night up the trestles of London Bridge
where they'd stuck her father's head on a spike,
and hunting among the stinking and bloody heads,
of criminals, till she found her father's head,
his beard matted and hard with blood.
And climbing down with it, and taking it home.
To bury in the garden, perhaps.
Would they fix my head up on London Bridge?
No. Even Henry would object to that.
I've been his queen. He's kissed my lips.
He wouldn't want it. I'll lie in lead—or brass. Meat. Dead meat.
But if my head were on the bridge he wouldn't climb to take it down.
Nobody'd climb for me. I could stay and face up the river,
and my long hair blow out and tangle round
the spikes—and my small neck.
Till the sea birds took me,
and there was nothing but a wisp of hair
and a cup of bone.
I must think of something to say when the time comes.
If I could say it—with the ax edge toward me,
Could I do it? Could I lay my head down—
and smile, and speak? Till the blow comes?

They say it's subtle. It doesn't hurt. There's no time.
No time. That's the end of time.

HENRY (*rising—the paper in his hands*)—Shall I tear this?

ANNE—
No.
Go your way, and I'll go mine.
You to your death, and I to my expiation.
For there is such a thing as expiation.
It involves dying to live.

HENRY—
Death is a thing the coroner can see.
I'll stick by that.

ANNE—
A coroner wouldn't know you died young, Henry.
And yet you did.

HENRY (*turning away*)—Burn these records! (*He kicks the clerk's book, which lies on the floor, and goes out.*)

The lights black out.

SCENE VIII

Henry is at his desk, as he was in the beginning of the play. He has been working all night, and now daylight comes. A cannon booms once. "Nan is dead. Well, so much for Nan," he sighs. "That's over."

But is it? For now he begins to think and to talk aloud to himself once more. "Open that bag you lug behind you, Henry. Put in Nan's head." That head, those eyes, those lips he kissed—they'll follow after him now. . . .

He seems to see her as she was, standing over there. Well, he tells the apparition, no doubt he'll see her often when he is alone, whenever he is weary. The old days and ways will come back to him, and the things she said. But it will wear out, will erase—

"—Why do you smile?
—I can hear you saying, 'Nothing's ever forgiven,
nothing's ever forgotten or erased,—
nothing can ever be put back the way it was.
The limb that was cut from Rome won't graft to that trunk again.'
What we were will be permanent in England;
It may be then what we were will be permanent in me.
It may be all other women will be shadows

and I'll be angered,
and turn from one white face to another,
striking left and right like an angry snake
spewing venom,
striking down,
till I'm old and drained of venom.
It may be I shall seek you forever down the long corridors of air,
finding them empty, hearing only echoes.
It would have been easier to forget you living
than to forget you dead."

THE CURTAIN FALLS

THE MADWOMAN OF CHAILLOT *
A Comedy in Two Acts
By Jean Giraudoux; English Adaptation by Maurice Valency

THE arrival of "The Madwoman of Chaillot" at the Belasco Theatre on December 27, 1948, provided one of the two most stimulating premieres of the season. One group of reviewers greeted it with such descriptives as scanty, perplexing, tepid, confused and self-conscious. The other and smaller section of the paid first-nighters found it rare, exhilarating, original and inspired. This historian ventured the prediction that it would be more fun to talk about than any other play of the season, and events seem to have borne him out. "The Madwoman" began with no advance sale and had a touch-and-go career at the beginning; but, slowly, little groups and then lines began to form at the ticket window and the comedy became a solid popular hit. It also was voted the best foreign play at the Critics' Circle meeting.

The late Jean Giraudoux had been known to Americans as a poet, novelist and philosopher, more than as a playwright. He had dramatized one of his stories of World War I under the title of "Siegfried" and this had been produced by the Civic Repertory Theatre in 1930. In 1937 the Theatre Guild produced his "Amphytrion 38," as adapted by S. N. Behrman, for the Lunts.

In 1942 the Germans were in Paris, Giraudoux was safe in Switzerland and Louis Jouvet, the noted French actor-producer, was in Rio de Janeiro. Giraudoux telephoned Jouvet across the South Atlantic, telling him of a play. " 'The Madwoman of Chaillot' will be ready for you when you return to Paris," he said. Several months before he died in 1944, Giraudoux inscribed on the title page of his completed scrip, " 'The Madwoman of Chail-

* Copyright, 1947, by Maurice Valency, under the title of "La Folle de Chaillot," by Jean Giraudoux. English version by Maurice Valency.
Published by Random House, New York, and Random House of Canada, Toronto.
Authors' agent, Liebling-Wood (in association with Mme. Ninon Talon), 551 Fifth Ave., New York.

lot' was presented on October 15, 1945, by Louis Jouvet at the Theatre de l'Athenee." He was not too far wrong in his prediction. Jouvet did present the play at the Athenee on December 19, 1945.

Maurice Valency, an associate professor of comparative literature at Columbia University, made the adaptation for the New York stage. Of this task he wrote in *Theatre Arts Magazine* that the work of a translator is more than merely pouring a play carefully out of one language into the other. "It is not easy to say why, but a little French seems to go a long way in English. . . . There is a marked tendency in contemporary French dramatic literature to explore the penumbral regions of thought and feeling far beyond anything in our current practice. It is this technique that gives extraordinary richness of overtone to such a play, for example, as 'The Madwoman of Chaillot.' But the American audience, it is said, will resist with indignation any tendency on the author's part to linger upon matter that does not advance the action. I have absolutely no faith in this preconception. . . ." In his adaptation, Valency has, as he says, compressed, interpreted, abstracted and invented—and he also has managed to preserve the extraordinary richness of overtone of the original work.

The late Christian Berard, noted artist who was credited with giving his dress-designing friend, Dior, the idea for the "new look," designed the settings for Jouvet's Paris production, and these settings were brought to New York. The first of the two is the sidewalk café terrace Chez Francis, on the Place de l'Alma in the Chaillot quarter of Paris. This time is "a little before noon in the Spring of next year," and a good many of the tables already are occupied for lunch. A blonde with ravishing legs is toying with an aperitif and trying to engage the attention of The Prospector, who is taking little sips of water and rolling them over his tongue like a connoisseur. A policeman is lounging about, finding it not difficult to keep the peace in the neighborhood. Two gentlemen, The President and The Baron, take a table, and this party obviously is on The President, who begins offering special port and cigars.

"Tell me about yourself," he invites The Baron.

THE BARON—Well, where shall I begin? (*The* STREET SINGER *enters. He takes off a battered black felt with a flourish and begins singing an ancient mazurka.*)

STREET SINGER (*sings*)—
>Do you hear, Mademoiselle,
>Those musicians of hell?

THE PRESIDENT—Waiter! Get rid of that man.

WAITER—He is singing *La Belle Polonaise*.

THE PRESIDENT—I didn't ask for the program. I asked you to get rid of him. (*The* WAITER *doesn't budge. The* SINGER *goes by himself.*) As you were saying, Baron . . . ?

THE BARON—Well, until I was fifty . . . (*The* FLOWER GIRL *enters through the café door, center.*) my life was relatively uncomplicated. It consisted of selling off one by one the various estates left me by my father. Three years ago, I parted with my last farm. Two years ago, I lost my last mistress. And now—all that is left me is . . .

THE FLOWER GIRL (*to the* BARON)—Violets, sir?

THE PRESIDENT—Run along. (*The* FLOWER GIRL *moves on.*)

THE BARON (*staring after her*)—So that in short, all I have left now is my name.

THE PRESIDENT—Your name is precisely the name we need on our board of directors.

THE BARON (*with an inclination of his head*)—Very flattering.

THE PRESIDENT—You will understand when I tell you that mine has been a very different experience. I came up from the bottom. My mother spent most of her life bent over a washtub in order to send me to school. I'm eternally grateful to her, of course, but I must confess that I no longer remember her face. It was no doubt beautiful—but when I try to recall it, I see only the part she invariably showed me—her rear.

THE BARON—Very touching.

THE PRESIDENT—When I was thrown out of school for the fifth and last time, I decided to find out for myself what makes the world go round. I ran errands for an editor, a movie star, a financier. . . . I began to understand a little what life is. Then, one day, in the subway, I saw a face . . . My rise in life dates from that day.

THE BARON—Really?

THE PRESIDENT—One look at that face, and I knew. One look at mine, and he knew. And so I made my first thousand—passing a boxful of counterfeit notes. A year later, I saw another such face. It got me a nice berth in the narcotics business. Since then, all I do is to look out for such faces. And now here I am—president of eleven corporations, director of fifty-two companies,

THE MADWOMAN OF CHAILLOT

and, beginning today, chairman of the board of the international combine in which you have been so good as to accept a post. (*The* RAGPICKER *passes, sees something under the* PRESIDENT'S *table, and stoops to pick it up.*) Looking for something?

THE RAGPICKER—Did you drop this?

THE PRESIDENT—I never drop anything.

THE RAGPICKER—Then this hundred-franc note isn't yours?

THE PRESIDENT—Give it here. (*The* RAGPICKER *gives him the note, and goes out.*)

THE BARON—Are you sure it's yours?

THE PRESIDENT—All hundred-franc notes, Baron, are mine.

THE BARON—Mr. President, there's something I've been wanting to ask you. What exactly is the purpose of our new company? Or is that an indiscreet question . . . ?

THE PRESIDENT—Indiscreet? Not a bit. Merely unusual. As far as I know, you're the first member of a board of directors ever to ask such a question.

THE BARON—Do we plan to exploit a commodity? A utility?

THE PRESIDENT—My dear sir, I haven't the faintest idea.

THE BARON—But if you don't know—who does?

THE PRESIDENT—Nobody. And at the moment, it's becoming just a trifle embarrassing. Yes, my dear Baron, since we are now close business associates, I must confess that for the time being we're in a little trouble.

THE BARON—I was afraid of that. The stock issue isn't going well?

THE PRESIDENT—No, no—on the contrary. The stock issue is going beautifully. Yesterday morning at ten o'clock we offered 500,000 shares to the general public. By 10:05 they were all snapped up at par. By 10:20, when the police finally arrived, our offices were a shambles. . . . Windows smashed—doors torn off their hinges—you never saw anything so beautiful in your life! And this morning our stock is being quoted over the counter at 124 with no sellers, and the orders are still pouring in.

THE BARON—But in that case—what is the trouble?

THE PRESIDENT—The trouble is we have a tremendous capital, and not the slightest idea of what to do with it.

The President looks and acts just the way he should; he is quietly but impressively dressed, and so sure of his position as a ruler that the lesser characters who frequent a café are annoying to him and always are rudely treated. The Baron is just the way he sounds—gullible. But The Prospector, on the other hand, is quite obviously a forceful character, with his saturnine face and his coldly humorous eyes. The President observes him and decides he will be of use; he may be the answer to The President's newest profitable problem. Though he has never laid eyes on this man before, he feels he would entrust to him his inmost secrets—which are more than he ever trusted to his wife, his daughter, his closest friend or his secretary.

One of the lesser characters who frequent but cannot afford this café interrupts The President's contemplation of The Prospector by placing small envelopes before each customer. He is the Deaf Mute, and to The President's great irritation he talks only in sign language—a form of communication which only Irma, the waitress in the inside part of the café, can understand. Irma is imperiously summoned to do some interpreting. Irma is 20 and has the face and figure of an angel. She watches the Deaf Mute's wigwags, then tells the irascible guest that all the Deaf Mute wanted to say was that it is an exceptionally beautiful morning.

"But he says," Irma adds, "it was nicer before the gentleman stuck his face in it."

The next wandering irritant is a shoelace peddler, who is brushed off as another of the riffraff. Something more to the liking of The President is the arrival of The Broker, whose enthusiasm about the progress of the market almost overshadows the appearance of another itinerant—a Street Juggler. While The Juggler is unpacking a suitcase of paraphernalia, The Broker burbles about the day's action on the market . . . up, up, up, then down, down, down, then up, up again—but, by 11:30, there is a profit of three and a half million francs. Curiously, the rise and fall of The Broker's story, and its rise again, are illustrated by the rise and fall of The Juggler's dumbbells. It is a symbolic and spectacular illustration of a morning on the stock market—and it so impresses a Little Man who has been watching nearby that he dumps a sackful of money on The President's table.

"It's my life's savings," says the Little Man. "I put it all in your hands." The Broker casually sweeps up the money and the Little Man is grateful.

After a moment The Prospector leaves his own table and glass of water and stands, sardonically, over The President's table. "Well?" he inquires—as though he knows exactly what is going to be said.

"I need a name," says The President.

THE MADWOMAN OF CHAILLOT

"I need fifty thousand," says The Prospector. "Cash." The name he offers is International Substrate of Paris, Inc. This sounds perfect, and with no further dickering The Prospector is paid what he wants by The Broker—who uses the Little Man's life savings.

After this transaction the gentlemen introduce themselves and The Prospector explains what he has been doing and what his company should be. He has been looking for oil—not in Indo-China or Morocco, but right here in Paris.

"But why has nobody ever thought of this before?" queries The Baron.

THE PROSPECTOR—The treasures of the earth, my dear sir, are not easy to find nor to get at. They are invariably guarded by dragons. Doubtless there is some reason for this. For once we've dug out and consumed the internal ballast of the planet, the chances are it will shoot off on some irresponsible tangent and smash itself up in the sky. Well, that's the risk we take. Anyway, that's not my business. A prospector has enough to worry about.

THE BARON—I know—snakes—tarantulas—fleas. . . .

THE PROSPECTOR—Worse than that, sir. Civilization.

THE PRESIDENT—Does that annoy you?

THE PROSPECTOR—Civilization gets in our way all the time. In the first place, it covers the earth with cities and towns which are damned awkward to dig up when you want to see what's underneath. It's not only the real-estate people—you can always do business with them—it's human sentimentality. How do you do business with that?

THE PRESIDENT—I see what you mean.

THE PROSPECTOR—They say that where we pass, nothing ever grows again. What of it? Is a park any better than a coal mine? What's a mountain got that a slag pile hasn't? What would you rather have in your garden—an almond tree or an oil well?

THE PRESIDENT—Well . . .

THE PROSPECTOR—Exactly. But what's the use of arguing with these fools? Imagine the choicest place you ever saw for an excavation, and what do they put there? A playground for children! Civilization!

THE PRESIDENT—Just show us the point where you want to start digging. We'll do the rest. Even if it's in the middle of the Louvre. Where's the oil?

The Prospector—Perhaps you think it's easy to make an accurate fix in an area like Paris where everything conspires to put you off the scent? Women—perfume—flowers—history. You can talk all you like about geology, but an oil deposit, gentlemen, has to be smelled out. I have a good nose. I go further. I have a phenomenal nose. But the minute I get the right whiff—the minute I'm on the scent—a fragrance rises from what I take to be the spiritual deposits of the past—and I'm completely at sea. Now take this very point, for example, this very spot.

The Baron—You mean—right here in Chaillot?

The Prospector—Right under here.

The President—Good heavens! (*He looks under his chair.*)

The Prospector—It's taken me months to locate this spot.

The Baron—But what in the world makes you think . . . ?

The Prospector—Do you know this place, Baron?

The Baron—Well, I've been sitting here for thirty years.

The Prospector—Did you ever taste the water?

The Baron—The water? Good God, no!

The Prospector—It's plain to see that you are no prospector! A prospector, Baron, is addicted to water as a drunkard to wine. Water, gentlemen, is the one substance from which the earth can conceal nothing. It sucks out its innermost secrets and brings them to our very lips. Well—beginning at Notre Dame, where I first caught the scent of oil three months ago, I worked my way across Paris, glassful by glassful, sampling the water, until at last I came to this café. And here—just two days ago—I took a sip. My heart began to thump. Was it possible that I was deceived? I took another, a third, a fourth, a fifth. I was trembling like a leaf. But there was no mistake. Each time that I drank, my taste buds thrilled to the most exquisite flavor known to a prospector—the flavor of—(*With utmost lyricism.*)—petroleum!

The President—Waiter! Some water and four glasses. Hurry. This round, gentlemen, is on me. And as a toast—I propose International Substrate of Paris, Incorporated. (*The Waiter brings a decanter and the glasses. The President pours out the water amid profound silence. They taste it with the air of connoisseurs savoring something that has never before passed human lips. Then they look at each other doubtfully. The Prospector pours himself a second glass and drinks it off.*) Well . . .

The gentlemen now believe they detect the taste of oil. Oil, The Prospector explains, right beneath this café, which has soaked

THE MADWOMAN OF CHAILLOT

into the iron pipes of the water system and is discernible to educated taste buds. It is, indeed, a magnificent discovery—but the authorities won't let The Prospector drill a single well! However, he has a little plan of his own, and is about to explain it when . . .

The Madwoman strolls in. She is dressed in the grand fashion of 1885—taffeta skirt with an immense train, ancient button shoes, a Marie Antoinette hat, a lorgnette, an enormous cameo pin at her throat. On her arm she has a basket. "Are my bones ready, Irma?" she inquires of the waitress.

"There won't be much today, Countess," Irma answers. "We had broilers. Can you wait? While the gentleman inside finishes eating?"

The Countess pursues, "And my gizzard?"

"I'll try to get it away from him."

"If he eats my gizzard, save me the giblets. They will do for the tomcat that lives under the bridge. . . ."

Irma goes back into the café and The Countess saunters up to The President's table and examines him, very deliberately, with undisguised disapproval. To him she is one more of the annoying streetfarers and he snaps to the waiter, "Ask that woman to move on."

"Sorry, sir," apologizes the waiter. "This is her café."

"Is she the manager?"

"She is the Madwoman of Chaillot."

The President, wanting to get things straight, asks, "She's mad?"

"Who says she's mad?" bristles the waiter. "You asked who she was. And I told you. What's mad about her? She's the Madwoman of Chaillot."

It's too much for The President. "Call a policeman!"

The Countess promptly whistles through her fingers—but not for the policeman. The doorman runs out of the café with three scarves in his hands and offers them to her. "Have you found it?" she inquires eagerly. "My feather boa?"

DOORMAN—Not yet, Countess. Three scarves. But no boa.

COUNTESS—It's five years since I lost it. Surely you've had time to find it.

DOORMAN—Take one of these, Countess. Nobody's claimed them.

COUNTESS—A boa like that doesn't vanish, you know. A feather boa nine feet long!

DOORMAN—How about this blue one?

Countess—With my pink ruffle and my green veil? You're joking! Let me see the yellow. (*She tries it on.*) How does it look?

Doorman—Terrific. (*With a magnificent gesture, she flings the scarf about her, upsetting the* President's *glass and drenching his trousers with water. She stalks off without a glance at him.*)

The President—Waiter! I'm making a complaint.

Waiter—Against whom?

The President—Against her! Against you! The whole gang of you! That singer! That shoelace peddler! That female lunatic! Or whatever you call her!

The Baron—Calm yourself, Mr. President. . . .

The President—I'll do nothing of the sort! Baron, the first thing we have to do is to get rid of these people! Good heavens, look at them! Every size, shape, color and period of history imaginable. It's utter anarchy! I tell you, sir, the only safeguard of order and discipline in the modern world is a standardized worker with interchangeable parts. That would solve the entire problem of management. Here, the manager. . . . And there—one composite drudge grunting and sweating all over the world. Just we two. Ah, how beautiful! How easy on the eyes! How restful for the conscience!

The Baron—Yes, yes—of course.

The President—Order. Symmetry. Balance. But instead of that, what? Here in Chaillot, the very citadel of management, these insolent phantoms of the past come to beard us with their raffish individualism—with the right of the voiceless to sing, of the dumb to make speeches, of trousers to have no seats and bosoms to have dinner bells!

The Baron—But, after all, do these people matter?

The President—My dear sir, wherever the poor are happy, and the servants are proud, and the mad are respected, our power is at an end. Look at that! That waiter! That madwoman! That flower girl! Do I get that sort of service? And suppose that I—president of twelve corporations and ten times a millionaire—were to stick a gladiolus in my buttonhole and start yelling—(*He tinkles his spoon in a glass violently, yelling*)—Are my bones ready, Irma?

The Baron and The Prospector cool The President off, and presently The Prospector secretively unfolds his plan. Right across the river, he points out, is the office building of the city

THE MADWOMAN OF CHAILLOT

architect—the man who wouldn't give a permit for oil drilling. Well, there is a bomb. . . .

Once again there is an interruption from a passerby—this time a self-styled Dr. Jadin, a foot doctor and a "former specialist in the extraction of ticks and chiggers. My office is here, second row, third table, week days twelve to five." The Doctor gives The Countess a warm greeting, takes his table and gets immediate attention from the waiter.

"This is impossible! Let's go somewhere else," fumes The President.

But The Prospector says "No" and explains why: At noon—in five minutes—the city architect and his building across the river are going to blow up—Boom! Within two minutes an agent of The Prospector is going to drop a bomb in the coal bin over there, and in three more minutes there will be hope of a more reasonable city architect.

Noon strikes. There is no explosion. Instead, The Policeman staggers in carrying a limp and unconscious young man. "It's Pierre, my agent!" exclaims The Prospector.

"Drowned man," says The Policeman—but the young man's clothes are dry. The officer puts his burden on a bench, begins administering artificial respiration, and explains that he found the young man about to jump off the bridge and slugged him. Since the patient probably thinks he is drowning, The Policeman is giving him artificial respiration, just as it is prescribed in Rule 5 of the Life Saving Manual. A serious and dutiful cop, this one. "I've got to go by the book," he declares.

The Prospector points out that some of the book details are missing, and suggests that The Policeman make a perfect rule-book case by taking the young man back to the bridge and throwing him in the river. Then the life-saving job can be done properly from start to finish. He is so persuasive that The Policeman shoulders the unconscious young man and is about to start for the bridge when Dr. Jadin interrupts to point out that, should the officer drop his man over and then go to the rescue, it might be the officer who would drown.

The burden is replaced on the bench, and The Policeman and Dr. Jadin get into a pleasant chat about medics. Obviously, The Prospector's young man, who is dangerous alive, is going to stay alive, unless something is done about it.

The thing to do is to lure The Policeman and Dr. Jadin away, and this is done by telling the simple gendarme that two women are calling for help on the Avenue Wilson. The officer hastens to the rescue and takes the doctor with him. The Prospector moves with obvious evil intent toward the young man—whose name is Pierre—but Irma, the waitress, crosses in front of him and takes Pierre's hand.

"How beautiful he is!" she marvels. "Is he dead?"

The waiter gives her a pocket mirror which she holds to Pierre's mouth. It clouds over. "He's alive," the waiter pronounces.

The Prospector is still edging around, but The Countess' eagle eye drives him off. Now Pierre opens his eyes, sees Irma—and it is his turn to exclaim "How beautiful!" But before anything more can be made of this, Irma is summoned into the café by the loud voice of an impatient patron, and The Countess takes Irma's place on the bench—and Pierre's hand.

When Pierre notices that he is no longer looking at Irma's face, but at the very peculiar countenance of The Countess, his blissful expression changes—but she seems to pay no heed to this and begins an amiable and disconnected chatter about the iris she is wearing, and how the Sergeant of Police admired it. At the mention of a Sergeant, Pierre struggles to escape—but The Countess holds him firm. "When you let someone go," she says, "you never see him again." She never saw Charlotte Mazumet again. Or Adolphe Bertaut.

Correction: She did see Adolphe once again, thirty years later, in the market. He had changed a great deal and he didn't know her. . . .

The Countess is most often vague, but occasionally sharp. When the Sergeant appears to note down the details of the suicide, she exhorts him, as a guardian of the State, to speak out in praise of life—but all the Sergeant wants is the facts, beginning with the young man's name.

"His name is Roderick," supplies The Countess, and when Pierre starts to object, she continues, firmly, "It's noon. At noon all men become Roderick."

"Except Adolphe Bertaut," suggests the Sergeant.

The officer's idea of speaking out in praise of life is to demand of Pierre, "What was the idea of jumping off the bridge, anyway?" Suicide, he lectures, is a crime against the State. As for his own pleasure in life—well, he does enjoy a nice little game of casino with a nice cold glass of beer. . . .

The Countess sees that it is she who must persuade Pierre that life is worth living. She begins by hinting that he has fallen in love with Irma and Irma has fallen in love with him—something that he does not quite dare believe. Suddenly and craftily she

THE MADWOMAN OF CHAILLOT 129

shifts for a moment to another tack, saying she knows why "Roderick" tried to drown himself. "It's because The Prospector wanted you to commit a horrible crime."

Pierre is astonished that she should know this, but to her the divination is simple. "He stole my boa and now he wants you to kill me."

"Not exactly," he counters.

COUNTESS—They can't kill me because—I have no desire to die.

PIERRE—You're fortunate.

COUNTESS—To be alive is to be fortunate, Roderick. Of course, in the morning, when you first awake, it does not always seem so very gay. When you take your hair out of the drawer, and your teeth out of the glass, you are apt to feel a little out of place in this world. Especially if you've just been dreaming that you're a little girl on a pony looking for strawberries in the woods. But all you need to feel the call of life once more is a letter in your mail giving you your schedule for the day—your mending, your shopping, that letter to your grandmother that you never seem to get around to. And so, when you've washed your face in rosewater, and powdered it—not with this awful rice-powder they sell nowadays, which does nothing for the skin, but with a cake of pure white starch—and put on your pins, your rings, your brooches, bracelets, earrings and pearls—in short, when you are dressed for your morning coffee—and have had a good look at yourself—not in the glass, naturally—it lies—but in the side of the brass gong that once belonged to Admiral Courbet —then, Roderick, then you're armed, you're strong, you're ready —you can begin again. (PIERRE *is listening now intently. There are tears in his eyes.*)

PIERRE—Oh, Madame . . . ! Oh, Madame . . . !

COUNTESS—After that, everything is pure delight. First the morning paper. Not, of course, these current sheets full of lies and vulgarity. I always read the *Gaulois,* the issue of March 22, 1903. It's by far the best. It has some delightful scandal, some excellent fashion notes, and, of course, the last-minute bulletin on the death of Leonide Leblanc. She used to live next door, poor woman, and when I learn of her death every morning, it gives me quite a shock. I'd gladly lend you my copy, but it's in tatters.

SERGEANT—Couldn't we find him a copy in some library?

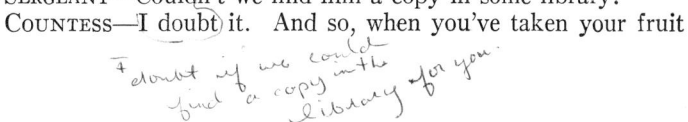

COUNTESS—I doubt it. And so, when you've taken your fruit

salts—not in water, naturally—no matter what they say, it's water that gives you gas—but with a bit of spiced cake—then in sunlight or rain, Chaillot calls. It is time to dress for your morning walk. This takes much longer, of course—without a maid, impossible to do it under an hour, what with your corset, corset-cover and drawers all of which lace or button in the back. I asked Madame Lanvin, a while ago, to fit the drawers with zippers. She was quite charming, but she declined. She thought it would spoil the style. (*The* DEAF MUTE *comes in.*)

WAITER—I know a place where they put zippers on anything. (*The* RAGPICKER *enters.*)

COUNTESS—I think Lanvin knows best. But I really manage very well, Martial. What I do now is, I lace them up in front, then twist them around to the back. It's quite simple, really. Then you choose a lorgnette, and then the usual fruitless search for the feather boa that the prospector stole—I know it was he: he didn't dare look me in the eye—and then all you need is a rubber band to slip around your parasol—I lost the catch the day I struck the cat that was stalking the pigeon—it was worth it—ah, that day I earned my wages!

THE RAGPICKER—Countess, if you can use it, I found a nice umbrella catch the other day with a cat's eye in it.

COUNTESS—Thank you, Ragpicker. They say these eyes sometimes come to life and fill with tears. I'd be afraid. . . .

PIERRE—Go on, Madame, go on. . . .

COUNTESS—Ah! So life is beginning to interest you, is it? You see how beautiful it is?

PIERRE—What a fool I've been!

COUNTESS—Then, Roderick, I begin my rounds. I have my cats to feed, my dogs to pet, my plants to water. I have to see what the evil ones are up to in the district—those who hate people, those who hate plants, those who hate animals. I watch them sneaking off in the morning to put on their disguises—to the baths, to the beauty parlors, to the barbers. But they can't deceive me. And when they come out again with blonde hair and false whiskers, to pull up my flowers and poison my dogs, I'm there, and I'm ready. All you have to do to break their power is to cut across their path from the left. That isn't always easy. Vice moves swiftly. But I have a good long stride and I generally manage. . . . Right, my friends? (*The* WAITER *and the* RAGPICKER *nod their heads with evident approval.*) Yes, the flowers have been marvelous this year. And the butcher's dog on the

Rue Bizet, in spite of that wretch that tried to poison him. is friskier than ever. . . .

Pierre has begun to take heart—but The Prospector returns and grimly commands, "All right, Pierre. Come along now." The young man weakens and starts to obey, but The Countess clings to his hand. "Madame," says the icy Prospector, "will you oblige me by letting my friend go?"

"I will not oblige you in any way."

The Prospector pushes The Countess aside. She catches up a soda water siphon and squirts it in his face. When he makes a second attempt to drag Pierre away, she cracks him on the head with the bottle and he begins to fight in earnest.

Once more The Countess whistles between her fingers, and the Doorman, the vagabonds and the Sergeant flock to the scene. In a hullabaloo in which The Prospector is demanding the Madwoman's arrest, the Deaf-Mute is wigwagging frantically. Irma, his only interpreter, announces, "He says the young man is in danger of his life. He mustn't go with The Prospector."

The Prospector is full of dark threats, but The Countess steadfastly holds Pierre, explaining, "I've never really held anybody before, and I'm making the most of it. And because so long as *I* hold him, he's free."

The Sergeant muscles the murderous Prospector down the street, and The Countess addresses Pierre. "They're blackmailing you, are they?" He nods, and tells his story.

Once Pierre had forged a signature—his father's—to a note, and The Prospector has the paper and is trying to force him to help in a scheme to destroy the whole city of Paris.

"Fantastic!" laughs The Countess.

Not at all, insists Pierre. The man may be mad, but he is powerful and he has friends. He has his machines all waiting, and soon the city may be a forest of derricks and drills, looking for the lake of oil that The Prospector is convinced lies beneath Paris.

"What do they want with this oil?"

"They want to make war, Countess."

Such men and such things are horrible and best forgotten, she says, lightly. To her the world is beautiful and happy and no man can change it. She would forget, too, as she has before— but the Waiter, the Ragpicker, and her other friends figure it is time to tell her about the world.

The Ragpicker begins. Old clothes used to be as good as new, he points out—so good that clothes which were thrown away thirty years ago now are being sold in the shops as new. And garbage! "There was a time when garbage was a pleasure. . . . If it smelled a little strange, it was because it was a little confused—there was everything there—sardines, cologne, iodine, roses. An amateur might jump to a wrong conclusion. But to a professional—it was the smell of God's plenty."

The Ragpicker earnestly advises The Countess that she is living in a dream. The world is not happy or beautiful, and people are not the same—they are from another planet. They are faces without a face—not human. His own belief is that they are models out of shop windows, animated by a secret process.

The Countess is obviously impressed. "What work do they do?" she asks.

THE RAGPICKER—They don't do any work. Whenever they meet, they whisper, and then they pass each other thousand-franc notes. You see them standing on the corner by the Stock Exchange. You see them at auctions—in the back. They never raise a finger—they just stand there. In theatre lobbies, by the box office—they never go inside. They don't do anything, but wherever you see them, things are not the same. I remember well the time when a cabbage could sell itself just by being a cabbage. Nowadays it's no good being a cabbage—unless you have an agent and pay him a commission. Nothing is free any more to sell itself or give itself away. These days, Countess, every cabbage has its pimp.

COUNTESS—I can't believe that.

THE RAGPICKER—Countess, little by little, the pimps have taken over the world. They don't do anything, they don't make anything—they just stand there and take their cut. It makes a difference. Look at the shopkeepers. Do you ever see one smiling at a customer any more? Certainly not. Their smiles are strictly for the pimps. The butcher has to smile at the meat-pimp, the florist at the rose-pimp, the grocer at the fresh-fruit-and-vegetable pimp. It's all organized down to the slightest detail. A pimp for bird-seed. A pimp for fish-food. That's why the cost of living keeps going up all the time. You buy a glass of beer—it costs twice as much as it used to. Why? 10 percent for the glass-pimp, 10 percent for the beer-pimp, 20 percent for the glass-of-beer pimp—that's where our money goes. Personally, I prefer the old-fashioned type. Some of those men at least were loved by the women they sold. But what feelings can a pimp

arouse in a leg of lamb. Pardon my language, Irma.
Countess—It's all right. She doesn't understand it.
The Ragpicker—So now you know, Countess, why the world is no longer happy. We are the last of the free people of the earth. You saw them looking us over today. Tomorrow, the Street Singer will start paying the song-pimp, and the garbage-pimp will be after me. I tell you, Countess, we're finished. It's the end of free enterprise in this world!
Countess—Is this true, Roderick?
Pierre—I'm afraid it's true.
Countess—Did you know about this, Irma?
Irma—All I know is the doorman says that faith is dead.
Doorman—I've stopped taking bets over the phone.
Juggler—The very air is different, Countess. You can't trust it any more. If I throw my torches up too high, they go out.
The Ragpicker—The sky-pimp puts them out.
Flower Girl—My flowers don't last over night now. They wilt.
Juggler—Have you noticed, the pigeons don't fly any more?
The Ragpicker—They can't afford to. They walk.
Countess—They're a lot of fools and so are you! You should have told me at once! How can you bear to live in a world where there is unhappiness? Where a man is not his own master? Are you cowards? All we have to do is to get rid of these men.

She is enigmatic, but she has a scheme, if everybody will help. "We shall drive the whole machine into a ditch."
The others are dubious, but The Countess is decisive. The first thing she wants, from Irma, is a little kerosene in a dirty bottle. She commands The Street Singer to go find Madame Constance and tell her to be at The Countess' house by two o'clock. "And tell her to bring Mademoiselle Gabrielle and Madame Josephine with her. Do you know how to get in to speak to Madame Constance? You ring twice, and then meow three times like a cat."
Irma has found the kerosene in the café and has put some in a perfume vial. Now The Countess dictates a letter to the Deaf-Mute, with Irma as the wigwagging relay. It is to The President. "I have personally verified the existence of a spontaneous outcrop of oil in the cellar of Number 21, Rue de Chaillot, which is at present occupied by a dignified person of unstable mentality," the letter begins. It invites The President to verify this outcrop

himself by calling at that address at 3 P.M. today.

As for a signature? Simple enough. Pierre is a forger, isn't he? And he is familiar with The Prospector's signature, isn't he? "One forgery wipes out the other," she comforts.

The Doorman is to deliver this note, and then give a message to The Prospector at his office that The President expects to see him at 21, Rue de Chaillot at three.

So far, so good—but The Ragpicker points out that this takes care of only two of them. The Countess is confident. They are all connected like the works of a machine, and if one comes the rest will follow. And now for home, with Pierre. "Roderick," she tells him, "you shall escort me. . . . I have some old Chartreuse at home. I always take a glass each year. Last year I forgot. You shall have it. . . ."

They all go on their missions and errands except Irma, who still is on duty at the café. Alone, she soliloquizes, "I hate ugliness. I love beauty. I hate meanness. I adore kindness. It may not seem so grand to some to be a waitress in Paris. I love it. A waitress meets all sorts of people. She observes life. I hate to be alone. I love people. But I have never said I love you to a man. Men try to make me say it. They put their arms around me—I pretend I don't see it. They pinch me—I pretend I don't feel it. They kiss me—I pretend I don't know it. They take me out in the evening and make me drink—but I'm careful, I never say it. If they don't like it, they can leave me alone. Because when I say I love you to Him, He will know just by looking in my eyes that many have held me and pinched me and kissed me, but I have never said I love you to anyone in the world before. Never. No. (*Looking off in the direction in which* PIERRE *has gone, she whispers softly.*) I love you.

Inside, a patron calls her, and she moves off.

The curtain falls.

ACT II

Now it is two o'clock and The Countess is awaiting the first of her callers in her home. It is as weird as she is—a deep, vault-cellar of mossy, sweating masonry. In its corners are piled packing cases, bird cages and other odds and ends—the accumulation of centuries. In the center of this vast place some furniture has been assembled to give the impression of a sitting room of the 1890s—an ancient chaise longue piled with once-gay cushions, armchairs, a table with an oil lamp and a bowl of flowers, a shaggy rug.

Irma, who seems to be performing as a kind of upstairs maid, calls down the stair from somewhere near the street level, "The Sewer Man is here!"

This gentleman is permitted to descend. He carries his hip boots in his hand. "Etiquette, Countess," he explains after a punctilious exchange of greetings.

The Countess has made her plan carefully, and this is why she has summoned The Sewer Man. She needs some information, but she moves obliquely—almost deferentially. She reminds her caller of the time she found him here in the cellar looking half dead, and how she gave him some brandy. "That night," she says, "you promised if ever I should need you—you would tell me the secret of this room."

"The secret of the moving stone?"

"I need it now."

He dissembles, saying that only the King of the Sewer Men knows this secret. Blandly she assures him, "I'm sure of it."

The Sewer Man locates a brick in the masonry and pushes it. A huge block of stone flooring swings upward, uncovering a trap from which a circular staircase winds into the bowels of the earth. In reply to The Countess' obvious question, The Sewer Man says that the stairs lead nowhere—they just go down. "There's no end to it, Countess. Once you start you can't stop. . . ." He was the only one who ever stopped and came up again, and that is when he got the brandy. He shows the Madwoman how to swing the flooring stone back into place.

She knows he is the King of the Sewer Men, but they both pretend there is no such person, and he solemnly disavows many of the legends of the original Parisian Underground—such as the one about a race of girls down there who never see the light of day. This is not true, he maintains; they come up every Christmas and Easter.

As he departs, boots in hand, Madame Constance and Mademoiselle Gabrielle are announced by Irma and invited down. Constance, known as the Madwoman of Passy, is all in white, and she wears an enormous hat graced with ostrich plumes and battened down by a lavender veil. Gabrielle is primly attired in severely tailored black, and as she minces down the stair with a macabre coyness she seems a remorseless parody of blushing innocence.

The Countess greets each, and her welcome to Gabrielle is purposely loud. "You needn't shout today, my dear," huffs Gabrielle. "It's Wednesday. Wednesdays, I hear perfectly."

"It's Thursday," observes The Countess.

Constance is not interested in the day of the week; her attention is absorbed by an imaginary dog. "Come along, Dickie. And stop barking," she admonishes this invisible and soundless pet.

The girls think this is just another visit to chat about Adolphe Bertaut and the nine-foot feather boa which has been stolen, and to have a dish of tea. But The Countess advises them that this is a serious conclave about the future of the human race. And there isn't a moment to lose.

The Madwomen of Passy and St. Sulpice are not immediately serious. Constance seems to be having trouble with Dickie, who seems to be acting up. She divines the trouble. "You want to sit in Aunt Aurelia's lap. All right, darling. Go on. Jump, Dickie!"

The Countess has a little time to kill, for she still is waiting for Josephine, another of her cronies, and Josephine is sitting on her bench in front of the Palace waiting for President Wilson to come out; but the moment is too serious for The Countess to be fussing about Dickie. She gently informs Constance that, much as everybody loves her and much as everybody loves Dickie, it's no time to be childish. The dog may be a sacred memory— "But please don't plump him in my lap when I'm settling the future of mankind."

Constance bridles, but The Countess is firm. Dickie is a beautiful convention, she agrees—but the convention doesn't have to bark all the time. Besides, he is spoiled. The last time he was left with The Countess while Constance was off on a visit he didn't bark . . . or even eat.

Gabrielle seeks to smooth things over by offering to take Dickie in *her* lap—but the offended Constance will have none of this. "There's plenty of times," she announces, "that I make believe Dickie is here, when really I've left him home, and you cuddle and pet him just the same."

And as for Gabrielle—Gabrielle has her own conventions. They are people. People who exist only in her imagination, and she invites them to tea, Constance explodes.

Gabrielle objects, "I don't invite them at all. They come by themselves."

Constance defends herself on the subject of Dickie. "Don't you suppose I know about him? Don't you think I'd rather have him here alive and woolly and frisking around the way he used to? . . . Do you think I'd be so silly about him if it

THE MADWOMAN OF CHAILLOT 137

wasn't that it's only by pretending that he's here all the time that I get him to come sometimes, really? Next time I won't bring him!"

The Countess, even with a world problem on her mind, gives in to her friend's whim and offers to have Irma take Dickie for a nice walk. "No," shouts Constance. "He doesn't want to go. Besides, I didn't bring him today. So there!"

The Countess explains to her friends about the plot to tear down Paris. Men are always destroying things—even space with telephones and time with airplanes. The virginal Gabrielle offers a word in praise of males, saying they are big and beautiful and as loyal as dogs.

"Men," pronounces The Countess, "are changing us back into beasts."

CONSTANCE—I think Gabrielle is perfectly right about men. There are still plenty who haven't changed a bit. There's an old Senator who bows to Gabrielle every day when he passes her in front of the palace. And he takes off his hat each time.

GABRIELLE—That's perfectly true, Aurelia. He's always pushing an empty baby carriage, and he always stops and bows.

COUNTESS—Don't be taken in, Gabrielle. It's all make-believe. And all we can expect from these make-believe men is itself make-believe. They give us facepowder made of stones, sausages made of sawdust, shirts made of glass, stockings made of milk. It's all a vulgar pretense. And if that is the case, imagine what passes, these days, for virtue, sincerity, generosity and love! I warn you, Gabrielle, don't let this Senator with the empty baby carriage pull the wool over your eyes.

GABRIELLE—He's really the soul of courtesy. He seems very correct.

COUNTESS—Those are the worst. Gabrielle, beware! He'll make you put on black riding boots, while he dances the can-can around you, singing God knows what filth at the top of his voice. The very thought makes one's blood run cold!

GABRIELLE—You think that's what he has in mind?

COUNTESS—Of course. Men have lost all sense of decency. They are all equally disgusting. Just look at them in the evening, sitting at their tables in the café, working away in unison with their toothpicks, hour after hour, digging up roast beef, veal, onion. . . .

CONSTANCE—They don't harm anyone that way.

COUNTESS—Then why do you barricade your door, and make

your friends meow before you let them come up? Incidentally, we must make an interesting sight, Gabrielle and I, yowling together on your doorstep like a couple of tomcats!

CONSTANCE—There's no need at all for you to yowl together. One would be quite enough. And you know perfectly well why I have to do it. It's because there are murderers.

COUNTESS—I don't quite see what prevents murderers from meowing like anybody else. But why are there murderers?

CONSTANCE—Why? Because there are thieves.

COUNTESS—And why are there thieves? Why is there almost nothing but thieves?

CONSTANCE—Because they worship money. Because money is king.

COUNTESS—Ah—now we've come to it. Because we live in the reign of the Golden Calf. Did you realize that, Gabrielle? Men now publicly worship the Golden Calf!

GABRIELLE—How awful! Have the authorities been notified?

COUNTESS—The authorities do it themselves, Gabrielle.

GABRIELLE—Oh! Has anyone talked to the bishop?

COUNTESS—Nowadays only money talks to the bishop. And so you see why I asked you to come here today. The world has gone out of its mind. Unless we do something, humanity is doomed! Constance, have you any suggestions?

Constance's suggestions are not very practical, and neither are Gabrielle's. Gabrielle could go home and consult her voices, of course, which used to be in her sewing machine but now have passed into her hot water bottle, where they talk in gurgles.

But The Countess doesn't really need any suggestions. She has her plan. "I've baited a trap," she informs her friends. "In just a few minutes the rats will be here." But there is an ethical doubt in her mind. Suppose she does get all the rats in her cellar —does she have the right to exterminate them?

And little Gabrielle has her own worries. If the men are killed, she declares, they're bound to be missed. "And then we'll be fined. They fine you for every little thing these days."

Discussions of philosophy and the realities of imagination finally are cut short by Irma's announcement from above that Madame Josephine has arrived, and The Countess breathes a "Thank heaven!" Josephine, the Madwoman of La Concorde, sweeps in majestically in a getup somewhere between the regal and the priestly—and she's a bit of both.

"My dear friends," says Josephine, "today once again I waited for President Wilson—but he didn't come out."

To which the almost always practical Countess replies, "You'll have to wait quite a while longer before he does. He's been dead since 1924."

Josephine remains unruffled. "I have plenty of time."

The Countess gets down to business. It's a legal problem for Josephine. Suppose they had all the world's criminals in this room, and had a way of getting rid of them—would they have the right to do it?

Decidedly yes, opines Josephine—if there had been a fair trial. Her legalistic mind comes to bear, and she expounds on the rights of the accused, including the right to an attorney for the defense. The Countess is with her—but it will be a trifle difficult to find an attorney in the next ten minutes.

Of course, there are all the people waiting upstairs—but the Deaf-Mute, for instance, wouldn't be much good in the job. Considering all the prospects, they finally decide upon The Ragpicker, and he is summoned. He descends with a stately air and bestows stately greetings upon the women. Hovering behind him on the landing half-way down from the street are the other vagabonds.

The Countess posts The Ragpicker on his task. He has been appointed attorney for the defense. "Do you know the defendants well enough to undertake the case?"

Solemnly he replies, "I know them to the bottom of their souls. I go through their garbage every day."

The Ragpicker comes up with a good idea. He suggests, "Instead of speaking as attorney, suppose you let me speak directly as defendant. It will be more convincing, and I can get into it more." Josephine approves heartily of this notion, but The Countess warns, "We don't want you to be too convincing, remember."

Josephine briefs him by explaining that he has millions, billions, and that he most likely got them by murder and embezzlement. The trial is now to begin, and Josephine invites all the vagabonds to come down and be the public—for this is a public trial."

"You are charged," pronounces Judge Josephine, "with the crime of worshiping money."

The Ragpicker begins a masterly defense. He does not worship money—money worships him, and he can't avoid it. When he was a little boy, he found a gold brick in some garbage, and swapped the brick for a rundown railroad, and the railroad increased a hundredfold in value. . . . So he just had to keep on buying things, and they all increased in value, and now he is stuck with them. He begins to weep. Is it the fault of the rich if they're rich?

Countess—Dry your tears. You're deceiving nobody. If, as you say, you're ashamed of your money, why is it you hold onto it with such a death-grip?

The Ragpicker—Me?

Street Peddler—You never part with a franc!

Juggler—You wouldn't even give the poor Deaf-Mute a sou!

The Ragpicker—Me, hold onto money? What slander! What injustice! What a thing to say to me in the presence of this honorable, august and elegant Court! I spend all my time trying to spend my money. If I have tan shoes, I buy black ones. If I have a bicycle, I buy a motor car. If I have a wife, I buy . . .

Josephine (*rings*)—Order!

The Ragpicker—I dispatch a plane to Java for a bouquet of flowers. I send a steamer to Egypt for a basket of figs. I send a special representative to New York to fetch me an ice-cream cone. And if it's not just exactly right, back it goes. But no matter what I do, I can't get rid of my money! If I play a hundred to one shot, the horse comes in by twenty lengths. If I throw a diamond in the Seine, it turns up in the trout they serve me for lunch. Ten diamonds—ten trout. Well, now, do you suppose I can get rid of forty millions by giving a sou to a deaf-mute? Is it even worth the effort?

Constance—He's right.

The Ragpicker—Ah! You see, my dear? At last, there is somebody who understands me! Somebody who is not only beautiful, but extraordinarily sensitive and intelligent.

Countess—I object!

Josephine—Overruled!

The Ragpicker—I should be delighted to send you some flowers, Miss—directly I'm acquitted. What flowers do you prefer?

Constance—Roses.

The Ragpicker—You shall have a bale every morning for the next five years. Money means nothing to me

Constance—And amaryllis.

The Ragpicker—I'll make a note of the name. (*In his best lyrical style.*) The lady understands, ladies and gentlemen. The lady is no fool. She's been around and she knows what's what. If I gave the Deaf-Mute a franc, twenty francs, twenty million francs—I still wouldn't make a dent in the forty times a thousand million francs that I'm afflicted with! Right, little lady?

CONSTANCE—Right.

JOSEPHINE—Proceed.

THE RAGPICKER—Like on the Stock Exchange. If *you* buy a stock, it sinks at once like a plummet. But if *I* buy a stock, it turns around and soars like an eagle. If I buy it at 33 . . .

PEDDLER—It goes up to a thousand.

THE RAGPICKER—It goes to twenty thousand! That's how I bought my twelve châteaux, my twenty villas, my 234 farms. That's how I endow the Opera and keep my twelve ballerinas.

FLOWER GIRL—I hope every one of them deceives you every moment of the day!

THE RAGPICKER—How can they deceive me? Suppose they try to deceive me with the male chorus, the general director, the assistant electrician or the English horn—I own them all, body and soul. It would be like deceiving me with my big toe.

CONSTANCE—Don't listen, Gabrielle.

GABRIELLE—Listen to what?

THE RAGPICKER—No. I am incapable of jealousy. I have all the women—or I can have them, which is the same thing. I get the thin ones with caviar—the fat ones with pearls. . . .

COUNTESS—So you think there are no women with morals?

THE RAGPICKER—I mix morals with mink—delicious combination. I drip pearls into protests. I adorn resistance with rubies. My touch is jeweled; my smile, a motor car. What woman can withstand me? I lift my little finger—and do they fall?—Like leaves in Autumn—like tin cans from a second-story window.

CONSTANCE—That's going a little too far!

COUNTESS—You see where money leads.

THE RAGPICKER—Of course. When you have no money, nobody trusts you, nobody believes you, nobody likes you. Because to have money is to be virtuous, honest, beautiful and witty. And to be without is to be ugly and boring and stupid and useless.

COUNTESS—One last question. Suppose you find this oil you're looking for. What do you propose to do with it?

THE RAGPICKER—I propose to make war! I propose to conquer the world!

COUNTESS—You have heard the defense, such as it is. I demand a verdict of guilty.

The Ragpicker—What are you talking about? Guilty? I am never guilty!

Josephine—I order you to keep quiet.

The Ragpicker—I am never quiet!

Josephine—Quiet, in the name of the law!

The Ragpicker—I am the law. When I speak, that is the law. When I present my backside, it is etiquette to smile and to apply the lips respectfully. It is more than etiquette—it is a cherished national privilege, guaranteed by the Constitution.

Josephine—That's contempt of court. The trial is over.

Countess—And the verdict?

All—Guilty!

The Countess now has what she wants—the full and ethical authority to carry out the sentence. The jury shouts "Yes" to her query, "I have the right to exterminate them?" Then, with fine solemnity, she congratulates The Ragpicker on his marvelous and impartial defense.

The crowd departs, to the music of The Street Singer's Polonaise—"Do you hear, Mademoiselle, those musicians of hell? . . ." The Countess, weary, stretches on the chaise longue, and Irma, last to leave, tiptoes out. In a moment Pierre tiptoes down, the long-sought feather boa in his hands. He kneels beside The Countess and without opening her eyes she asks, "Is it you, Adolphe Bertaut?"

"It's only Pierre."

"Don't lie to me, Adolphe Bertaut. These are your hands. Why do you complicate things always? Say that it's you."

Pierre falls in with the fancy and makes gentle love to her, calling her Aurelia and parrying her questions about another woman who seems to have been named Georgette. Had he taken Georgette, too, to hear *Denise?*

Pierre—No one hears *Denise* any more.

Countess—It was on the way home from *Denise*, Adolphe Bertaut, that I first took your arm. Because it was windy and it was late. I have never set foot in that street again. I go the other way round. It's not easy, in the Winter, when there's ice. One is quite apt to fall. I often do.

Pierre—Oh, my darling—forgive me.

Countess—No, never. I will never forgive you. It was very bad taste to take her to the very places where we'd been together.

Pierre—All the same, I swear, Aurelia . . .

Countess—Don't swear. I know what you did. You gave her the same flowers. You bought her the same chocolates. But has she any left? No. I have all your flowers still. I have twelve chocolates. No, I will never forgive you as long as I live.

Pierre—I always loved you, Aurelia.

Countess—You "loved" me? Then you too are dead, Adolphe Bertaut?

Pierre—No. I love you. I shall always love you, Aurelia.

Countess—Yes. I know. That much I've always known. I knew it the moment you went away, Adolphe, and I knew that nothing could ever change it. Georgette is in his arms now—yes. But he loves me. Tonight he's taken Georgette to hear *Denise*—yes. But he loves me. . . . I know it. You never loved her. Do you think I believed for one moment that absurd story about her running off with the osteopath? Of course not. Since you didn't love her, obviously she stayed with you. And, after that, when she came back, and I heard about her going off with the surveyor—I knew that couldn't be true, either. You'll never get rid of her, Adolphe Bertaut—never. Because you don't love her.

Pierre—I need your pity, Aurelia. I need your love. Don't forget me. . . .

Countess—Farewell, Adolphe Bertaut. Farewell. Let go my hand, and give it to little Pierre. (Pierre *lets go her hand, and after a moment takes it again. The* Countess *opens her eyes.*) Pierre? Ah, it's you. Has he gone?

Pierre—Yes, Countess.

Back to earth again, she sees the feather boa and exclaims over it. Pierre explains that he found it in the wardrobe when he took off the mirror—a task she had set him at when she brought him home. "You can take the mirror off the wardrobe door," she had said, "and deliver me once and for all from the old harpy that lives in the mirror." And with the boa he had found a purple shopping bag.

To The Countess this is a clear indication that "they" are trembling for their lives and have quietly begun to put back all the things they have stolen . . . but they haven't yet put back the little sewing box she had when she was a child. Looking far back into the years she describes it, with its green cardboard and paper lace, and the gilt thimble in it. The fact that the sewing box still is missing firms her resolve.

"I'm under no obligation to be merciful," she decides.

Irma runs down, excitedly. They are here! But all of them, just as The Countess predicted, and the street is full of limousines and taxis. The Countess checks with Irma to make sure the girl poured the kerosene into some water, and Irma gives her a bottle. The Madwoman puts finishing touches on makeup and prepares to meet her visitors. "I don't have to be merciful—but, after all, I do want to be just," she counsels herself.

Irma goes up to admit the guests and The Countess presses the special brick which opens the trap in the floor. A greenish light comes from below, and from above comes Irma's voice repeating, "Yes, Mr. President, come in, Mr. President, this way, Mr. President . . ." Several Presidents descend, all looking alike, all dressed alike, all smoking long cigars. "The Countess is quite deaf, gentlemen," Irma advises them. "You'll have to shout."

The President—the one from Chez Francis—greets The Countess effusively and she pretends not to hear well. He keeps raising his voice until finally he shouts just one word, "Oil?" She nods, smiles and points down the trap. He produces a legal paper and a pen and shouts, "Sign here." It is a waiver of rights, and she signs it. In return he presents her with a gold brick.

"Are you going to give her that?" another President queries.

"Don't worry. We'll pick it up again on the way out."

They all jockey for first place at the subterranean stair, but are halted by The Countess, who asks if any of them happened to bring along a little sewing box. Or a little gold thimble. None has.

"What a pity!" she sighs—and permits them to descend.

They go down hurriedly and soon Irma announces a new batch —the Prospectors. The Prospector from Chez Francis heads the delegation, and his keen nose smells oil. He and all his delegation look alike—long noses and Western hats. The Countess signs another paper—an agreement for division of profits, she is told. But *sotto voce* The Prospector informs one of his doubles that it is an application to enter a lunatic asylum.

They all go down.

Next come the Gentlemen of the Press, and after them the Public Relations Counselors. The Countess signs a publicity contract and then points to the descending stair. Here comes the first hitch in her scheme. "We don't have to see it to write about it," says the First Press Agent. But, for another ten percent on her contract, they will condescend to have a look.

"It's worth it," she agrees—and they go down. One of them

steals The Countess' gold brick on his way.

Now there is another unscheduled development—the arrival of three chattering women who push in despite Irma's objections. "We are," one of them announces to The Countess, "the most powerful pressure group in the world." And they want to see the oil well. They are tall, slender, and as soulless as if they were made of wax. As they, too, descend, the first one warns, "Put out your cigarettes, girls. We don't want any explosions. Not with my brand-new eyelashes."

This is the lot—the catch—the works. The Countess starts to close the trap when a man runs breathlessly in. He just makes the closing door in time. He never is identified.

Irma enters and sees with astonishment that The Countess is alone. Little by little the dismal cellar is suffused with light, as if the very walls were glowing with the quiet radiance of universal joy. "They've vanished!" exclaims Irma.

"They've evaporated, Irma. They were wicked. Wickedness evaporates."

Pierre and the vagabonds come down, and they, like the very walls, seem to be glowing. Life has become beautiful again. Pigeons can fly, the juggler can throw his fireballs high and they won't go out, strangers are shaking hands with each other on the street. . . . They all have come to thank The Countess. Voices of others who are not even present join in the chorus of thanks. And, miraculously, the Deaf-Mute talks: "Sadness flies on the wings of the morning, and out of the heart of darkness comes the light."

From the shadows of the cellar three men appear—all alike, all shabby, dressed in the fashion of 1900. "We are the Adolphe Bertauts of the world," one of them proclaims. Says another, "We are no longer timid." Says the first, "From this day on, we shall hold fast to what we love."

COUNTESS (*sadly*)—Too late! Too late! (*She waves them aside. They take up their melons sadly and vanish. The voices of the vagabonds are heard again, and the music dies.*) Too late! Too late!

PIERRE—Too late, Countess?

IRMA—Too late for what?

COUNTESS—I say that it's too late for them. On the twenty-fourth of May, 1881, the most beautiful Easter in the memory of man, it was not too late. And on the fifth of September,

1887, the day they caught the trout and broiled it on the open fire by the brook at Villeneuve, it was not too late. And it was even not too late for them on the twenty-first of August, 1897, the day the Czar visited Paris with his guard. But they did nothing and they said nothing, and now—kiss each other, you two, this very instant!

IRMA—You mean . . . ?

PIERRE—You mean . . . ?

IRMA—But, Countess . . .

COUNTESS—It's three hours since you've met and known and loved each other. Kiss each other quickly. (PIERRE *hesitates*.) Look at him. He hesitates. He trembles. Happiness frightens him. . . . How like a man! Oh, Irma, kiss him, kiss him! If two people who love each other let a single instant wedge itself between them, it grows—it becomes a month, a year, a century; it becomes too late. Kiss him, Irma, kiss him while there is time, or in a moment his hair will be white and there will be another madwoman in Paris. Oh, make her kiss him, all of you! (*They kiss*.) Bravo! Oh, if only you'd had the courage to do that thirty years ago, how different I would be today! Dear Deaf-Mute, be still—your words dazzle our eyes! And Irma is too busy to translate for you. (*They kiss once more*.) Well, there we are. The world is saved. And you see how simple it all was? Nothing is ever so wrong in this world that a sensible woman can't set it right in the course of an afternoon. Only, the next time, don't wait until things begin to look black. The minute you notice anything, tell me at once.

THE RAGPICKER—We will, Countess. We will.

COUNTESS (*puts on her hat. Her tone becomes businesslike*)— Irma. My bones. My gizzard.

IRMA—I have them ready, Countess.

COUNTESS—Good. (*She puts the bones into her basket and starts for the stairs*.) Well, let's get on to more important things. Four o'clock. My poor cats must be starved. What a bore for them if humanity had to be saved every afternoon. They don't think much of it, as it is.

THE CURTAIN FALLS

DETECTIVE STORY *

A Melodrama in Three Acts

By Sidney Kingsley

OF all the able dramatists we have, Sidney Kingsley may be the most deliberate. His first produced play, "Men in White," arrived in 1933, and there have not been a great many since then. There was "Dead End," in 1935, which created a group of boy actors known as the Dead End Kids. Some of the Dead End Kids went to Hollywood and have remained there, to grow up and become one day—one supposes—Dead End Grandfathers. Mr. Kingsley once had a quick failure, "Ten Million Ghosts." In 1943 he had an artistic and popular success, "The Patriots." In 1949 he had "Detective Story."

Mr. Kingsley certainly may be described as a careful writer, taking his time and getting his facts before he goes to work, and working meticulously after that. He spent many months visiting station houses and traveling around with detectives and cops in preparation for "Detective Story." He listened and looked, and had the fine ear and eye of a good reporter. On the stage, his melodrama possesses so much naturalism and realism, and performs so easily, that a careless onlooker might use a film term on it and call it a documentary.

"Detective Story" has a deceptive naturalness which conceals the know-how of an experienced and intelligent dramatist. To those of us who saw it at the first New York performance, it seemed as well made as could be; but Mr. Kingsley was not satisfied. Months later he was still to be found watching performances from the back of the house and writing new lines for his play—not to keep it up to date with the day's headlines, for it is not timely in the sense that "State of the Union" was, but to try to make it even more effective.

The setting is the detectives' squad room on the second floor of the 21st Precinct police station in New York. As a matter of record, Manhattan does not have a 21st Precinct station

* Copyright, 1949, by Sidney Kingsley and Madge Evans.
Published, 1949, by Random House, New York.
Author's agent, Liebling-Wood, Inc., 551 Fifth Avenue, New York City.

house. There is a 20th, on West Sixty-eighth Street, and a 22d, on the Transverse Road in Central Park. But, to an old police reporter like the editor of this volume, Mr. Kingsley's 21st station house is typical of them all. The main portion of the stage is the squad room, and to its right is part of the Lieutenant's private office. "The rooms are three quarters of a century old, with an effluvium of their own, compounded of seventy-five years of the tears and blood of human anguish, despair, passion, rage, terror and violent death." They also are as drab and dirty as a station house can get. The high windows have iron grilles on them, and the entrance to the squad room is marked by an iron railing and a swinging gate. The squad room's equipment includes a chart on the wall for measuring a client's height, a fingerprint shelf, a bulletin board with rogues' gallery pictures on it, battered desks, battered typewriters and battered telephones. The barred windows give a view of the city's skyscrapers.

Nick Dakis, detective, second grade, is at the typewriter desk making out a form and interrogating a woman who has been picked up for shoplifting. At the phone desk his partner, Tom Gallagher, detective, third grade, is writing up some squeals, or complaints from citizens. In brusque routine Nick snaps questions at the shoplifter and types the answers on his form—color of hair, color of eyes, weight, height. At the phone desk Gallagher makes notes of a squeal; then there is another call from the lieutenant, wanting to know what's doing.

"Hello, Loot. No, nothing. A shoplifter. Best's. A pocketbook worth six bucks."

The shoplifter hears Gallagher's conversation as well as Nick's questions as to her pedigree. "My God," she says, "the times I spent twice as much for a pocketbook."

"Well," says Nick, coldly, "you took it."

"I didn't need it. I didn't even like it. Crazy!"

A uniformed patrolman comes upstairs to the squad room; name of Keogh, who sings opera to himself. He has come up to get from Gallagher form slips known as 61s. A Mrs. Farragut comes in, demanding protection, and Gallagher soothes her, saying he has doubled the guard on her and now has twenty-five men watching day and night. Mrs. Farragut goes away, relieved, for she knows all about the foreigners next door to her who are making atom bombs and blowing atomic vapor through the walls at her. She is in some danger, for the foreigners have discovered that she has electronic vision and can see everything.

DETECTIVE STORY

Joe Feinson, a small, thin police reporter, arrives in time to see Gallagher put a comforting hand on Mrs. Farragut's arm and ease her away. Joe comments, "You give the customers a good massage."

"Hell," Gallagher grins, "this job is ninety percent salesmanship!"

The small routine goes on. Joe is looking for a story, but there isn't one—certainly not in the shoplifter. The shoplifter is fingerprinted and sent into the washroom to clean her hands. Two more detectives enter—one, Callahan, youngish and exuberant, dressed in a red hunting shirt and baggy trousers; the other, O'Brien, older, spectacled, neatly dressed and soft-spoken. Callahan makes a joke about a barrel of beer falling out of a truck on Thoid Avenue and falling on a baby carriage—but it didn't hurt the baby because it was light beer, ha, ha.

Still another detective, Lou Brody, comes up with several containers of coffee, cokes, and a bag of sandwiches. They all fall to, including the shoplifter. She wants to pay for it but Brody says it's on the house.

A middle-aged man, well dressed, carrying a brief case, announces himself at the swinging gate as Endicott Sims, an attorney. He has come on behalf of a client, one Kurt Schneider, for whom a warrant has been issued. Mr. Sims says Mr. Schneider is prepared to surrender.

"Hey, Lou, that's Jim's squeal, ain't it?" asks Dakis.

"Yeah," says Lou Brody. "I'll take it." And, to the lawyer, "This is my partner's case."

Sims produces some pictures of a naked man—his client, who is willing to surrender. These pictures were taken a half hour ago, as evidence. "I don't want any rubber hoses used on him," the lawyer warns. "Who's handling this case here?"

Brody explains that it's his partner, James McLeod. At this moment Jim himself comes in, his huge hand grasping the arm of a young man with a sensitive face. The young man is guided to a chair in the squad room and Jim turns his attention to the lawyer. He has seen him, he tells his partner coldly, and he is very clever in court. Brody volunteers, "He's here for Kurt Schneider."

"Oh, yes," says McLeod to Sims. "I had the pleasure of arresting your client a year ago." The client poses as a successful truck farmer from New Jersey, but Detective McLeod knows and hates him for being the operator of an abortion mill in New York. The lawyer again offers the nude pictures of the man who wants to surrender and McLeod grimaces, commenting, "There's no doubt the process of evolution is beginning to reverse itself." He invites the attorney to take a chair while he turns his attention to the young man he has just brought in—a young man named Arthur.

McLeod, all of a sudden, has a number of things on his mind at once. He is told to call his wife. He has the lawyer waiting. He has the prisoner, Arthur. He has a phone call from the Lieutenant, whom he most evidently does not like. And he has Joe, the reporter, hanging around for a story. That is the way things some times go in a station house, and McLeod handles them. He has a joke for Joe, whom he likes; a proper "Yes, sir" for the Lieutenant on the phone, and a professional way of frisking Arthur and advising the young man not to try to run for it. He notes that his partner, Brody, seems to be scrutinizing young Arthur carefully, and asks if Brody knows him. The partner shakes his head, "No . . . no . . . I . . ."

McLeod goes into the Lieutenant's office and calls his wife. Up to now he has been hard and efficient, but as he talks his voice takes on warmth and tenderness and his whole being seems to undergo a metamorphosis. "What did the doctor say? Yeah? Good. Thank God! Mm. Nothing organic? Sure, now, Mary? Just how does he explain those palpitations? Psychosomatic?" A little more medical discussion, and then he laughs, "Oh, Mary, you're wonderful. I love you! . . . I'll call you later."

In the squad room Arthur has turned greenish and is clutching his stomach. Brody, who has been studying him, goes over to the young man's chair and points to the washroom, where Arthur quickly goes and is sick. When he comes out, Brody has a bottle and a paper cup ready. "Have a bomb?" he invites. Arthur declines, and Brody takes the drink himself.

The desk phone rings and Gallagher reaches for it once again, but Brody says he will take over and Gallagher can go on home. Brody is taking down a squeal when McLeod comes out of the office after his call to his wife and addresses Sims, "Now, Counselor?"

SIMS (*presenting him with the photographs*)—You will observe there are no scars or lacerations of any kind! (*Points to photos.*) This is the way I'm delivering my client to you, and this is the way I want him back.

McLEOD—I should think that any change whatsoever would be an improvement, Counselor.

Sims—I want you to know I'm not going to allow you to violate his constitutional rights. You're not to abuse him physically or degrade his dignity as a human being, do you understand?

McLeod (*bites this off*)—Counselor, I never met a criminal yet who didn't wrap himself in the constitution from head to toe, or a hoodlum who wasn't filled to the nostrils with habeas corpus and the rights of human dignity. Did you ever see the girl your client operated on last year—in the morgue—on a marble slab? Wasn't much human left of her, Counselor—and very little dignity?

Sims—My client was innocent of that charge. The court acquitted him.

McLeod—He was guilty.

Sims—Are you setting yourself above the courts of the land?

McLeod—There's a higher court, Counselor.

Sims—I'm sure there is, Officer. Are you qualified to speak for it? I'm not. God doesn't come down and whisper in my ear. But when it comes to the man-made law on terra firma, I know it, I obey it, and I respect it.

McLeod—What do you want to do?—Try the case here? This isn't a court. Save it for the Judge. Now, Counselor, I'm busy. Your client will be treated with as much delicacy as he is entitled. So bring him in—or get off the pot.

Sims—I've heard about you. You're quite an anomaly, McLeod, quite an anomaly. It's going to be a real pleasure to examine you on the witness stand.

McLeod—Anything to give you a thrill, Counselor.

Sims—We may have a thrill or two in store for you.

McLeod—Meaning?

Sims—For over a year you personally have been making my client's life a living hell. Why?

McLeod—I beg your pardon.

Sims—Why?

McLeod—Because I'm annoyed by criminals that get away with murder. They upset me.

Sims—You're easily upset.

McLeod—I'm very sensitive. To me your client is just another criminal. (*Turns away, dismissing* Sims.) O.K., Arthur! In there! (*He indicates the* Lieutenant's *office.* Arthur *rises, enters the office.*)

Sims—That's your story. At considerable expense we have investigated and discovered *otherwise*. (McLeod *turns to stare at him.* Sims *smiles knowingly and goes.*)

BRODY—What the hell's he driving at?

McLEOD—A fishing expedition. That's a shrewd mouthpiece. I've seen him operate. (*He enters the* LIEUTENANT'S *office. To* ARTHUR.) Arthur, empty your pockets! Take everything out! Put them on the desk! (ARTHUR *empties the contents of his pockets on the desk.*) That all?

Yes, that's all. As for the money, Arthur says he spent it, all of it. He has been doing the hot spots on the $480 his employer claims he has taken.

"Why'd you take the money?"

Arthur evades, "What's the difference? I took it, I admit it, I took it!"

In the squad room life remains at once incongruous and real, as it so often does in a police station. It is incongruous, for instance, that a city detective, Callahan, should get a parking ticket—and that little Joe, the reporter, should fix it with a phone call. "A free press," Joe pronounces, "is the tocsin of a free people. The law keeps you in line, we keep the law in line, the people keep us in line, you keep the people in line. Everybody kicks everybody else in the ass! That way nobody gets too big for his britches. That's democracy!"

Life is real when the little shoplifter is sitting there, on and on under the eye of her captor, Dakis, wondering what will happen next. Night court at nine is the next move for her. Has she got a lawyer?

"My brother-in-law's a lawyer."

"Call him up."

"Gee, I hate to. He's kind of a new brother-in-law. If my sister finds out, oh, God, she'll die! And she's in the fourth month, too."

In the Lieutenant's room Arthur is being put through a brisk, cold examination by McLeod. Short questions calling for short answers. They reveal that Arthur has never been arrested before. He can't return the money because it is gone. The pawn ticket that was in one of his pockets was for text books. No, he didn't graduate from college.

"What stopped you?"

"World War Two, the first time."

"And the second time?"

"World War Three."

"Foolish question, foolish answer," shrugs McLeod, and he goes on. An identifying mark is a name, J-O-Y, with a heart

DETECTIVE STORY

tattooed on Arthur's left wrist. "Whose girl?" Arthur shrugs, "What's the difference?" He is unmarried, twenty-seven, from Ann Arbor, former chief petty officer, an orphan. His father taught the history of music. In the address book Arthur has turned out on the table is that name Joy again—Joy Carmichael. "Why drag her into this?" pleads the young man. "She doesn't know anything about it."

Mockingly, McLeod queries, "You wouldn't lie to me, would you, Arthur?"

Brody, McLeod's partner, is informed that Arthur has made an admission but the money is gone. But McLeod has an angle and he goes into the squad room to make a phone call. Brody remarks gently to Arthur that he looks like a nice boy, and how did he get into this mess? At first the young prisoner is resentful, but Brody's easy questioning draws him out a bit. Arthur doesn't know how he got into it; he just got trapped. . . . He had wanted to be a history teacher, but the war washed it up. . . .

McLeod doesn't have time to make a phone call outside, for a policeman is hauling in two burglars, handcuffed to each other, followed by a disheveled, hysterical woman. She is the complainant and she speaks in a French accent. She had gone to her apartment, and the door had been broken open, and these men were inside. When she started to run one of them grabbed her and choked her. Patrolman Barns was across the street when he heard her scream, and he collared the pair as they ran out.

The First Burglar, a tough character, screams it's all a lie. He was just walkin' down the stairs mindin' his own business. But the Patrolman had found a jimmy and a loaded .22 revolver on the second one. The second one is a phlegmatic character.

Brody abandons Arthur and joins his partner, and the detectives go through a pointed bit of routine before beginning to question the prisoners. McLeod takes his revolver out of its holster and puts it in his pants pocket, and Brody puts his gun in the desk drawer.

BRODY (*to* 1ST BURGLAR)—What's your name? Stand up! (*Searches him more thoroughly.*)

1ST BURGLAR—Gennini. Charles Gennini. And I don't know nothin'. I don't even know this guy. Ask him! Do I know you? No!

BRODY—Take it easy, Charley. Sit down! (*To other* BURGLAR.) What's your name?

2ND BURGLAR—Lewis Abbott.

BRODY (*brandishes revolver and jimmy*)—Were you carrying these, Lewis?

LEWIS (*matter of fact*)—Ya.

WOMAN (*begins to cry*)—By the throat he grabbed me! How can this happen in New York?

MCLEOD (*gently*)—Take it easy, madame. You're all right, now. Sit down, madame. I'll get you a glass of water.

WOMAN—Oh, please, please! (MCLEOD *crosses into bathroom.*)

BRODY (*searches* LEWIS)—You're a bad boy, Lewis, and what's more, you're a bad thief. Don't you know a good thief never carries a loaded pistol? It means five years added to your sentence, Lewis.

LEWIS—I'd never use it.

BRODY—That's what you think, Lewis. But it'd happen. You're lucky you were picked up. Probably saved you from a murder rap. Just once you'd walk in, a woman, she'd scream, resist, you'd get scared. . . .

CALLAHAN—Boom! Boom! (*Sings a funeral dirge.*) Ta da de da da de da de da de dum. . . .

BRODY—You like the smell of burning flesh? Your own?

LEWIS—Na. (MCLEOD *returns with glass of water, gives it to the* WOMAN.)

BRODY—Getting dropped today was the luckiest thing ever happened to you, Lewis. (*Turns to* CHARLEY.) Now, you! (CHARLEY *rises.* BRODY *searches him more carefully.*)

CHARLEY—I got nothing to do with this, I swear. You think I got rocks in my head?

BRODY (*producing a large wad of bills from* CHARLEY'S *pockets*)—Look at this!

MCLEOD—Quite a bundle! How much is here, Charley?

CHARLEY—Fourteen hundred bucks.

MCLEOD (*digs into his own pocket, takes out a tiny roll of bills*)—Eleven! Why is it every time one of you bums comes in, you've got fourteen hundred dollars in your kick and I've got eleven in mine?

BRODY—You don't live right.

MCLEOD—No, evidently not. (*To* CHARLEY.) Where'd you get this?

Charley maintains he earned it as a bricklayer—but his hands are soft. . . . Charley swears to God he never was in jail. . . .

Charley wants his lawyer. "Print him," orders McLeod. "You'll find he's got a sheet as long as your arm!" Charley, almost weeping, falls on his knees, swearing innocence. Callahan joins in the questioning with "How many women you raped?"

Callahan is near the prisoner and his gun is in its holster. Charley looks at it and licks his lips and McLeod warns, "Watch that roscoe!" Callahan puts his gun in his pocket.

McLeod gets rid of the still-fearful woman by sending Patrolman Keogh to escort her home.

The Shoplifter has decided she'd better call her brother-in-law, and dials a number while the partners bend attention to Lewis, the second burglar. Lewis won't answer any questions. In an agony of embarrassment, the Shoplifter gets her sister's home, forces a moment's idle conversation, then asks for her brother-in-law. "Jack," she whispers hoarsely, as if her sister Milly might overhear, "I'm in a jam. . . . Don't let on. . . . I'm at the police station. . . . I took a bag. I *had* to admit it, Jack, it was on my arm. . . . Thanks, Jack! 101 Center Street." The girl hangs up and sighs, "Boy, am I relieved!"

Lawyer Sims comes back with Kurt Schneider to surrender the latter. He warns McLeod that he has advised Schneider of his legal rights, and Kurt will answer no questions except to give his name and address. "When are you going to book him?"

"In a couple of hours, when we get around to it."

"I want to arrange his bail bond."

"You'll have to get Judge Crater to stand bail for him."

The lawyer leaves and McLeod orders Kurt to a seat. He even offers coffee, sandwiches, doughnuts, but Kurt declines them. McLeod goes back to that phone call he had in mind and is looking up a number as Brody and Callahan begin to soften up the untalkative Lewis. They hint to Lewis that Charley double-crossed him by making him carry the gun and jimmy and that he is the one who will take the big rap.

Lewis admits he got out of Elmira in March, after three and a half years for burglary. He has committed nine or ten burglaries in New York. He gave the stuff to Charley. Charley gave him four hundred dollars.

Callahan and Brody are amazed. The latter exclaims, "This stuff was worth thirty to forty thousand dollars!" McLeod interjects, "Lewis, you've been robbed."

"Ya," says Lewis. He tells the detectives that he can show them where Charley lives on West 129th Street. Charley is brought back from a visit to the washroom just as Lieutenant

Monoghan arrives. Monoghan is a tough, experienced, stern police officer. He looks the squad room over and comments, "Busy house!"

Callahan and another detective, O'Brien, get ready to take Lewis to Charley's house. They show the Lieutenant the gun and jimmy, brief him on what they are up to, and indicate Charley as the other burglar. "Print him," Monoghan orders. And to the attesting patrolman, Barnes, "Nice goin'."

The Lieutenant is introduced to another of the guests, Schneider. "Mm," says Monoghan to McLeod. "That mouthpiece of his got hold of me downstairs, chewed my ear off. I wanna have a talk with you." They go into the office, while Dakis prints Charley.

In the office is Arthur. "The Pritchett complaint," McLeod explains. Arthur is told to go into an anteroom. McLeod shuts the door, and, after taking off his hat and jacket, the Lieutenant queries, "On Schneider—what's your personal angle?"

McLeod resents the question; in fact, he resents the Lieutenant, who now is taking off and hanging up his shoulder holster and putting his revolver in a hip pocket.

LIEUTENANT—What have you got? (*Takes off his shirt, hangs that up.*)

McLEOD—Girl—Miss Harris in the hospital. Critical. I called the D.A.'s office. I'm taking Schneider over to the hospital for a positive identification. I got a corroborating witness. I phoned her. She's on her way over here. And I want to get a signed statement from Schneider.

LIEUTENANT—How?

McLEOD—Persuasion. (JOE *saunters into the outer office.*)

LIEUTENANT—Keep your big mitts off. That's an order.

McLEOD—Were you ever in those railroad flats of his? Did you ever see that kitchen table covered by a filthy bloodstained oilcloth on which Kurt Schneider performs his delicate operations?

LIEUTENANT (*crosses to desk, opens drawer, takes out shaving articles and towel*)—This is an impersonal business! Your moral indignation is beginning to give me a quick pain in the butt. You got a Messianic complex. You want to be the judge and the jury, too. Well, you can't do it. It says so in the book. I don't like lawyers coming in here with photos. It marks my squad lousy. I don't like it—and I won't have it. You understand?

DETECTIVE STORY

McLeod—Yes, sir.

Lieutenant—Can't you say, "yes, sir," without making it sound like an insult? (*Pause.*)

McLeod—Yes, sir.

Lieutenant—You're too damn superior. That's your trouble. For the record, I don't like you any more'n you like me; but you got a value here and I need you on my squad. That's the only reason you're not wearing a white badge again.

McLeod (*reaches in his pocket for his shield*)—You wouldn't want it back now, would you?

Lieutenant—When I do, I'll ask for it.

McLeod—Because you can have it—with instructions.

Lieutenant—Get what you can out of Schneider, but no rough house! You know the policy of this administration.

McLeod—I don't hold with it.

Lieutenant—What the hell ice does that cut?

McLeod—I don't believe in coddling criminals.

Lieutenant—Who tells you to?

McLeod—You do. The whole damn system does.

Lieutenant—Sometimes, McLeod, you talk like a maniac.

McLeod (*starts to speak*)—May I. . . .

Lieutenant—No. You got your orders. That's all.

McLeod—May I have the keys to the files, *sir?*

Lieutenant—You got to have the last word, don't you? (*Throws keys on desk, exit off-right.*)

Dakis has finished printing Charley and waves him to the washroom, and the reporter has begun getting the story of the burglaries from Brody when a handsome young girl enters, looking about for help. She asks for Detective McLeod and is told he is busy. "Please tell him Miss Susan Carmichael is here," she says to Callahan.

McLeod, in the office, is looking over burglary sheets and fuming at the Lieutenant when the girl is announced and he goes into the squad room. He orders O'Brien to round up eight or ten fellas for a lineup. A couple of the men downstairs could get into civvies. Then he invites the girl into the office.

"Are you the officer who phoned?" she asks. He is. Frantic, she demands where Arthur is and what has happened to him.

"Did you contact your sister?"

"N . . . no. . . . I couldn't reach her."

McLeod begins the sharp questioning routine again. Susan has known Arthur Kindred all her life. They used to live next door to each other. He was always a very serious boy.

"Did he give your sister any money?"

"My sister earns $25 an hour. She's a very successful model. She averages $300 to $400 a week for herself. Will you please tell me what this is about?"

"Let me ask the questions, do you mind?"

Arthur was in the Navy five years. Cited four times. Silver star. Carried a sailor up three decks of a burning ship. Had two ships sunk under him.

"Is he in love with your sister?"

"My sister is one of the most beautiful girls in New York. A lot of men are in love with her. May I talk to Arthur now, please?"

Almost brutally, McLeod informs Susan that Arthur is a self-confessed thief, and she won't believe him. He calls Arthur in, and the girl exclaims, "Jiggs! What happened?"

Arthur indignantly asks the detective, "Did you have to drag children into this?" He admits to Susan that he took some money from the man he works for—but as to why, it's none of her business.

Brody calls his partner aside for a moment and Arthur whispers urgently that Susan must get out of here, and she whispers back, "Have you got a lawyer?"

"No."

"I'll phone Joy and tell her."

"Do you want to get her involved? You want to ruin her career?" Again he urges her to leave, but she asks McLeod how much the young man has taken. It is $480. Arthur begs the detectives to send the girl away, and she leaves, almost in tears, with instructions to have her sister get in touch right away.

Brody wants to know if it's true about his carrying a wounded sailor up three decks, and Arthur admits it. He also admits that he could use that drink now. Brody gets a bottle and a glass out of the filing cabinet and pours, while McLeod takes up the problem of Kurt in the squad room.

McLeod inserts a form sheet in the typewriter and begins to question Kurt—but about farming in New Jersey, and the crops he has. Kurt imperturbably sips coffee from a container.

"How much can a man average a year?"

"Varies," says Kurt. "Two thousand a good year." Kurt has had his own farm eleven years.

"And you average two thousand a year?"

"What . . . ?"

DETECTIVE STORY 159

"Then how'd you manage to accumulate $56,000 in the bank, Kurt? Hm? . . . Hm, Kurt? How?"

McLeod has the dope in his notebook—so much in Passaic, so much in Oakdale and Newark. Kurt refuses to tell how he got it, except that he got it honestly.

McLeod drives hard at him about the abortion mill and an operation on a certain Miss Harris. Kurt knows nothing about it.

"She identified your picture." Kurt shrugs. McLeod rips the statement from the typewriter and orders, "Sign that."

"What is it?"

"An admission."

"You think I'm crazy."

The grim and angry detective informs his prisoner that this time they've got him dead to rights. Miss Harris is waiting in the hospital to identify him, and there is a corroborating witness downstairs right now.

Schneider, instead of being frightened, laughs softly to himself, and the detective calls downstairs for the lineup.

In the other room Brody is looking at Arthur with sweet compassion. "My boy was in the Navy, too," he says. But his boy went down on a cruiser. His only boy. . . .

McLeod organizes his lineup out of cops in civilian clothes and plainclothesmen, and puts Kurt in the group. The corroborating witness is called from downstairs—a Miss Hatch.

She looks cheap and is wearing a new fur stole. McLeod butters her by saying it was nice of her to come down and help, and she replies, "Don't mention it."

But when it comes to going down the line of men and pointing out one of them she draws a blank. "He isn't here," she announces. Since she has already identified a picture of Kurt, McLeod becomes angry, and she sasses him back.

Brody takes a phone call, listens, then tells McLeod in subdued tones, "That was the D.A.'s office. The Harris girl died."

McLeod is hopeless. "There goes the case."

"The D.A. says just go through the motions. He can't get an indictment now. Just book him and forget it, he says."

McLeod bitterly congratulates Kurt and sneeringly advises Miss Hatch that she has earned her fur piece. The lineup filters away, the girl leaves muttering about seeing her lawyer, and Callahan and O'Brien get ready to take Lewis to 129th Street.

"Why am I wasting my life here?" McLeod asks Joe, the reporter. "I could make more money driving a hack." Joe and the detective discuss the case. McLeod is convinced it is a phony, and says Joe can judge for himself—but Joe is reminded of a judge he knows who has become a nervous wreck since attaining the bench, sentencing men to death and asking himself, "Who am I to judge? It takes a God! To know! To really know!"

McLeod—Bunk!

Joe—I'm quoting Judge Mendez.

McLeod—Then he's a corrupt man himself. All lawyers are anyway. I say hang all the lawyers, and let justice triumph. (*Washes down aspirin with a drink, sits, takes off his tie, rolls up his sleeve, slowly reflecting.*) Evil has a stench of its own. A child can spot it. I know. . . . I know, Yussel. My own father was one of them. No good he was . . . possessed. Every day and every night of my childhood I saw and heard him abuse and maliciously torment my mother. I saw that sadistic son-of-a-bitch of a father of mine with that criminal mind of his drive my mother straight into a lunatic asylum. She died in a lunatic asylum. (*Pause.*) Yes, I know it when I smell it. I learned it early and deep. I was fourteen and alone in the world. I made war on it. Every time I look at one of these babies, I see my father's face! (*Phone rings in outer office.* Brody *answers.*)

Brody—2-1 Squad. Brody. (*Pause.*) Lock the door. Don't let him out! I'll be right over. (*Rushing to inner office for his hat and coat.*) Say, Jim, there's a guy at O'Donovan's bar with a badge and gun, arresting a woman. Claims he's a cop. Might be, might be a shake-down. I'll be right back. Catch the phone for me! (*Takes his gun out of the drawer and runs off.*)

Joe (*runs after him*)—Might be shooting. Wait for me, baby! (*Exit.*)

(McLeod *comes out of* Lieutenant's *office, his face grim, black, the veins in his temple standing out.*)

McLeod (*to* Kurt)—You're a lucky man, Kurt. Kissed in your cradle by a vulture. So the girl died, Kurt.

Kurt—That's too bad.

McLeod—What have you got, Kurt, in place of a conscience? (Kurt *starts to speak.*) Don't answer!—I know—a lawyer. I ought to fall on you like a sword of God.

Kurt is smiling and self-confident. He knows there are no witnesses and he can't be convicted. McLeod's righteous fury increases. He advises Kurt that, as soon as he is freed, he get out of New York. "You butcher one more girl in this city— and law or no law, I'll find you and I'll put a bullet in the back

DETECTIVE STORY

of your head, and I'll drop your body in the East River, and I'll go home and I'll sleep sweetly!"

KURT—You have to answer to the law the same as I. You don't frighten me. Now, I'll give you some advice. I've got plenty on you, too. I know why you're so vindictive. And you watch your step! Because I happen to have friends, too, downtown . . . with pull, lots of pull!

McLEOD—Have you? What do you know? Aren't you the big shot! *Pull!* Have you got any friends with *push!* Like *that!* (*Kicks him*—KURT *goes over, chair and all.*)

KURT—Cut that out! You let me alone now. . . . (McLEOD *grabs him by the lapels, pulls him to his feet.*) You let me go! Let me go!

McLEOD—No, Kurt! Everybody else is going to let you go. You got it all figured . . . exactly. The courts—the juries—the judges— (*He slaps him.*) Everybody except me. . . . (*He slaps him.* KURT *starts to resist, growls and tries to push* McLEOD *away.* McLEOD *hits him in the belly.* KURT *crumples to the floor.* McLEOD's *rage subsides. He sighs, disgusted with himself for losing his temper.*) Why didn't you obey your lawyer and keep your mouth shut? All right! Get up, Kurt! Come on! Get up!

KURT (*moaning and writhing*)—I can't. . . . I can't. . . . Something inside . . . broke! (*He calls feebly.*) Help! Help!

McLEOD—Get up! You're all right. Get up! (KURT's *eyes roll up exposing the whites and he groans something unintelligible.* LIEUTENANT MONOGHAN *enters.*)

LIEUTENANT—What's going on? (*He sees* KURT, *goes to him, bends down.*)

KURT—Inside! It broke. He hurt me. . . . (DAKIS *rushes in.*)

LIEUTENANT—Take it easy, son; you'll be all right.

KURT—I feel terrible.

LIEUTENANT—Quick! Quick! Get an ambulance.

DAKIS—Yes, sir. (*Goes to phone, puts in a call.*)

LIEUTENANT—Did he resist you? (GALLAGHER *enters.*)

McLEOD—No.

LIEUTENANT—No? You lunatic! Didn't I just get through warning you to lay off. (*To* KURT *who is on the floor, moaning in agony.*) What happened?

KURT (*gasping for breath*)—He tried to kill me!

LIEUTENANT—Why should he do that?

Kurt—Tami Giacoppetti! . . . Same thing! . . . She got after me too. . . . Tami Giacoppetti. . . . (Kurt's *mouth opens and closes like a fish with barely any sound emerging.*)

The Lieutenant demands who Tami Giacoppetti is. McLeod has no idea. But Gallagher has; Tami is a black market guy who runs a creep joint in the Village.

The Lieutenant is worried. If Kurt is really hurt, this can be a hot potato and the big brass will be after him. "What plays between you two guys?" he demands of McLeod, and the detective answers, "Nothing."

"Then what was his mouthpiece yellin' and screamin' about?"

"Red herring. Red herring!"

The Lieutenant announces that he is going to god damn well find this out for himself. If McLeod is concealing something—. He orders Gallagher to find Giacoppetti and bring him in, and Gallagher departs on the double.

The curtain falls.

ACT II

The dirty clock on the wall says it is twenty-four minutes later. In the squad room the Shoplifter is reading comics, Arthur is sitting quietly, the Janitor is in a huddle with Gus, the singing cop, and Brody is talking to an excited man and woman who are glaring at a tough-looking specimen who is seated nearby. In the office Lawyer Sims is laying down the law to the Lieutenant and McLeod. "How dare you take the law into your own hands?" he fulminates at the detective. Outside, Brody makes note of a call from the hospital, and inside the Lieutenant is trying to soothe Lawyer Sims.

But Sims won't be soothed. He is going to press a felonious assault charge and will see McLeod in jail. The detective, undisturbed, seems preoccupied with repairing a hangnail. He suggests that *he* will be seeing Sims in jail, for subornation of a witness, Miss Hatch.

Sims insists that McLeod has personal motives against Schneider—motives which he is not at liberty to divulge at the moment. "Legal bull," comments McLeod, and the Lieutenant is inclined to agree with him. Brody knocks, opens the office door and says, "Phone, Lieutenant."

Monoghan takes the call, from the hospital, and after hanging up says, "See, Counselor, it always pays to wait the event. There are no external lacerations on your client that would warrant a felony assault. They're now making X-rays and tests to see if there are any internal injuries. So far you haven't got a leg to stand on."

McLeod shouts for Sims to bring his felony charge, and the Lieutenant orders him out of the room. "What kind of an officer is that?" Sims asks.

"Detectives," says the Lieutenant, "are like fingerprints. No two alike. He has his quoiks. . . . We all got 'em. He has a value here. He's honest. He ain't on the take. I stand up for him on that."

"I wasn't saying he had."

Then what was it the lawyer was trying to say, the Lieutenant inquires. Sims declines to discuss it; the Lieutenant should discuss it with McLeod—or his wife.

Monoghan looks up sharply at the mention of "wife" and tries to learn what the lawyer was hinting at, but Sims adopts silence. He'd like to go now and see his client at the hospital.

McLeod has joined Brody in the squad room. Brody's clients, the man and the woman, have been the objects of an attempted shake-down by a surly-looking individual who was posing as an officer. Just one of the little incidents that might happen in any police station.

Monoghan summons McLeod to the door of his office and once again asks what the hell this is about, and once again the detective assures him, "I give you my solemn word of honor. . . ." Monoghan dismisses him and McLeod turns to a man who has come to the gate to report that his pants pocket has been cut and his wallet removed. His best suit, too. Just business as usual in a police station, and McLeod notes down the facts. The Shoplifter lays down her comic page and tries to make time and conversation with her captor, Dakis.

"Gee, I think I'm getting a reaction," she says, feeling her pulse. "Emotions are bad for me. I got diabetes."

Dakis belches and replies, "I got ulcers—I'm not supposed to eat sandwiches. A hot meal was waiting for me at home. Do me a favor. Next time get yourself arrested before four o'clock. Let a fellow eat a home-cooked meal."

The Shoplifter is genuinely contrite. She's sorry she has made Dakis do all this waiting and fill out all these forms and go to night court on his own time.

In the office, the Lieutenant fishes an address book out of his desk drawer and dials a number. "Mrs. McLeod? This is Lieutenant Monoghan at the 21st. No, no! He's all right. . . ."

The rest of his conversation is drowned out by the arrival in the squad room of Callahan, Barnes, O'Brien and the burglar, Charley. They have been to Charley's home and have brought back two suitcases and several pillow cases filled with loot. Callahan opens the Lieutenant's door, holds up some of the loot and calls, "Look what we found, boss."

Patrolman Barnes unlocks Charley's handcuffs and pushes him into a chair, and they all begin examining Charley's possessions and asking where he got them. Charley's answers are very vague.

"I yam getting a reaction. Emotions are bad for me," announces the Shoplifter.

McLeod discovers a monogram, J.G., on a silver item, and declares this must be some of the Gordon stuff. Charley ain't talking. Detective Dakis tries a little praise—Charley is a good thief. He's no bum. Bums wear sweaters, and Charley has a hundred-dollar suit on. He admires the jacket, looks at the label inside and commands, "Take it off, you bum! Stolen! The name's still in it!"

Charley shucks the jacket, seemingly surprised that it is stolen goods, and begins to talk fast. This fellow Lewis, he makes out like he is a dummy, but he ain't. Charley got here from Pittsburgh two weeks ago, and loses his valise, and runs into Lewis in a poolroom, and Lewis takes him to his flat and lends him this suit. . . .

Nobody believes him, of course, and Callahan orders him into the washroom to take off the pants. Willie, the janitor, will provide the prisoner with a pair of his old trousers. The detectives continue checking their burglary lists against Charley's loot. Charley raises the washroom shade and tries the iron grillwork. "The only way you can get out of there, Charley," McLeod calls to him, "is to jump down the toilet and pull the chain."

Monoghan beckons Dakis to his office door and instructs, softly, "Wait downstairs for Mrs. McLeod. When she gets here, let me know foist."

The reporter has noticed that Kurt Schneider was removed in an ambulance a while ago, and he sidles up to McLeod and asks what gives. There are angles here that are bothering him. "Kurt Schneider," the detective informs him, "was a butcher who murdered two girls and got away with it. High time somebody put the fear of God in him. The law wouldn't, so I did. Print it, Yussel. You don't like cops."

But Joe won't. He is a police buff, and says, "If I got fired tomorrow, you'd still find me here, hanging around, running errands for you guys happy as a bird dog."

A short, stout, timid man, Mr. Pritchett, Arthur's boss, approaches the gate. McLeod invites him to a chair and tells him Arthur has spent all the money on women and plush saloons. "You'll be in court tomorrow?" Indeed Mr. Pritchett will.

McLeod is interrupted by having to answer the phone at the phone desk. Charley, looking disgusted in an ancient, ill-fitting pair of trousers, is led by Patrolman Barnes back out of the washroom and made to sit down. Mr. Pritchett asks Arthur why he did it. Just now Susan comes upstairs to the gate and at McLeod's nod walks in.

Mr. Pritchett is asking Arthur, "You spent my money on fast women?"

Susan walks up and declares, "You'll get it back. I promise you." She takes $120 from her purse and hands it to Mr. Pritchett. It was all she could scrape together tonight, but she will have the rest tomorrow. "Susan, take that back!" Arthur commands —but Susan wants no interference from him.

McLeod—Where'd you get that cash, Miss Carmichael?

Susan—I had some. And I pawned some jewelry. Here are the tickets. Do you want to see them?

McLeod—If you don't mind. (*Takes them, examines them.*) Anything of your sister's here?

Susan—Nothing. Not a bobby pin.

Mr. Pritchett—Is this the young lady who . . . ?

Arthur—No. She doesn't know anything about it.

Susan—I know all there is to know. (*To* Mr. Pritchett.) Mr. Pritchett, this whole mess you can blame on my sister.

Arthur—What's the matter with you, Suzy? What are you dragging Joy into this for? She's got nothing to do with it.

Susan—Hasn't she?

Arthur—No.

Susan—I've got news for you. I just spoke to her on the phone. (*Pause.*)

Arthur—You didn't tell her?

Susan—Of course I did.

Arthur—What'd she say?

Susan—She was upset.

Arthur—Naturally, she would be. You shouldn't have. . . .

Susan—Naturally!? My blue-eyed sister was in a tizzy because she didn't want to get involved in your troubles. You know where I called her? At Walter Forbes in Connecticut. She's afraid this might crimp her chances to be the next Mrs. Forbes. . . . Big deal!

ARTHUR—I know, Suzy. That's not news to me. I know.

SUSAN—Till ten minutes ago, I thought my sister was the Cherubim of the world. There wasn't anything I wouldn't have done for her. But if she can do this to you—to you, Jiggs—then I don't want any part of her. And I mean that. I'm through with her.

ARTHUR—Suzy! Take it easy.

SUSAN—All my life everything I wanted Joy got. All right! I didn't mind. I felt she was so special. She was entitled to be Queen. But now I'm through.

ARTHUR—Suzy, maybe you don't understand. Like everybody else, Joy is frightened. She wants to grab a little security. Don't blame her for it. I don't.

SUSAN—Security? You've seen Walter Forbes. He's had four wives. He gets falling down drunk every single night of his life. Some security!

ARTHUR—He's very rich. You can't have everything.

SUSAN—Jiggs! Don't! Don't you be disgusting, too. (*To* MR. PRITCHETT.) Should I make out a note for the rest?

MCLEOD—Wait a minute. (*He hangs up phone, crosses to* MR. PRITCHETT, *takes the money from him and hands it back to* SUSAN.) We don't run a collection agency here! This man is a thief. We're here to prosecute criminals, not collect money. (DETECTIVE DAKIS *comes in, crosses into the* LIEUTENANT'S *office.*)

SUSAN—He's not a criminal.

MCLEOD—Miss Carmichael, you seem like a very nice young lady. I'm going to give you some advice. I've seen a thousand like him. *He's no good!* Take your money and run.

Dakis tells the Lieutenant that Mrs. McLeod is downstairs, and Monoghan gets rid of her husband by sending him to look up some files on an old case in an inside room.

Mr. Pritchett, who might have softened, has been made firm by McLeod's harsh judgment of Arthur. Pritchett once saw a dandy picture, "Less Miserables," about one Gene Valjeane, who was jailed for stealing a loaf of bread. But Arthur, now, wasn't starving. . . .

Softly, Arthur declares, "I did it because I was hungry. Hungry. You can be hungry for other things besides bread. You've been decent to me, Mr. Pritchett. You trusted me, and I let you down. I'm sorry. It's hard to explain, even to myself. I'd been separated from my girl for five years—five long, bloody years! The one human being in the world I loved. She's very beautiful, Mr. Pritchett. Tall, a silvery blond girl. . . . Warm, understanding. At least she was. She was, Susan. We all change. When I came back from the war, I tried going back to school, but I couldn't get myself settled. I came to New York just to be near her. She'd moved on into a new world. She was out of my reach. I should have accepted that. I couldn't. To take her out to dinner and hold her hand cost a month's salary. I hung on anyway. Last Wednesday I had to face it. I was going to lose my girl. She told me she wanted to marry someone else. I made a final grand-stand play for her. Late collections had come in. Your money was in my pocket. I blew the works on her. I didn't give a damn about anything except holding on to her. It was my last chance. I lost anyway. . . ."

The sympathetic Brody prompts Arthur to promise he will make restitution—and Susan promises the money tomorrow. Brody further softens Pritchett by mentioning the boy's fine war record. He takes the employer aside for a private talk, and Susan, too.

Dakis brings Mrs. McLeod up and Joe recognizes her. She seems highly disturbed, and worried about her husband. The reporter assures her he is all right, and in the office there. She goes on into the Lieutenant's office, and demands of Monoghan, "He hasn't been shot? I had a terrible feeling that he . . ."

The Lieutenant assures her that her husband is all right and she will see him in a few minutes, after she answers some questions. He lays out his cards frankly. He does not get along with her husband, but right now he is sticking his neck out a mile to save him—and he wants her help.

He explains that a prisoner has been assaulted. If it develops that he is badly hurt it could mean McLeod's job and maybe jail. Is she willing to help by answering his questions truthfully?

"Yes, of course."

"Did you ever run into a man named Kurt Schneider?"

She utters a hoarse "No" and coughs. Answering many direct questions, she reveals that she has been married for three years, left her home in Highland Falls in 1941, got a job in a defense plant in Newark in 1941.

"This doctor was practicing in Newark about that time," the

Lieutenant comments—but draws no reaction. She never met him.

"He knows you. He said so. . . . Are you sure a Dr. Schneider never treated you?" She is positive, and indignant. Monoghan is getting nowhere.

"Did Dr. Schneider ever perform an abortion on you?"

"You've no right to ask me that." And she categorically denies it.

He continues: Does the name Tami Giacoppetti mean anything?

"No."

Gallagher has found Tami and brings him in. Tami sees the woman and softly greets her, "Hello, Mary." She withers, all evasion gone. She is invited into the anteroom and Monoghan goes to work on Tami—not business this time, he advises the wise and wary man—just some questions off the record. . . .

In the squad room, Lewis has been brought back from a tour of burglary sites. Callahan has taken off his coat and put his gun in its holster again and Charley tries to edge toward it—but Callahan bids him be seated. "Mike, watch the roscoe," Dakis warns. Callahan and O'Brien begin telephoning robbery victims, asking them to come down and try to identify property. McLeod returns with the old records he has been sent for, and Brody informs him, "Say, Jim, I had a long talk with Mr. Pritchett and he's willing to drop the charges." Pritchett confirms this; he'd like to give the boy another chance.

"To steal from someone else?" asks the aroused McLeod. The detective is like an avenging angel; it's not Brody's case, but his, and it sticks. Brody can do nothing about it.

In the office, Tami asks the Lieutenant, "What's on your mind, Champ?"

"The woman you just said hello to."

Tami earnestly vouchsafes that the girl's a hundred percent and he wouldn't say a word against her. "Mind if I phone my lawyer?"

"It ain't necessary."

"My lawyer gets mad."

"Nothing you say here will be held against you, understand?" Monoghan is after somebody else, and the girl is only a witness.

"O.K. Shoot!"

The short, direct questions and answers begin. Tami has been married fifteen years. No children. Yes, he knows what he's missing. "I got a wife as big as the Sahara Desert—and twice as sterile." He's got nine brothers and four sisters, all on his payroll, and they got kids like rabbits. But not Tami, and the Lieutenant has hit him right on his spot.

"When did you know this girl?" Monoghan demands.

"Seven years ago. . . . I was crazy about her. . . . I'd a married her if I could a gotten a divorce."

"What broke it up?"

"Aah, she give me the air. She got caught . . . and that soured her on me."

"Send her to a doctor?"

"Me? I wanted that kid. . . . Next thing I know I hear she went to some doctor. If I'd a found her I'd a broken her neck. I found him, though. I personally beat the hell out of him. Sent him to a hospital."

"What was his name?"

"A Dutchman. Schneider . . . something."

"Thank you, Tami!" The Lieutenant beckons Mary in from the anteroom, and tells her, "Mr. Giacoppetti has told me everything." She begins to weep.

It is getting dark in the squad room as McLeod is looking over Charley's criminal record sheet. Burglary, assault, mugging, rape, extortion, two arrests for murder, three jail sentences. . . . To Patrolman Barnes he says, "This crumb is a four time loser. You have a club. If he makes one false move—you know what to do with it."

As Joe comes in and listens, the detective begins a lecture on criminals to Mr. Pritchett. They are a different breed, and they don't need sympathy. Once he made a mistake and let two weeping young car thieves go, and two nights later they held up a butcher and killed him. McLeod's anger is rising as he says, "When you are dealing with the criminal mind, softness is dangerous, Mr. Pritchett." Susan is aghast at the detective's viciousness.

"But if I get paid . . ." Mr. Pritchett objects.

In a neurotic frenzy McLeod shouts, "I don't care about that. This is a criminal action." He will not let Arthur go, and if Pritchett fails to bring charges the detective will subpoena him into court. The baffled and unhappy Pritchett gives in, and goes home.

"Humble yourself, sweetheart! Humble yourself!" It is Joe, warning McLeod. "You're digging your own grave. A bottomless pit, baby. It's right there in front of you." Joe looks searchingly at his friend's face and finds it hard as granite, with all friendship gone out of it. Smiling sadly, he shakes his head and goes away.

The Lieutenant thinks he has cleaned up the Schneider beating now. McLeod has been persecuting Kurt because of what he knows about Mary—but again Mary confounds him: she swears her husband never knew of this part of her past. Monoghan sends for the detective and moves for a showdown.

"Why'd you lie to me?" he demands of McLeod. The detective insists he has not lied, and Mary breaks in, "Jim, the Lieutenant won't believe me that you knew nothing about this . . . Dr. Schneider."

Her husband looks blankly at her. "What's he got to do with you?"

"I . . . had occasion to see him once."

It takes some moments for McLeod to put things together. He notices Tami and demands what he's got to do with it.

"We were going together."

He is getting the picture, and grimly he asks to talk alone with his wife. Tami is dismissed and the Lieutenant goes into his anteroom.

"I'm terribly sorry, Jim," she says, touching him. He moves away from her. He questions her as a detective would, sharply and shortly. She went with Tami about four months. No, he didn't give her money. Yes, he did give her presents.

McLeod—Expensive ones?
Mary—I don't know.
McLeod—What do you mean you don't know?
Mary—I don't know. What difference does it make?
McLeod—This difference. I'd just as soon Schneider died. I'd sooner go to jail for twenty years—than find out this way that my wife was a whore.
Mary—Don't say that, Jim.
McLeod—That's the word, I didn't invent it. That's what they call it.
Mary—I don't care about "they." I only care about you, Jim, and it isn't true. You know it isn't true.
McLeod—Why didn't you tell me?
Mary—I wanted to, but I didn't dare. I would have lost you.
McLeod—I thought I knew you. I thought you were everything good and pure. . . . And with a pig like that! Live dirt!
Mary—Jim, don't judge me. Try and understand. Right and wrong aren't always as simple as they seem to you. I was

on my own for the first time in a large city. The war was on. Everything was feverish! I'd only been out with kids my own age until I met this man. He paid me a lot of attention. I was flattered. I'd never met anyone like him before in my whole life. I thought he was romantic and glamorous. I thought I was in love with him.

McLeod—Are you trying to justify yourself in those terms?

Mary—Not justify! Just explain. It was wrong. I know it. I discovered that for myself.

McLeod—When? Just now? (*The phone rings.* Dakis *answers it.*)

Mary—Jim, my darling. My beloved! I love you. Try and understand. I'm trying to make my life everything you want it to be. If I could make my past life over I'd do that, too, gladly. But I can't. No one can. I made a mistake. I admit it. I've paid for it . . . plenty. Isn't that enough?

Dakis (*crosses to* Lieutenant's *office, enters*)—Where's the Lieutenant?

McLeod—Inside.

Dakis (*shouting off*)—Lieutenant!—Hospital's on the phone.

Lieutenant (*enters—picks up phone*)—Yeah! . . . Put him on! . . . Yeah? You're sure? O.K., Doc. Thank you. (*He hangs up.*) The Devil takes care of his own! . . . It looks like Schneider is all right. They can't find anything wrong with him. (*There is a long pause.*)

Mary—May I go now?

Lieutenant—Yes, Mrs. McLeod. (*Exit* Lieutenant *off right.*)

Mary—Jim, I beg you. Please understand.

McLeod—What's there to understand? . . . You got undressed before him.

Mary—Jim!

McLeod—You went to bed with him.

Mary—Jim! I can't take much more of this.

McLeod—You carried his child a while inside you . . . and then you killed it.

Mary—Yes. That's true.

McLeod—Everything I hate . . . even murder . . . what the hell's left to understand! (Mary, *completely stunned, looks at his face, swollen with anger. The face of a madman, backs up to the door, suddenly opens it, turns, flees.*)

The curtain falls.

ACT III

Eight-thirty at night, and out the window signs flash. The office is dark, but the squad room is humming with men and women identifying stolen property. A patrolman is watching Charley closely. McLeod is typing Arthur's confession, and Susan is hovering over Arthur like some impotent guardian angel. The Shoplifter is enjoying the whole scene. A photographer is making a shot of a man and woman in evening dress identifying some of the loot. Now McLeod is taking Arthur's pedigree—age, height, weight, identifying marks. . . . He tells Susan to go home, but she pleads for a few minutes more.

The phone rings and Callahan answers it. "A jumper? Fifty-thoid Street. Her name? Mc . . . ? What?"

McLeod tenses with apprehension . . . until Callahan says the name was McFadden, an old lady. "That's my street," says McLeod, wiping his brow.

Brody fingerprints Lewis and sends him to the washroom, and Arthur is next.

Callahan, checking records, finds a case he feels sure Charley and Lewis did, and asks Charley if he did it. "You do us a favor . . . we might help you."

Charley snarls, "What the hell you gonna help me? I'm a four-time loser. I'm gone to jail for life."

Arthur has finished being fingerprinted and goes to wash. Susan crumples in a chair and the Shoplifter comforts her with, "It don't hurt. Just gets your hands a little dirty. . . . Are you married?" Susan shakes her head, and the Shoplifter continues, "Me, neither. Everybody tells you why don't you get married. You should get married. My mother, my father, my sisters, my brother—'Get married!' Like I didn't want to get married. Where do you find a man? Get me a man, I'll marry him. *Anything!* As long as it's got pants. Big, little, fat, thin. . . . I'll marry him. You think I'd be here? A lousy crocodile bag? I'd be home, cooking him such a meal. Get married!!? It's easy to talk!"

The photographer wants a picture of the burglars and their captor, and the prisoners are lined up in front of a desk with some of the loot on it. Lewis mutters to Charley, "You louse. I ought to kill you." He has seen the list of the loot—thirty grand, and all he got was four hundred. And how about the fourteen hundred Charley had on *him?* Charley offers him the whole fourteen hundred and Lewis says he will be satisfied.

McLeod has begun pressing his temples, as if annoyed. He has Arthur sign his fingerprint card, and Susan is quickly behind the boy, saying, "I believe in you, Arthur. . . ." The detective asks Joe if he has any aspirin and the reporter curtly says "No" and walks away. The photographer makes a picture of Arthur, and Susan appeals hysterically to Brody, "They're not going to print that in the papers, are they?" Brody beckons the photographer and Joe out through the gate and they disappear.

Time for the Shoplifter to go to night court, and Dakis takes her. She bids all a nice farewell: "So long, everybody! You been very nice to me. . . . And I'm sorry I caused you all this trouble."

McLeod would like to get rid of Susan, but she begs two minutes alone with the boy. He handcuffs Arthur to a chair and goes into the Lieutenant's darkened office, and Susan tries tenderly to buck Arthur up. He got mixed up; everybody gets mixed up some time or other, and he's coming out of it fine.

ARTHUR (*shakes his head*)—Look around, Susan. Look at this. (*Indicates his handcuffs.*) The dreams I had—the plans I made . . . to end like this?

SUSAN—This isn't the end of the world, Jiggs.

ARTHUR—It is for me. (*He studies the handcuffs.*) All I ever wanted was to live quietly in a small college town . . . to study and teach. No! (*Bitterly.*) This isn't a time for study and teachers . . . this is a time for generals.

SUSAN—I hate that kind of talk, Jiggs. Everywhere I hear it. . . . I don't believe it. Whatever happens to you, you can still pick up and go on. If ever there was a time for students and teachers, this is it. I know you can still make whatever you chose for your life. (*She pauses, sees his black anguish.*) Arthur! Do you want Joy? Would that help? Would you like to see her and talk to her?

ARTHUR—No.

SUSAN—I'll go to Connecticut and bring her back.

ARTHUR—I don't want her.

SUSAN—I'll get her here. Say the word. I'll bring her here, Arthur. She'll come. You know she will.

ARTHUR—I don't want her, Suzy. I don't want Joy.

SUSAN—You're sure?

ARTHUR—Yes. (*Pause.*) For five years I've been in love with a girl that doesn't exist. I wouldn't know what to say to her now. (*The noises of the city outside rise and fall.*) That's finished. Washed up.

SUSAN—Oh, Arthur! Why couldn't you have fallen in love with me?

ARTHUR (*looks at her, for a long time, then, tenderly*)—I've always loved you, Suzy. You were always . . . my baby.

SUSAN—I've news for you. I voted for the President in the last election. I'm years past the age of consent.

ARTHUR—Just an old bag?

SUSAN—Arthur, why didn't you fall in love with me? I'd have been so much better for you. I know I'm not as beautiful as Joy, but . . .

ARTHUR—But you are. Joy's prettier than you, Susan, but you're more beautiful.

SUSAN—Oh, Jiggs, you fracture me! Let us not . . . (*She almost cries.*)

ARTHUR—Let us not be emotional. We were going to be realists. Remember?

SUSAN—Yes.

ARTHUR—Suzy, when I go to jail . . . (*Her lip quivers again.*) Now . . . Realists?

SUSAN—I'm not going to cry.

ARTHUR—Be my senible Susan!

SUSAN—Jiggs, I can't be sensible about you. I love you.

When it's over they'll go back home again. The love scene appears to amuse Charley, who screeches "Hearts and Flowers" and pretends to play a violin. He taunts the boy about facing five to ten and what will happen to him in jail, and Arthur moves, chair and all, to attack Charley. Susan screams for Brody, and Barnes runs over to Charley. Brody, entering quickly, calms the boy down. In his hand is a photographic film which he crumples. "Here's your picture." He goes into the office, looking for McLeod, and switches on the light. He pours himself a stiff drink and offers his partner one, but Jim doesn't want any.

For thirteen years, Brody begins, he has been McLeod's sidekick, and never asked a favor. Now he wants one—give the kid outside a break. . . . He thinks Arthur's a good kid . . . reminds him of his own boy. It is a touching plea, but McLeod says he can't drop the charges.

"You coulda let him go two hours ago. You still can. The complainant left it up to you."

McLeod (*a moan of anguish*)—For Christ's sake, stop it, Lou, will you? My nerves are like banjo strings.
Brody—Well, play something on them. Play "Love's Old Sweet Song."
McLeod—Shut up! Lay off! God damn it! I'm warning you. Lay off! (*Silence.*)
Brody (*studies him, then . . . softer*)—What's the matter?
McLeod—I'm drowning, Lou. I'm drowning. That's all. I'm drowning in my own juices.
Brody—I wish I could understand what makes you tick.
McLeod—I don't expect you to understand me, Lou. I know I'm different than the others. I think differently. I'm not a little boy who won't grow up, playing cops and robbers all his life, like Callahan; and I'm not an insurance salesman, like you, Lou. I'm here out of principle!! Principle, Lou. All my life I've lived according to principle! And, goddamit, I couldn't deviate even if I wanted to.
Brody—Sometimes you gotta bend with the wind . . . or break! Be a little human, Jim! Don't be such a friggin' monument!
McLeod—How, how? How do you compromise? How do you compromise, Christ!—convictions that go back to the roots of your childhood? I hate softness. I don't believe in it. My mother was soft—it killed her. I'm no Christian. I don't believe in the other cheek. I hate mushiness. You ask me to compromise for this kid? Who the hell is he? Now, right now, Lou, I'm faced with a problem of my own that's ripping me up like a 22 bullet bouncing around inside, and I can't compromise on that. So what do I do? What do I do? (*A long pause.* Joe *has entered quietly and has been standing in the doorway, listening.*)
Joe—Try picking up that phone and calling her.
McLeod—Who?
Joe—Mary. (*Tosses aspirin box onto desk.*) Here's your aspirin.

The reporter reveals that he knew Mary when he worked in Newark, years before McLeod did, and she is one in a million. Brody takes Joe's cue and reminds his partner what life was like before he got married. "Pick up that phone," he urges.

There is no need to, for Mary arrives and goes to the office. "I'm leaving now, Jim," she says in a low voice. . . . "Here are the keys." She has a taxi waiting with her valises and trunk.

Her husband begs her to take her things back home. He'll be there at 8 A.M. and they can work it out then. But she has worked it out over and over, and to her their life is finished. "I know the way your mind works. It never lets go. The rest of our days, we'll be living with this. . . . I couldn't take it. I'd dry up and die."

He keeps pleading, almost pitifully, that he loves her and needs her. "Mary, you just don't stop loving someone."

MARY—I wouldn't have thought so. I wouldn't have believed it could happen. But, there it is. I suppose in this life we all die many times before they finally bury us. This was one of those deaths. Sudden, unexpected, like being run over by a bus. It happens.

McLEOD—Who do you think you're kidding?

MARY (*cracks*)—No one! (*Begins to cry.*) Least of all, myself.

McLEOD (*takes her in his arms*)—Mary, I love you.

MARY (*clinging to him, sobbing*)—Then help me! I'm trying to be a human being. I'm trying to bundle myself together. It took every bit of strength to go this far. Help me, Jim.

McLEOD—It's no use, sweetheart, it's no use. I couldn't go home if you weren't waiting for me with the radio going and the smell of coffee on the stove. I'd blow out my brains. I would, Mary, if I went home to an empty flat—I wouldn't dare take my gun with me. (*He gives her his handkerchief. She dries her eyes.*) Now powder your nose! Put on some lipstick. (*She kisses him.* SIMS *appears at the gate, outside.*)

CALLAHAN (*crosses to* SIMS)—Yes, Counselor?

SIMS—I want to see Detective McLeod.

Mary, smiling now, wants to go home, but he asks her to wait a minute. He leaves her in the office and meets Sims outside. Sims says he is lucky he isn't facing a murder charge.

"I could always get you to defend me," the detective sneers.

The lawyer admits he probably could. Every man has a right to counsel, a right not to be arbitrarily judged, particularly by men in authority. As for the Harris girl . . . he doesn't know if Schneider killed her, and it is not his job to judge. It is his job to defend his client, not judge him. That remains with the courts. . . . It is a straightforward statement of straightforward ethics, but McLeod sneeringly reminds the lawyer of bought witnesses and perjured testimony.

Stung, Sims shouts, "If you're so set on hanging Schneider, why don't you ask Mrs. McLeod if she can supply a corroborating witness?"

McLeod looks as if he'd been hit with a meat ax. Face twitching, he returns to Mary in the office, and begins another cross-examination of the desperately puzzled woman. Did her parents know? How long was she in New York before she met him? How many other men were there?

"None," she answers, and, alarmed, asks, "What's the matter with you, Jim?" He is trying to control the insane turbulence inside—but he can't. He tells her he would like to take out his brains so he could wash away the dirty pictures she put there tonight.

"You're a cruel and vengeful man. You're everything you've always said you hated in your own father." She knows now that she must leave him, and when he says he will take her home himself she screams, "What for? To kill me the way your father killed your mother?" She pulls away from him.

"Where are you going?"

She looks at him sadly. "Far away. . . . You won't find me." She goes, and McLeod dazedly returns to the squad room and tells Susan her two minutes are up. Brody, Joe and the Lieutenant come in, and Monoghan can see that something is wrong with McLeod. He'd better go home and buzz his doctor. When McLeod argues that he has a squeal to finish off first, the Lieutenant orders him home. McLeod, sitting at the desk, confides to Brody that Mary has left him for good. Again the Lieutenant orders him home. "I haven't got any," says the anguished man.

Fiercely, Joe cries, "I tried to warn you, you damn fool!"

A woman has come to the gate to complain of a purse-snatching and Callahan moves over to attend to her. He invites her in, bends over to pick up a letter—and, like a cat, Charley lunges for Callahan's gun, gets it, knocks the detective insensible with the butt, and then whirls, snarling, on the rest of them. He aims at Barnes and orders him to drop his club. "Drop it," Brody advises. "He's a four-time loser. He'll kill you."

"Goddam right," Charley yells. "Rot in jail the rest of my life! I take five or six a you bastards with me first."

McLeod begins to laugh. Rising, he says, "Give me that gun!"

Charley warns him not to move, but the detective keeps coming, reaching for his own gun. Charley fires point-blank—three shots; McLeod staggers, sinks back into a chair.

Barnes leaps into action, knocking the gun from the burglar's hand, and others swarm over him with drawn billies. Charley screams twice and is silent.

Brody puts a supporting arm around his partner, and asks if he's hurt.

"Slightly. . . . Oh, Mary, Mary, Mary. . . . Slightly killed, I should say." McLeod manages a crooked smile. The Lieutenant orders him taken inside to bed—but there is something he wants to finish first. Never mind a doctor—get a priest, he suggests. And to Brody, "Give me Buster's prints. . . . I don't know. I hope you're right, Lou. Maybe he'll come in tomorrow with a murder rap. I don't know any more. . . ."

Brody goes for the prints as the half-conscious and moaning Charley is dragged off. To Joe, McLeod gasps, "Find her! Ask her to forgive me. And help her . . . will you?"

When Brody returns with the prints McLeod tears them up. "Unchain him, Lou." Then he explains to the Lieutenant that the complainant withdrew. Now, with all done that he wanted to do, he crosses himself and begins a prayer—"In the name of the Father and the Son and the Holy Ghost. Oh, my God. I'm sorry for having offended thee. . . ." He topples into Brody's arms, dead. The Lieutenant completes the prayer—"I firmly resolve with the help of Thy Grace . . ." and at the end crosses himself.

Brody frees Arthur, urges him and Susan to get the hell out. Gallagher is on the phone to St. Vincent's, asking for a priest. The Lieutenant is on the phone, telling the Communications Bureau to notify the Commissioner, the D.A., homicide squad . . .

THE CURTAIN FALLS

EDWARD, MY SON *
A Play in Three Acts
By Robert Morley and Noel Langley

WHEN most British actors achieve a personal success in New York, they manage to return every season or so—and some of them, like Maurice Evans, become American citizens. After his appearance in the play, "Oscar Wilde," Robert Morley could have appeared on Broadway as often as he chose. He did not choose to return until eleven years later, when he came with his hand-tailored London hit and its carefully picked company in "Edward, My Son." Broadway gave "Edward" an enthusiastic greeting as an actors' play—an ideal display for the talents of Mr. Morley, Peggy Ashcroft, Leueen MacGrath and others.

Miss Ashcroft went back to London before the New York run was over, and so did Mr. Morley. Miss MacGrath remained to become the wife of George S. Kaufman.

Mr. Morley's profession is that of an actor, but he has written plays before now. Two of them seen in London were "Short Story" and "How Sad," produced in 1935 and 1937, respectively.

The other author of "Edward, My Son" is strictly in the writing business—but once he was a broadcast announcer in his native South Africa. He is the author of "Queer Cargo," "No Regrets" and other plays, and has done a number of Hollywood scripts.

When the play begins, the curtain does not rise, as it would upon a scene. Instead, Arnold Holt comes before the curtain to offer an explanation, an apology . . . perhaps a plea. "My name, ladies and gentleman, is Arnold Holt," he begins.

He is a large, genial man of about sixty, "With the easy charm of a man who has long been accustomed to being accepted by

* Copyright, 1948, by Robert Morley and Noel Langley.
Published in the United States by Random House, New York.
Published in England by Samuel French, Ltd., London.
Amateur rights controlled by Dramatists Play Service, 14 East 38th Street, New York City 16.
Authors' American agents, MCA Management, 444 Madison Avenue, New York City 22.

others at his own valuation." It can be noted instantly that he is a man of importance and individual character. His long, black overcoat with its astrakhan collar, his black homburg and his bearing mark him a public figure. And he suavely admits to the audience that he *is* a public figure—the owner of a great newspaper, of a brewery, of a chain of stores, of a match company, of six or eight cracker bakeries. . . .

But this is just background, he explains. What he has come here for is to ask the audience its opinion. When it has learned the facts, he wants to know what it would have done—gone on, as he did, or gone back? It is, of course, rather an academic question now, considering that Edward, his son, has been dead for some time—killed at the age of 23. But here is the way it was. . . .

The curtain rises on a little maisonette in Brighton. It is November 11, 1919—the first anniversary of the Armistice of World War I, and the first birthday of Edward Holt, son of Evelyn and Arnold Holt. Evelyn, very pretty, is preparing for a party—just herself and her husband and the baby and Dr. Parker, who brought this wonderful baby into the world.

Arnold, a young and ambitious husband and father, comes home, bearing an inexpensive bottle of champagne for the party and a string of imitation pearls for his wife. "One day, my darling, you'll have real pearls," he declares. It isn't a boast, but a statement. Besides the bottle and the baubles, he has news: he has left his employer and has taken a little office. They will be a bit tight for money for a month or two until he gets started.

Arnold has been a house agent; now he is going into the hire-purchase business. "It's an American idea," he explains to his young wife. "Instead of saving up to buy something, you buy it right away and pay for it gradually." Furniture, chiefly. And he has found a partner with the necessary money for stocks—Harry Soames, an ex-convict who is anxious to reinstate himself in the world.

All of this—even the taking on of Harry Soames—is for Edward. Arnold Holt's fatherhood has hit hard and made him fiercely ambitious as well as proud. His boy is going to have nurses and fine prams and later will attend the best school in the world. Therefore, Arnold Holt is impelled to become very rich. *And* famous.

Dr. Parker, a kind and sensible medic, comes to the birthday party, bringing a Teddy bear for the infant he delivered. Harry

EDWARD, MY SON 181

Soames comes, too—a large, florid, foreign-looking fellow who wears his good clothes and his smile as though he were aware of a certain feeling of distrust which he evokes. Harry is introduced to Dr. Parker as Arnold's new partner in Holt & Co.

When Evelyn takes Soames up to have a look at the baby for a moment, Dr. Parker frankly tells Arnold that the other guest makes him uneasy—too much charm, perhaps, charm being a nice asset but not being a trustworthy stock in trade. Evelyn and Harry return and the party begins; a candle is lighted on the cake and Soames expertly slips the cork out of Arnold's champagne bottle. Arnold toasts the infant upstairs: "Sleep safe, Edward, the world shall be your oyster." The lights fade. . . .

Scene II

It is three years later, in the same ugly room. Dr. Parker has come to attend Edward and has brought with him a consultant specialist, Dr. Waxman. Parker is explaining that young Edward, now upward of four, was perfectly healthy until he complained of pain in his side about a month ago and showed a hesitancy about walking.

There is no doubt in Waxman's mind about what it is: it is Manders Atrophy. There is a specialist, Schmitt, in Switzerland, who will take a case like this and operate, but it is expensive and it takes a whole year. The ordinary treatment, for those who have not the money, is a plaster of Paris cast and a diet heavy with glucose and iron.

Dr. Waxman breaks the news to Evelyn and Arnold—that Edward has an atrophy in the nerves of the hip and is in for a bad year in a plaster cast. Perhaps, after that, the boy might not limp much.

"Isn't there anything else—an operation, some sort of electric treatment?" pleads Arnold. "If there's anything he needs . . . I mean *anything at all* . . . we want him to have the best."

Evelyn gallantly conquers her own grief and shock and goes to see her son. The busy consultant physician departs. Dr. Parker ventures a question: "Could you raise a thousand pounds?"

Arnold doesn't think so, the way things are going. Why? Parker tells him of the Swiss specialist. "For Edward," says Arnold, "I could raise a million." Dr. Parker departs to make arrangements in Switzerland by telegraph, and passes the incoming Harry Soames.

Soames is weighted with care. The way things have gone,

the shop might just as well be closed up for a couple of months. He hints that Arnold might have put a little more effort into selling those rugs and Arnold, bristling, offers a startling suggestion: "How would you like to buy me out?" He will sell for what he put into the enterprise—fifteen hundred pounds.

"Gee," moans Soames, "if I could get out from under that business today, I'd *give* fifteen hundred."

"All right," Arnold counters. "Write me a check for fifteen hundred and I'll take over your liabilities."

Harry now realizes that his partner is desperate for money, and is told why; but he has none. They discuss a petition of bankruptcy, but Harry shies at Arnold's suggestion that they sell the stock before going bankrupt. He, personally, has had enough of prison.

Over a drink, Arnold has another idea. "Do you know a man called Ethrington?"

Soames does not.

Ethrington is a friend of Arnold's and would do a good deal for him—and he is a fire assessor. How about increasing the fire insurance?

Soames flatly announces, "I want no part of it."

"Then suppose you leave it to me?" Just leave it to Arnold for a week or two before shutting up the shop, and put a couple of hundred in the bank for carrying on until then. The reluctant Soames agrees, and takes his leave.

Evelyn comes down. She has made up her mind to a long period of nursing her son in bed, but Arnold announces that there isn't going to be any bed—she and the boy are going to Switzerland for the operation. And when they return, Edward will be well, and they'll send him to a fine school like Graingerry. . . .

Arnold puts in a call for Ethrington—but Ethrington has moved to Glasgow. Arnold abandons the call.

"When are we leaving?" Evelyn asks.

"Right away. Next week."

The lights go down.

Scene III

Arnold comes into the room, in the dark, turns up the light, hangs up his coat. It is a few weeks later. He gets a bottle of beer and is about to apply himself to a cold meal lying on the table when he winces and notices that his hand is burned. A momentary panic seizes him—but he puts some butter on the burn and wraps it with a handkerchief.

Harry Soames drops by. He notices that Arnold is alone, and is told that the missus and the kid are away for the night.

"This fire-raising scheme of yours is off, see?" Harry declares. He never did like it and never exactly agreed to it.

"Then why did you give me two hundred pounds to square Ethrington?"

Soames protests he did not know this was what the money was for; he thought it was to keep the shop going—and now he wants the money back. Ethrington has a good job, and it's not worth his while risking a stretch.

ARNOLD—You're suddenly very solicitous for his welfare, Harry.

SOAMES—Yes, maybe I am. Maybe I'm thinking about myself too. I've been doing a lot of thinking this last week, and I don't like it.

ARNOLD—I shouldn't worry, Harry. A lot of people don't like thinking.

SOAMES—Don't try and get smart with me, Holt. You get your hat and coat and go round and see Ethrington. Tell him there isn't going to be a fire. And bring me back my two hundred.

ARNOLD—That's going to be a bit difficult, Harry. I didn't give him your two hundred.

SOAMES—You mean the scheme's off. . . . Why didn't you tell me? I never liked it, anyway. Gee, that's a relief.

ARNOLD—The scheme isn't off, Harry. I've started the fire.

SOAMES—You've done what?

ARNOLD—I decided to go ahead without Ethrington. . . . Besides, I needed that two hundred to send Edward and Evelyn to Switzerland.

SOAMES—You swine. . . .

ARNOLD—We'll see. . . . I think I've done a pretty good job . . . as long as they don't discover it too soon. . . . (*He looks at his watch.*) It's had half an hour already . . . another fifteen minutes we should be all right.

SOAMES—You won't get away with it. . . . I'll tell them the truth.

ARNOLD—Will they believe you? Remember, you start at a slight disadvantage.

SOAMES—I'm getting out of here.

ARNOLD—Just wait another quarter of an hour . . . see what

happens. . . . You'll sleep so much better.

SOAMES—How will you know when it happens?

ARNOLD—The police will probably ring up. We shall hear the fire-engines, they come round this corner. By the way, how much exactly are we insured for?

SOAMES—We increased it to five thousand.

ARNOLD—There, now, I hope we haven't been greedy.

SOAMES—I think you've gone mad . . . taking a chance like this.

ARNOLD—So do I. . . .

SOAMES—Then why in God's name did you do it?

ARNOLD—I did it because I was pushed, Harry . . . and if it comes off . . . I'll never complain of my luck in the future whatever happens. . . . I'll use it all up tonight gladly. This is how I want it to be. If you want anything enough I believe you get it. . . . I want Edward to walk through life without a limp . . . that's all I ask. Nothing else matters in the very slightest.

SOAMES—So it seems.

ARNOLD—Have a drink; it's going to be all right. Something tells me this is my lucky night. (*The phone rings.*) Damn, that's a bit soon—

SOAMES—Well, answer it; for God's sake act surprised.

ARNOLD (*picking up the phone*)—Hullo. Yes, this is Mr. Holt speaking. Yes. Yes. . . . Thank you.

SOAMES—Say you're coming along right away.

ARNOLD—Be quiet. Will you repeat that, please? I didn't quite get it. Thank you. Good-by. (*He puts down the phone.*)

SOAMES—That's tremendous. Is that how you think a guy acts when they ring up to tell him his place is on fire? Get your hat and get down there fast.

ARNOLD (*shaking his head*)—That was from Switzerland, a telegram from Evelyn. It said "Operation performed successfully. . . . Schmitt very confident. Love from us both, Evelyn." (*The noise of a fire-bell is heard.*)

SOAMES—Listen. It's started.

ARNOLD—No, no, it's all over. . . . I'm telling you. . . . Operation performed successfully. I knew it would be all right. Schmitt very confident. Let's have a little air. (*He goes to the window and opens it. The noise of fire-engines is very loud.*) Why, Harry, come and look—there's quite a glow in the sky. (*But* SOAMES *has fainted.*)

The lights go down.

Scene IV

The years have gone on during the dimming of the lights. Now it is 1930 and the setting no longer is the dingy maisonette—it is the handsome study of the headmaster of Graingerry School, where two assistant masters are waiting for Mr. Hanray, the headmaster. They have been summoned rather urgently, and they don't know what for.

Mr. Hanray, a well-tailored lion tamer with twenty years of experience as a headmaster, tells his assistants what for when he arrives. Mr. Arnold Holt has arrived. "We know, of course, what he's here for, and although I fear there is no hope of a reprieve for his son, in certain circumstances I may need your support. . . . We are, I take it, all agreed on the wisdom of the course I have seen fit to adopt?"

As far as Ellerby, the first assistant, is concerned, "the sooner we get rid of the little stinker the better." The other assistant, Cunningham, is of the same mind. He is the one who has the information about Edward—that the little blighter tried to bribe a lad named Townsend with ten shillings.

Hanray dismisses the two men after giving them final instructions in case they are sent for. They are not to argue with Mr. Holt; Ellerby will confine his remarks to Edward's classroom behavior, and Cunningham will report on his conduct in the House. As they leave, Arnold steps through the French window, and one could suspect that he had overheard the conversation.

Arnold is bland and affable. He admires the study, the view, the books. Suddenly he queries, "Why do you want to expel my son?"

Hanray tries to make it easy by equivocation. It isn't expulsion, exactly; the boy will finish his term, and then, perhaps, his parents can find him "a more congenial milieu."

Arnold protests that Edward finds the milieu here most congenial. Under direct questioning, the headmaster admits that he feels Edward should leave for the good of the school, because he is a corrupting influence on his companions. This, Arnold will not believe.

Hanray takes a paper from his drawer and throws it across his desk to Arnold. "This is your small son's handwriting, Mr. Holt." It is a smutty piece of writing, and Arnold is taken aback for a moment—but only for a moment. He inquires if the headmaster ever thought of thrashing the boy and is informed that one thrashing already has been administered.

"How did he take his punishment?"

"Not very well, I'm afraid. He bit me in the hand."

"What did you do?" Arnold asks, suppressing a laugh.

"What would *you* have done, Mr. Holt?"

"I would have put on a pair of thick gloves and started again."

Gloves had not occurred to Hanray. What has occurred to him is that Edward is a misfit in the school. To be blunt about it, Edward has stolen another boy's wrist watch. Arnold can't believe it—the lad has three watches of his own; but the headmaster is quite sure of his facts. "There are a number of excellent schools," he suggests, "which specialize in dealing with boys who—shall we say—do not quite conform to the more conventional standards. . . ."

Arnold is not interested. If Edward has learned to write smut and to steal, he must have learned it here. "This is your responsibility and you shall not shelve it. . . . You are the one who is going to teach him, whether you like it or not."

HANRAY—I'm sorry, but I really cannot be spoken to like this.

ARNOLD—If you know what's good for you, Hanray, you'll listen, and listen carefully.

HANRAY—Are you threatening me?

ARNOLD—I am. There is only one condition on which I will remove my boy from Graingerry, and that is that Graingerry has ceased to exist. Do I make myself clear?

HANRAY—I'm afraid not.

ARNOLD—Very well. We are living in an age of slump, Mr. Hanray. In an age of unemployment and discontent, at a time when parents are finding it increasingly difficult to afford the fees which you, and other schools like you, have to charge. Admirable though your administration of Graingerry as a seat of learning has been, your financial handling of the situation has been less than adequate. Before the war, you embarked on an ambitious rebuilding program here, the capital for which was advanced in equal parts by a firm named Dobson & Blacker, who were acting for a Mr. Christopherson, and by the Westminster Bank. Don't interrupt. (HANRAY *subsides*.) Neither of these mortgages has been repaid; nor are you in a position to repay them; consequently, anyone holding the mortgages can, by calling them in, place the school and yourself in bankruptcy. I hold the mortgages.

Hanray—But I don't understand. How did you get hold of them?

Arnold—I acquired them when Edward came here, in order to prevent the possibility of someone else doing what I now propose to do myself.

Hanray—What you propose to do yourself? Even supposing this plan of yours was feasible, and I do not admit for a moment that it is, do you think that when the story got out it would really benefit your boy?

Arnold—I shall do my best to see that it doesn't get out. The mortgages are not in my name, and those acting for me are discreet. I assure you I have given this matter every consideration, Mr. Hanray. I am fighting for the good name of my boy. I have two alternatives: either I submit tamely to your decision to expel him, or I fight you with every weapon I can lay my hands on. I prefer to fight.

Hanray—I am amazed, Mr. Holt, at the line you've taken, and deeply shocked. The only possible excuse for your conduct is that you are acting in what you mistakenly believe are your son's interests. I would be doing less than my duty if I allowed myself to be influenced by the preposterous threats you have made. (*The telephone bell rings.*) Excuse me. (*Into the telephone.*) Yes, good morning, Arbuthnot. It's not very convenient just at the moment. Can you give me some idea what it's about? Proceedings have already started? But I don't understand. Don't they have to give notice? I see. No, of course, I wasn't prepared for it. (*He puts the phone down.*) I can't believe it, suddenly, like this. Have you started proceedings? I don't understand.

Arnold—Perfectly easy to understand, Hanray. You're a bankrupt. I was afraid you'd take up this attitude. Few schoolmasters, even the most enlightened ones, regard their own judgment as fallible. I suppose that is in the nature of their calling. I see no point in wasting time. What has to be, has to be. It would be hypocritical to add my condolences. Graingerry was a fine school. I shall make it possible for you to carry on until the end of the term. In doing so I am only returning the compliment, as it were. I wonder what will happen to all this, Hanray? What will happen to the playing fields, the swimming pool and the library, of which you were so justly proud? Building land d'you think, or a factory site, or a luxury hotel? Or do you think there will be someone hardy enough to try and start a school here again? If so, perhaps they'd let you come back here one day, when the scandal's died down, of course, and when you've got your discharge. To come back—not as headmaster, but as a junior. You'd be rather old to be a junior master, but I expect you'll manage. Not quite the old age you'd planned for yourself, but then it wasn't quite the youth I'd planned for Edward. What is it they say? "The best laid schemes of mice and men gang aft agley."

HANRAY—I don't believe it. I don't believe that here in England in 1930 one man can destroy another's life, his career, a whole tradition as calmly as if . . . What's happening? Nothing's safe any more. No standard, no principle, no law, counts any longer. If it's true, we're all of us lost.

ARNOLD—Good-by, Mr. Hanray. (*He goes out, shutting the door behind him.*)

HANRAY—No, wait a moment. (*He goes to the door and calls.*) Mr. Holt, please, just a moment. (ARNOLD *comes back.*)

ARNOLD—Well?

HANRAY—You win.

ARNOLD—There is no question of victory, or of defeat, Hanray. We have merely worked out the solution together. It is agreed then that Edward shall remain here, and that you and your staff will renew your efforts to curb his exuberances and make him a decent, sober young citizen.

HANRAY—Very well.

ARNOLD—I believe that when you think it over you will realize that this is a duty which you owe to yourselves as much as to him. I know that in my business at any rate the difficulties and the problems make the job worthwhile.

HANRAY—If you put it like that, Mr. Holt, I suppose there is a possibility that we haven't done all that we might. It's fatally easy to get discouraged.

ARNOLD—I can quite understand that. And now about these mortgages. I think that the best plan would be for you to pay them off, you know.

HANRAY—But . . . I thought you wouldn't want repayment immediately.

ARNOLD—Well, I do and I don't, Hanray. I think it's unwise that you should ever again be put in the position in which you were this morning. I, therefore, propose to write you a check for £27,000, which will clear up the matter once and for all. (*He sits in* HANRAY'S *chair.*) Do you mind if I sit here? It's the twelfth, I think, isn't it?

HANRAY—I don't quite follow, Mr. Holt. You wish to make some other arrangement?

ARNOLD—This is a gift, Mr. Hanray. An unconditional gift. One that I do not wish ever referred to again.

HANRAY—I am overwhelmed by your generosity, but I couldn't possibly accept it.

ARNOLD—Come, Mr. Hanray, that would be churlish. Besides, it is in the interests of Graingerry that you should accept. We both, you know, have them very much at heart.

HANRAY—You are an extraordinary man, Mr. Holt.

ARNOLD—I'm a practical man, Mr. Hanray. (*He hands him the check.*) Please, no thanks. You know this is really the most delightful room. I wonder if you'd mind if I had it copied?

Hanray is hurt and beaten, but gallant in defeat. He sends for an assistant to take Arnold on a tour of the campus, and bids another one to bring him Holt Junior. He tears up the boy's dirty paper, then arranges a chair by his desk to accommodate a kneeling boy. On his desk he notices a thick pair of motoring gloves which Arnold has left. He puts one on, and fetches a cane from the corner. . . .

The curtain falls.

ACT II

Four more years have gone by. Evelyn is in Arnold's fine office and Miss Perry, his attractive young personal secretary, is on the phone.

"I'm afraid we don't know where Sir Arnold is," she is telling some caller. And to Evelyn she suggests, "Perhaps he's gone to the station to see you off, Lady Holt." This Evelyn doubts—and it doesn't really matter anyway, because she can ring him up from Paris tonight. Too bad Arnold can't be going with her.

Miss Perry is efficiently briefing Evelyn on the arrangements for her trip, including being met as usual in Paris, when Dr. Parker is announced and is bidden in. The doctor's date is with Arnold. He is pleased to see Evelyn again, and he admires her smart appearance.

"How is Edward?"

"Oh, he's very grown up now. He shaves every other day. They say he's going to be captain of cricket next year. Of course, Arnold spoils him dreadfully. I'm so afraid sometimes he'll never have any real sense of values."

Quite evidently, Evelyn is a disturbed mother. Edward isn't

quite straight about money, for one thing. For another he—well, he doesn't get exactly drunk on port some times, but he seems a little too fond of it. . . .

"Worthy of Arnold," comments Parker, drily. He protests that he still likes Arnold, but doesn't approve of many of the things he gets up to, like his last business with Harry Soames. "I'm not defending Soames, but he had been Arnold's partner way back in the hire-purchase days at Brighton and right up to six months before this happened. There's no doubt Arnold could have saved him if he'd chosen to. Instead, he did just the opposite. There are people who say Arnold was the one who should have gone to prison."

Evelyn remains the loyal wife. Whatever her husband has done has been for her and their son, and she will hear nothing against him. But Evelyn is not prepared to hear what follows.

"I know," says Dr. Parker about Arnold. "He's made a most unholy mess of it, hasn't he?"

Before Evelyn can get too indignant, Parker continues, "I know I'm only a poor fool of a doctor who's in love with the wife of his best patient."

Evelyn pretends she hasn't known—but she *has* known, for a long time. "What ought I to do?" she begs. And then pretends that the question is what should she do about Edward.

Arnold breezes in, full of apologies and importance. He's been stuck with the Prime Minister's secretary for the last hour and a half. And now he wants to be sure that Evelyn is all set for her trip—money, passports, tickets. . . .

Yes, Evelyn has it all. One man will meet her at Victoria Station, another will meet her and Edward in Paris, and undoubtedly a brass band will meet them in Zurich. Her irony is lost upon her husband, and so is that of Dr. Parker, who remarks that the only traveling he ever does is on his week's vacation to the Isle of Wight. This causes Arnold to half-remember something. "Who did we know," he asks his wife, "who always took their holidays in the Isle of Wight?"

"Mr. Soames," she replies.

"He still does," says Dr. Parker. "Parkhurst"—a prison on the Isle of Wight.

Evelyn departs for the station, to go to Paris and then to Switzerland with her son, and now Arnold gets down to the business of his appointment with Dr. Parker. "I just thought perhaps you'd like to check my heart and my blood pressure."

The doctor's reply is short and ironic. "Like to?" he asks.

Parker has no worries about his patient; he's as fit as a horse—but he does talk too much for a fat man. Before going about the business of measuring blood pressure, Parker pops a thermometer in his patient's mouth—not to get a temperature reading, but just to keep Arnold quiet for a minute or so. During one of these silent minutes there is a phone call and the doctor takes it. It is only Miss Perry, in the outside office, to bring Arnold a written message.

Dr. Parker would like to have Arnold dine with him at "the Club," and Arnold makes the date. When the physician has gone, he refers to the message Miss Perry has brought. "Soames, is he out?" he queries. "Has he escaped?"

Miss Perry is an efficient young woman who prepares for questions by preparing their answers. She already has read the paper and knows that Soames was released from prison this morning. Resignedly, Arnold tells his secretary to let Harry in . . . but to give him a minute. In this minute Arnold rather oddly looks around the room for a weapon. He tests a paperweight and discards it; then finds in a desk drawer a heavy, black ruler, which he puts beside him handily.

Harry Soames looks much older now, when he comes in—and he does have things on his mind—things like being sold out to the police.

ARNOLD—I think you'd be wiser to forget it, Harry . . . all of it.

SOAMES—Maybe.

ARNOLD—How are the family?

SOAMES—I guess they're fine, thanks. Mabel has a job in a tea shop and Arthur is a van boy. Making good money, too, all of two pounds a week.

ARNOLD—I wrote to Mabel, you know, offering her any help I could give. . . . I never got a reply.

SOAMES—She told me. It was good of you. I guess she's got more pride than I have. Fiona, the little one, remember?

ARNOLD—Of course I do.

SOAMES—She got a scholarship to the London University.

ARNOLD—Oh, that was splendid.

SOAMES—She couldn't afford to go, so she's working in a shop now. Gee, I'd like to see them again!

ARNOLD—Well, you will soon.

SOAMES—No, I don't expect to see them for quite a time, Arnold, not till I've got one or two things straightened out. I think I've caused them enough harm to be going on with.

Arnold—Now, Harry, you mustn't feel like that. (*The telephone rings.*) Hullo. Yes. Put him through. (*To* Soames.) Excuse me. Hullo, Edward? Where are you? At the station? Good. What? Oh, nonsense, you'll have a whale of a time. I wish I could have, old man. Well, yes, maybe. What? But you had fifty pounds last week. All of it? Yes, that's all very well, what's your mother going to say? (*He laughs.*) I expect she will. What do you want me to do? That's no use, she'd see the letter. Certainly I'd have to register it. I could do that, I suppose. Do you think there's more than one Post Office? Oh. Well, I suppose we boys have to stick together. But, Edward, do try and be a bit more careful. That's all right. Have a good time. Oh, I say, while you're out there you might go and see Schmitt. You remember him? Might be the smart thing to do. Oh, Edward, give my love to your mother. Oh, yes, I forgot, so she would. Well, good-by then. (*He rings off.*) He'll be a wonderful business man. . . . He never misses a trick. . . . (*He turns to* Soames.) What were we talking about?

Soames—Our children.

Arnold—Yes. Well, look, if there's anything I can do for them, you only have to ask.

Soames—Thanks, I'll remember that.

Arnold—And now the next question is, what can we do for you? Just a moment—(*Into the dictaphone.*)—Miss Perry, wire Mr. Edward fifty pounds Poste Restante, St. Moritz. Yes, that's right. No, not the Hotel. Better make it seventy-five pounds. (*To* Soames.) Got any plans?

Soames—No, not a great many. I don't find it quite so easy to make them as I did. I'm getting old, I suppose.

Arnold—Nonsense!

Soames—Perhaps just discouraged. Mind you, I'm not kicking against my trial or my sentence, they were fair enough. What gets me is that twice in my life I've been fool enough to try and get away with it, each time I told myself that I wouldn't be the one to get caught. All around me I saw other men taking the chances I took; they got through all right. Why shouldn't I? I know men and so do you, not a hundred yards away from this desk who are much bigger crooks than I ever was; who break the law over and over again. And they do worse than that, they get round the law and squirm under it and climb above it, and what happens to them? Nothing. That's what burns me up. It's so damned unfair—I only wanted what they wanted, not as much as most of 'em. I wanted money for my wife and kids and a decent home and a respectable old age.

ARNOLD—What you need, my boy, is work.

SOAMES—What sort of work would you suggest?

ARNOLD—Well, how about starting a little business somewhere? An antique shop, or a tobacconist; that's one of the things there's still money in, they tell me.

SOAMES—Who are they, Arnold?

ARNOLD—Why, people. . . . What's the matter now?

SOAMES—Nothing's the matter. I just don't like being fobbed off. . . . They have never told you anything of the kind. Shall I tell you why? Because *they* are all the people you've never asked about the questions that never interested you. *They* tell me you should buy Kaffirs. *They* tell me you should sell Oil. *They* tell you there's money in tobacco. All lies, my friend.

The one thing the embittered Harry wants is his old job back in the Arnold Holt Trust; it's his one chance to be able to hold his head up again, and here he is begging the great Arnold Holt for the chance.

Arnold affects sympathy, but is cagey. He'd like to do it for Harry, personally, but now he has his associates to consider and he does not know how the associates would feel. It might be better if Harry tried other fields, outside the city, and perhaps even changed his name. Maybe they can talk more about it at lunch one day next week.

Soames is agreeable in a defiant way. "Which day?" he demands, and Arnold, caught short for an answer, mumbles about Miss Perry having his engagement book. He suggests that Harry ring him up in the morning so they can fix a date. "By the way, how are you fixed for cash?"

Harry declares he is all right, thanks, and says he will call in the morning. In departing he adds, "You can put that ruler away now. You haven't drawn a straight line for years."

When Miss Perry enters the office with letters to be signed, Arnold is for the moment miles away, pondering Soames' parting remark. But soon he comes to, checks over the remaining business to be done, then asks his secretary to mix him a whisky and soda. He invites her to have one, too, but she declines; so he orders her to sit down and at least talk and listen and answer questions.

Miss Perry has been Arnold's secretary for two years. Likes the job very much. At the moment, no other interests in life than the progress of Arnold Holt & Co. Evenings, she goes home. She lives alone in Islington.

Arnold asks, "Would you like to have dinner with me tonight?" Miss Perry remembers that Arnold already has a date with Dr. Parker at the doctor's club, and reminds Holt of this. "Ring him up and tell him I've got mumps."

Miss Perry accepts the date and writes her home address, where Arnold can pick her up. The scene ends, and now Arnold comes once more before the curtain, as he did at the beginning of the play. "Well, ladies and gentlemen, that's how it started," he admits. "I'm not apologizing for the next scene. . . ."

The lights fade, and then they go up on

Scene II

which is the living room of Eileen Perry's flat in Islington. A year has gone by since Arnold asked Miss Perry to have dinner at the end of that day when Evelyn left for Paris and Zurich and Dr. Parker took his blood pressure and Harry Soames tried to get back into the firm.

Miss Perry is most obviously a mistress now, in negligee. In her living room she checks over a supper table, turns on a phonograph for soft music, opens a bottle of champagne, pours herself a drink and sits down to eat. This moment on the stage is a dramatist's ideal of how to picture sin in pantomime, for soon Arnold emerges from the bedroom in a dressing gown worn over a dress shirt and trousers.

"Good morning, my love." He gives her a perfunctory kiss.

And it does seem to be morning—or, anyway, three o'clock. The food is stale and the ice has melted in the champagne bucket. Arnold pours himself a glass and toasts, "Here's to us. A year ago today." He waxes affectionate: She never fusses and is always the same.

MISS PERRY—You think that's a virtue?
ARNOLD—I know it is.
MISS PERRY—*How* do you know?
ARNOLD—Well, anyway, I like it.
MISS PERRY—That's something quite different, Arnold. You like it because it suits you. I don't question what you do and where you're going. I accept things, but I oughtn't to accept them, Arnold, not all the time. It's not good for you to have your own way always, I know that, but I don't do anything

about it because I'm in love with you. I'm in love with you and not what you might be or ought to be. . . . I'm a gangster's moll, Arnold.

Arnold—Thank you very much. . . . Well, here's to our next hold-up. And may you never stop feeling the way you do. The great thing is to be happy. You are happy, aren't you?

Miss Perry—Yes, I'm happy.

Arnold—So am I . . . happier than I've been for years, and younger. Do you think I'm younger?

Miss Perry—Yes, much younger.

Arnold—What I like about you is that you never flatter me. Would you like a pearl necklace?

Miss Perry—Very much.

Arnold—Then this seems as good a moment as any to give you one. Don't look so surprised. (*He takes out a case.*) May I put them on?

Miss Perry—No.

Arnold—Yes.

Miss Perry—What on earth would I do with a pearl necklace? (*She has her back to him and cannot see his face.*)

Arnold—You could pretend they were Ciro . . .

Miss Perry—What's the matter?

Arnold—Nothing. I couldn't fasten the catch. (*He puts them on.*)

Miss Perry—They are lovely. I don't think I've ever seen real pearls close to before. Is it true they dissolve in vinegar?

Arnold—If you've got the vinegar and a little courage, now's the time to try.

Miss Perry—I haven't. Thank you very much, but you shouldn't have done it.

Arnold—I feel very honored that you've accepted them. Will you believe me when I tell you that nothing I've ever given you or could give you would not leave me in your debt?

Miss Perry—Darling, I do love you. We're being very sentimental tonight.

Arnold—It's the warm champagne; have some more?

Miss Perry—Yes, please. (*She has drawn the curtains.*) What would you do if someone were to find out about us?

Arnold—I shouldn't care. Probably lots of people have found out already. Why? Have we anything to be ashamed of?

Miss Perry—Not ashamed of exactly.

Arnold—There are a great many things in my life I wish I hadn't done . . . but loving you will never be one of them.

Miss Perry—You're not being very practical, Arnold. Supposing your wife knew about me. What would she do?
Arnold—I haven't the slightest idea.
Miss Perry—Do you think she'd divorce you?
Arnold—Good heavens, no!
Miss Perry—Why are you so sure?
Arnold—For one thing, there's Edward.
Miss Perry—Edward's seventeen. . . .
Arnold—What of it?
Miss Perry—You don't think your wife might consider him old enough to make up his own mind?
Arnold—I don't think it would be a nice thing for a boy of seventeen to be confronted with. He's got a very happy home. I don't think he'd want to see it broken up.
Miss Perry—Is that what your wife thinks? About the happy home?
Arnold—I imagine so.
Miss Perry (*getting up and going back to the window and arranging the curtains*)—Then you're quite safe, aren't you, Arnold? The best of both worlds.
Arnold—What's the matter? Why do you keep fussing with the curtains? Why are you so restless?

The matter is, Miss Perry informs, that Arnold is a fool. There is someone watching the flat—a man in a raincoat and a bowler hat who has been under the lamp post all evening. "What are you going to do?" she challenges.

Arnold pulls back the curtains a bit and takes a look. "He's there, all right," he agrees. "Of course, he may be watching the flat below." She knows he doesn't mean it and so does he. The man must be a private detective watching Miss Perry's abode. Arnold asserts that instinct tells him he should try and get out of here—but how?

There is no easy escape, his secretary informs him. No fire escape, and the service lift is only big enough for small parcels. It might be a good idea to ask the man in the raincoat and the bowler to come in and identify himself. Not a bad idea, agrees Holt—and he parts the curtain, opens the window and calls, "Hullo, you down there, sir, under the lamp post. Won't you come up?"

The man does come up. His name is Mr. Prothero—Walter Prothero. He introduces himself, and he does not wait for return introductions because he knows who his hosts are. Miss

Perry and Sir Arnold. And a very cozy bit of co-operation they have offered him, too—a bit irregular, perhaps, but he will be guided by whatever Mr. Wilson thinks."

Arnold demands, "Who's Mr. Wilson?"

"Mr. Wilson is acting for Lady Holt, I understand."

The efficient Mr. Prothero begins making notes of the layout of the apartment, and Arnold's anger rises very swiftly. "Get out of here!" he orders. Mr. Prothero has just been invited up and now he is being thrown out . . . but this is one of the strange things a private detective comes to expect of life. He bids Miss Perry and Arnold a polite good-night and cheerily expects that Sir Arnold will be hearing from Mr. Wilson in a day or two.

For a sophisticated man, Holt becomes strangely and suddenly indignant—and puzzled, even. "Get me Whiteman on the phone," he snaps to Miss Perry—for now she is not his mistress, but his secretary. "Do you know his private number?"

Good secretaries always know all private numbers, and Miss Perry promptly supplies Whiteman's. Arnold rings it and gets the man out of bed. A man has been watching Miss Perry's flat, he explains, and he just happens to be spending the evening here. The man is invited up, and right away he begins making notes. "She can't start proceedings without telling me," Arnold shouts. Mr. Whiteman is quite obviously Arnold's lawyer, and quite dutifully he agrees to see Arnold at his office in the morning.

Now Holt turns to Miss Perry. If it weren't for Edward he'd let Evelyn get away with this—but on account of Edward he must fight the divorce.

MISS PERRY—Suppose you lose?

ARNOLD—I won't lose . . . the issue's too big. I'm afraid it means the end of us, for a time.

MISS PERRY—Of course.

ARNOLD—It was fun while it lasted, wasn't it?

MISS PERRY—Great fun.

ARNOLD—I think I'd better get out of here now. (*He goes into the bedroom. Off.*) I'll give you a call, when I've seen Whiteman in the morning.

MISS PERRY—A call? (*Suddenly realizing.*) Oh, yes, of course, I'll be here. (ARNOLD *enters, putting on his jacket.*)

ARNOLD—I don't know how on earth I'm going to manage without you at the office. God, what a mess all this is!

MISS PERRY—You'll manage all right. Don't worry about me. I shan't throw myself under a train like Harry Soames.

ARNOLD (*shocked*)—I suppose I deserved that.

MISS PERRY—I'm sorry, I shouldn't have said it. Go along and put your coat on. (*He goes into the bedroom.*) What did you do with the pearl box?

ARNOLD (*returning*)—The what?

MISS PERRY—The box. The case . . . the pearls were in?

ARNOLD—Isn't it there? (*He is putting on his overcoat.*)

MISS PERRY—Oh, yes, how silly of me. (*She puts the pearls in it and holds it out.*)

ARNOLD—Why?

MISS PERRY—I'm sure Mr. Whiteman will agree with me, it simplifies matters.

ARNOLD—Don't let's make it too easy for Whiteman; he charges too much, anyway. Besides, I'd like you to have them if you would.

MISS PERRY—Very well.

ARNOLD—I don't know how to say good-by.

MISS PERRY—Don't you? Do you think Prothero is still there? (*Going to the window and looking out.*) Yes, still at it. Getting very wet. The gloomy sentry. But I suppose in a way he's the winner, you know. Let's give him three cheers. (*Suddenly opening the window and leaning out.*) Three cheers for Mr. Prothero. Hip, hip, hooray. Hip, hip, hooray. (*She closes the window.*) Do you know, he actually raised his hat! (*She turns round*—ARNOLD *has gone.*)

The lights fade, and when they come up again it is Scene III, a hotel bedroom in the Italian Riviera. Evelyn is the occupant, and it is the next day after Mr. Prothero's call on Miss Perry's flat. Evelyn is talking on the phone. She is ready to check out, but her son is missing, and she has been trying to get the hotel to track him down at sundry clubs and bars. She is beginning to fear that Edward has been in an accident.

As she talks, Arnold eases through the doorway, and when she hangs up he greets her with a suave "Good evening, my dear." He looks as though he has traveled for a day—and of course he has. To his surprised wife he explains that he has managed to snatch a short holiday . . . and now he finds that Evelyn is getting ready to leave the hotel as soon as she finds her son.

"I wouldn't worry about Edward," he advises. "He's perfectly safe, at the pictures."

To the surprised and puzzled Lady Holt Arnold explains that he telephoned Edward from the Paris airport on his way down and suggested that the young man go see a movie. "I planned to join you and wanted it to be a surprise. I also suggested that the best way of delaying your departure was for him to disappear."

Evelyn, angry, denounces this maneuver as underhand—and Arnold counters with the charge that having him investigated by a private detective is equally underhand. "You won't win, you know," he warns.

Evelyn thinks her chances of winning are good, but Arnold announces that he has no intention of giving her a divorce.

"I'm delighted to hear you say so."

"Why?" He is, for once, puzzled.

"Because I should like you to fight and lose. That is part of my plan for Edward. . . . I want him to realize that with all your money and power there are still some things you can't get away with."

In Evelyn's mind, a divorce is the only thing which will bring Edward to his senses—and Edward certainly needs bringing. For instance, he was very drunk last night and then he was very sick, and he was rude to everybody, including a waiter. This morning he apologized all around and gave the waiter five pounds. Result: everyone in the hotel calls him "Milord." "He's seventeen," says his mother. "If he goes on like this, what will he be like when he is twenty?"

The doting Arnold tries to imagine excuses for his son, but Evelyn's mind is firm. She is frightened for her boy, and she is going to take him away—abroad somewhere, after she has won her divorce. Abroad somewhere where he can learn what it is to work for his own living and have responsibilities.

ARNOLD—But even if you won this divorce you still couldn't take him out of England without my consent.

EVELYN—Mr. Wilson thinks that under the circumstances the Courts might give permission. . . .

ARNOLD—Does he, indeed?

EVELYN—. . . and if you force me to stay in England I can always change my name. Mrs. Soames did.

ARNOLD—Why do you hate me so much?

EVELYN—I don't hate you. I'm sorry. I shouldn't have said that about Mrs. Soames. I'm very tired. Do you mind if I go to bed?

ARNOLD—Go ahead. I'm still your husband. We're not divorced yet, you know.

EVELYN—How long did you tell Edward to stay out?

ARNOLD—No particular time. I just wanted a chance to talk to you.

EVELYN—Now you've had that, perhaps you'll leave.

ARNOLD—Not just yet. Won't you sit down? Evelyn, I never realized that you cared so much. I thought that that side of marriage wasn't important to you nowadays. I'm not excusing what I've done—I'd have done it, I expect, whatever the circumstances might have been. I didn't realize that my taking a mistress would make you so terribly bitter. I'm sorry.

EVELYN—You haven't understood one word of what I've been saying, have you?

ARNOLD—Only that you think the best way of dealing with Edward is to break up his home.

EVELYN—His home! When did he last have a home? A real home? Something that wasn't a cross between the toy department of Harrod's and the Bank of England. Presided over by a perpetual fairy godfather who granted his every wish before he even thought of it himself.

ARNOLD—Some wives would be grateful to a husband who tried to be just that.

EVELYN—Possibly, but I'm not. I've had enough, Arnold. I've seen the fairy godfather when he's off duty. I think it's time Edward should too, time he got to know his father, and all his father stands for.

ARNOLD—You don't think it's rather late to introduce us? I think Edward knows a good deal more about me than you suspect. It's true he doesn't know about Eileen, but I'm perfectly prepared that he should know if you really think it necessary. But while we're being so very frank with him, perhaps he should know about Larry too.

EVELYN—What do you mean?

ARNOLD—Larry's in love with you. I think you're in love with him. I think that's why you want a divorce.

Devilishly, Arnold pursues his point. He knows that Dr. Parker is in love with Evelyn, and with this knowledge he can wreck the doctor's career—for the British Medical Council has very definite views about physicians who seduce their patients. He has no evidence, he admits—"but you should know what private investigators can do once they start. This is going to be a very dirty case. . . ."

For the first time, Evelyn really despises her husband. She

orders him out of her hotel room, but he blandly declines to leave. The telephone rings, and he answers it. "Oh, yes. . . . Yes, we're all staying. You may send my luggage up here." He cradles the phone and tells his wife, "Edward's back. I'd better go and look after him. He's just been a little sick in the lift."

The curtain falls.

ACT III

It is 1938, and Lord Holt has a house in Charles Street and in it is a very grand room called the Gainsborough Room because it is hung with Gainsboroughs. Burton, Arnold's private secretary, and Dr. Parker are in this room at the moment. Parker, who has been reading *The Times*, wonders aloud if there is going to be a war.

"His Lordship is very hopeful," says Burton, ambiguously. Then he explains what he meant was that Lord Holt hopes a war can be avoided and that those who think Britain ought to fight are irresponsible hotheads.

Burton has been with Arnold for three years. Miss Perry, his predecessor? She's still with the organization, in the Paris office.

Evelyn, on whom the years have begun to tell, brings in a very pretty girl of about 20, Phyllis Maxwell. Phyllis is Edward's fiancée, Dr. Parker is told, and he says the proper things. A butler brings in a tray of drinks, as if he knew that Evelyn would be wanting one, and they quaff a toast to the affianced couple. Phyllis flies off to dress.

"We're having a little party at the Berkeley," Evelyn explains to the doctor. "Won't you join us, Larry?" He begs off, saying he has more patients to see when he has finished with Lord Holt.

When Evelyn and Parker are alone he is properly complimentary about Phyllis. "She's what Edward needs," says the young man's mother. "Sensible, down to earth, frank." And then: "Is there anything wrong with Arnold?"

Parker doesn't think so—just another bee in his bonnet, and wanting another checkup.

"How do you think I'm looking?" she asks.

He lies, "Fine . . . fine!"

She helps herself to another cocktail. "When I get Edward and Phyllis married, I'll try taking a cure. . . . Do you think people know I drink?"

When Arnold arrives he orders Evelyn off to dress for the party, in spite of her protest that she may not be going because she thinks she is going to have one of her headaches. He gets down to business with Parker. It's not himself he wants a consultation about this time; it is a girl. From a locked desk drawer he removes a packet of letters and shows them to the doctor. They are Edward's letters, and they are addressed to somebody named Bettikins. "Miss Betty Fowler," Arnold explains.

"You want my opinion on them? I think he should see a psychologist!"

But what Arnold wants is for Dr. Parker to see Bettikins, and she is here now. She is going to have a child and she claims Edward is the father.

Miss Fowler, nice-looking enough, is brought in by the butler. "It was nice of you to come and see me," says Arnold at his pleasantest.

Betty replies, "I've always wanted to meet Edward's father. I've seen pictures of you, of course."

"I only wish we could have met under happier circumstances. . . . I've told Dr. Parker that you think you're going to have a child."

Betty doesn't think—she's quite sure. She has been to a doctor and the tests are positive.

Parker questions the girl and learns that she has known Edward for nearly a year. She works in a shop and one time Edward came in there to buy a postcard, and then they began going out. . . . "And then one night he suggested we should be lovers, and—well—I was afraid of losing him if I said no."

Betty insists that she is in love with Edward and wants to marry him—but Edward has stopped seeing her and that is why she sent Arnold the letters. "It's not that he's really weak, it's just that he hates having to make up his mind," she explains.

Arnold breaks the bad news to her. Edward *has* made up his mind—to marry another girl. Betty takes it gamely. He then suggests, "Supposing you weren't going to have this child, the position would be a good deal easier, would it not?" This she admits, but says, simply, "But I *am* going to have it."

"Not necessarily, eh, Larry?"

Not necessarily, the doctor agrees. "If she doesn't take proper care of herself—there's always a risk."

That isn't what Arnold meant, and Dr. Parker very well knows it "What Lord Holt is now suggesting is that you have an illegal operation," Larry tells the girl. She will have none of it— and neither will Dr. Parker, whose ethics are solid.

Arnold is casting about in his mind for some other plan, and he very pointedly dismisses Parker. The physician agrees to leave only on one condition—that Betty promise him that the next time Lord Holt suggests she have an abortion, she will get right up and walk out. She promises and Parker goes.

ARNOLD—Thank heaven for that. Now we can get on. Larry's a nice fellow, but he's apt to get rather excited, a bit of an old woman. Would you like a drink?
BETTY—No, thank you, I'm not drinking just now.
ARNOLD—Oh, nonsense, one won't do you any harm.
BETTY—Really, I won't.
ARNOLD—Well, come and sit down. The trouble is he's very fond of Edward, thinks I'm not strict enough with him. Perhaps he's right. But it is difficult to be strict with Edward—you've found that out, haven't you? Now, Betty, suppose you tell me why you're so keen on having this baby.
BETTY—I'm not keen on it exactly, but—well, I don't approve of what Dr. Parker said just now.
ARNOLD—I'm certainly not going to suggest that again because if I did you'd have to get right up and walk out of here. Remember? Although if you did there's nothing to prevent me getting up and walking out with you. Why, that's quite an idea. How about you and I talking about this over a bit of dinner, eh?
BETTY—If you like to.
ARNOLD—Go on, have a drink. Mustn't look so tragic, you know. Pretty girls ought to smile. Where would you like to eat? They tell me there's a new place opened in Compton Street, run by a Greek. When Greek meets Greek they always open a restaurant, eh?
BETTY—Yes. (*She smiles.*)
ARNOLD—You know, I've got an idea you and I will get on famously. The great thing is not to be afraid of anything. Eh?

The curtain falls.

SCENE II

Three years have passed. Evelyn is in the Gainsborough Room, finishing a meal from a tray and drinking champagne. One of the windows has been boarded up; there are sounds of air raid warnings, airplanes and gunfire. The butler clears away the tray, leaving the champagne, and then brings in Dr. Parker.
"Hallo, Larry. In at the birth, in at the death, my friend.

... It happened thirteen days ago. It's his birthday, remember?"

They toast the departed Edward. She looks back over the years to that first birthday party, when Arnold had toasted his son and told him the world was his oyster. Then, breaking, she says, "I'm a maudlin, drunken old woman." It has been hard on Phyllis, too, for she is pregnant—but she is game, Evelyn says.

Arnold returns from a visit to Edward's aerodrome. He has seen the commanding officer, and "he said that he was just about the best pilot in the squadron, that he didn't know what fear was, that he never took a chance with anybody's life but his own, that he was a born leader of men—I liked that best of all."

Bitterly Evelyn comments what an extraordinary life the Commanding Officer must have—sitting there all day telling parents fairy stories about their children.

"Hadn't you better go to bed?" Arnold queries, darkly.

"No, Arnold. I want to hear what the Commanding Officer said. I want to find out about Edward. Twenty-three years isn't very long to get to know anyone. I never really knew him properly. Not like his Commanding Officer. He summed him up in thirty seconds. Thirty seconds. Just as long as it takes a sparrow to fall to the ground. . . . They said it would have taken about thirty seconds for Edward to fall. He wasn't very high. I wonder what he thought about . . . what his Commanding Officer would say, I suppose. A born leader of men, like his father. I thought that would please you, Arnold. He didn't say where you thought of leading them, by any chance. He didn't know the real joke, did he? He didn't know that the leader himself had lost all sense of direction. It's an extraordinary thing, but I can't find that damned staircase. There you are. Do you know how many stairs there are, Larry? I do. I've counted them. You see, sometimes one can't see quite as clearly as one would wish and then it's a great help to count. (*She starts to walk upstairs.*) One, two, three—that's the funny one—four, five, six, seven—good-by, Larry. . . . (*She has gone.*)

Arnold, too, reminisces about his son to Dr. Parker—a bloody hero now, but one who had got into much trouble, like the time at school and the adventure with Betty Fowler. (The Fowler business turned out all right in the end.) "Maybe," he muses, "if I'd been another sort of man things would have been different—who's to say? I did what I thought was best for my boy because I loved him. You can't do more than that—can you?"

The lights fade.

Scene III

It is a dim, foggy morning in 1948 and there are no lights in the Gainsborough Room. There has been a power cut, and Burton is gamely peering at a stack of papers.

"Fancy not being able to turn the lights on in your own house," mutters the butler.

"Fancy not classing Lord Holt as an essential industry," Burton retorts.

The household is upset. Arnold has decided to sell the house—has been wanting to ever since Evelyn died, in the butler's opinion. Burton is more realistic. "Lady Holt's death has nothing whatever to do with this. His Lordship's decision has been dictated solely by necessity. He can no longer afford to live in this house. That is why he is going to Palm Beach and taking his grandson with him."

Arnold comes down the stairs and is informed everything is ready—hand luggage in the hall, the rest of it already at the station, and the car dispatched to fetch Mrs. Holt and Master Holt. Arnold makes one more try to get Burton to go with him, but Burton declines because his mother won't go.

"What is her objection to America?"

"I think it's the Americans, my Lord."

Dr. Parker arrives—with a message from Phyllis. "Arnold, she asked me to tell you that she isn't coming with you to Palm Beach."

"You mean she wants me to take the boy on my own?"

"No, Arnold. She wants the boy to stay here."

Arnold is becoming angry, and he suspects, correctly, that at least some of this is Dr. Parker's doing. Parker admits that he has told Phyllis that if she isn't careful, Edward's son will have the same disastrous childhood that his father had.

Arnold is in a complete fury. He tries to get Phyllis on the phone, but the phone isn't working. He goes round to her house to fetch her and her boy to the station—and if they refuse to come he will cut them off without a shilling.

When he leaves, Parker calls up the stair, "All right, you can come down now. He's gone." Phyllis and her son have been in the house all the time, because Parker felt they'd be safer here.

"Won't he come back when he finds we're not at the station?" she asks.

"No. He'll never come back. He's on his way out, and he knows it."

Parker mounts a few of the stairs and calls, "All right, Edward, you can come down now—there's a good boy."

The lights black out.

EPILOGUE

Arnold appears before the curtain, as he had in the beginning. "Well, ladies and gentlemen, that's how it all happened. I wonder what you would have done. . . ." He lifts his hat, waves cheerily and

THE CURTAIN FALLS

LIFE WITH MOTHER *

A Comedy in Three Acts

By Howard Lindsay and Russel Crouse

EVER since the fabulous "Life with Father" ended its fabulous run, people have hounded the authors, Lindsay and Crouse, and the producer, Oscar Serlin, for a sequel. People knew that the late Clarence Day, son of the "Father" of the first play, had written a great deal more about life with his family—certainly enough to warrant more for the stage.

But a sequel to so extraordinary a success was admittedly a risky proposition. It could not follow the original success too soon afterward, and when it did follow it had better be very, very good; for people would be bound to ask, "Is it as good as 'Life with Father'?"

Lindsay, Crouse and Serlin took their time and weighed all the angles. At last, on October 20, 1948, they presented "Life with Mother" at the Empire Theatre. Mr. Lindsay and Dorothy Stickney again were Father and Mother Day. One of the acts took place in the original Stewart Chaney setting of the Days' town house—a setting which has lasted longer than many real houses erected since Mr. Chaney's establishment was moved into the Empire in time for the opening on November 8, 1939.

No play could have got happier notices from the critics than did "Life with Mother." It was a warm and expert comedy, so well made and so well played that it would stand out in any season. People wise in the Broadway trade felt certain that, although it probably would not run as long as had its phenomenal predecessor, it would be good for at least a couple of years. But "Mother" confounded the experts by barely running out the season. In other times such an engagement would have been a respectable hit, but in days when hits range upward of a thousand Broadway performances a single season is disappointing. Various reasons have been advanced, but nobody will ever know for sure.

* Copyright, 1938, by Howard Lindsay, Russel Crouse and Katherine B. Day.
Published by Alfred A. Knopf, Inc., New York.

One theory is that the public, seeing the title in the ads and on the theatre marquee, mistook the play for the old "Life with Father" and said to itself, "Oh, we've seen that one." Another is that the booking of many theatre parties at the beginning of the run discouraged the cash-carrying public from visiting the box office. Still another is that a sequel is a chancy enterprise.

The box-office adventures of "Life with Mother" do not detract from its fine qualities as an American family comedy. This time, we discover the Day family—Father, Mother and all the boys—at their country home in Harrison, N. Y. (The house still is in Harrison, in battered condition, an object of mild interest to an occasional sightseer.) It is the middle of the afternoon of Friday, August 31, 1888, and the scene is the corner room of the house, which is decorated in pale pastels, pink brocade and beige woodwork. A veranda, topped by a striped awning, runs along outside. A large arch leads out of the room into a hall, and four high windows open on the veranda. Important in the Victorian clutter of furniture are Vinnie's sewing table, Father's desk and chair, and a bulky wall telephone.

Father, knees crossed, is enthroned in the middle of the sofa, pince-nez on, reading with some impatience a handsomely bound book. "Bah!" he exclaims. "Trash!"

Two of his sons, Whitney (whose left arm is in a sling) and Harlan, the youngest, come looking for their mother and find she isn't here. Perhaps Father could speak to Mother for them. They have been around the neighborhood trying to sell vegetables from the garden—but Mother has been ahead of them in the dog cart *giving* vegetables away. They would like Father to tell Mother to stop doing that. Father will do no such thing. He advises the boys to start out ahead of their mother tomorrow, for "you have to get there first in this world." Mr. Day examines Whitney's broken arm and the boy is fearful—not that it hurts now, but the last time his father looked at the arm he broke it again.

Little Harlan wants to know what book his parent is reading and is informed, with an accompanying snort of disdain, that it is "Memoirs of the French Court." Harlan jumps to an erect position, salutes briskly and begins to recite, with gestures,

> "You know we French stormed Ratisbon,
> A mile or so away.
> On a little mound Napoleon
> Stood on our storming day."

It is Harlan's new piece, but Father doesn't want any more of it now.

Whitney, too, is interested in his father's book. "Oh, that's what Mother gave you for your birthday."

"There are twenty-four volumes, Whitney. They were bought on the installment plan . . . $10 a volume. Your mother gave me the first volume. It turns out I'm giving myself the other twenty-three."

"Is it good, Father?"

"I have never read such nauseating balderdash in all my life!"

Whitney marvels, "Twenty-four volumes!" and Harlan asks, "Are you going to read them all, Father?"

"So help me God!"

He sends the boys off to look for Margaret and tell her to come here, and is reading and snorting over the French memoirs when John, another of the Day sons, comes looking for still a fourth, Clarence, but Clarence isn't there. Margaret appears and asks what was it Mr. Day is wantin'.

"It's about dinner tomorrow night, Margaret."

"This bein' the first time you've had your anniversary in the country, are the children to have dinner with you, too?"

"Margaret, you know Mrs. Day and I always dine alone on our anniversary."

The boys, then, will have their dinner early. Father has summoned Margaret to talk about the anniversary repast. He is having Dorlon's send out the first oysters of the season. He will choose the wines. And for dessert there might be something Mrs. Day particularly likes, maple mousse.

Clarence, the fourth son, comes in through one of the windows, looking for his mother. Michael, the coachman, also comes in a window heading for the arched doorway and carrying a large cake of ice on a piece of wet burlap. He is in livery and his hat is pushed back on his head.

Father is indignant at Michael coming through the living room, but Michael alibis that the screen door was latched and he had to. He is carrying the ice because the ice company didn't deviller . . . uh . . . devill . . . didn't leave any again today. Father sniffs at Michael and accuses, "You've been drinking again."

"Ha . . . how can you say that, sir, after I signed the pledge right in front of you?"

Father lays down the law. This has got to stop. He pays Michael and Bridget good wages, and Bridget is a very good maid. Michael must not take another drink as long as he is in

Father's employ. The coachman retreats through the window with his ice, for Margaret has unlatched the screen door in back. Father calls after the retreating servant, "And have Brownie saddled and in front of the house at four o'clock sharp."

Clarence deferentially suggests that Father can't ride today at four because Mother has invited some ladies to tea—ladies who were invited especially to see Father. Mrs. Willoughby and—. Mr. Day is not having any tea with that family; Willoughby is a scalawag and that wife of his is just a climber.

"Well, sir," Clarence interposes, "their daughter is a very fine girl."

"She looks like a little snip to me."

"Sir, you are speaking of my fiancée."

Father goggles a moment, then yelps, "Oh, God!!" He won't have it. At his outcry Mother runs into the room, wondering what's wrong. When she is told she takes it calmly, for she knew it already and she thinks it's wonderful. Father forbids the engagement, commands Clarence to remain in Yale and announces he is going for his ride.

"Clare, you can't go for your ride now," says his wife. "I have a surprise for you. We have guests coming." It's no surprise to him—but, he says, he has a surprise for Vinnie: he won't be there. He will not ruin his day listening to a lot of cackling females.

"Clare, Mrs. Willoughby is bringing an old acquaintance of yours. . . . A Mrs. . . . Logan." Clarence Jr. helps her remember the name. Father never heard of any Mrs. Logan, and he yells to John to tell Michael to have the horse ready—at five minutes past four. He has weakened by five minutes. "Damn Mrs. Logan! Damn the Willoughbys! Damn everything an inch high and a year old!"

Vinnie is pleased with the way things are working out. Since Father has decided to stay for five minutes, he can meet Hazel Willoughby and they'll all have a nice visit. She tells John to warn Michael that Mr. Day will be a little late for his ride. Now, she wants to hear all about the engagement from Clarence. "When did you first know?"

"Last night . . . when I kissed her." Clarence is transported.

"Clarence! You didn't kiss her before you were engaged?"

No, he hadn't. Hazel was making fudge in the chafing dish and Mrs. Willoughby had gone to the kitchen to butter some pie pans. . . . "Mother, I don't know whether you will understand this, but I'll never smell fudge again without thinking of Hazel."

This clinches it with Vinnie. Clarence is in love, all right. The young man is grateful for his mother's understanding, and wishes his father would understand, too—"because I *have* to give Hazel an engagement ring." He gets a sudden idea. "Mother, could I borrow yours?"

Vinnie turns away in embarrassment. She . . . ah . . . she hasn't got one. Father never gave her one, so she knows why it is so important to Clarence. "It wasn't his fault, I suppose. We were married so quickly I didn't really have the experience of being engaged." She fingers a ring on her right hand. "He's given me lots of other rings, you *know*. But to this day, when people talk about engagement rings, I catch myself hiding my hand."

Vinnie begins dreaming a scheme. Tomorrow is their wedding anniversary, and she has bought a surprise for her husband—a music box that plays the same tune the band was playing in Pleasantville when he asked her to marry him. They call it "their" tune. Perhaps, tomorrow night, when the music box begins to play . . .

Her speculation is interrupted by the arrival of the Willoughbys, and she takes them for a turn through the garden. Bridget is bringing in tea and lemonade when John appears to tell her that Michael is packing to leave and she'd better go see him. Michael has a bottle. Bridget drops her work and runs off on the porch as Father is heard yelling, "Vinnie! *Vinnie!*"

Hazel has come in with Clarence. She is pretty and knows it; she also knows what she wants and how to get it. "What a lovely house! . . . Oh . . ." says Hazel—and claps a hand over her mouth. "I have to be careful not to say that in front of Mother unless . . . well, have you told your family about it yet?"

Clarence assures Hazel his family knows about "it." And hers does, too. Her father thinks it's wonderful, but her mother doesn't want it mentioned today unless Mrs. Day also knows about it. Clarence doesn't think today would be a good time to talk about it, in front of Father. "He isn't used to the idea yet."

"My father says your father thinks he's God Almighty."

Clarence, righteous and indignant, proclaims, "My father's a very fine man. He deals in railroad stocks!"

Since everybody seems to know about it, Hazel would like Clarence's fraternity pin. She sent Charley Noble's back to him. "A girl always wears her fiancé's fraternity pin . . . unless he gives her a ring right away."

Clarence regretfully gives up his pin. She offers him a kiss but he doesn't want it—not here in this house.

Mrs. Logan—Bessie Fuller Logan—makes an imperious entrance. She is a busty middle age, and she prides herself on her sense of humor, of which she has none. She is followed by Mrs. Willoughby, who is the kind of woman who enjoys Bessie's humor. Vinnie, the hostess, joins them, and the visitors make compliments about the garden. Bessie's first joke is about the mums; other people say chrysanthemums, but with her "mums" the word.

Clarence is sent upstairs to tell his father that the guests have arrived, and Hazel beams after the young man. "Clarence is such a nice boy," says Mrs. Willoughby. In return Vinnie says something nice about Hazel and how they hope they will be seeing more of her. With laborious significance, Mrs. Willoughby asks her daughter, "This is the first time you've been in Clarence's home, isn't it?" Hazel ignores the cue for the line about what a lovely house and answers something polite and vague.

Father is heard above, shouting at Clarence. "Mr. Day is changing," Vinnie explains.

"He hasn't changed much," says the funny Bessie, and Vinnie goggles a bit. Mrs. Willoughby explains, "Before you met Mr. Day, Mrs. Logan was engaged to him."

Vinnie makes a close study of the visitor and decides she must be Bessie Fuller. "Well, for pity's sake! I've always wondered what you *looked* like. . . . Well . . . Sit down!" There is an element of relief in her cordiality. "I'd always imagined you as looking quite different."

BESSIE—I imagine I look quite different . . . until I see myself in the mirror. (*She hoot-laughs, and breaks off to point vigorously at* VINNIE.) Of course, I've been curious about you.

VINNIE—Well, I should think your husband would be curious about Mr. Day. Is Mr. Logan in the East with you?

BESSIE—My husband passed on some years ago.

VINNIE (*with sincere sympathy*)—Oh, I'm so sorry . . . tsk, tsk, tsk . . . to lose Mr. Day and then to lose your husband.

BESSIE—I survived the loss of Clare surprisingly well. (*She hoots with laughter.*)

MRS. WILLOUGHBY—Bessie! I wonder whether Mr. Day will

recognize you. (BESSIE *looks complacent*.) Mrs. Day, I have an idea! Let's not tell him and see what happens.
  VINNIE—Yes, he may not know you at all.
  BESSIE—Oh, I think he will. After all, I was his first love.
  VINNIE (*not relishing* BESSIE's *phrase*)—But after all, he married me.
  BESSIE (*confidently*)—Clare will know me.
  VINNIE—Well, *I* didn't recognize you . . . but then, of course, I'd never seen you before.

The visitors learn that Vinnie and Clare will have been married twenty-two years tomorrow. Not to be topped, Bessie recalls that it was twenty-two years ago this Summer that Clare and she had their last pitched battle. It was on the Fourth of July. "You must have had a short engagement," she observes to Vinnie.

Mrs. Willoughby thinks this is a good time to talk about engagements, and how short ones mean long marriages, but Vinnie edges away from the topic. Clarence comes down to say Father will be there directly—he thinks, and his mother suggests pointedly that he take Hazel out for a good look at the garden.

Father comes down, dressed for riding, just in time to be introduced to Hazel before the young couple leave for the garden tour. He puts his hat, gloves and crop on a table and is presented to Mrs. Willoughby. "And," says Vinnie, "this is your old friend, Mrs. Logan." Father gives her a formal how-d-you-do.

"It's nice seeing you after all these years," says Bessie, and Father looks frantically at his wife for some hint as to what he should do or say. Laughing gaily, Vinnie says, "Clare, do you mean to say you don't recognize Mrs. Logan?"

He pretends he does. "How is Mr. Logan these days?" Vinnie whispers that Mr. Logan has passed on. "Oh, of course," Father catches himself. "A great loss to the country, the death of General Logan."

Father supposes that the girls have been talking about old times, and tries to make a break—but Vinnie halts him. He is informed they haven't been talking old times, they have been talking about engagements and how people who are engaged sometimes don't get married to each other. This doesn't interest him much, but he tries to be polite.

Vinnie asks him if the Fourth of July means anything to him, and if it does, he should be talking to Mrs. Logan. "Very well. Mrs. Logan, *what* would you like to *know* about the Fourth of July?"

Vinnie is having her triumph. Bessie demands that Clare take a good look at her, which he does, and he finally recognizes her as Bessie Fuller as she hoots with laughter. They shake hands violently and Vinnie and Mrs Willoughby go into gales of merriment. It certainly was a good one on Clare.

"Well," says he, "no wonder I didn't recognize you, Bessie. You've changed." And to the others he says, "She used to be the prettiest little thing you ever saw."

Bessie bridles, "Well, the worst thing I can say about you, Clare, is that you *haven't* changed."

He asks her where she has been keeping herself. In Colorado. Until her husband died. They were married only three years. "What was your husband doing out in Colorado?" "Mining his own business"—and Bessie hoots appreciatively at another of her own jokes.

Father would dearly love to get away, and when he sees John come in he hopes that John has come to tell him the horse is ready. Vinnie tries to keep him, because he hasn't had a chance to talk to Mrs. Logan. Mrs. Willoughby comes up with a good idea: why don't Mr. and Mrs. Day come to her house for Sunday dinner?

Father quickly squelches the suggestion; they've guests of their own coming. Monday, then? No, they're dining in town. He explains to his wife, who has begun to look uncertain, "I forgot to tell you, Vinnie, your cousin Cora and her husband are in New York on their honeymoon."

Tuesday? Mrs. Willoughby pursues. No, the Days are moving back to the city on Tuesday.

Vinnie is interested in the news of Cora, and Father explains that Cora dropped into the office to see him this morning. He doesn't know what her husband is like because he didn't meet him. Always the polite hostess, Vinnie excuses herself for talking family matters in front of her guests by explaining that Cora Cartwright is her favorite cousin—a Mrs. Clyde Miller now.

Bessie knows Cora. She would. They went to school together, and she *does* hope to see her. Father explains to Vinnie that Cora came in to ask him to invest "that thousand dollars" for her. Vinnie explains to the others, "Our grandfather died recently and left my cousin and me each a thousand dollars."

Margaret comes through to serve lemonade on the veranda and is followed by Whitney, carrying a cake, and young Harlan, chanting, "Lemonade, made in the shade, stirred with a spade, by an old maid." The women move toward the veranda and Father makes a break for his ride, but Bessie catches his hand and stops him. "You can't desert me for your horse. . . . After all, I haven't seen you for over twenty years."

Father counters, "As I remember it, Bessie, you never wanted to see me again." But he agrees to have a glass of lemonade and puts down his riding things as she goes on to the porch. He tells John to tell Michael to hold the horse, and he'll be there directly.

"Michael didn't saddle the horse, sir," says John. "He's packing up to leave."

"You tell Michael I want to see him. You tell him to come here this instant!" John goes obediently on his errand, and Vinnie rushes in from the porch to remind her husband that they have guests and he should talk quietly.

"Damn! Damnation!" he fumes. The telephone rings and he barks another "Damn!" at it, then answers in a bellow. Yes, this is Clarence Day. What? One dozen deviled eggs? Ridiculous. "Madam," he concludes in hanging up, "I have better use for my time than attending a beach picnic. Bah!"

Clarence wants to know who it was on the telephone and is told it was some silly female inviting Father to bring deviled eggs to a beach picnic.

"I think it was for me, Father."

"Then why didn't she say so?" Father demands.

Bessie comes in from the porch and offers Father a glass of lemonade and a suggestion to cool off. "How," she asks flirtatiously over her own glass, "could you possibly have lived all these years without me?"

FATHER (*chuckling*)—Let's not go into that, Bessie. With us it was just a case of the irresistible force meeting the immovable object. (VINNIE *hovers in the window.*)

BESSIE—It's a little late, Clare, to be telling me *I'm* irresistible. (VINNIE *marches past a window again, with raised eyebrows.*)

FATHER—You were immovable.

This banter is interrupted by young Harlan, who marches in with a plate of cake, walks between Bessie and Father and says, "Excuse me! Mother told me to bring in this cake to you."

They both decline, and Harlan plops himself on the sofa, puts one plate of cake beside him and begins eating the other.

FATHER—Bessie, I remember the day you got that new sunshade. You wanted to parade around town showing it off, and the sun had been down so long it was dark.

HARLAN (*jumping erect, plate in hand*)—

> "Between the dark and the daylight,
> When the night is beginning to lower . . ."

FATHER—Not now, Harlan. (HARLAN *subsides and returns to eating.*) Harlan, take that cake out on the veranda.

HARLAN—*Mother* said if you didn't want it, *I* could *stay here* and eat it.

FATHER—Harlan, did you hear me tell you to take that cake outside?

HARLAN (*looking up*)—Yes, sir. (*He rises, picking up second plate.*)

BESSIE—Harlan, when your father speaks to you like that, you bow and you answer very politely, "Yes, Mr. Do-As-I-Say." . . . Clare, do you remember how mad you used to get when I would call you Mister Do-As-I-Say?

FATHER—Harlan, take that cake outside.

HARLAN (*bowing deeply*)—Yes, Mister . . .

FATHER (*exploding*)—Do as I say!

Bessie is laughing merrily when Margaret appears to tell Mr. Day that Michael is here, and Father explains to Bessie that he must talk to his coachman, who has given notice. She advises him not to let Michael leave and gets in one more joke before going back on the veranda. "You need somebody around here to help you off your high horse."

Michael, on unsteady legs, confirms the report that he is packing to leave. He's got feelings, and he's not going to stay where he isn't wanted. Father roars that he can't quit without giving due notice, and Michael weakens.

"You go saddle my horse!" Father commands.

"Yes, sir." The coachman starts out.

"The trouble with you, Michael, is that you have no strength of character."

"No, sir."

"Then you'd better get some."

Michael, surprisingly, flares up. "I don't want any! Mr.

Day, you're a strong character. You *enjoy* being a strong character. Me, I'm a weak character. I *enjoy* being a weak character. And by God, I'm going to *stay* being a weak character!" Michael marches out, leaving Father half in amazement and half in delight.

Vinnie comes from the veranda, shushing her husband, and is nonplused to learn that it was Michael who had been raising his voice. She is followed by the guests, who announce they are leaving, much to Father's relief. Mrs. Willoughby still has the dinner date on her mind, and Vinnie promises she will talk it over with Mr. Day tonight. It's a chance for Bessie, who says, "Just so you don't talk it over with Mr. Night today."

The ladies depart, but Hazel and Clarence linger. They are going to walk to Hazel's house, instead of taking the carriage. She wants to know if salt water might hurt the fraternity pin, because she plans to wear it to the beach picnic tomorrow, right on her bathing dress.

"Maybe you shouldn't go to that beach picnic," says Clarence. "Charley Noble will be there."

"That's why I think it's important that we should be there together," announces Hazel. Father, having sped the departing guests, returns to the room. "Mr. Day," Hazel queries, "did you belong to Psi U when you were in college?"

"I didn't go to college."

"Really!" she snoots. "My father graduated from Harvard . . . cum laude." She leaves and Clarence follows, but his father ominously warns him, "I shall want to see you later, Clarence."

Margaret comes in to clear off, now that the guests have gone, and suggests that Mr. Day arrange things on his desk for the move back to the city. He dons his gold spectacles and goes to work on the job. He is engrossed at his desk when Vinnie flutters in and finally gains his attention. She says it must have been exciting for him to see his first love again.

"Don't ever invite that woman into this house again," he commands—and goes back to his papers. But Vinnie won't give up. Did seeing her again upset him? Has he any regrets? She must feel very badly about what she's missed. Why didn't Cora ever mention Bessie? And where is Cora?

Clare informs his wife that Cora and husband are seeing the Brooklyn Bridge and that Cora said she'd telephone as soon as they got back to the hotel. Yes, Cora seemed happy, and Clare is looking forward to seeing her husband, who seems to be quite a substantial citizen.

John tells his father that Michael is ready outside with the horse, and Clare says he will be there in a minute. Vinnie still has Bessie on her mind. In what way did she upset Clare? She must have been *very* pretty. . . .

"Vinnie, she wasn't half as pretty as you were. . . . And *you* still are." Delighted, she puts her arms around his neck and coos, "Clare, for a man who is so outspoken, you keep the strangest things to yourself." He pats her clasped hands and murmurs, "Twenty-two years tomorrow . . ."

Vinnie continues her feminine speculation. Bessie Fuller's still in love with him. . . . She couldn't wait for a chance to be alone with him. . . . And the way she was flirting with him!

Clare denies the woman was flirting.

"How can you say that? I saw the two of you through the window. The way she was ogling you over her glass of lemonade. I suppose you don't call *that* flirting!"

Father has finished with his desk work and tosses a final crumpled paper into the waste basket. He dismisses the flirting charge as nothing at all. "She was just trying to flash that ring in my face."

"*What* ring?"

"The engagement ring I gave her."

"Clare, did you give Bessie Fuller an engagement ring?"

"Of course."

"But you never gave *me* one."

"That's why."

"What's why?"

"She didn't give it back. I discovered engagement rings were damn bad investments. If she'd given it back, you'd have had an engagement ring."

Vinnie makes up her mind soon enough. "Then that ring rightfully belongs to me." The enormity of Bessie Fuller wearing *her* engagement ring! "Clare, you ride right over to the Willoughbys' and get my ring back!"

Father can't see the reason for so much fuss and is glad when the telephone rings with a call for his wife—but Vinnie is not to be sidetracked. She declares that the next time he sees Bessie Fuller he's got to ask her for it. After a moment's hesitation, and just as he breaks away to take his long-delayed ride, he consents. "Because," he adds, "I'm never going to see her again."

The call is from Cousin Cora. Yes, Vinnie knows they are dining with them on Monday. Did Cora ever know a Bessie

Fuller? Yes, that's what Bessie said. She's visiting a neighbor. She said she'd love to see Cora, too. . . .

Vinnie gets an idea during the conversation. "Cora," she suggests, "if you were out here, I could invite . . . no, that is, *you* could invite her over here. Cora, why don't you and your husband come out here for over Sunday?" She arranges for Cora and husband to take the morning train and get to Harrison tomorrow before Clare gets home. Vinnie will meet them at the station.

Vinnie gives a cocky nod in the direction of her vanished husband, and, singing to herself, goes to Father's desk and begins a note. "Dear . . . Mrs. . . . Logan . . . ha! 'Dear'!" She still is writing when Clarence comes in.

She finishes writing, then tells her son that Cousin Cora and her husband are coming out tomorrow for a visit. And she wants Clarence to run right over to the Willoughbys' with this note for Mrs. Logan—an invitation from Cousin Cora. Old school friends . . . dying to see each other . . . invitation to have tea tomorrow.

Clarence takes the note and starts on his errand, but at the door he halts and says, "Oh, Mother, you won't forget to speak to Father, will you?"

"What about, Clarence?"

"My engagement ring for Hazel."

His mother pats him comfortingly. She can't do it today, but she will do it tomorrow—when she gets hers.

"Mother, is Father going to give you an engagement ring tomorrow?"

"Yes, Clarence, but don't you tell him. It's going to be a surprise!"

The curtains falls.

ACT II

Next afternoon, Saturday. Whitney is at the table behind the sofa, burning an outline of the head of President Cleveland on a wooden plaque. Harlan has been on the sofa, studying from an open book. He rises and starts to recite:

> "Let us then be up and doing
> . . . up and doing . . .
> With a heart for any fate.
> Still . . . achieving, still pursuing. . . .
> Learn to labor and to wait."

He gets the last line over with very fast and is sure he has it all by heart now. Will Whitney listen? Whitney, very bored, grumbles that he knows it himself by this time—but Harlan is not to be deterred. He begins: "A Psalm of Life" by Henry Wadsworth Longfellow.

> "Tell me not in mournful numbers,
> Life is but an empty dream . . ."

He stops, ignoring Whitney's prompting of "For the soul . . ." "Whitney," he asks, "what are 'mournful numbers'?"

"Maybe the multiplication table."

Satisfied, Harlan goes back to his recitation, and Father comes home through a porch window, wearing a straw hat, carrying his gray leather gloves and carrying a fancily wrapped quart of champagne and a small tissue-wrapped package. In the hall he calls, "Vinnie, I'm home!" His sons greet him and Harlan offers to recite his piece. "Not now, Harlan."

Father unwraps the small package and reveals a velvet jewel case, which he puts in a desk drawer. He'd like to be rid of the boys, and suggests that they should be out in the air on a day like this. With malice aforethought, Whitney announces that there isn't any ice—the ice man didn't come again. Father's temper rises with a "Damn!" and he shouts for Bridget. Then he cranks the telephone, gets the operator, and demands the man who runs the Coal and Ice Company. "I don't know the number," he shouts. "That's your business. You live here, don't you?"

Bridget comes on the double. Father begins, "You tell Michael to—" when the Coal and Ice Company comes on the wire. He identifies himself as Clarence Day and demands what they mean by not delivering his ice again today. He wants two hundred pounds right away—and he hangs up violently. Then he instructs Bridget to tell Michael to drive down to the butcher's and bring back the largest cake of ice they'll sell him.

Bridget says it's a good idea to have plenty, because there is something wrong with the ice box. A man of action, Father once more seized the telephone and shouts himself into a connection with the Davis Furniture Company. "I want to buy an ice box, the largest one you have . . . I don't want it Monday morning. I want it this afternoon. . . . See that you do. . . . Hello! Hello! I want that ice box delivered full of ice. . . . If you haven't got the gumption to sell your damn goods to a customer who wants them delivered in condition to use, you'd better shut up shop and have done with it!"

Harlan is plodding on with his piece:

> "For the soul is dead that slumbers
> And things are not what they seem . . ."

Bridget's back, just as the telephone rings. Bad news from her: Michael can't go for the ice because Clarence drove off in the trap on some errand for his mother. Good news from the telephone: the Davis people will deliver a full refrigerator not later than six o'clock. Father gives the maid the champagne to be iced for tonight's dinner. "I was just wondering, sir, will it be enough for four?"

"Mrs. Day and I are dining alone, Bridget."

"Oh, no, sir. You have guests. They're upstairs now. A Mr. and Mrs. Miller."

Father looks at Bridget for a moment of horror before exploding, "Oh, God!!"

This always brings Vinnie running, and it does now. She confirms the news of Cousin Cora. Yes, she knows that for over twenty years they've dined alone on their wedding anniversary—and that is why she thinks it will be nice to have the honeymooning couple this time; it may influence their whole lives, seeing how happy the Days are.

"Vinnie," he roars, "this is the worst thing that's happened to me since my baptism!"

Clyde appears in the arch. He knows all about everything. He has the middle-Westerner's suspicion of New York and is determined not to be outsmarted. He also has the heartiness and geniality of the middle West. Father meets him stiffly, and in a moment he also meets Cora, a married spinster and happy about it.

Clyde has been hearing about the Days for years from Cora—and the Days have been hearing about Clyde for years from Cora. Vinnie is sure that Clyde and Clare are going to be great friends. Cora exclaims over the beauties of the place and the forthright Clyde asks Father how much he paid for the place. "Too much," snaps Father.

Mr. Day tries to make conversation. He . . . ah . . . hopes they are enjoying their visit to New York.

"Can't say as I am," says Clyde. Seems that when they got in from Niagara Falls at the Grand Central depot they took a cab to the Murray Hill Hotel and were driven around for the better part of an hour and were charged a dollar. Next morning they looked out the window and there was the depot practically across the road. "What beats me is—how did he know we were from out of town?" says Clyde, to Father's horror.

Cora has brought her thousand dollars from Grandpa Ebbets' estate; Vinnie will get hers in the mail any day. Cora archly hints that Father is going to make her a wealthy woman. But then, Clyde is quite a business man, too—hay, grain and feed.

"He's also a notary public," Cora adds.

Vinnie is delighted. "When were you elected?" she asks.

CLYDE—You're appointed by the court. (*To* FATHER.) Clare, you'd be surprised how much you have to know in my business. For instance, is that your horse that drove us up from the depot?

VINNIE—Oh, yes. That's Brownie. He's by . . . somebody. Out of . . . somewhere.

CLYDE (*enjoying himself*)—Well, I don't know what you paid for him, but you got stung.

FATHER—He's not properly a carriage horse. I bought him to ride.

CLYDE (*in his element*)—You still got stung. I know all about horses. And another thing . . . that lawn of yours . . . you used the wrong kind of seed.

VINNIE (*desperately*)—We think it's a very nice lawn.

CLYDE—You got stung.

VINNIE (*after a moment*)—Well, there's one thing Clare can be proud of . . . that's our vegetable garden.

CLYDE—I noticed as we drove up you were trying to grow some vegetables. Say, come on out there a minute, Clare. There's something I want to show you. (*He starts, turns back to see that* FATHER *hasn't moved.*) Come on, Clare. Here's your chance to learn a thing or two.

VINNIE (*sotto voce*)—Clare! (FATHER *doesn't move.*)

CLYDE (*indicating*)—Let's see . . . this must be north.

VINNIE (*appealing to* FATHER's *good manners*)—Clare, our guests want to see the vegetable garden. (FATHER *stalks slowly out after* CLYDE.) Cora, I've never seen you looking better. Marriage certainly agrees with you.

CORA (*proudly*)—It's Clyde, Vinnie. He has a way of making people happy.

Vinnie confides that she has invited Bessie Fuller over and she ought to be here any minute. Conspiratorially Vinnie suggests that Cora go to dress just before Bessie comes in—and take Clyde with her. Vinnie wants Clare to have a chance to be alone with Bessie for a few minutes. Cora doesn't get it; if Bessie's anything like she used to be, Clare should not be left alone with her. But Vinnie says she has a very good reason.

On the porch Clyde can be heard telling Father he'd better do what Clyde has shown him, and Father snaps that he'll do as he pleases.

"But I'm from the corn country and I know what I'm talking about. Now you won't get any corn out of *that* garden."

"We've already *had* corn out of that garden." Father has had enough. He comes off the veranda and stands at the fireplace, his angry back to everybody. It's a good time for Cora to go change, and she manages to drag Clyde with her. "I'll try to be ready by the time Bessie Fuller gets here," she calls.

Father's cup now is slopping over. "Did you invite that woman back into this house?" he demands. "Damn! Damn!"

Vinnie explains that it was Cora who wanted to see her—and now a "sudden idea" strikes her—this is just the opportunity for Clare to get the ring back as he promised. Father points out that he promised he was never going to see her again—and he won't. "I'm going to lock myself in my room and stay there until that woman is gone."

He stalks off, Vinnie after him, pleading, just before Bessie and Clarence arrive. Bessie teases Clarence about Hazel. Taking off her left glove, she says, "It isn't much fun for a girl to be engaged if it's a secret. . . . It ought to be announced formally."

Clarence protests it can't be announced until he gives Hazel an engagement ring—and he doesn't know when that will be. "Father seems to have a very unusual attitude toward engagement rings. He says they're not safe investments."

Bessie looks at her own ring and, to Clarence's puzzlement, starts hooting. She explains she is not laughing at Clarence, but at his father. "I'm going to talk to him about this. I just love to tease your father." The appalled Clarence says, "Mrs. Logan, no one teases Father."

Clarence takes a phone call. It's a message from the depot, and as Vinnie comes in to greet Bessie, he goes up to tell his father. There's a package at the depot and they won't be responsible because it is leaking and it's time to lock up the baggage room. Father is heard to explode and in a moment he marches in and calls the depot. He explains that the package is oysters, and it isn't leaking—it's just ice melting. "No, you can't lock up until I get down there. . . ."

Vinnie whispers urgently to Clarence to drive right down for the oysters and the protesting boy obeys. By the time Father has finished his call Clarence has gone—and Father is trapped. Vinnie sidles out to see Cora, but first Bessie gives her a written invitation for dinner at the Willoughbys' tonight.

"Didn't they know we have guests?" Father asks.

"Oh, yes. Cora and her husband are included."

Father's desire to get away somewhere is so obvious. Teasingly, Bessie says, "Clare, you used to love to be alone with me."

"Bessie, I don't think either one of us should presume upon our past acquaintance."

"Of course, I've had something all these years to keep your memory fresh. You know you asked me to wear this forever." She flashes the ring.

"I withdrew that statement later," he points out.

"Yes, and you *tried* to withdraw the ring. Clare, that was no way to get the ring back . . . to write me that I was 'lost to shame and dead to honor.' You also said you'd never ask me for it. . . . But, maybe after all these years and under the present circumstances—"

She tells him all he has to do is ask her for it. "Give it to me," he commands.

She takes it off and is about to hand it to him. "And I might add," he says, reaching, "it's about time you gave it back."

She snatches the ring back. Now he won't get it until he says "pretty please." He will be damned if he will. She warns that if he doesn't say it right away she will make him say "pretty please with sugar on it."

He will make no such concession. Instead, he summons Harlan and tells the boy to inform Vinnie that Mrs. Logan is still here. Vinnie and Cora come down, and Cora and Bessie fall into each other's arms. Clyde arrives.

Bessie was hoping they'd have a nice long visit at the Willoughbys' tonight, "but Clare won't hear of it." Vinnie explains that Clare has taken particular pains with tonight's dinner. Bridget announces that the ice has come, and the new ice box, full, too. Father instructs her to tell Margaret not to ice the champagne until he says to, and he will bring up the other wines later and let her know which are to be chilled.

Vinnie explains to Bessie that she has to leave everything about the wine to Clare. "If a wine has to be at room temperature, I never know what temperature the room should be." That gives Cora a chance to say that her Clyde knows all about wines.

"If you're serving any wine, pass me up," says Clyde. "Wine is just European belly-wash."

"Mr. Miller," says Father, rising ominously, "we have finally hit upon a subject that you apparently don't know all about."

Clarence, frantic to get to the beach picnic, rushes in to get the keys to the wine cellar for Margaret. She needs some of the best sherry for the sweetbreads.

Clyde is horrified. "Do you people eat sweetbreads? . . . You know what they are, don't you?"

Clarence is given the keys, and tells his father he has brought back the oysters and put them on ice. "I never eat 'em," announces Clyde. "Know too much about 'em."

Father towers over Clyde. "I see. Oysters are something else you know all about."

"You know what they call 'em, don't you? Scavengers of the sea."

The telephone has rung and Vinnie has been taking the call. "Just a minute," she says. She halts a possible physical assault by Father upon Clyde by saying, "It's Mrs. Willoughby. It's about dinner tonight."

Father goes to the instrument. "How do you do, Mrs. Willoughby. . . . I'm sorry, but Mrs. Day and I cannot possibly dine with you tonight. . . . However, Mr. and Mrs. Miller will be delighted."

The curtain falls.

Scene II

Twilight outside. Just before dinner. The room is lighted only by a kerosene lamp on the sofa table. Margaret is arranging flowers, and Bridget brings in a lamp for the desk. The servants already have decorated the dining room. They talk some about Michael, who hasn't taken a drop since yesterday—and this puzzles Bridget. Speak of the devil—in comes Michael, off the veranda because the screen door has been locked again to keep out flies. He has brought Mr. Day's paper to put on his desk. "Mr. Day is the kind of a man who wants things the way they ought to be, and I respect him for it."

Clarence, entering, tells Michael to be ready with the trap because they'll be leaving as soon as Mr. and Mrs. Miller come down. Michael goes jauntily on his way. He'll have to clean up the trap first, because those oysters leaked all over it.

Whitney and Harlan come in, having finished their supper, and wonder where Clarence was. "I'm dining out tonight," he tells his brothers, loftily. And John hasn't come back from the beach picnic yet.

Whitney settles down to read and Harlan gets out his jacks and begins to play with them on the floor. Clyde comes in and wanders around. He picks up the book Father has been reading. "'Memoirs of the French Court'?" Clarence explains it's a set of books Father has been reading. Sounds like him, says Clyde—trying to read twenty-four books all at once.

Now Cora is ready and comes down. She tells Whitney to go on with his reading. "And little Harlan's playing jacks," she notices.

That's his cue. He jumps erect and demands, "Want me to recite for you?" Clarence is disgusted but Cora is polite, and Harlan begins:

"'An Incident of the French Camp,' by Robert Browning. *(Saluting.)*

"You know we French stormed Ratisbon,
A mile or so away.

(Pointing stiff right arm.)

On a little mound Napoleon
Stood on our storming day.
With neck out-thrust . . ."

Vinnie comes in, wearing a beautiful beige silk evening gown. "Not now, Harlan." He goes back to his jacks. Cora exclaims over Vinnie's gown. "Are you wearing that just to have supper alone with your husband?" Clyde demands incredulously. He is downright suspicious when Father appears in white tie and tails. "You two just eating alone with each other? Well, I'll be darned."

Father would like the guests to be on their way, but Clarence explains that Michael is harnessing the trap. Father reluctantly offers a glass of sherry—then takes it back as he chuckles and remembers Clyde's opinion on wine. Vinnie suggests they all sit down, and Father takes his paper. Harlan thinks now would be a fine time for him to finish his piece, but his mother staves him off with, "Some other time, dear."

Clyde, looking out the window, tells Father he'd better do something about that elm tree outside. Father, preferring not to listen, fastens on his pince-nez and opens the paper. Vinnie throws Harlan into the breach. "Now you may recite, Harlan."

The boy leaps to it . . . and goes doggedly on to the end, with all the gestures, no matter what else is happening. And plenty else is happening. Something in the paper has made Father say "Damn!" and Clyde takes a look to see what it was.

"That was Chesapeake & Ohio, wasn't it? That stock you bought for Cora . . . Well, it's gone down three points!" Clyde is stunned, but Father assures him it is nothing to worry about.

Clyde is angry. "We thought you knew your business." And to Cora, "Well, you've lost thirty dollars in twenty-four hours." Now Cora is alarmed. Father tries to soothe her. She might lose thirty if she sold right away, but he wouldn't let her.

Clyde demands, "I'd like to know why you wouldn't let her."

"Because she'd lose thirty dollars . . . plus my commission."

"You mean to say she has to pay you to lose money for her?"

By now Harlan has got about up to "Scarce any blood came through" in the long Browning poem.

Father is steaming. "I didn't charge her for buying the stock, but if she sells it, by God, I will."

"Cora's going to sell that stock first thing Monday. She's lost enough money already." Placatingly, Vinnie says if Cora loses any money Clare will pay out of his own pocket. "I'll do nothing of the kind!" he roars.

Clyde says he could have told Clare not to buy any railroad stock—he knows all about railroads. Vinnie begs, "Clare, give Cora the thirty dollars." Almost apoplectic, Father is fed up. He informs them that the stock may be selling for more than Cora paid for it next week—and he goes to the end of his room and turns his back on them all. Harlan reaches his end, too:

"Smiling, the boy fell dead."

And Harlan, saluting, falls on the floor.

There is a long, frozen silence, finally broken by Clarence saying the carriage is ready. As the party leaves, Father starts to find Bridget and some sherry. All this time Harlan has been lying "dead," and now his mother notices him. "That was just fine, Harlan. You may get up now."

The young elocutionist and his brother Whitney are hazed off to bed, and at last the anniversary celebrants are alone. Father, relieved and mellowing, chuckles, "I never thought I'd be grateful to the Willoughbys." They toast each other in sherry, and he says she looks beautiful tonight in that dress. He always has liked it. Vinnie smiles wistfully at him and gives him a pat; this is the first time she has ever had the gown on.

"I have something to give you later which I think will please you."

Happy and melted, she replies, "Yes, dear, I know."

Vinnie suggests that they make an exception this year and give their presents now. She goes out to get his, and he resumes his paper and is absorbed in it when Vinnie tiptoes back with the music box, puts it on the sofa table and turns it on. He stirs restlessly at his reading, then says, "Vinnie, will you stop that damn racket." With a wail she collapses into a chair, and he asks what has he done now.

He is contrite when he realizes that the music box is his present, and asks her to play it again.

"Clare, you remember it, don't you?"

"Oh, yes, I've heard that."

She laughs nervously. "Clare, that's 'our tune.'"

"Our tune?"

"The one the band was playing . . . across the lake . . ."

"Oh, Switzerland!"

She is nearly in tears.

"It wasn't Switzerland?" he asks.

"Clare, that's the tune the band was playing when you asked me to marry you."

"Oh, that was in Pleasantville."

He has put his foot in it, but now he is contrite and grateful. "Well," he says, jovially, "let's see what I have for you." He takes the jewel case from the desk, opens it, and removes a diamond necklace. "This is something I happen to know you want."

"But, Clare . . ."

"Don't you like it?"

"Why, yes, dear, it's lovely, but where's my real present?" He is baffled. "Bessie Fuller's ring . . . my engagement ring."

"Damn it, Vinnie, this is a diamond necklace."

But she wanted the ring, and he promised. That's why Vinnie left him alone with Bessie today. Didn't he get it?

He is baffled and getting angry. Making a fuss about one diamond when here's a whole necklace of them. "Very well, if you don't want it." He replaces the necklace in its box and slams the box into the desk drawer.

"You wouldn't even ask her for it today," she pursues.

"I did ask her for it."

"And she wouldn't give it to you?"

"I couldn't accept it on her terms. . . . I considered the whole incident an indignity."

Father calls, "Bridget, when dinner is ready let me know. I'll be in my room." And he goes there. Vinnie can scarcely believe what has happened . . . and now she is angry. She takes the jewel box and without opening it transfers it to her sewing table. Then, curiosity getting the better of her, she removes it from the table, goes to the sofa, takes out the necklace and starts counting the diamonds when her son John arrives from the beach picnic.

John wants permission to stay at Charley Noble's. "Clarence and Hazel wouldn't even speak to me at the picnic, just because I was with Charley Noble," he informs her. "She was walking Clarence around as if she owned him. Gosh, I hope she doesn't marry him."

"That couldn't happen for years, John."

"You don't know Hazel. She's so mad at Charley Noble that she'd even marry somebody else, just to spite him."

This is something shocking to Vinnie. Slowly, she asks John if anyone would get married just for spite.

"Well, Merle Willoughby married that Clark girl just to spite Harriet Gardner. Everybody knows that."

John notices the music box, turns it on and asks where it came from. "Never mind," his mother commands with agonized sharpness. "You run along, dear."

Alone, she slowly replaces the necklace, snaps the box shut just as the tune finishes. She returns it, not to the sewing table, but to the desk, just as Father, upstairs, yells, "Oh, God!" Automatically she starts to go to him—then halts herself and returns to the sofa. At first she sits defiantly; then, as the tears start, she speaks as only a lady could:

"Damn!"

Shocked, she covers her mouth, then collapses, weeping.

The curtain falls.

ACT III

The Day tribe and servants have come back home to 420 Madison Avenue. The Summer is over and the boys must be shipped off to school or college. The setting is the old, familiar morning room, and it is the old, familiar time for breakfast. The table is about ready. Margaret hears the postman's whistle and two rings on the doorbell, and fetches two letters and the *Times*, which she puts at Father's place. Kathleen, a young Irish maid, brings in the rest of the breakfast things. It's obvious she's new, for she puts the cream and sugar in the middle of the table.

"No, no, not there, Kathleen. The cream and sugar go down at this end. Mr. Day sits here. . . . And remember, always serve Mr. Day first. He's a fine man, but you have to get used to him."

"Arrah," says Kathleen, "I've worked in houses where him and her couldn't stand the sight of each other."

"Oh, it's not like that here. Mr. and Mrs. Day never hold a crossness for one minute to the next. At least up to now they haven't. But this time . . ." Margaret gives her head a worried shake. Kathleen observes happily that she's only been here an hour, so they can't blame her.

The boys begin assembling. Clarence first, asking if his shirts will be ready in time for him to leave a little after five. They will—but Master Whitney's train leaves at one and his things must be got ready first. John comes down cheerfully and is warned by Clarence not to get chipper with Father—the paper says the stock market is going even lower.

"So that's what's been the matter with Father," Clarence adds. "But what's been the matter with Mother?"

Harlan slides down the bannister with a whee! and marches around the table reciting, with gestures, a verse admonishing a little man to take his meals like a gentleman, and at the end he plops into his chair. Father comes down and admonishes Harlan not to be seated before his mother and father are seated.

Clarence gives Father his mail. "Well," says Father, "you and John are off to New Haven today. John, I expect you to make a better record than your brother did." He opens an envelope, sees it's a bill and throws it in the fireplace, muttering, "What's the matter with that fellow?" The second envelope he gives to Harlan to put at his mother's place.

Vinnie and Whitney aren't here yet because Dr. Humphreys is upstairs looking at Whitney's arm. Father looks at the headlines and gives off an "Oh, God!" Vinnie, in negligee, is coming down the stairs, and her instinctive reaction is to leap to his aid—but she quite consciously resumes a serene walk and bids everybody a serene good morning. Father tries to pull her chair out for her, but she beats him to it by sitting, and when he tries to push the chair in she pulls it in ahead of him. Father goes to his own place in defeat. They will start without Whitney.

The doorbell rings; Kathleen answers and reports it's a Mr. Noble to see Mr. John Day. "Well," says Father, "doesn't he know enough not to come around at breakfast time? Send him away!"

But Vinnie cuts calmly in. "See him at the door, John." Father is at first astounded, then hurt.

Clarence talks stock market. His father says the drop is serious, but business is in a perfectly sound condition. Clarence is glad of that, because he . . . he is a junior this year . . . and certain things will be expected of him—

Vinnie has opened her envelope and cries, "It's my check from Grandpa Ebbets's estate. One thousand dollars."

"That's fine," says Father, holding out his hand. "Harlan, hand me that check."

Vinnie won't give it up. He needn't bother depositing it. She is going to cash it and spend it. Kathleen serves Father his scrambled eggs. What is Vinnie going to buy with it?

"I'm going to buy an engagement ring for my son."

"Vinnie, you can't spend a thousand dollars on an engagement ring!"

"If there's any left over, I'm going to buy him a chafing dish. . . . It's for his room at college. He's going to make fudge." Father is aghast. Fudge at Yale!

Whitney runs downstairs, his sling gone, and is followed by Dr. Humphreys. As Kathleen is pouring the coffee around, Father halts the doctor and goes and picks the crumpled bill out of the fireplace. "This Dr. Somers keeps sending me a bill for five dollars," he says to Dr. Humphreys. Humphreys explains it is for services as a specialist the time Mrs. Day was seriously ill. Humphreys had called him in.

Indignantly Father declares, "That's the whole point. *I* didn't send for him." If Humphreys has to send for other men to help him out, why should Father have to pay for them? Patiently Humphreys tries to explain that Somers is a specialist and Father counters with, "Now see here, we can't let a thing like that get started. A man might have to have more than one doctor. Besides, he's trying to charge more than you do. Don't you pay him any five dollars. If he only knows part of his business, he shouldn't get more than a dollar."

Dr. Humphreys is getting mad, but Vinnie blandly and cleverly tells him that Mr. Day is a very reasonable man . . . about business matters. He has never disputed one of Humphreys' bills, has he? And he knows that anything he charges for coming to see Whitney will be paid without question. The doctor gets the point. "I'll see that this bill is paid," he says to Father.

Clarence works around to himself again. He hopes Father will increase his allowance. Father weakens. It's expensive keeping Clarence and John in Yale and now Whitney in St. Paul's, but he wants Clarence to keep up his end. A thought strikes him—after today Harlan will be the man of the house.

Says Vinnie, "If Harlan's going to be the man of the house, you ought to increase Harlan's allowance."

"Yes, I like fudge, too," says the boy.

Father snorts, "Fudge!" Pointing a finger at Clarence, he declares, "You don't get another penny!" He takes an angry mouthful of egg. It's cold—as well it might be by now. "Take it away," he orders. "Clarence, any young man who's foolish enough to give a girl an expensive engagement ring doesn't deserve an allowance at all."

The young man points out that his mother is getting the ring. John returns from the door with an envelope.

FATHER—What have you got there, John?

JOHN—It's a note for Clarence, Father. Charley Noble brought it. (*He gives the envelope to his brother, who opens it and starts reading.*)

VINNIE—Clarence, I've been thinking. With a solitaire as valuable as that, Hazel really ought to have a guard ring, too.

FATHER—Now she has to have two rings. Vinnie, let's be practical about this.

VINNIE—An engagement is not a practical matter.

CLARENCE (*having reached the crux of his letter*)—Mother, before you go any further . . .

FATHER—Vinnie, an engagement ring is a damn bad risk. I know that out of my own experience . . .

VINNIE—There are some things you don't know, Clare, and one of them is how a woman feels. . . .

CLARENCE—But, Mother . . .

VINNIE—No, Clarence, you and I are going to pick out the ring this afternoon.

CLARENCE (*holding up the letter*)—But, Mother, I couldn't give it to her if we did. Hazel has broken the engagement!

VINNIE (*incredulous*)—What!

FATHER (*laughing uproariously*)—Vinnie, that's certainly a joke on you. That's the funniest thing that's happened in this house in years. (*He goes on laughing.*)

VINNIE—Clarence Day, how can you be so unfeeling in front of your broken-hearted son?

FATHER (*as* CLARENCE *is discovering his fraternity pin at the bottom of the envelope*)—That's a lot of folderol. Clarence is a very lucky young man.

CLARENCE—Yes, I got my fraternity pin back!

Father continues to laugh until the indignant Vinnie orders him to get out of this house and go to his office. Genially he says, "I guess now you'll let me take that check with me." She will not. Vinnie turns to Clarence, with sympathy, and asks if Hazel gave any reason.

"Yes, she said she was going to marry Charley Noble."

Father, hat on and cane in hand, marches toward the door in slow and silent dignity—but he has to bring his dignity back into the room when Whitney reminds him he hasn't said good-by yet, and they won't be seeing each other soon.

Father begins giving Whitney some advice. To do better than John did at St. Paul's. And then, noticing Vinnie at the window, he quotes, "Neither a borrower nor a lender be . . ."

Whitney points out that he can't very well *not* be a lender unless he has some money *not* to lend, and Father had promised . . . Father gives him five dollars to last until Thanksgiving.

Father turns and makes what he considers an impressive exit. Vinnie, searching her mind, asks herself, "Now what can I buy for a thousand dollars that I don't need most?"

The curtain falls.

SCENE II

It is late afternoon. Clyde is reading the financial page of the *Sun* and Cora is looking anxiously out the window. She tells her husband they can't wait much longer because she has all that packing to do. Clyde shakes the paper he is holding and says, "According to this paper, you've lost a hundred and fifteen dollars . . . and there's no telling how much more since this came out." Clyde has grimly decided that Cousin Clare is going to guarantee that Cora won't lose a penny, and they won't leave the house until he does. And another thing—they can't get him to believe they got all dressed up that time just to have supper by themselves. They must have had some other guests. Clyde and Cora weren't fancy enough. But it worked out all right. "What we learned about him over at the Willoughbys' . . . that was a fine scandal."

Cora begs him not to mention it. Kathleen comes in with a letter. She explains she is new here, and she doesn't know which one of the young men is Mr. Clarence. The eldest, Cora tells her, and Kathleen takes the letter up to Clarence's room.

Cora has an idea. She fishes in her reticule and brings up a diamond solitaire ring on a red ribbon. It's the ring Bessie Fuller asked her to give to Clare. "Let's give him this first," she suggests.

"You hang onto that," her husband warns. "Don't you give him the ring until he promises you ain't going to lose any money!"

Father appears, gives Cora a how do you do, is told Vinnie isn't home yet. "She's probably shopping," Cora suggests. Remembering the check, Father thinks it possible.

Cora announces that they are leaving for Ohio at six and Father suddenly becomes very expansive. "Oh! So this is a farewell visit! How nice of you!"

Clyde is in no mood for niceties. "We came to talk about Cora's stock. How much has she lost today?"

"When the market closed, Cora's stock would have sold for seven hundred and eighty dollars."

It's a kick in the stomach to Clyde. Now Cora has lost two hundred and twenty dollars—and she isn't going to leave the house until Clare gives it to her. Doing his own cousin out of two hundred and twenty dollars!

Father points out coldly that Cora is Vinnie's cousin—and that he resents the implication that he is doing her out of anything. Cora, hoping to make peace, fishes in her reticule and says, "Just a minute . . ." She dangles the ring on the ribbon. Clare and Clyde are nearing blows when Kathleen comes down the stairs. Father halts her and with calm dignity informs her, "You will show Mr. Miller to the door, Bridget." Looking closer, he sees it isn't Bridget. "Nora . . . Maggie . . . whatever your name is!"

But Cousin Cora is welcome to stay, he adds. Clyde storms out, vowing he'll get the money if he has to go to law. Cora, weeping and defiant, follows him, and the front door slams.

Father is reading the *Sun* and saying "Damn!" when Clarence comes down, looking worried. He is holding an open letter. "Father, I want to apologize to you. I'm afraid I've opened a letter of yours by mistake." He explains that Kathleen had given it to him, saying it was for him, and naturally he read it before he realized it wasn't.

"This letter from Mrs. Logan puts me in a rather awkward fix," the young man continues. "She has sent back the engagement ring you gave her. Her idea was that I should give it to Hazel, but now . . ."

"No, Clarence, that ring belongs to your mother, and it'll make me very happy to turn it over to her. Let me have it."

Clarence explains the ring didn't come in the letter, as he'll see when he reads it. He reads and utters an "Oh, God!"

He rushes to the hall, gets his hat and is about to dash out when he hears the voices of Cora and Vinnie. Vinnie is insisting, "You come right in! I'm not going to have my cousin treated like this." Father returns to the morning room and soon Vinnie appears, arm around Cora, followed by Clyde. "This happens to be my home, too," Vinnie reminds her husband. Good thing she saw Cora and Clyde getting into a cab. "I brought them back here to receive your apologies."

Remembering Bessie's letter, Father controls himself enough to say he is very sincerely glad to see Cora back. He would like to talk to her. "I'm the one that was insulted!" yelps Clyde. Father coldly informs him that if there are any apologies to be exchanged, they will have to come from Clyde. Clyde wants to leave, but Vinnie won't allow it.

"In that case, I'm leaving," says Father. He won't stay in the same room with a man who called him a swindler. Now Vinnie is getting indignant. Desperately Father explains that Cora hasn't lost any money—that in his considered judgment the stock is still worth a thousand dollars. "You can take my word for it."

"Your word," jeers Clyde. "We heard all about you over at the Willoughbys'. There's a name for a man like you! . . . You're . . . a jilt!"

Vinnie begins, "Don't you dare call my husband a . . . What did you say?"

Clyde bellows that Father would like his wife to think Bessie Fuller broke off their engagement. Well, *he* broke it off and told it all over town. That's the kind of man Vinnie is married to.

Father starts to go again, but Vinnie demands, "Clare, is this true?" He goes upstairs and she calls up after him, "Did you jilt Bessie Fuller?" From above he calls, "I wasn't going to marry a woman I was damn good and sick of."

Vinnie's face reflects the sun that is shining in her heart. She is happy again . . . and she has a splendid idea for satisfying Clyde and Cora. She will buy Cora's stock with her thousand dollars, for didn't Father say it was worth it? Cora and Vinnie go into the library to endorse the check and the stock and complete the deal.

Clarence comes down and tells the now-genial Clyde that he and John are about to start off for Yale. In that case, Clyde has a cab outside and they'll be glad to drop the boys off at Grand Central. Clarence calls the news up to John and tells him to hurry—but the one who hurries down is Father. He still has to see Cousin Cora about something.

After a moment's gaze at Clyde he announces, "My sons can afford their own cabs." There is no hurry, and he wants a word with the boys before they go.

Cora and Vinnie come in from the library. Vinnie is holding the stock and happily announces that everything is all right. Father would like a word alone with Cora, so Vinnie takes Clyde on out to the cab. "Didn't Bessie Fuller give you something to give me?" Father asks the cousin. She had almost forgotten it, but she fishes it out of her reticule and hands it over. "I remembered it as being larger," he observes.

Peace has been made. "Don't feel bad about Clyde," Cora urges. "He'll get over this. You'll see. I'll get him back to New York."

"Cora," he replies, "I want you to be happy, and the basis of a happy marriage is to keep your husband happy. Don't force Clyde to leave Ohio *ever*. Good-by."

She leaves, and Harlan scampers down to the hall to say good-by, too. Clarence is ready to say good-by to his father. "Clarence, I've been thinking," says his parent. "I've decided to increase your allowance." John comes down just as Vinnie returns, and there are more good-bys, including some from Margaret. Finally the boys are off.

Father, fingering the ring in his vest pocket, is truly in fine fettle. He bids Margaret ice the champagne they didn't drink that night in the country. He asks Harlan how much spending money he is giving him these days. "Ten cents a month, Father." "From now on, it will be fifteen cents. Do you think you can manage on that?"

"Oh, yes, sir," says the boy, "with that and with what Mother gives me . . ." Vinnie shoos him off, picks up the stock certificate she has put on the desk and begins admiring it.

FATHER—Vinnie, what have you got there?
VINNIE—Cousin Cora's stock. I bought it from her.
FATHER—You bought it! What did you give her for it?

VINNIE (*matter-of-factly*)—My thousand dollars.
FATHER (*horrified*)—Oh, God!
VINNIE (*running to him*)—What's the matter, Clare? What's wrong?
FATHER—Vinnie, today that stock is only worth seven hundred and eighty dollars.
VINNIE—Clare, you said yourself it was worth a thousand.
FATHER—I said it would be. I knew you couldn't be trusted with that thousand dollars. Vinnie, how could you take a step like that without consulting me?
VINNIE (*sitting on sofa, almost tearfully*)—But, Clare, I did it just to prove my faith in you.
FATHER—Why should you have to?
VINNIE—Mr. Miller didn't believe in you as a business man, so I bought the stock just to show them I did.
FATHER—Vinnie, this moves me very much. . . . But let this be a lesson to you. You've just thrown away two hundred and twenty dollars.
VINNIE—Well, Clare, it's all in the family. It just means— (*Gesturing with stock from him to herself*)—you owe me two hundred and twenty dollars.

Father begins to boil again—but then he remembers there *is* something he owes his wife. He puts the engagement ring on her finger. She is overjoyed—her ring! She kisses him and he feels pleased, saying, "Should I ask you to marry me all over again?"

"Well, Clare," she remembers, "you never did ask me to marry you. You just informed me I was *going* to."

They both are laughing, sentimental, reminiscent, as they sit on the sofa. The moon on the lake that night . . . the band . . . "their" tune. . . . He turns on the music box.

"Vinnie, there's never been a woman in this world who could hold a candle to you."

"Clare, it's nice to hear you say that."

"There's no need to say it, Vinnie. You must know how I feel about you."

"Yes, dear, I know," she says softly, tumbling her head against his shoulder. "But it's nice to know that you know too."

THE CURTAIN FALLS

LIGHT UP THE SKY *
A Comedy in Three Acts
By Moss Hart

IN 1930 a stage-struck gentleman of 24 submitted to Sam H. Harris the script of a comedy about Hollywood—concerning which locale he knew nothing first-hand. The young man had written for and acted with school, neighborhood, church and amateur theatre groups and more recently had been an $18-a-week secretary for the late Gus Pitou, booking boss of the Erlanger empire. Harris took the comedy, "Once in a Lifetime," and enlisted George S. Kaufman to point it up here and there. Thus Moss Hart became a wealthy playwright.

In 1938, after an unbroken string of successes, stage-struck Hart attempted with Kaufman a drama about the theatre, "The Fabulous Invalid," which was not a great work. He went on, with a success here and a disappointment there, and in 1948 he again took the theatre as subject-matter for a play titled "Light Up the Sky." It was a fortuitous coincidence that what happened *in* the play also happened *to* it.

When it started on its tryout, "Light Up the Sky" looked to its author like a comedy which had some serious things to say about the stage. When it arrived in Boston, first audiences found that the funny things in it were quite funny, but they were less impressed with the serious parts. Audience reaction and the Boston critics both indicated that "Light Up the Sky" was good, but it "needed work." The coincidence of this is that the play itself was about a tryout in Boston which revealed that the drama being tested had possibilities—but needed work.

After the well-praised New York opening of "Light Up the Sky," Elliot Norton, drama critic of the Boston *Post,* wrote to the editor of this yearbook. "I'm glad the play is a hit," said Norton. "Moss Hart did a terrific job of rewrite on it here,

---

* Copyright, 1948, as an unpublished work, by Moss Hart.
Copyright, 1949, by Moss Hart.
Published by Random House, New York, and Random House of Canada, Toronto.
Amateur acting rights controlled by Dramatists Play Service, New York.

much of it while running a temperature of 101. That he was able to rewrite it successfully is to his credit. The remarkable thing is that he not only ironed out the difficulties in the play but also managed to find new comedy as he went along. What he had had originally was a much more serious play, which was very interesting—but it failed to hold most of the audience when he turned away from rough comedy. So he junked a great deal of dialogue which, I am sure, was rather important to him as a man, and gave it to them the way they liked it."

It is 5:30 P.M. in Irene Livingston's flower-bedecked suite at the Ritz-Carlton Hotel in Boston. One might imagine that at this hour, just before the first performance of a Boston tryout, the suite of a star might be a shambles and the star herself in hysteria; but the only ones in the well-ordered sitting room are Nan Lowell, who is quietly working at a portable typewriter, and a parrot, Orson, who is not so quiet.

"Oh, so you've got a parrot!" exclaims Orson, loudly. "SRO, darling, SRO! No seats till January. Bless you, darling!" When Nan shushes him Orson subsides for a moment, then snarls, "Think you're smart, don't you? Think you're George Jean Nathan!" Nan quiets him for good by covering his cage just as Carleton Fitzgerald knocks and comes in.

Carleton doesn't merely enter; he pervades the room. Even his battered hat and old mackintosh have dramatic value. Sighing heavily, he inquires if Irene is asleep and learns that she is having a massage.

"I could cry," observes Carleton. "Five-thirty, six-thirty, seven-thirty. Eight-thirty. The footlights dim. The curtain rises. These next three hours, Miss Lowell, I could cry."

It isn't his nerves; it's "magic time"—those few magic hours when a play belongs only to the author and the actress who will bring it alive. And this, he portentously advises Nan, is a shattering and beautiful play. "I cried when I read it, I cried when I directed it and last night the cast could hear me sobbing. I had to move back."

Carleton continues a while talking softly about himself, shows a flash of anger when he notices from the window that the theatre sign is not yet lighted, and receives a phone call from his wife in New York. "Tremble for us, darling, and call me here in Irene's room about one," he murmurs. Then, to Nan, "Would you call the theatre? Tell them to light that sign immediately. It's very bad luck, you know. And tell Irene I'll stop by. I have a talisman for her to wear tonight. . . . Magic time! Feel it, Miss Lowell?"

"Not exactly. This is all quite new to me, you know."

"You will, my dear. Suddenly you'll want to cry. You *will* phone those bastards, won't you?"

He leaves and in a moment Frances Black bounces in, arms full of packages. Her vitality is something fearful.

FRANCES—Hi ya, honey. I thought maybe Sidney was here. I called the room and the barber shop, but no dice, so I thought maybe he was up here. Where's everybody? Dead or something?

MISS LOWELL—Miss Livingston's having a massage.

FRANCES—Boy, I could stand somebody to pound my behind right now. I'm beat.

MISS LOWELL—Been shopping?

FRANCES—You said it, honey. If Sidney can sink three hundred thousand bucks into a play, I can shop—and when I say shop, honey, I ain't kidding. Get a load of that. (*She stretches out her hand, one finger bearing a huge topaz ring.*) I didn't have it when I went out, honey. And I got a little platina fox cape to wear to the opening tonight that's real yummy. Sidney'll drop dead, but so what? He buys Renoirs and Utrillos—I buy stuff to hang on myself—not the walls. Say, honey, is Stella around? We got a gin game to finish.

MISS LOWELL—She went out about an hour ago.

FRANCES—You know something, honey? That old bag plays a real gutsy game of gin. Yattata, yattata, yattata, all the time—she don't even hold her cards right—and then "boffo"—she slips it to you. Gin. If she comes back, tell her I'm just parking this junk—maybe we can get in a fast game before dinner. (*To the parrot.*) Hi ya, kid! What do you hear from the mob?

MISS LOWELL—I'll tell her, Mrs. Black.

FRANCES (*stopping at the door*)—Say, honey, did *you* see the dress rehearsal last night?

MISS LOWELL—I wasn't allowed in, Mrs. Black.

FRANCES—Me too, honey. Some big deal. A guy puts up three hundred thousand bucks and his wife ain't allowed in the theatre. It's gonna melt, or something, if somebody looks at it.

MISS LOWELL—I believe it's an unshakeable rule of Mr. Fitzgerald's.

FRANCES—Oh, honey, is he kidding? Honest, I sit and listen to him sometimes with my mouth hanging open, and I look around and everyone else is taking it deadpan, and Sidney, who's a mugg like me, is drinking it in and lapping it up and giving out with that "I-could-cry" routine, so that I think maybe *I'm* nuts. Don't get me wrong, Miss Lowell, my husband's a great guy—but I don't want to see him step out of his class. He's running in the long-haired derby tonight, and I don't want to see him get hurt. Well, honey, they gotta let the common people in for a gander tonight, so we'll see. Tell Stella I'll be right down. S'long. Say, it'll be a hell of a note if that curtain goes up and nobody cries but Mr. Fitzgerald. (*She goes out. With a sigh,* Miss Lowell *goes back once more to the papers, but not for long. Again there is a knock at the door. This time* Miss Lowell *puts down the papers very carefully, folds her arms and speaks almost cooingly.*)

"Come in . . ."

This next caller is Owen Turner, a quiet, urbane gentleman in his late forties whom Irene has asked to drop by for a good-luck drink along about this time. Nan recognizes his name and says she is an old admirer of his plays—even acted in two or three of them in college. But she is not an actress, she explains. "I'm that repellent literary invention, a ghost writer. Miss Livingston's autobiography."

"Is there a title yet?" Owen asks.

"This is today's title. We change it every day. 'With a Bow to the Moon.'"

"A suggestion of Mr. Fitzgerald's?"

"How did you know?"

"Scar tissue. He directed two plays of mine for Irene."

"He's quite an emotional man, isn't he?"

"Indeed. He cries at card tricks."

Nan and Owen talk pleasantly of show business for a bit, until he interjects, "By the way, is Miss Livingston's mother up here with her?"

"Stella? Yes, indeed."

"Good. A breath of foul air in the middle of magic time. What else is here, Miss Lowell? I'd enjoy knowing the full cast."

Nan ticks them off: Sidney Black and his wife, Frances; Miss Livingston's husband is due to arrive for dinner; and Mr. Fitzgerald.

Owen points out that Miss Lowell has left someone out, and it's always the same one who is left out—the author.

Filling in this omission, Nan describes the author as young and nice and shy and not talkative.

There is a raucous laugh outside the door. "That is unmistakably Stella," Owen remarks—and it is.

She is "almost a perfect specimen of that redoubtable old pirate and saboteur, the mother of the star . . . she is quite a handsome old hoodlum and she has retained, undaunted through the years, the spirit and ethics of a Dead End Kid." She greets Turner ebulliently, and asks if he has a new play up his sleeve for Irene.

"She's going to need one, dear," Stella advises. "By eleven o'clock tonight, if you ask me." She elaborates on her prediction until Owen points out that she hasn't even seen the play yet.

"Like hell I haven't seen it! I saw it till half-past twelve last night—then I came home and cut down my Christmas list and Irene's contribution to the Actors' Fund."

This information is amazing, for Carleton Fitzgerald never permits anybody at his rehearsals.

"I got in myself and I saw and heard the whole thing, including that sonofabitch sobbing," Stella relates. "I got up at seven o'clock in the morning yesterday and left a note for Irene saying I was going to Brookline for the day to visit an old friend. Instead I went to the theatre and went in with the cleaning women. I gave one of them five dollars to give me her clothes—and I stayed up in the balcony with a mop and pail and a rag around my hair. Saw the whole dress rehearsal. I damn near starved."

She makes for the bar, vowing that she's never going to see that play sober again, when Peter Sloan, the author, arrives. He is in his middle thirties, with the body and face of a good-humored longshoreman and the brooding, deep-set eyes of a poet. Stella introduces him to Turner and Turner tries to draw him out.

Peter confesses he is surprised at having an upset stomach, considering that when he was driving a truck and eating in every two-bit hash joint between Omaha and Chicago his stomach was fine.

"Always glad to welcome a new member of the Dramatists' Guild," laughs Owen, and he continues to query Peter about his writing career.

"It's a two-day drive to Chicago and then you get two days off," Peter explains. "I slept one whole day and then I had all the next day free to work. . . . I wound up soda jerking and dish washing before I finished the damn play. Trucking was easy."

Peter is not indifferent to his premiere, but he says he will be happy if he never sees a performance because he never expected to see his play produced. It's all velvet up to now. "The big kick for me, no matter what happens tonight, is the humanity of these people. . . . It's a damn nice thing to see."

Owen—Indeed—though I'm not quite sure I understand what you mean.

Peter—I mean—here they are—all of 'em—working like horses, pouring out money, staking their reputations, pushing aside all thoughts of personal gain and self-interest—why? For what? They like this play of mine—but that's not the whole answer. Irene's playing an old woman of seventy and doesn't speak a line for the whole first act. Fitzgerald postponed his wife's play and paid off the cast to get this on right away. Sidney Black planked down three hundred thousand dollars. That's more than just liking or believing in a play, for my money, Mr. Turner. It's deeper than that. These people are good in heart . . . They have the wonderful courage of dreamers and fools. And there's not too much of that around. (*He stops, startled.*) My God, an upset stomach makes you talk a lot!

Owen—Not for a minute, Mr. Sloan, not for a minute. And how I shall contain myself until 8:30 tonight, I don't know! (*There is a knock at the door, but this time the door is opened without waiting for an invitation to come in.* Sidney Black *stands in the doorway. He is a short man in a dark-blue suit with a dark-blue tie and hat, but this dark-blue façade, from which he never varies, conceals a blazing dynamo of lightning-blue sparks beneath. He comes quickly into the room, waving a "hello" to* Peter *and* Miss Lowell.)

Sidney—Weather clear, track fast, the flag is up. Where is our lovely lady? I found this Georgian silver baptismal cup I would like to place in her hands. Where is she, Miss Lowell?

Miss Lowell—She's having a massage, Mr. Black.

Sidney—Good. The heavy honey dew of slumber before an opening. Peter, my dear boy, this is your night! (*He stops, seeing* Owen.) Owen! Nobody told me you were in Boston. Well! This begins to look like what Frances calls a very stylish affair. Glad to see you. (*He inclines his head toward* Peter *as they shake hands.*) Did I interrupt you two fellows who make with the words? Go right ahead. Me, I'm just a crepe-paper moon over the Taj Mahal waiting for Scheherazade to start the entertainment. I always listen when Toscanini gives the downbeat. Go right ahead.

Owen—I think you came in on Deems Taylor, Sidney—we're all finished. But Mr. Sloan has me practically panting for the curtain to go up tonight.

Sidney—You mean our tattered Tolstoy has been talking, Owen? Why, that's like picking diamonds out of the herring at Lindy's. What did I miss, Peter?

Peter—Nothing.

Sidney—You see? I'm lucky to get a two-syllable word. Here's a fellow who takes a yellow sheet of paper, Owen, and makes it sing like a first folio—you try and *talk* to him and he makes the doorman downstairs sound like Bernard Shaw drinking vodka instead of vegetable juice. Now Mr. Turner talks like a playwright, Peter. You put a nickel in the slot and out comes playwright talk. This I understand. This is my type playwright.

Owen (*laughing*)—That's not what the audience cares about, Sidney.

Sidney—I'm only kidding. This is our big private joke. When I went to meet Peter for the first time after I read the play, I said to Frances: "How do you say hello to the Salzburg Festival? How do you shake hands with Tchaikowsky's Fifth?" Then I meet our tongue-tied friend and I realize I'm talking to Coolidge with a head cold. I finally had to turn to Irene and say: "You're sure this is the fellow who wrote it?" Remember, Peter?

Peter—Yes.

Sidney—See, Owen? We're right back to the one-syllable words.

Owen—Irene sent you the play?

Sidney—She didn't send it to me—she brought it to me—like Joan of Arc bringing the King the crown and a hot corned beef sandwich. And both bad bets. Owen, I'm a guy who parts very slowly from a buck.

Owen—I've heard tell.

Sidney—When I let go that eagle not only screams—it goes back to the mint with a double rupture. What's more, I'm all set once again to invade most of the forty-eight States with my Ice Show. This is a razzamatazz I know from, Owen. A sweet and sure annuity—it's like taking a bath at Fort Knox. I know when I put Frances on her skates and let the fans see her spangled panties swinging low against the ice while that orchestra plays, "I Wonder Who's Kissing Her Now," I'm good for at least a Cézanne and maybe a Matisse and we're not going to eat rye bread in the country this Summer, either. What do I need with the theatre—a business where you get one roll of the dice from seven middle-aged men on the aisle who hated Mickey Mouse when they were kids. I need them like a hole in the head. So what happens? I read the play, I write out a check for three hundred thousand dollars, and Frances keeps her can warm this Winter. That's what Silent Sam here does to a smart money boy—just by putting wonderful words together on a piece of paper. And to give it the real, corny, Technicolor schmaltz, me, the sucker, I'm happy. I don't regret one dollar of it. You happy, too, Peter? Like what we've done with your baby?

PETER—Yes. Very.

SIDNEY—He must be. Two words. Well, in a little while we'll take the curtain up, Peter, and give Mr. Turner and Miss Lowell a look, eh? We're sticking a Roman candle into the tired face of show business tonight, Owen, and the sparks that fly are going to light up the theatre like an old-fashioned Fourth of July. Me, I'm only the guy who paid for the ink on the Declaration of Independence—I just lurk in the light of the rocket's red glare—but I'm proud to have standing room. Signed, Sidney Black. Say, it's a quarter of six! Shouldn't somebody wake up Irene? At a quarter to— (MISS LOWELL *starts to rise, but as she does so, the door of* IRENE'S *room opens, and a masseur, carrying a little black bag and a massage table, comes out.*)

They all rise, awaiting Irene's entrance—and it is a fitting one: the ineffable essence of a great star. For an instant she poses in the doorway, blinking her eyes as if to get the sleep out of them—then suddenly she covers her face with her hands and begins to sob. There is consternation in the group and they all try to find out what is the matter; but all Irene does is sob that she is "so very sorry." Sidney Black is close to panic when Owen takes command.

"Sidney," says Owen, "I think if you would all just move upstage—I mean, if you would all just clear away for a moment and let Irene—that is, if you would just let her be quite quiet for a moment or two, I'm sure she'll be able to tell you."

This is the correct maneuver. Irene recovers and assures Sidney that she is all right for tonight. As for what was the matter—it's gone, completely gone. It was only a nightmare while she was dozing on the massage table.

"Darling," she explains to Sidney, "I don't speak a line for the entire first act—not a syllable! That's one of our surprises! Isn't it staggering?"

Quietly, Owen comments that it is historical.

"Well, my dears, suddenly I was dreaming that I was on the stage and the curtain was going up. . . . And then I began to speak. I took the lines from all the other actors and nobody spoke but me. I couldn't stop. It was horrible." And the nightmare went on, with Peter weeping because she had ruined his beautiful play.

"Where was I?" demands Sidney. "For three hundred thousand dollars I should at least be in there *some place!*"

"Sidney, darling, you were," Irene coos. "You were chasing me with a pair of ice skates." She goes to the bar and pours drinks for the good-luck toast. Noting that Sidney still looks upset, she begs him not to worry.

"I'm not worried," replies the producer. "I was having a dream about your dream. How I watched you take the lines from all the other actors, then I climbed over the footlights and hit you over the head with a Coca-Cola bottle."

They have lifted their glasses for a toast to Peter when Frances throws wide the outside door and waits there to be admired; she is literally covered with diamonds and platina fox. "They're gonna know there's an opening up here tonight," she exults, "and it ain't a grocery store, either."

"Baby," her husband pleads, "it's an opening—not a coronation! You don't have to put *everything* on."

"Everything? I got enough left over for a complete change during intermission." Half mournfully, half in awe, Sidney says, "My wife moves into a store like the Soviets into occupied territory. She dismantles it and sends it home bit by bit." But he loves her and she can wear anything she wants.

When Stella comes out of her room, not quite as glitteringly dressed as Frances, Frances nabs her to finish up a game of gin rummy. Says Sidney, "You know, if ever the Bomb falls, I can just hear Frances saying, 'Here it comes, kid—gin!'"

When Carleton arrives, the company is complete—or so Irene thinks at the moment, and she now proposes a toast. But Carleton must first make a presentation. Slowly he approaches Irene and brings from a pocket a paper package. "Inside this paper, Irene, are some little glass beads—a little peasant necklace—but these tiny bits of glass glow with the light of immortality, for this great lady wore them, too, on the night of an opening. I give you the necklace of Eleanora Duse."

Irene is effusively overcome as Carleton unwraps the package and reverently places the necklace over her head.

"Oh, Carleton, darling, bless you, bless you. I'm going to cry."
"So am I, my dear, so am I!" And so they do, in an embrace. The toasts begin. Irene toasts Owen as an old co-worker. Owen replies with "Success to you all." Irene toasts Peter whose play has meant so much to them all, and after much urging Peter returns it.

PETER—I used to think that actors were just people who liked to put make-up on their faces every night. That producers, directors, and all the rest were part of the whole absurd foolishness and vanity. I was wrong. If there's a debt owed, it's my debt to you—to all of you—for showing me a new world—a new frontier—the real democracy of the theatre. Thank you for that.

IRENE—Bravo, Peter, bravo! That was beautiful.

PETER—Would you drink a toast with me to my girl?

IRENE—Of course.

PETER—She's not here tonight, but she's as much a part of this play as I am. She's suffered through every line of the play with me for two solid years. I don't think I'd ever have finished it without her. She's waited a long time for this and I know she's looking at the clock right now. So—to Helen!

SIDNEY, IRENE—To Helen!

CARLETON—I could cry. (*There is a knock at the door.*)

IRENE—Oh, damn! Come in! (TYLER RAYBURN, *carrying his bags, stands smiling in the doorway.*)

TYLER—Hello, everybody! All ready to open?

IRENE—Oh, Tyler dear, you *do* always manage to break into things. You all know Tyler Rayburn, don't you—my husband? Darling, put your bags down, and fix yourself a drink. Hurry, darling—we're toasting the play, and it's very bad luck to break the chain.

SIDNEY—Irene, can a guy who loves the Chase National Bank like a brother say a few words?

IRENE—Darling, none of this would have been possible without you. We owe this very moment to your generosity and your great heart, Sidney. Bless you, darling, always for that. Of course, you must speak.

SIDNEY—Irene—I don't know from words like generosity and great heart. With me generosity is something my relatives expect every Saturday night, and Great Heart is the name of a very good dog food. When a guy coughs up three hundred thousand dollars for a show, he doesn't deserve any thanks—he should run, not walk, to the nearest psychiatrist. So unless I'm nutty as a fruit cake, why did I do it? I'll tell you. Because when I read the play I forgot about money, and being a smart operator, and all the cute tricks I know, I only knew I had to see this play get on a stage, to be part of getting it on, and for the first time in my life, Mammy's little baby loves canceled checks . . . Prosit!

IRENE—Oh, Sidney dear, that was just lovely. Touching and kind and warm. Bless you, darling.

TYLER—Very nice, very well said.

IRENE—I do think a toast before an opening makes everything so much better. Takes away nerves and jitters and that dreadful feeling in the pit of the stomach. Don't we all feel better now, hmm? (*There is a loud, intensely annoyed clearing of the throat from* CARLETON.) Oh, my God, how *could* I? Carleton's toast! Only the most important toast, that's all I forgot. Only the one we're all waiting for.

CARLETON (*with icy sweetness*)—No, no. It's not important. Everything's been said quite adequately. I'm sure we all feel warm and cozy without me.

IRENE—Darling, do you think I would open tonight without your toast? Oh, please, my dear, do forgive me! It was Tyler bursting in in the middle of everything that made me . . . Really, Tyler, I do think that with all the trains running out of Grand Central Station you might find one that doesn't dump you into the Ritz at a perfectly ridiculous moment. Oh, darling, please. I shall be so upset! Sidney, make him.

SIDNEY—Come on, Carleton—it's even better this way. Yours is the bell on the wedding cake—the angel on top of the Christmas tree. Come on! Glasses high, everybody!

IRENE—Carleton's toast, always the best toast, my darlings, Carleton's toast! (*There is a moment of silence as* CARLETON *waits for all eyes to turn his way. Then.*)

CARLETON—Mine is not a toast—not a toast to ourselves. It is, instead, a grateful bow to a little old lady—a little old lady unknown to me—unknown to any of us—but who will be forever enshrined in my memory. Last night, during the dress rehearsal, there came a moment when I could no longer look at the stage. My eyes, I am not ashamed to admit, were dim with tears. I rose from my seat and walked up the aisle to the back of the theatre, and, as I did so, I saw a shadowy figure in the balcony. I was about to stop the rehearsal and have the intruder put out, when I looked again, and discovered it was a scrubwoman—a scrubwoman who had stayed behind after the others had gone, her own work not finished, and then the play had started, and she had been caught up in it. I watched her—she did not see me —her eyes were glued to the stage. There she stood, a shapeless, dirty old harridan, her face ravaged by time, her greasy hair stringing out from the rag tied around her head. My own eyes were too clouded to see her face clearly, but suddenly I knew that this withered crone, this hapless bag of bones, had discovered beauty. For in her trembling hands she held a mop—and she was tearing it to bits with emotion. So it is not to us that I raise this toast—but to her! To an unknown and unforgettable bit of human wreckage who found beauty and a moment of rapture in our play.

STELLA (*wrathfully*)—Gin, goddammit to hell, gin! (*As the others raise their glasses—the curtain falls.*)

ACT TWO

About 11:45 in the evening Stella and Frances come back from the premiere. Without a word, Stella goes to the bar and pours two drinks, handing one to her companion. They sink into a sofa and sip in silence. Suddenly the parrot, whose cage has been uncovered, cries, "SRO, darling, SRO. Bless you, darling! No seats till January!"

"You should live so long," snorts Stella. Then, "Cheer up, Frances, it's only money. Sidney's lucky. You've still got your ice skates."

The ladies are indeed low, and most evidently the first performance has been a dismal event—and half of that $300,000 belonged to Frances. "Do you realize how many times I have to fan my tail around an ice rink for that kind of dough?" she complains.

Stella can't understand why Frances would risk so much, and the young woman bitterly explains that it is Sidney's fault. For years he has been driving her crazy with his successes. He buys antique silver by the truckload and in two or three years it is worth two or three times what he paid for it. Or he buys Old Masters and turns a profit. And so on down the line—the 97-room house in the country ("I think there's still a St. Bernard dog lost up on the third floor.") turns out to be a wonderful buy, with its wine cellar and kitchen furniture that is genuine French provincial. And now all Frances gets for her $150,000 share is one shove. "What the hell is that play all about?" she demands.

"It's an allegory," Stella offers. "That's what the man in back of me said. In the middle of the first act he said 'This play is either an allegory or the biggest joke ever played on the City of Boston.'"

What Stella can't understand is how her daughter, who is crazy like a fox, ever got into it. No, it wasn't to get even with Sidney for something, because if you want to get even with a producer you talk him into doing an Ibsen revival. This doesn't make any more sense than when Irene married Tyler.

"But he's something big in Wall Street, isn't he? I thought that was why she married him," says Frances.

"Irene didn't have to marry Wall Street money, dear—we've socked away plenty. *I* saw to that. Why, before she was old enough to *read* she knew how to order two breakfasts from Room Service and only pay for one." But Irene had Tyler all figured out and her mother was too dumb to catch on. Irene married for comfort and it worked out fine—and now even Stella is fond of Tyler.

Speak of the devil—in comes Tyler. "Hello, Mother. Went extremely well tonight, didn't it?"

"What theatre were you at?" Frances demands.

"I went to see 'Oklahoma!'"

Stella explains that the play didn't go very well, and he tries to comfort her. A play never goes too well the first time, he points out, and anyway people like Stella and Frances are always too critical.

"Now me—I'm just John Q. Public. You artists! Now, just supposed we behaved this way down in Wall Street every time a stock didn't do well, hm? I mean, you see, that *we* have our dreams and our disappointments, too. I often say it's very much like the theatre. Same thing! For instance, you float an issue of Canandaigua Copper, you manipulate it on the Board three ways from Sunday, and the public won't buy a share of it. Finally you split it two for one. Just like the theatre, isn't it? What?"

Sidney comes in, hat over eyes, coat collar turned up, hands in pockets—a picture of dejection. Sweetly his wife needles him, "Well, you sure stuck a Roman candle in the tired face of show business, Daddy."

Daddy glares murderously at his wife and at Stella, then picks up the phone and asks for the chief night operator of the hotel, to whom he gave a pair of passes for the opening. He wants to know what the plain public thinks. In this case, the plain public was the chief night operator's parents, to whom she had given the tickets and who, she tells Sidney, asked afterward, "What *is* it?" Another blow.

The bickering continues between Sidney, Frances and Stella,

with Tyler trying in his mild way to pacify them, until Carleton arrives. Carleton is no less than a martyr now; he has been sitting alone in the dark in his room for the last half hour, brooding about the great days of the Greek drama and fuming at "that dreadful, stupid audience. This play escaped them completely. This play is completely Greek." He gives a nice lecture about the true Greek and Latin meanings of such words as drama, theatre and audience, but nobody listens much and there is a welcome new interest when Irene, the star, comes home.

She is resplendent in a shimmering, low-cut dress, furs and diamonds—and in one hand she holds six colored balloons. "Aren't they fun?" she asks. "Peter bought them for me on the way in tonight." It is as though Irene had never been to the play, let alone acting the stellar role; at the moment, the balloons are the most important and amusing things in the world, and they mean good luck.

Sidney is not interested in toys. There are problems to face and he wants to talk about them. And when Peter, a haggard author, comes in, Sidney would like to talk to him, too, about $300,000 worth of trouble. Stella and Frances prefer another game of gin rummy. The bickering rises in pitch, with even Irene breaking out into short insults when Sidney comments on her bad performance.

IRENE—Tyler, did you hear that? Mother, you heard it, of course? Our little friend is judging acting now. My dears, not figure eights—*acting!* Darling, don't open your mouth and show everybody what rink you come from!

SIDNEY—I'll tell you what kind of a rink I come from, Miss Livingston! I've got three hundred thousand dollars sunk in this jamboree, but that wouldn't stop me from closing it tonight. Not tomorrow night—tonight! That's the kind of a rink I come from.

IRENE—Tyler, darling, did you hear what the little man said? We're closing tonight! Do you know what that means, dear? You can take me duck-shooting with you this year, darling, just as we've always planned.

TYLER—That's smashing, Irene. . . .

IRENE—We'll lie in the blinds together, Tyler, and laugh at all the silly people getting ready to play matinees. Break a balloon with me, darling, we're closing. (*She pops a balloon.*) Bang! Got him, Tyler. . . . (*She pops another.*) Bang! There's a brace of them.

STELLA—Bang! That's gin, Frances.

SIDNEY—Shut up, shut up, SHUT UP! All of you! Now, listen to me! And not a word out of any of you! (*Strangely enough, there is silence. His face is so violent that they all stare at him fascinated.*) We're going to stop talking about everything else and we're going to talk about this play! Nothing but this play! I'll hear from you one at a time, and anyone who interrupts can pick up his teeth outside. All right. You're first, Peter. You wrote it. Got anything to say?

PETER—I believe in this play. And I'll work like hell to fix it. All I need to know is that *you* still do.

SIDNEY—Never mind whether we believe in it—we're stuck with it, Bub! And I don't intend to be stuck with it, ladies and gentlemen! Not for a minute. Before that wise mob gives *me* the horse laugh, I'll laugh it up *for* 'em! I'll put a line of girls in it and Olsen and Johnson, if necessary. So let's quit horsing around with what we believe in and get down to cases. Okay. Irene, you got anything to say?

IRENE—Plenty! But to start with, is there any earthly reason, in that first scene, why I should not be wearing a simple but smart afternoon dress instead of those rags Mr. Fitzgerald has me walking around in? Second, is there any reason why . . .

CARLETON—I am not interrupting—I am merely pointing out that the first scene of this play is the ruins of Radio City, and the bomb has fallen just one hour before.

IRENE—What of it? She might have just been coming out of the Stork Club and been caught in the crowd. All they saw tonight was a great mob of extras groaning and dying. It was twenty minutes before they knew I was on the stage at all.

CARLETON—What do you want to do, dear? Rush on in a smart afternoon dress to the ruins of Radio City and say: "Is anything the matter?" Talk sense, my dear.

IRENE—Sense—sense!

PETER—Wait please, everybody! I know you're disappointed and upset . . .

IRENE—Just a trifle upset!

PETER—All of this is my fault. . . .

CARLETON—Really? I thought it was all my fault!

PETER—After all, this is my first play.

IRENE—We know, dear.

PETER—I had to learn what you can give an audience and what you can't.

CARLETON—We did, too.

PETER—Look—I'm trying. Let me speak. There are things I can do that will help this play. When they laughed they were right. I was being pompous and they saw through me. I can say the same things and make it simpler and more honest. I know I can.

SIDNEY—Look, Jack. Simplicity and honesty we got plenty of in this play. What we need are a few laughs and a little schmaltz.

PETER—Laughs?

SIDNEY—Yes, laughs. What's the matter with laughs? To hell with telling 'em anything—let's give 'em a show.

PETER—Look—all this play has got—the thing that made you do it—work the way you all did is what it had to say. If you try to make it into something else, we'll be left with nothing!

IRENE—As against what we've got now, of course!

PETER—That's all we've got—believe me! That's what made you want to do the play! That's what made me want to write it. Good or bad, don't run out on that now, or we haven't got a chance.

Even Orson, the parrot, chips in with "Bless you, darling! Bang! Bless you, darling! Bang!" Thin-lipped and just about at the end of his string, Sidney orders somebody to get that talking vulture out of the room—both talking vultures, in fact, the other one being Stella. He wants the room cleared of everybody but the star, the author and the director, so they can get down to fixing the play.

In an instant, Irene's mood changes again to one of silky sweetness. "Tyler, dear," she invites her husband, "would you fetch that nice mystery book you brought up with you? We're going to bed." She makes as if to go and stops before Carleton. "Here," she says, "is Duse's necklace! Hang it around a neck more worthy than mine. Hang it around your wife's neck, dear. If it doesn't fit, I know a number of people who will be glad to tighten it."

Just one more insult in a happy gathering, and Carleton, livid, begins demanding that Sidney make Irene offer a public apology. "Take me away, Tyler, oh, Tyler, take me away from all this and give me a child," sighs the actress. "A child that won't turn on me—at least until it's older. Let me have a few good years— I need them—I deserve them—all my life I've worked and slaved —and for what?" Continuing in this vein, she achieves her bedroom door and slams it behind her.

Stella, the old hoodlum, knows her daughter backward and knows what the next mood will be. "The spirits of ammonia are in the medicine chest, the hot water bag is in the closet and you can get ice from Room Service for the cold compresses, Tyler."

By now even the impassive Tyler is worked up. "Some day, Mother," he threatens, "I'm going to put my foot down! Some day I'm going to forget I'm a Harvard man—Mother." And he follows his wife into their room. The decks are cleared enough now for Frances to try to get into action against her husband. Up to now has just been the warmup, she advises him, and now she'd like to see his footwork in the main event.

So would Carleton, who announces as he flounces out the entrance door, "Since I have no intention of ever speaking again to anyone connected with this play for the rest of my life, I shall say what I intend to say. Mr. Black, I think—you stink!"

"Isn't he cute, Daddy? He thinks you only stink," Frances jeers.

Sidney gives up, for the moment. He doesn't want to talk now; he is going for a walk. "When I decide what to do with this $300,000 worth of sheep dip I'll let you know"—and he storms out after Carleton.

The next one out is Stella, who takes a bottle of whiskey with her to her room—but not before giving Peter some motherly information. "If I know my daughter, Mr. Sloan, she's getting laryngitis right now. Stick around, Mr. Sloan, and you'll hear coughing start from that bedroom in a few minutes that'll make Camille sound like she had nothing but hay fever."

When the phone rings Stella answers. It's a call for Peter so she turns the instrument over to him, gathers up her bottle and retires, leaving Peter alone. The call is from Helen.

"Hello, darling! I couldn't call you—I've been up here in Miss Livingston's room. (*A pause. Then.*) Brace yourself, baby. It's a bust—a complete and absolute failure. Now take it easy—you've got to believe it—it's true. No—not *any* of it. I didn't even see the third act—they started to laugh and I couldn't stand it. (*He listens for a moment.*) No, Helen—please, don't! Please! I don't want you to come up—I don't want you to see it! It's just—too painful, that's why. I didn't know what it was like—it's awful, Helen. A kind of naked, personal exposure. Oh, to hell with it! So I can't write! Maybe it's better to get it this way and stop fooling yourself. I'll talk to you tomorrow—it won't seem so bad tomorrow—I just can't talk about it now. Sure, I'll call every day—it helps. It's helped right now. Baby, sure it would help to have you here—but I don't want you to come up—I kinda have to go through this part of it alone. Okay, I promise. As soon as I open my eyes in the

LIGHT UP THE SKY

morning. Good night, darling. (*A slow smile comes over his face as he listens.*) Good night, baby.

A drunken Shriner breaks into the room, wanting to know if it's Jim Unger's. Peter gets rid of him and Owen Turner and Nan Lowell appear in the doorway. They bring with them the only heartening words about the play Peter has heard yet.

"Your play is a lot better than it looked," says the experienced Owen. "A lot of it was very touching and true." Miss Lowell confesses she was very moved. Owen counsels, "It's the work you do on the play from now on, Peter, that's going to make all the difference between success and failure."

"Is it?" queries the unhappy young author. "Well, I'm *not* going to do any work on this play, Mr. Turner."

Peter has been crushed and flabbergasted by the scenes he has witnessed. He is ashamed of his own wide-eyed idealism. He is not just walking out on the play—he's walking out on a lot of his own half-baked ideas that make him want to laugh now. Sidney Black & Co. have shown him what the score is.

Owen tries to tell him that this is no new experience. Turner's own first play, 22 years ago, had just such a first performance, right here in this hotel. He had his own Sidney, his own Irene, his own Carleton. But he stuck it out. "And if you walk out that door now, Peter, there's a very good chance that you may never write another line."

Peter won't listen. It was all over for him half an hour ago. He's got a girl, and they want to get married, and they've been waiting for two years for this play—and now he has learned the score and now he is going to walk out. He calls the airport and makes a reservation for the 4:30 A.M. plane to New York.

Owen makes one more try. Peter can't leave without making one final bow to an old tradition of the Dramatists' Guild—having griddle cakes at Childs around 3 o'clock. It's always done after an opening, and afterward, Owen and Nan will drive him to the airport. The young ex-dramatist agrees, and also agrees to let Turner deliver his note of resignation to Sidney.

Peter goes to his own room to pack and Owen and Nan depart. For a long moment the room is in darkness and silence; then there is a hubbub outside in the corridor—drunken, singing voices and a trumpet. There is coughing from Irene's room. Tyler stumbles out and knocks at Stella's door. Mother had better come out, because Irene is losing her voice—losing it faster than she ever did before. Mother comes out to take over, and, hearing the noises outside, opens the hall door and tries to chase the roisterers away.

"Go away from this door—go be funny some place else."

"Hello, Peachy," a Shriner greets her.

The doughty Tyler comes to the rescue. "Stand aside, Mother! I'll handle these ruffians. . . . Now look here, you fellows . . ."

"Oh, a spoilsport!" jeers a celebrant—and Tyler staggers back holding his eye.

The racket has aroused Irene, who emerges from her room and wants to know what it's all about.

"I got hit! A Shriner hit me!"

Irene, the martyr, chides her spouse with, "I do think, Tyler, that with your wife very ill you might do me the courtesy of not indulging in vicious street brawls."

Sidney now flings in through the door, full of purpose. "It's a cold night and I came to a cold decision," he announces. "The show is opening in New York as per schedule. I'm in so deep a few thousand more won't make any difference. All I want now out of this whole thing is to read those notices the next morning on you and Carleton Fitzgerald." Irene gives out with a cough, but Sidney is unimpressed. "You're coming in clear as a bell, but you're under contract to me and you're going to open."

Huskily, Irene defies him. "You'll never get me to New York in this show. You're lucky if I play tomorrow night."

"Careful, Irene, you'll lose your voice," Tyler soothes.

"That's what I'm trying to do, you fool," she screams at top lungpower. "Oh, my God, I'm married to Mortimer Snerd. Pneumonia! That's what I want, pneumonia. The peace and quiet of an oxygen tent where I can't hear any of you!"

Sidney, unmoved, grates, "You'll play this show, Miss Livingston, if you have to do it with your head in an iron lung! Three of my nephews are doctors and they'll be there at every performance!" He huffs out, and Irene and Stella commence yelling recriminations at each other.

The curtain falls.

ACT III

Some time has passed now; the suite is deserted, with only one lamp lighted—but there is plenty going on outside in the hall.

First Man—Good night, Jack.

Second Man—Good night, Ed.

Third Man—Good night, Jim. You say you were from Saginaw, Michigan, Jack?

LIGHT UP THE SKY

FIRST MAN—That's right, Saginaw. Moved to Saginaw from Moline, Ill., about eleven years ago. You from Elkhart, Ind.?

THIRD MAN—That's right, Elkhart. Ever run into a feller called Ben Gitzel in Moline? Hardware supplies. Used to be a feller called Ben Gitzel in Moline about eleven years ago.

FIRST MAN—No. There was a Ben Whittaker in Moline 'bout eleven years ago. He was in machine tools. Can't remember any Ben Gitzel. Well, good night.

SECOND MAN—Good night, Jack.

THIRD MAN—Good night, Ed.

FIRST MAN—Good night, Jim. Say, was Ben Gitzel a short fat feller with a mustache who switched over into plywood?

THIRD MAN—That's right. That's Ben Gitzel.

FIRST MAN—Why, sure I know Ben Gitzel! What the hell ever happened to him?

THIRD MAN—He's got a factory in Elkhart. We sell him all his paper cups.

FIRST MAN—You don't say! Little old Ben Gitzel! Little fat feller with a mustache who switched over into plywood?

THIRD MAN—That's right. We sell him all his paper cups. Well, good night, Jack.

SECOND MAN—Good night, Ed.

FIRST MAN—Good night, Jim. Say, will you be seeing Ben Gitzel when you get back to Elkhart?

THIRD MAN—Sure. We sell him all his paper cups.

FIRST MAN—Well, ask Ben Gitzel if he remembers Jack Ebinger, will ya?

THIRD MAN—Sure will. Well, good night, Jack.

SECOND MAN—Good night, Ed.

FIRST MAN—Good night, Jim. (STELLA, *during the latter part of this exchange, has come sleepily out of her room. Now she picks up a bottle from the bar and marches determinedly toward the door. She opens it to find* FRANCES *in the doorway, hand upraised to knock.*)

FRANCES—Hold it, Stella—I'm on your side! (*She closes door.*)

STELLA—They got *you* up, too, huh? (*She snaps on the lights.*)

FRANCES—Oh, it's ducky up on our floor! They're tossing fire crackers into the bathrooms. This is nice and quiet. Better give up on the sleep department, honey, and play some gin with me. The boys are really living tonight!

STELLA—Gin? I won't be able to see the cards, Frances.

Frances—Then I got a fighting chance. Come on, Stella—you won't be able to sleep! Let's get some sandwiches and a bottle of beer and make a night of it.

Stella makes a try for Room Service, but it's closed. Frances, the loser at the gin game by quite a lot of money, makes her friend a sporting proposition—three games across for whatever she owes against half her interest in the show.

Stella grumpily guesses that a half interest in the show would be worth about $11, and Frances becomes indignant. All that scenery—the staircase and the mountain with the faces of Washington, Jefferson and Lincoln carved on it—and all those costumes. "You gotta get something back, don't you?"

Pityingly, Stella tells this debutante angel the facts of life. The scenery isn't saleable, and she can't even walk away and leave it. She must have it carted away and pay somebody to burn it. And as for the costumes—"Well, in an ordinary show, Frances, a costume that cost $200 they buy back for about $2—but this is an allegory, dear. The costumes in this show are mostly rags the survivors of the world are walking around in. Right?"

"Do people who put money into shows know about this, Stella?"

"Well, usually a backer gets some kind of a souvenir for his dough. He gets a lamp to take home or his wife gets a pocketbook. You see anything in this show you can take home? You got any place in your house for the mountain, or the rain effects?"

"Sidney's bedroom," Frances answers promptly. He should wake up every morning and look at it and the rain should pour down on him. . . . Boy, I can't wait now to run into Irving Berlin. 'There's no business like show business.' He ought to be arrested."

The girls have barely begun their game when they are interrupted by another Shriner, who sticks his head in the door. He won't shoo. This is a different kind of Shriner—sober and earnest—and he knows where he is. He wants to apologize to Miss Livingston. "I want to apologize to her on behalf of all Shriners—and particularly for those Shriners who were at the theatre tonight. I was ashamed of them—ashamed of being a Shriner myself. That beautiful play!"

Frances can't believe her ears as the visitor goes on about it being the most beautiful play he ever saw, with a message in it for all of us. He doesn't know what it says, it's true—but he was choked up all the time. And now he is standing right in Irene Livingston's room, and he recognizes Frances Black, the skater, too. He can hardly wait to tell his wife about it!

By now the astounded women have become fascinated.

FRANCES—Go ahead, Mr. . . .

SHRINER—Gallegher. William H. Gallegher. Excuse me. Just forgot all my manners, I'm so excited.

FRANCES—You were saying how you loved the theatre.

SHRINER—Yessir, I missed the bus somewhere along the line. Always wanted to be in the theatre—but my father died while I was still in college, and there I was with four big factories in Elkhart, Indiana. What could I do?

FRANCES—Four factories? You still got 'em?

SHRINER—Five now. Big success—and never did what I really wanted to do! You people are the lucky ones. The theatre! What I wouldn't give to be a part of it!

FRANCES—You know, Mr. Gallegher, you're just saying something that strikes close to home. I was saying to my husband, Sidney Black—he produced the show you saw tonight—I was saying to him just this afternoon—"Sidney," I said, "the trouble with the theatre today is that it's a closed corporation. A few big shots run it, and nobody else can get a look-in. You ought to let more people in—real American folks from out of town"—like yourself, Mr. Gallegher—"those people ought to have a chance to come into the theatre. New faces—new blood—new money!" I think my husband would be very interested in meeting you, Mr. Gallegher. Let me get him up here.

SHRINER—Oh, I wouldn't want to trouble him, Mrs. Black. It's very late.

FRANCES—This is no trouble. He'll shoot up here for this. Like a Roman candle.

STELLA—Frances, you make me proud of being a woman!

FRANCES—Operator, get me Mr. Black. Keep ringing until he answers. This is Mrs. Black.

STELLA—Can I give you a drink, Mr. Gallegher? Scotch, bourbon, rye—anything you want.

SHRINER—No, thanks. I'm drunk enough with just the smell of the theatre!

STELLA—Chanel Number Five—that's what it is!

FRANCES—Hello? Daddy? I'm with Stella. Can you come up here for a minute, Daddy? I want you to meet somebody. A Mr. Gallegher, from Elkhart, Indiana. (*She makes a face.*)

No, Daddy, I'm not. He's sitting right here and he wants to get into the theatre. He wants to get into the theatre, Daddy—in the worst way—he loves this show—I told him you might think about letting him in. Come on up, Sidney. (*She hangs up.*) He didn't quite understand at first. He was asleep.

SHRINER—Oh, I could have talked to him tomorrow. (*He remains silent for a moment. Then suddenly he bursts out.*)

"O what a rogue and peasant slave am I.
O that this too, too solid flesh would melt."

Hamlet. Did it in high school.

FRANCES—I'll bet you were just wonderful.

SHRINER—Oh, just adequate. Tell me something, Mrs. Black. Just what kind of play would you say this is? I loved it, mind you, but it's a very strange play, isn't it?

FRANCES—Why, no. It's an allegory.

SHRINER—Oh. I see.

STELLA—Ever see "Life with Father," Mr. Gallegher?

SHRINER—Oh, yes.

STELLA—That was an allegory.

SHRINER—Was it?

FRANCES—Sure. "Oklahoma!"? Big allegory. (*The door opens and* SIDNEY *appears.*)

SIDNEY—If this is some kind of joke I'm going to hit you both over the head with Orson!

FRANCES—Honey, this is Mr. William H. Gallegher.

SHRINER (*shaking him by the hand*)—Mr. Black, this is a privilege—to meet the man who put on that wonderful show! What a message! And your wife says you agree with her about getting new people in the theatre. New faces—new blood—new money! It's a kick meeting you all, I can tell you. I'm just a great big, stage-struck businessman, Mr. Black.

SIDNEY (*getting it*)—Oh, yes! *yes!* Sit down, Mr. Gallegher! Make yourself comfortable. Did you offer Mr. Gallegher a drink, Frances?

Mr. Gallegher thinks it would be nice if Sidney, when he's doing his next show, would open the door a little and let some outside people in like William H. Gallegher of Elkhart, Ind. He wouldn't want to take advantage of Sidney on this show, because this one is a sure thing.

But Sidney will give his all for art. "Take advantage of me! Trap me! Come on! Take advantage! Who cares?" And a thought occurs. "What makes you so sure this is a sure thing, my friend?"

"Why—haven't you seen the papers, Mr. Black? The morning papers?"

Sidney hasn't—but take Gallegher's word for it, the papers say the play is wonderful. He has them right in his pocket. Sidney makes a grab for them and begins reading. One notice says that, although "The Time Is Now" is not exactly a good play, its best moments have a kind of singing poetry, a lyric quality of exultation and hope, that makes it a stirring and exciting experience.

Frances and Stella snatch other papers and there is a chorus of reading. The notices all sound wonderful. Irene Livingston's performance makes theatrical history. . . . Fitzgerald's direction is a dazzling experiment in modern stagecraft. . . . And one critic enthusiastically advises star, author and director to get to work and make the play live up to its best.

Stella calls Carleton Fitzgerald on the phone and tells him about the reviews. "Don't cry for a couple of minutes yet and get in here," she admonishes.

Sidney goes to Irene's door, calls out to ask if she is awake, then reads loudly such lines about her as, "She gave the play and her part her glorious best." Irene comes out like a shot, grabbing for papers and reading more about herself in a very fine voice.

The Shriner is beside himself with pleasure at being in on so intimate and thrilling a scene. "Wait till I tell Milly about this," he keeps saying—until Sidney unceremoniously propels him out the door with, "Listen, Jack, we're very busy, thanks. Call me in the morning and I'll send you an autograph."

Tyler has come out too, and it dawns on him that something has happened. "Does this mean everything is all right, Irene? That we're not going duck shooting? . . . But, Irene, I've already wired Abercrombie & Fitch!"

When Carleton enters, Irene reads him a quote about himself— long and distinguished career . . . sensitive directorial hand . . . pure stage magic. Carleton could cry.

Sidney manages to find a mention of himself, too—deserving some kind of Academy Award for wonderful courage and staggering lavishness. And in another paper he finds:

"To paraphrase Mr. Churchill, we see nothing ahead for 'The Time Is Now' but blood, sweat, toil and tears, but with another little bow to Mr. Churchill, we should like to remind the star, the author, the director and the producer that this may be their finest hour. That's how good we think it could be."

The group's happiness about themselves is such that it is some time before anybody thinks of the author. It is Irene who remembers him, and is about to phone when Sidney halts her. That boy will need every bit of sleep he can get, and all his strength, because he's got work to do. "My friends, we're going to mother him, father him, laugh with him, cry with him, rock him to sleep, massage him awake, buy him strange foods and if necessary strange women. . . . It's D-Day, folks; be nice to General Eisenhower!"

All enmities are forgotten and there are waves of forgiveness and salvos of kisses. They want to call Peter right now and get to work, so Sidney gives in and calls the playwright's room. What he hears is a blow! "He checked out. He's gone!"

The meaning of this dawns on the others and they are thunderstruck.

Owen Turner and Nan Lowell come in without knocking and Sidney regards them searchingly. He figures they know something about Peter's disappearance, and he is right. "We left him at the airport. He's taking the 4:30 plane to New York to pick up his girl and tomorrow afternoon he'll be in Wisconsin."

With the brusqueness and efficiency of a Walter Burns, Sidney calls the manager of the airport, who owes him a favor. "Listen. Remember what you told me in Union Station last Summer? Well, now I'm ready. There's a guy going out on the 4:30 plane. Peter Sloan is the name. I need him back here. How? Throw him off the plane and get one of your special deputies to bring him over here. No, no, don't worry about false arrest. I'll take the responsibility."

This reminds Owen that he has a note from Peter to all the rest of them. Sidney, Irene and Carleton read it together. It's unbelievable to Irene—"Accusing us of pettiness and selfishness!" In the note are such phrases as "strange insincerities you call loyalties." The man must be crazy. "Are *you* crazy?" Sidney asks Owen. "Are all authors crazy?"

OWEN—A little. No sane person could stand this for long. But Sloan isn't crazy, Sidney. There's something touching and young and rather admirable about him. And I'm not even sure he isn't right.

SIDNEY—Right about what? What did we destroy? His play? Him? Because a few snappy words were exchanged? Is that it?

Because we were all trying to save our necks, and his, too, for that matter! What were we supposed to do—hit the trail and be saved—get religion or something? What are you handing out? A new commandment?

OWEN—No. It's just that he's found out we're dubious people—and he can't accept that. Me—I made my bed with you a long time ago—I'm one of you—I even enjoy it now. But we've all forgotten what it is to be young, to be sensitive, and to be hurt. This was his first play—his baby—and you were its mother and father all rolled into one. Well, the baby was born and it wasn't a very pretty child. So what did Mama and Papa do? They kicked it in the head—stepped on it—and threw it out the window. What do you expect, Sidney? Flowers?

IRENE—You're unfair, Owen. You're bitterly unfair. We loved this play—we always have. We knew what a chance it was—

SIDNEY—And we blew it! He's right! We blew it—all of us. Nobody more than me! The only thing he didn't say was that we deserve this—we deserve that kid walking out on us—to hell with whether he's right or wrong or crazy. We deserve it! You know something, Owen? You know what makes it funny? This was the one time I wasn't showing off—showing the world how smart I was—this was something I was doing for myself—putting my chips down quietly on the one thing that always had me bug-eyed with wonder and respect—talent—like Sloan's. It's maybe the first time in my life I ever did something like this—for my insides—for me—to be a big man to myself. Just that and nothing else. And I blew it. So I guess I won't keep on kidding myself any more.

FRANCES—You keep right on, Sidney. With every cent I've got or you've got. And that includes this junk—and hocking those ice skates if necessary.

SIDNEY—Shut up, Frances. (*The phone rings,* SIDNEY *grabs it.*) Yes. Yeah! Okay. (*He hangs up.*) Peter's coming up!

IRENE—He's back!

CARLETON—Wonderful! Wonderful!

SIDNEY (*slowly*)—I don't think we've got much chance. Folks, will you just leave the three of us alone to talk to him?

There is a knock, and when Sidney calls "Come in" a plainclothesman hauls Peter in by the arm—a disheveled Peter who is white with rage. "He's given me lots of trouble," says the officer.

Peter grimly promises he will be all right now and the officer goes. There is a chorus of apology and cajolery, but the young playwright is unaffected by it.

Sidney tries a new tack—a dejected giving up—but Peter just laughs at him. Sidney gives him a long look, then, at the desk, quickly writes a document relinquishing all his rights to "The Time Is Now" to the author. He thrusts it into Peter's hand and snaps, "Okay. You got your play back. And this gives me the privilege of telling you just what I think of you. You write like an angel but you're a bit of a jerk. And maybe a little yellow, too. You turned just as much as we did—even more; you walked out on yourself. . . . Get on your plane."

Peter laughs heartily, exclaiming, "This is the biggest switch of all! And I've got one for you . . . There'll be no laughing it up—no Olsen and Johnson—and no idiotic shenanigans from you, you or you"—pointing to Irene, Carleton and Sidney. "Especially you, you crazy little bastard."

Sidney flings his arms about the playwright. "Peter, darling, this is my type talk!"

PETER (*pushing his arms away*)—But watch out—all of you. I've just graduated! I've got diploma scars all over me. Now, let's get to work!

SIDNEY—All right! Act one. Scene one! Let's fix the show!

IRENE (*to* PETER)—Oh, bless you, darling, you know how I love this play—how I'd give my life for it—but I cannot have three hundred sweaty extras lying on top of me during—

CARLETON—If you'd stay in the place you're supposed to stay in, Irene, instead of wandering all over the damn stage, you wouldn't—

SIDNEY—Let the woman finish a sentence, can't you?

CARLETON—Just a moment, Mr. Black—my contract says you are not to even *talk* to me unless I allow it, and I have no intention of tearing my contract up, believe me! I can also bar you from the theatre!

PETER—Shut up! Shut up, all of you, shut up! I'll tell you what's wrong with that first scene. Shut up and let the man who wrote it tell you. Now come on, all of you. (*These last few remarks have not been made quietly. They have been shouted, and if* PETER *had not shouted just a little more loudly they would all have been at one another's throats. The noise has brought the others out of the bedroom, however, and they stand listening, sensing somehow that everything is going to be all right.*)

IRENE—Oh, bless you, darling—if you can just fix the first scene, I'm sure everything else will fall into place.

SIDNEY—Sh! Irene! Do you interrupt a salmon swimming upstream? Do you interrupt Dr. Ehrlich at experiment 605? Talk, Peter, talk! Take a wire to Lee Shubert, Miss Lowell: "Dear Lee, I want two weeks in Philadelphia, two in Detroit and two in Pittsburgh!"

STELLA—Six more weeks of gin, Frances!

CARLETON—I could cry!

FRANCES (*calling across the room*)—Daddy—it's the same old story! You're coming out of that sewer covered with honey! Deal 'em up, Stella!

THE CURTAIN FALLS

THE SILVER WHISTLE [*]
A Comedy in Three Acts
By Robert E. McEnroe

AT the age of 33, Robert Edward McEnroe, an employee of the research department at the United Aircraft plant in Hartford, Conn., found that his first play was a hit on broadway. But his was not an overnight success; he had written eleven plays before this one and nothing had happened to ten of them. The eleventh was optioned by three different producers, but nobody produced it. The Theatre Guild optioned the dozenth work, under the title of "Oliver Erwenter." Mr. McEnroe chose this name for his principal character because he—Mr. McE.—is a southpaw, and "Erwenter" is very easy to spell with the left hand on a typewriter.

A day or two before the Summer theatre tryout of the comedy in Westport, Conn., it was decided that it should have a new title. Somebody thought "The Silver Whistle" sounded good, although there was no mention of such an instrument in the script. McEnroe obligingly wrote a fanciful couplet for Erwenter to recite:

The old dog crawled away to die and hid amid the thistle;
Then joy and youth came back to him on the note of a silver
    whistle.

The play opens in the small garden of a church adjoining a home for the aged—a run-down and battered little garden. To the right of it is the lower part of the building in which the old people live. To the left is a wall of the church, the Church of John. The rest of the space is taken up by an eight foot wall

---

[*] Copyright, 1949, by Robert Edward McEnroe.
Copyright, 1948, as a dramatic composition under the title of "Oliver Erwenter," by Robert Edward McEnroe.
Dramatists Play Service, Inc., 14 East 38th Street, New York 16, N. Y., is the exclusive publisher of the entire play. It also has the exclusive rights to authorize nonprofessional productions.
Author's agents, Claire Leonard and Carl Cowl, 516 Fifth Avenue, New York City.

with a big, heavy door set in an archway. Up on the back wall of the church is one of those "churchy" windows. There is a scrubby tree in the garden close to the wall. Old mended furniture is scattered about in the center.

It is afternoon and three of the home's inmates, Mr. Beebe, a gentle, white-haired old man, Mrs. Hanmer and Miss Hoadley are seated around a table. Mrs. Hanmer is a waspish-looking woman in her late sixties. Miss Hoadley, big and florid and agreeable, is deaf. She wears a hearing aid which happens now to have fallen to the ground. Always vague, Miss Hoadley is frequently, as now, under the influence of alcohol.

Mr. Beebe shakes his head slowly, experimentally, reporting to the two ladies that he is starting to get dizzy again—that things are going 'round and 'round—a condition he attributes to a disturbance of his inner ear. Mrs. Hanmer, however, is far more concerned about her appendix than Mr. Beebe's ear. It is Mrs. Hanmer's belief that the organ should have been removed a long time ago and that it is only sheer penuriousness on the part of the home that obliges her to suffer. "It's terrible," she rasps shrilly. "We're all sitting here waiting to die." She addresses Mr. Beebe point-blank. "Do you want to sit here and die?"

Mr. Beebe is resigned. "Well, as long as we have to wait, I suppose we may as well sit."

The reply serves only to goad Mrs. Hanmer into a self-pitying harangue that nobody cares about her which seems perfectly true as far as Miss Hoadley is concerned. A silent third of the group until now, Miss Hoadley continues to nod vaguely, oblivious to the conversation in a drunken stupor. "They're willing to let me sit here and rot," Mrs. Hanmer shouts at Miss Hoadley. The latter fails to comprehend until Mrs. Hanmer shouts again, louder this time, then she belches and mumbles something about being all right.

Miss Tripp, the superintendent of the old people's home, comes into the garden. She is in her early thirties, plain, prim and proper. One has the feeling that if Miss Tripp took some trouble to improve her appearance, she would look quite fetching—but also that she isn't likely to do so.

"You've got the top of the table littered again," Miss Tripp chides the elderly trio fondly. "You know you're supposed to keep things neat." Bending down she recovers Miss Hoadley's hearing aid, admonishing her gently to try not to keep on losing it. Opening the bottle, she reminds Mr. Beebe that it is time for his pills. The old gentleman, who eyes the pills with mild dislike, tries to divert her attention. "Miss Tripp, the flowers have wilted again."

"They have wilted, haven't they? I was sure these were going to last." But Miss Tripp is not to be outwitted—just yet. She hands Mr. Beebe the glass of water and a pill before turning to look at the flowers. "Their heads are dropped right down," Mr. Beebe continues with calculated concern, throwing the pill away. "I guess they're dead like all the others."

"Never mind, Mr. Beebe," Miss Tripp consoles. "Some day we'll have a wonderful garden. We'll have green grass and pretty flowers."

"Flowers won't grow here," Mrs. Hanmer breaks in belligerently. "The whole place is old. Even the ground is old. This is an old dump. You should be ashamed to run an old dump."

Miss Tripp notices that Miss Hoadley has been drinking again. Something ought to be done about her, Mrs. Hanmer persists. She's on church property and can't be kept sober. What's more, she can't see why the Reverend Watson stands for it. He wouldn't if he knew about it, Miss Tripp declares, but decides that this is a little secret between all of them and that the Reverend mustn't see Miss Hoadley in her present condition. "Mr. Beebe," she orders, "run in the house and get some ammonia." The old gentleman hastens out on the errand.

Eyeing his departure, Mrs. Hanmer asks Miss Tripp confidentially if she's noticed Mr. Beebe lately. "He's aged," she remarks. "He won't last much longer." "Mr. Beebe?" queries Miss Tripp. "He's getting ready to die," Mrs. Hanmer informs her decisively. "They don't last long once they're here." Miss Tripp is doubtful. She feels that in Mr. Beebe's present state of health he's good for another twenty years. But Mrs. Hanmer is not to be dissuaded from her prophecy of doom. "Mark my words, he'll be dead in a week."

At this moment, the Reverend Watson, pastor of the Church of John, enters through the garden door. He is thirty-six or seven and appears slim and ascetic. Actually, he is dull, plodding, conventional and righteous even at the expense of others. He carries a number of letters in one hand and is examining them. They are mostly bills.

He bids the ladies good afternoon then addresses himself specifically to Miss Tripp. "More bills. Religion's become so expensive that only the wicked can afford it. My dear, thank you for straightening up my study and thank you for the little dish of fruit."

THE SILVER WHISTLE

Obviously pleased at the acknowledgment, Harriet examines the Reverend's jacket. One of the buttons is missing from his coat. "Sometimes," she says fondly, "I think you need as much attention as the guests."

Watson smiles at her, then returns to the mail. There is a letter from the Bishop. It's almost time for his monthly tour of inspection—a trying experience. The minister inquires as to everybody's health.

MRS. HANMER—There's not much use in telling you, but my appendix is bad again.

WATSON—Your side is bothering you, Mrs. Hanmer?

MRS. HANMER—Of course it's bothering me. Everybody knows I need an operation.

WATSON—Now, Mrs. Hanmer . . .

MRS. HANMER—Operations cost money, so everybody knows I'm not going to get one. You spend just enough money on us to keep us alive so you can brag about the charity the church does.

WATSON—Mrs. Hanmer, we live in a very poor parish. Our parishioners cannot afford to spend money on unnecessary operations. The Bishop has already complained about our expenses.

MRS. HANMER—The Bishop will be sorry if I die doubled up in a knot.

WATSON—Please, Mrs. Hanmer. (*To* TRIPP, *as he crosses to church door.*) My dear, I'll be in my study if you need me.

MISS TRIPP (*taking a step or two after him, starting to speak, then changing her mind, stopping and turning back*)—All right, Reverend.

MRS. HANMER—What you see in that man I don't know. Did he propose yet?

MISS TRIPP—Propose what?

MRS. HANMER—Marriage. He's a minister, what else could he propose?

MISS TRIPP—I think we have an understanding, Mrs. Hanmer.

MRS. HANMER—You may have an understanding, but you haven't got a ring.

MISS TRIPP—Rings aren't important, Mrs. Hanmer. It's how people feel that matters.

MRS. HANMER—You can marry him if you want to. It's your life. But personally I think you're making a mistake. You could do a lot better. There's not much to him. You couldn't say he was big-hearted. You couldn't say he was kind. You couldn't say he was generous. I wouldn't even say he was a red-blooded man.

Miss Tripp does not contradict Mrs. Hanmer, reproaching her instead by pointing out how good the Reverend Watson has been to all of them, including herself. At this moment, a pretty, little old lady—the kind they show on candy boxes—puts in an appearance. This is Mrs. Sampler, and she appears upset. She has run into Mr. Beebe inside the house and heard that the flowers have wilted.

She then sees for herself. "Oh, they did!" she wails piteously. "Those lovely flowers all wilted. They were so beautiful. Look at them. Their little heads are drooping to the ground. Every flower we plant grows up and dies. I think I'm going to cry."

"Don't start that again," Mrs. Hanmer snaps, ignoring a warning look from Miss Tripp. Every time there's someone around to watch, she remarks spitefully, Mrs. Sampler puts on a great big helpless little girl act. "Watch Mr. Beebe when he comes out with the ammonia," Mrs. Hanmer taunts. "He'll run to her like a fly goes to molasses. She didn't get three husbands by being brave and self-sufficient."

"Mrs. Hanmer, that isn't a nice thing to say," Miss Tripp reproves, patting Mrs. Sampler whose eyes are brimming with tears. Mr. Beebe returns with the bottle of ammonia and goes running instantly to Mrs. Sampler's side. "I told you, I told you," Mrs. Hanmer cackles.

Distressed in the extreme, Mr. Beebe begs to know what has made Mrs. Sampler cry. "Tell us what makes you feel sad," he coaxes. It is the flowers, of course. Mrs. Sampler guesses they didn't want to live here with all the ugly old people.

Mrs. Hanmer snorts. "Fishing for compliments again. She's seventy-eight years old and she acts coy. Who ever heard of a seventy-eight-year-old minx?

Mrs. Sampler bridles. She's not coy, she insists and what's more, she's only seventy-four years old. "You're seventy-eight and you look every damned day of it," Mrs. Hanmer continues derisively. A bee interrupts Mrs. Sampler's indignant protestations, terrifying her and causing Mrs. Hanmer to express the hope that it stings her.

Gallant Mr. Beebe takes off his hat and starts waving it at the bee. He cautions Mrs. Sampler not to worry, that he'll get rid of it. This involves dancing around in a little circle and backing over near Miss Hoadley who is sitting with her eyes closed and oblivious of the general consternation. The bee alights on Miss Hoadley's hat. Mr. Beebe tries to brush it off with his own hat. But the bee falls down on to Miss Hoadley's neck and down the front of her dress. A tremendous shudder, silent and awful, suddenly goes through Miss Hoadley, but she makes no sound. The others crowd around her as the Reverend Watson re-enters the garden.

Two more guests of the home enter the garden. These are Mr. Cherry and Mrs. Gross. Mr. Cherry, a slow, deliberate, earnest and precise little man is pushing Mrs. Gross in her wheel chair. The woman is a bit senile.

Reverend Watson bows acknowledgment to Mrs. Gross, who cries out: "Sin—sin—the whole world's gone crazy with sin."

"Mrs. Gross is referring to the average woman on the street," Mr. Cherry, a self-appointed interlocutor, explains. Mrs. Gross doesn't approve of modern clothes. To her, they are shamefully immodest. "Clothes were meant to cover a person up. What makes all these women stick out so far in front? God has nothing to do with it."

"Neither did the devil," the minister parries, reminding Mrs. Gross that one must be fair.

"There's nothing on them," Mrs. Gross thrusts back. "You can see everything a good woman hides."

Watson comments that styles have changed. Mrs. Gross is not impressed. It is still vulgar sinning. Why, just a little while ago, she and Mr. Cherry had seen a woman sitting in the park with her legs crossed and exposed right up to her knees. And she had felt called upon to exhort Mr. Cherry not to look. Mr. Cherry confirms the statement, whereupon Mr. Beebe asks if he did look. Soundlessly, Mr. Cherry nods "yes."

Reverend Watson interrupts the exchange by recalling what he had come to tell them in the first place. He has just received a phone call from the Bishop regarding a Mr. O. T. Erwenter. Mr. Erwenter is seventy-seven years old, but according to the Bishop, is very spry and young. Mr. Erwenter also has traveled all over the world and has many interesting stories to tell. Mr. Erwenter is coming to stay at the home.

Miss Tripp's first reaction is concern over another mouth to feed. There is scarcely enough for everybody now. Watson piously quotes the Bishop as having said that their charity must be stretched to its fullest limits. But they can't take care of anybody else, Miss Tripp argues, unless they have more money. Doesn't the Bishop know this? Watson admits that the Bishop does, but that when asked for more money had seen fit only to remind him of what the Lord accomplished with the loaves and fishes.

"If the Lord were feeding these people, I wouldn't worry," Miss Tripp counters with some bitterness. "But the Lord and the Bishop leave it up to me."

"Harriet, we must try to help everyone who needs our help."

"But these people have nothing, and yet you're perfectly willing to take in someone else."

"What they have is better than nothing," the minister maintains.

"You're stretching charity so thin, it isn't charity," is the crushing reply.

"Please, Harriet." Watson advances to placate her when for no particular reason, Miss Hoadley—who has been silent all this time—starts to laugh. "What is the matter with Miss Hoadley?" Watson demands to know as he lifts her head. The awful truth dawns upon him instantly. The woman has been drinking. "Are we serving whiskeys to these people? Do we have a bar for cocktails? Are we to cut down on the number of people we have here so that we can keep the remainder in their cups?" He orders Miss Hoadley taken inside and cold water thrown on her until she sobers up. He then takes his leave in a fit of righteous indignation.

Now the problem is how to get Miss Hoadley indoors. She is too heavy for Mr. Cherry and Mr. Beebe to carry. Mrs. Gross supplies the answer—standing Miss Hoadley on the footboard of her wheel chair and wheeling her in. The maneuver is accomplished with Beebe and Cherry on either side of the wheel chair, propping Miss Hoadley up, and Miss Tripp pushing the whole entourage inside.

This leaves Mrs. Hanmer and the kittenish Mrs. Sampler alone outside. "She looks like the prow of a ship that hit a reef," Mrs. Hanmer says maliciously. "Isn't it a shame she took to drink?" Mrs. Sampler moralizes. "Isn't it a shame we don't know where she took it from?" Mrs. Hanmer corrects, just as O. T. Erwenter, carrying a rooster in a cage, comes through the door in the wall.

Erwenter appears to be about forty and is quite attractive. He is very tanned, with a devil-may-care air about him. He stops and takes in the scene, holding the rooster aloft.

"Good afternoon, ladies," Erwenter commences.

Mrs. Sampler becomes all girlish sweetness. "Good afternoon."

"Is this the Church of John?"

"There's a bell outside that door," Mrs. Hanmer observes drily.

The newcomer ignores the snub. "A home for the aged. You have a home for the aged?"

Mrs. Hanmer folds her hands together. "You're supposed to ring the bell."

Mrs. Sampler comes to the stranger's rescue. "This is the Church of John."

He introduces himself as Oliver T. Erwenter, who has come to stay at the home for a short time. Mrs. Hanmer sets him right. He'll never get out. He'll be there till he dies.

The ladies express joint amazement at Erwenter's youthful appearance for a man seventy-seven years old. The secret, Erwenter tells them, is his heart—the heart of a youth. Mrs. Sampler summons Miss Tripp while Mrs. Hanmer explains that Miss Tripp is the superintendent and that she'll tell him what to do, which, to hear Mrs. Hanmer tell it, is nothing, just waiting around to die.

When Miss Tripp appears, Erwenter produces a letter from the Bishop identifying himself. Miss Tripp is nonetheless incredulous about his age. To allay her doubts, Erwenter produces a birth certificate which finally convinces her.

The whereabouts of Erwenter's luggage is the question posed next. He explains that due to a disastrous fire which wiped out his effects, he has nothing left in the world but his rooster. The bird he introduces as Omar—the world's greatest living fighting cock. Omar, Erwenter claims, can subdue any feathered creature that moves on two legs.

There is some doubt in Miss Tripp's mind as to whether Erwenter will be allowed to keep the rooster with him. For one thing, she thinks fighting cocks are against the law—to which Erwenter replies that a fighting bird is obviously not a fighting bird unless he fights. For another, she's sure that Reverend Watson won't want any kind of bird—much less a fighting cock—on church premises.

Mrs. Hanmer and Mrs. Sampler, however, favor keeping the rooster and Miss Tripp agrees to let Omar stay after making the ladies promise not to breathe a word to the Reverend about its being a fighter. She then calls out to Mr. Beebe and Mr. Cherry, introducing the two to Erwenter as they come rushing on from inside.

Mr. Beebe, Miss Tripp explains, used to work in an insurance company in Hartford, Connecticut. Beebe himself adds promptly that he worked there forty-five years. Erwenter wonders why after forty-five years, Mr. Beebe finds himself in a home. The answer is that at sixty-five, one is obliged to resign. But, Mr. Beebe emphasizes, they give you a free policy. When he dies, he'll have a beautiful funeral. He'll have a casket lined in silk. And it's all free!

Mr. Beebe has invited all of them to the funeral Mrs. Hanmer imparts, and everybody's going to go. At this point, Beebe tenders a similar invitation to Erwenter, who thanks him without particular relish.

Mr. Cherry collects stamps. He has always been interested in traveling, having worked as a clerk in a shipping firm, but never had the opportunity to go. Mr. Cherry understands that Mr. Erwenter has done considerable gadding about the world in his time—and so Oliver has. By his own admission, he has sought diamonds and orchids in Africa, traded in blacks, blown glass in Italy, raised grapes on the shores of the Mediterranean, sailed before the mast on the seven seas—to list only a few of his life's endeavors.

"Weren't you ever in love?" Mrs. Sampler ventures.

Oliver finds it hard to say. He's had affairs, of course, with women in most of the countries of the world—but as for love, he doesn't know. A woman is thrilling, he opines, until you've had her—then you start to dream about something else.

As for his youthful appearance, Oliver declares that being young is the way one thinks. The main trick, he counsels, is never to let yourself get into a rut. And don't dream! Live! Live every moment as if it were going to be the last. Doing just that is the main thing that has kept him young, and, of course, having his full sexual powers has helped some.

"What?" Mrs. Sampler is taken aback.

"Mr. Erwenter," Miss Tripp steps in. "There are some things we don't talk about here."

"No offense, ladies."

"Let him talk," Mrs. Hanmer insists. "The man's the damnedest liar I ever met, but it's a change."

"Forgive me." Oliver addresses himself to Miss Tripp. "I had forgotten that one so young and lovely was listening. You're a very attractive woman. Far too attractive to be trapped in such a dingy place."

Mrs. Sampler—Tell us more about keeping young, Mr. Erwenter.

THE SILVER WHISTLE

ERWENTER—Yes. Well, back in 1916 when I was forty-five years old, I made a trip into Outer Mongolia.

BEEBE—What were you looking for then?

ERWENTER—Nothing. Not a thing. I'd never been to Outer Mongolia and I was forty-five years old, so I decided it was high time I got there. High time.

BEEBE—So you just went.

ERWENTER—I was on a small freighter plying the waters of the South China Sea. We pulled into the Bay of Tongking and I jumped ship and started out on foot. The trip across China was a nightmare. I'll never forget it, I'll tell you that.

MRS. SAMPLER—You poor man.

ERWENTER—When I reached the mountains my strength was almost gone. Some kindly monks took me into their monastery and nursed me back to health. It was in that monastery that I first met Lao Chin Po, the man who set my sights on destiny.

CHERRY—Were you near Lhasa at the time?

ERWENTER—Lhasa? I was a thousand miles from Lhasa. In the wildest, bleakest country that man has ever seen. At the end of the world. Lhasa. (MRS. GROSS *enters*.)

MRS. SAMPLER—Please go on, Mr. Erwenter.

BEEBE—Lao Chin Po.

ERWENTER (*resuming as if he had never stopped*)—Spring came and the snows melted into the valley. Warmth crept into the ground and Lao Chin Po and I walked through the vastness and talked of man and God.

CHERRY—He spoke English?

ERWENTER—I speak Chinese. One day as we walked, we looked into each other's eyes and had knowledge. We swore friendship and he gave me the great gift . . . the potion of Twingsti. No man can give another more.

MRS. GROSS (*to* ERWENTER)—Foreign devils. Worshipers of heathen idols.

MISS TRIPP—Mrs. Gross . . .

MRS. GROSS—Sin has come into the garden.

MISS TRIPP—Mrs. Gross. Mrs. Gross has been with us a long time.

ERWENTER—She's been somewhere a long time.

MRS. GROSS—Young man, I've been right here in the Springfield Public Library for fifty-five years and I never signed out a dirty book.

MRS. SAMPLER—Mr. Erwenter, what was the potion for?

ERWENTER—The potion?

CHERRY—The potion of Twingsti, I believe?

ERWENTER—In the youth of man, his blood runs swift and hot. After man has crossed the meridian of life the passions cool. The lusts within him cease to flame and die to but a simmer. The potion of Twingsti brings to life that force within a man that makes him flame.

MRS. GROSS (*shouting at church*)—Reverend Watson . . . Reverend Watson. This is mad talk. This man has heathen dreams. Reverend Watson . . . Reverend Watson.

WATSON (*entering*)—Did someone call me?

MISS TRIPP—Reverend Watson . . . this is Mr. Erwenter.

WATSON—It is difficult to believe that you are seventy-seven years old, Mr. Erwenter. You must have lived a healthy, wholesome life to look so fit.

ERWENTER—Let me explain—I once taught Freshman English in an Eastern University. I was an Associate Professor at the age of thirty-four. I had developed a substantial pot about my middle, was starting to show a double chin and jowls, regularly took cathartics, had trouble breathing and was engaged to a very proper and rather boring young woman named Amanda Newberry. (REVEREND WATSON *tries to interrupt.*)

WATSON—Yes—very interesting . . .

ERWENTER—One day as I read the Rubaiyat of Omar Khayyam aloud to a class, one of my students raised his hand and said: "Professor, what would happen to a man who tried to follow Omar's doctrines in our modern world?" As I paused to frame an answer I thought of Omar's joyous affinity for nature and the jug in relation to my own dull, staid life. I suddenly decided that Omar was right and that my entire existence was completely futile. Throwing the book into the wastebasket, I turned to the blackboard and wrote: "By God, I'll find out!" I then climbed out the nearest window and set out to search the world to find the true joy of living.

By now even Watson has become fascinated, and Erwenter continues his flight of fancy by offering to take twenty-five years off every guest in the home. They all are for this, of course, but Mrs. Gross has a reservation: If it involves sin, she won't do it.

Watson wants some details of this plan, and Erwenter confides that he will begin by playing upon a silver whistle. "The old dog crawled away to die and hid amid the thistle. Then joy and youth came back to him on the note of a silver whistle," he quotes, as if from a poem. He rather horrifies the minister by talking of the Pipes of Pan, pagan madness in a moonlight mist, little men with jugs containing wondrous tiny beverages. . . .

But now it is supper time, and there won't be any tiny beverages. The inmates always are ready to eat, and they troop inside, leaving the Reverend brooding about his strange and somehow fascinating new guest.

The curtain falls.

Scene II

It is nine-thirty the same evening. A full moon shines down on the little garden. There is a touch of midsummer night's madness in the air. One looks about for Tweedledee and Tweedledum. Erwenter is sitting alone at the table. The rooster is on the chair to his right.

"Omar," Oliver reflects aloud, "as you follow me about, I will tell you various things about the world. You will become a wise bird and other birds will hold you in high esteem. Look about you. What do you see? Nothing but dingy squalor and hopelessness. No color, no laughter, no beauty. Bird, I tell you we are in the darkened lair of the living dead. . . ."

The soliloquy is interrupted by Miss Tripp's voice from offstage calling out that it's ten more minutes to bedtime and time to wash and say prayers.

Oliver turns back to apostrophizing the rooster. "Bird, believe me, I can halt this march toward death and bring these people back to life. You shrug. You are not interested. Then you are a foolish bird. However, you, my friend, shall have a better fate than dragging out your later years in misery. For a short time you will live well. You will become round and fat and jolly, and then . . . and then, you feathered bastard, I will eat you."

A snatch of whistling is heard, soft and from far off—the tune is "Annie Laurie." Oliver stiffens and turns toward the wall. The head and top part of the body of a man appear over the wall. The stranger is Emmett—a tramp. Although dressed in old clothes and a battered hat, Emmett gives off an aura of well-being, happiness and contentment. His position behind the wall makes him appear to be suspended in mid-air. The moonlight makes him seem unreal . . . even more so because he is calmly examining an egg.

An egg has no sides, Emmett decides, which he finds very reassuring. Every part of an egg is curved, and it's so nice to know that there's something one can depend on. Oliver greets him by name but Emmett continues in his own vein, this time remarking upon the fact that everybody knows how Dick Whittington felt about his cat, but did they ever stop to wonder how the cat felt?

Oliver wants to know what on earth Emmett is standing on. It's a ledge that runs along the wall. But you can't see it from the street because there are bushes in front of it.

How did Emmett find him? Oliver inquires. His friend's reply is that it was a nice bit Oliver gave the old people about Lao Chin Po. Oliver is disconcerted. So Emmett heard that, did he? Correct him, if he is wrong, Emmett goes on. But Oliver's name is not Oliver T. Erwenter. It is Wilfred Tasbinder and he was unkind enough to steal Emmett's rooster. Oliver denies this. He only borrowed Omar—borrowed him for a week or two.

Emmett shakes his head. "Wilfred, I'm afraid that you are something of a scoundrel."

Oliver protests, pointing out that nothing but good can come of his present situation. The rooster will be well fed. Its plumage will become sleek and glossy. It will regain its courage and confidence. One need not mention, Emmett concludes, the food that will find its way into Oliver's own tummy.

Oliver then confides that he found the birth certificate in an ash can, that the idea of being old before his time intrigued him, and that he's going to find out if there is any point in living to be seventy-seven.

"Frankly, Wilfred," Emmett speculates, "I find the situation fantastic. You are not even fifty and yet these people are willing to believe that you are seventy-seven years old. What are they going to think?"

"How are they going to find out?"

Through Emmett—unless Oliver supplies him with food to avoid exposure. "Blackmail?" "Blackmail."

Emmett doesn't think Oliver can help them a bit and says so. Oliver then confides that under a wild plum tree on the top of Sugar Loaf Hill he has a jug of elderberry wine hidden away. He offers to put up said jug against Emmett's rooster that he can do what he claims. Emmett accepts the wager and disappears from the wall at the sound of Mr. Beebe's voice calling for Oliver.

Mr. Beebe trots into the garden followed by Mr. Cherry. "My, my, my," Mr. Beebe chortles appreciatively, "isn't it a nice night." Indeed it is. It was on such a night as this, Oliver reminisces off-handedly, that he climbed the trellis outside Maude

THE SILVER WHISTLE

Adams' window. The statement has the desired effect and then some.

Mr. Cherry nudges Mr. Beebe and whispers to him to get on with their mission. What both old men are after is the potion of Twingsti. Does Oliver have any of it left . . . does he have any with him? No, he is out of it at the moment, but informs Beebe and Cherry that he sent to Tibet six weeks ago for a fresh supply.

The session is interrupted by the appearance of Miss Tripp who chides the two old gentlemen and orders them to bed. Oliver, she tells him when they are alone, is supposed to be in bed, too. But he never goes to bed until two or three in the morning, Oliver protests. What is he going to do in bed?

MISS TRIPP (*somewhat annoyed and tapping her foot*)—We stay up until twelve on Christmas and New Year's. The rest of the time we go to bed at nine-thirty.

ERWENTER—And you yourself go to bed at nine-thirty?

MISS TRIPP—It takes me a few minutes to lock up, but I'm in bed by ten.

ERWENTER—My God! How long have you been doing that?

MISS TRIPP—I've been here three years.

ERWENTER—And you've been in bed by ten o'clock every night? You can't expect me to go to bed at the same time these old fogies do.

MISS TRIPP—Mr. Erwenter, if you are old enough to be a guest here, you are old enough to go to bed.

ERWENTER—But I don't feel old. I'm alive. I'm full of life!

MISS TRIPP—I don't care what you're full of or how you got full of it. You're seventy-seven years old and you have to go to bed.

ERWENTER—This is terrible. (*Suddenly.*) Look, when was the last time you were kissed by a man?

MISS TRIPP—Mr. Erwenter, I don't think that's any of your business.

ERWENTER—Don't be afraid to tell me, my child. I'm an old, old man.

MISS TRIPP—Well, which is it? Do you stay up late because you're young or do you pry into my private life because you're an old, old man?

ERWENTER—The moonlight does something to your hair and eyes. You're very beautiful. Why are you hiding here? What are you running away from?

MISS TRIPP—Mr. Erwenter, I don't know you. I've never seen you before today. I have no intention of examining my motives with you.

ERWENTER—Can you stand there and tell me you'd just as soon go to bed at ten o'clock on a moonlit night?

MISS TRIPP (*sighing with annoyance*)—It's the only way I know of to get a good night's sleep.

ERWENTER—Sleep! Do you want to sleep your life away? You're hiding in this place sleeping your life away.

MISS TRIPP—I'm not hiding, and furthermore . . .

ERWENTER (*interrupting*)—You are hiding. Outside that wall life is going on. People are loving, hating, being born, dying, wounding, healing, killing, creating; and what are you doing? Spending your waking hours with old people and sleeping your nights away. Tell me, what makes you stay here?

MISS TRIPP (*shrugging her shoulders*)—The same things that keep most people in one spot.

ERWENTER—Habit, being in a rut, losing faith in yourself, depending on security . . . things like that.

MISS TRIPP (*deciding to talk and sitting down*)—No, there's more to it than that. Everybody wants to be needed. Each of us wants to feel important to someone. These people need me. They're like children; they depend on me, and, in a way, they love me.

Erwenter may be odd, but he is persuasive, the girl discovers. He urges her to live each moment from now on—and at this moment to allow him to take her hand while they look at the moon. "Keep looking," he urges . . . and something seems to be happening within her—a kind of closeness to the world. She feels so strange and wonderful . . .

He turns her to him, takes her in his arms and bends to kiss her. She breaks away and runs into the house.

The curtain falls.

ACT II

It is evening some time later and Emmett, who has had no lunch during the day, rebukes Oliver for his neglect.

"Were you so busy chasing that vapid Tripp wench that you forgot my lunch?"

"I will not hear Miss Tripp referred to in those terms."

"You forget, Wilfred, that your security depends on my good

THE SILVER WHISTLE

will. I warn you, do not tamper with my appetite. Where have you been?"

"Though it is none of your business," Oliver proceeds cavalierly, "I will tell you. I have been to the Post Office." He produces a small package, which, he explains he had to prepare himself.

"Did that take all day?"

"Since this package is presumed to have come from Tibet it was necessary for me to find a piece of paper with the proper canceled stamp on it. You forget that there is a philatelist in residence here."

Inside the package is the precious potion of Twingsti. But the contents do not impress Emmett as having been of sufficient importance for Oliver to have neglected his lunch in order to prepare an imaginary aphrodisiac. Oliver waves aside his protests announcing that he has some chores for Emmett to perform—simple tasks that will not tax his time or spirit. But Emmett is skeptical. Oliver has not acted like this since the time he offered to donate a live water buffalo to the Children's Museum . . . or the time he thought up a cure for baldness . . . or the Hopi Indian with the four brains . . . or the brassière with the little springs.

Furthermore, all of Oliver's fantastic schemes have caused nothing but trouble in the past. But Oliver is convinced he can really do something worth while for these old people. Miss Tripp is a lovely woman, he opines, and feels kindly toward the old souls, but doesn't understand their needs.

Which reminds Emmett that Oliver appears to be growing very fond of Miss Tripp and that so far in his life he has been engaged to five women and that it has been Emmett who extricated him from all five predicaments. Besides, Emmett concludes, he doesn't think the Reverend approves—he likes her himself.

Oliver dispenses with the Reverend as a monster, a creature who should have been born a machine for making buttons rather than a man. He has no soul, no understanding.

"Wilfred, let's not stay here any longer," Emmett implores. "Let's be on our way to see what's over the top of the next hill."

But Oliver ignores the entreaty, commencing to talk again about the chores . . . then changing his attitude suddenly as Reverend Watson appears at the door of the home.

ERWENTER—For the third and last time, your dog isn't in here. Kindly remove yourself from our wall. (EMMETT *disappears. To* WATSON.) He's looking for an old white dog he claims is supposed to be here.

WATSON—I'm very glad to find you alone, Mr. Erwenter. I've wanted to have a talk with you.

ERWENTER—An evening chat, Reverend. What could be more delightful?

WATSON—Mr. Erwenter, I have noticed an attachment growing between you and Miss Tripp.

ERWENTER—An attachment, Reverend?

WATSON—Let us say that she has become interested in you.

ERWENTER—We find each other attractive, Reverend.

WATSON—Miss Tripp is a very likeable young woman, Mr. Erwenter.

ERWENTER—I find the word "likeable" inadequate, Reverend. I would prefer "gorgeous." Miss Tripp is a gorgeous woman. A luscious creature.

WATSON—I see. I see. Miss Tripp has led a very sheltered life. Very sheltered.

ERWENTER—Too sheltered.

WATSON—Perhaps it may have been. But the fact remains that she has led a sheltered life.

ERWENTER—Sheltered and wasted. A waste of desirable womanhood.

WATSON—Since we both agree that she has been sheltered, I think we'll both agree that her judgment in matters of love may not be developed.

ERWENTER (*briskly*)—Then we should make every effort to develop it. We should find experiences for her.

WATSON—Mr. Erwenter, you are an older man. You have lived your life. It is not fair to this young woman to encourage her in her foolish infatuation.

ERWENTER—Foolish infatuation? And why is it foolish? If it brings her happiness, then it justifies itself.

WATSON—There can be no real happiness between an old man and a young woman.

ERWENTER—Oh, but if there were a younger man, such as yourself, it would be perfectly proper.

WATSON—She would have a better chance of finding happiness with a man nearer her own age. Yes.

ERWENTER—Reverend, you're jealous. You have the bug yourself.

WATSON—As long as I do not demonstrate them, my feelings for Miss Tripp are my own affair.

ERWENTER—Then you admit you care for her.

WATSON—I admit nothing. (*Annoyed.*) Mr. Erwenter, I did not join you to discuss my emotions. I'm here to discuss yours.

ERWENTER—I have nothing to conceal. I find Miss Tripp most attractive and desirable and luscious.

WATSON—So it would seem.

ERWENTER—And I feel quite capable of bringing love into her life.

WATSON—In spite of the fact that you are an old man.

ERWENTER—In spite of the fact that I am an old man.

WATSON—You refuse to discourage the girl?

ERWENTER—Of course I refuse to discourage her. Reverend, I'm afraid you're acting a bit stuffy; loosen up. Forget some of your codes. You're making life too grim.

WATSON—Thank you for your advice, Mr. Erwenter.

ERWENTER—Not at all, Reverend. Any time at all. (WATSON *goes.*)

Miss Tripp comes into the garden with Mr. Beebe, Mr. Cherry, Mrs. Hammer and Mrs. Sampler—all helping to carry a dining room table. The old people spot Erwenter and rush toward him, eager for news of what happened at the Post Office. Oliver waves them back to the table with "Later . . . later." It has been Oliver's idea for the old people to eat outdoors and he apprises them that during supper he will tell them of big things in store for each and every one. Anxious to find out, they troop willingly indoors to wash up at Miss Tripp's bidding.

When he is alone, Oliver whistles and Emmett appears on the wall. He tells Emmett that the chores he has in mind for him are the least they can do to repay these people for their kindness. But Emmett wants a more detailed explanation, which Oliver gives. To help these people, money is needed, and the way to get it is to hold a church social—a bazaar. The first thing that must be done is to make the bedraggled little garden look attractive—bright green grass, gaily colored flowers, perhaps a bird bath and a shiny croquet set. Once the proper setting is achieved, it will be simple to prepare a stand for lemonade and sandwiches to which Oliver's and Emmett's customers may turn when they tire of playing a game called Bingo.

But this is not all. Among his other activities of the day, Oliver managed to squeeze in reconnaissance of one sort or another. He has located a bird bath not far from the home, a promising flower bed and on the lawn of a neighboring hospital, a croquet set. Emmett is to fetch these and together they will work on the garden under cover of darkness.

Emmett suspects Oliver of going to all this trouble more for Miss Tripp's sake than for his advertised purpose of bringing joy to the old people. "You've fallen in love. Let me warn you that love holds hidden dangers. Love leads to marriage. Marriage leads to work. Work is living death. Think of it and be warned. Leave while you can still get away."

Oliver doesn't even deign acknowledgment of the advice. He instructs Emmett to go to the hospital to fetch the croquet set first. It's on the lawn. They are to meet later on. But Emmett wants his dinner first, otherwise, no croquet set. Oliver's promise that he will be fed later gets a dubious reception—but Emmett drops out of sight when Oliver warns that someone is coming. The "someone" is Mrs. Sampler and Mr. Beebe carrying a cloth and silver for the outdoor dining table.

BEEBE—We're going to set the table, Mr. Erwenter.

ERWENTER (*briskly*)—Then time is short. Dinner will be upon us. I must go and prepare myself for the feast.

BEEBE—Mr. Erwenter, did you go to the Post Office?

ERWENTER (*just before he goes off*)—I did. I have wonderful things to tell all of you as soon as we are gathered.

BEEBE (*as he and* MRS. SAMPLER *spread the cloth*)—Isn't Mr. Erwenter a wonderful man?

MRS. SAMPLER (*sighing*)—Just having him here has made so big a difference. He's so vibrant and alive.

BEEBE (*adjusting the cloth*)—I think it's the potion he takes.

MRS. SAMPLER (*as to a conspirator*)—Do you really think so, Mr. Beebe?

BEEBE (*leaning over the table*)—What else could it be?

MRS. SAMPLER (*leaning over the other side of the table*)—I don't know. Do you think . . . he takes it himself?

BEEBE (*shakes his head*)—He couldn't have, so far. He didn't have any.

MRS. SAMPLER (*edging around the table toward* BEEBE)—Oh. Do you think he brought it back with him?

BEEBE (*looking about quickly*)—He won't say so, but I think he did.

MRS. SAMPLER (*thrilled*)—Do you think he has it now?

BEEBE (*nodding*)—I think so, I'm not sure, but I think so.

MRS. SAMPLER (*simpering*)—I'd be afraid to try it. Wouldn't you?

THE SILVER WHISTLE

BEEBE (*standing up very straight*)—I'd try it. I wouldn't be afraid to try it.

MRS. SAMPLER (*pretending to be shocked*)—You wouldn't. You wouldn't dare.

BEEBE (*importantly*)—Yes, I would.

MRS. SAMPLER (*whispering*)—You would.

BEEBE (*waving the silver in his hand*)—I'd try it in a second.

MRS. SAMPLER (*eyeing him*)—It might change you completely. (*Archly.*) You'd chase after young girls and forget all about us old people.

BEEBE (*surprised*)—Why, I wouldn't at all! I'd chase right after you, Mrs. Sampler.

MRS. SAMPLER (*putting hands to cheek*)—Mr. Beebe!

BEEBE (*stoutly*)—That's just what I'd do. I'd chase right after you, Mrs. Sampler.

MRS. SAMPLER (*with mock fear*)—Mr. Beebe, I'll be frightened to death if you take the potion. I won't feel safe. (MRS. HANMER *enters the garden. She surveys the table,* MR. BEEBE *and* MRS. SAMPLER, *then sniffs.*)

MRS. HANMER—Are you frozen in that position? Are you staring into the deep blue wells of her eyes, Mr. Beebe? Isn't it cozy?

Miss Hoadley staggers into the garden much the worse for alcoholic wear. "Where's the party? . . . Where's the party? Goin' to a party—wheeee!" Miss Hoadley then announces drinks for the house—on her. Mr. Beebe grabs her by the arm and shouts into her ear, asking her where her whiskey is so he can fetch it for her to pass around. Miss Hoadley screams, "Thief! Murderer!" as Miss Tripp comes dashing in with her arms full of cups and saucers. "What happened?" Mr. Beebe explains that he just asked Miss Hoadley where she kept her bottle of whiskey. Miss Tripp pats the drunken woman's shoulder. "It's all right, Miss Hoadley," she comforts, "nobody will touch your whiskey." Miss Hoadley subsides. "Drinks on the house," she smiles again. Mr. Beebe is all for taking her up on the offer somehow, but Miss Tripp discourages the notion. Miss Hoadley is a handful by herself without all the rest of the guests getting drunk.

Mr. Cherry enters pushing Mrs. Gross in her wheel chair. Miss Tripp leaves instruction for them all to fix the table while she goes in for a surprise she has ready for them. Mrs. Sampler casts about for Mr. Erwenter. They can't start supper without Oliver, who appears at the window, his face lathered for shaving and a wet shaving brush in his hand.

"Is the feast of Apollo ready? Are the lute players, handmaidens and dancing girls prepared? Does the wine of Bacchus flow for the bacchanale?"

"It's only stew, Mr. Erwenter," Mr. Cherry discloses. "You'll have to pretend the rest."

"Why, Mr. Cherry, use your imagination . . . Look . . . ice cream . . ." and Oliver pretends to lick the shaving brush as one would a cone.

Miss Tripp returns carrying a cake. Mrs. Sampler points to the cake. "She has a shortcake!"

And a strawberry shortcake at that . . . something the old people haven't had in months. Only Oliver is missing from the table. When he appears, he is nominated guest of honor by Miss Tripp, who now addresses him by his given name, and he, her, as "darling," the scandalous possibilities of which are not lost on Mrs. Hanmer.

Standing before the gathering, Oliver says that while they eat, he would like to tell them of his plan. He thinks all will agree that Miss Hoadley ought to have a new hearing aid—with batteries; that Mr. Cherry should have new stamps; that Mrs. Sampler should have flowers that grow; Mrs. Hanmer, an operation and that Mrs. Gross should have her mind adjusted. Mr. Beebe inquires if there is any provision in the plan for him. Yes, Oliver replies, but they'll discuss it later, in private. Mr. Beebe understands.

Then Oliver proposes the bazaar as a means of raising money by their own efforts. Immediate consternation results. Neither Miss Tripp nor any of the others think the Reverend Watson would allow such a thing.

Erwenter then leads the group in a spirited rendition of "Little Brown Jug," which ceases abruptly with the appearance of Reverend Watson in the doorway. To Watson, the whole outdoor dining business is an unseemly demonstration and he orders the table carried inside immediately. He asks Miss Tripp, however, to remain behind. Oliver offers to stay with her, but she declines the offer, and he leaves with the rest.

"Why did you make those people take that table in?" she asks the Reverend.

"I lost my temper. I'm sorry I was so disagreeable. Tell them that they can bring it back out."

"It's too late now."

What he wanted to see her about, Watson explains, was Erwenter, who seems to be an upsetting influence on the guests. "Just the guests?" Miss Tripp thrusts. Who else could he upset, Watson wants to know—and Miss Tripp tells him. The Reverend denies having any personal objection to Oliver Erwenter. He simply wants to know if Mr. Erwenter is aware of the fact that he and Miss Tripp are engaged.

"How could he? There is no ring on my finger—no date set—and the last time you told me you loved me was four months ago."

"People who are in love don't have to keep proving it to each other," Watson counters defensively.

"What are they supposed to do? Keep it bottled up inside them?"

The Reverend stomps off as the soft whistle of "Annie Laurie" filters through the dusk and Emmett appears over the wall. Peering about the garden, he fails to perceive Miss Tripp standing in the shadow of the tree. After satsifying himself that the garden is empty he produces a number of croquet mallets and balls, sits on the wall and starts throwing the mallets down, one by one. Miss Tripp steps forward into the moonlight and demands what Emmett is doing. Oliver makes the same demand when he strolls in with his rooster.

EMMETT—It depends on the point of view. To the wall I am a burden. To the lawn I represent a striking force. To the croquet balls I am momentum. To the owner of this place I am a messenger.

ERWENTER—A messenger? This is very unconventional, sir. Please explain your actions.

EMMETT—Catch. (*He throws a ball to* ERWENTER.) No doubt you've heard of Wilfred Tasbinder, the philanthropist?

ERWENTER (*nodding*)—A name well known to all.

EMMETT (*throwing another ball*)—You are then familiar with his secret charities.

ERWENTER—Of course. Who hasn't heard?

EMMETT—Then I must tell you that I am one of his agents.

MISS TRIPP (*utterly confused*)—A philanthropist? What did you say his name was?

EMMETT (*swiveling and standing on the ledge facing them*)—Both at once. (*He throws two balls at once—one to* ERWENTER, *the other to* MISS TRIPP, *then disappears.*)

MISS TRIPP—What did he say the man's name was?

ERWENTER—Wilfred Tasbinder. He's mad as a hatter . . . gives things away.

MISS TRIPP—It's crazy, but it's wonderful.

ERWENTER—My dear, it's a stroke of good fortune that has come in the nick of time. We can use a croquet set. For that matter we can use almost anything.

MISS TRIPP—They're new and strong. And they're ours. Think of it.

ERWENTER—He may leave more things during the night.

MISS TRIPP (*sitting*)—It's just as if they dropped out of the air.

ERWENTER (*coming behind her*)—They came from the other side of the wall. That's where things happen—where life is lived instead of wasted. There's more to the world than odds and ends that dribble over walls.

MISS TRIPP—Perhaps I've waited too long.

ERWENTER—The more the palate dries, the more it tingles when it touches wine. Listen . . . I can show you where a golden cockatoo sits in a little crooked tree . . . where green and copper fishes lunge through a cobalt pool . . . where a shaft of saffron yellow sunlight illuminates a single blood-red rose . . . to strange enchanted places where mystic things can happen to the soul . . . and I can give you love.

MISS TRIPP—Perhaps I don't know any more about love than I do about the world.

ERWENTER—I can show you a love that has no limits to its ecstasy. . . . I can give you a love that does not fear its own awakening.

MISS TRIPP (*starting*)—Oliver, please . . . Oliver, there's somebody at that window!

Indeed there is; none other than the Reverend Watson, and he is in a righteous fury. Miss Tripp must have lost her reason, listening to a man like this, whose intentions are carnal. And as for the man—might not the Reverend point out to him that the Reverend and Miss Tripp are engaged?

Watson withdraws from the window and closes it, while Erwenter disbelievingly pursues this report of an engagement. Well, she falters, it is an understanding, and some day Watson will put a ring on her finger.

"If you want a ring, I'll give it to you now." Oliver produces a cigar band.

"But, Oliver, how can I know my mind on such sudden notice?"

The tryst is interrupted by the appearance of Mr. Beebe and

THE SILVER WHISTLE

Mr. Cherry. Miss Tripp whispers that she will come to Oliver later, and withdraws.

Miss Tripp looked, Mr. Beebe observes, as if she were carrying a croquet mallet. What's more, Mr. Cherry elaborates, she also looked as if she didn't know she was carrying it. They drop the subject of Miss Tripp simultaneously to attend to the business at hand—the potion of Twingsti—and whether or not it has come. It has, and Oliver produces a small package. Mr. Cherry peers at the stamp and pronounces it in excellent condition; the perforations aren't torn at all, as they sometimes are. Mr. Beebe notes that the package is addressed to Mr. Erwenter in English. Oliver explains that someone must have addressed it for Lao Chin Po, this not being his friend's writing. Mr. Cherry inquires about the Tibetan stamp and Oliver presents it to him for his collection. Just as the men are about to split the potion three ways, Mr. Beebe cautions them to put it away—that Miss Hoadley is coming. Quick, out the garden door, Oliver instructs—he has a reason for wanting to hide.

Oliver peers over the wall while Miss Hoadley comes into the garden and heads for the tree. She looks about then reaches up into the tree and pulls out a bottle, and takes a nip. Wiping her mouth, she puts the bottle back and leaves the garden. Oliver goes to the hiding place, brings forth the bottle and notes that "by the shortest of kilts it turns out to be Scotch," as Mr. Cherry and Mr. Beebe gather 'round.

Oliver takes the first swig while Mr. Beebe asks him to open the package. Whiskey and the potion of Twingsti—the boys are really in for a wild night. The bottle and the open box containing pellets are passed from hand to hand. They may look like rolled-up bread crumbs, but in reality, they are pellets of passion, Oliver assures the two elderly men.

Mr. Beebe and Mr. Cherry each sample a pellet. But they don't have any instantaneous reaction. Have patience, Oliver counsels. The potion, after all, is up against enormous odds. The bottle and pellets are passed rapidly back and forth between the two old men and Oliver until all of a sudden Mr. Beebe is seized with a desire to yell dirty words . . . for the fun of it.

Mr. Cherry agrees. Standing beneath the church window, Mr. Beebe shouts: "Hell!" "Think of a worse one," Oliver encourages him. Returning to the window, Mr. Beebe shouts even louder: "Hell and damnation!" He retires from this feat very pleased with himself. Give it a real bad one, Oliver suggests. He'll make this one good and loud, Mr. Beebe promises, and shouts: "Damn it to hell."

The window opens suddenly and Reverend Watson appears. Both Mr. Beebe and Mr. Cherry jump as if they had been shot. The minister orders them to bed. They exit running while Erwenter stays where he is. The Reverend appears at the door and addresses Oliver from the threshold. His grandfather, Watson informs him, built this church. Two of his uncles have been pastors here. He and his predecessors have tried to set up standards their parishioners might be guided by. He, Watson, does not pretend that their way of life is absolute—or even the only correct approach to living—but it is theirs and by their standards, what Oliver has just done was anything but proper. He will have more to say in the morning and he goes out.

Oliver soliloquizes that to some his action might appear a low and cunning trick without a purpose—but there is more to come, and when all the pieces are in place, its value will be seen. His monologue is interrupted by the appearance of Miss Tripp in the window above him.

Miss Tripp—Oliver.
Erwenter—You've come at last. The Capulets are tucked away, the Montagues aslumber while two lovers woo in a clandestine covenant I tremble with the fear that you are but a lovely apparition and I a creaking ancient who dreams while he's awake. Come, we'll find a rendezvous, for love's embarrassed when two lovers are apart, and I can no longer wait to take you in my arms.
Miss Tripp (*shaking her head*)—I'm still afraid of silly things that women think of. Of what is sure, of what is safe.
Erwenter—I ask a question and beg an answer from your lips red wine incarnadine against the snow. I ask for the three small words that spin the universe.
Miss Tripp (*smiling*)—Most women prefer to have their lovers say it first.
Erwenter—Then I say at once I love you and damn myself for having tarried. The world is full of women of all shapes and sizes who have love to peddle for security, but none have I ever seen to move me until now. I only ask of you to whisper once you love me.
Miss Tripp—It seems a bold thing to say: I love you, Oliver.

And now, the young woman points out, it is time to be practical. How are they going to live? Oliver will have to find work of some sort.

THE SILVER WHISTLE

He reassures her—just leave it to him.

And they will have to have a home, because there might be more than two of them sometime.

A loud call from Mrs. Gross for Miss Tripp brings an end to this colloquy. Alone again, Erwenter muses, "Babies! What does society expect of a seventy-seven-year-old man?"

The curtain falls.

ACT III

It is morning and the garden looks entirely different. Many kinds of flowers have been set into beds along the wall. A small cedar tree with a wheel of chance nailed to it has been planted in the corner. There is a bird bath in the center, and the croquet set has been installed to the left.

It is a complete surprise to the old people, who flock at Mr. Beebe's bidding to view the metamorphosis. They can hardly believe their eyes. Nobody can figure out how it happened, or who was responsible. Mrs. Hanmer hazards a guess that the credit is due one Oliver T. Erwenter. Mrs. Gross claims that God did it.

The seeming miracle of the garden imbues the old men and women with a glorious sense of well-being. Mr. Beebe, who made the fabulous discovery, cries out that they're all getting younger . . . getting younger by the minute. He nudges Cherry to ask if he doesn't feel it, too . . . which he does. Beebe rhapsodizes that he feels alive from his head to his toes—as wild as a tiger cub —like a whippersnapper. His exhilaration prevents him from keeping his mind on a game of croquet with Mr. Cherry. He's going to start courting Mrs. Sampler this morning. He invites Cherry to court her, too, and make it a triangle.

To Mrs. Gross, it's all proof that when you cast out sin, the angels can get at a place to fix it up. It's decency does this sort of thing to a place—cleans it up and makes it shine.

Mrs. Hanmer tugs at Miss Hoadley's sleeve and draws her aside to inquire if anybody tried to "get at her" last night. Miss Hoadley is slow to understand. Mrs. Hanmer wants to know if anybody—a man—tried to get into Miss Hoadley's room last night. The answer is a mystified no. Well, somebody tried to get at Mrs. Hanmer, all right—rattled the door handle, and all. Miss Hoadley is properly awed.

The little conference is interrupted by the appearance of Mrs. Sampler on the newly landscaped scene. "It's a fairyland!" she gushes. "Oh, lovely, lovely fairyland!" And it isn't long before

Mr. Beebe lets fall his croquet mallet to gaze reverently at the sight of Mrs. Sampler among the flowers. Just to look at her, he declares, is like looking at a picture painted by a painter. Mrs. Sampler preens herself archly, carrying on a coy back-and-forth exchange with Mr. Beebe, until he rushes over and embraces her—to the astonishment of Reverend Watson, who has just entered the garden.

Mr. Beebe explains hastily that they weren't doing anything, but the minister's attention is focused on the garden. "What's happened? Who put those flowers there? Where did this croquet set come from?"

Mr. Cherry answers that nobody knows—that everything was here when they came out of the house this morning.

Reverend Watson allows that it's all very nice, but he'd feel a lot better if he knew where it all came from. He then scrutinizes his elderly charges, remarking that they all seem different today.

"The damn fools all think they're young," Mrs. Hanmer scoffs.

But Reverend Watson has to admit that they all look younger —much younger.

Mr. Cherry announces that they all feel better too, thanks to Mr. Erwenter.

The minister wonders if, perhaps, he's been wrong about Erwenter. "What's that wheel for?" He points at the cedar tree. "That round thing with the numbers?"

Mrs. Gross volunteers the information that it is for the bazaar. Reverend Watson doesn't take her seriously. "Mrs. Gross is fooling, of course," he addresses the company at large.

But no, Mrs. Gross is not fooling, he learns, and there isn't much he can do about it at this late date. Posters advertising the bazaar are up all over the city . . . without permission. The posters tell the location and time of the bazaar—which is in the garden of the Church of John—today—and promise the public Bingo.

Reverend Watson is stricken. They don't realize what they have done. Neither he nor they can hold a bazaar or anything like a bazaar without permission from the Bishop. But the bazaar simply *must* go on, the old people plead. Miss Hoadley has made cookies . . . Mrs. Sampler, marmalade . . . Mrs. Hanmer baked bread . . . and the Messrs. Cherry and Beebe worked very hard making the booths.

Reverend Watson is moved, but doesn't see any way out. The old people accede graciously to the ultimatum, too graciously.

THE SILVER WHISTLE 293

The minister as a further apology adds that if he personally could get permission from the Bishop, he'd do it. But the old folk tell him never to mind . . . that they understand. Whereupon Reverend Watson is so moved that he decides to take the bull by the horns. The bazaar will go on as scheduled. He doesn't know how he's going to talk the Bishop into it, but he'll certainly try.

All the early morning's exhilaration is quickly restored and the old people troop off happily. They are gone by the time Oliver enters the garden, carrying Omar's cage in one hand and a box in the other, leaving him to face the Reverend Watson alone.

The minister asks where the flowers and croquet set came from, and Oliver asks in return why he wants to know. Watson explains that he's been wrong about Oliver and wants to make amends now by helping him all he can with the bazaar—but although it is Oliver who has given the home's guests a new lease on life, Watson is still running the church and the home and wants to know where all the stuff came from.

"You must realize, Mr. Erwenter, that I will have to explain this to the Bishop."

In that case, Mr. Watson need not worry. Oliver and the Bishop are close, warm friends. He'll run over to see him and get his consent over a glass of his tawny port and a pair of his big cigars. Mr. Watson informs Oliver that the Bishop is on his way over to the home right now to examine the records, but that when he arrives, he, Watson, will do the talking.

The Reverend's departure cues the appearance of Emmett on the wall. Emmett is sick and tired of the whole business. "Fill your pockets with food for us and grain for the bird," he adjures his friend, "and let's be on our way."

But Oliver cannot go . . . he has a moral commitment he must abide by. He has to stay three days longer. The moral commitment is the Church of John bazaar, today, tomorrow and the next day.

Emmett is incredulous. "You're not going ahead with it?"

ERWENTER—Emmett, I am not the same man who came here two days ago.
EMMETT—Then who are you?
ERWENTER—I have just discovered that bringing happiness to these old people gives one a feeling of rich reward. When I came here, a bed and board was all I needed. Three square meals

and a downy bed was the extent of my desires. Then I saw them grow young before my eyes and something happened to me. I felt the warm glow of satisfaction. I tell you, Emmett, I have grown very fond of these old people."

EMMETT—It's worse than I thought. Wilfred, you're going to find yourself in a Salvation Army uniform holding a tambourine.

ERWENTER—I have even more news. . . . I have made a splendid deal with the rooster man.

EMMETT—You've been diddled by . . . what rooster man?

ERWENTER—There is only one rooster man. The dean of fighting bird breeders hereabouts. He is justly famous.

EMMETT—What has he got to do with all this?

ERWENTER—I have induced him to enter his rooster against my rooster as a feature attraction for the male guests at the bazaar. To adopt the nomenclature of the gaming cognoscenti, we will have a cockfight.

EMMETT—A cockfight? You can't have a cockfight at a church bazaar.

ERWENTER—Nonsense, it's the very thing you need at a church bazaar.

EMMETT—In case it's slipped your mind, that rooster belongs to me.

ERWENTER—Have you forgotten your wager? The jug of wine against the rooster. The bird is almost mine. Today it will be mine if I fulfill my promise and make these people laugh and sing and dance.

EMMETT—Wilfred, you are now only one jump ahead of the man from the happy house. You'll be holding hands with yourself in a strait-jacket. Are you going to stay here the rest of your life taking care of these old people?

ERWENTER—Of course not. Once the bazaar is over the three of us will take the bird and be on our way.

EMMETT—Did you say the three of us?

ERWENTER—Miss Tripp is the third. I forgot to tell you: I'm engaged.

In Emmett's opinion, Wilfred has lost his mind again. He can't support anybody. If he marries her, he'll have to go to work. Why not seduce her and be done with it?

Miss Tripp, Oliver makes very clear, is no common wench to tickle in the hay. She is the most wonderful woman he's ever met; her heart is lovelier than all other women's beauty.

THE SILVER WHISTLE 295

Emmett tries to point out that Oliver has bought the bill of goods he tried to sell these people. He's let his emotions take over while his mind has snapped the switch. He simply can't marry Miss Tripp.

Oliver doesn't see why not. Is marriage for a tramp outlawed? What's wrong with a Mrs. Hobo to smooth the wrinkles in her husband's coat, sew his buttons, patch his pants and fix him a stew? A hobo's wife, in fact, would be better at begging, better at stealing and better able to induce the world to furnish transportation for her husband.

Emmett threatens to turn Oliver in for stealing if he doesn't listen to reason. Far better for his friend to spend a short time in jail than be a prisoner to a woman for life.

Oliver calls Emmett's bluff. "A married tramp would have more stability and poise," he maintains. "He would be surer of himself and better able to resist the temptations of responsibility. And it would be splendid for the woman. She would avoid the weary years of washing pots and pans. No mops and pails, no scrubboard in a tub for her. No babies to . . . Ah, there's the catch."

And so it is. As all pitchmen know, there has to be a catch. In this case it's the little tot in pointed pants. Ah, well, Oliver sighs resignedly, another dream exploded into stardust.

The old people re-enter the garden carrying frames for booths, colored streamers, signs, banners and bunting—all fixings for the bazaar. Oliver signals to them to start, directing them in their tasks. He is in the midst of this when the Bishop enters the garden unnoticed and overhears Oliver's instructions to his group in the dubious professional ethics of making change.

The Bishop is a big, heavy, stern-looking man. He listens in until Oliver sees him and breaks off his spiel, then demands, "What are all these gaudy drapes doing in this churchyard?"

"It's a bazaar, Bishop," says Mr. Cherry.

"Is Reverend Watson here?"

"He's in his study, Bishop. I think he's expecting you," Erwenter volunteers.

"Would you ask him to step out here, please?"

The Bishop begins to fume as he examines the gaudy paraphernalia of the bazaar, and when Watson appears he demands who put this nightmare up.

"I had it put up, Bishop." On his own responsibility, Watson continues. Something had to be done for the guests and he is sorry he didn't do it sooner. "It might do a great deal of good.

They ask little of the world. Some little thing to hope for, some reason they can tell themselves for still being alive."

It is a fine, inspired statement, but the Bishop is stern and unmoved. "We're dispensing charity, not metaphysics."

Reverend Watson now is fighting for the cause—a cause which was brought to them by this man Erwenter here.

"Bishop," says Erwenter, "you have forgotten how much fun can be had at silly games." He produces three shells and a pea and challenges the Bishop to accept a demonstration. "A nickel will pay you five to one, if you name the shell the pea is under."

The Bishop allows he is a fair-minded man, and puts up a nickel. Erwenter manipulates the shells—and, of course, the Bishop wins. A second time, and Erwenter lets him win again. The Bishop now is excited about the game, but he doesn't see how anybody is going to make money for the home this way.

"Not everyone has as quick an eye as you have," Erwenter smoothly says. "The odds are with the house."

"Make sure you win."

"Then we can have the bazaar?" Watson asks.

"You can have it."

The Bishop goes off with Reverend Watson to examine the books. The old people cluster around Oliver congratulating him on his skill in winning a reprieve for the bazaar. Miss Tripp comes in with bread, cheese, ham, hot dogs, hamburgers and prizes. She tells Oliver that the garden looks wonderful, that everything seems to be happening at once—the garden's been changed, the bazaar and their engagement.

No, she hasn't told Reverend Watson yet that she's broken her engagement to him, but right now, all that's important is for Oliver and herself to plan their lives. Oliver disapproves. But Miss Tripp wants a home. She doesn't want to wander all over the world sleeping in the open or hanging from a cliff or staring tigers in the eye. There's more to life, she feels, than that, and realizes that it was because Oliver had offered her beauty and escape that she fell a little bit in love with him the night before. But things seem different now.

Oliver understands. She is in love with her minister, was last night and is now. She was smitten last night by the words he spoke—not by the man. But that's all right because Oliver has changed his mind about the Reverend Watson. He's apparently quite a man beneath that chilly armor. Just a little while ago, he tells her, Watson took a stand against the Bishop and pumped for the bazaar.

"He did!" Miss Tripp is thrilled.

Not only that, Oliver goes on, he also admitted Oliver was right and he was wrong about finding youth and happiness for these old people.

Watson steps out on the threshold of the Church door and asks to speak to Harriet. Erwenter excuses himself. Miss Tripp confesses to the minister, before he can interrupt her, that she had agreed to marry Oliver last night—that she had accepted a paper cigar band ring which had subsequently got wet and come off.

The Reverend tenders his best wishes, remarking that he thinks the whole thing is incredible, particularly on the grounds of the difference in age.

Mr. Watson points out that he has emotions, too.

"But you're afraid to show them," wails Miss Tripp. "You're even afraid to tell me that you love me."

"That's absurd. I love you and I'm not afraid to tell you."

"Then say it."

"I love you." (*Hard.*) "I love you." (*Soft.*)

"More."

"I love you."

"More."

"I love you more than all the Erwenters in the world could ever love you."

"Lots more."

"If you want to stay up all night and look at the moon, I'll stay up with you. If you want to look at fishes in a pool I'll look at them with you. If you want to get married, I'll marry you right now. If you—"

"That's enough," Miss Tripp announces, and he kisses her as the old people come on and watch.

Their joy is short-lived. Emmett appears on the wall bearing ill tidings, tidings of peril about to come screaming down on the little garden. Emmett reveals that Oliver T. Erwenter is an impostor—that his right name is Wilfred Tasbinder.

"The philanthropist?" Miss Tripp inquires.

Wilfred is not a philanthropist, Emmett enlightens her. He is nothing unless being a liar counts for something. Wilfred, it seems, doesn't work, having retired from the competitive struggle for existence at the age of thirty-four. Wilfred has no job or income, nor any place to lay his head. Wilfred is very close to being a tramp.

The old people rally to Oliver Erwenter's defense, their faith being shaken only after Emmett tells about the birth certificate in the ash can and the rolled-up bread crumb pellets of Twingsti. What's more, Mr. Tasbinder never has set foot outside the country!

Miss Tripp senses the impact of the blow upon the elderly folk. "Please don't feel bad," she implores. "Remember what Mr. Erwenter said. Remember how happy you were."

But Emmett isn't through yet. All the bazaar properties are stolen goods, he beams. The croquet set and flowers came from St. Vincent's Hospital . . . a Catholic hospital! . . . the bird bath belongs in front of the Yale Club (Wilfred didn't think it looked well there) . . . the cedar tree is from the Greenlawn Funeral Home.

She had known Erwenter was a fake the moment she laid eyes on him, Mrs. Hanmer rejoices at the expense of her stricken circle. She had told them all that he was crooked, he and his potion!

Oliver comes into the garden with his bird cage and box. "The bazaar has opened," he announces. "Please forgive me for being late." He quickly learns the reason for the downcast faces and hurt expressions. To the old people, he makes a last stand:

"So perhaps I did tell you a few lies. You're not going to let that get you down, are you? I showed you a way of life—they can't take that away from you. After all I've done for you, are you going to turn against me?"

"You made us get all tired out," Mr. Beebe whimpers.

Emmett suggests that he and Oliver get out as fast as possible.

"Go ahead," Mrs. Hanmer sniffs. "You're just a nut. Nobody wants you here anyway." She starts to cry. "Nobody likes you any more."

Have they all forgotten how they felt last night and this morning? Oliver pleads. It was wonderful while it lasted, they admit, but they don't feel that way now. To Cherry this sounds as if Oliver were just saying that a person is as old as he feels. Of course that's what he's telling them, Oliver explains impatiently, but he's also telling them what to do about it—how to feel young, not old. And if he's "just a tramp"—well, so were Walt Whitman, Omar Khayyam and François Villon, for they, too, found the magic that men had long forgotten—the haunting thrill of Nature's beauty and the enchantment of the world. "I say that be we nine or ninety, these wonders should be ours."

Erwenter's great eloquence is removing some of the doubt

that has grown among his erstwhile friends, but it is halted by Emmett's warning that the constabulary is at hand. A priest, an undertaker and a secretary of the Yale Club march in through the wall door to reclaim their stolen properties, accompanied by an officer.

Once again Reverend Watson takes the rap. The man who did the stealing is not to be blamed, he argues, for he saw what these people needed and got it for them. It is Watson, who would not give them these things, who is to blame—and he will pay whatever debt the thief owes to society.

Miss Tripp is thrilled beyond words. Erwenter speaks up and confesses to the thefts and the constable is about to haul him away when one more strange and wonderful scene develops. It begins when Mr. Beebe asks Mr. Reddy, the undertaker, "Do you mean that because a little cedar tree is here instead of somewhere else, Mr. Erwenter has to go to jail?"

Mrs. Hanmer demands of the Yale Club man how old the bird bath is and how much it cost originally. It is fourteen years old and it cost $15. Mrs. Hanmer reasons that it should be worth about $1 now—and for this and merely transplanting a tree must Erwenter go to jail?

Mrs. Sampler asks the priest what he has lost and he replies, "If what I have seen here today is true, then I have gained instead of lost. Reverend, if a few flowers and a croquet set can bring happiness to your people, then you are welcome to them."

The Yale secretary, not to be outdone but still grudging, says they can keep the bird bath for at least a couple of days until he can find out if he has the authority to give it to them. The undertaker declares, "I'd like to give you the tree. As Father Shay said, if the tree makes anyone happy—well, it's all right with me."

The strangers and the officer depart, and the guests of the home turn excitedly toward Erwenter. "You see," he smiles at them, "you forgot about being old."

BEEBE—I feel all right.

CHERRY—I confess I am starting to feel younger.

MRS. HANMER—Let's go to work on the bazaar. What are we waiting for?

CHERRY—Everybody get busy. We've got work to do.

MRS. HANMER—No use being young if you're broke. Now get every nickel you can.

ERWENTER (*turning to* EMMETT)—Well, Emmett, the time has come for us to boot the stirrup. We must away to start work on the middle-aged. (*Takes* OMAR *from* BEEBE.)

MRS. SAMPLER—Mr. Erwenter, we'll miss you.

ERWENTER—No, you won't. From now on you'll be too full of mischief to think of me.

BISHOP (*comes on as* ERWENTER *is about to leave*)—Here! Where are you going—are you leaving us?

ERWENTER—I came here to find out if there is any point in living to be seventy-seven. I have learned that a ripe old age is well worth while . . . so, having learned, I'm leaving.

MRS. HANMER—Where are you going now?

ERWENTER—Under wild plum tree on the top of Sugar Loaf Hill, I have a jug of elderberry wine secreted. I will relax beneath that tree and tope the grape while mine eyes and nose regard a bed of coals and a brown and tender bird upon a spit. Omar, your days are numbered. Good-by, and God bless you.

BEEBE—God bless you, too, Mr. Erwenter. (ERWENTER *kisses* MRS. SAMPLER *and* MISS HOADLEY, *starts to kiss* MISS TRIPP *and is intercepted by a handshake from* WATSON. *He laughs and turns to leave.*)

THE CURTAIN FALLS

TWO BLIND MICE *

A Comedy in Three Acts

By Samuel Spewack

SAMUEL SPEWACK, an old hand at reporting, play writing and scenario writing, was the only author who had two hits on Broadway last season. With his wife, Bella, he did the libretto for Cole Porter's songs in "Kiss Me, Kate," and on his own he wrote a comedy about Washington, "Two Blind Mice." As has many a dramatist Spewack began as a newspaperman, so it is not surprising that a newspaperman is the focal character in his most recent comedy. The theme of his play might have been taken from the words of the former Supreme Court Justice, James F. Byrnes—"The nearest approach to immortality on earth is a government bureau."

The setting is what once was the drawing room of what once was a mansion in Georgetown, near Washington, D. C. Now, pretty obviously, the place has been taken over by the Government, for the room has two typewriters and filing cases in it. The place breathes age, but not mustiness, and it has dignity; the same may be said of its occupants, Mrs. Letitia Turnbull and Miss Crystal Hower. These ladies are in their middle fifties and they have been in government service for many years. Crystal, the spinster, is a little more timid and gentle than her widowed colleague. At the moment, Crystal is typing while Letitia dictates as she strolls.

"The Office of Seeds and Standards," Letitia recites, "formerly known as the Office of Medicinal Herbs, is always willing to be of service. We are happy to have accommodated you. I particularly appreciate your tribute to the founder of the office, my late husband."

The ring of the telephone seems to disturb the women unduly.

* Copyright, 1949, by Samuel Spewack.
Dramatic Composition, copyright, 1948, by Samuel Spewack.
Dramatists Play Service, Inc., 14 East 38th Street, New York City 16, is the exclusive publisher of the entire play. It also has the exclusive right to authorize nonprofessional productions.
Author's agent, Monica McCall, 457 Madison Avenue, New York City.

"No one's telephoned this office in four and a half years," says Letitia. Crystal suggests that it might be answered, but Letitia is against this. It will stop ringing eventually—and it does stop eventually. To Crystal this has been an event, and she burbles "It's rather exciting, isn't it?" It is almost as exciting as the dream she had last night, in which she and Letitia were being defended in court by Letitia's late husband, who pleaded, "Don't send them to prison."

There is another series of rings on the telephone and Crystal practically insists that it be answered—so Letitia uncradles the instrument, sharply demands, "What is the meaning of this unseemly disturbance?" . . . and hangs up.

Mr. Murray, an exceedingly shy man, enters the office. "You've come for your rumba lesson, haven't you?" Letitia queries. She presses a button and in a moment Miss Johnson, a young woman with a good figure, appears from one of the inner government sanctums and leads the suffering Mr. Murray off for his lesson.

A mailman arrives, bringing a packet of letters and two other envelopes which he has held separately because he knows what they are—the monthly good news, the pay, from the U. S. Treasury. When he has gone, the ladies engage in a stealthy ritual commencing with the locking of all doors and windows and the transfer of a brass bowl from a stand near the fireplace to their desk. Letitia then reads out the serial numbers of the checks to Crystal, who records them in a small ledger. When this is done, Letitia holds the checks over the brass bowl while Crystal strikes a match, dropping them into the bowl when they start to burn.

Crystal wonders if it isn't about time they consulted someone— someone they could trust, like Letitia's niece, Karen, who is coming to the office this very afternoon. "But what are we going to do?" she wails when Letitia is against involving Karen in the situation.

A knock is heard on one of the doors and the ladies bestir themselves to unlock the other doors and the windows, hastening back to their seats before asking the visitor to come in. This turns out to be Tommy Thurston who enters with hat in one hand and a bouquet of roses in the other. Neither of the ladies recognizes him and are noticeably cool in their acknowledgment of his presence.

"Is this the Office of Seeds and Standards?" the stranger inquires.

Letitia says that it is and Crystal adds that it is also known as the Office of Medicinal Herbs.

"You're Crystal, of course," the stranger identifies the astonished woman. "And *you're* Aunt Lettie." Five years ago, he reminds them, they sent him a wedding present all the way to London—a waffle iron.

The women recall this, realizing that the visitor is the divorced husband of Letitia's niece, Karen. Being such a poor letter writer, Thurston explains, as most newspapermen are, he's come to thank them in person. Will they forgive him? To Crystal, who melts immediately, he gives the bouquet which she arranges in an herb jar on her desk. Letitia, however, remains aloof.

"By the way," Thurston asks about Karen, "when's she coming?" He gets no specific reply but he knows that she *is* coming because he called her office . . . State Department . . . Information, New York.

"Did you really drink so much?" Crystal wants to know.

"I've been on the wagon for fourteen months."

"Isn't that nice!" Crystal beams. Karen, it seems, had never sent them a snapshot of her husband because he never stood still long enough.

"I've changed," Thurston announces soberly. "I'm cautious—careful. I no longer act on impulses. Judicial, you might call me."

Crystal thinks that's wonderful. "Letitia, he's judicial now!"

But Thurston's easy-going charm still cuts no ice with Letitia who recalls that Karen told her Tommy had pawned the waffle iron. It is true, Tommy allows, that a house guest—an old friend of his in the Air Force—happened to exchange the waffle iron for a bottle of Scotch and he, Thurston, happened to share the bottle with him. "You see how the truth can be distorted."

What is he after, Letitia demands.

"Aunt Lettie—"

"Please don't call me Aunt Lettie."

"I can't very well call you ex-Aunt Lettie!"

What is it he wants, Letitia repeats, unmoved. Her love, is the reply. His is a very lonely life. Do they know what it means to be a Washington newspaperman? Why, there are days when he sees no one but Congressmen. They have no idea how lonely one can get with four hundred and thirty-five Congressmen.

At this juncture, Crystal has a brainstorm. Doesn't Letitia think Thurston might be the right one to consult . . . "for advice about . . . you know!" He sees Congressmen, after all.

But Letitia immediately rejects the idea.

A man comes into the office asking who he sees about parking his car in the field outside. Crystal indicates herself, rising to put on a long white parking coat that is hanging from a tree. "That'll be fifty cents, please."

"I thought this was a government office," the man expostulates. Oh, it is, Crystal avers, but they like to accommodate the public. Government, Letitia backs her up, is public service. They'd have free parking, Crystal explains apologetically to Thurston, but they need the money. She goes out, followed by the man.

When did the Office of Medicinal Herbs go into the parking business, Tommy wants to know. During the war, Letitia replies, and business is very good. Within a few minutes, an elderly colored man enters, carrying a bundle of clothes. This turns out to be Simon, who rents the basement where he conducts a tailoring business. The sound of rumba music elicits the information that Miss Johnson also is a tenant of the Office of Medicinal Herbs.

By this time, Thurston is frankly curious about the setup, and when Crystal returns, asks both women if it isn't rather unusual for a government agency to teach the rumba and press pants. Letitia replies blandly that they distribute literature and seeds and rent space to private enterprises. Noticing the brass bowl Tommy asks if they've been burning papers. They have, something they wanted to get rid of.

"Don't tell me the Office of Medicinal Herbs has top secret papers, too? Are we sending poisoned sassafras to Russia?"

The telephone rings again but neither Letitia nor Crystal makes any move to answer it, which puzzles Thurston. "We never answer the telephone," Crystal explains. "Naturally not," Tommy concedes after the phone has stopped ringing.

She wants to ask Tommy something, Crystal ventures hesitantly. If he were in the liquidating agency of O.S.S. . . . and he came in here . . . would he think there was anything—*odd*—about this office?

"Why, no—of course not!" Thurston reassures her heartily.

"Oh, that's such a relief! Letitia, we've nothing to worry about. Those strangers will never guess we've been abolished!"

The secret is out, to Letitia's considerable annoyance, and Thurston's amazement. The Office of Medicinal Herbs, it seems, was abolished on the fifteenth of March, 1944—the Ides of March. But Letitia and Crystal were never notified officially, hence have been carrying on all these years. Thurston understands. Some weary file clerk put the notification in File A instead of File C so the Budget Bureau and the Treasury haven't been notified either.

This office, Letitia informs him, was Mr. Turnbull's lifework. It was founded by her late husband together with President Theodore Roosevelt . . . Mr. Turnbull's warm, personal friend. Mr. Turnbull once cured the President, in fact, of indigestion with a strong dose of camomile tea. What's more, Mr. Turnbull's original research and classifications in herbology are recognized all over the world. Hence, her determination to carry on his work under any circumstances.

They burn their checks and buy their own stamps, Crystal discloses. And whatever surplus they accumulate, they send to the Conscience Fund, U. S. Treasury . . . anonymously, of course. Last year they sent $28.66.

"Which undoubtedly went directly to the House Un-American Activities Committee!" Thurston jests.

"We are quite prepared to face the consequences," Letitia announces.

Crystal confirms this, adding that she's even sewn a dress for the penitentiary—with stripes.

The occasion of the crisis is a letter which Letitia hands Thurston. "May I ask what advice, if any, you have to give us?"

THURSTON (*reading*)—Department of Public Buildings? They want four of your offices for—what is this?—the O.S.S. Liquidating Agency? . . . Ah, yes—they're still liquidating the war agencies. The other day I heard of an agency that was liquidating an agency that was supposed to liquidate an agency of World War I. However, we're all caught up on the War of 1812.

LETITIA (*impatiently*)—The point is—we can't have a strange agency in this building.

CRYSTAL—They can't have four of our offices—everything's rented!

THURSTON—I see your dilemma.

CRYSTAL—We could give them the library, of course.

LETITIA—I won't have strangers prying into our affairs.

CRYSTAL—That reminds me . . . I must see if Mrs. Frawley is all right. (*She goes to a wall phone, pushes a button and speaks.*) Mrs. Frawley?

MRS. FRAWLEY'S VOICE—Yes?

CRYSTAL—Are you all right?

Mrs. Frawley's Voice—Oh, I'm fine . . .
Crystal—You'll buzz—won't you . . . if . . . if . . .
Mrs. Frawley's Voice—Yes, I will!
Crystal—Keep your spirits up!
Thurston (*putting the letter in his pocket*)—Are you keeping someone chained up in the attic?
Crystal—Oh, no—that's Mr. and Mrs. Frawley—they're—they're expecting a little one.
Thurston—You also conduct a maternity service? There's no limit to your versatility!
Crystal—Well—they couldn't find a place with the housing shortage, you know . . . and Mr. Frawley's only a CAF One, poor man. He can't pay very much. He was in the Bureau of Labor Statistics—now he's in Reclamation.
Thurston—I understand.
Crystal—Oh, you do, don't you. What do you suggest we do?
Thurston—Forget it!
Crystal—Forget?
Thurston—You are now in my hands.
Letitia—I beg your pardon?
Thurston—Fortunately, this is my day off. A Lost Department! Just think what you can do with a lost department! Think of the rumors you could start buzzing . . . around the Pentagon . . . around the Press Club! (*Dreamily.*) A new top secret agency—a new development in warfare—Herbs! Herbological warfare—the Herbological age!
Letitia—What?
Thurston—Think of the fun you could have—with the Army—the Navy—to say nothing of the State Department.
Letitia—We don't wish to have fun with the State Department!
Crystal—We just want to know what to do.
Thurston—What to do? What to do? Have faith in me!

Oh, they do indeed, Crystal assures him. He'll get them back into Agriculture if it's the last thing he does, Thurston promises. They were in Interior, Letitia corrects. But how, Crystal implores. He doesn't know that himself, yet, Thurston replies—but just have faith in him.

Just then Karen Norwood, an attractive, intelligent young woman, enters the office. She kisses Letitia, her aunt . . . greets Crystal fondly, then freezes when she spots Thurston. "What the hell are you doing here?"

He's come to thank Aunt Lettie for that waffle iron, Tommy confides.

"Karen," Crystal speaks up in Thurston's behalf, "he's judicial now. He's not drinking."

"Will you please go!" Karen demands.

"You're looking very lovely," Tommy answers. "Is it the State Department—or New York?"

Momentarily ignoring Karen, Tommy tells Letitia he's been thinking that if he's to deal with these strangers when they come, he'll have to take the oath of office. Letitia doesn't immediately comprehend. They are now looking, Thurston explains, at the new supervisor of the Office of Medicinal Herbs, CAF 16 P9, salary $9,500 a year, when and if . . . Tommy asks Crystal to swear him in, but as she appears nonplused, does it himself.

"I hereby pledge allegiance to the United States Government and swear I have never read the *New Republic,* the *Nation* or the *Sioux City Bugle,* and will defend the Office of Medicinal Herbs against all enemies, including the Pure Food Act, so help me, Hannah!"

Karen is beside herself. "Get out of here!" she rages. Get him out, she begs Letitia. This brings back everything she's wanted to forget. The fish heads!

"Fish heads?" asks Crystal.

"In London—at Lady Astor's . . . She was sweet enough to give us our wedding breakfast, and he called her and told her I was raised in Japan and that I ate only raw fish! And that's what I got! Horrible little fish heads staring up at me!"

He was just trying to make her interesting, socially, Tommy reveals modestly.

Karen doesn't know what he's up to now, but she warns Letitia that whatever it is—she should have nothing to do with it. One of these days, Tommy is going to wake up and not be able to move his arms. There'll be a man in a white coat bending over him. And she hopes he'll spit in Tommy's eye.

Karen's vituperative outburst shocks both Letitia and Crystal. Thurston seizes upon the advantage to say in a hurt tone that he's not complaining, mind you, but that's a small sample of what he had to put up with. "And to think when we were married, she said she was mad about me."

Karen asks him to leave again, but Tommy simply settles himself on the sofa with a book. She's asked a friend to the office to meet Aunt Lettie, Karen explains, and she doesn't want Tommy here when he comes.

"A friend?" Thurston queries.

"Well, if you must know—my fiancé!"

"Your fiancé?" Letitia is surprised.

"I wrote you about—the Doctor—Aunt Lettie."

But she didn't say she was engaged, Crystal recalls. Well, she wanted them to meet him first, Karen explains. Even Tommy would understand why she'd rather he weren't here when the Doctor comes.

"Why?" Tommy inquires blandly.

"Well, *you* might not be embarrassed, but he would!"

But Tommy doesn't know about that. The Doctor may be a quack but he hasn't killed any of Tommy's friends, after all.

"Oh, what's the use! Will you please go!" Karen pleads.

Tommy throws the book down on the sofa and rises, grasping Karen's arms. "Listen, Hellcat, I will now whisper." And he tells her about the Lost Department and the predicament Letitia and Crystal are in. "By the way," he asks, "who swung the ax? Senator Kruger?"

"That monster!" Crystal shudders.

Letitia confirms the situation, also the fact that they have placed themselves in Tommy's hands. Karen can hardly believe it. She never even suspected . . . but how could she, Crystal points out. They didn't begin renting out rooms until after she had left for New York. Up to that time they were still living on their savings.

It is time for lunch and Letitia and Crystal go out to wash up, leaving Tommy and Karen alone.

THURSTON—Why did you keep them from me? Huggable—that's what they are—huggable!

KAREN (*miserably*)—Look—go away.

THURSTON—And desert two blind mice? What kind of a heel do you think I am?

KAREN—No matter what trouble they're in, you'll only make it worse . . . I know you! All you can do is to take a calamity and turn it into a disaster.

THURSTON—You never did have any faith in me. I'm a changed man, Karen—you wouldn't know me.

KAREN—I don't want to know you— Why did they have to tell you? Why did they have to bring *you* into it?

THURSTON (*suddenly*)—Miss me?

KAREN—NO!

THURSTON—We had some lovely moments.

KAREN—*I* never thought so!
THURSTON—I kind of liked our honeymoon, as honeymoons go. Didn't you? I mean—off the record.
KAREN—No!
THURSTON—Funny! I could have sworn you did.
KAREN—Please, don't say anything!
THURSTON—I thought it was really lovely . . . that inn on the Thames—and that beautiful bed with the saxophone springs—
KAREN—I remember nothing!
THURSTON—I'll always remember your waking up in the morning with a half smile on your lips and your eyes still closed, and your arms very warm, and your voice drowsy and tender as you said: "Has she brought that God-damn coffee?"
KAREN—I haven't sworn since I left you.
THURSTON—Congratulations! Of course, I'll admit it was pretty bad coffee.
KAREN—And I haven't cried since I left you.
THURSTON—Sure?
KAREN (*looking at him, then away*) —Positive.

Why did he come here, today, Karen wants to know. Tommy sticks to his story about thanking Aunt Lettie for the waffle iron. Just a minute, Karen recalls . . . was he in New York on Friday night? Tommy doesn't follow her. He followed her, all right, *that* night Karen realizes—when she was with Henry—to the French restaurant, to the theatre and later to the Plaza. He had found out about Henry, she accuses him. And that's why he's here—to break it up!

He's got better things to do, Tommy retorts, than interfering with Karen's love-life . . . such as extricating Letitia and Crystal from the clutches of the O.S.S. Liquidating Agency. At any moment, he points out, the following members of the Liquidating Agency may appear . . . Wilbur F. Threadwaite, Department of State—Commander Thomas Jellico, U. S. Navy—Major John Groh, U. S. Army—and Lieutenant Colonel Robbins, U. S. Air Force. Any one of these men may notice that there is something wrong with the Office of Seeds and Standards. Any one of them may also know Senator Kruger—or run into him—and tell him about the office he abolished four and a half years ago.

There is one fact in his favor, Tommy suggests . . . the fact that most human beings in government do not think for themselves. They know how to do things but seldom stop to ask why they're doing them. What is he cooking up, Karen inquires dubiously. He has a notion, Tommy answers mysteriously, he has a notion . . .

Just then, Threadwaite, State Department, enters, carrying a small briefcase. Threadwaite is amiable, comfortable and plush-lined. He says good-morning and identifies himself.

He's been expecting Threadwaite, Tommy acknowledges. He's Thurston and this is his secretary, Miss Norwood. Karen darts a suspicious glance at him, but goes along with the gag.

Threadwaite is followed by Major Groh and Lieutenant Colonel Robbins, each carrying a briefcase. Introductions follow to be interrupted, then resumed with the appearance of Commander Jellico, who also carries a briefcase.

Major Groh looks at the other officers and lodges a protest. He didn't know the Navy was assigning a *full* commander to the O.S.S. Liquidating Agency. That means he's outranked by both the Air Force *and* the Navy. Tommy informs the Major cavalierly that he'll take care of that . . . that Groh might as well buy his eagles now, that those oak leaves are coming off, *Colonel*.

Identifying himself as the Civilian Administrative Director of the Office of Medicinal Herbs, Tommy informs the group that the O.S.S. Liquidating Agency to which they've been assigned, is just a blind—a security cover. As a matter of fact, Tommy goes on, not even their superiors know the real nature of the project— or the actual assignments of their men.

This announcement is received with considerable surprise.

THURSTON—You have all been carefully selected for very special qualities. Aptitude, leadership, executive ability, but above all things—discretion. *The ability to keep your traps shut.* Discipline. *The ability to take orders without question.* We've combed the lists for each one of you. We weren't satisfied with mere competence. We wanted men of *brilliance*— (*Looking at them to see the effect, then to* KAREN.) I think we've got them! (*The men look pleased.*)

GROH—What's the project?

THURSTON—A very innocent seeming agency known as the Office of Medicinal Herbs—O.M.H.

GROH—Huh?

THURSTON—O.M.H. (KAREN *rises as* CRYSTAL *and* LETITIA *re-enter.*)

CRYSTAL—Oh—excuse me.

TWO BLIND MICE

THURSTON—Gentlemen, Mrs. Turnbull and Miss Hower are the scientists attached to this section. Mr. Threadwaite of State. Major Groh, Colonel Robbins. Commander . . .

COMMANDER—Jellico.

THURSTON—These scientists have now completed their research and are now ready to co-ordinate their efforts with the services. That right, ladies?

CRYSTAL (*uncertainly*)—Yes—I think so. Well, welcome to the Office of Medicinal Herbs.

THURSTON—O.M.H.

CRYSTAL—Yes. We're very happy to have you. Sometimes we've been awfully lonesome here. (*The door opens and the* MAN *and* MISS JOHNSON *enter.*)

MISS JOHNSON—You're doing beautifully, Mr. Murray—just beautifully!

CRYSTAL—Did you have a nice lesson?

MR. MURRAY (*on his way out*)—Yes, ma'am.

CRYSTAL—He's so shy. Oh, this is Miss Johnson. (*The men look at* MISS JOHNSON *and nod, then turn back to* CRYSTAL.) She teaches the rumba. (*The officers really give* MISS JOHNSON *a "take."*) Very conscientiously.

MISS JOHNSON (*cooing*)—How do you do? (*She leaves and the officers look at* THURSTON *for some explanation.*)

THURSTON—Security cover Number Two. (SIMON *enters carrying coat on hanger and trousers.*)

SIMON—Oh, excuse me, gentlemen . . . (*He leaves.*)

THURSTON—Security cover Number Three.

CRYSTAL—He does lovely work. I recommend him.

THURSTON—Before we venture—oh, sit down, gentlemen— Before we venture into the exact nature of the project, we have many problems of procedure and organization. We are functioning, of course, on both a policy AND an operational level.

CRYSTAL—It sounds fascinating. (HENRY *enters.* HENRY *is Dr. McGill. Obviously no setup, he's attractive, intelligent and devoted to* KAREN.)

HENRY—Excuse me—

KAREN (*rising*)—Henry!

HENRY—Hello, Karen—I finally got here.

CRYSTAL (*to* LETITIA)—This is Henry!

HENRY—Sorry I'm late. I tried to phone you. I must have had the wrong number. No one answered.

CRYSTAL—We never use the telephone.

KAREN (*taking* HENRY *by the arm*)—Crystal, this is Henry . . . Aunt Lettie, this is Henry. Dr. McGill.
CRYSTAL—Welcome, Henry.
LETITIA (*graciously*)—I'm very glad to meet you, Doctor.
HENRY—Well, Aunt Lettie, I've been looking forward to this minute . . .
THURSTON (*sternly*)—Commander, will you arrange to have a marine stationed at the door to check all visitors?

The Commander will. Turning to Karen, Thurston demands the data on the newcomer. Henry is puzzled. He thought he had made it clear, Tommy admonishes Karen, that no visitors were permitted in the Office for obvious security reasons. Then, assuming the manner of a bureaucratic inquisitor, Thurston puts the bewildered Doctor through a dizzy cross-examination, and dismisses him peremptorily. "That's all. Good afternoon, Doctor!"

Henry glares at Thurston, then smiles at Karen, asking if she's ready to go, and if Aunt Lettie and Crystal will join them. He's reserved a table at the Mayflower and rented a drive-yourself-car. He thinks they'd all like to look at the cherry blossoms.

"We can't take too long," Letitia worries. "We have our mail."

"Oh, let's play hooky today!" Crystal burbles.

"There's your typical scientist," Tommy laughs, turning to the officers, "charming . . . lovable . . . irresponsible. Run along and play, ladies. Take good care of them, Doctor. By the way, I recommend the creamed chicken at the Mayflower."

As Karen starts to go out with Henry, Letitia and Crystal, Thurston calls her back with instructions to get her book. Swallowing her rage, Karen obeys. Henry reminds Karen that she told him she was in Washington on leave. Thurston breaks in with the information that Miss Norwood is no longer a free agent. Furious, Karen is obliged to submit and tell Henry that she'll see him later . . . at five. Henry and the ladies start to go when Tommy interrupts the departure with a request that Henry send in sandwiches and coffee for five . . . er, six . . . people, including Karen. The State Department officer rises to amend the order to milk for him, and Henry goes.

Turning to a blackboard, Tommy picks up a piece of chalk and proceeds to draw, at the top, an outline of the White House. Next he draws a short perpendicular line from the White House, continuing with a horizontal line to the right and another short perpendicular line, at which point he draws the insignia of the

Joint Chiefs of Staff. Drawing a second short perpendicular line from the White House, he continues with a horizontal line to the left and another short perpendicular line ending in the symbol for Atomic Energy. Then, with lines indicating a juncture of the Joint Chiefs and the Atomic Energy Commission, Tommy illustrates his point by drawing a flower pot with a small leafy bush in it at the bottom of the board. Turning to the officers he announces, "I S S O M H S C." During all the above business, Threadwaite has been busy taking notes.

THURSTON—Now, gentlemen—may I have your undivided attention? You all know as well as I do how explosive the situation is.

THREADWAITE (*still busy taking notes*)—Oh, yes!

THURSTON—In the words of one V.I.P.—in fact one of the most distinguished men in the country—(*He taps his drawing of the White House.*)—what we do in ISSOMHSC may very well determine the fate of these United States in the next decade! (*He sees* THREADWAITE *busy with pencil and says sternly.*) Mr. Threadwaite.

THREADWAITE (*half-rising*)—Sir?

THURSTON (*ominously*)—May I have your notes?

THREADWAITE—Notes? (*Realizing that* THURSTON *means his notebook, he tears the leaves out of it and hands them to him.*) Sorry. (THURSTON *takes the papers over to the brass bowl on the desk.*) I'm awfully sorry.

THURSTON—I'm afraid I'll have to burn them. (*He takes a cigarette lighter out of his pocket and ignites the papers over the bowl.*) Miss Norwood will take the only notes. (*He drops the burning papers into the bowl, warming his hands over them.*) Eighteen copies, Miss Norwood.

Karen slams her steno notebook down on the sofa as . . .
The curtian falls.

ACT II

It is several days later and Crystal and Letitia are busy at their desks. Letitia is stuffing enclosures into envelopes and handing them one at a time to Crystal with instructions. Crystal inserts into each the proper seeds from a row of cans on her desk.

A Sergeant comes in and hands a dollar and fifty cents over to Crystal. The money is for three parking tickets, a job to which the Sergeant is now assigned. Shortly after the Sergeant's departure, Thurston enters carrying a large black briefcase to which is attached a chain with a small padlock and key. He describes it to the ladies as a courier's briefcase—one where the case is chained to the courier's wrist. Their very own courier, in fact, will be there any minute and Tommy has to prepare his first mission. He has picked the ideal man, he boasts, the ideal man . . . Ensign Jamison.

Groh, wearing a pair of "Eagles," comes in to tell Thurston that he's been having trouble with his report, that he can't write it because there is something about the setup he doesn't get . . . namely, what all this stuff, indicating the herbs, has got to do with the Army. Crystal remarks archly that curiosity killed the cat. Threadwaite, of the State Department, enters to report that he stopped off after lunch to pick up a few pictures for his little cubbyhole.

THREADWAITE—Do you like them?
THURSTON—Charming.
THREADWAITE—Just a few familiar Chinese prints that have traveled everywhere with me.
THURSTON—Threadwaite, are you having trouble with your report?
THREADWAITE—Trouble with my report? Good God, no.
GROH—What are you saying in yours?
THREADWAITE—Well, what do you ever say in a report? Just generalities. A Council was formed to function on an operational as well as a policy level. Harmonious relationships are established between State, Army, Navy et cetera . . .
GROH—Yeah, but—
THREADWAITE—I don't commit myself, of course. I never do. It's all very well to commit yourself and get a reputation for brilliance . . .
THURSTON—Which is ruinous in the long run in the State Department.
THREADWAITE—I'd rather stick to generalities and get a reputation for soundness.
THURSTON—Exactly. Threadwaite, why don't you show the Major your report?
GROH—Will you?
THREADWAITE—Delighted!
GROH—Thanks . . . I've seen security in my time, but this one! Brother!
THURSTON—I don't know what you're beefing about.

TWO BLIND MICE 315

Groh—Oh, I'm not beefing.

Thurston—Your promotion's coming through any day now, and you'll be able to wear those eagles in public.

Groh (*embarrassed*)—I was just trying them on.

The two officers go out as Miss Johnson enters with her rumba student, Mr. Murray. But things have changed and Crystal asks Murray if she may have his *pass*. When he hands it to her, she stamps it with a rubber stamp then returns it to him with instructions to give it to the Sergeant on his way out. The Air Force Colonel, Robbins, enters and is spirited off by Miss Johnson for *his* rumba lesson.

Crystal wonders wistfully if learning the rumba is very difficult. Letitia inquires suspiciously if Crystal's thinking, at her age . . . but Crystal protests that she was just wondering. Letitia hands Crystal a packet of sassafras as Commander Jellico comes in.

The Commander tells the ladies that Sassafras is wonderful stuff for the old stomach, that he's a new man. To Thurston, who asks if arrangements for the courier have been made, the Commander says that Ensign Jamison is in the library. Tommy tells the Air Force officer to have Jamison wait, and the Commander leaves to convey this message and to get back to work on his report.

Thurston now tackles the problem of what the courier is to carry. Calling in Simon, he asks the tailor if he has a pair of old pants that somebody never called for. Simon has. Simon also serves notice that the ladies and gentlemen of his choir are coming for practice, today. If they make too much noise, Letitia and Crystal are just to holler.

As Simon leaves, Tommy is putting through a long distance call to New York—to Dinty's Tavern in West Forty-third Street. He contacts a "Mike" at the other end of the line and launches into a description of "Operation Trousers." Ensign Jamison, the courier, Tommy tells Mike, is leaving Washington on the Congressional and will get to Dinty's Tavern about eight-fifteen. Mike's instructions are to open the briefcase—take out what's in it—put it back—lock it—give it back to Jamison. A photographer, Tommy informs Mike, one Joe Girocoli, will also be there. Everything, Tommy emphasizes, everything depends on Operation Trousers—and he hangs up.

Thurston asks the Sergeant to send Ensign Jamison in, and subjects the new courier to a long silent scrutiny when he arrives. This is an important mission, Thurston tells the young man. It may also be a dangerous one. He is to tell no one, to follow orders without question and, if need be, to defend the contents of the briefcase with his life. With all his heart, Jamison replies that he is prepared to do so. Whereupon Thurston snaps the briefcase chain on Jamison's left wrist and locks it. "That's all, Jamison. And Godspeed!"

When Jamison goes, Thurston asks the Sergeant to admit a newspaperman, Charlie Brenner, of the *Times,* who has also been waiting outside. Brenner, he explains to Letitia and Crystal, once was his city editor. He fired Tommy, in fact . . . on Christmas Eve, 1938—just because he'd written Brenner's obituary and it got into the paper by mistake.

Charlie comes in and is presented to the ladies as "the greatest living authority on every conceivable subject under the sun." Brenner utters a mechanical laugh. Except one subject, Tommy amends the introduction—how to live like a gentleman on a newspaper salary. Brenner is glad that Tommy has settled down and congratulates him on his new job.

THURSTON—What's on your mind, Charlie?

BRENNER—You know what's on my mind. Those rumors! About this office.

THURSTON—Which ones?

BRENNER—Now don't put on that poker face. I happen to KNOW.

THURSTON—You do?

BRENNER—We've licked herbological warfare!

THURSTON—Have we?

BRENNER—The Nazis couldn't do it in '44. University of Heidelberg. The French had a project at the Sorbonne under the Deuxième Bureau. The British had a crew working at the University of London. We did it at Smith!

THURSTON—No comment.

BRENNER—Correct me, if I'm wrong. The basic principle is the use of gases shot from rockets that will destroy every inch of vegetation in the enemy country. That right, Madame?

CRYSTAL—No comment.

BRENNER—Which one of you scientists was connected with Smith? Both?

CRYSTAL—Letitia was in the daisy chain.

THURSTON (*chuckling*)—You can't pry anything out of THEM!

TWO BLIND MICE

Brenner—Are we using the V 2 to deliver the herbological projectile?
Thurston—No comment.
Brenner—Where's the laboratory? Upstairs?
Crystal—Oh, it's right here. (*She indicates her desk.*)
Thurston—Our new man's lavatory is straight through that door to the right.
Brenner—Now, look, Thurston . . . I happen to know.
Thurston—What, Charlie?
Brenner—The whole damn story!
Thurston—Where'd you get it?
Brenner—I've got friends in the Pentagon. I can't tell you more than that. And I can put two and two together, as you know, from past experience!
Thurston—By God! Joe Stalin is going to be a happy man tonight!
Crystal—Do you think so? Really?
Thurston—You can't keep a secret in Washington!
Brenner—Hell, the *President* practically confirmed it!
Crystal—He did?
Thurston—When?
Brenner—At the press conference this morning. Didn't you know?
Thurston—Just what did he say?
Brenner—I asked him a honey of a question. I whipped it right in. Timed it right. It was at the end of the conference. I'll admit he was pretty weary—Russia, China, Palestine, inflation, housing. And then I said: Mr. President, when do you think Russia will catch up with us on herbological warfare?
Thurston (*apprehensively*)—Just what did he say?
Brenner (*smiling knowingly*)—He asked me to repeat the question.
Thurston—And then?
Brenner (*smugly*)—Then he said: No comment.

Tommy, relieved, agrees that this statement by the President is fraught with significant implications. Brenner rises to the bait and adds that his own private source, unidentified, of course, tells him the President really thinks the Russians will catch up with us on herbological warfare in 1952. Crystal disagrees with the President's estimate. She didn't support him anyway last election because as soon as Senator Kruger came out for him, she knew where she stood.

The house telephone rings and it is Mrs. Frawley. She is feeling a little . . . funny. Letitia tells Crystal to say they'll be right up. "I do hope Mrs. Frawley's all right," Crystal says. "You don't think it's—time?" Letitia allows that it may be and that they'll call the hospital if such is the case.

Brenner, who has listened meaningfully to the conversation, asks Tommy what's up when the ladies take their departure. A little experiment, Tommy reveals. It has been going on for nine months. Who's Mrs. Frawley, Brenner inquires. One of the subjects in the experiment, Tommy replies. "How many subjects are there?" "It takes two."

Brenner now has it all figured out. He knows this much at least. They're trying out the effects of something—call it X—on the human system. That's the Frawley experiment. No comment, is Tommy's retort.

Brenner declares that he now has practically everything he needs to break the story. Tommy affects an attitude of extreme concern. Brenner gloats that he hasn't told Tommy half of what he knows. Tommy's concern becomes anxiety as he begs Brenner to tell him where he got it. "Wouldn't you like to know!" Brenner says smugly. "Such are the ways of a democracy," Tommy observes gloomily. "In a police state you'd get shot. In our country they'll probably punish you by giving you the Pulitzer Prize." Yes, Brenner might as well print the story—let all the security go down the drain. If he doesn't, someone else will. Brenner agrees. That's the sensible way of looking at it, and he departs with Tommy congratulating him lugubriously on the scoop.

Now whistling cheerfully, Thurston picks up the phone and dials the City Desk. His voice becomes suddenly bronchial as he coughs out an explanation to his city editor that his cold is much worse, that he can hardly talk, but will be all right by tomorrow. Karen enters in the middle of the conversation and Tommy signals her for quiet. She waits impatiently while he winds up the phone call thanking his editor for the extra day off.

What does he mean, Karen launches into him indignantly, by offering Henry a job as Medical Attaché to the O.M.H. in Paris? And telling him to buy his State Department wardrobe which he's already gone and done! Ten thousand mythical dollars a year, Karen storms, for a mythical job. So what, Thurston shrugs, Henry likes it and he, Tommy, incidentally, also likes Henry. They didn't hit it off at first—but after last night, they really got together. He sees exactly what Karen sees in the

Doctor. Henry is attractive, substantial, able and interesting. But he's not going to be made a fool of, Karen warns.

Henry, who has been parking the car outside, comes in, togged out in full State Department rig, feeling quite the boulevardier. Tommy thinks the Doctor looks positively splendid. Henry then lets them in on a little secret. The suit was really made for the Lithuanian press attaché who never called for it . . . and it fits perfectly. The Homburg, of course, he bought the regular way.

"Henry, you're not going to Paris," Karen blurts out.

But Henry doesn't see why she keeps saying that inasmuch as he has already taken the physical and passed it, and Tommy has just handed him his passport and said that he's arranging air passage on a B-29. The Doctor supposes that he can amend the passport—to have it stamped: And wife, meaning Karen, of course.

She's not going to Paris, Karen retorts, and neither is he.

"Don't you like Paris?" the bewildered Henry inquires.

"I love it!"

"Well, then! It seems to me it would be an ideal place for a honeymoon. And we'll have a chance to save half my salary. Why, in two years I'll have enough to go into private practice."

Karen insists that Thurston is just trying to humiliate him, that there is no job at all. But Henry cannot believe this. He has seen the full Civil Service job description, after all.

"Do you know who he is?" Karen rages, pointing to Thurston.

"HE," Tommy chuckles, "is her ex-husband."

This comes as a complete surprise and shock to Henry who wants to know why Karen has never told him that she was once married to Thurston. Not that it matters, for they're all adult. And Henry thinks Tommy is behaving very decently.

"I know *him*," Karen declares meaningfully.

"She never liked me, Doctor. At no time. Always suspicious. Always reading the most sordid motives into my simplest actions."

"You know you're giving Henry a mythical job."

"That's an example of what I mean," Thurston says gently.

"I saw the papers, honey," Henry protests. And why have the Army, Navy, the Air Force and the State Department assigned officers here? Karen *must* be wrong.

The telephone rings. It is the White House for Thurston. The President, it seems, is really interested in O.M.H. and wants to have tea with the two women scientists. Thurston is able to arrange an appointment for that very afternoon.

Karen is completely stunned, her arguments obviously shattered in the eyes of Henry who observes that with the President entertaining Aunt Lettie and Crystal, don't tell *him* that there's anything fishy about the deal.

Henry then recalls that he happened to run into his Senator last night at the dinner of the Virginia Society. He has told his Senator, who is quite a power on the Hill, that he was going abroad for O.M.H. and that the legislator was extremely interested. Karen is aghast. The lawmaker is none other than Senator Kruger who abolished the office in the first place. No wonder he was interested when his talkative constituent revealed where O.M.H. made its headquarters, who was in charge and so forth. Henry, who still has no notion of the enormity of his indiscretion, is only slightly hesitant for fear that he may have violated security regulations. But Thurston reassures him, telling him to forget it. He is not the only offender.

The Doctor thanks Tommy, remarking that he has been awfully decent and can't see why Karen doesn't think so too. He's in the peculiar position, Henry notes, of defending her first husband. Utterly defeated, Karen is glad the boys are so chummy. So glad. It's going to help a lot when the deluge comes—the one Tommy has been cooking up.

Crystal re-enters and goes immediately to the phone to dial the operator, but flashes the operator thereby cutting herself off. Then she notices Henry for the first time. "Oh, Doctor, thank goodness you're here. The hot water is boiling—the towels are out—I was just going to call the hospital, but I'm afraid it's too late for the hospital."

The stork is fluttering over O.M.H. with a bundle for Mrs. Frawley. Tommy orders Henry upstairs. The flabbergasted Doctor protests that he's no obstetrician, but will do what he can, of course.

Crystal is so excited she can hardly breathe. Then Tommy breaks the really *big* news that she and Letitia are expected to tea at the White House at four-thirty! Letitia, who has just come in, thinks Tommy is joking until Karen, in spite of herself, has to admit that she heard the call.

THURSTON—An invitation to the White House is a command! Aunt Lettie, this is your chance to tell your story to the highest authority in the land!

CRYSTAL—What'll I wear?

LETITIA—Your black silk.

CRYSTAL—But it's so gloomy! I wouldn't want to depress the President.
THURSTON—You haven't too much time!
CRYSTAL—I think we ought to wear something gay!
THURSTON—I would. I'm going to have the Sergeant drive you in state! (*To* KAREN.) He can get a limousine from the Navy pool. (*He goes out.*)
CRYSTAL—What are you going to wear, Letitia?
LETITIA—My black silk!
CRYSTAL—I wonder if the first lady will be there. Do you think she'll trust him to entertain us—alone?
KAREN—Now—look—you can't go. You just can't. You know this whole thing is one gigantic hoax!
LETITIA—Of course I know it.
KAREN—Then why . . . ?
CRYSTAL—An invitation from the White House is a command. And they have such lovely china.
LETITIA—I've been waiting to tell the story of the Office of Medicinal Herbs to the proper official. I know no one better than the Chief Executive. This is my chance. Mr. Turnbull would think pretty poorly of me if I didn't take full advantage of it.
CRYSTAL—Oh, he would, dear, he would.
LETITIA—I knew we couldn't go on forever this way. Especially when all the other agencies began interfering with us—the Army, and the Navy! If I'm eloquent enough—and I'm relying on Mr. Turnbull to inspire me—we may yet win!

They've had tea at the White House before, Crystal recalls, with the Roosevelts—the Theodore Roosevelts. She wonders if the cookies will be as nice as they were then.

Karen announces that she's licked as Letitia sweeps out to dress. Crystal goes to the house phone and calls Henry, but he is busy and no, he doesn't need any help. "What a day! What a day!" Crystal marvels, going out and leaving Karen sitting disconsolately on the sofa until Tommy re-enters. He has not only arranged for the limousine but for the Sergeant to drive it . . . to lend color.

This starts Karen off on another tirade about making a laughing stock of her aunt—her fiancé—herself that is interrupted by the telephone. Karen answers. It is the French Embassy for Thurston, to inform him that the Republic of France desires to award the Legion of Honor to Madame Turnbull and Mademoiselle Hower in recognition of their services to science. Vive la France!

Karen is trying to figure out this new turn of events when two colored men and a woman enter the office. Thurston directs them to where choir practice is taking place—in the basement. They file out as Threadwaite and Groh come in.

The State Department man hands his report to Karen instructing her to make ten copies. Thurston asks the Major if he found Threadwaite's report helpful. Groh is glum. He thinks maybe he has combat fatigue. Maybe he's had it all along and the docs didn't catch it. But he still can't figure out how the Hell you can beat the enemy's brains out with wild garlic.

"You're not going to get ahead in the Army with that attitude, Major," Thurston rebukes meaningfully.

The Major doesn't understand. What attitude? He's not a West Pointer. He came up the hard way. Thurston reverses his approach, takes Groh's report and pronounces it an excellent one, handing it to Karen for ten copies to be made. "But you never even read it," Groh protests. Has the Major ever heard of a government report being *read?* Thurston asks. Why doesn't Groh take a tip from Threadwaite, the Colonel and the Commander who don't ask questions—just follow orders? The Commander comes in with *his* report, submitting it to Karen for typing, followed within moments by a man with a forbidding face and a paunch—Senator Kruger! Obviously no fool.

Thurston, who has started a gin rummy game with Threadwaite, looks up and directs the stranger to choir practice in the basement.

KRUGER—Choir practice? I'm Senator Kruger!

KAREN (*frightened*)—Oh! (*She rushes over to the typewriter and starts typing furiously.*)

KRUGER—What's this about choir practice?

THURSTON (*rising from game*)—Come in, Senator— Come in. Welcome to O.M.H. You remember me? I'm Thurston, civilian administrative director. Used to be on the *Post!*

KRUGER (*half-smiling and shaking hands with* THURSTON)— Oh, yes.

THURSTON—Miss Norwood, will you please stop that clattering? I can't hear myself think!

CHOIR (*heard offstage as* KAREN *stops typing*)—
               Throw out the life line.
               Throw out the life line.
               Someone is drifting away.

(*Starting the second phrase as* CRYSTAL *and* LETITIA *enter.* CRYSTAL *joins in the singing*)—
>Throw out the life line.
>Throw out the life line.
>Someone is sinking today.

(*The* CHOIR *repeats, singing the first phrase again.*)

KAREN (*warningly*)—Crystal—this is Senator Kruger! (*She crosses to the door, opens it and calls offstage.*) Quiet, please—quiet, please!

SIMON'S VOICE (*offstage*)—Quiet, folks! (*The* CHOIR *stops.*)

CRYSTAL (*clouding as she stares at the* SENATOR)—I know that face!

KRUGER (*quietly, puzzled*)—What's that singing? Why are you playing cards during office hours? (*To* CRYSTAL.) What do *you* do here, Madame?

CRYSTAL (*coldly*)—I have no wish to talk to you.

LETITIA—You ridiculed Mr. Turnbull on the floor of the Senate!

CRYSTAL—Anything we have to say, we shall say to the President!

THURSTON—Senator—Miss Hower and Mrs. Turnbull are two of the top scientists in their field. They report directly to the White House!

HENRY (*who enters, panting, with shirtsleeves rolled up*)—Karen! Aunt Lettie! Karen!

KAREN—What's wrong, Henry?

HENRY—It's a boy—seven pounds, two ounces.

THURSTON—Swell!

HENRY—Hello, Senator . . . Sorry, I've got to get back to my patient. She's doing fine. Haven't delivered a baby since I was an interne, but the old hand hasn't lost its cunning. I'll be back.

May he ask, Kruger commences, if it's not too much to ask . . . But he is interrupted by Major Groh who informs the Senator that "they don't let you ask anything around here." But the Senator makes another try when Miss Johnson enters with Colonel Robbins. She's sorry, she tells the Air Force officer, but there'll be no more rumba lessons. There is nothing more she can teach him, except self-restraint! Spotting the Senator, Miss Johnson mistakes him for a new pupil she has not yet seen, but expects. "Oh, you must be Mr. Geller! And how are we today—loose limbed—rubbery, springy? Right on the balls of our feet?"

"I beg your pardon, Madame?"

Miss Johnson tugs at Kruger's arm. "Now—now don't be shy! You want your wife to be proud of you, don't you? You don't want to be just a stick in the mud all your life, do you?"

"Madame," the exasperated Senator requests, "will you please stop mauling me!?" What's more, he has no wife. He has been a bachelor for fifty years!

"Naturally!" Crystal says spitefully. "No woman would be mad enough to marry a monster!"

A strange man wanders in asking who he should see about parking his car since the Sergeant doesn't seem to be around. Thurston indicates Senator Kruger. "Fifty cents." The man puts the coin in Kruger's hand and departs. Threatening to look into the extraordinary activities of O.M.H., the Senator absent-mindedly puts the coin in his trousers pocket.

"Did you see that?" Crystal shrills to the gathering at large. "How dare you!" she scolds the Senator. "How dare you pocket our conscience money?"

"Conscience money?" Kruger is puzzled.

"Grafter!" Crystal denounces.

Just then the Sergeant enters to announce that transportation to the White House for the ladies is ready.

Crystal and Letitia start to go. But Crystal fires a parting shot at the Senator. "We have witnesses! They saw you! They all saw you! I'm going to tell the President about you!"

The Choir resumes singing "Throw out the life line," as the ladies stalk out. Thurston shakes his head reprovingly at the Senator as . . .

The curtain falls.

ACT III

It is the next morning and Threadwaite is talking to his State Department chief on the phone. He explains to the superior that Senator Kruger was in, yesterday afternoon, asking all sorts of questions and finally leaving in a huff. The legislator has evidently gone over to the State Department to find out what goes on in O.M.H. Threadwaite suggests showing the Senator his report.

As he hangs up, Major Groh and Colonel Robbins come in asking for Thurston. Groh is all steamed up. He wants to get down to cases with Thurston on the function of O.M.H.

Ensign Jamison enters, dazed, with a portion of the chain from the courier's briefcase still locked to his wrist. He turns aside the officers' queries with the statement that he can't talk about anything until he sees Thurston, which only infuriates Major Groh even more. He follows the Colonel out.

Thurston enters through a window, wearing a hat and carrying the courier's briefcase with the other half of the chain attached. Seeing Jamison, he quickly places the briefcase in the kneehole of the desk, then turns and hangs his hat on the tree as if just coming in.

Jamison makes a clean breast of the situation. The briefcase was stolen. He was drugged. He reported to Dinty's Tavern in New York as per Thurston's instructions, Jamison relates, and asked for Mike. He was offered a drink, but being a teetotaler, ordered some gingerale. The aforesaid Mike then conducted him to the men's room where a photographer was waiting. Mike opened the briefcase and took out a pair of trousers. Then Mike took his own trousers off and put the others on. But the trousers brought by Jamison didn't fit so he put his own back on again. The photographer kept taking pictures all the while. Then the photographer said he had instructions for the Ensign which were to proceed to the Waldorf and wake up a Mr. Egan. A newspaper publisher, Jamison believes.

Tommy winces. The boys have been adding a few touches of their own. He was to tell Mr. Egan, Jamison goes on, that Thurston sent him. The password was: "How's Margie?" And how *was* Margie? Tommy asks. Jamison doesn't know. Mr. Egan opened the door just a crack and began shouting, and he heard a woman scream. He then proceeded back to Dinty's Tavern where Mike said: "Have a drink," and he ordered gingerale again. The next thing he knew he was on the Congressional bound home for Washington and the briefcase was gone.

Jamison doesn't know what else to say. He was following orders.

Thurston dismisses the Ensign, then takes the briefcase from its hiding place. Opening it, he removes the trousers and several 8 x 10 photographs. The pictures make him chuckle with satisfaction. Reaching for the phone, he dials the City Desk, and puts on his bronchial voice. But the ruse is to no avail. Mr. Egan has ordered him fired.

The Sergeant ushers in Charlie Brenner of whom Thurston ruefully inquires if there are any newspaper jobs around. Brenner laughs the question off as ludicrous and brandishes a newspaper containing his piece on O.M.H. What does Tommy think of the A.P. trying to throw it down. Thurston is incredulous. Why, Brenner's piece has some of the finest imaginative pseudo-scientific writing he's read in years. Brenner is indignant. What does Thurston mean—imaginative? Pseudo-scientific? Was the piece supposed to be fact, Tommy inquires innocently. What does he think it was supposed to be. . . . It was he who told Brenner, after all. This isn't quite true, Tommy reminds his former boss. He told Brenner nothing—Brenner told him!

Major Groh, Threadwaite, Colonel Robbins and Commander Jellico enter in a body in time to overhear Brenner demand to know just one thing—just what does O.M.H. do? That's what he's been trying to find out ever since he got here, Groh volunteers. Brenner is amazed. Hasn't Thurston even told the Army? Tommy says no—if they're going to have security, let them have it.

GROH (*thumbing through a sheaf of papers*)—Look! From the White House to the Chief of Staff. From the Chief of Staff to General McElton. From General McElton to General Haas. From General Haas to General Swayne. From General Swayne to Colonel Rowland. From Colonel Rowland to Colonel Jensen. From Colonel Jensen to Major Groh—

THURSTON—That's a darn interesting chain of command.

GROH—They all want to know who authorized ISSOMHSC. What does it do? Who appointed you? Who issued the directive? And *I* want to know—right now.

THURSTON (*finishing a piece of candy he has taken from a box on the table*)—That's easy. Nobody authorized it. Nobody issued the directive. Gentlemen, ISSOMHSC is a hoax.

GROH—A hoax?

BRENNER—Wait a minute. You mean my piece?

THURSTON—Un-huh.

BRENNER—You told me I'd get the Pulitzer Prize!

THURSTON—Could be.

GROH—Wait a minute—

THURSTON—I want to congratulate you, Major. You were the only man to think for himself. What's it all about? you asked plaintively. Congratulations, Major. We need more men like you.

GROH—Don't you try to soft soap me.

BRENNER—What are you trying to do? Cover up? I know intelligence techniques. Standard deception routines.

THURSTON—I don't understand, Charlie—

BRENNER—The White House doesn't want to confirm the story. Doesn't want the Russians to know. It was an old trick in the war. Marshal Zhukov used it at Stalingrad. General Haas used it in North Africa. Let the enemy get an authentic piece of intelligence and then throw it down. Confuse him. Routine deception tactics.

Brenner's reasoning convinces the others and Thurston is unable, try as he may, to peddle his hoax. It is finally decided among the officers that an executive session is in order. They file into the library—all except the newspaperman, Brenner—followed by Thurston who by now is almost tearful from frustration and indicates his hopelessness by taking the pack of cards along.

Letitia and Crystal enter, wearing their Legion of Honor medals and engage in conversation with Brenner who tries to pump them. Just what does this office do, Brenner commences. Oh, they told the President all about that yesterday, Crystal replies. Do they mean to say the President didn't know either? Naturally not! But he was very impressed, Crystal assures. What did they tell the President, Brenner perseveres. Everything they've been through, Letitia declares. They weren't with him very long, Crystal discloses. The President didn't finish his tea, in fact. He was called away for an urgent conference and the ladies had tea with two secret service men. These later escorted them out the back way—so the newspaper reporters wouldn't bother them.

Brenner tries a new tack, holding out his newspaper to Crystal and asking if she's read his piece. She has and says it's ridiculous.

BRENNER—What do you mean—ridiculous? What's ridiculous about it?

CRYSTAL—All that war stuff! Our work is constructive—not destructive!

LETITIA—Exactly!

CRYSTAL—As Letitia told the President—and Letitia, dear, I thought you were positively inspired. She said—What did you tell the President?

LETITIA—I said a pinch of pipsissewa is worth more to suffering humanity than a ton of nitroglycerine.

CRYSTAL—Isn't that wonderful?

BRENNER—What's pipsissewa?

CRYSTAL (*taking a handful of seeds from a jar and pouring them into* BRENNER'S *hand*)—Just one of God's gifts—that's all!

BRENNER—What do you do with it?

LETITIA—Brew it, and drink it.

BRENNER—How do you get the enemy to drink it? Put it in his coffee?

CRYSTAL—We don't make it for our enemies. We make it for our friends.

BRENNER (*putting seeds into his pocket*)—Look—

CRYSTAL—Besides, we haven't any enemies except Senator Kruger. Really, I wish you would all stop talking about enemies so much. Major Groh is always talking about the enemy.

BRENNER—I've met a lot of scientists but I never met one who talked like you before!

CRYSTAL—The President said we were different, too.

LETITIA—He said YOU were different.

CRYSTAL—Well, I don't want to take all the credit.

The conversation is interrupted by the appearance of Thurston, distraught and still unable, despite the executive conference, to convince his staff that ISSOMHSC is a hoax. He even tried to abolish the office as a last resort—but the officers wouldn't leave.

Karen comes in with the information that Senator Kruger has returned and is now just outside, interviewing the Sergeant. Her unsolicited reference to the setup as a hoax finally convinces Brenner that this really is just another of Tommy's frightful stunts. He begins to feel a little sick. Brenner's condition becomes contagious as Karen recounts what she has learned from a lawyer—one of the best lawyers in Washington, to whom she has told everything. According to Karen, the lawyer had just whistled, then begun adding up the penalties. One year for contempt of Congress—five years for impersonating a Federal employee—two years for burning Federal checks—three years for fraud—five years for conspiracy—a grand total of thirty years.

Henry makes an entrance at this moment, singing "La Marseillaise." He has just come from the hospital where Mrs. Frawley and son are blooming. He has also made arrangements for Karen to take her first series of shots in the afternoon.

Brenner can take no more and leaves.

Karen now undertakes to break the news to Henry announcing finally that they're all going to the penitentiary. Tommy assures the Doctor that he, however, is safe, not having drawn any of the taxpayers' money. Henry doesn't quite see it that way. He's done nothing but spend money so far.

Letitia and Crystal decide they might as well go up to their rooms and get ready for the penitentiary. Tommy reminds them that they haven't been indicted yet. "Does that take long?" Crystal asks. "Ages," is the reply. But she and Letitia don't like to be kept waiting, Crystal tells Thurston. They'd like to get it over with. There's no use putting it off. It's like going to the dentist's. Letitia is quite as prepared as Crystal to take the consequences. She always has been. Karen is not to fret about them. No matter what happens, Mr. Turnbull will understand.

Henry's most urgent problem is what to do with his State Department suit which, considering what he paid for it, merits attention—even at a time like this. But the wrath-propelled entrance of Senator Kruger cuts short his deliberation.

KRUGER—Herbological warfare! Rumba teachers, choir singers, expectant mothers! Running a department that I abolished! The greatest conspiracy against Congress in the history of the United States.

HENRY—Senator, I didn't know—

KRUGER—Somebody's going to the penitentiary for this, or I'll personally see to it that our soft-hearted, soft-headed Attorney General is impeached!

THURSTON—You wouldn't send a man to the penitentiary for running a model bureau?

KRUGER—A model bureau?

THURSTON—You're always shouting economy! We are the very model of economy. Our budget is zero. We've only four in personnel. Miss Hower, Mrs. Turnbull, myself and . . . my secretary . . . Miss Norwood. Why, most government bureaus couldn't operate a peanut stand with less than a hundred!

KRUGER—How long have you been on the public payroll?

THURSTON—Two days. I think I'm retiring.

KRUGER—You bet you're retiring!

THURSTON—I'm applying for a pension.

KRUGER—Pension?

THURSTON—Why, of course. A man gives two of the best days of his life to his government. Do you propose to cast me off without a penny?

KRUGER—I want to see this layout from top to bottom!

THURSTON—May I suggest, Senator, that you start with the bottom? Our trousers section?

KRUGER—Your what?

THURSTON—You'll meet our courier down there. He must be lonely!

Kruger—Courier?
Thurston—Get him to tell you about his trip to New York.

The Senator leaves by a door Thurston has opened. Tommy, Henry and Karen now are alone and Henry opens up on Tommy, accusing him point-blank of being a liar, a fraud and a cheat. If the law doesn't take care of Thurston, Henry swears, he personally will horsewhip the man. Karen is all for the latter, offering, in fact, to help Henry any way she can.

Thurston offers no resistance to Henry's attack save to explain that he had no motive for wanting to hurt the Doctor but was forced into the whole charade in order to protect Karen's family. In a subtle undercut, Tommy inquires of Karen artlessly why she didn't confide in Henry who is her fiancé, after all. He, himself, couldn't have told the Doctor. He hadn't the right.

This makes sense to Henry who seeks refuge in the role of a much-aggrieved man. Not only did Karen fail to confide in him, she let him accept a mythical post—let him make a fool of himself—let him tell his family, buy clothes, get a passport, take his booster shots— Didn't she try to warn him, Karen bridles, beg him not to listen to Thurston? She hinted, Henry allows, but she wasn't forthright about it. A man expects his wife to confide in him.

What's more, Henry has found out that Karen has a pretty foul temper. Now they're quarreling, Karen tries to make clear, because Tommy is egging them on. Can't Henry see? Tommy wants to break them up—that's what he's been trying to do all along. Henry doesn't see. He wants a wife who is responsible, forthright, frank, practical and . . . frankly, Karen doesn't quite fill the bill. He's terribly sorry but a man's got to be practical, especially one in his position who is just starting out. He can't let love blind him. Karen returns his ring. Mutual good-bys are exchanged and Henry leaves.

"I wonder what it is," Tommy remarks in mock bewilderment. "Why can't you hold a man?"

"God, how I hate you—" Karen snarls.

"You lost a fine fellow."

"You know what you do to me?"

"No. Tell me. What?"

Karen is venomous. "You make me want to use all the four letter words I'm not supposed to know!"

Henry was quite right, Tommy opines. Karen is not forthright. She's not direct—like himself, for example.

"If you don't stop talking to me," Karen threatens, "I'll begin to throw things."

"Your love life has really been shot to hell," Tommy observes righteously. "You messed up *my* life." And now she has messed up Henry's. She's a femme fatale, that's what she is. Just goes around breaking hearts!

Karen picks up a book from the desk and is just about to hurl it at Tommy's head when Crystal enters, followed by Letitia carrying a suitcase. Crystal is dressed in the striped garment she has sewn in advance for the penitentiary. They are ready, she announces. Tommy takes the suitcase away from Letitia. They are not going to the penitentiary, he assures. They're going back to Interior under the personal auspices of that watchdog of the Treasury—none other than Senator Kruger himself.

Karen throws up her hands. "He's mad—it's come—it's here. I've known it all along! Time to call the man in the White Coat."

An offstage bellow is heard from Senator Kruger, followed by a rather plaintive note of protest from Ensign Jamison. The Senator appears holding the broken chain on Jamison's wrist and dragging the youth behind him.

KRUGER—What the hell do you mean by making a courier out of MY NEPHEW!?

KAREN—Your nephew!?

THURSTON—Our courier. Senator, you should be proud of that young man. You've been voted the Senator most likely to succeed in getting all his relatives on the payroll. He managed to get on without your influence.

JAMISON—Does the Navy have to know, Uncle Robert?

THURSTON—Does the Navy have to know, Uncle Robert, that your nephew was courier for the office you abolished? Does the Navy have to know that your nephew carried top secret pants for the office you abolished?

JAMISON—I was just following orders, Uncle Robert!

KRUGER—Who's orders?

JAMISON—Mr. Thurston's.

KRUGER—You idiot!

THURSTON—Senator, I want to present you with a pictorial record of your nephew's historic mission. (*He picks up from the desk the photographs that he took from the briefcase.*) You know, Senator, you're the one man who can get the Office of Medicinal Herbs back into Agriculture—pardon, correction, Interior!

KRUGER—I'll see you in hell first!
THURSTON—I thought we could make a deal.
KRUGER—Sir, I don't make deals.
JAMISON—Uncle Robert—you made a deal for father!
KRUGER (*to* JAMISON)—Get out of my sight!
JAMISON (*backing up*)—But where'll I go, Uncle Robert?
KRUGER—I don't care. Get out of my sight!
JAMISON—Yes, sir. (*He exits.*)
KRUGER—Damn that family of mine. If it weren't for them, I'd be President today.
CRYSTAL—Thank God we've been spared that calamity!
THURSTON—Senator, you have my sympathy! I've always maintained all politicians should be born orphans.
KRUGER (*taking the photographs with him*)—I'll see you in my office. (*He goes.*)
LETITIA—We're very grateful to you, young man.
CRYSTAL—Oh, yes.
THURSTON—Not at all. I'm very grateful to you. This has been an interesting experiment in government. (THURSTON *kisses* CRYSTAL. *He looks at* LETITIA, *who invites him to kiss her. He does so—then he looks at* KAREN. *She turns away.* THURSTON *goes over to her.*) I've been thinking; I lost a job, you lost a man. I'm a man, you've got a job. How would you like to support me? (KAREN *wheels facing him.*)

THE CURTAIN FALLS

GOODBYE, MY FANCY *

A Comedy in Three Acts

By Fay Kanin

THE Kanin family appears to be working itself up to the status of a dynasty in the worlds of the theatre and the motion picture. Garson Kanin, the young and beardless patriarch of the tribe, is a playwright—a sample of whose work is the hit, "Born Yesterday"—and a director of both plays and pictures. His wife, Ruth Gordon, is an actress and dramatist who was briefly on a stage during the season in her own "The Leading Lady," and in her husband's "The Smile of the World." Miss Gordon's happiest writing-and-acting hit was "Years Ago."

A younger brother of Garson's, Michael, is a screenwriter, and Michael married Fay Mitchell, an actress and radio and movie author. Fay Mitchell Kanin paid a visit to her alma mater, Elmira College, N. Y., about three years ago and out of it came the urge to write a play with a college background. "The visit affected me strangely," she remembers. "What is this curious thing, I asked myself, that happens to people when they remember the past? What is this nostalgia that has so much power over us all? And what happens to the man or woman who goes back to look at the past—to recapture it?"

When she had answered these self-imposed questions and a few more—the hardest work she ever did, she says—she had her play, "Goodbye, My Fancy." Her husband accommodatingly produced it for her on Broadway, in association with the firm of Aldrich & Myers.

Mrs. Kanin's alma mater was Elmira, but the institution she tells about in her comedy is "Good Hope College for Women in Good Hope, Mass." The time is Commencement weekend, June, 1948, and the scene is a ground-floor dormitory sitting room, where "there is no relationship closer both spiritually and physically than that peculiar educational phenomenon known as 'room-

* Copyright, 1947, under title of "Most Likely to Succeed," by Fay Kanin. Copyright, 1949, by Fay Kanin and Michael Kanin.
Published by Samuel French, New York.
Author's agent, William Morris Agency, Inc., 1270 Sixth Ave., New York.

mates.' Outside the U.S.S.R., communal living has no purer form."

Hope Hall, the dormitory, was endowed by an alumna with a love for Gothic architecture, so the room has a stone fireplace and a seat beneath a leaded bay window. Ordinarily the room would be in good order, but on this Friday morning it's bedlam, with suitcases, packing cartons and such items of outdoor equipment as skis and riding boots spilled here and there. The condition of the room is surprising to Ginny Merrill, an alert, intelligent and sensitive 19-year-old who comes in carrying a book.

At this moment, Amelia, an excited senior, races in from the adjoining bedroom carrying an armload of clothes, and is followed shortly by Ginny's roommate, Mary Nell, carrying skis and looking very pretty even in faded jeans and run-over moccasins. It's about time Ginny showed up, Mary Nell and Amelia inform her—and where has she been, anyway? Already they have packed up most of her things.

"What's the rush?" Ginny inquires. "We've got another three days on campus."

Evidently Ginny does not know what has happened and Mary Nell is bursting with the information. "Guess who's going to stay here—right in these rooms?"

"Agatha Reed?" Ginny guesses—correctly. She has been at the library looking up this Agatha Reed, and in her hand is a book by Miss Reed. "Women in the Vanguard," which tells about her college days right here in these rooms, with the bay window facing the willow trees. And now, apparently, Miss Reed is going to stay here instead of at the Dean's—and they are trying to make the rooms look the same as they were in her day, even to getting back the old furnishings.

"I wonder what she's like," Ginny muses.

"Busty, probably," Mary Nell hazards. "Most women with brains, I notice it goes right to their bust."

But this isn't what Ginny means. She wonders what kind of person Agatha Reed is. Her coming up to get an honorary degree doesn't mean anything, necessarily, for honorary degrees are a racket—a celebrity gets some fancy letters after his name and the school gets publicity or a new wing. Just because Agatha Reed wrote for all those papers and now is in Congress is not necessarily important to the cynical Ginny, either; anyone can be in Congress these days.

These speculations are interrupted by Miss Shackleford and two janitors; the lady is a faded old-timer, the Alumnae Secretary, and the gentlemen are carrying a faded love seat—the very seat on which Miss Reed sat when she was a student. Ginny tests this hallowed *meuble* and wincingly observes, "Spring's broken."

"Well," says Miss Shackleford, "they can't expect sentiment *and* comfort. I've just spent the morning tracking it down—to one of the basement rooms." It is very generous of the girls to give up their rooms, she continues—but it's quite an honor and something they can tell their children about. Of Ginny she inquires, "Did your father happen to mention what time her plane might be arriving?"

Ginny freezes and replies, "I don't see father except on holidays, Miss Shackleford." The Alumnae Secretary bustles off in search of more men and more furnishings and Ginny comments, "She's a finger-down-the-throat if I ever saw one."

"Oh, alumnae secretaries have to gush around," says Mary Nell. "Besides, you're too sensitive about your father, Ginny. If *my* father was president of this college, I'd have lived in a penthouse on top of the Libe and never taken gym . . . and had men imported from Princeton every weekend."

Miss Shackleford herds the janitors back, this time with a ladder, a framed reproduction of a painting and a chair. "Why," exclaims Ginny as she sees the picture, "that's Uncle Willy!" The Alumnae Secretary corrects her. "That's the Laughing Cavalier, by—"

"Franz Hals," says Ginny helpfully. "I know. But father has one just like it in his study. We always called him Uncle Willy."

"This *is* your father's," Miss Shackleford reveals. "We borrowed it. Somebody remembered one like it used to hang in this room."

The business of carrying-out and carrying-in continues. The room is going to be just the way it used to be, except for the added convenience of a telephone which a telephone man has just connected. Mary Nell speculates on how wonderful it would have been to have had that phone all year—"there's something about talking to a man when you're lying down"—and has draped herself on the window seat for an imaginary conversation with a man named Da-arling, when the instrument actually rings.

Gingerly, Mary Nell answers, listens and exclaims with wide-eyed awe, "It's *Life Magazine!*" She takes down a message for Agatha Reed to the effect that *Life* is sending up a man to cover the whole weekend—a man named Matt Cole. She has just hung up when a woman in her late forties and plenty busty appears, carrying a briefcase, a small suitcase and a portable typewriter.

Mary Nell recognizes her as Agatha and hands her the message about the magazine and Matt Cole. The newcomer is unexcited. Ginny introduces herself and Mary Nell. The newcomer walks toward the inner door, asks, "This the bedroom?" and goes on in. It seems odd to the girls that she doesn't remember. And it's still odder when she comes back and is unimpressed by the sofa and the picture.

A little angrily, Ginny says, "We'd better go, Mary Nell, and leave Miss Reed alone—with her memories."

"Miss Reed *is* alone with her memories. Outside, under a tree," says the visitor.

"Then who—?" puzzles Mary Nell.

"Me? I just carry the typewriter." She is, in fact, Miss Reed's secretary—Grace Woods. Better known in Washington as Woody.

The girls dash for the window for a look at the celebrity under the willows, so not much of them except two excited behinds is visible as Agatha Reed arrives. She is "undoubtedly the best thing that's happened to the United States Congress in a long time."

"Your reception committee," says Woody, indicating the two behinds, and at the sound of the voice the girls turn. Agatha doesn't even notice them, for she is suffused with nostalgia. She drinks in the room, touching the sofa, fingering the desk, looking at Uncle Willy and finally wafting spellbound into the bedroom. Woody has watched this performance with disgust, but it has made Mary Nell feel as though she were in church.

Ginny and Mary Nell hurry out to inform the reception committee that the celebrity has arrived, and Woody goes to work at the telephone, checking on all-night switchboard and Western Union service. Agatha emerges from the bedroom, wiping her eyes. "I haven't cried in years. It feels wonderful," she says.

Woody—It looks lousy.

Agatha—You don't understand. You just see a collection of buildings, a gate, some ivy—

Woody—What do *you* see?

Agatha—Myself at eighteen—eager, expectant, a little frightened. Asking—what is life? What am I? This is where it all starts.

Woody—You sound like an alumnae bulletin.

Agatha—Don't you even believe in colleges?

WOODY—I don't believe in looking at the past. I was born in Newark, New Jersey. Every time I go through on a train, I pull down the shade.

AGATHA—You ought to see a psychoanalyst.

WOODY—I just don't get it, that's all. A crowded calendar, two important bills coming out of committee, an election just four months off—and we're braiding a daisy chain.

AGATHA—Look, Woody, let's get this settled right now. I've come down here to *enjoy* this weekend. I'm going to cry, I'm going to be silly, I'm going to be sentimental, I'm going to walk barefoot down memory lane with ivy entwined in my hair. If you don't like it you don't have to look.

WOODY (*shrugs and picks up her notebook*)—What do you want to do about that Madison Square Garden rally? There's a choice of dates.

AGATHA (*plaintively*)—Not now—

WOODY—The world doesn't stop, even for Honorary Degrees.

AGATHA (*with a sigh*)—All right, tell them I think it should be the earliest date they can get. (*Sitting on the sofa, she winces.*) They never fixed it!

WOODY—Fixed what?

AGATHA—The spring. Ellie broke it when she got her junior grades. She thought old Dennis was going to flunk her. When she got the C, she jumped up and down on the sofa for ten minutes.

WOODY—I'll wire them you'll speak—if they can make it next week. Who's Ellie?

AGATHA—My roommate, Ellen Thatcher. She was a beautiful girl. They called us Sugar and Spice. (*Crossing to the window seat.*) We used to sit over here—on this window seat—Spring nights after Lights Out and talk about Life. (*Smiling.*) We had a pact. Wherever in the world we were, we'd send each other a telegram when we lost our respective virginities.

WOODY—Well?

AGATHA—Whatever happens to all girlhood pacts?

WOODY (*grunting eloquently and turning over to the next sheet of paper*)—Mrs. S. Arthur Poinceford invites you for a cruise on her yacht the week of the twenty-ninth. Down to Florida—back by Monday.

AGATHA—That's the oil lobby. Tell her oil and water don't mix. (*At the desk.*) There's a little secret panel in this desk. (*She pulls out a drawer and feels around behind it.*) I used to hide brownies in it. You share your clothes, your perfume, even your themes with your roommate. But not your brownies. Not the—(*She reacts suddenly, draws out a small box, opens it.*) Brownies!

WOODY—God, they must be stale.

AGATHA (*tasting one, relieved*)—Fresh this week. (*She offers the box to* WOODY.)

WOODY (*grimacing*)—Horrible stuff. Sticks to the roof of your mouth.

AGATHA—Now I *know* you need a psychoanalyst.

WOODY (*consulting the paper in her hand*)—Hope you feel photogenic. *Life's* covering the weekend.

AGATHA—Oh, that's nice.

WOODY—You *must* be getting important. They're sending Matt Cole down.

AGATHA (*abruptly turning*)—Who?

WOODY—Matt Cole, the war photographer.

AGATHA—You're joking.

WOODY—That's what it says here. (*Reading.*) "Matt Cole delayed." One of the kids took the message.

AGATHA—Why should they send *him* down here? This isn't his kind of thing at all. It's—it's ridiculous.

WOODY (*shrugging*)—Maybe he needs a vacation.

AGATHA (*obviously perturbed*)—You call Henry Luce. They've got twenty men that can do a better job on this sort of things. Tell him I *don't want Matt Cole*—I'd consider it a personal favor if he'd see to it.

Woody can't see why all the bother, but she puts in the call and is told the circuits are tied up. Ginny reappears, explaining that she has forgotten something.

"I'm afraid I found them," Agatha confesses. She extends the remainder of the box of brownies. But this isn't what Ginny forgot; it's a book she has left in the desk—Walt Whitman's "Leaves of Grass."

Agatha Reed is fond of Whitman, too. Her favorite poem, she tells Ginny, is a rather obscure one—"Goodbye, my fancy. Farewell, dear mate, dear love. I'm going away, I know not where—"

And Ginny finishes it for her: "Or to what fortune, or whether I may ever see you again. So goodbye, my fancy."

This intellectual interchange puts the young girl and the Congresswoman on friendly terms, and Ginny explains that she hadn't known much about Whitman until Dr. Pitt, the physics prof, gave her the book. Pitt apparently is a teacher who knows more than one subject.

Agatha realizes that she doesn't know the girl's name, and asks it. Merrill. She has started for the bedroom to fix up for the reception committee, and suddenly she stops.

"Your parents—will they be here for Commencement?"

"There's just my father," Ginny explains.

"You're Jim Merrill's daughter!"

Ginny uncomfortably admits it, and the delighted Agatha recounts that Merrill was *her* favorite professor, in History 101 A. He was very handsome and all the girls were in love with him. And he was a very good teacher, with a way of making history come to life.

Pensively, Ginny wishes aloud that her father were still a teacher.

A woman appears in the doorway—one with the look of a beauty who has eaten too many finger sandwiches at too many afternoon teas. She is wearing an expensive print dress and a much-too-fancy hat, and is carrying a large paper hat box. She is Ellen Griswold, nee Thatcher—Agatha's old roommate. The two alumnae fall upon each other with glad and emotional cries, and Ginny gets out as soon as she can.

In the hat box, Ellen has brought some mementoes—a sketch of a boy, a stuffed red Clara Bow doll and their favorite Victrola record, "Betty Boop." Ellen would like to play it right now on the machine Ginny and Mary Nell have left in the room, but Agatha would rather talk and catch up on Ellen.

This is not difficult, for Ellen is not much to catch up on—a perfectly satisfied, overweight empty-head. Married to Claude Griswold, and if there is anything she wants to know she just asks him; it's convenient having a husband.

"You know," Ellen apologizes, "I never did send you that telegram—like we promised. I guess I figured the wedding invitation would—"

"It did," says Agatha.

"I've never gotten one from you, either," pursues Ellen.

"Must have slipped my mind at the moment." Agatha goes on with her questioning and listening. Ellen has two boys. And a big barn of a house—eighteen rooms, and maybe Agatha can come to dinner with just a few people like the Mayor and the Falkners of Falkner Tools and the college trustees. Claude, of course, is chairman of the board of trustees.

"It's so cute—the interest he takes in the school," says Ellen.

"Gets a big kick out of it when the girls call him Daddy Griswold. He's always giving them things. This year it's a projection booth and movie equipment. They're renaming the theatre the *Griswold* Theatre."

This reminds Agatha that Miss Shackleford had asked her to bring down a documentary film from Washington, so she has brought her own—a picture based on a speech of hers entitled "Fight to the Finish."

Ellen is impressed. "Isn't that wonderful? You know, I always talk about how I knew you when. How we all voted you the girl most likely to succeed. . . . Of course, I never say anything about your being expelled."

Agatha is amused. "Thank you. I guess there won't be much said about that this weekend."

"I never did understand it, Agatha. Student court was so hush-hush about it. . . . Of course, everybody knew there was a man connected with it. You don't get expelled for staying out all night unless there's a man. . . ."

Agatha stares at her old and vacuous roommate. "You know, I've got the most peculiar feeling, Ellen. That you haven't changed—at all."

The reception delegation, which had planned an elaborate welcome at the railroad station, swarms into Ellen's sight through the window, Miss Shackleford, leading the way. The student committee. Miss Birdeshaw.

"Old Fun-in-Bed Birdeshaw?" Agatha asks.

"Still here. And still teaching physiology. Only now they call it Sex Hygiene."

Suddenly, Ellen is surprised to descry a man—none other than Dr. Pitt, the physics professor. This is a boner for sure, having him on the reception committee. "Claude," explains Ellen, "says he is a troublemaker. Jim's going to get rid of him next year. You knew they made Jim Merrill president the year after you left?" Yes, Agatha had read about it.

Now, with the delegation imminent, the cozy little chat is over. Just like old times to Ellen. And to Agatha, too, in a way; wryly, she says, "It's the first time in years I've been alone with anyone that I haven't been asked what's going on in Washington."

Ellen's reply causes Agatha to stare at her almost as if she can't believe her ears: "Oh, you never have to worry about that from me. I always say the less women worry about the government, the better."

The welcoming business is started off resoundingly by Miss Shackleford, who announces, "Welcome home, Agatha Reed!"

AGATHA—Thank you, Miss Shackleford.
MISS SHACKLEFORD—Or should I call you—the Honorable?
AGATHA—Definitely not.
MISS SHACKLEFORD (*chidingly*)—I see Mrs. Griswold's been the early bird. But I'm sure she's been telling you how honored Good Hope is to welcome back one of its *favorite* graduates.
AGATHA—Not *quite* a graduate.
MISS SHACKLEFORD (*thrown for a moment*)—Well—practically. (*Turning quickly to the rest who have grouped themselves inside the door.*) You remember Miss Birdeshaw? (MISS BIRDESHAW *flutters forward.*)
AGATHA—Of course. (*As* MISS BIRDESHAW *shakes her hand.*) How could I forget Miss Birdeshaw? She taught me the facts of life.
MISS BIRDESHAW (*embarrassed*)—I never really thought of it that way.
AGATHA—You look wonderful, Miss Birdeshaw.
MISS BIRDESHAW—So do you, Agatha. Of course, a bit older —I mean, a woman instead of a—
MISS SHACKLEFORD (*hastily*)—Miss Birdeshaw means you look so *young* to be in Congress.
AGATHA—Maybe Congress was equally deceived, Miss Birdeshaw. At least for the first few months.
DR. PITT—September fourteenth, to be exact, wasn't it? (AGATHA *turns to look at him in surprise.*) Your atom-bomb speech on the House floor.
MISS SHACKLEFORD (*delighted at the coup*)—I don't believe you know Dr. Pitt, Agatha. Our physics professor. He came to us a little after your time.
AGATHA—How do you do, Dr. Pitt. (*They shake hands.* DR. PITT *is around fifty—tall, a little drawn. There is the look about him of a man who knows a great deal, so much that there is no necessity to be constantly proving it.*) It's very gratifying your knowing my speech. Sometimes you get a feeling on the floor of Congress, something like being on the radio—you're not sure anyone's listening.
DR. PITT—I know what you mean. Get somewhat the same feeling in my classroom. (*There is a general laugh at this, especially from the student committee.* MISS SHACKLEFORD *beckons them forward. The girls are eager and excited.*)

Miss Shackleford—And this is your "honor guard"—chosen to represent the activities of the college this weekend.

The speeches of the girls are typical, formal and stilted, and as each speaks her piece, she hands Agatha a bouquet until the Congresswoman has an unmanageable armload. Student Government's speech is about Woman taking her rightful place beside Man. Physical Education praises Agatha's good sportsmanship with a handshake that makes Agatha wince. May Queen praises Womanhood Glorified. Dramatics Club is in favor of the Theatre of Life. And, at last, there's Graduating Seniors, in the person of Ginny Merrill. Graduating Seniors think Agatha's important presence is giving them courage when they need it most.

Agatha replies easily and gracefully, and at the end of her little speech, Dr. Merrill appears in the doorway. He is handsome and has virility and charm; the dignity of the presidency is on his shoulders, but a sense of humor seems to go with it.

"We're very pleased to have you back, Miss Reed," he greets her, and he extends his hand. Agatha drops some of the bouquets; Merrill tries to help recover them—and it's an awkward moment until Woody steps in and gathers all the flowers, including those Agatha still holds. Woody meets the president, and now Miss Shackleford takes charge again, for there is a full day ahead. She herds her brood out the door, and Dr. Pitt is last to go.

Agatha thanks Pitt for coming. Looking pointedly at Merrill, Pitt says it was a pleasant surprise to have been put on the committee—that he'd never expected it. When he has gone, Ellen Griswold bristles, "Well, that certainly was uncalled for! Now I see what Claude means—"

Politely, but firmly, Merrill reminds Ellen that she is in charge of the luncheon seating list, and she departs. Miss Shackleford now reminds Agatha of the film she is supposed to bring and Agatha says that it was sent a few days ago.

"What does it look like?"

"It's round—in a tin can," says Woody.

"Like sardines?"

Miss Shackleford hurries out to see if the film has arrived at the theatre, and Woody goes along to help her recognize it. Agatha explains to Merrill that Woody knows more about Washington than the FBI.

There is a silence for a moment—a rather awkward one, as if these two people are very aware that they are alone in a room

GOODBYE, MY FANCY 343

together. Merrill ventures to say that Agatha looks very well, and soon they are talking about how it feels to be president, and about Ginny. Merrill speaks deprecatingly of his post as requiring a few good Latin phrases, one slightly risqué story for Alumnae Dinners and a cap and gown in fairly good condition—but Agatha knows there must be more to it than that.

"I have a pretty vivid recollection of your contempt for educators with banquet-side manners. What was it you called them—Educaterers?"

He is surprised that she'd remember. "You've heard a lot of people say a lot of things."

Agatha agrees—then, quietly: "Only you were the first. The first who ever said anything that mattered."

On the other hand, Merrill seems to be up on everything Agatha has done and written; he has read all her articles, from Spain, Poland, China, Russia, Washington . . . He knows all she has done—except the first thing. "All these years I've wondered—what happened. Why you—just disappeared."

"It was very stupid of me to get caught climbing in my window at 6 A.M.," she smiles. And then, earnestly now, "It would have made no difference to the trustees that you were the man and that we were planning to be married. I would have been kicked out just the same, only you would have been kicked out with me. Not many young professors would have been so willing to give up a chance to be president."

"We'd decided to take that chance."

"I know. But I couldn't let you, Jim."

Agatha recounts how she'd hidden with an aunt in Detroit, and had made her mother promise to tell no one where she was. And then, after a time, she had read about Jim's marriage. Merrill tells her about it—a woman at Columbia, a little older than he was. They had much in common, though . . . and she died when Ginny was born.

The attraction between the two has become irresistible, and they have begun to move toward each other when Woody bursts in with the announcement that the film has been found. Agatha and Jim turn away from each other with elaborate casualness, but the secretary looks sharply from one to the other.

WOODY—I've got orders to tell you the Alumnae look hungry.
AGATHA (*to* MERRILL)—Creamed chicken and peas?
MERRILL—You learn to accept the inevitable.
AGATHA (*crossing toward the bedroom*)—I'd better fix my face.

MERRILL (*coming up to her*)—Miss Reed, did I tell you—it's wonderful to have you back?

AGATHA—Yes, Dr. Merrill. But it's good to hear it again. (*They smile at each other. Then* MERRILL *turns and starts toward the door.*)

MERRILL—It's wonderful to have you, too, Miss Woods. (*He exits.* WOODY, *looking after him curiously, crosses to the door and closes it. There is a silence.*)

WOODY—Nice-looking—

AGATHA—Who?

WOODY—Prexy. (AGATHA *is fixing her hair at the mirror.*)

AGATHA—Yes, isn't he?

WOODY—Looked mighty cozy in here when I came in.

AGATHA—Mmm.

WOODY—Talking over old history exams?

AGATHA (*laughing*)—You know what's wrong with you? You're spoiled. You're so used to having your thumb in every Washington pie you can't stand missing—

WOODY—Stop filibustering.

AGATHA—All right. (*She sits down deliberately.*) It's so.

WOODY—What's so?

AGATHA—Just what you're thinking.

WOODY—Oh. Well, I guess you've got to do something to give this weekend a lift. Has he got a friend for tonight?

AGATHA (*laughing*)—You're warm, darling. But not warm enough.

WOODY—Wait a minute! Let me get this straight—

AGATHA—It's quite simple. He was the first man I ever loved. Maybe the only one. (*As* WOODY *stares at her.*) Don't look so shocked. I'm going to marry him.

WOODY—*Marry* him?

AGATHA—He hasn't asked me yet. But he will—tonight.

WOODY (*hopefully*)—You're kidding.

AGATHA—Why? Are you against marriage, too?

WOODY—Good God, Agatha, I'm not against marriage. But there's a time and place for everything. You're smack in the middle of an election campaign—a *hundred* things. Your life's too busy.

AGATHA—There's quite a difference between a busy life and a full one.

WOODY (*shaking her head*)—That's funny—coming from you. Do you know what you are to millions of American women? The embodiment of an ideal. The woman they think they'd like to be. Not just reading about history, but helping to shape it.

AGATHA—Am I all that? Sounds wonderful.

WOODY (*belligerently*)—It *is* wonderful!

AGATHA—You've missed the point, Woody. I don't want to be any less. I'm greedy. I want to be more.

WOODY—And he's the man to do it?

AGATHA—Yes.

WOODY—For God's sake, Agatha, when I was fourteen I fell in love with the fellow who sold peanuts on our block. I'm not going to marry him.

AGATHA—Maybe you should. Maybe you have a deep and consuming need for peanuts. (*There is a silence.* AGATHA *turns away.*) I'm a little—disappointed. I hoped you'd be happy for me.

WOODY—What did you expect? I don't even *know* the guy.

AGATHA—Well, *I* know him. (*Earnestly.*) Woody, this isn't a whim. It's something I've waited for—thought about for twenty years. It may be the most important thing in my whole life. That's why I don't want anything to spoil it. I don't— (*She stops suddenly.*) What about that telephone call?

WOODY—Telephone—?

AGATHA—To *Life*. Henry Luce. About Matt Cole.

Agatha herself takes the telephone and learns that the call can be put right through now. Woody can't understand why all the rush. Agatha gets *Life* on the wire, identifies herself, and says she must speak with Henry Luce about something very important. Yes, she will wait . . .

A student, Susan, runs in excitedly. "Oh, Miss Reed! Mr. Cole just came and he's taking pictures of everybody! He wants one of you . . ."

Agatha's hand with the phone in it drops slowly to her side and she sinks into a desk chair. The squeak of a voice is heard in the instrument. It seems to be saying, "Hello, hello."

Woody takes the phone from Agatha and into it says, "Hello, Mr. Luce? You'll be delighted to know. We're renewing our subscription."

The curtain falls.

ACT II

It is late afternoon the next day—Saturday. Some of the flowers from the day before have been arranged around the room and they give it a kind of festive air. Through the open corridor door can be heard voices and the tinkle of glass—Agatha's "tea," going on in the lounge of Hope Hall. After a moment, Agatha comes into the room with two excited Merry Larks—a Merry Lark being a girl dressed in a maroon flannel blazer with large yellow notes appliquéd on it. The girls are chattering, and it seems to be about Miss Birdeshaw.

Out of the bedroom comes Professor Dingley, who teaches botany and looks it. He reports that Miss Birdeshaw is resting on the bed inside but looks quite pale. He has asked the janitor to bring his car alongside—to the service entrance, he hopes—so Miss Birdeshaw can be taken home.

An inkling of what has happened comes from the Merry Larks, who are talking almost in unison. All of them were lined up in the hall, ready to serenade Miss Reed, when Miss Birdeshaw came along and insisted on singing with them. The Larks didn't know what to do about that, but Miss Birdeshaw solved the problem by just sort of collapsing.

"Well," soothes Agatha, "don't worry about it. She probably forgot to eat lunch." She shoos the two girls out as Woody also emerges from the bedroom, carrying a wet towel. "Poor little Birdeshaw," sympathizes Agatha. "I'm afraid she never had a cocktail before . . . How is she?"

"Stinking!" reports Woody.

Dingley returns, reporting that the car has arrived, and goes back to the bedroom. Woody remarks that Birdeshaw certainly had been snuggling up to this butterfly chaser, and Agatha explains that this has been a crush since way back when she was in the college.

The botanist emerges, carrying the limp form of the teacher of sex hygiene. He doesn't need any help, thanks—except that, when he gets her to her home, well—

"Okay," says the efficient Woody. "You put her *on* the bed. I'll be along in a few minutes and put her *in* it."

"You're a regalla Florence Nightingale," jeers Agatha.

Woody has a thing or two to say about her employer. One—turning the tea into a cocktail party was something nobody else could get away with. Two—keeping the president of the college out until 3 A.M. isn't done.

"It's all right, Woody," Agatha reassures her. "You're now speaking to the future Mrs. James Merrill."

Woody has her own private feelings, but she masters them and loyally offers congratulations. "But what was all that fuss about Matt Cole?" "Forget it," says Agatha.

GOODBYE, MY FANCY

Merrill appears, having heard of Miss Birdeshaw's "accident," and is told what he has already guessed.

MERRILL—It's a good thing the *Life* man wasn't around. . . . He told me you worked together in China.
AGATHA—Yes.
MERRILL—Is he discreet?
AGATHA (*shaking her head*)—I'm afraid no, but don't worry. He specializes in major indiscretions. I don't think he'll make anything of it.
MERRILL—Oh, yes, he wants a picture of you, Miss Woods. Said you'd been dodging him.
WOODY—I hate *Life* photographers. They're always trying to catch you picking your nose. (*She exits, pointedly closing the door.* AGATHA *and* MERRILL *stand looking at each other.*)
AGATHA—You can lock the door, if you want to.
MERRILL—It's against dormitory rules. (*He crosses the room and catches her in his arms.*) And so is this. (*He kisses her.*)
AGATHA—I hate dormitory rules.
MERRILL—So do I.
AGATHA—Who makes them, anyway?
MERRILL—I do. (AGATHA *laughs.*) I can't believe it.
AGATHA—What?
MERRILL—That you're here. That everything's the same. You won't run away again?
AGATHA—Not a chance. Never on second proposals.
MERRILL—Incidentally—how did they compare?
AGATHA—Well, the first one was a bit more colorful. It had one lovely quotation from Shelley.
MERRILL—Shelley! I don't believe it!
AGATHA—Would you like me to quote?
MERRILL—No! Women have such frighteningly long memories.
AGATHA—*Some* women—for the words of *some* men. Have you any idea how many times I remembered things you said?
MERRILL—No . . .
AGATHA—That's how I got into politics. (*As he looks at her questioningly.*) I have a little farm in Pennsylvania where I go whenever things get too complicated. Some women change their hairstyle or take an ocean voyage. I put up chow-chow. In jars. With labels. (*Suddenly.*) Do you *like* chow-chow?
MERRILL—Very much.

AGATHA (*relieved*)—It's lucky. We have four hundred jars. Anyway, I was up there when a local delegation called on me. They wanted to run me for Congress—with an assist from Mr. Roosevelt. There wasn't any machine, or much money, but there seemed to be a lot of plain people who wanted to go out and ring doorbells for me. (*She pauses, remembering.*) It was all very flattering—but I didn't want to run for Congress. I just wanted to relax and get some sleep for a while. Only all that night I kept remembering something you'd once said when there was first talk of their offering you the presidency. You were a teacher, you said, and you wanted to teach. I asked you if that meant you'd turn it down, and you said, of course not. You said that "not to go forward was to go back. That no man could afford the luxury of standing still, no matter how comfortable it was." (*A pause.*) Do you remember?

MERRILL—Yes.

AGATHA—I called them up the next morning and told them they had a candidate.

MERRILL (*quietly*)—That's quite a responsibility. I'm not sure I would have wanted it. (*He rises.*) I think we'd better get back in there.

AGATHA—Maybe *everybody's* passed out by now.

MERRILL—I wouldn't count on it. I'm sure Miss Shackleford hasn't passed out.

AGATHA—Or Claude Griswold.

MERRILL—What do you think of Claude?

AGATHA—He's a charm-boy, all right.

MERRILL—Well, he has his faults. But he's pleasant—and he's really interested in the school. Oddly enough, he's a great admirer of yours.

AGATHA—Oddly enough is right. My voting record can't exactly have endeared me to him.

MERRILL (*laughs*)—No, but he seems to like you in spite of it. (*Then.*) Maybe I'll go on ahead. It'll look less— (*He searches for the correct word.*)

AGATHA (*kissing him*)—Is that what you mean?

MERRILL—That's what I mean. (*There is a knock on the door.* MERRILL *releases her quickly.*)

AGATHA—Yes?

GINNY'S VOICE—It's Ginny, Miss Reed. Are you busy? (MERRILL *reacts to this information nervously. He gets out his handkerchief and dabs at his lips.*)

MERRILL—I'd rather we didn't mention anything about this to Ginny at the moment. I'd like to tell her later—in my own way.

AGATHA—Of course, Jim. Just as you like. (*Crossing to the door, she opens it.*) Come in, Ginny.

Ginny has an urgent favor to ask Miss Reed, but stops short when she sees her father. Agatha senses a tension between these two, but Merrill eases it by excusing himself after giving Ginny an aimless and wrong compliment about her dress. Ginny's urgent news for Miss Reed is that Dr. Pitt is coming to see her.

"I hope you don't mind," explains the girl. "I did it without asking you—but I had to get him away. Claude Griswold is there, sounding off all about 'the next war' and Dr. Pitt's getting mad." To Ginny, Pitt is what all teachers should be, and she is worried about their trying to get him out. "You *will* pretend you asked to see him?" she pleads, and Agatha agrees.

Dr. Pitt arrives, Ginny excuses herself, and Agatha says amiably that she wanted another talk with a physics professor who would give his students Whitman to read.

Pitt is in no mood for blandishment. "I teach physics, Miss Reed. Only sometimes I don't. Sometimes I talk about other things. The daily headlines—the atom bomb—the world. You see, I have the dangerous misconception that the object of education is to teach the young to think."

And now he has been given an ultimatum—to teach what is inside the physics book and no more. Do that or resign. He has tried for another job in Texas, but the friend he has relied on there has "resigned" too. So now he is becoming resigned in the other sense. He will obey orders. "If they don't care enough about it, why should I? Let their daughters bring their knitting to classes and read movie magazines inside their notebook covers. Let them all be wiped off the face of the earth without even knowing why . . ."

Agatha counsels courage. All Dr. Pitt has to do is get the support of his president and make a real fight of it.

Pitt is taken aback by this suggestion. "Have you seen our library, that monument to learning? And the shiny gymnasium? Our eminent president gave up battles for buildings a long time ago."

Agatha won't believe him. "I *know* Jim Merrill," she says, and Pitt shrugs in defeat.

Unannounced through the door comes Miss Shackleford, conducting a sightseeing tour for the benefit of Matt Cole, the *Life* photographer. Matt wants to bow out when he sees who is in the room, but Dr. Pitt bows out instead. Miss Shackleford has a splendid idea for another picture for Mr. Cole—a shot of the present roommates and the old ones, Agatha and Ellen, together—and she hastens out to round up the other subjects, leaving Matt and Agatha alone.

Matt, coldly and expertly, cases the room—noticing the Betty Boop record, snapping a picture here and there, finally asking Agatha to pose on the sofa. His work seems to be distasteful to him, for he cannot see this woman in an atmosphere like this.

"I got a shot yesterday of some of the girls here—how old are they, nineteen, twenty? They were rolling hoops down the lawn. Very cute. I've got a picture I took in Rome five weeks ago. A couple of fourteen-year-old girls, soliciting on the streets. I'd like to print them side by side—'Higher Education, 1948.'"

Agatha and Matt begin to talk about their own old times covering the world. Did she get the pictures he sent her from China—and did she like the one of herself?

"I'm not sure. The one place you don't expect to be photographed is in bed—asleep . . . The occasion wasn't exactly the kind of thing I want recorded for posterity."

"Can I quote you on that, Miss Reed?" Matt puts his question quietly.

"I'm sorry. I didn't mean that quite the way it sounded. But it's true, isn't it, Cole? It's what I tried to say that day in Paris—but didn't. That it was a nice snapshot, but never a family portrait."

Matt drily offers her the negative for a wedding present—for he has been observing and he has been talking to Woody and has guessed pretty well what is in the wind.

"Who're you kidding?" he demands. "You can't bury yourself in a graveyard like this. Or on a corpse like Merrill. Anyone can see he's got no blood. They've sucked him dry."

"Will you get out of here!" Agatha orders.

"Sure. But here's another memento." He pulls her to him and kisses her, which increases her fury. She is in the midst of advising him to mind his own business when Miss Shackleford gaily returns with Ellen Griswold, Ginny and Mary Nell.

"I'm awfully excited," burbles Mary Nell, "to get my picture in *Life*."

Matt replies, "Just stick around long enough and *Life's* bound to catch up with you." He goes about arranging a suitable pose for the quartet, with Agatha co-operating icily. He sneaks a shot of Ellen when she isn't expecting it, and she wails, "But you didn't say when. I wasn't even trying to look nice."

"I have a theory about women, Mrs. Griswold"—and he looks at Agatha. "I think they look nicest when they're not trying."

Cole goes about shooting this one and that one and making notes for his captions. When Miss Shackleford explains that Ginny is the daughter of the president, Ginny pleads that the connection not be mentioned.

"Oh, I meant to ask you, Mrs. Griswold," Matt says casually, "did your husband ever get hold of Dr. Merrill?"

Ellen replies that she thinks so, and to Agatha she explains, "Claude was a little worried about the movie you brought down. Mr. Cole was telling him something about it."

Agatha looks sharply at Matt. Innocently, he says he was telling Griswold the film is one of the few pictures he's seen with real guts. And Ellen chimes in that Claude just wanted to be sure it was all right for the girls to see. Both Agatha and Ginny can see the direction events are taking, but bravely Agatha announces, "I'm sure Dr. Merrill is quite capable of handling the situation."

Merrill himself appears, and Miss Shackleford wails, "I hope there isn't any trouble about the movie."

"Oh," says Merrill, trying to take it all in. He admits, awkwardly, that Griswold has been a little concerned. Cole pointedly suggests to Miss Shackleford and his other picture subjects that they go somewhere else and make more pictures. When they have left, Merrill says to Agatha, "Darling, I'm sorry this happened. I forgot to ask you about the picture . . ."

"You don't think I'd have brought anything unsuitable?"

"Of course not."

"You know what I feel about what another war would mean. That's what this movie is—some newsreel film, illustrating a speech I once made."

Merrill speaks soothingly. It's just that Claude is a little ruffled about Agatha springing a cocktail party instead of a tea. Now, they can both go look at the picture.

But Agatha declines, pleading weariness, and a puzzled and worried Merrill departs after a tender kiss. The disconsolate Agatha wanders over to the phonograph, lifts the needle over the Betty Boop record and starts it. It sounds pathetically and irretrievably dated, and suddenly she shuts it off and slams down the lid.

The curtain falls.

Scene II

Two hours later and the lamps are on. The corridor door is open and the noise of a dormitory can be heard . . . a radio, occasional voices. Woody is at a desk, typing briskly. The student, Susan, comes in carrying two corsage boxes, coughs politely, finally gains Woody's attention by knocking. The flowers are for Woody and Miss Reed, Susan explains, and the twenty-two-man orchestra has arrived. And, if Miss Reed needs anything, Susan will be on the switchboard all night.

Woody sets down her own orchid box and examines Agatha's, trying to read the card dangling from it—right through the envelope—when Cole appears outside the window, leans on the sill and chides, "Uh-uh-uh!" Woody jumps guiltily.

"Why don't you try a little steam?" he suggests.

Matt swings into the room, but he is not welcome, for Woody has learned to mistrust him. She cannot, however, figure out what he is in this for—starting the business about Griswold and the picture. His reply is candid. "I'm in it for the same thing you are. I think she's making a mistake. I'd like to stop her."

"But why should *you* care?" asks Woody. Then she catches on. "Oh, God! It all adds up." She stares at him. "How long has *this* been going on? Twenty-*five* years?"

Matt tells her a bit. It started in Jugoslavia, where he found Agatha up to her hips in mud in a shell hole. She was the only reporter he ever knew who could sit in a poker game, win the biggest pot and still have every guy wondering what she'd be like in bed.

"How long did it take you to find out?"

Matt gives her a look. "I'll write my biography some day. You can read it."

But Woody won't be put off. She doesn't just work for Agatha—she likes her and cares what happens to her. So Cole begins, quietly:

"I haven't seen her since Paris—August 26, 1944. The day of the liberation. Me and every other newspaper hack in Europe had 'liberated' the city—with a little help, of course, from the Allied Forces. I shot 241 pictures by six o'clock and sent them off. Then I went over to the Scribe Bar. The 'cream' of American Journalism was there—and all way ahead of me. The place was a madhouse—I wanted to get out fast. . . . Then I saw Agatha. I hadn't seen her in six months. She had a red flower in that blonde hair—it stood out against the khaki and smoke. She was talking with some officer. She saw me and she stopped talking—I could tell it was in the middle of a sentence. It took us ten minutes to push our way through to each other, and another five minutes to get outside. That was even more hectic. The French people were celebrating outside—with champagne they'd hoarded in cellars for four years. Men wept in the streets, strangers kissed like lovers. Nobody talked—they yelled. (*He stops, remembering.*) I had to fight off two French Maquis to hang on to Agatha. Then I saw two more coming. I pushed in a door and pulled her after me. It was a barber shop. I could smell the hair tonic when I kissed her. And when I did, I knew it didn't matter that she'd ducked out on me in China—that she'd been a little remote in Algiers. I knew I wasn't going to ask her why—I was just going to ask her to marry me. She knew it, too. She had a room at the Ritz and she gave me the key while she went to her office to file her story. I bought up all the flowers I could find in ten blocks and sent them up to the room. Then I went up. (*Wryly.*) I sprinkled rose petals in the doorway— (*A long pause.*) They were a little brown around the edges when I got the cable from London. It said there'd been an urgent message calling her back to New York. Would I have the hotel send her bag on to her? (*He stops, smiles without humor.*) Well, I did. But I looked in it first. She traveled light. A toothbrush, a clean khaki blouse, a pair of stockings, two cakes of soap, her newspaper credentials, a flashlight—and a snapshot of a man. Not a very good one—overexposed. But good enough for me to remember. I recognized the face last week in a New York newspaper announcing the return of the 'Honorable Agatha Reed' to her college for an honorary degree."

Matt is confident that he will win out; Merrrill is no competition—just a memory, like something pressed in a book. "She can lie to herself just so much. Then she'll see him for what he is. And then she'll see me."

Woody is not nearly so hopeful—but she does admit that Agatha is getting worried already.

There is a phone call which Woody answers in a curious manner—somebody named George, and she's glad he has the stuff for her, and they'll be back next week. Matt is suspicious of what Woody is up to, and she confesses that she had George do a little research on Merrill for her. Matt is trying to guess what this information might be, when a girl is heard outside in the hall offering Miss Reed some candy.

Woody forces Matt to hide in the bedroom. "If she sees you in here she'll blow her top. She thinks we're in cahoots as it is."

Agatha comes in with Mary Nell and three other girls in evening dresses—Clarisse, Amelia and Carol. Mary Nell still is offering candy from a box she holds, and the other girls are greatly excited. Woody doesn't understand why until Agatha explains that it's an old school custom for a girl to pass the candy to announce her engagement. Mary Nell has got herself a man—one Sam Carter, All-American, 1947. "And we're going to live in Bangor, Maine, and have a woodburning fireplace in every room, practically."

When a girl outside shouts, "The men are here!" Mary Nell and her companions make a dash.

Agatha has been in the dormitory's "date room" giving an interview to the local press. The usual questions.

WOODY—Did you tell them?

AGATHA—I went easy.

WOODY—Easy? Since when have you started pulling your punches?

AGATHA—Well, after all, I'm not down here for political purposes.

WOODY—I know, but—

AGATHA—Well, I'm not. It would just create more embarrassment— (WOODY *stares at her, then turns abruptly and walks to her desk.*)

WOODY—I finished typing the notes you dictated for your Commencement speech. You better look them over tonight. (*She pulls the sheet out of the typewriter.*)

AGATHA—Good idea. (*She takes the pages, then sets them down absently.*)

WOODY (*suddenly making up her mind*)—I have some other notes you might like to look over. (*She picks up her shorthand pad.*)

AGATHA—Other notes?

WOODY—I called George Cameron and asked him to see what dope there might be around on Merrill.

AGATHA—You did—what?

WOODY—Yeah, I'm funny that way. I like to know everything I can about everybody. You always said that's what makes

GOODBYE, MY FANCY

me such a good secretary.

AGATHA—Stop making excuses. It's inexcusable! (*As* WOODY *shrugs and starts to put down the pad.*) What did he find out?

WOODY (*handing her the pad*)—It's right here. You can read it. (*Almost unwillingly* AGATHA *crosses to her, takes the pad. She looks at it, turns over the page, goes back to the first one in confusion.*)

AGATHA—I don't understand.

WOODY—Just what you see there.

AGATHA (*looking again*)—There's nothing there.

WOODY—That's what I mean. Nothing. An unblemished record. (*As* AGATHA *relaxes.*) That's what bothers me.

AGATHA—Bothers you?

WOODY—Yes. Don't you think it's funny? He's a prominent educator. Yet he's never been a member of one committee that took a stand on any issue. Not a single endorsement of anything the least bit political, controversial. Never even been investigated *once*.

AGATHA—What are you trying to say?

WOODY—We've just been through a war. People took stands on things. *You've* been investigated.

AGATHA (*icy*)—Very nice, Woody. Only don't forget. I've seen you work before.

WOODY—For God's sake, Agatha. If you want to get married, it's your own business. I just want you to be happy.

Agatha's anger has mounted, but a quarrel with her secretary is averted by the appearance of Ginny, seeking a talk with Miss Reed. Woody withdraws to the bedroom after having remembered to tell her employer that there are some flowers for her on the table. Agatha opens them; they are orchids, and she tells Ginny they are from her father. "He's my date," she explains, "and he's late."

Ginny knows this. "They're having a meeting over there," she explains. Then, abruptly, "Is it a good picture?"

"Yes, I think it is."

"Would you call it—propaganda?"

"It's a picture against war. If that's propaganda, it's like propaganda against cancer . . . Why, Ginny?"

After a moment's hesitation, Ginny blurts out that some people think the president of a college has the right to make decisions—but her father doesn't. He has to check everything with the trustees.

Ginny's perturbation mounts. Her father has done wonderful things for the school, she says, bitterly. Seven new buildings in ten years. The most successful college administrator east of the Rockies. "Isn't that something to be proud of? I'm so proud I could—" Ginny fights to hold back the sobs but they won't stay back, and Agatha tries to soothe her. "I'm so ashamed," the girl exclaims, and starts for the door.

"Where are you going?"

"I don't know. Anywhere—away from here. . . . Why should I stay? To stand up and let him hand me a diploma when I know it doesn't mean anything?"

Agatha argues that the diploma is for what Ginny already has learned here, and Ginny counters, "What have I learned? That my father's a coward?" She pulls away from the arms of Miss Reed. "Dr. Pitt wasn't the first, and your movie won't be the last."

Agatha asks point-blank if they have decided not to show the picture, and Ginny admits no, not yet, but . . . Agatha clings to hope; sometimes a man needs a certain moment for decision and maybe this is it. Ginny still tries to pull away.

"Ginny, you must listen! You probably know I was expelled from this college. I want you to know why. Because I stayed out all night with a man. We were very much in love—we were planning to be married. But I ran away—so I wouldn't hurt his chances of becoming president. (GINNY's *face pales*.) Even at eighteen, I felt it was important for a man like him to be the president of a college. I think your father remembers that today. Whatever's happened in between, I think he'd like to be that man again. (GINNY *crosses away from her*.) Maybe you resent me now. That was the chance I had to take. But I want you to know why I told you this. It's because I've grown very fond of you. You have a good mind and a whole life ahead of you. You mustn't throw it away by being bitter and disillusioned."

This puts a new light on things for the girl. Now she knows why her father always seemed different when he talked about Agatha Reed and why that picture of Uncle Willy was always in his study and things like that. Ginny feels better. She will go and get dressed now.

A moment later, Merrill appears—in tails, distinguished, handsome and apologetic for the delay. "Claude and Ellen dropped by. They thought we might as well make it a foursome." And the Griswolds enter behind him. Claude is a personable, jovial man in the late forties, impeccably dressed and having the air of wealth and power. Ellen wears an evening gown that seems carefully designed to accentuate the worst points of her figure. Quite evidently she has kept up the pace since the afternoon's cocktail party and now is really sailing. To Ellen this is just like old times—her and Ag going on double dates. She'd like to start the party right now, right here, with a phonograph record. Overriding Claude's objections that there's plenty of time for dancing to the orchestra, she puts on a hot Stan Kenton number and firmly swings her husband into a fox trot—which soon has him puffing a bit.

Agatha considerately turns off the machine. Directly, she asks Claude how he liked her picture, and he dissembles. "Well, it's not Abbott and Costello." "They're Claude's favorites," informs Ellen. Merrill tries to stir the group along to the party, but Agatha isn't ready to budge yet. She wants a showdown with Griswold and she begins it cleverly and amiably by complimenting him on his interest in the college.

Claude warms to the flattery. The motion picture theatre was really Jim's idea, of course, because visual education has become important—but what made Claude reach his hand in his pocket was the thought of the kick the kids would get at seeing movies right on the campus. He has no daughter of his own, but he regards "the kids" as six hundred and twenty-two daughters—"all spoiled silly. And why not? They've got time enough to start worrying their heads when they're out of college."

Again Agatha steers Claude toward the subject of her own movie—what did he think of it? It's a good thing to make pictures about outlawing war, he admits—as long as you're careful who you show them to. "For instance, if I'd known some of those strong scenes were going to be in the picture, I wouldn't have wanted Ellen to see it."

Ellen chimes in, "That's all right, Claude. I turned my head away at the bad parts."

Claude goes on with his subject. Agatha, after all, is a very special kind of woman. She's been on the war fronts and has gotten a kind of toughness. He finally comes right out with it and says he doesn't like propaganda, no matter where it comes from. "There's too much scaremongering going on. You can't stop wars that way."

"How *are* you going to stop them?"

"There've always been wars. There always will be."

Something explodes inside Agatha. She remembers aloud that Claude owns Great Northern Textiles—and points out that she sits on the Jameson Committee, which has been reviewing war profits.

Griswold catches the threat and smiles steadily. He admits that he made money out of the war, sure—but if she's accusing him of doing anything to start another one . . .

Agatha assures him she doesn't mean that—but what is he doing to stop one?

"That's beyond my power."

"Maybe. Maybe it's in the power of your six hundred and twenty-two daughters. But only if they know what war means. If they look at it—if they understand it."

Griswold won't be caught or moved. Life is tough enough and he isn't going to cheat those kids out of their youth. *"We know what's best for our school."*

Frequently Merrill has been trying to head off this discussion and he tries once more, but Griswold has the bit between his teeth. He announces flatly that the picture has been cancelled.

"And the president, did he agree?" asks Agatha. Merrill's face is strained as Griswold smugly replies, "The president and trustees always agree."

Merrill now begs to be allowed to speak to Miss Reed alone and Griswold, though annoyed, takes Ellen off. As they go, Ellen seems to be looking at her husband, for the first time in their marriage, with the suspicion that he may be less than perfect.

When they are alone, Agatha says to Merrill, "I feel a little sick." He expostulates, "You're not giving me a chance to explain."

He is in for a bad time. She forces him to admit that he thought the picture was all right for the seniors to see. But Claude is the man who foots the bills and he is generous, Jim argues.

"Yes, I know," sneers Agatha. "Give a college a science building—then tell the professors what they can say in it. Give them a motion picture machine but tell them what to run on it. That's not generosity. That's an investment—with damned good dividends."

Merrill, stung and desperate, cries, "All right. It's a business deal. He gives money. He wants his say. It's as simple as that." He pleads for her to understand that he must compromise on smaller things in order to win on larger ones. And if he fought Griswold to a showdown he'd be out tomorrow—and he has Ginny to think of.

Agatha observes that he doesn't know his daughter very well. In fact, he is going to lose her. Stand up to Griswold, she urges; but not for Agatha nor for Ginny, but for himself! Agatha can see that she is beginning to reach Merrill when they are interrupted by a student paging him from outside with a message to hurry from Mr. Griswold. Once again Merrill tries to escape and asks, harshly, "Are you coming?"

AGATHA—In a moment. I have a few more things to say.

MERRILL—Agatha, I'm sorry, but there's no use in pursuing the matter any—

AGATHA (*rising*)—Oh, I'm not going to plead with you any more. No more appeals to your better nature. I know when I'm licked. (*She smiles.*) I'm going to make a deal with you. A business deal. That's more in your line.

MERRILL—What are you talking about?

AGATHA—A few minutes ago I assured your daughter that you'd run this picture tomorrow. I don't like to think of her finding out that you won't. So I'm afraid you're going to do it. With or without Mr. Griswold's consent. I'll leave procedure up to you.

MERRILL—Is this your idea of a joke?

AGATHA—And in exchange for that small service, I'll give you my personal guarantee that the *Life* article won't even hint at the colorful events leading up to my expulsion from this seat of higher learning. (MERRILL *stares at her.*) You can imagine how excited Cole would be, stumbling across such a juicy morsel. Such a beautiful tale of love and sacrifice. A daring young girl caught climbing in her dormitory window—see picture of window on preceding page—braving the perils of expulsion rather than blight the budding career of her lover. And now, twenty years later—the girl, a Congresswoman, asked back to her college for an honorary degree. And the lover—hold on to your hats, now, folks—the president of the college!

MERRILL—I can't believe you'd . . .

AGATHA—Why not? You see, I'm willing to take a chance on you, Jim. I know now that you're a coward, and with a coward it's only a question of the lesser of two evils. Whether you *risk* being removed from here by running the picture or whether you accept the *certainty* of being removed when this story breaks.

MERRILL—You'd really do a thing like this?

AGATHA—Yes. You learn all kinds of dirty tricks in my work. The most important one being never to play fair except when you respect the man you're playing with. (*She picks up her scarf from the chair. From outside, the clear young voices of the senior class have broken into the Alma Mater as the step-sing obviously begins.*)

VOICES (*off*)—

"Good Hope, Our Alma Mater,
Thy wisdom and thy truth
Shall grow forever greater
In the years beyond our youth—"

AGATHA—The Alma Mater. Appropriate, isn't it?

VOICES—

"Whate'er may be our station,
Whate'er the storm and strife—"

(MERRILL *stands there for a second. Then he turns without a word and goes out.*)

"Thy shining inspiration
Shall light our way through life—"

(AGATHA *looks after him. Then she walks slowly to the door, turns off the lights and exits. The room is in darkness except for the moonlight streaming in the windows.*)

"So we raise up our voices and we shout Good Hope.
Good old Good Hope—
All the praise of our voices is about Good Hope,
Good old Good Hope—"

(*The bedroom door opens and* COLE *comes out. There is a calm satisfaction about even his silhouette which makes it obvious that he hasn't missed a word.*)

"We hope to be
Worthy of thee
And we plight love undying
To thy bright colors flying
In our hearts, brave and bold—"

(COLE *lights a cigarette and starts slowly across the stage toward the window.*)

"Maroon and Gold—
Good old—
GOOD HOPE!"

The curtain falls.

ACT III

It is early Sunday afternoon, half an hour before the Commencement procession. Woody is alone in the room and on the telephone explaining to Miss Shackleford that she hasn't seen Miss Reed since eight o'clock in the morning when she went out for a walk. Miss Birdeshaw comes in looking for Agatha and sits down to wait, because she wants to apologize. "I didn't get to her film showing this morning. I had a little—ah, headache."

With grim satisfaction Woody informs her that the show was canceled, and Miss Birdeshaw is glad—glad, that is, that she didn't miss it. Something else is worrying Miss Birdeshaw, and finally she screws up the courage to mention the tea party yesterday afternoon. "Did I leave with anyone? I mean—it was very nice of Professor Dingley to accompany me, wasn't it?"

Woody—Very. He wouldn't let anyone else carry you.

Miss Birdeshaw—*Carry* me? (Woody *nods*. Miss Birdeshaw *emits a little moan*.)

Woody—You felt a little—sleepy. We took you home.

Miss Birdeshaw—We? *You* undressed me?

Woody—Yes.

Miss Birdeshaw (*sinking back with a sigh of relief*)—Thank you, Miss Woods.

Woody—Not at all. Some day you can return the favor.

Miss Birdeshaw—I must have acted pretty silly yesterday.

Woody—Don't you remember?

Miss Birdeshaw—I remember some things.

Woody—You told some great stories. About your Aunt Deborah. The time she locked herself in the carriage house all night with two of the stable boys . . .

Miss Birdeshaw—Oh, no! (*Faintly.*) Did Professor Dingley laugh at that?

Woody—He choked. That was when you took him out in the garden for some deep breaths of fresh air. Do you remember that?

Miss Birdeshaw—A little. (*Blushing.*) I suppose I ought to be ashamed of myself.

Woody—Why?

Miss Birdeshaw—At my age— (*Then, remembering.*) But I had a wonderful time. The best time I ever had in my life.

Woody (*touched*)—Good. That's the way to talk.

Miss Birdeshaw—I wonder—maybe you'd tell Agatha I'm sorry. In case she feels badly about yesterday. I've been worrying about that.

Woody—Sure, I'll tell her.

Miss Birdeshaw—Thank you. Then I think I'll be running along. (*Rising.*) Professor Dingley's waiting for me outside. We're walking in the procession together, you know.

Woody—No, I didn't.

Miss Birdeshaw—He dropped by this morning, to see how I felt. He brought me some roses—yellow roses. Two dozen.

Woody—That was very thoughtful.

Miss Birdeshaw—Wasn't it? (*Then.*) Do you know something, Miss Woods? Professor Dingley and I have walked in twenty-three Commencement processions at this college. But this is the first time we'll have ever walked—together.

When Miss Shackleford bustles in, Miss Birdeshaw is bright-eyed, flushed and almost pretty. Miss Shackleford is still worried about where Agatha is, and she'd like to be rid of the professor of sex hygiene. Pointedly she tells this lady that the Associate Professors are standing in line right now for the procession, and she'd better get going.

Quietly, Miss Birdeshaw informs Miss Shackleford, "Professor Dingley and I are walking together in the procession."

This is ridiculous. Why, full professors are several hundred feet ahead of associates. Miss Birdeshaw says she knows this—but that she and Professor Dingley prefer it the other way. Furthermore, there's no rule that says they can't—and she exits in triumph.

This weekend is getting Miss Shackleford down, with everybody acting so strangely. Dr. Merrill, for instance, and the whole film business. "Last night he tells me to cancel it. Then this morning he says I'm to go ahead."

Woody is dumbfounded at this news, and her puzzlement isn't helped any by the appearance of Matt Cole in high spirits. Miss Shackleford flutters off once more and Woody, looking narrowly at Matt, wonders why he feels so good if he has just come from the movie showing—as she correctly presumes he has. He feigns being philosophical: "Got to take the bad with the good."

Susan bounces in with a report that she's been asking around casually, like Miss Woods said to do, and has heard a report that Miss Reed was seen about an hour ago walking toward the railroad station. Woody shoos her out with advice to keep on the trail, real casual-like. Woody is troubled, and decides she'll go out hunting for Agatha herself.

As soon as she has gone, Cole's pose of unconcern disappears. On the phone he checks the railroad station, makes sure that a tall blonde hasn't bought a ticket within the last hour. Then there is a phone call. It is Susan, with a message: Miss Reed has been sighted coming through the Ivy Arch. At this news he begins acting like an expectant lover examining the scene of the rendezvous. He opens the door a bit wider, turns the Clara Bow doll's face to the wall, tosses a rumpled pillow into the bedroom, puts on the phonograph. It is the Betty Boop record, which he breaks immediately and finds in a stack a more suitable one for background music—a love song, low. From a vase he takes a couple of roses and strews a handful of their petals in the doorway, then makes a path of petals to the window seat. Here he stretches out, waiting.

When Agatha arrives, she is tense, jittery and weary, and does not notice the petals or the man. She starts when Matt inquires, "Tired?" He explains that he is holding the fort while Woody is out looking for Agatha. He congratulates her on the film showing, and she tries to show pleasure.

COLE—You were right about Merrill. Weren't you?

AGATHA (*crossing away from him*)—Really, there's no need to . . .

COLE—Eat crow? Oh, I don't mind. Where you're concerned, I've got no pride. You ought to know that by now. I gave it up when I came down here. (*Approaching her again.*) Of course, I did have a feeling you might like it. . . .

AGATHA (*eluding him again*)—We went through all this yesterday.

COLE (*coming round to face her*)—I know. But that was so long ago. I thought you might have changed your mind.

AGATHA—Why should I?

COLE (*gently*)—People do. All the time. (*Brushing his face against her hair.*) Besides, I saw it once in a movie—how the bride turned at the last minute and ran off with the best man. (*For one moment,* AGATHA *stands there. Then she breaks away from him.*)

AGATHA—Cole, leave me alone. . . . (*There is a pause as* COLE *looks at her, unable to believe that she isn't going to tell him the truth.*)

COLE—You mean—you've got nothing to say to me?

AGATHA—I thought we said it all.

COLE (*slowly*)—Yeah, but I'm stupid. I've got to have it spelled out for me. He's a great guy. He's all you've dreamed about—waited for—for twenty years. You're gonna go right ahead and marry him—?

AGATHA (*her back to him*)—The date hasn't been set—yet.

COLE—But it will be?

AGATHA (*turning desperately*)—I don't see that this is any of your business!

COLE—You don't? (*Abruptly he crosses, turns off the victrola; then he strides to the telephone and picks it up.*) Get me Dr. Merrill's office.

AGATHA—What are you doing?

COLE—I'm gonna ask Merrill to come over here. I'd like to congratulate him. (*Into phone.*) Is Dr. Merrill there? I'd like to talk to him— (AGATHA *runs across the room and wrenches the phone out of his hand, slams it down on the desk.* COLE *stands looking at her.*) You couldn't face that, could you? Because you know it's a lie. You threw away six years we could have had together because of a lie, but you can't be honest enough now to admit it to me. You've got to hang on to your precious ego. Well, you can keep it. I'm a big boy now. I've got bigger and better things to do with my life. (*He turns and goes out.*)

Agatha bangs up the phone when it squeaks hello, picks her Commencement speech off the desk, reads a few lines, and with violent disgust crumples it and throws it into the wastebasket. She checks her suitcase to be sure it is packed, gets her hat, jacket and purse out of the bedroom and is in flight when Merrill enters. It is obvious to him what she is about to do and she makes no attempt to conceal it. The speech is in the basket, where it belongs; she can send a telegram saying she is sick or needed in Washington, and he can read the speech, she suggests.

"Just like twenty years ago, isn't it, Agatha? Running away again." This brings her to a halt. She tries to tell him that she was wrong last night—that she shouldn't have thought she could "save" his daughter. "I can't blackmail you for the rest of your life. It's better for her to know the truth—now, while she's young."

GOODBYE, MY FANCY

And the chance for Ginny to know is, indeed, right now—for Ginny comes into Agatha's room. She is radiant as she smiles at the Congresswoman and her father. The motion picture, she feels, was the best graduation present that could have been given the senior class—and to her. She kisses her father without shyness or apology and is about to take flight again when he stops her.

"You kissed me just now," he says. "You haven't done that in a long time. I'm very grateful. But I can't accept it under false pretenses. . . . I had the movie shown—but not for the reasons you think. I did it because Miss Reed forced me to. . . . I don't want any more lies between us. . . . I'm sorry."

Ginny begins to weep and her father gently tells her that he hasn't meant to hurt her. Ginny, facing him, says, "You've forgotten a lot of things about me, haven't you? That I just don't cry when I'm sad. That I cry just as much when I'm happy." She embraces him and continues, "I don't care why you showed the picture. I just wanted you to be honest. With me. And with yourself."

A happy time for father and daughter is interrupted by the breathless entrance of Ellen Griswold, demanding to know what this resignation nonsense is. First it was the movie, and now the resignation, and Claude is terribly upset. The letter of resignation came a half hour ago, and Ellen read it on Claude's desk. "And it was just beautiful. Especially the part about self-respect."

The astounded Agatha can't understand what has motivated Merrill until he explains it to her. He had stood in the back of the theatre watching the picture and he realized he almost hadn't let the students see it. "That's when I knew everything you said about me last night was true. That I had no right to be president of this college—or any college."

This statement is shocking to Ellen, who argues that the college would be nothing without Jim—and what a row the students would raise! "I just wanted to come and ask you to reconsider, Jim. . . . You won't mention this to Claude, will you? He'll like to think it was his own idea."

Commencement is really under way, now. The joyful Ginny has gone, and Ellen follows. Agatha begs Jim to reconsider his resignation, arguing that it is important to the college that he stay on. But he has a lot of thinking to do. When he came in here just now it was to tell her that he is in love with her, but he doesn't have much hope for it after last night.

Agatha, as he talks, has seen a rose petal on the floor. She picks it up and smiles in sudden appreciation as she listens. "I know we're different people than we were twenty years ago," he pleads. "I know a lot of things have changed. But I won't want to kick myself for the rest of my life—for not trying. Do I have a chance?"

Agatha's answer is not immediate, but it comes. "You might have had a hell of a chance, Jim. Except that I've had a standing offer for six years. And I think I'd better take it up before it runs out. If it hasn't run out already."

Jim accepts the inevitable and leaves for the Commencement just as Woody comes back. To Agatha, he says, "See you in a few minutes?" She assures him she'll be there, and Woody goes to the bedroom to get the cap and gown.

Agatha inspects the room—the faded, broken sofa and all the rest of it—and laughs to herself. Suddenly she feels free! Briskly she calls to Woody, "What arrangements did you make for getting us out of here?" To the amazed secretary, it's a new Agatha Reed—or the old one, full of plans for committee meetings and a speaking tour. Woody is still trying to figure out the change when Cole appears, looking angry and charged with resolve. Brusquely, he orders Woody out.

COLE—You're the stubbornest dame I ever saw in my life. You're so goddam stubborn, you'd go ahead and *marry* him— (*With grim resolution.*) But you're not going to do it!

AGATHA (*enjoying it*)—Really?

COLE—Look, let's get one thing straight. I don't expect you to fall into my arms. I wouldn't even catch you if you did. One thing I found out this weekend. I *don't like women!*

AGATHA (*if she could only laugh*)—Then why all the bother?

COLE—Because I'm neat! I straighten pictures—I put the tops on toothpaste tubes. I don't like leaving unfinished things around. You're not going to go through with this!

AGATHA—Aren't you being a little overconfident?

COLE—I don't think so. I'm offering you a deal. A business deal. (AGATHA's *smile fades.*) In exchange for such a small service, I'm giving you my personal guarantee that the *Life* article won't even hint at the colorful events leading up to your expulsion from this seat of higher learning. (AGATHA *takes an angry step toward him. He holds up his hand.*) See pictures on preceding page.

AGATHA—So you even eavesdrop!

Cole—Sure. (*With a smile.*) You learn all kinds of dirty tricks in *my* work, too. (*There is a moment while* Agatha *struggles between anger and appreciation. The latter wins, but* Cole *doesn't know it.*)

Agatha (*elaborately*)—Well, then it seems I have no choice. (*She crosses to the door, opens it and calls.*) Woody! (Woody *enters almost immediately. She looks toward* Cole *eagerly.*) Woody, there's been a change of plans. We'll drive into Boston and catch the seven o'clock plane. And call Wister tonight to set up that committee meeting in the morning. Oh, yes—call Senator Haines and tell him I'll make a swing through the whole state before the election.

Woody (*bewildered*)—But you just told me to—

Agatha—I know. But there's been a *change of plans*.

Four girls, capped and gowned, announce themselves as Miss Reed's honor guard. The campus bells start ringing. Agatha retrieves her speech from the wastebasket, puts on her cap. "Got everything now?" asks one of the honor guard.

Agatha, marching out, gives Cole a meaningful little smile as she passes. "Everything," she says.

It's all too much for Woody, who stands shaking her head. "A woman couldn't go crazy in one weekend, could she?" she asks Cole.

"What's so crazy about changing her mind?"

Woody howls, "Changing her mind? She told me the *same damned thing* five minutes ago!"

Comprehension slowly sweeps over Cole. He seizes Woody and gives her a resounding kiss. When she can come up for air she expostulates, "Hey, what's the matter with *you?*"

"Sweetheart, don't try to understand it. Just relax and enjoy it." And he heads for the door like crazy as

THE CURTAIN FALLS

THE PLAYS AND THEIR AUTHORS

DEATH OF A SALESMAN, by Arthur Miller

Arthur Miller, whose "Death of a Salesman" tops the current list of Ten Best Plays, may hold all records as an award and prize-winning playwright. His career was founded and furthered by cash prizes, the first being an Avery Hopwood Award of $250 while he was an undergraduate at the University of Michigan. A year later he won another Hopwood Award, and, out of college in 1944, a $1,250 Theatre Guild prize. After college he then joined the Federal Theatre Project, which folded before he had finished his first play. He tried again and the result was "The Man Who Had All the Luck," which folded a week after it reached Broadway in 1945. In 1947 he won the Drama Critics' Circle prize with "All My Sons."

Miller was born October 17, 1915, in New York City and brought up in Brooklyn. He graduated from high school in 1932, during the depression, and went to work in a warehouse for auto parts for $15 a week. It took him two years to earn enough to start his freshman year at Ann Arbor. He has held such tiring jobs as truck-driver, waiter, crewman on a tanker, and even now spends a few weeks each year working in a factory so he will remember what it feels like to stand on one's feet in one place eight hours a day.

He lives an average family life in Brooklyn with his wife, whom he met in college and who as Mary Slattery encouraged him to write plays for the Hopwood contests. Later, as Mrs. Miller, she helped the family finances with her salary as a secretary. They have two children and four acres in Connecticut where he built his work shack with his own hands. In addition to his plays, Arthur Miller has written for the radio, a few short stories for the magazines and two novels. He collected material for the movie, "GI Joe," during the war. In 1944 he wrote "Situation Normal," a story of army camps, and in 1946 "Focus," a novel about anti-Semitism.

ANNE OF THE THOUSAND DAYS, by Maxwell Anderson

Maxwell Anderson is the most prolific of our major playwrights; as soon as one work is done and upon the stage, he begins another—and he tries to vary his pace. Following his seriously literary and dramatic history, "Anne of the Thousand Days," he began with Kurt Weill, the composer, on a musical, "Cry the Beloved Country," based on Alan Paton's novel about South Africa. Anderson does most of his work at his home near High Tor, the Hudson Valley mountain about which he wrote a play.

In 1923, when he was on the editorial staff of the *New York World*, he wrote "What Price Glory?" with fellow-staffer Laurence Stallings, and has been a dramatist ever since. He developed his yearning to write in verse, or measured prose, feeling that it was the best medium for emotion. He hoped that this medium, so familiar in the tales of the kings and queens and gods of the classics, could be used on the modern scene and about ordinary people—and he proved to himself it could be done with "Winterset." But he also likes the heroic figures of olden times, and "Anne" is the latest in a series of dramas about kings, queens and saints.

The playwright was born in Atlantic, Pa., in 1888, the son of a minister.

THE MADWOMAN OF CHAILLOT, by Jean Giraudoux; English play by Maurice Valency

Jean Giraudoux wrote "The Madwoman of Chaillot" during the German occupation of Paris when few Frenchmen could see with certainty that France might be again liberated. The play's posthumous production and success would have neither surprised nor annoyed him. Though he wrote the play in 1943 during the time of darkest occupation, he refused to have it presented while his country was in the grip of the enemy.

Giraudoux, popular in France as both dramatist and novelist, was born in 1882 at Bellac (Haut Vienne) and educated at the Ecole Normale in Paris. In 1918 he spent some time in America as an officer-instructor and afterward wrote a book of American experiences called "Amica America." His play, "Amphitryon 38," was produced by the New York Theatre Guild in November, 1937, following the original French presentation by eleven years. Another play of his called "Siegfried" was tried briefly by Eva Le Gallienne at the Civic Repertory Theatre in 1930.

Maurice Valency, who made the English adaptation of "The Madwoman of Chaillot," is an associate professor of Comparative Literature at Columbia University. He has written three original plays and though none has had a New York production, two have been presented in other American cities and in Europe.

Detective Story, by Sidney Kingsley

Sidney Kingsley in his current melodrama displays the same thorough and deliberate qualities which have characterized the playwright all through his career. He was born in New York City in 1906 and did well enough in his preliminary studies to be awarded the State Scholarship to Cornell University. While in college he took all the courses offered in public speaking and drama and showed early promise as a writer. He became an outstanding debater, was in the dramatic club, played in numerous productions and contributed a number of sketches in the annual revues of the club. He won the Director's Prize in 1928, the year of his graduation, for his play, "Wonder-Dark Epilogue." After college he gained experience as an actor, playreader and scenario writer. His first produced play, "Men in White," won the Pulitzer Prize for the season of 1933-34. His second play, "Dead End," was an immediate success. He wrote, produced and directed two plays, "Ten Million Ghosts" and "The World We Make." "The Patriots," a play about Thomas Jefferson and his home, Monticello, was produced in 1943.

Since it was necessary to report in 1933 at the time of "Men in White" that Sidney Kingsley was not a physician, let us make it clear that he is not a member of the detective squad and his own Monticello is a 50-acre farm near Oakland, N. J., where he lives in contentment with his wife, Madge Evans, whom he married in 1939.

Edward, My Son, by Robert Morley and Noel Langley

Robert Morley, who wrote the successful play, "Edward, My Son," in conjunction with Noel Langley, has with brilliant results spent most of his life refuting conservative plans and generally accepted axioms. In 1908 he was born at Semley in Wiltshire, England, though he prefers to say he was born outside of London. His family had him educated at Wellington, a military school, but he never arrived at Sandhurst. They sent him abroad to learn languages in preparation for a diplomatic calling, but he did not do well in them, though he is a master of fluent spoken and written English. He did shine at selling beer and vacuum cleaners and took the proceeds to enter the Royal Academy of

Dramatic Art. In spite of his youth and because of his appearance, he played a surprising number of butlers in touring English comedies and only the elderly, portly gentlemen in Shakespeare. After writing the play, "Short Story," he decided to give up acting and then received the role of Oscar Wilde which established his reputation in London in 1937 and New York, 1938. He did say playwriting was his ultimate ambition but never considered writing a play for himself, until he made another sensation playing the main role in his "Edward, My Son."

Noel Langley, who wrote "Edward, My Son" with Robert Morley, is listed in two previous Burns Mantle compilations. In 1939 his drama, "Farm of Three Echoes," was produced with Ethel Barrymore acting and lasted 48 performances. In 1941, "The Walrus and the Carpenter," described as comedy on the mad side without music when it was first put on in Southern California, performed also at the Cort to 9 paying audiences. As stated elsewhere in this volume, he was born in Natal, South Africa, in 1911; went to Natal University College; has been engaged in broadcast announcing and film writing; authored a novel, "There's a Porpoise Close Behind Us."

Life with Mother, by Howard Lindsay and Russel Crouse

Howard Lindsay and Russel Crouse, the happy writing team whose "Life with Mother" sequeled their "Life with Father," had both collaborated with other writers before joining their talents on the musical, "Anything Goes," in 1934. Together they did three musicals before the first "Life," then more musicals and "State of the Union," for which they received the Pulitzer Prize in 1946. They also co-produced "Arsenic and Old Lace," and "The Hasty Heart" and "Detective Story."

Howard Lindsay, author, actor, director and producer, was born in Waterford, N. Y., in 1889. His family had never been theatrically inclined but he got a taste for the boards when Howard became the recipient of elocution lessons in lieu of cash owed to his mother. He was educated at Edward Everett Grammar School, Dorchester, Mass., Boston Latin School, won a scholarship to Harvard where he spent a year, then six months at the American Academy of Dramatic Art. His first job was in "Polly of the Circus." His first important role was in "Dulcy." He is married to Dorothy Stickney, for whom he tailored the role of "Mother."

Russel Crouse was conducting a newspaper column on the

New York Evening Post when he did his first theatrical writing, "The Gang's All Here," a musical. It ran two weeks. He also served as press representative for the Theatre Guild for a number of years. He was born in Findlay, Ohio, in 1893, attended public and high schools in Toledo, held reportorial jobs—sports, political and general—on the *Kansas City Star, Cincinnati Post* and several New York papers. His column "Left at the Post" was noted for his wit. He is married to the former Anna Erskine and they have a son named Timothy.

LIGHT UP THE SKY, by Moss Hart

Moss Hart, a native New Yorker, wanted to be part of the theatre since he saw his first play at the age of seven. Besides having the theatre in his blood and caring about the success of his own efforts to the point of being nauseated on opening nights, he is a gifted, conscientious, brilliant craftsman who has had experience in many of the phases which make up the Broadway scene. His first theatre job was as office boy and typist at the age of 18 for a play producer to whom he submitted anonymously the manuscript for a melodrama called "The Holdup Man." It was produced and resulted in loss to the producer and some small extra revenue to Hart. At one time his ambition was to be an actor. He directed amateur theatre groups in New York in the Winter and at Summer camps, the Borsch Circuit, in the Summer. Then he rang the bell with his play, "Once in a Lifetime," George S. Kaufman collaborating. As librettist, he did "Face the Music" and "As Thousands Cheer" with Irving Berlin.

"You Can't Take It with You," another Kaufman collaboration, was awarded the Pulitzer Prize in 1935. Other outstanding contributions by Moss Hart include: "The Man Who Came to Dinner" (with Kaufman), "Lady in the Dark," "Winged Victory" and "Christopher Blake." He has had financial interests in several plays and has directed a number of Broadway successes. Mr. Hart married Kitty Carlisle, singer and actress, in 1946. They have a son, a New York apartment and a Bucks County farm.

THE SILVER WHISTLE, by Robert E. McEnroe

For the records, this is Robert E. McEnroe's first play. Actually it is his twelfth, no producer having nibbled at any of the others which he wrote in his spare time while working in a factory. To those who call his playwriting an avocation, he replies that it is nice to have a job and gives credit to the United Aircraft Corp. in Hartford, where he worked in the research department, for being wonderfully kind in giving him time off to work with the Theatre Guild when it became interested in "The Silver Whistle."

Mr. McEnroe was born in New Britain, July 1, 1916, but grew up in Florida. His father was an insurance and real estate man and moved his family there each Winter, so most of the playwright's education was obtained in the southern state, though he did attend schools in Connecticut and the Middle West. Eventually he settled in Hartford and gave up his job at the factory only when his play was an established hit.

Two Blind Mice, by Samuel Spewack

Samuel Spewack wrote "Two Blind Mice" alone, though the well-known husband-and-wife writing team of Sam and Bella Spewack is represented in New York by the musical, "Kiss Me, Kate." Since they have written many successes together, notably "Boy Meets Girl," the fact that their last two plays, "Woman Bites Dog" and "Miss Swan Expects," ran only 5 and 8 performances, respectively, most likely has no bearing upon the situation.

Samuel Spewack was born in Russia in 1899. He was brought up on the East Side in New York, educated in New York public schools and Columbia University. He became a reporter on the *New York World* at the age of 18, covering the Genoa Conference in 1922. He and Bella had just been married, so they shared the experience of being sent to various foreign bureaus, including two years in Moscow and another two in Berlin. He returned to this country in 1926 and devoted his energies to writing for Hollywood and the New York stage until 1941, when he again went abroad, this time to England for *Look* and the *New York Evening Post*. In 1942 he headed the Domestic Film Unit of the Office of War Information. In 1943 he was press attaché to the U. S. Embassy in Moscow for the Moscow Conference, and headed the Russian division for Overseas Office of War Information. In the Summer of 1949 he was again back in Europe, making a documentary film for the U. S. Government.

Goodbye, My Fancy, by Fay Kanin

Fay Kanin, born Fay Mitchell in New York City, graduated from the University of California at the age of 19 but it was a visit to her former Alma Mater, Elmira College, New York, which gave her the idea for her first full-length play. This successful production was accomplished by the time she was 30. She had wasted no time in accumulating a solid background for playwriting. A few months after her college graduation she was working for RKO Studios in Hollywood. While she was in the story department on that lot she also wrote originals for pictures, sold several magazine stories and acted in plays, including a short one of her own, for the RKO Studio Club. She continued her acting with a year at the Hollywood Actors' Lab and found time to co-author a novelette which appeared in *American Magazine*. She calls herself a feminist and her theories, which take the angle that women are just as good as men, may have taken shape while she organized, wrote the script for and did the commentary on a network radio program called "The Woman's Angle" at the beginning of the war.

In 1940 she married Michael Kanin, young screen-writer, who became a legitimate theatre producer to stage her play. They have a son, Joel, aged 4, and make their home in one of the Los Angeles movie suburbs.

PLAYS PRODUCED IN NEW YORK

June 1, 1948—June 1, 1949

(Plays marked "continued" were still playing June 1, 1949)

SLEEPY HOLLOW

(12 performances)

Musical comedy in two acts, presented by Lorraine Lester at the St. James Theatre, June 3, 1948. Book and lyrics by the late Russell Maloney and Miriam Battista (Mrs. Maloney); music by George Lessner; orchestrations by Hans Spialek, Ted Royal and Mr. Lessner; directed by John O'Shaughnessy and Marc Connelly; dances by Anna Sokolow, costumes by David Ffolkes, settings by Jo Mielziner; musical conductor, Irving Actman.

Cast of characters—

Ike	William Ferguson
Roelf	Larry Robbins
Mrs. Van Brunt	Laura Pierpont
Mrs. Van Tassel	Ruth McDevitt
Mrs. Van Ripper	Jean Handzlik
Wilhelmina	Ellen Repp
Mr. Van Brunt	Bert Wilcox
Mr. Van Tassel	Tom Hoier
Mr. Van Ripper	Morley Evans
Jacob Van Tassel	Bobby White
Willie Van Twiller	Walter Butterworth
Hans Van Ripper	Alan Shay
Martin Van Horsen	Richard Rhoades
Stuyveling Van Doorn	Lewis Scholle
Teena	Doreen Lane
Hilda	Robin Sloan
Greta	Sylvia Lane
Brom "Bones" Van Brunt	Hayes Gordon
Katrina Van Tassel	Betty Jane Watson
Hendrick	Ward Garner
Eva	Mary McCarty
Luther	Russell George
Ichabod Crane	Gil Lamb
Annie	Margery Oldroyd
Lena	Peggy Ferris
Nick	Franklin Wagner
Piet	Shaun O'Brien
Balt	Ray Drakeley
Walt	James Starbuck
Chris	John Ward
Bertha	Margaret Ritter
Margaret	Jo Sullivan
Elizabeth	Kaja Sumdsten
Jenny	Ann Dunbar
Mr. Van Hooten	Ken Foley

```
Joost..................................................John Russel
Conscience............................................Ty Kearney
Indian................................................Kenneth Remo
Cotton Mather.........................................William Mende
The Lady from New Haven..............................Dorothy Bird
    Act I.—Scene 1—The churchyard.  Noontime.  2—The river bank.
3—The schoolroom.  4—Kitchen of the Van Tassel house.  5—The
river bank.  6—The churchyard.  Act II.—Scene 1—The Van Tassel
barn.  2—Attic room in Eva's house.  3—The kitchen.  4—The church-
yard.  5—The churchyard.
```

Principal musical numbers—Act I.—"Time Stands Still," "I Still Have Plenty to Learn," "Ask Me Again," "There's History To Be Made," "Here and Now," "Why Was I Born on a Farm?", "If," "My Lucky Lover," "A Musical Lesson," "You've Got That Kind of a Face," "I'm Lost."   Act II.—"Pedro, Ichabod," "Poor Man," "The Things That Lovers Say," "Ichabod."

(Closed June 12, 1948)

THE INSECT COMEDY

(14 performances)

Play in three acts, by Josef and Karel Capek, adapted by Owen Davis. Revived by the New York City Theatre Company at the City Center of Music and Drama, June 3, 1948.

Cast of characters—

PROLOG
```
The Vagrant......................................George Coulouris
The Professor....................................Robinson Stone
```

THE BUTTERFLIES
```
Felix............................................Jose Ferrer
Young Butterflies: Annabelle Lyon, Jane White, Betty Low, Claire Hale
Iris.............................................Phyllis Hill
Victor...........................................Tom Avera
Clythia..........................................Rita Gam
Otakar...........................................Thomas Poston
```

THE MARAUDERS
```
Chrysalis.................................Mildred Joanne Smith
Male Beetle...............................Stanley Carlson
Female Beetle.............................Paula Laurence
Another Male Beetle.......................Bobby Busch
Ichneumon Fly.............................Robert Carroll
Its Larva.................................Chevi Colton
Male Cricket..............................Ray Walston
Female Cricket............................Annabelle Lyon
Parasite..................................Bert Whitley
```

THE ANTS
```
Blind Ant.................................Leonardo Cimino
1st Engineer..............................Alexander Scourby
2nd Engineer..............................Robert Carroll
An Ant....................................Sidney Walters
Another Ant...............................Ted Allegretti
Inventor..................................Robinson Stone
Another Messenger.........................Mack Busch
```

Quartermaster	Thomas Poston
Wounded Man	Bert Whitley
Telegrapher	Ray Walston
Journalist	Tom Avera
War Worker	Joyce Hill
Bond Salesman	Chevi Colton
A Traitor	George Hall
Yellow Commander	Jose Ferrer

EPILOG

1st Moth	Jane White
2nd Moth	Betty Low
3rd Moth	Claire Hale
4th Moth	Annabelle Lyon
1st Snail	Bobby Busch
2nd Snail	Mack Busch
Wood Cutter	Arthur Newman
Woman	Nan McFarland

Staged by Jose Ferrer; sets by Herbert Brodkin; costumes by Emeline Roche; dances by Hanya Holm.

(Closed June 12, 1948)

HOWDY, MR. ICE!

(406 performances)

An ice revue presented by Sonja Henie and Arthur M. Wirtz at the Center Theatre, June 24, 1948. Production director, William H. Burke; staged by Catherine Littlefield. Settings by Bruno Maine; costumes by Billy Livingston and Katherine Kuhn; skating direction by May Judels. Lyrics and music by Al Stillman and Alan Moran.

Principal skaters—

Skippy Baxter	Rudy Richards
Eileen Seigh	Paul Castle
Freddie Trenkler	James Sisk
Cissy Trenholm	Fred Werner
Jinx Clark	Buster Grace
Harrison Thomson	Snookums and Buck Pennington

Principal singers—

Nola Fairbanks	Fred Martell
Dick Craig	William Douglas

Act I.—Scene 1—Overture. 2—In the Pink. 3—Bovine Capers. 4—Landscape Artists. 5—Celebration: Easter, Fourth of July, Thanksgiving, Yuletide. 6—Safari. 7—Little Bo-Peep. 8—Sir Frederick Werner. 9—Trinidad Wharf. 10—Mercury. 11—Bouncing Ball of the Ice. 12—48 States. Act II.—Scene 1—Sleeping Beauty. 2—Highland Laddies. 3—The Bluebirds. 4—The Cradle of Jazz. 5—Himalayan Wonder. 6—Leaps and Bounds. 7—In the Dark. 8—Variations on a Romantic Theme. 9—Fireman, Save That Tramp. 10—The World's Greatest Show.

(Closed April 23, 1949)

SUNDOWN BEACH

(7 performances)

A play in three acts by Bessie Breuer. Produced by Louis J. Singer as sponsor for the Actors Studio at the Belasco Theatre, September 7, 1948.

Cast of characters—

Cecil	Nehemiah Persoff
Merle	Martin Balsam
Hazel	Treva Frazee
Vanilla	Jennifer Howard
Tourist	Ellen Mahar
Helen	Vivian Firko
Pop	Ralph Cullinan
Thaddeus Long	Steven Hill
Otis	Don Hanmer
Buster	Joe Sullivan
Grits	Michael Lewin
Nadine	Joan Copeland
Nona	Anne Hegira
George Washburn	Edward Binns
Arthur Bond	Warren Stevens
Henry	Tom Avera
Ella	Lenka Peterson
Belle	Kathleen Maguire
Nancy	Phyllis Thaxter
Tommy	Joseph Fallon
Ida Mae	Julie Harris
Muriel	Cloris Leachman
Major Paul Walters	John Sylvester
Psychiatric Captain	Ira Cirker
Sheriff	Robert Simon
1st Airforce Pilot	Alex Nicol
2nd Airforce Pilot	George Joseph
Lou	Lou Gilbert

The scene is the Sundown Café, near an Air Forces hospital on an island off the Florida Gulf Coast. The time is 1945. Act I.—A Saturday afternoon. Act II.—Three weeks later. Act III.—Two weeks later.

Staged by Elia Kazan; setting by Ben Edwards.

An episodic drama of the lives and loves of a number of combat-weary fliers, wives, waitresses, and a WAC. The coldness of one wife drives her husband to suicide. Another upsets her husband by joining him and bringing along a child which is hers but not his. The WAC, impatient at the indecision of the flier she loves, takes over the proposing and this couple is headed for a happy life.

(Closed September 11, 1948)

SHOW BOAT

(15 performances)

A musical comedy presented by Richard Rodgers and Oscar Hammerstein 2d at the New York City Center of Music and Drama. Music by Jerome Kern; book and lyrics by Oscar Hammerstein 2d, based on a novel by Edna Ferber.

Cast of characters—

Windy	George Spellman
Steve	Fred Brookins
Pete	Gerald Prosk
Queenie	Helen Dowdy
Parthy Ann Hawks	Ruth Gates
Captain Andy	Billy House
Ellie	Clare Alden
Frank	Sammy White
Rubber Face	Gordon Alexander
Julie	Carol Bruce
Gaylord Ravenal	Norwood Smith
Vallon	Fred Ardath
Magnolia	Pamela Caveness
Joe	William C. Smith
Backwoodsman	Howard Frank
Jeb	Gerald Prosk
Sam	La Verne French
Sal	Gloria Smith
Barker	Walter Russell
Fatima	Sylvia Myers
Sport	Robert Fleming
Dahomey King	La Verne French
Landlady	Sara Floyd
Ethel	Assota Marshall
Mother Superior	Lorraine Waldman
Kim (Child)	Danice Dodson
Jake	King Brill
Jim	Seldon Bennett
Man with Guitar	Albert McCary
Doorman at Trocadero	Walter Mosby
Drunk	Walter Russell
Lottie	Sara Dillon
Dolly	Elaine Hume
Sally	Janet Van Derveer
Old Lady on Levee	Ann Lloyd

This was the 1946 revival which played the Ziegfeld Theatre for a year and which had been on tour since then. After playing the City Center the production again had a season-long tour.

(Closed September 19, 1948)

HILARITIES

(14 performances)

A vaudeville show presented by Ken Robey and Stan Zucker at the Adelphi Theatre, September 9, 1948. Music and lyrics by Buddy Kaye, Stanley Arnold and Carl Lampl; sketches by Sidney Zelinka, Howard Harris and Morey Amsterdam.

The principals—

Morey Amsterdam	The Herzogs
Harold and Lola	Al Kelly
Sid Stone	Gil Maison
Gali Gali	Connie Sawyer
Holloway Sisters	Raul and Eva Reyes
Betty Jane Watson	Victoria Crandall
Larry Douglas	Moreland Kortkam
George Tapps	Connie Stevens
Calgary Brothers	Enid Williams

(Closed September 18, 1948)

SMALL WONDER

(134 performances)

Revue produced by George Nichols 3d at the Coronet Theatre, September 15, 1948. Music by Baldwin Bergersen and Albert Selden; lyrics by Phyllis McGinley and Billings Brown; sketches by Charles Spalding, Max Wilk, George Axelrod and Louis Laun; sets by Ralph Alswang; costumes by John Derro; dances by Gower Champion, and direction by Burt Shevelove.

The players—

Tom Ewell	Alan Ross
Alice Pearce	Jack Cassidy
Hayes Gordon	Bill Ferguson
Joan Mann	Marilyn Day
Chandler Cowles	J. C. McCord
Virginia Oswald	Kate Friedlich
Evelyn Taylor	Mort Marshall
Mary McCarty	Joan Diener
Tommy Rall	Devida Stewart
Jonathan Lucas	

Principal song numbers—"The Commuters' Song," "Ballad for Billionaires," "No Time," "Flaming Youth," "Show Off," "Pistachio," "When I Fall in Love," "Saturday's Child" and "William McKinley High."

(Closed January 8, 1949)

HEAVEN ON EARTH

(12 performances)

Musical comedy presented by Monte Proser in association with Ned C. Litwack at the New Century Theatre, September 16, 1948. Book and lyrics by Barry Trivers; music by Jay Gorney; dances by Nick Castle; sets and costumes by Raoul Pene duBois; production supervised by Eddie Dowling and directed by John Murray Anderson.

Cast of characters—

James Aloysius McCarthy	Peter Lind Hayes
Friday	Dorothy Jarnac
Punchy	Danny Drayson
Fannie Frobisher	Caren Marsh
Florabelle Frobisher	Ruth Merman
Mrs. Frobisher	Nina Varela
Commissioner Frobisher	Irwin Corey
Officer Clabber	Claude Stroud
John Bowers	Robert Dixon
Mary Brooks	Barbara Nunn
The Lovers	{ June Graham / Richard Darcy }
Lieut. Sullivan	Wynn Murray

```
Officer Jonesy..................................Dorothy Keller
Officer Blandings................................Betty George
Sailor..........................................Billy Parsons
H. H. Hutton.....................................David Burns
Magistrate Kennedy................................Dick Bernie
Sailor with Trumpet..............................Steve Condos
Officer O'Brien..................................Bert Sheldon
Radio Engineer...................................Jack Russell
Slim.............................................Remi Martel
Dippy............................................Jack Russell
Butch.............................................Bill Hogue
```
Act I.—Scene 1—Central Park—noon. 2—The Housing Commissioner's Office—that afternoon. 3—Central Park—that afternoon. 4—The Hutton Home of Tomorrow—that evening. Act II.—Scene 1—Central Park—next morning. 2—A cell block in the Park jail—that morning. 3—Police Court in the Park jail—that morning. 4—Fifth Avenue—immediately afterwards. 5—Interior of Hutton Home—late that day. 6—Central Park—immediately afterwards.

A boy and a girl—the boy so poor he has to live in a tree in Central Park, are befriended by a genial horse-hack driver, who is friendly with all the denizens of the park, including a pixy named Friday who is his silent and admiring secretary. McCarthy arranges a wedding for the lovers, installs them in a model house for their wedding night. The builder of the house causes the arrest of McCarthy and his friends, but relents when McCarthy frightens him by imitating Hollywood stars.

Principal song numbers—Act I.—"In the Back of a Hack," "So Near and Yet So Far," "Don't Forget to Dream," "Bench in the Park," "Push a Button in a Hutton," "Home Is Where the Heart Is," "Heaven on Earth." Act II.—"What's the Matter with Our City?", "First Cup of Coffee in the Morning."

(Closed September 25, 1948)

MAGDALENA

(88 performances)

"Musical adventure" in two acts. Produced by Homer Curran at the Ziegfeld Theatre, September 20, 1948. Book by Frederick Hazlitt Brennan and Homer Curran; pattern and lyrics by Robert Wright and George Forrest· music by Heitor Villa-Lobos.

Cast of characters—

```
Padre Josef....................................Gerhard Pechner
Manuel............................................Peter Fields
Solis..............................................Melva Niles
Ramon.............................................Henry Reese
Maria.........................................Dorothy Sarnoff
Pedro..............................................John Raitt
Major Blanco..................................Ferdinand Hilt
Doctor Lopez..................................Carl Milletaire
General Carabana...................................Hugo Haas
Chanteuse.........................................Betty Huff
Cigarette Girl................................Christine Matsios
Zoggie.........................................John Schickling
```

Danseuse	Lorraine Miller
Teresa	Irra Petina
The Old One	Gene Curtsinger
Chico	Patrick Kirk
Juan	Leonard Morganthaler
Conchita	Betty Brusher
Major Domo	Roy Raymond
Bailadora	Marie Groscup
Bailador	Matt Mattox

Act I.—Scene 1—The courtyard of Padre Josef's chapel near the Magdalena River, Colombia, about 1912. 2—Private dining room in a café in Paris. 3—Boat landing at the Muzo village. 4—At the shrine of the Madonna. Act II.—Scene 1—At the Singing Tree. 2—Kitchen of General Catabana's hacienda. 3—Terrace of the General's hacienda. 4—Floor of a nearby canyon. 5—The chapel courtyard.

Staged by Jules Dassin; sets by Howard Bay; costumes by Sharaff; dances by Jack Cole; musical direction by Arthur Kay; choral direction by Robert Zeller. Production by Edwin Lester.

Principal musical numbers—Act I.—"The Omen Bird (Teru, Teru)," "My Bus and I," "The Emerald," "The Civilized People," "Food for Thought," "Come to Colombia," "Plan It by the Planets," "Bon Soir, Paris," "Travel, Travel, Travel," "Magdalena," "The Broken Pianolita," "Greeting," "River Song," "Chivor Dance." Act II.—"The Singing Tree," "Lost," "Freedom!", "Vals de Espana," "Piece de Resistance," "The Broken Bus," "The Seed of God."

(Closed December 4, 1948)

A STORY FOR STRANGERS

(15 performances)

Fantasy in two parts by Marc Connelly. Produced by the Wico Company (Dwight Deere Wiman) at the Royale Theatre, September 21, 1948.

Cast of characters—

Newt Fender	Joseph Sweeney
Audrey	Joann Dolan
George Hubinder	Paul Huber
A. J. Kissle	Frank Tweddell
Mr. Mercer	Edward Nannary
Sophie Whiting	Jane Hoffman
Hector Whiting	George Cotton
Norman Hunt	James Dobson
Bessie	Joan Gray
Policemen	{ Richard McMurray { Victor Parber
St. Elmo Ottley	John McGovern
Mrs. Patoon	Grace Valentine
Mayor Orrin Sully	Tom Hoier
Vincent Gatling	Joseph L. Graham
Dunbar Stote	Lauren Gilbert

Townspeople who crowd doorways

The locale is Huntsville, Mich., in 1934. Part I.—Scene 1—A barbershop, September fourteenth. 2—A porch, the previous July. 3—An office, the same day. 4—A stable, the same day. Part II.—Scene 1—The barbershop, September fourteenth. 2—The porch, September

BURNS MANTLE BEST PLAYS OF 1948-49   383

eighth. 3—The stable, the same afternoon. 4—The barbershop, September fourteenth.
Staged by Marc Connelly; settings by Ralph Alswang; costumes by Millie Sutherland.

A talking horse, belonging to young Norman Hunt, reforms the denizens of a small town. Flabbergasted by the miracle of a horse that talks wisdom, crooked folk become honest and unpleasant ones become kindly. The story is told, in flashback style, to a stranger—a traveling salesman—who happens into the local barbershop for ministrations and finds all of Huntsville in a warm glow of sanctity.

(Closed October 1, 1948)

GRANDMA'S DIARY

(6 performances)

Comedy by Albert Wineman Barker, in three acts. Produced by the American Theatre Group at Henry Miller's Theatre, September 22, 1948.

Cast of characters—

```
Harrison........................................Augustus Smith
Peter..........................................Herbert Evers
Alice..........................................Eileen Prince
Linda..........................................Gertrude Rozan
Cary...........................................George Neise
Boris..........................................Leonard Elliott
Gaines.........................................Robert E. Griffin
```
Spring, in the penthouse of Linda Perdue. Act I.—Late afternoon. Act II.—That night. Act III.—The next morning.

Linda Perdue is a successful writer of radio soap operas. She gets her plots from her grandmother's diary. One of the most thoroughly denounced comedies of the season.

(Closed September 25, 1948)

TOWN HOUSE

(12 performances)

Comedy in three acts by Gertrude Tonkonogy, based on a series of magazine stories by John Cheever. Produced by Max Gordon at the National Theatre, September 23, 1948.

Cast of characters—

```
Lucille Tremaine................................June Duprez
Jack Tremaine..................................James Monks
Pete Murray....................................Hiram Sherman
Esther Murray..................................Mary Wickes
Ramona Murray.................................Roberta Field
```

Carol Hyler	Peggy French
Larry Hyler	Reed Brown, Jr.
Mrs. Osgood	Margaret Dale
Katherine Levy	Elizabeth Dewing
Vince Barber	Henry Jones
Putnam Phelps	Edwin Jerome
A Man	Klock Ryder
A Woman	Vera Fuller Mellish

The setting is a one-time mansion in New York. Act I.—A Spring evening. Act II.—Scene 1—A few weeks later. 2—Several days later. Act III.—A few days later.

Staged by George S. Kaufman; setting by Donald Oenslager; costumes supervised by John Derro.

A once-grand New York town house has been taken over by several couples of various beliefs, occupations and temperaments. They try to make it a smooth co-operative venture but they clash continually. However, when they are faced with splitting up, they realize they have been enjoying life.

(Closed October 1, 1948)

TIME FOR ELIZABETH

(8 performances)

Comedy in three acts by Norman Krasna and Groucho Marx. Produced by Russell Lewis and Howard Young at the Fulton Theatre, September 27, 1948.

Cast of characters—

Mr. Robinson	Kenneth Patterson
Walter P. Schaeffer	Russell Hicks
Miss Greene	Eleanor Lawson
Ed Davis	Otto Kruger
Harrison Oglethorpe	John Arthur
Lily Schaeffer	Leila Bliss
Mr. McPherson	Leonard Mudie
Kay Davis	Katherine Alexander
Anne Davis	Ottilie Kruger
Richard Coburn	Dick Hogan
Mr. Jasper	Harlan Briggs
George Zwilling	Edward Clark
Amy Zwilling	Theresa Lyon
Vivian Morgan	Sheila Bromley

Act I.—Office of Ed Davis, boss of the Snowdrift Washing Machine Co.; 6 P.M. in early December. Act II.—Scene 1—Living room of an apartment in Florida, two weeks later. 2—The same, six weeks later. Act III.—Scene 1—The same, four days later. 2—The same, three months later.

Staged by Norman Krasna; sets by George Jenkins.

Ed Davis decides to retire and go to Florida and deservedly suffers the kind of dull life one has to live in Florida on a retirement income. So he goes back to work again at more pay.

(Closed October 1, 1948)

EDWARD, MY SON

(260 performances)

Play in three acts by Robert Morley and Noel Langley. Produced by Gilbert Miller and Henry Sherek at the Martin Beck Theatre, September 30, 1948.

Cast of characters—

Arnold Holt	Robert Morley
Evelyn Holt	Peggy Ashcroft
Larry Parker	Ian Hunter
Harry Soames	Torin Thatcher
Dr. Waxman	Dayton Lummis
Cunningham	Waldo Sturrey
Ellerby	Godfrey Kenton
Hanray	D. A. Clarke-Smith
Eileen Perry	Leueen MacGrath
Prothero	Richard Newton
Burton	Godfrey Kenton
Summers	Waldo Sturrey
Phyllis Maxwell	Dorothy Beattie
Betty Fowler	Patricia Hicks

Prologue.—In the theatre at the present. Act I.—Scene 1—Arnold's flat in Brighton, 1919. 2—The same, 1924. 3—The same, a few weeks later. 4—The head master's study, Graingarry School, 1930. Act II.—Scene 1—Offices of Arnold Holt & Co., 1934. 2—Eileen Perry's flat, 1935. 3—A hotel room in Alassio, next day. Act III. Scene 1—Lord Holt's house, 1938. 2—The same, 1941. 3—The same, 1948. Epilogue.—In the theatre at the present.

Staged by Peter Ashmore; settings supervised by Raymond Sovey.

(Closed May 14, 1949)

PRIVATE LIVES

(248 performances)

Comedy in three acts by Noel Coward. Revived by John C. Wilson at the Plymouth Theatre, October 4, 1948.

Cast of characters—

Sibyl Chase	Barbara Baxley
Elyot Chase	Donald Cook
Victor Prynne	William Langford
Amanda Prynne	Tallulah Bankhead
Louise, a maid	Therese Quadri

Act I.—Terrace of a hotel in France on a Summer evening. Act II.—Amanda's flat in Paris a few days later; evening. Act III.—The same, next morning.

Staged by Martin Manulis; settings by Charles Elson.

Mr. Coward's comedy about a quarrelsome divorced couple was first produced in New York by Charles B. Cochran at the Times Square Theatre on January 27, 1931, where it had a run of 256 performances. The cast included Mr. Coward, Gertrude Lawrence, Laurence Olivier and Therese Quadri—the last-named being the only member of the original company to play in the revival. Mr. Wilson's revival, with Miss Bankhead, had a highly successful tour of the U. S. in 1947 and 1948 before opening in New York.

(Closed May 7, 1949)

SUMMER AND SMOKE

(100 performances)

Play in a prologue and two parts by Tennessee Williams. Produced by Margo Jones at the Music Box Theatre, October 6, 1948.

Cast of characters—

```
Alma as a Child..............................Arlene McQuade
John as a Child..............................Donald Hastings
Rev. Winemiller...........................Raymond Van Sickle
Mrs. Winemiller............................Marga Ann Deighton
John Buchanan, Jr..................................Tod Andrews
A Girl...............................................Hildy Parks
Dusty.............................................William Layton
Dr. Buchanan...................................Ralph Theadore
Alma Winemiller..............................Margaret Phillips
Rosa Gonzales...................................Monica Boyer
Nellie Ewell......................................Anne Jackson
Roger Doremus.................................Earl Montgomery
Mrs. Bassett................................Betty Greene Little
Vernon...........................................Spencer James
Rosemary..........................................Ellen James
Papa Gonzales......................................Sid Cassel
Mr. Kramer........................................Ray Walston
```
The town of Glorious Hill, Mississippi, from the turn of the century to 1916. Prologue.—"Early Sorrows." Part I.—A Summer. Part II.—A Winter.

Staged by Margo Jones; setting by Jo Mielziner; costumes by Rose Bogdanoff; music by Paul Bowles.

Alma Winemiller, prim vocal teacher, is at once repelled by and in love with Dr. John Buchanan, Jr., free-living young medic whose home is next door. Her sense of propriety is stronger than her feminine instinct and she becomes a frustrated female. . . . Mr. Mielziner's imaginative setting was acclaimed as one of the best stage-designing works of the season.

(Closed January 1, 1949)

LOVE LIFE

(252 performances)

Musical comedy in two parts. Produced by Cheryl Crawford at the Forty-sixth Street Theatre, October 7, 1948. Book and lyrics by Alan Jay Lerner; music by Kurt Weill.

BURNS MANTLE BEST PLAYS OF 1948-49

Cast of characters—

Part I—Act 1
THE MAGICIAN

The Magician	Jay Marshall
Susan	Nanette Fabray
Sam	Ray Middleton

Act 2—THE COOPER FAMILY
Scene: Outside the Cooper home, Mayville, 1791

Mary Jo	Holly Harris
Tim	Evans Thornton
George Crockett	David Thomas
Jonathan Anderson	Gene Tobin
Charlie Hamilton	Victor Clarke
Will	Mark Kramer
Hank	Robert Byrn
Ben	Lenn Dale
Child	Vincent Gugleotti
Sam Cooper	Ray Middleton
Susan Cooper	Nanette Fabray
Elizabeth Cooper	Cheryl Archer
Johnny Cooper	Johnny Stewart

Act 3—EIGHT MEN

Act 4—THE FAREWELL
Scene: Outside the Cooper home, Mayville, April, 1821

Susan	Nanette Fabray
Elizabeth	Cheryl Archer
Johnny	Johnny Stewart
Sam	Ray Middleton
Walt	Evans Thornton

Act 5—QUARTETTE

Act 6—THE NEW BABY
Scene: The bedroom of the Cooper house. September, 1857

Susan	Nanette Fabray
Sam	Ray Middleton

Act 7—THE THREE TOTS AND A WOMAN

Three Tots	Rosalie Alter, Vincent Gugleotti, Lenn Dale
Trapeze Artist	Elly Ardelty

Act 8—MY KIND OF NIGHT
Scene: The porch and living-room of the Cooper home. The early 1890's

Sam	Ray Middleton
Elizabeth	Cheryl Archer
Johnny	Johnny Stewart
Susan	Nanette Fabray
Two Women Soloists	Lily Paget, Faye Elizabeth Smith

Act 9—LOVE SONG

Hobo	Johnny Thompson

Act 10—THE CRUISE
Scene: The main dining-room of an ocean liner. In the 1920's

Entertainer	Virginia Conwell
Harvey	David Thomas
Sam	Ray Middleton
Boylan	Victor Clarke
Slade	Larry Robbins
Leffcourt	David Collyer
Susan	Nanette Fabray
William Taylor	Lyle Bettger

388   BURNS MANTLE BEST PLAYS OF 1948-49

PART II—Act 1—RADIO NIGHT
Scene: The living-room of the Coopers' New York apartment. The present time

Sam	Ray Middleton
Johnny	Johnny Stewart
Elizabeth	Cheryl Archer
Susan	Nanette Fabray

Act 2—MADRIGAL SINGERS

Leader	David Thomas

Act 3—FAREWELL AGAIN

Act 4—"PUNCH AND JUDY GET A DIVORCE"

Act 5—A HOTEL ROOM

Sam	Ray Middleton

Act 6—"THE MINSTREL SHOW"

Interlocutor	Victor Clarke
Sam	Ray Middleton
Susan	Nanette Fabray
Miss Horoscope	Holly Harris
Miss Mysticism	Carolyn Maye
Mr. Cynic	David Thomas
Girl	Josephine Lambert
Girl	Marie Leidal
Miss Ideal Man	Sylvia Stahlman

Staged by Elia Kazan; dances by Michael Kidd; settings by Boris Aronson; costumes by Lucinda Ballard; musical director, Joseph Littau.

Susan and Sam Cooper, a typical young American couple, remain typical, young and American from Colonial days to the present. As mechanical and business civilization expands, their love life becomes more complex and difficult. But in the end it all boils down to Boy Needs Girl and Girl Needs Boy.

Principal song numbers—"Here I'll Stay," "Progress," "I Remember It Well," "Green-Up Time," "My Kind of Night," "Love Song," "Ho, Billy O!" "This Is the Life," "Madame Zuzu," "Mr. Right."

(Closed May 14, 1949)

WHERE'S CHARLEY?

(256 performances)
(Continued)

Musical comedy in two acts, based on Brandon Thomas' "Charley's Aunt." Produced by Cy Feuer and Ernest H. Martin in association with Gwen Rickard (Mrs. Ray Bolger) at the St. James Theatre, October 11, 1948. Book by George Abbott; words and music by Frank Loesser.

Cast of characters—

Brassett	John Lynds
Jack Chesney	Byron Palmer
Charley Wykeham	Ray Bolger

Kitty Verdun	Doretta Morrow
Amy Spettigue	Allyn Ann McLerie
Wilkinson	Edgar Kent
Sir Francis Chesney	Paul England
Mr. Spettigue	Horace Cooper
A Professor	Jack Friend
Donna Lucia D'Alvadorez	Jane Lawrence
Photographer	James Lane
Patricia	Marie Foster
Reggie	Douglas Deane

Act I.—Scene 1—A room at Oxford University. 2—A street. 3—The garden. 4—Where the nuts come from. Act II.—Scene 1—The garden. 2—A street. 3—Where the ladies go. 4—A garden path. 5—The ballroom.

Staged by George Abbott. Sets and costumes by David Ffolkes; dances by George Balanchine, assisted by Fred Danielli; vocal arrangements and direction by Garry Dolin; musical director, Max Goberman; orchestrations by Ted Royal, Hans Spialek and Phil Lang.

Principal musical numbers—Act I.—"The Years Before Us," "Better Get Out of Here," "The New Ashmolean Marching Society and Students' Conservatory Band," "My Darling, My Darling," "Make a Miracle," "Serenade with Asides," "Lovelier Than Ever," "The Woman in His Room," "Pernambuco." Act II.—"Where's Charley?", "Once in Love with Amy," "The Gossips," "At the Red Rose Cotillion."

THE LEADING LADY

(8 performances)

Play in three acts by Ruth Gordon. Produced by Victor Samrock and William Fields at the National Theatre, October 18, 1948.

Cast of characters—

Maudie	Margot Stevenson
Clyde	James MacColl
Clara	Elizabeth Dewing
Annie	Margaret Barker
Lester	Harry Worth
Ida	Sonia Sorel
Williams	Mildred Dunnock
Clarissa	Brooke Byron
Trem	Ossie Davis
Everett	Emory Richardson
Stoatsie	Guy Spaull
Gerald	Ian Keith
Gay	Ruth Gordon
Harry	Wesley Addy
Benjy	John Carradine
Mrs.	Laura Pierpont
Old Carter	Wm. J. Kelly
Mrs. Gilson	Ethel Griffies
Eugene	Douglas Watson
Mr. Beckwith	Harry Sheppard

Acts I, II and III.—The home of Gerald and Gay Marriott, 60 West 27th Street, New York. Act I.—December 30, 1899. Act II.—October, 1901, late afternoon. Act III.—January, 1902, early afternoon.

Staged by Garson Kanin; set by Donald Oenslager; costumes by Mainbocher; production associate, David M. Pardoll.

Gerald and Gay Marriott, great stars, have returned to the stage and a new success after Gerald's illness. Gerald dies in a fit of anger at a dramatic critic. Gerald has always dominated Gay, although she is the better artist, and her stage career goes to the grave with him—until a young playwright who loves her persuades her to resume work and hope.

(Closed October 23, 1948)

MY ROMANCE

(95 performances)

Musical play in a prologue, three acts and an epilogue, based on Edward Sheldon's "Romance." Produced by the Shuberts at the Shubert Theatre, October 19, 1948. Book and lyrics by Rowland Leigh; music by Sigmund Romberg.

Cast of characters—

Bishop Armstrong (Tom)	Lawrence Brooks
Suzette Armstrong	Joan Shepard
Alice	Marion Bradley
Harry Armstrong	William Berrian
Miss Potherton	Hildegarde Halliday
Cornelius Van Tuyl	Melville Ruick
Susan Van Tuyl	Hazel Dawn Jr.
Percival Hawthorne-Hillary	Tom Bate
Mrs. DeWitt	Barbara Patton
Veronica DeWitt	Gail Adams
Octavia Fotheringham	Luella Gear
Sir Frederick Putman	Rex Evans
Lady Putman	Doris Patston
Rupert Chandler	Melton Moore
Vladimir Luccachevitch	Nat Burns
Miss Joyce	Natalie Norman
Bertie Wessel	Lawrence Weber
Georgianna Curtright	Verna Epperly
Margaret Fears	Mary Jane Sloan
Lawrence Riley	Andy Aprea
Thyra Winslow	Lou Maddox
DeWitt Bodeen	Donald Crocker
Rosella	Allegra Varron
Mme. Marguerita Cavallini (Rita)	Anne Jeffreys
Charlotte Armstrong	Madeleine Holmes
Tosatti (The Organ Grinder)	Tito Coral
1st Maid	Edith Lane
2nd Maid	Patricia Boyer
Page Boy	Norval Tormsen

Prologue.—Bishop Armstrong's library in the rectory of St. Giles Church, New York, the present. Act I.—Home of Cornelius Van Tuyl, New York, 1898. Act II.—The rectory, six weeks later. Act III.—Mme. Cavallini's suite at the Brevoort, four hours later. Epilogue.—The library, the present.

Staged by Rowland Leigh; settings by Watson Barratt; costumes by Lou Eisele; orchestrations by Don Walker; dances by Fredric N. Kelly.

"Romance" told the story of a minister who fell in love with an opera diva. Edward Brewster Sheldon, who died in 1946 at the age of 60, wrote this sentimental drama in 1913 and it made the actress Doris Keane a memorable figure in the American theatre.

(Closed January 8, 1949)

LIFE WITH MOTHER

(265 performances)

Comedy in three acts by Howard Lindsay and Russel Crouse, based on Clarence Day's family reminiscences. Produced by Oscar Serlin at the Empire Theatre, October 20, 1948.

Cast of characters—

Father	Howard Lindsay
Whitney	David Frank
Harlan	Robert Wade
John	Robert Antoine
Margaret	Dorothy Bernard
Clarence	John Drew Devereaux
Michael	Michael Smith
Vinnie	Dorothy Stickney
Bridget	Mary Diveny
Hazel Willoughby	Jo Anne Paul
Bessie Fuller Logan	Gladys Hurlbut
Mrs. Willoughby	Amy Douglass
Clyde Miller	Robert Emhardt
Cousin Cora	Ruth Hammond
Kathleen	Marguerite Morrissey
Dr. Humphreys	A. H. Van Buren

Acts I, II and III.—Mid-afternoon on the last day of August in the 1880s. Act I.—Living room of the Day country home at Harrison, N. Y. Act II.—The same. Act III.—The Day house on Madison Avenue, New York.

Staged by Guthrie McClintic; country home setting by Donald Oenslager; town house setting by Stewart Chaney.

(Closed June 4, 1949)

MINNIE AND MR. WILLIAMS

(5 performances)

Comedy in three acts by Richard Hughes. Produced by John Gassner and David Dietz at the Morosco Theatre, October 27, 1948. Originally titled "A Comedy of Good and Evil," this play was produced in Britain in 1924.

Cast of characters—

The Reverend John Williams	Eddie Dowling
Minnie	Josephine Hull
Scraggy Evan	Gwilym Williams
Timothy Ysgairnolwen	Paul Anderson
Mari Jones	Lee Wilcox
Gladys	Elizabeth Ross
Owain Flatfish	Clarence Derwent
Mrs. Jones Bakehouse	Grace Mills
Mr. Gas Jones	Geoffrey Lumb

Mrs. Resurrection Jones..........................Gwyneth Hughes
    Kitchen of the Williams' cottage in a Welsh village at the turn of the century. Act I.—Scene 1—About 9 o'clock of a September evening. 2—About 7:30 the next morning. Act II.—Immediately following. Act III.—A year later.
    Staged by Eddie Dowling. Setting and costumes by Mordi Gassner.

The Reverend John Williams and his wife, Minnie, wish they had company in their modest cottage. They get it—in the shape of Gladys, a young girl who is an emissary of the devil. Gladys' mission is to bag the Rev. Williams for hell, but the couple are so nice to her that when he dies she reneges on her mission and allows him to go to heaven, where he should be.

(Closed October 30, 1948)

SET MY PEOPLE FREE

(36 performances)

Play in three acts by Dorothy Heyward. Produced by the Theatre Guild at the Hudson Theatre, November 3, 1948.

Cast of characters—

    George, Head Slave.................................Canada Lee
    Rose..Mildred Joanne Smith
    Denmark...Juano Hernandez
    Captain Wilson...................................Blaine Cordner
    Phyllis..Marion Scanlon
    Eliza...Gail Gladstone
    Gullah Jack.......................................Leigh Whipper
    Trader Henri......................................Somer Alberg
    Morris Brown......................................Frank Wilson
    Patrolman...Tyler Carpenter
    The Mauma...Bertha T. Powell
    Pompey..Alonzo Bosan
    Tina..Edith Atuka-Reid
    Aneas...William Warfield
    Pharaoh...William McDaniel
    Benbow..Wanza L. King
    Rachel..Fredye Marshall
    Adam..Merritt Smith
    Cuppy...Theodore Hines
    Belleisle...Harry Bolden
    Lot...Louis Sharp
    Jemmy...George Dosher
    Sinah...Musa Williams
    Blanche...Urylee Leonardos
    Peter Poyas.......................................Earl Sydnor
    Jesse Blackwood...................................Thomas Anderson
    Ned Bennett.......................................Earl Jones
    Rolla Bennett.....................................William Marshall
    Monday Gell.......................................Charles McRae
    Perault Prioleau..................................John Bouie
    Mingo Harth.......................................Eric Burroughs
    Blind Philip......................................Harold Des Verney
    Frank Ferguson....................................Richard Silver
    1st Drummer.......................................Samuel Brown
    2nd Drummer.......................................Moses Mianns
        Act I.—Scene 1—Breakfast room in the house of Captain Wilson, Charleston, S. C., an evening in 1810. 2—Room in the slave quarters of Trader Henri. 3—African church. Act II.—Scene 1—Room

in Denmark Vesey's house, April, 1822. 2—Captain Wilson's breakfast room. 3—Vesey's room. 4—Wadmalaw Island. Act III.—Scene 1—The breakfast room. 2—Vesey's room. 3—George Wilson's cabin.

Staged by Martin Ritt; settings by Ralph Alswang; choral direction by Joshua Lee; costumes by Ernest Schraps; associate producer, Allyn Rice.

Denmark Vesey, a slave who once was an African prince, is religiously inspired to become the deliverer of the slaves of Charleston. He plots an uprising in which the whites will be massacred and the slaves will take the city. The plot is unwillingly revealed to his master, Captain Wilson, by George, head slave of the Wilson household. George is torn between loyalty to his master and loyalty to his race. The uprising fails to come off.

(Closed November 27, 1948)

BRAVO!

(44 performances)

Play in three acts by Edna Ferber and George S. Kaufman. Produced by Max Gordon at the Lyceum Theatre, November 11, 1948.

Cast of characters—

```
Vilna Prager.........................................Janet Fox
Rudy................................................Oliver Cliff
Martin Link.........................................Edgar Stehli
Zoltan Lazko.......................................Oscar Homolka
Rosa Rucker.........................................Lili Darvas
Lew Gilbert........................................Morton Havel
Jimmy Flint........................................Arthur Havel
Kurt Heger........................................Kevin McCarthy
Stephanie..........................................Zolya Talma
Anna Zinsser.......................................Elena Karam
Lisa Kemper...................................Christiane Grautoff
Jeffrey Crandall..................................Frank Conroy
Sophie Marelle.....................................Fritzi Scheff
Wallace............................................King Calder
Black..............................................George Cotton
Jane Velvet........................................Jean Carson
```

An old brownstone house in New York's West Sixties; time, the present. Act I.—December. Act II.—February. Act III.—April.

Staged by George S. Kaufman. Setting by Leo Kerz; costumes by Rose Bogdanoff; evening gowns by Castillo.

Zoltan Lazko and his mistress, Rosa Rucker, are displaced Hungarians having a hard time. He had been a rich and famous romantic playwright; she a stage star. In the brownstone house with them are other once-important folk. They ultimately find new hope in their newly adopted country—and the authors of the play express a hope for the return of the romantic drama.

(Closed December 18, 1948)

AS THE GIRLS GO

(228 performances)
(Continued)

Musical comedy; book by William Roos; lyrics by Harold Adamson; music by Jimmy McHugh. Produced by Michael Todd at the Winter Garden, November 13, 1948.

Cast of characters—

Waldo Wellington	Bobby Clark
Lucille Thompson Wellington	Irene Rich
Kenny Wellington	Bill Callahan
Mickey Wellington	Betty Lou Barto
Tommy Wellington	Donny Harris
Guard	John Sheehan
Kathy Robinson	Betty Jane Watson
Barber	Hobart Cavanaugh
White House Visitor	John Brophy
Miss Swenson	Cavada Humphrey
Butler	Curt Stafford
Daughter of the Boston Tea Party	{ Claire Grenville / Claire Louise Evans / Lois Bolton / Marjorie Leach }
Floyd Robinson	Douglas Luther
Diane	Mildred Hughes
Photographer	Kenneth Spaulding
Ross Miller	Jack Russell
Daphne	Dorothea Pinto
Photographer	William Reedy
Blinky Joe	Dick Dana
Darlene	Rosemary Williamson
Secret Service Women	{ Gregg Sherwood / Truly Barbara }
Children	{ Marlene Cameron / Pauline Hahn / Norma Marlowe / Joanthan Marlowe / Clifford Sales / Eugene Steiner }
Secretary	Ruth Thomas
President of Potomac College	Douglas Luther
Premiere Danseuse	Kathryn Lee

Act I.—Scene 1—Roxy Theatre, January 20, 1953. 2—The White House (Truman) balcony. 3—The White House barber shop. 4—White House grounds. 5—The chartreuse room, in Springtime. 6—A corridor. 7—The rumpus room. 8—A hotel room. 9—White House grounds. 10—The American Cannes Beach Club. 11—The corridor. 12—The barber shop. 13—Kathy's bedroom. 14—Lobby of the Mayflower Hotel. 15—Union Depot. Act II.—Scene 1—Union Depot. 2—The Campus Inn. 3—A street in Washington. 4—Chartreuse room, June 3. 5—A college campus. 6—The gold room.

Staged by Howard Bay; vocal direction by Hugh Martin; dances by Hermes Pan; costumes by Oleg Cassini; orchestrations by Ted Royal; orchestra conducted by Max Meth.

Lucille Thompson Wellington has become the first woman president of the U. S. Waldo Wellington, her husband, has thus become the first First Gentleman, and he takes advantage of his position to chase girls.

Principal song numbers—Act I.—"Nobody's Heart But Mine,"

BURNS MANTLE BEST PLAYS OF 1948-49   395

"Brighten Up and Be a Little Sunbeam," "Rock, Rock, Rock," "It's More Fun Than a Picnic," "American Cannes," "You Say the Nicest Things, Baby," "I've Got the President's Ear," "Holiday in the Country." Act II.—"There's No Getting Away from You," "Lucky in the Rain," "Father's Day," "It Takes a Woman to Get a Man."

FOR HEAVEN'S SAKE, MOTHER!

(7 performances)

Comedy by Julie Berns, in two acts. Produced by David Kay at the Belasco Theatre, November 16, 1948.

Cast of characters—

```
Henry Wheeler.............................St. Clair Bayfield
Bob Lawrence..................................Alfred Garr
Dick Lawrence.................................Robert White
Lucinda Lawrence..............................Nancy Carroll
Edward Lawrence............................Herschel Bentley
Lavinia....................................Jacqueline Andre
Jack Warren................................Stiano Braggiotti
Deedee Warren.................................Peggy Romano
Susan Beresford..............................Marian Russell
Emily Bland....................................Jean Pugsley
Milton Rubin...................................Richy Shawn
Joe Keneaghan..................................Ted Plummer
Mrs. Rubin.....................................Molly Picon
Sara Louise................................Margaret Draper
```

The home of the Edward Lawrences in Larchmont. Act I.—Scene 1—Noon, late August. 2—November. 3—Late afternoon, Christmas Eve. Act II.—Scene 1—Three days later. 2—The following September.

Staged by Julie Berns. Set by Leo Kerz.

Lucinda Lawrence, mother of two army-age boys, is glamorous, does not look her age, and would like to get back on the stage. Instead, she is surprised by becoming a mother again. This is agreeable to her husband, who is a stage star.

(Closed November 20, 1948)

GOODBYE, MY FANCY

(226 performances)
(Continued)

A comedy in three acts by Fay Kanin. Produced by Michael Kanin in association with Aldrich & Myers at the Morosco Theatre, November 17, 1948.

Cast of characters—

```
Ginny Merrill..................................Bethel Leslie
Amelia.........................................Sally Hester
```

396   BURNS MANTLE BEST PLAYS OF 1948-49

```
Clarisse...............................................Gerrianne Raphael
Mary Nell...............................................Mary Malone
Miss Shackleford..............................Eda Heinemann
Janitors........................................{ Andrew George
                                               { John Ware
Telephone Man....................................Tom Donovan
Susan.......................................................Patty Pope
Grace Woods....................................Shirley Booth
Agatha Reed..................................Madeleine Carroll
Ellen Griswold..............................Lulu Mae Hubbard
Prof. Birdeshaw..................................Lillian Foster
Carol.........................................Betty Lou Holland
Jo...............................................Lenore Garland
Dr. Pitt.........................................George Mitchell
James Merrill......................................Conrad Nagel
Prof. Dingley....................................Ralph Bunker
Matt Cole........................................Sam Wanamaker
Claude Griswold..................................Joseph Boland
```
   Act I.—Friday morning of June, 1948, in a dormitory room of Good Hope College for Women, in Good Hope, Mass. Act II.—Scene 1—Saturday afternoon. 2—Saturday evening. Act III.—Sunday afternoon.
   Staged by Sam Wanamaker; setting by Donald Oenslager; costumes by Emeline Roche.

THE YOUNG AND FAIR

(48 performances)

Play in three acts by N. Richard Nash. Produced by Vinton Freedley in association with Richard W. Krakeur at the Fulton Theatre, November 22, 1948.

Cast of characters—
```
Emmy Foster....................................Frieda Altman
Frances Morritt..........................Mercedes McCambridge
Patty Morritt..................................Patricia Kirkland
Sara Cantry.......................................Frances Starr
Laura Cantry....................................Betty Morrissey
Lee Barron.......................................Lois Wheeler
Selma Keeney...................................Lenka Peterson
Nancy Gear.........................................Julie Harris
Mil Cheaver...................................Frances Freeman
Drucilla Eldridge.....................................Doe Avedon
Mary Louise...................................Patricia Bouchard
Sylvia...........................................Peggy O'Connor
Sally..................................................Ann Sorg
Helen............................................Vicki Carlson
Gloria..............................................Rita Gam
Sue...............................................Ann Murphy
Mathilda.......................................Elaine Bradford
Boots McGregor...................................Sally Moffet
Georgetta.....................................Mary Lou Phelan
Pauline..........................................Lee Truhill
Carol............................................Bette Stanley
```
   Act I.—Scene 1—Miss Cantry's Office in Fairchild Hall. An afternoon in late September. 2—A Bedroom in Fairchild Hall. Immediately following. 3—The Lounge in Fairchild Hall. Friday afternoon, a week later. Act II.—Scene 1—The Office. The following afternoon. 2—The Bedroom. Immediately after. 3—The Office. Later, the same afternoon. Act III.—Scene 1—The Bedroom. An hour later. 2—The Office. A half hour later.
   Staged by Harold Clurman; setting by Paul Morrison; costumes by Eleanor Goldsmith.

The action of the play takes place in the Brook Valley Academy, a girls' Junior College not far from Boston. Frances Morritt returns to the school where she had been a student ten years before in the capacity of teacher and personnel director. Her younger sister, a student, is falsely accused of stealing, thereby unwinding a plot involving the kleptomaniac daughter of one of the school's trustees in the clutches of a nasty ringleader, also a trustee's daughter whom the owner of the school hesitates to discipline. When she sees the state of affairs, she and her sister are glad to leave.

(Closed December 11, 1948, at Fulton; reopened December 27, 1948, at International. Closed January 8, 1949)

LIGHT UP THE SKY

(216 performances)

Comedy in three acts by Moss Hart. Produced by Joseph M. Hyman and Bernard Hart at the Royale Theatre, November 18, 1948.

Cast of characters—

```
Miss Lowell.....................................Jane Middleton
Carleton Fitzgerald.............................Glenn Anders
Frances Black..................................Audrey Christie
Owen Turner......................................Philip Ober
Stella Livingston................................Phyllis Povah
Peter Sloan......................................Barry Nelson
Sidney Black......................................Sam Levene
Sven................................................S. Oakland
Irene Livingston................................Virginia Field
Tyler Rayburn..................................Bartlett Robinson
A Shriner.......................................John D. Seymour
William H. Gallegher..........................Donald McClelland
A Plainclothes Man...............................Ronald Alexander
```
    Acts I, II and III.—Living room of Irene Livingston's suite at the Ritz-Carlton Hotel, Boston; the present. Act I.—5:30 P.M. Act II.—The following 12:30 A.M. Act III.—3:30 A.M.
    Staged by Moss Hart; setting by Frederic Fox; costumes by Kiviette.

(Closed May 21, 1949)

THE SILVER WHISTLE

(219 performances)

Comedy in three acts by Robert McEnroe. Produced by the Theatre Guild at the Biltmore Theatre, November 24, 1948.

Cast of characters—

```
Mr. Beebe........................................William Lynn
Mrs. Hanmer......................................Doro Merande
Miss Hoadley...................................Frances Brandt
```

```
Miss Tripp......................................Eleanor Wilson
Reverend Watson................................Robert Carroll
Mrs. Sampler..................................Kathleen Comegys
Mrs. Gross.......................................Jane Marbury
Mr. Cherry.....................................Burton Mallory
Oliver Erwenter..................................Jose Ferrer
Emmett........................................George Mathews
Father Shay......................................Charles Hart
Mr. Beach.......................................Edward Platt
Mr. Reddy......................................Charles Kuhn
Policeman........................................Chase Soltez
Bishop..........................................Franklin Fox
```
Acts I, II and III.—The garden of a church adjoining an old people's home. Act I.—Scene 1—Afternoon. 2—Evening. Act II.—Evening, next day. Act III.—Morning, following day.

Staged by Paul Crabtree. Setting by Herbert Brodkin; costumes by Ernest Schraps; production supervised by Lawrence Langner and Theresa Helburn.

(Closed May 28, 1949)

RED GLOVES

(113 performances)

Drama in a prologue, three acts and an epilogue, by Jean-Paul Sartre, adapted by Daniel Taradash. Produced by Jean Dalrymple at the Mansfield Theatre, December 4, 1948.

Cast of characters—

```
Reich.........................................J. Anthony Penna
Johanna...........................................Anna Karen
Loutec..........................................Guy Thomajan
Munster.......................................Horace McMahon
Hugo.............................................John Dall
Jessica..........................................Joan Tetzel
Marochek.........................................Jesse White
Kirtz.........................................Martin Kingsley
Hoederer......................................Charles Boyer
The Prince...................................Francis Compton
Karsky...........................................Royal Beal
```
Prologue.—Johanna's flat in a country in Middle Europe, early Spring, 1945. Act I.—A room in a villa in Hoederer's courtyard; Spring, 1943. Act II.—Hoederer's quarters in an old palace a few days later. Act III.—The same, the following morning. Epilogue.—Johanna's flat an hour or so after the prologue.

Staged by Jed Harris; settings by Stewart Chaney; costumes by Emeline Roche; New York presentation by arrangement with Gabriel Pascal.

Hugo, scion of a wealthy family, has joined a revolutionary party and has been given the mission of assassinating Hoederer, current party leader. He becomes Hoederer's secretary, and his wife falls in love with the leader and his ideals. He cannot bring himself to commit his assigned assassination, but when he discovers his wife kissing the leader's hand he shoots Hoederer. The dying leader exonerates Hugo as an assassin, says it was only a *crime passionnel.*

(Closed March 12, 1949)

THE MEDIUM and THE TELEPHONE

(40 performances)

Musical plays by Gian-Carlo Menotti. Produced by the New York City Center, by arrangement with Chandler Cowles, Efrem Zimbalist, Jr., Edith Luytens and the Ballet Society, at the New York City Center of Music and Drama, December 7, 1948. Music and words by Gian-Carlo Menotti; settings and costumes for "The Medium" by Horace Armistead; musical director, Emanuel Balaban.

Cast of characters for "The Telephone"—

```
Lucy..............................................Maria d'Attili
Ben...............................................Paul King
```

Cast of characters for "The Medium"—

```
Monica............................Evelyn Keller or Derna de Lys
Toby..............................................Leo Coleman
Madame Flora...................Marie Powers or Margery Mayer
Mrs. Gobineau.....................Derna de Lys or Maria d'Attili
Mr. Gobineau......................................Paul King
Mrs. Nolan.......................................Virginia Beeler
```

A return engagement of Mr. Menotti's works which were first presented in New York in the Spring of 1947.

(Closed January 9, 1949)

ANNE OF THE THOUSAND DAYS

(198 performances)
(Continued)

Drama in two acts by Maxwell Anderson. Produced by the Playwrights' Company and Leland Hayward at the Shubert Theatre, December 8, 1948.

Cast of characters—

```
Anne Boleyn.......................................Joyce Redman
Henry.............................................Rex Harrison
Cardinal Wolsey...................................Percy Waram
Thomas Boleyn..................................Charles Francis
Servant...........................................Ludlow Maury
Henry Norris....................................Allan Stevenson
Mark Smeaton.....................................John Merivale
Duke of Norfolk..................................John Williams
Percy, Earl of Northumberland.....................Robert Duke
Elizabeth Boleyn..................................Viola Keats
Serving Woman..................................Kathleen Bolton
Servant..........................................Cecil Clovelly
Mary Boleyn......................................Louise Platt
Madge Shelton.................................Margaret Garland
Jane Seymour.....................................Monica Lang
Sir Thomas More..................................Russell Gaige
```

```
Thomas Cromwell..............................Wendell K. Phillips
Bishop Fisher.......................................Harry Irvine
Prior Houghton..................................George Collier
Messenger..........................................Harry Selby
Bailiff........................................Fred Ayres Cotton
Bailiff...........................................Harold McGee
Clerk..........................................Terence Anderson
Singers............Richard Leone, Frank Myers and Donald Conrad
Musicians..........Harold McGee, Malcolm Wells and Charles Ellis
```
The play takes place in England between the years 1526 and 1536.

Staged by H. C. Potter; setting by Jo Mielziner; costumes by Motley; music by Lehman Engel.

LEND AN EAR

(190 performances)

(Continued)

Revue with sketches, lyrics and music by Charles Gaynor. Produced by William R. Katzell, Franklin Gilbert and William Eythe at the National Theatre, December 16, 1948. Moved later to the Broadhurst Theatre.

The list of players—

Yvonne Adair	Bob Herget
Anne Renee Anderson	Beverly Hosier
Dorothy Babbs	Jenny Lou Law
Carol Channing	Arthur Maxwell
Al Checco	Tommy Morton
Robert Dixon	Gene Nelson
William Eythe	Bob Scheerer
Nancy Franklin	Jeannie Smith
Antoinette Guhlke	Lee Stacy
George Hall	Larry Stewart
Gloria Hamilton	

Staged by Gower Champion; directed by Hal Gerson; costumes and settings by Raoul Pene duBois; musical direction by George Bauer; additional sketches by Joseph Stein and Will Glickman; orchestrations by Clare Grundman; pianists, George Bauer and Dorothy Freitag.

Principal songs—Act I.—"Neurotic You and Psychopathic Me," "I'm Not in Love," "Power of the Press," "Friday Dancing Class," "Ballade," "Join Us in a Cup of Tea," "Where Is the She for Me," "I'll Be True to You," "Doin' the Old Yahoo Step," "A Little Game of Tennis," "In Our Teeny Little Weeny Nest." Act II.—"Santo Domingo," "I'm on the Lookout," "Three Little Queens of the Silver Screen," "Molly O'Reilly," "Who Hit Me?", "Words Without Song."

MAKE WAY FOR LUCIA

(29 performances)

Comedy in three acts by John van Druten, based on the novels by E. F. Benson. Produced by the Theatre Guild at the Cort Theatre, December 22, 1948.

Cast of characters—

```
Major Benjamin Flint..............................Philip Tonge
Grosvenor.........................................Cherry Hardy
Miss Mapp.....................................Catherine Willard
Georgie Pillson...................................Cyril Ritchard
Mrs. Emmeline Lucas (Lucia)........................Isabel Jeans
Mr. Wyse..........................................Ivan Simpson
Mrs. Wyse..........................................Essex Dane
Rev. Kenneth Bartlett...............................Guy Spaull
Mrs. Bartlett....................................Doreen Lang
Godiva Plaistow...................................Viola Roache
Signor Cortese....................................Kurt Kasznar
```

The locale is Tilling, a small town in England; the time is around the Summer of 1912. Act I.—Scene 1—Morning. July. 2—Morning, four weeks later. Act II.—Scene 1—Afternoon, two weeks later. 2—Afternoon, ten days later. 3—Evening, a week later. Act III.—Scene 1—Morning, next day. 2—Evening, same day. The action takes place in the drawing-room of a house.

Staged by John van Druten. Set and costumes by Lucinda Ballard.

Mrs. Emmeline Lucas, who calls herself Lucia with the Italian pronunciation, takes a Summer rental of the home of Miss Mapp. A rivalry and feline enmity develops between the two women as to who shall be the leader of such civic enterprises as art exhibits and charity garden parties. Miss Mapp is forceful and blunt; Lucia is wily and devious. Lucia wins.

(Closed January 15, 1949)

JENNY KISSED ME

(20 performances)

Comedy in three acts by Jean Kerr. Produced by James Russo, Michael Ellis and Alexander H. Cohen, in association with Clarence M. Shapiro, at the Hudson Theatre, December 23, 1948.

Cast of characters—

```
Father Moynihan.................................Leo G. Carroll
Michael Saunders....................................Alan Baxter
Mrs. Deazy.......................................Frances Bavier
Sister Mary of the Angels............................Sara Taft
Shirley Tirabossi..................................Bonnie Alden
Miss Stearns.......................................Ruth Saville
Mary Delaney.......................................Bette Howe
Harry.............................................Jean Jordan
Jo ..........................................Winnie Mae Martin
```

```
Owen Parkside..................................Brennan Moore
Jenny...........................................Pamela Rivers
A girl..........................................Camilla de Witt
Another girl....................................Dorothy King
Mr. Parkside....................................William A. Lee
```
The living-room of St. Matthew's rectory; time, the present. Act I.—An afternoon in the Fall. Act II.—Scene 1—Five weeks later, afternoon. 2—The following night. Act III.—Next morning.

Staged by James Russo; set by Ralph Alswang; costumes by Eleanor Goldsmith.

Father Moynihan takes into his rectory the mousy, pathetic, orphaned, 18-year-old niece of his housekeeper, Mrs. Deazy. He decides that the girl, Jenny, would be improved by some attractive clothes and a new hair-do. He even picks a neighborhood boy, Owen, as a husband for her—but Jenny fools him and picks her own man, Michael Saunders.

(Closed January 8, 1949)

OH, MR. MEADOWBROOK!

(64 performances)

Comedy in three acts, by Ronald Telfer and Pauline Jamerson. Produced by John Yorke at the John Golden Theatre, December 26, 1948.

Cast of characters—

```
Constance Vye...............................Grace McTarnahan
Harland Vye.................................Harry Ellerbe
Sophie MacDonald............................Sylvia Field
Japhet Meadowbrook..........................Ernest Truex
Nesta Madrigale.............................Vicki Cummings
James Howells...............................Morton L. Stevens
```
Scene, the Vyes' living room in Connecticut. Act I.—A Friday afternoon in early Summer. Act II.—The next afternoon. Act III.—Next morning.

Staged by Harry Ellerbe; setting by Wolfgang Roth; costume supervision by Lucille Little.

Japhet Meadowbrook, an inoffensive English taxidermist, has been advised by his psychiatrist to become more venturesome toward females, and he comes to the Connecticut home of a playwright and his sophisticated wife to do so. He winds up with the maid.

(Closed February 5, 1949)

THE MADWOMAN OF CHAILLOT

(177 performances)
(Continued)

Comedy in two acts by Jean Giraudoux, adapted by Maurice Valency. Produced by Alfred de Liagre, Jr., at the Belasco Theatre, December 27, 1948.

Cast of characters—

The Waiter	Ralph Smiley
The Little Man	Harold Grau
The Prospector	Vladimir Sokoloff
The President	Clarence Derwent
The Baron	Le Roi Operti
Therese	Patricia Courtley
The Street Singer	Eugene Cibelli
The Flower Girl	Millicent Brower
The Ragpicker	John Carradine
Paulette	Barbara Pond
The Deaf Mute	Martin Kosleck
Irma	Leora Dana
The Shoe-Lace Peddler	Maurice Brenner
The Broker	Jonathan Harris
The Street Juggler	John Beahan
Dr. Jadin	Sandro Giglio
Countess Aurelia, *The Madwoman of Chaillot*	Martita Hunt
The Doorman	William Chambers
The Policeman	Ralph Roberts
Pierre	Alan Shayne
The Sergeant	Richard Sanders
The Sewer-Man	James Westerfield
Mme. Constance, *The Madwoman of Passy*	Estelle Winwood
Mlle. Gabrielle, *The Madwoman of St. Sulpice*	Nydia Westman
Mme. Josephine, *The Madwoman of La Concorde*	Doris Rich
The Presidents	Clarence Derwent / Jonathan Harris / Le Roi Operti
The Prospectors	Vladimir Sokoloff / William Chambers / Maurice Brenner
The Press Agents	Archie Smith / Sandro Giglio / James Westerfield
The Ladies	Patricia Courtley / Barbara Pond / Sonia Sorel
The Adolphe Bertauts	Paul Byron / Harold Grau / William Chambers / Gilbert Smith

Time, the present. Act I.—The café terrace of Chez Francis in Paris. Act II.—The Countess' cellar at 21 Rue de Chaillot.

Staged by Alfred de Liagre, Jr.; settings and costumes by the late Christian Berard.

DON'T LISTEN, LADIES

(15 performances)

Comedy in two acts by Sacha Guitry, translated by Stephen Powys. Produced by Lee Ephraim and Jack Buchanan at the Booth Theatre, December 28, 1948.

Cast of characters—

Daniel Bachelet	Jack Buchanan
Henriette	Joan Seton
Madeleine	Moira Lister
Baron De Characnay	Hugh Miller
Blandinet	Ian Lubbock
Julie Bille-En-Bois	Ivy St. Helier
Valentine	Adele Dixon
A Porter	Bartlett Mullins
Michel Aubrion	Austin Trevor

Time, the present; scene, Daniel Bachelet's antique shop in Paris. Act I.—Monday morning. Act II.—Friday afternoon. (The curtain is lowered during Act II to denote the passage of time from Friday afternoon to the following Monday.)

Staged by Willard Stoker; setting by Leon Davey.

Daniel Bachelet, fashionable antiquarian, is married to his second wife. He suspects her of infidelity and she suspects him of the same weakness. Sensing the breach, the first wife tries to move back in—but the second love is the true love. It is Verdi's old song hit, "La Donna e Mobile," made into a play.

(Closed January 8, 1949)

THE RAPE OF LUCRETIA

(23 performances)

Opera in two acts; libretto by Ronald Duncan; music by Benjamin Britten. Produced by Marjorie and Sherman Ewing and Giovanni Cardelli at the Ziegfeld Theatre, December 29, 1948.

Cast of characters—

The male chorus	Edward Kane
The female chorus	Brenda Lewis
Collatinus	Holger Sorensen
Junius	Emile Renan
Tarquinius	George Tozzi
Lucretia	Kitty Carlisle
Bianca	Vivian Bauer
Roman woman	Lidija Franklin
Lucia	Marguerite Piazza
Soldiers	Kazmir Kokic / Lucas Hoving
Roman man	Robert Pagent
Roman youth	Stanley Simmons
A prostitute	Bunty Kelley

(Note: This was the opening night company. At varying performances subsequently other principals alternated with those listed above. Thus, Donald Clarke and Patricia Neway also sang the male and female chorus roles; Edwin Steffe was Collatinus; Andrew Gainey was Tarquinius; Eunice Alberts was Bianca; Adelaide Bishop was Lucia, and Belva Kibler was Lucretia.)

The period is Rome, 509 B.C. Act I.—Scene 1—The Generals' tent in the camp outside Rome. 2—Lucretia's house in Rome, the same evening. Act II.—Scene 1—Lucretia's bedroom. That night. 2—Lucretia's house. The next morning.

Staged by Agnes de Mille; musical director, Paul Breisach; vocal director, John Daggett Howell; costume supervision by Frank Thompson; settings by John Piper.

Ronald Duncan, poet; Benjamin Britten, composer, and John Piper, artist, collaborated in making this operatic version of the violation, remorse and suicide of Lucretia, chaste wife of a Roman general. The legend first appeared in Livy; Shakespeare used it, and so did, most recently, André Obey. Thornton Wilder made an adaptation of Obey's "Le Viol de Lucrèce" for Katharine Cornell, who appeared in it at the Belasco Theatre in December, 1932.

The opera was first produced in England, where it had 150 consecutive performances. It has been presented in many European capitals, and its first American performance was in Chicago in the Spring of 1947.

(Closed January 15, 1949)

KISS ME, KATE

(174 performances)
(Continued)

Musical comedy in two acts, produced by Saint Subber and Lemuel Ayers at the New Century Theatre, December 30, 1948. Music and lyrics by Cole Porter; book by Bella and Samuel Spewack.

Cast of characters—

Fred Graham	Alfred Drake
Harry Trevor	Thomas Hoier
Lois Lane	Lisa Kirk
Ralph	Don Mayo
Lilli Vanessi	Patricia Morison
Hattie	Annabelle Hill
Paul	Lorenzo Fuller
Bill Calhoun	Harold Lang
First man	Harry Clark
Second man	Jack Diamond
Doorman	Bill Lilling
Harrison Howell	Denis Green

Act I.—The scenes are, in order, the stage of the Ford Theatre, Baltimore; the corridor backstage; Fred's and Lilli's adjoining dressing rooms; Padua; a street in Padua; backstage; the dressing rooms, and the exterior of a church. Act II.—The alley of the theatre; before the curtain; Petruchio's house; the corridor backstage; the dressing rooms; the corridor; backstage, and Baptista's home.

Staged by John C. Wilson; settings and costumes by Lemuel Ayers; dances by Hanya Holm; musical director, Pembroke Davenport; orchestrations by Robert Russell Bennett.

Fred Graham and Lilli Vanessi, who have been divorced, are stars of a troupe playing Shakespeare's "The Taming of the Shrew." Taking a tip from Shakespeare, Fred conquers Lilli again by using considerable force.

Principal musical numbers: Act I.—"Another Op'nin', Another Show," "Why Can't You Behave," "Wunderbar," "So in Love Am I," "We Open in Venice," "Tom, Dick or Harry," "I've Come to Wive it Wealthily in Padua," "I Hate Men," "Were Thine that Special Face," "I Sing of Love," "Kiss Me, Kate." Act II.—"Too Darn Hot," "Where Is the Life that Late I Led?", "Always True to You (In My Fashion)," "Bianca," "Brush Up Your Shakespeare," "I Am Ashamed that Women Are So Simple."

THE SMILE OF THE WORLD

(5 performances)

Play in three acts by Garson Kanin. Produced by the Playwrights' Company at the Lyceum Theatre, January 12, 1949.

Cast of characters—

```
Josef Boros....................................Boris Marshalov
Mrs. Boros....................................Elizabeth Dewing
Petey.........................................Sam Jackson
Evelyn........................................Ruby Dee
Sara Boulting.................................Ruth Gordon
Sam Fenn......................................Warren Stevens
Justice Reuben Boulting.......................Otto Kruger
Stewart.......................................Ossie Davis
Alice Widmayer................................Laura Pierpont
```

Act I.—The home of Justice Boulting, Washington, October, 1923. Act II.—A few months later. Act III.—A week later.

Staged by Garson Kanin; setting by Donald Oenslager; Miss Gordon's clothes by Mainbocher; other costumes by Forrest Thayer.

With middle age and his rise to pre-eminence as a jurist, the once-eager, once-rebellious Reuben Boulting has become a stuffed shirt, and his wife, Sara, finds she has lost the man whom once she loved. She finds this man again in Sam Fenn, a young lawyer who has come to be the Justice's clerk.

(Closed January 15, 1949)

ALONG FIFTH AVENUE

(158 performances)
(Continued)

Revue in two acts, produced by Arthur Lesser at the Broadhurst Theatre, January 13, 1948. Music by Gordon Jenkins; lyrics by Tom Adair; additional music and lyrics by Richard

Stutz, Milton Pascal and Nat Hiken; sketches by Charles Sherman and Nat Hiken; settings by Oliver Smith; costumes by David Ffolkes; dances and musical numbers staged by Robert Sidney; additional direction by Charles Friedman.

Principal players—

Nancy Walker	Joyce Mathews
Hank Ladd	Dick Bernie
Carol Bruce	George S. Irving
Donald Richards	Zachary Solov
Viola Essen	Lee Krieger
Johnny Coy	Wallace Seibert
Virginia Gorski	Louise Kirtland
Judyth Burroughs	Jackie Gleason

Principal songs: Act I.—"Fifth Avenue," "Sweet Surrender," "A Window on the Avenue," "If This Is Glamour!", "I Love Love in New York," "The Fugitive from Fifth Avenue." Act II.—"Weep No More," "Chant D'Amour," "Call It Applefritters," "A Trip Doesn't Care at All."

THE SHOP AT SLY CORNER

(7 performances)

Melodrama in three acts by Edward Percy (Smith). Produced by Gant Gaither at the Booth Theatre, January 18, 1949.

Cast of characters—

Archie Fellowes	Jay Robinson
Descius Heiss	Boris Karloff
Margaret Heiss	Mary McLeod
Joan Deal	Jane Lloyd-Jones
Mathilde Heiss	Ethel Griffies
Mrs. Catt	Una O'Connor
Robert Graham	Philip Saville
Corder Morris	Emmett Rogers
Steve Hubbard	Alfred Hyslop
John Elliot	Reginald Mason

A room at the back of a London antique shop. Act I.—A Friday evening in August. Act II.—A Sunday evening, the following Winter. Act III.—The next Tuesday morning.

Staged by Margaret Perry; setting and costumes by Willis Knighton. (Note: This play was tried out in Boston and Princeton in 1941 under the title of "Play with Fire," with Henry Hull in the leading role. It was produced in London in 1945 and ran two years.)

Decius Heiss, former Devil's Island convict, is running an antique shop as a blind to cover his operations as a fence. A young shop assistant, Archie Fellowes, learns his secret, begins to blackmail him and is strangled. When a police inspector calls, Heiss poisons himself and dies laughing when he learns that the inspector does not suspect him, but merely wants to buy an antique suit of armor.

(Closed January 22, 1949)

LEAF AND BOUGH

(3 performances)

Play in three acts by Joseph Hayes. Produced by Charles P. Heidt at the Cort Theatre, January 21, 1949.

Cast of characters—

Bert Warren	Anthony Ross
Myra Warren	Dorothy Elder
Attie Warren	Louise Buckley
Mary Warren	Mary Linn Beller
Grandpa Nelson	William Jeffrey
Laura Campbell	Alice Reinheart
Frederick Campbell	David White
Glenn Campbell	Charlton Heston
Mark Campbell	Richard Hart
Nan Warren	Coleen Gray
Harlan Adams	Jared Reed
Dr. Vincent Cullen	Tom McElhany

Side by side on the stage are the kitchen of the Warren farmhouse and the living room of the Campbell home in a small town. Act I.—An Autumn evening. Act II.—Next morning. Act III.—Next day.

Staged by Rouben Mamoulian; settings by Carl Kent.

Nan Warren, daughter of a respectable but frustrated farm family, falls in love with the moody and sensitive son of a generally dissolute town tribe. It's tough going, but love conquers.

(Closed January 22, 1949)

ALL FOR LOVE

(141 performances)

Revue in two acts, produced by Sammy Lambert and Anthony B. Farrell at the Mark Hellinger Theatre, January 22, 1949.

Principal players—

Grace and Paul Hartman	Kathryn Mylorie
Bert Wheeler	Milton Frome
Patricia Wymore	Paul Reed
Milada Mladova	Budd Rogerson
Dick Smart	June Graham
Leni Lynn	Richard d'Arcy

Music and lyrics by Allan Roberts and Lester Lee; sketch editor, Max Shulman; staged by Edward Reveaux; dances by Eric Victor; settings by Edward Gilbert; costumes by Billy Livingston; Clay Warnick, musical director.

Principal musical numbers: Act I.—"My Baby's Bored," "Why Can't It Happen Again," "My Heart's in the Middle of July," "It's a Living." Act II.—"Run to Me My Love," "Mary Maggie McNeil," "No Time for Love."

(Closed May 7, 1949)

CAROUSEL

(48 performances)

Musical play in two acts. Revived by the Theatre Guild at the New York City Center of Music and Drama, January 25, 1949. On February 22 it moved to the Majestic Theatre.

Cast of characters—

Carrie Pipperidge	Margot Moser
Julie Jordan	Iva Withers
Mrs. Mullin	Louise Larabee
Billy Bigelow	Stephen Douglass
First Policeman	Kenneth Knapp
David Bascombe	Ross Chetwynd
Nettie Fowler	Christine Johnson
June Girl	Mavis Ray
Enoch Snow	Eric Mattson
Jigger Craigin	Mario De Laval
Hannah	Dusty Worrall
Boatswain	Kenneth MacKenzie
Arminy	Bobra Suiter
Penny	Evelyne Ross
Jennie	Audrey Sabetti
Virginia	Jean Rogers
Susan	Ruth Devorin
Second Policeman	Richmond Page
Captain	Warren Harr
Heavenly Friend (Brother Joshua)	Jay Velie
Starkeeper	Calvin Thomas
Louise	Diane Keith
Carnival Boy	Kenneth MacKenzie
Enoch Snow, Jr.	Anthony Aleo
Principal	Kenneth Knapp

This musical version of Ferenc Molnar's "Liliom," with book and lyrics by Oscar Hammerstein II and music by Richard Rodgers, was first presented in New York April 19, 1945. Since April, 1947, the company listed above had been on tour.

(Closed March 5, 1949)

FORWARD THE HEART

(19 performances)

Drama in two acts by Bernard Reines. Produced by Theatre Enterprises Inc. and Leon J. Bronesky at the Forty-eighth Street Theatre, January 28, 1949.

Cast of characters—

Mrs. Marian Gibbs	Natalie Schafer
David Gibbs	William Prince
Dr. George Whiting	Harry Bannister
Julie Evans	Mildred Joanne Smith

Spring, in the Gibbs house in a fashionable Boston suburb. Act I.—Scene 1—A Monday morning toward the end of May. 2—The following day. 3—Early afternoon, two days later. Act II.—Scene 1—Three weeks later. 2—One week later.

Staged by Peter Frye; setting by Perry Watkins.

David Gibbs, blinded in the war, returns home with little hope for his future. He discovers that to the blind, color makes no difference—and he falls in love with his mother's Negro maid, Julie; and Julie with him. He wants to marry her, but she sadly arrives at the conclusion that the world is not yet ready to accept a union such as theirs would be.

(Closed February 12, 1949)

DIAMOND LIL

(24 performances)
(Continued)

Play in three acts by Mae West, based on a play by Jack Linder. Revived by Albert H. Rosen and Herbert J. Freezer at the Coronet Theatre, February 5, 1949.

Cast of characters—

Jim	Billy Van
Bill	Jack Howard
Porter	James Quinn
Ragtime	Dick Arnold
Spike	George Warren
Jerry	Harry Warren
Card Players	{ Fred Catania { Patsy Perroni
Kitty	Harriet Nelson
Frances	Sheila Trent
Flo	Sylvia Syms
Maggie	Louise Jenkins
Flynn	Charles G. Martin
Kane	Mike Keene
Gus Jordan	Walter Petrie
Sally	Frances Arons
Rita	Miriam Goldina
Juarez	Steve Cochran
Mike	James Fallon
Diamond Lil	Mae West
Charlie	Peter Chan
Bessie	Buddy Millette
Violet	Margaret Magennis
Barbara	Marilyn Lowe
Captain Cummings	Richard Coogan
Pete the Duke	Lester Laurence
Doheney	Ralph Chambers
Jacobson	Louis Nussbaum
Chick Clark	Jeff Morrow
Sailor	Jerry Tobias
Cop	F. Ben Miller
Singer	Michael Edwards
Miss West's Accompanist	David Lapin

Cyclists, Customers, Bowery Characters, Policemen, Society Women, Society Men: John Quigg, Robert Behr, Frederic Meyer, James Wiler, Robert Allender, William H. Miller, Hiram Breckenridge, Harry Miller, Curtis Karpe, Hyacinth Melon, Ethel Curtis, Lawrence Holmes, Marjorie Dalton, Lucille Perroni, Joli Coleman, Lillian Martin.

Bowery Pianist .... Arnold New

Staged by Charles K. Freeman; sets by William De Forest and Ben Edwards; costumes by Paul Du Pont.

This comedy melodrama was first produced at the Royale Theatre, April 9, 1928. (See Best Plays for 1927-28.) In 1947-48 Miss West had a run of ten months in a London production of the play. In the 1949 New York revival two members of the cast, Louis Nussbaum and Jack Howard, played their original roles—as, indeed, did Miss West. Miss West broke her ankle in a fall in her hotel suite February 26, 1949, and performances were not resumed until early in June, 1949.

RICHARD III

(23 performances)

Shakespeare history, arranged in three acts and seventeen scenes. Produced by Herman Levin at the Booth Theatre, February 8, 1949.

Cast of characters—

Richard, Duke of Gloucester, later Richard III	Richard Whorf
George, Duke of Clarence, his brother	Will Kuluva
Brackenbury	Alan Frost
Hastings, the Lord Chamberlain	Robert H. Harris
Anne, widow of the son of Henry VI, later Richard's queen	Frances Reid
Tressel	Robert Carricart
Berkeley	Milton Selzer
Queen Elizabeth, wife of Edward IV, king as the play opens	Polly Rowles
Rivers, her brother	Glenn Wilson
Grey, Dorset, her sons by a previous marriage	{ David Clive { Douglass Watson
Vaughan, friendly to the Queen's party	Warren Burmeister
Duke of Buckingham	Philip Bourneuf
Stanley, married to Richmond's mother	Orrin Redfield
Catesby, Ratcliff, Lovel (followers of Richard)	{ William Nichols { Ray Walston { Charles Nahabedian
Queen Margaret, widow of Henry VI	Grace Coppin
Edward IV, Richard's oldest brother, who took the throne from Henry VI	Joseph Foley
Lord Mayor of London	Walter F. Appler
Tyrell, later Earl of Surrey	Nehemiah Persoff
Richmond, head of the house of Lancaster, later Henry VII	Michael Sivy
Citizens	{ Connie Lessard { Ed Hoffman

Staged by Richard Barr; settings and costumes by Richard Whorf.

(Closed February 26, 1949)

MY NAME IS AQUILON

(31 performances)

Comedy in two acts by Jean Pierre Aumont, adapted by Philip Barry. Produced by the Theatre Guild at the Lyceum Theatre, February 9, 1949.

Cast of characters—

Paulette	Phyllis Kirk
Pierre Renault	Jean Pierre Aumont
Christiane Benoit-Benoit	Lilli Palmer
Denise	Doe Avedon
Victor Benoit-Benoit	Lawrence Fletcher
Madeleine Benoit-Benoit	Arlene Francis
Toto	Donald Hanmer
Bascoul	Louis Sorel
Rondet	Richard Hepburn

Act I.—Scene 1—A Paris apartment, April, 1948. 2—The apartment, two months later. 3—A room in a small hotel. Evening of the same day. Act II.—Scene 1—The apartment, late August. 2—The hotel room, the following morning.

Staged by Robert B. Sinclair; settings by Stewart Chaney; gowns by Valentina and Castillo.

Pierre Renault, who lives by his wits and tells vast imaginary tales about his exploits, becomes secretary to Victor Benoit-Benoit, an outwardly respectable dealer in black market currency. Pierre falls in love with his employer's daughter, Christiane, and she accepts him even when she learns he is a penniless liar.

(Closed March 7, 1949)

DEATH OF A SALESMAN

(126 performances)
(Continued)

Play in two acts by Arthur Miller. Produced by Kermit Bloomgarden and Walter Fried at the Morosco Theatre, February 10, 1949.

Cast of characters—

Willy Loman	Lee J. Cobb
Linda	Mildred Dunnock
Happy	Cameron Mitchell
Biff	Arthur Kennedy
Bernard	Don Keefer
The Woman	Winifred Cushing
Charley	Howard Smith
Uncle Ben	Thomas Chalmers
Howard Wagner	Alan Hewitt
Jenny	Ann Driscoll
Stanley	Tom Pedi
Miss Forsythe	Constance Ford
Letta	Hope Cameron

The action of the play is in two parts. It takes place in Willy Loman's house—its bedrooms, kitchen, basement, front porch and back yard, and in various offices and places he visits in New York City and Boston today.

Staged by Elia Kazan; settings by Jo Mielziner; incidental music by Alex North; costumes by Julia Sze.

THEY KNEW WHAT THEY WANTED

(61 performances)

Comedy in three acts by the late Sidney Howard. Revived by John Golden at the Music Box Theatre, February 16, 1949.

Cast of characters—

Joe	Edward Andrews
Father McKee	Charles Kennedy
Ah Gee	Francisco Salvacion
Tony	Paul Muni
The R.F.D.	Bruno Wick
Amy	Carol Stone
Angelo	Danny Leone
Giorgio	Victor Rendina
The Doctor	Henry Burk Jones
First Italian Mother	Eole Gambarelli
Her Daughter	Dolores Brown
Second Italian Mother	Delores Badaloni
Her Son	Joseph Italiano
Third Italian Mother	Eole Gambarelli
Her Daughter	Dolores Brown

Tony's farmhouse in the Napa Valley, California. Act I.—Morning, early Summer. Act II.—Evening, same day. Act III.—Three months later.

Staged by Robert Perry; setting by Frederick Fox.

This play was first produced by the Theatre Guild at the Garrick Theatre, November 24, 1924, with Richard Bennett and Pauline Lord as the principals. It won the Pulitzer prize. (See Best Plays of 1924-25.) It was revived by Leonard Sillman at the Empire Theatre, October 2, 1939, with Giuseppe Sterni and June Walker in the leads. It had 24 performances. RKO made it into a film with Charles Laughton and the late Carole Lombard.

(Closed April 9, 1949)

THE BIG KNIFE

(108 performances)

Drama in three acts by Clifford Odets. Produced by Dwight Deere Wiman at the National Theatre, February 24, 1949.

Cast of characters—

Russell	Frank Wilson
Buddy Bliss	William Terry
Charlie Castle	John Garfield
Patty Benedict	Leona Powers
Marion Castle	Nancy Kelly
Nat Danziger	Reinhold Schunzel
Marcus Hoff	J. Edward Bromberg
Smiley Coy	Paul McGrath
Connie Bliss	Mary Patton
Hank Teagle	Theodore Newton

Dixie Evans..Joan McCracken
Dr. Frary..John McKee
    The playroom of Charlie Castle's house in Beverly Hills. Act I.—A Summer afternoon. Act II.—Late night, the following week. Act III.—Scene 1—Afternoon, four days later. 2—An hour later.
    Staged by Lee Strasberg; setting by Howard Bay; costumes by Lucille Little.

Charlie Castle, movie star, wants to get away from Hollywood because his wife, Marion, wants him to. But he is bound to a fourteen-year contract worth $3,400,000, and the studio warns him that if he tries to break loose from his comfortable bondage it will expose him for a drunken-driving killing. The only way out of the contract is for Charlie to kill himself, which he does.

(Closed May 28, 1949)

ANYBODY HOME

(5 performances)

Romantic drama in two acts by Robert Pyzel. Produced by Phyllis Holden (Mrs. Pyzel) at the John Golden Theatre, February 25, 1949.

Cast of characters—

Franklin..Jimmy Dutton
Joah..Emory Richardson
Bill Gordon.....................................Roger Clark
Kay Howard.....................................Phyllis Holden
Julia Henley...................................Katherine Anderson
Harry..Lloyd Holden
Taylor...Valerie Valaire
John Howard....................................Donald Curtis
    Act I.—The Westchester County home of the Howards. Scene 1—A Sunday afternoon in late August. 2—Afternoon, Tuesday. Act II.—Scene 1—Early evening, Wednesday. 2—Late that night and early Thursday morning.
    Staged by Ralph Forbes. Setting by Louis Kennel.

The Howards, of the horsy country set, have marital misunderstandings and Mrs. Howard has an admirer. A well-intentioned little play, but one of the most inexpert of the season.

(Closed March 1, 1949)

TWO BLIND MICE

(103 performances)
(Continued)

Comedy in three acts by Samuel Spewack. Produced by Archer King and Harrison Woodhull at the Cort Theatre, March 2, 1949.

Cast of characters—

Mrs. Letitia Turnbull	Laura Pierpont
Miss Crystal Hower	Mabel Paige
Mr. Murray	Roland Wood
Miss Johnson	Jane Hoffman
Mailman	Howard Fischer
Tommy Thurston	Melvyn Douglas
A Visitor	Robert P. Lieb
Simon	Alonzo Bosan
Karen Norwood	Jan Sterling
Wilbur F. Threadwaite, Dept. of State	Geoffrey Lumb
Major John Groh, U.S.A.	Raymond Bramley
Lt. Col. Robbins, U.S.A.F.	Walter Brooke
Commander Thomas Jellico, U.S.N.	Robert Pike
Dr. Henry McGill	Richard Kendrick
Sergeant	Robert Webber
Charles Brenner	Howard St. John
Ensign Jamison, U.S.N.	Elliott Reid
Senator Kruger	Frank Tweddell

Act I.—The Office of Herbs and Standards, Washington. Act II.—The same, several days later. Act III.—The same, next morning.

Staged by Samuel Spewack; setting by Albert Johnson; costumes by Natalie Barth Walker.

AT WAR WITH THE ARMY

(97 performances)
(Continued)

Comedy in three acts by James B. Allardice. Produced by Henry May and Jerome E. Rosenfeld in association with Charles Ray McCallum at the Booth Theatre, March 8, 1949.

Cast of characters—

Captain Ernest Caldwell	William Mendrek
Second Lieutenant Davenport	Kenneth Forbes
T/5 Corporal Clark	Mitchell Agruss
Corporal Di Ruccio	Ernest Sarracino
Staff Sergeant Krieger	Jerry Jarrett
A Soldier	Alfred Leberfeld
Another Soldier	Joseph Keen
First Sergeant Robert Johnson	Gary Merrill
Staff Sergeant McVay	Mike Kellin
A Lost Private	George Mosel
Private Jack Edwards	Bernard Kates
First Lieutenant William Terray	Ty Perry
Millie	Maxine Stuart
Mrs. Caldwell	Sara Seegar
Private First Class Alvin Hawkins	William Lanteau
Colonel Davies	John Shellie
Helen Palmer	Sally Gracie

A company orderly room in a training camp in Kentucky. Act I.—Afternoon, late in 1944. Act II.—Scene 1—Early evening, same day. 2—The following morning. Act III.—That afternoon.

Staged by Ezra Stone; setting by Donald Oenslager.

A farce about the boredom of war in a training camp, in which everybody from privates first class to the colonel have their troubles. What story there is in a play consisting mostly of farcical pranks and situations involves First Sergeant Robert Johnson, who deceives himself into believing he is the father of the child that Millie, a PX waitress, expects.

DETECTIVE STORY

(79 performances)

(Continued)

Melodrama in three acts by Sidney Kingsley. Produced by Howard Lindsay and Russel Crouse at the Hudson Theatre, March 23, 1949.

Cast of characters—

Detective Dakis	Robert Strauss
Shoplifter	Lee Grant
Detective Gallagher	Edward Binns
Mrs. Farragut	Jean Adair
Joe Feinson	Lou Gilbert
Detective Callahan	Patrick McVey
Detective O'Brien	John Boyd
Detective Brody	James Westerfield
Mr. Sims	Les Tremayne
Detective McLeod	Ralph Bellamy
Arthur Kindred	Warren Stevens
Patrolman Barnes	Earl Sydnor
1st burglar (Charlie)	Joseph Wiseman
2nd burglar (Lewis)	Michael Strong
Mrs. Bagatelle	Michelette Burani
Dr. Schneider	Harry Worth
Lieut. Monoghan	Horace McMahon
Susan Carmichael	Joan Copeland
Patrolman Keogh	Byron C. Halstead
Patrolman Baker	Joe Roberts
Willy	Carl Griscom
Miss Hatch	Maureen Stapleton
Mrs. Feeney	Sarah Grable
Mr. Feeney	Jim Flynn
Crumb-Bum	Archie Benson
Mr. Gallantz	Garney Wilson
Mr. Pritchett	James Maloney
Tami Giacoppetti	Alexander Scourby
Photographer	Michael Lewin
Lady	Ruth Storm
Gentleman	John Alberts
Mr. Bagatelle	Joseph Ancona
Indignant citizen	Jacqueline Paige

Act I.—5:30 P.M. on a day in August in the detective squad room of a New York precinct police station. Act II.—7:30 P.M. Act III.—8:30 P.M.

Staged by Sidney Kingsley; setting by Boris Aronson; costume supervision by Millie Sutherland.

THE BIGGEST THIEF IN TOWN

(13 performances)

Farce comedy in three acts by Dalton Trumbo. Produced by Lee Sabinson at the Mansfield Theatre, March 30, 1949.

Cast of characters—

Bert Hutchins	Thomas Mitchell
Horton Paige	Russ Brown
Laurie Hutchins	Lois Nettleton
Buddy Gwynne	Robert Readick

BURNS MANTLE BEST PLAYS OF 1948-49

```
Dr. Jay Stewart..................................Walter Abel
Miss Tipton.....................................Charity Grace
Sam Wilkins....................................Rhys Williams
Dr. Rolfe Willow...............................Brent Sargent
Col. Jared Rumley................................Fay Roope
John Troybalt................................William J. Kelly
First nurse................................Alexander Lockwood
Second nurse........................................Ben Metz
```
Act I.—Bert Hutchins' undertaking parlor in Shale City, Colorado. A Spring evening. Act II.—A half hour later. Act III.—Twenty minutes later.

Staged by Herman Shumlin; setting by Leo Kerz; costumes by Eleanor Goldsmith.

The meanest and richest old man in town, John Troybalt, is pronounced dead. His fancy funeral would normally be handed over to a big Denver undertaking firm. With the help of a number of drinks the local undertaker, Bert Hutchins, abetted by his physician friend, Dr. Stewart, abducts the corpse and clinches the funeral deal. But the corpse revives.

(Closed April 9, 1949)

THE TRAITOR

(67 performances)

Melodrama in two acts by Herman Wouk. Produced by Jed Harris at the Forty-eighth Street Theatre, April 4, 1949.

Cast of characters—
```
Professor Tobias Emanuel.....................Walter Hampden
Jane Bailey.......................................Louise Platt
Margaret......................................Georgia Simmons
Professor Allen Carr..............................Wesley Addy
Eva McKeon........................................Jean Hagen
Lieutenant Henderson.............................Richard Derr
Mr. Fislinger...................................James Van Dyk
Captain Gallagher..................................Lee Tracy
Reynolds..................................William Thunhurst, Jr.
Chief Mate Wilson..............................Maurice Manson
Lieutenant Smith...............................James Davidson
Hammontree.....................................Michael Abbott
First Man........................................Gene Blakely
Second Man.....................................Larry Sherman
Stricko........................................Michael Dreyfuss
A Man..........................................Phillip Coolidge
Another Man......................................John Wengraf
Pharmacist's Mate.................................Don Doherty
```
Act I.—Scene 1—The living room of the ground floor apartment of Prof. Tobias Emanuel in upper Manhattan; an afternoon in March. 2—That evening. Act II.—Scene 1—Five minutes later. 2—11:05 that night.

Staged by Jed Harris; setting by Raymond Sovey; costumes by Joseph Fretwell III.

Professor Emanuel has a protégé, Professor Allen Carr—an atomic scientist who is about to turn over atom bomb secrets and a sample of fissionable material to a Russian spy ring. Naval Intelligence gets wind of it and Captain Gallagher and a trained crew of investigators move in. A Geiger counter gives them proof that Carr has had possession of radioactive material and he confesses that he has been dealing with the spies because he believes world safety lies in both sides having the bomb. He redeems his mistake by leading the chief spy into a trap—and is killed by the spy.

(Closed May 28, 1949)

THE IVY GREEN

(7 performances)

Play in two acts by Mervyn Nelson. Produced by Hall Shelton at the Lyceum Theatre, April 5, 1949.

Cast of characters—

Martin	Barnard Hughes
Martha Tripham	Ruth White
Baroness Angela Burdette-Coutts	Neva Patterson
Daniel MacLise	Oliver Cliff
John Forster	Hurd Hatfield
John Dickens	Ernest Cossart
Mary Hogarth	Joy Reese
Charles Dickens	Daniel O'Herlihy
Georgina Hogarth	Carmen Mathews
Maria Beadnell	Leta Bonynge
Harriet	Mary Lou Taylor
Ellen Ternan	June Dayton
Charles Dickens, Jr.	Donald White
Catherine Dickens	Judith Evelyn

The action takes place in the drawing room of Tavistock House, London, between 1836 and 1870. Act I.—Scene 1—A night in Spring. 2—Dusk, one year later. 3—Four years later, a Summer afternoon. 4—Christmas Eve, eight years later. Act II.—Scene 1—A Summer afternoon, ten years later. 2—A Summer evening one year later. 3—Sunset, June 16, 1870. 4—8 A.M., two days later.

Staged by Roy Hargrave and Richard Barr; set and costumes by Stewart Chaney.

Charles Dickens brings his young wife, Catherine, to their fine new house. In the ensuing years he gradually abandons her, first finding favor in her sister, Georgina, and becoming devoted to an actress in his old age. A chronological drama ending with Dickens' death.

(Closed April 9, 1949)

SOUTH PACIFIC

(60 performances)
(Continued)

Musical play in two acts. Produced by Richard Rodgers, Oscar Hammerstein 2d, Leland Hayward and Joshua Logan at the Majestic Theatre, April 7, 1949. Music by Richard Rodgers;

lyrics by Oscar Hammerstein 2d; book by Oscar Hammerstein 2d and Joshua Logan, based on James A. Michener's "Tales of the South Pacific."

Cast of characters—

Ngana	Barbara Luna
Jerome	Michael Deleon or Noel DeLeon
Henry	Richard Silvera
Ensign Nellie Forbush	Mary Martin
Emile de Becque	Ezio Pinza
Bloody Mary	Juanita Hall
Bloody Mary's Assistant	Musa Williams
Abner	Archie Savage
Stewpot	Henry Slate
Luther Billis	Myron McCormick
Professor	Fred Sadoff
Lt. Joseph Cable	William Tabbert
Capt. George Brackett, U.S.N.	Martin Wolfson
Cmdr. William Harbison, U.S.N.	Harvey Stephens
Yeoman Herbert Quale	Alan Gilbert
Sgt. Kenneth Johnson	Thomas Gleason
Seabee Richard West	Dickinson Eastham
Seabee Morton Wise	Henry Michel
Seaman Tom O'Brien	Bill Dwyer
Radio Operator Bob McCaffrey	Biff McGuire
Marine Cpl. Hamilton Steeves	Jim Hawthorne
Staff Sgt. Thomas Hassinger	Jack Fontan
Seaman James Hayes	Beau Tilden
Lt. Genevieve Marshall	Jacqueline Fisher
Ensign Dinah Murphy	Roslyn Lowe
Ensign Janet MacGregor	Sandra Deel
Ensign Cora MacRae	Bernice Saunders
Ensign Sue Yaeger	Pat Northrop
Ensign Lisa Minelli	Gloria Meli
Ensign Connie Walewska	Mardi Bayne
Ensign Pamela Whitmore	Evelyn Colby
Ensign Bessie Noonan	Helena Schurgot
Liat	Betta St. John
Marcel, Henry's Assistant	Richard Loo
Lt. Buzz Adams	Don Fellows

Islanders, Sailors, Marines, Officers: Mary Ann Reeve, Chin Yu, Alex Nicol, Eugene Smith, Richard Loo, William Ferguson.

The action takes place on two islands of the South Pacific during the recent war. There is a week's lapse of time between the two acts.

Staged by Joshua Logan; sets by Jo Mielziner; costumes by Motley; orchestrations by Robert Russell Bennett; musical director, Salvatore dell' Isola.

Among the American forces stationed on a South Pacific island is Ensign Nellie Forbush, a nurse, who falls in love with Emile de Becque, wealthy French planter. When she learns he has two children by a Polynesian first wife, now dead, she breaks off the affair. But when he returns from a dangerous spying mission she again accepts him. There is a concurrent love story involving Lt. Joseph Cable, Marine aviator, and Liat, a Polynesian girl. Cable is killed on the spying mission.

Principal musical numbers: Act I.—"Dites-Moi Pourquoi," "A Cockeyed Optimist," "Some Enchanted Evening," "Bloody Mary Is the Girl I Love," "There Is Nothing Like a Dame," "Bali Ha'i," "I'm Gonna Wash That Man Right Outa My Hair,"

"I'm in Love with a Wonderful Guy," "Younger Than Springtime." Act II.—"Soft Shoe Dance," "Happy Talk," "Honey Bun," "You've Got To Be Taught," "This Nearly Was Mine."

MAGNOLIA ALLEY

(8 performances)

Comedy in three acts by George Batson. Produced by Lester Cutler at the Mansfield Theatre, April 18, 1949.

Cast of characters—

Angel Tuttle	Julie Harris
Laura Beaumont	Jessie Royce Landis
Andy Hamill	Jackie Cooper
Maybelle	Bibi Osterwald
Tom	Robert White
Joadie	Hildy Parks
Miss Eels	Francis Bavier
Nita	Anne Jackson
Cravin	Brad Dexter
Col. Stacey	Fred Stewart
The doctor	Don Kennedy
Mr. Albus	Douglas Rutherford

Act I.—Living room of Laura Beaumont's home in a small Southern town. Mid-afternoon, early Summer. Act II.—Scene 1—Late afternoon, a week later. 2—Two weeks later. Act III.—Scene 1—Early the next afternoon. 2—The following afternoon.

Staged by Carl Shain; set by Edward Gilbert; costumes by Guy Kent.

Laura Beaumont takes in roomers, including a professional floozy named Maybelle. Visitors to and inhabitants of the house include Angel Tuttle, who is very religious; Andy Hamill, a prize fighter whose head is his weak spot; Nita, Andy's no-good wife, and Joadie, a nice girl who loves Andy. This play was quite generally denounced for its bad taste.

(Closed April 23, 1949)

THE HAPPIEST YEARS

(8 performances)

Comedy in three acts by Thomas Coley and William Roerick. Produced by Gertrude Macy at the Lyceum Theatre, April 25, 1949.

Cast of characters—

Martha Johnson	Judy Parrish
Richard Johnson	Douglas Watson
Alida Wentworth	Jessie Busley
Clara Graves	Peggy Wood
Bertram Graves	Richard Bishop
Roger Littlefield	James Goodwin

Joan Miller	Louisa Horton
Florence Graves	June Walker
Morton Graves	Loring Smith

Act I.—A late January evening in the living room of the Graves home in a small midwestern college town. Act II.—Scene 1—7:45 the next morning. 2—That evening. Act III.—Noon the next day.

Staged by James Neilson; setting by James Russell.

Richard and Martha Johnson, newlyweds, are living with Martha's parents while Richard continues a belated college career under the GI Bill. Richard is a grind, and a fellow grind is an attractive female student, Joan Miller. Martha's mother, Clara, suspects that Joan and her son-in-law are studying biology in something besides books, but her suspicions are narrow and groundless.

(Closed April 30, 1949)

MEDEA

(16 performances)

Adaptation in verse by Robinson Jeffers of Euripides' tragedy, in two acts. Presented by Guthrie McClintic at the New York City Center of Music and Drama, May 2, 1949.

Cast of characters—

The Nurse	Hilda Vaughn
The Tutor	Don McHenry
The Children	{ Peter Monsen { James Francis McArdle
First Woman of Corinth	Mary Servoss
Second Woman of Corinth	Marian Seldes
Third Woman of Corinth	Martha Downs
Medea	Judith Anderson
Creon	Frederic Worlock
Jason	Henry Brandon
Aegeus	Bruce Gordon
Jason's slave	Theodore Marcuse
Attendant to Medea	Mary Adams
Soldiers	{ Anthony Radecki { James Doyle

The action of the play takes place before Medea's house in Corinth.

Staged by Guthrie McClintic; setting by Ben Edwards; costumes by Castillo.

At the end of a season-long tour of the country, Miss Anderson returned for a limited engagement in the production which was first offered at the National Theatre, October 20, 1947, and which ran for 214 performances. Principal cast changes included the substitution of Hilda Vaughn for Florence Reed as The Nurse; of Frederic Worlock for Albert Hecht as Creon, and of Henry Brandon for John Gielgud as Jason.

(Closed May 21, 1949)

MRS. GIBBONS' BOYS

(5 performances)

Comedy in three acts by Will Glickman and Joseph Stein. Produced by George Abbott at the Music Box Theatre, May 4, 1949.

Cast of characters—

Myra Ward	Glenda Farrell
Mrs. Peggy Gibbons	Lois Bolton
Rudy Gibbons	Tom Lewis
Mr. Rausch	Richard Taber
Lester MacMichaels	Francis Compton
Woodrow Grupp	Edward Andrews
Francis X. Gibbons	Richard Carlyle
Rodla Gibbons	Ray Walston
Ernie "Horse" Wagner	Royal Dano
Coles	William David
Pearl	Helen Mayon

Act I.—Living room of Mrs. Peggy Gibbons' home, 8:30 in the evening. Act II.—The following morning. Act III.—Ten minutes later.

Staged by George Abbott. Setting by John Root; costumes by John Robert Lloyd.

Mrs. Peggy Gibbons has a warm heart and no brain. To her, her three sons can do no wrong, even though two have broken out of a penitentiary and the other is on parole.

(Closed May 7, 1949)

GAYDEN

(7 performances)

A play in two acts by Mignon and Robert McLaughlin. Produced by Gant Gaither at the Plymouth Theatre, May 10, 1949.

Cast of characters—

Emily Archer	Carol Wheeler
Agnes	Hazel Jones
Grace Sibley	Fay Bainter
Dr. Ned Whitaker	Clay Clement
Gayden Sibley	Jay Robinson
Polly Dalton	Gloria Stroock

Act I.—Scene 1—A day in early July in the Sibley house in New York. 2—The following afternoon. Act II.—Scene 1—An evening six weeks later. 2—Midnight, the same night.

Staged by Lex Richards; setting by Willis Knighton; costumes by Emeline Roche.

Gayden Sibley, an effeminate young dilettante, lives with his mother, Grace. In the opinion of Grace's brother, Dr. Whitaker, Gayden is insane—a criminal sadist. When Grace finally admits that what he says is true, she still loves her son so much that she continues to live with him.

(Closed May 14, 1949)

MAN AND SUPERMAN

(16 performances)

Comedy in three acts by Bernard Shaw, produced by Maurice Evans at the New York City Center of Music and Drama, May 16, 1949.

Cast of characters—

Roebuck Ramsden	Malcolm Keen
Maid	Dorothy Eaton
Octavius Robinson	Chester Stratton
John Tanner	Maurice Evans
Ann Whitefield	Frances Rowe
Mrs. Whitefield	Josephine Brown
Miss Ramsden	Phoebe Mackay
Violet Robinson	Nan McFarland
Henry Straker	Morton DaCosta
Hector Malone, Jr.	James Daly
Hector Malone, Sr.	Victor Sutherland

This was a fortnight's return engagement of Mr. Evans' production, at the end of a season-long tour. It was first presented October 8, 1949, and ran for 295 performances.

(Closed June 4, 1949)

MR. ADAM

(5 performances)

Comedy in two acts by Jack Kirkland, based on a novel with the same title by Pat Frank. Produced by Jack Kirkland at the Royale Theatre, May 25, 1949.

Cast of characters—

Mary Ellen Adam	Elisabeth Fraser
Mrs. Brundage	Effie Laird
Homer Adam	James Dobson
Steve Smith	Frank Albertson
Joe	George Ramsey
Colonel Phelps-Smythe	Howard Freeman
Sergeant Carlson	John James
Sergeant Donetti	Robert Gray
Nate Gabelman	Ted Thorpe
Percy Klutz	Emory Parnell
Jane Zitter	Maxine Semon
Obadiah Latch	Oliver Blake

Act I.—Scene 1—About 4 P.M. on a June 22nd. 2—That night. Act II.—Scene 1—Next day. 2—The following morning. The action takes

place in the living room of Homer Adam's home on the outskirts of Tarrytown, N. Y.
Staged by Jack Kirkland; setting by Phil Raiguel.

An atomic explosion has made sterile every male in the world except Homer Adam, who happened to have been in a lead mine at the time. The ladies, however, still are vigorous, and the nation drafts Homer as a repopulation project. Another notable candidate for the Worst Play of the Season honors.

HOWDY MR. ICE OF 1950

(9 performances)
(Continued)

Revised edition of the skating revue which opened June 24, 1948, and closed April 23, 1949. Produced by Sonja Henie and Arthur M. Wirtz at the Center Theatre, May 26, 1949.

Principals engaged—

Skippy Baxter	John Kasper
Eileen Seigh	Buck Pennington
Eddie Barry	Cissy Trenholm
The Bruises	Arthur Erickson
The Prestons	John Walsh
Jinx Clark	Nola Fairbanks
Harrison Thomson	Dick Craig
Sid Krofft	Fred Martel
Paul Castle	Bill Douglas
Trixie	Freddie Trenkler
Buster Grace	

Staged by Catherine Littlefield; lyrics and music by Al Stillman and Alan Moran; settings by Bruno Maine; costumes by Grace Huston, Billy Livingston and Katherine Kuhn.

OFF BROADWAY

New York, the home of the professional, commercial theatre, also had 159 "off Broadway" groups at the end of the season, according to a compilation in the Summer Theatre Supplement of *Actors Cues*, a periodical published for the stage-struck. These groups ranged from professional and semi-professional to the amateur and the collegiate; they included organizations playing in Yiddish and Chinese, and a competent unit of blind players; their names ranged alphabetically from the Abbe Practical Workshop to the "Y" Drama Guild. Among the best known and most closely allied to the Broadway stage were the American National Theatre and Academy's Experimental Theatre, the Equity Library Theatre and New Stages.

Activity among these groups was feverish and frequent, and in them, doubtless, were stars, dramatists, technicians and managers of the future. But only one of them, during the season, managed to turn up something of interest to Broadway. This was the Neighborhood Playhouse production of Dorothy Heyward's "Set My People Free," which the Theatre Guild brought uptown for a brief and unprofitable run. New Stages, the new and vigorous Greenwich Village group which in a previous season made a hit with Sartre's "The Respectful Prostitute," failed to hit the commercial jackpot with any of its offerings.

Off-Broadway events in October included:

"The Minstrel Boy," by W. A. S. Douglas, produced by the Blackfriars Guild, a Catholic theatre group which makes several productions each season. This was a biographical drama about Tom Moore, the Irish poet. The author is a newspaperman.

Chamberlain Brown hopefully organized the Castle Square Players to present Charles Klein's "The Third Degree" in the auditorium at the top of the skyscraping Chanin Building—prices 10, 20 and 30 cents.

College drama groups helped celebrate New York's Golden Anniversary. Players at Fordham University offered Fitch's "Captain Jinks of the Horse Marines"; the Theatre Workshop of C. C. N. Y. presented Rice's "Street Scene"; Manhattan College Players contributed the Kaufman-Connelly "Beggar on Horseback"; Columbia Theatre Associates did "The Belle of

New York," by Gustave Kerker and Hugh Morton, and the dramatic group of Hunter College presented an original play by Eli Cantor, "Candy Store."

The Children's World Theatre, at the Barbizon Plaza Hotel, offered weekend performances of "King Midas and the Golden Touch," by Charlotte Chorpenning.

November activities included:

A production of Euripides' "Hippolytus" as the initial bill of the ANTA Invitational Series.

A production in German by the Players from Abroad of Goethe's "Egmont," at the Barbizon Plaza. Principals included Grete Mosheim, Hans Jaray, Leopoldine Konstantin and Reinhold Schunzel.

Shipstads and Johnson offered their annual "Ice Follies" at Madison Square Garden.

The New York Repertory Group revived Elmer Rice's "The Adding Machine" at the Cherry Lane Theatre, Greenwich Village.

Under the auspices of the National Theatre Conference, drama school graduates from all parts of the U. S. took part in three plays at the Hunter College Playhouse. The plays were Noel Coward's "Still Life," the Anderson-Stallings "What Price Glory?" and Garcia Lorca's "The House of Bernardo Alba."

The Blackfriars' second production was "City of Kings," a new play by Father Urban Nagle. It was about Martin de Porres, the mulatto saint of Lima, Peru.

The American Negro Theatre found new quarters at the Master Theatre on Riverside Drive and offered two one-acters—"Skeletons," by Nicholas Bela, and "The Fisherman," by Jonathan Tree.

The New York Repertory Group planned to alternate "Hamlet" and "The Taming of the Shrew" at the Cherry Lane in December.

New Stages offered, on the night after Christmas, another Jean-Paul Sartre melodrama, "The Victors." It concerned itself with existentialist philosophy among members of the French Underground.

In January the offerings among the city's dramatic outposts included:

"Rose of the Wilderness," by Rose Melcher, produced by the Abbe Practical Workshop. It concerned life in a Shaker colony in Civil War times.

The most ambitious work of the season by the Experimental Theatre was the production, at the Lenox Hill Playhouse, of

"Uniform of Flesh." It was a dramatization by Louis O. Coxe and R. H. Chapman of a minor Herman Melville novel, "Billy Budd."

On the last day of January Sonja Henie began her annual skating engagement at Madison Square Garden.

Events off Broadway in February included:

A performance by the American Negro Theatre of Synge's "Riders to the Purple Sea" and Kenneth White's "Freight." The latter was a new play about some Negroes escaping from a lynching in a box car.

The Players from Abroad, at the Barbizon Plaza, presented Albert and Elsa Bassermann in a German-language revival of "The Rape of the Sabine Women"—a pre-war German farce by Franz and Paul V. Schoenthian.

The Dramatic Workshop of the New School presented a new play by Roy Bradford, "Chameleon," concerning miscegenation.

New Stages made a production of Federico Garcia Lorca's "Blood Wedding." This play had had a 1935 production on Broadway under the title of "Bitter Oleander."

The Amateur Comedy Club began its sixty-fifth season with "Wings over Europe," by Robert Nichols and Maurice Browne. Melville Burke was the director.

A group calling itself the Six O'Clock Theatre offered "Madame Is Served," comedy by Joe Grenzeback, adapted from "l'Heritage," by de Maupassant. The season before, the Six O'Clock Theatre found and produced Richard Harrity's "Hope Is the Thing with Feathers," which became the curtain-raiser for "The Respectful Prostitute" on Broadway.

The Abbe Practical Workshop presented "Ninth Month Midnight," by Phil Bard.

The Dramatic Workshop tendered "Outside the Door," by Wolfgang Borchert. The play was first produced in Hamburg in 1946.

In March the Experimental Theatre produced "The Nineteenth Hole of Europe," by Vivian Connell—a play which many drama lovers had long been clamoring for. Connell, an Irishman, wrote his drama about the future of Europe—and wrote it pessimistically. A hoped-for Broadway run with a new production did not materialize.

In May, New Stages took over a comedy which had been held and dropped by Brock Pemberton. It was "Bruno and Sidney," by Edward Caulfield. It was a farce "about some screwball characters on a mouse hunt." Sidney is a scholar living in a tenement who pursues a mouse named Bruno, which he believes to be very valuable. Philip Loeb directed the production.

During the season Randolph Somerville's Washington Square Players of New York University gave twenty-one performances of twelve different plays—five Shakespearean, the rest modern revivals.

Also in May, Henry L. Scott, pianist, had a short engagement at the Mansfield Theatre in a one-man show called "Concerto for Fun."

The Experimental Theatre's final offering of the Invitational Series was "Me, the Sleeper," by Jack Balch, a director at the New York News' television station, WPIX. It concerned the tortured mind of a war veteran.

New York City Opera

The New York City Opera Company, at the City Center of Drama and Music, ended its Fall season on November 28. During the eight weeks beginning October 8 it gave forty-one performances of thirteen operas. Attendance approximated 110,000. The one new production was "The Marriage of Figaro," in English.

In December the opera company went to Chicago for a successful engagement.

On May 1 the company closed a Spring season of six weeks, during which it gave thirty-three performances and had an attendance of 85,000. The new production was William Grant Still's "The Troubled Island."

Ballet

The Ballet Russe de Monte Carlo returned to the Metropolitan Opera House after an absence of five years on September 18 and remained until October 10. "Associate" artists included Markova, Slavenska, DeMille, Dolin and Jose Torres. A world premiere of Ruthanna Boris' "Quelques Fleurs," based on music by Auber, was given.

On October 31 Harald Kreutzberg gave a single recital at the Ziegfeld Theatre.

The New York City Ballet Company, newly organized at the City Center under the direction of George Balanchine, opened its first season October 11 and gave two performances a week through November 23. Principals included Maria Tallchief, Marie-

Jeanne, Tanaquil Le Clerq, Beatrice Tompkins and Jocelyn Vollmar, among the ballerinas. Principal male roles were danced by Francisco Moncion, Nicholas Magallanes, Herbert Bliss and Todd Bolender. New productions were Balanchine's "Concerto Barocco," music by Bach; the Balanchine-Stravinsky "Orpheus," and Bolender's "Mother Goose" suite, music by Ravel.

Ted Shawn brought his Jacobs Pillow Dance Festival troupe from Lee, Mass., for a performance at Hunter College on December 29.

The New York City Ballet gave ten more performances beginning January 13 and ending January 23. A highlight was "The Guests," by Jerome Robbins, with music by Marc Blitzstein.

Valerie Bettis, who had done a ballet interpretation of the novel, "As I Lay Dying," for the Choreographers' Workshop in December, repeated her performance on January 23 at the Y.M. and Y.W.H.A.

The Ballet Russe de Monte Carlo had a popular-price season at the City Center, February 21 to March 20. Novelties were the New York premiere of "Love Song" and the revival of "Carnaval."

On Easter Sunday, April 17, Ballet Theatre opened a three-week engagement at the Metropolitan Opera House—at the popular price of $3 top. Principals included Youskevitch, Kaye, Gollner, Laing, Kriza, Tallchief, Tudor and Bambi Linn.

The Yiddish Theatre

By Jeanette Wilken

In one of its slowest seasons in recent history, the Yiddish theatre was sustained by its old standbys, most prominently Skulnik and Schwartz. Maurice Schwartz and his Yiddish Art Theatre came through with only two of a promised quartet of new plays, but these were the moderately successful "Voice of Israel" by Elias Gilner, and "Herschel, the Jester" by Moshe Livshitz. Schwartz staged the plays, Joseph Rumshinsky was musical director, and supporting actors were Charlotte Goldstein, Gustave Berger, Muni Serebrov and Anna Appel.

Menasha Skulnik bowed out of the Yiddish theatre (temporarily, at least) with two real hits, "What a Guy!" and "Leave It to Charlie," both enjoying respectable runs. Abe Ellstein and Isidore Friedman wrote scores and stories to fit Skulnik's talent like a glove; and he was supported by the usual group, Yetta

Zwerling, Lilly Lilliana, Anna Teitlebaum, Leon Liebgold, Jacob Susanoff and Ann Winters.

The Downtown Clinton and National Theatres specialize in weekend performances only, and a new show each weekend. In this fashion the Clinton displayed such succulent titles as "A Home for Mother," "The Singing Bridegroom," "Getzel at the Ball Game," "People Without Eyes," "Her Father's Melody," "The President's Jewish Friend" and "The Blacksmith's Daughter." The National countered with "The Romeo from Brooklyn," "The Golden Wedding," "I Want a Child," and so forth.

The Parkway Theatre began its season on October 13 with a melodrama, "The Lost Bride," by Louis Freiman, starring the popular Miriam Kressyn. Then came two shows featuring Leo Fuchs, "Mama's Boy" and "The Lucky Fool"; and the undistinguished season ended with Nathan Goldberg in "All in a Lifetime." The supporting cast in most of these were the same efficient team: Jacob Jacobs, Rose Goldberg, Hanna Hollander, Bettie Jacobs, Seymour Rechtzeit, Esta Saltzman and Leon Seidenberg.

The production with perhaps the greatest integrity of all came from a little-known group calling itself the Yiddish Theatre Ensemble, which showed Sholem Aleichem's "The Treasure Hunters" at the Barbizon Plaza Theatre in a wholly professional and engaging manner.

STATISTICAL SUMMARY

(Last Season Plays Which Ended Runs After June 1, 1948)

Plays	Number Performances	
Allegro	315	(Closed July 10, 1948)
Annie, Get Your Gun	1,147	(Closed February 12, 1949)
Ballet Ballads	69	(Closed July 10, 1948)
Brigadoon	581	(Closed July 31, 1948)
Command Decision	408	(Closed September 18, 1948)
Finian's Rainbow	725	(Closed October 2, 1948)
For Love or Money	265	(Closed June 20, 1948)
Harvey	1,775	(Closed January 15, 1949)
Hold It	46	(Closed June 12, 1948)
Inside U.S.A.	399	(Closed February 19, 1949)
Joy to the World	124	(Closed July 3, 1948)
Look, Ma, I'm Dancing	188	(Closed July 10, 1948)
Make Mine Manhattan	429	(Closed January 8, 1949)
Man and Superman	295	(Closed June 20, 1948)
Me and Molly	156	(Closed July 10, 1948)
Sally	36	(Closed June 5, 1948)
Strange Bedfellows	229	(Closed July 31, 1948)
The Heiress	410	(Closed September 18, 1949)
The Play's the Thing	244	(Closed December 18, 1948)
The Respectful Prostitute	348	(Closed December 18, 1948)

LONG RUNS ON BROADWAY

To June 1, 1949

(Plays marked with asterisk were still playing June 1, 1949)

Plays	Number Performances	Plays	Number Performances
Life with Father	3,224	Call Me Mister	734
Tobacco Road	3,182	Finian's Rainbow	725
Abie's Irish Rose	2,327	Claudia	722
Oklahoma!	2,248	I Remember Mama	714
Harvey	1,775	Junior Miss	710
The Voice of the Turtle	1,557	Seventh Heaven	704
Arsenic and Old Lace	1,444	Peg o' My Heart	692
Hellzapoppin	1,404	The Children's Hour	691
*Born Yesterday	1,396	*High Button Shoes	689
Angel Street	1,295	Dead End	687
Lightnin'	1,291	Dear Ruth	683
Annie Get Your Gun	1,147	East Is West	680
Pins and Needles	1,108	Chauve Souris	673
Anna Lucasta	957	The Doughgirls	671
Kiss and Tell	956	Irene	670
Carousel	890	Boy Meets Girl	669
Hats Off to Ice	889	Blithe Spirit	657
Follow the Girls	882	The Women	657
The Bat	867	A Trip to Chinatown	657
My Sister Eileen	865	Bloomer Girl	654
White Cargo	864	Rain	648
Song of Norway	860	Janie	642
You Can't Take It with You	837	The Green Pastures	640
Three Men on a Horse	835	*A Streetcar Named Desire	625
Stars on Ice	830	Is Zat So?	618
The Ladder	789	Separate Rooms	613
State of the Union	765	Star and Garter	609
The First Year	760	Student Prince	608
Sons o' Fun	742	Broadway	603
The Man Who Came to Dinner	739	Adonis	603
		Street Scene	601

BURNS MANTLE BEST PLAYS OF 1948-49

Plays	Number Performances	Plays	Number Performances
Kiki	600	*Mister Roberts	536
Blossom Time	592	The Red Mill	531
The Two Mrs. Carrolls	585	The Boomerang	522
Brigadoon	581	Rosalinda	521
Brother Rat	577	Blackbirds	518
Show Boat	572	Sunny	517
The Show-Off	571	Victoria Regina	517
Sally	570	The Vagabond King	511
One Touch of Venus	567	The New Moon	509
Happy Birthday	564	Shuffle Along	504
The Glass Menagerie	561	Up in Central Park	504
Rose Marie	557	Carmen Jones	503
Strictly Dishonorable	557	Personal Appearance	501
Ziegfeld Follies	553	Panama Hattie	501
Good News	551	Bird in Hand	500
Let's Face It	547	Sailor, Beware!	500
Within the Law	541	Room Service	500
The Music Master	540	Tomorrow the World	500
What a Life	538		

NEW YORK DRAMA CRITICS' CIRCLE AWARD

Continuing its one-ballot, majority-wins system of selection, the New York Drama Critics' Circle swiftly and overwhelmingly voted Arthur Miller's "Death of a Salesman" the best play of the 1948-49 season.

An almost equally heavy vote was cast for "The Madwoman of Chaillot," by the late Jean Giraudoux (adapted by Maurice Valency), as the best foreign play of the season. This ballot was somewhat in contrast with the newspaper reviews the day after the opening, in which only three critics found the play to their liking. Magazine reviews subsequently bolstered the opinions of the three daily reviewers, and "The Madwoman" became one of the season's hits.

"South Pacific," by Richard Rodgers, Oscar Hammerstein 2d and Joshua Logan (based on James A. Michener's "Tales of the South Pacific"), was voted the best musical by a rather close margin over "Kiss Me, Kate," by Cole Porter and Samuel and Bella Spewack (based on Shakespeare's "The Taming of the Shrew").

Previous Circle awards have been—

1935-36—Winterset, by Maxwell Anderson
1936-37—High Tor, by Maxwell Anderson
1937-38—Of Mice and Men, by John Steinbeck
1938-39—No award.
1939-40—The Time of Your Life, by William Saroyan
1940-41—Watch on the Rhine, by Lillian Hellman
1941-42—No award.
1942-43—The Patriots, by Sidney Kingsley
1943-44—No award.
1944-45—The Glass Menagerie, by Tennessee Williams
1945-46—No award.
1946-47—All My Sons, by Arthur Miller
1947-48—A Streetcar Named Desire, by Tennessee Williams
1948-49—Death of a Salesman, by Arthur Miller

PULITZER PRIZE WINNERS

Twice in a row now, and three times since the formation of the Critics' Circle, the Pulitzer Prize has fallen to a drama also chosen by the Critics—Arthur Miller's "Death of a Salesman." A year before, both groups had nominated Tennessee Williams' "A Streetcar Named Desire," and in 1940 they agreed upon William Saroyan's "The Time of Your Life."

Pulitzer Prize selections to date have been—

1917-18—Why Marry?, by Jesse Lynch Williams
1918-19—No award.
1919-20—Beyond the Horizon, by Eugene O'Neill
1920-21—Miss Lulu Bett, by Zona Gale
1921-22—Anna Christie, by Eugene O'Neill
1922-23—Icebound, by Owen Davis
1923-24—Hell-bent fer Heaven, by Hatcher Hughes
1924-25—They Knew What They Wanted, by Sidney Howard
1925-26—Craig's Wife, by George Kelly
1926-27—In Abraham's Bosom, by Paul Green
1927-28—Strange Interlude, by Eugene O'Neill
1928-29—Street Scene, by Elmer Rice
1929-30—The Green Pastures, by Marc Connelly
1930-31—Alison's House, by Susan Glaspell
1931-32—Of Thee I Sing, by George S. Kaufman, Morrie Ryskind, Ira and George Gershwin
1932-33—Both Your Houses, by Maxwell Anderson
1933-34—Men in White, by Sidney Kingsley
1934-35—The Old Maid, by Zoe Akins
1935-36—Idiot's Delight, by Robert E. Sherwood
1936-37—You Can't Take It with You, by Moss Hart and George S. Kaufman
1937-38—Our Town, by Thornton Wilder
1938-39—Abe Lincoln in Illinois, by Robert E. Sherwood
1939-40—The Time of Your Life, by William Saroyan
1940-41—There Shall Be No Night, by Robert E. Sherwood
1941-42—No award.
1942-43—The Skin of Our Teeth, by Thornton Wilder
1943-44—No award.

1944-45—Harvey, by Mary Coyle Chase
1945-46—State of the Union, by Howard Lindsay and Russel Crouse
1946-47—No award.
1947-48—A Streetcar Named Desire, by Tennessee Williams
1948-49—Death of a Salesman, by Arthur Miller

PREVIOUS VOLUMES OF BEST PLAYS

Plays chosen to represent the theatre seasons from 1899 to 1948 are as follows:

1899-1909

BARBARA FRIETCHIE, by Clyde Fitch. Published by Life Publishing Company, New York.
THE CLIMBERS, by Clyde Fitch. Published by the Macmillan Co., New York.
IF I WERE KING, by Justin Huntly McCarthy. Published by Samuel French, New York and London.
THE DARLING OF THE GODS, by David Belasco. Published by Little, Brown & Co., Boston, Mass.
THE COUNTY CHAIRMAN, by George Ade. Published by Samuel French, New York and London.
LEAH KLESCHNA, by C. M. S. McLellan. Published by Samuel French, New York.
THE SQUAW MAN, by Edwin Milton Royle.
THE GREAT DIVIDE, by William Vaughn Moody. Published by Samuel French, New York, London and Canada.
THE WITCHING HOUR, by Augustus Thomas. Published by Samuel French, New York and London.
THE MAN FROM HOME, by Booth Tarkington and Harry Leon Wilson. Published by Samuel French, New York, London and Canada.

1909-1919

THE EASIEST WAY, by Eugene Walter. Published by G. W. Dillingham, New York; Houghton Mifflin Co., Boston.
MRS. BUMPSTEAD-LEIGH, by Harry James Smith. Published by Samuel French, New York.
DISRAELI, by Louis N. Parker. Published by Dodd, Mead and Co., New York.
ROMANCE, by Edward Sheldon. Published by the Macmillan Co., New York.
SEVEN KEYS TO BALDPATE, by George M. Cohan. Published by Bobbs-Merrill Co., Indianapolis, as a novel by Earl Derr Biggers; as a play by Samuel French, New York.

ON TRIAL, by Elmer Reizenstein. Published by Samuel French, New York.
THE UNCHASTENED WOMAN, by Louis Kaufman Anspacher. Published by Harcourt, Brace and Howe, Inc., New York.
GOOD GRACIOUS ANNABELLE, by Clare Kummer. Published by Samuel French, New York.
WHY MARRY? by Jesse Lynch Williams. Published by Charles Scribner's Sons, New York.
JOHN FERGUSON, by St. John Ervine. Published by the Macmillan Co., New York.

1919-1920

ABRAHAM LINCOLN, by John Drinkwater. Published by Houghton Mifflin Co., Boston.
CLARENCE, by Booth Tarkington. Published by Samuel French, New York.
BEYOND THE HORIZON, by Eugene G. O'Neill. Published by Boni & Liveright, Inc., New York.
DÉCLASSÉE, by Zoe Akins. Published by Liveright, Inc., New York.
THE FAMOUS MRS. FAIR, by James Forbes. Published by Samuel French, New York.
THE JEST, by Sem Benelli. (American adaptation by Edward Sheldon.)
JANE CLEGG, by St. John Ervine. Published by Henry Holt & Co., New York.
MAMMA'S AFFAIR, by Rachel Barton Butler. Published by Samuel French, New York.
WEDDING BELLS, by Salisbury Field. Published by Samuel French, New York.
ADAM AND EVA, by George Middleton and Guy Bolton. Published by Samuel French, New York.

1920-1921

DEBURAU, adapted from the French of Sacha Guitry by H. Granville Barker. Published by G. P. Putnam's Sons, New York.
THE FIRST YEAR, by Frank Craven. Published by Samuel French, New York.
ENTER MADAME, by Gilda Varesi and Dolly Byrne. Published by G. P. Putnam's Sons, New York.
THE GREEN GODDESS, by William Archer. Published by Alfred A. Knopf, New York.

BURNS MANTLE BEST PLAYS OF 1948-49

Liliom, by Ferenc Molnar. Published by Boni & Liveright, New York.
Mary Rose, by James M. Barrie. Published by Charles Scribner's Sons, New York.
Nice People, by Rachel Crothers. Published by Charles Scribner's Sons, New York.
The Bad Man, by Porter Emerson Browne. Published by G. P. Putnam's Sons, New York.
The Emperor Jones, by Eugene G. O'Neill. Published by Boni & Liveright, New York.
The Skin Game, by John Galsworthy. Published by Charles Scribner's Sons, New York.

1921-1922

Anna Christie, by Eugene G. O'Neill. Published by Boni & Liveright, New York.
A Bill of Divorcement, by Clemence Dane. Published by the Macmillan Company, New York.
Dulcy, by George S. Kaufman and Marc Connelly. Published by G. P. Putnam's Sons, New York.
He Who Gets Slapped, adapted from the Russian of Leonid Andreyev by Gregory Zilboorg. Published by Brentano's, New York.
Six Cylinder Love, by William Anthony McGuire.
The Hero, by Gilbert Emery.
The Dover Road, by Alan Alexander Milne. Published by Samuel French, New York.
Ambush, by Arthur Richman.
The Circle, by William Somerset Maugham.
The Nest, by Paul Geraldy and Grace George.

1922-1923

Rain, by John Colton and Clemence Randolph. Published by Liveright, Inc., New York.
Loyalties, by John Galsworthy. Published by Charles Scribner's Sons, New York.
Icebound, by Owen Davis. Published by Little, Brown & Company, Boston.
You and I, by Philip Barry. Published by Brentano's, New York.
The Fool, by Channing Pollock. Published by Brentano's, New York.

MERTON OF THE MOVIES, by George Kaufman and Marc Connelly, based on the novel of the same name by Harry Leon Wilson.
WHY NOT? by Jesse Lynch Williams. Published by Walter H. Baker Co., Boston.
THE OLD SOAK, by Don Marquis. Published by Doubleday, Page & Company, New York.
R.U.R., by Karel Capek. Translated by Paul Selver. Published by Doubleday, Page & Company.
MARY THE 3D, by Rachel Crothers. Published by Brentano's, New York.

1923-1924

THE SWAN, translated from the Hungarian of Ferenc Molnar by Melville Baker. Published by Boni & Liveright, New York.
OUTWARD BOUND, by Sutton Vane. Published by Boni & Liveright, New York.
THE SHOW-OFF, by George Kelly. Published by Little, Brown & Company, Boston.
THE CHANGELINGS, by Lee Wilson Dodd. Published by E. P. Dutton & Company, New York.
CHICKEN FEED, by Guy Bolton. Published by Samuel French, New York and London.
SUN-UP, by Lula Vollmer. Published by Brentano's, New York.
BEGGAR ON HORSEBACK, by George Kaufman and Marc Connelly. Published by Boni & Liveright, New York.
TARNISH, by Gilbert Emery. Published by Brentano's, New York.
THE GOOSE HANGS HIGH, by Lewis Beach. Published by Little, Brown & Company, Boston.
HELL-BENT FER HEAVEN, by Hatcher Hughes. Published by Harper Bros., New York.

1924-1925

WHAT PRICE GLORY? by Laurence Stallings and Maxwell Anderson. Published by Harcourt, Brace & Co., New York.
THEY KNEW WHAT THEY WANTED, by Sidney Howard. Published by Doubleday, Page & Company, New York.
DESIRE UNDER THE ELMS, by Eugene G. O'Neill. Published by Boni & Liveright, New York.
THE FIREBRAND, by Edwin Justus Mayer. Published by Boni & Liveright, New York.

DANCING MOTHERS, by Edgar Selwyn and Edmund Goulding.
MRS. PARTRIDGE PRESENTS, by Mary Kennedy and Ruth Warren. Published by Samuel French, New York.
THE FALL GUY, by James Gleason and George Abbott. Published by Samuel French, New York.
THE YOUNGEST, by Philip Barry. Published by Samuel French, New York.
MINICK, by Edna Ferber and George S. Kaufman. Published by Doubleday, Page & Company, New York.
WILD BIRDS, by Dan Totheroh. Published by Doubleday, Page & Company, New York.

1925-1926

CRAIG'S WIFE, by George Kelly. Published by Little, Brown & Company, Boston.
THE GREAT GOD BROWN, by Eugene G. O'Neill. Published by Boni & Liveright, New York.
THE GREEN HAT, by Michael Arlen.
THE DYBBUK, by S. Ansky, Henry G. Alsberg-Winifred Katzin translation. Published by Boni & Liveright, New York.
THE ENEMY, by Channing Pollock. Published by Brentano's, New York.
THE LAST OF MRS. CHEYNEY, by Frederick Lonsdale. Published by Samuel French, New York.
BRIDE OF THE LAMB, by William Hurlbut. Published by Boni & Liveright, New York.
THE WISDOM TOOTH, by Marc Connelly. Published by George H. Doran & Company, New York.
THE BUTTER AND EGG MAN, by George Kaufman. Published by Boni & Liveright, New York.
YOUNG WOODLEY, by John Van Druten. Published by Simon and Schuster, New York.

1926-1927

BROADWAY, by Philip Dunning and George Abbott. Published by George H. Doran Company, New York.
SATURDAY'S CHILDREN, by Maxwell Anderson. Published by Longmans, Green & Company, New York.
CHICAGO, by Maurine Watkins. Published by Alfred A. Knopf, Inc., New York.

THE CONSTANT WIFE, by William Somerset Maugham. Published by George H. Doran Company, New York.
THE PLAY'S THE THING, by Ferenc Molnar and P. G. Wodehouse. Published by Brentano's, New York.
THE ROAD TO ROME, by Robert Emmet Sherwood. Published by Charles Scribner's Sons, New York.
THE SILVER CORD, by Sidney Howard. Published by Charles Scribner's Sons, New York.
THE CRADLE SONG, translated from the Spanish of G. Martinez Sierra by John Garrett Underhill. Published by E. P. Dutton & Company, New York.
DAISY MAYME, by George Kelly. Published by Little, Brown & Company, Boston.
IN ABRAHAM'S BOSOM, by Paul Green. Published by Robert M. McBride & Company, New York.

1927-1928

STRANGE INTERLUDE, by Eugene G. O'Neill. Published by Boni & Liveright, New York.
THE ROYAL FAMILY, by Edna Ferber and George Kaufman. Published by Doubleday, Doran & Company, New York.
BURLESQUE, by George Manker Watters and Arthur Hopkins. Published by Doubleday, Doran & Company, New York.
COQUETTE, by George Abbott and Ann Bridgers. Published by Longmans, Green & Company, New York, London, Toronto.
BEHOLD THE BRIDEGROOM, by George Kelly. Published by Little, Brown & Company, Boston.
PORGY, by DuBose Heyward. Published by Doubleday, Doran & Company, New York.
PARIS BOUND, by Philip Barry. Published by Samuel French, New York.
ESCAPE, by John Galsworthy. Published by Charles Scribner's Sons, New York.
THE RACKET, by Bartlett Cormack. Published by Samuel French, New York.
THE PLOUGH AND THE STARS, by Sean O'Casey. Published by the Macmillan Company, New York.

1928-1929

STREET SCENE, by Elmer Rice. Published by Samuel French, New York.

JOURNEY'S END, by R. C. Sherriff. Published by Brentano's, New York.
WINGS OVER EUROPE, by Robert Nichols and Maurice Browne. Published by Covici-Friede, New York.
HOLIDAY, by Philip Barry. Published by Samuel French, New York.
THE FRONT PAGE, by Ben Hecht and Charles MacArthur. Published by Covici-Friede, New York.
LET US BE GAY, by Rachel Crothers. Published by Samuel French, New York.
MACHINAL, by Sophie Treadwell.
LITTLE ACCIDENT, by Floyd Dell and Thomas Mitchell.
GYPSY, by Maxwell Anderson.
THE KINGDOM OF GOD, by G. Martinez Sierra; English version by Helen and Harley Granville-Barker. Published by E. P. Dutton & Company, New York.

1929-1930

THE GREEN PASTURES, by Marc Connelly (adapted from "Ol' Man Adam and His Chillun," by Roark Bradford). Published by Farrar & Rinehart, Inc., New York.
THE CRIMINAL CODE, by Martin Flavin. Published by Horace Liveright, New York.
BERKELEY SQUARE, by John Balderston. Published by the Macmillan Company, New York.
STRICTLY DISHONORABLE, by Preston Sturges. Published by Horace Liveright, New York.
THE FIRST MRS. FRASER, by St. John Ervine. Published by the Macmillan Company, New York.
THE LAST MILE, by John Wexley. Published by Samuel French, New York.
JUNE MOON, by Ring W. Lardner and George S. Kaufman. Published by Charles Scribner's Sons, New York.
MICHAEL AND MARY, by A. A. Milne. Published by Chatto & Windus, London.
DEATH TAKES A HOLIDAY, by Walter Ferris (adapted from the Italian of Alberto Casella). Published by Samuel French, New York.
REBOUND, by Donald Ogden Stewart. Published by Samuel French, New York.

1930-1931

ELIZABETH THE QUEEN, by Maxwell Anderson. Published by Longmans, Green & Co., New York.
TOMORROW AND TOMORROW, by Philip Barry. Published by Samuel French, New York.
ONCE IN A LIFETIME, by George S. Kaufman and Moss Hart. Published by Farrar and Rinehart, New York.
GREEN GROW THE LILACS, by Lynn Riggs. Published by Samuel French, New York and London.
AS HUSBANDS GO, by Rachel Crothers. Published by Samuel French, New York.
ALISON'S HOUSE, by Susan Glaspell. Published by Samuel French, New York.
FIVE-STAR FINAL, by Louis Weitzenkorn. Published by Samuel French, New York.
OVERTURE, by William Bolitho. Published by Simon & Schuster, New York.
THE BARRETTS OF WIMPOLE STREET, by Rudolf Besier. Published by Little, Brown & Company, Boston.
GRAND HOTEL, adapted from the German of Vicki Baum by W. A. Drake.

1931-1932

OF THEE I SING, by George S. Kaufman and Morrie Ryskind; music and lyrics by George and Ira Gershwin. Published by Alfred Knopf, New York.
MOURNING BECOMES ELECTRA, by Eugene G. O'Neill. Published by Horace Liveright, Inc., New York.
REUNION IN VIENNA, by Robert Emmet Sherwood. Published by Charles Scribner's Sons, New York.
THE HOUSE OF CONNELLY, by Paul Green. Published by Samuel French, New York.
THE ANIMAL KINGDOM, by Philip Barry. Published by Samuel French, New York.
THE LEFT BANK, by Elmer Rice. Published by Samuel French, New York.
ANOTHER LANGUAGE, by Rose Franken. Published by Samuel French, New York.
BRIEF MOMENT, by S. N. Behrman. Published by Farrar & Rinehart, New York.
THE DEVIL PASSES, by Benn W. Levy. Published by Martin Secker, London.

CYNARA, by H. M. Harwood and R. F. Gore-Browne. Published by Samuel French, New York.

1932-1933

BOTH YOUR HOUSES, by Maxwell Anderson. Published by Samuel French, New York.
DINNER AT EIGHT, by George S. Kaufman and Edna Ferber. Published by Doubleday, Doran & Co., Inc., Garden City, New York.
WHEN LADIES MEET, by Rachel Crothers. Published by Samuel French, New York.
DESIGN FOR LIVING, by Noel Coward. Published by Doubleday, Doran & Co., Inc., Garden City, New York.
BIOGRAPHY, by S. N. Behrman. Published by Farrar & Rinehart, Inc., New York.
ALIEN CORN, by Sidney Howard. Published by Charles Scribner's Sons, New York.
THE LATE CHRISTOPHER BEAN, adapted from the French of René Fauchois by Sidney Howard. Published by Samuel French, New York.
WE, THE PEOPLE, by Elmer Rice. Published by Coward-McCann, Inc., New York.
PIGEONS AND PEOPLE, by George M. Cohan.
ONE SUNDAY AFTERNOON, by James Hagan. Published by Samuel French, New York.

1933-1934

MARY OF SCOTLAND, by Maxwell Anderson. Published by Doubleday, Doran & Co., Inc., Garden City, N. Y.
MEN IN WHITE, by Sidney Kingsley. Published by Covici-Friede, Inc., New York.
DODSWORTH, by Sinclair Lewis and Sidney Howard. Published by Harcourt, Brace & Co., New York.
AH, WILDERNESS, by Eugene O'Neill. Published by Random House, New York.
THEY SHALL NOT DIE, by John Wexley. Published by Alfred A. Knopf, New York.
HER MASTER'S VOICE, by Clare Kummer. Published by Samuel French, New York.
NO MORE LADIES, by A. E. Thomas.
WEDNESDAY'S CHILD, by Leopold Atlas. Published by Samuel French, New York.

THE SHINING HOUR, by Keith Winter. Published by Doubleday, Doran & Co., Inc., Garden City, New York.
THE GREEN BAY TREE, by Mordaunt Shairp. Published by Baker International Play Bureau, Boston, Mass.

1934-1935

THE CHILDREN'S HOUR, by Lillian Hellman. Published by Alfred Knopf, New York.
VALLEY FORGE, by Maxwell Anderson. Published by Anderson House, Washington, D. C. Distributed by Dodd, Mead & Co., New York.
THE PETRIFIED FOREST, by Robert Sherwood. Published by Charles Scribner's Sons, New York.
THE OLD MAID, by Zoe Akins. Published by D. Appleton-Century Co., New York.
ACCENT ON YOUTH, by Samson Raphaelson. Published by Samuel French, New York.
MERRILY WE ROLL ALONG, by George S. Kaufman and Moss Hart. Published by Random House, New York.
AWAKE AND SING, by Clifford Odets. Published by Random House, New York.
THE FARMER TAKES A WIFE, by Frank B. Elser and Marc Connelly.
LOST HORIZONS, by John Hayden.
THE DISTAFF SIDE, by John Van Druten. Published by Alfred Knopf, New York.

1935-1936

WINTERSET, by Maxwell Anderson. Published by Anderson House, Washington, D. C.
IDIOT'S DELIGHT, by Robert Emmet Sherwood. Published by Charles Scribner's Sons, New York.
END OF SUMMER, by S. N. Behrman. Published by Random House, New York.
FIRST LADY, by Katharine Dayton and George S. Kaufman. Published by Random House, New York.
VICTORIA REGINA, by Laurence Housman. Published by Samuel French, Inc., New York and London.
BOY MEETS GIRL, by Bella and Samuel Spewack. Published by Random House, New York.
DEAD END, by Sidney Kingsley. Published by Random House, New York.

CALL IT A DAY, by Dodie Smith. Published by Samuel French, Inc., New York and London.
ETHAN FROME, by Owen Davis and Donald Davis. Published by Charles Scribner's Sons, New York.
PRIDE AND PREJUDICE, by Helen Jerome. Published by Doubleday, Doran & Co., Garden City, New York.

1936-1937

HIGH TOR, by Maxwell Anderson. Published by Anderson House, Washington, D. C.
YOU CAN'T TAKE IT WITH YOU, by Moss Hart and George S. Kaufman. Published by Farrar & Rinehart, Inc., New York.
JOHNNY JOHNSON, by Paul Green. Published by Samuel French, Inc., New York.
DAUGHTERS OF ATREUS, by Robert Turney. Published by Alfred A. Knopf, New York.
STAGE DOOR, by Edna Ferber and George S. Kaufman. Published by Doubleday, Doran & Co., Garden City, New York.
THE WOMEN, by Clare Boothe. Published by Random House, Inc., New York.
ST. HELENA, by R. C. Sherriff and Jeanne de Casalis. Published by Samuel French, Inc., New York and London.
YES, MY DARLING DAUGHTER, by Mark Reed. Published by Samuel French, Inc., New York.
EXCURSION, by Victor Wolfson. Published by Random House, New York.
TOVARICH, by Jacques Deval and Robert E. Sherwood. Published by Random House, New York.

1937-1938

OF MICE AND MEN, by John Steinbeck. Published by Covici-Friede, New York.
OUR TOWN, by Thornton Wilder. Published by Coward-McCann, Inc., New York.
SHADOW AND SUBSTANCE, by Paul Vincent Carroll. Published by Random House, Inc., New York.
ON BORROWED TIME, by Paul Osborn. Published by Alfred A. Knopf, New York.
THE STAR-WAGON, by Maxwell Anderson. Published by Anderson House, Washington, D. C. Distributed by Dodd, Mead & Co., New York.

SUSAN AND GOD, by Rachel Crothers. Published by Random House, Inc., New York.
PROLOGUE TO GLORY, by E. P. Conkle. Published by Random House, Inc., New York.
AMPHITRYON 38, by S. N. Behrman. Published by Random House, Inc., New York.
GOLDEN BOY, by Clifford Odets. Published by Random House, Inc., New York.
WHAT A LIFE, by Clifford Goldsmith. Published by Dramatists' Play Service, Inc., New York.

1938-1939

ABE LINCOLN IN ILLINOIS, by Robert E. Sherwood. Published by Charles Scribner's Sons, New York and Charles Scribner's Sons, Ltd., London.
THE LITTLE FOXES, by Lillian Hellman. Published by Random House, Inc., New York.
ROCKET TO THE MOON, by Clifford Odets. Published by Random House, Inc., New York.
THE AMERICAN WAY, by George S. Kaufman and Moss Hart. Published by Random House, Inc., New York.
NO TIME FOR COMEDY, by S. N. Behrman. Published by Random House, Inc., New York.
THE PHILADELPHIA STORY, by Philip Barry. Published by Coward-McCann, Inc., New York.
THE WHITE STEED, by Paul Vincent Carroll. Published by Random House, Inc., New York.
HERE COME THE CLOWNS, by Philip Barry. Published by Coward-McCann, Inc., New York.
FAMILY PORTRAIT, by Lenore Coffee and William Joyce Cowen. Published by Random House, Inc., New York.
KISS THE BOYS GOOD-BYE, by Clare Boothe. Published by Random House, Inc., New York.

1939-1940

THERE SHALL BE NO NIGHT, by Robert E. Sherwood. Published by Charles Scribner's Sons, New York.
KEY LARGO, by Maxwell Anderson. Published by Anderson House, Washington, D. C.
THE WORLD WE MAKE, by Sidney Kingsley.
LIFE WITH FATHER, by Howard Lindsay and Russel Crouse. Published by Alfred A. Knopf, New York.

THE MAN WHO CAME TO DINNER, by George S. Kaufman and Moss Hart. Published by Random House, Inc., New York.
THE MALE ANIMAL, by James Thurber and Elliott Nugent. Published by Random House, Inc., New York, and MacMillan Co., Canada.
THE TIME OF YOUR LIFE, by William Saroyan. Published by Harcourt, Brace and Company, Inc., New York.
SKYLARK, by Samson Raphaelson. Published by Random House, Inc., New York.
MARGIN FOR ERROR, by Clare Boothe. Published by Random House, Inc., New York.
MORNING'S AT SEVEN, by Paul Osborn. Published by Samuel French, New York.

1940-1941

NATIVE SON, by Paul Green and Richard Wright. Published by Harper & Bros., New York.
WATCH ON THE RHINE, by Lillian Hellman. Published by Random House, Inc., New York.
THE CORN IS GREEN, by Emlyn Williams. Published by Random House, Inc., New York.
LADY IN THE DARK, by Moss Hart. Published by Random House, Inc., New York.
ARSENIC AND OLD LACE, by Joseph Kesselring. Published by Random House, Inc., New York.
MY SISTER EILEEN, by Joseph Fields and Jerome Chodorov. Published by Random House, Inc., New York.
FLIGHT TO THE WEST, by Elmer Rice. Published by Coward-McCann, Inc., New York.
CLAUDIA, by Rose Franken Meloney. Published by Farrar & Rinehart, Inc., New York and Toronto.
MR. AND MRS. NORTH, by Owen Davis. Published by Samuel French, New York.
GEORGE WASHINGTON SLEPT HERE, by George S. Kaufman and Moss Hart. Published by Random House, Inc., New York.

1941-1942

IN TIME TO COME, by Howard Koch. Published by Dramatists' Play Service, Inc., New York.
THE MOON IS DOWN, by John Steinbeck. Published by The Viking Press, New York.

BLITHE SPIRIT, by Noel Coward. Published by Doubleday, Doran & Co., Garden City, New York.
JUNIOR MISS, by Jerome Chodorov and Joseph Fields. Published by Random House, Inc., New York.
CANDLE IN THE WIND, by Maxwell Anderson. Published by Anderson House, Washington, D. C.
LETTERS TO LUCERNE, by Fritz Rotter and Allen Vincent. Published by Samuel French, Inc., New York.
JASON, by Samson Raphaelson. Published by Random House, Inc., New York.
ANGEL STREET, by Patrick Hamilton. Published by Constable & Co., Ltd., London, under the title "Gaslight."
UNCLE HARRY, by Thomas Job. Published by Samuel French, Inc., New York.
HOPE FOR A HARVEST, by Sophie Treadwell. Published by Samuel French, Inc., New York.

1942-1943

THE PATRIOTS, by Sidney Kingsley. Published by Random House, Inc., New York.
THE EVE OF ST. MARK, by Maxwell Anderson. Published by Anderson House, Washington, D. C.
THE SKIN OF OUR TEETH, by Thornton Wilder. Published by Harper & Brothers, New York and London.
WINTER SOLDIERS, by Dan James.
TOMORROW THE WORLD, by James Gow and Arnaud d'Usseau. Published by Charles Scribner's Sons, New York.
HARRIET, by Florence Ryerson and Colin Clements. Published by Charles Scribner's Sons, New York.
THE DOUGHGIRLS, by Joseph Fields. Published by Random House, Inc., New York.
THE DAMASK CHEEK, by John Van Druten and Lloyd Morris. Published by Random House, Inc., New York.
KISS AND TELL, by F. Hugh Herbert. Published by Coward-McCann, Inc., New York.
OKLAHOMA!, by Oscar Hammerstein 2nd and Richard Rodgers. Published by Random House, Inc., New York.

1943-1944

WINGED VICTORY, by Moss Hart. Published by Random House, Inc., New York.

THE SEARCHING WIND, by Lillian Hellman. Published by Viking Press, Inc., New York.
THE VOICE OF THE TURTLE, by John Van Druten. Published by Random House, Inc., New York.
DECISION, by Edward Chodorov.
OVER 21, by Ruth Gordon. Published by Random House, Inc., New York.
OUTRAGEOUS FORTUNE, by Rose Franken. Published by Samuel French, New York.
JACOBOWSKY AND THE COLONEL, by S. N. Behrman. Published by Random House, Inc., New York.
STORM OPERATION, by Maxwell Anderson. Published by Anderson House, Washington, D. C.
PICK-UP GIRL, by Elsa Shelley.
THE INNOCENT VOYAGE, by Paul Osborn.

1944-1945

A BELL FOR ADANO, by Paul Osborn. Published by Alfred A. Knopf, New York.
I REMEMBER MAMA, by John Van Druten. Published by Harcourt, Brace and Co., Inc., New York.
THE HASTY HEART, by John Patrick. Published by Random House, Inc., New York.
THE GLASS MENAGERIE, by Tennessee Williams. Published by Random House, Inc., New York.
HARVEY, by Mary Chase.
THE LATE GEORGE APLEY, by John P. Marquand and George S. Kaufman.
SOLDIER'S WIFE, by Rose Franken. Published by Samuel French.
ANNA LUCASTA, by Philip Yordan. Published by Random House, Inc., New York.
FOOLISH NOTION, by Philip Barry.
DEAR RUTH, by Norman Krasna. Published by Random House, Inc., New York.

1945-1946

STATE OF THE UNION, by Howard Lindsay and Russel Crouse. Published by Random House, Inc., New York.
HOME OF THE BRAVE, by Arthur Laurents. Published by Random House, Inc., New York.
DEEP ARE THE ROOTS, by Arnaud d'Usseau and James Gow. Published by Charles Scribner's Sons, New York.

THE MAGNIFICENT YANKEE, by Emmet Lavery. Published by Samuel French, Inc., New York.
ANTIGONE, by Lewis Galantiere (from the French of Jean Anouilh). Published by Random House, Inc., New York.
O MISTRESS MINE, by Terence Rattigan. Published and revised by the author.
BORN YESTERDAY, by Garson Kanin. Published by Viking Press, Inc., New York.
DREAM GIRL, by Elmer Rice. Published by Coward-McCann, Inc., New York.
THE RUGGED PATH, by Robert E. Sherwood. Published by Charles Scribner's Sons, New York.
LUTE SONG, by Will Irwin and Sidney Howard. Published version by Will Irwin and Leopoldine Howard.

1946-1947

ALL MY SONS, by Arthur Miller. Published by Reynal & Hitchcock, New York.
THE ICEMAN COMETH, by Eugene G. O'Neill. Published by Random House, Inc., New York.
JOAN OF LORRAINE, by Maxwell Anderson. Published by Maxwell Anderson; distributed by Dodd, Mead & Co., New York.
ANOTHER PART OF THE FOREST, by Lillian Hellman. Published by Viking Press, Inc., New York.
YEARS AGO, by Ruth Gordon. Published by Viking Press, Inc., New York.
JOHN LOVES MARY, by Norman Krasna. Copyright by Norman Krasna.
THE FATAL WEAKNESS, by George Kelly. Published by Samuel French, Inc., New York and London.
THE STORY OF MARY SURRATT, by John Patrick. Published by Dramatists' Play Service, Inc., New York.
CHRISTOPHER BLAKE, by Moss Hart. Published by Random House, Inc., New York.
BRIGADOON, by Alan Jay Lerner and Frederick Loewe. Published by Coward-McCann, Inc., New York.

1947-1948

A STREETCAR NAMED DESIRE, by Tennessee Williams. Published by New Directions, New York.

MISTER ROBERTS, by Thomas Heggen and Joshua Logan. Published by Houghton Mifflin Co., Boston.
COMMAND DECISION, by William Wister Haines. Published by Random House, New York.
THE WINSLOW BOY, by Terence Rattigan.
THE HEIRESS, by Ruth and Augustus Goetz.
ALLEGRO, by Richard Rodgers and Oscar Hammerstein 2d. Published by Alfred A. Knopf, New York. Music published by Williamson Music, Inc., New York.
EASTWARD IN EDEN, by Dorothy Gardner. Published by Longmans, Green & Co., New York.
SKIPPER NEXT TO GOD, by Jan de Hartog.
AN INSPECTOR CALLS, by J. B. Priestley.
ME AND MOLLY, by Gertrude Berg.

WHERE AND WHEN THEY WERE BORN

(Compiled from the most authentic records available)

Abbott, George	Hamburg, N. Y.	1895
Abel, Walter	St. Paul, Minn.	1898
Adams, Maude	Salt Lake City, Utah	1872
Addy, Wesley	Omaha, Neb.	1912
Adler, Stella	New York City	1904
Aherne, Brian	King's Norton, England	1902
Anders, Glenn	Los Angeles, Cal.	1890
Anderson, Judith	Australia	1898
Anderson, Maxwell	Atlantic City, Pa.	1888
Andrews, A. G.	Buffalo, N. Y.	1861
Andrews, Ann	Los Angeles, Cal.	1895
Arliss, George	London, England	1868
Ashcroft, Peggy	Croydon, Eng.	1907
Astaire, Fred	Omaha, Neb.	1899
Bainter, Fay	Los Angeles, Cal.	1892
Bankhead, Tallulah	Huntsville, Ala.	1902
Barry, Philip	Rochester, N. Y.	1896
Barrymore, Diana	New York City	1921
Barrymore, Ethel	Philadelphia, Pa.	1879
Barrymore, John	Philadelphia, Pa.	1882
Barrymore, Lionel	Philadelphia, Pa.	1878
Barton, James	Gloucester, N. J.	1890
Beecher, Janet	Jefferson City, Mo.	1887
Behrman, S. N.	Worcester, Mass.	1893
Bell, James	Suffolk, Va.	1891
Bellamy, Ralph	Chicago, Ill.	1905
Bergman, Ingrid	Stockholm	1917
Bergner, Elisabeth	Vienna	1901
Berlin, Irving	Russia	1888
Blackmer, Sidney	Salisbury, N. C.	1898
Bolger, Ray	Dorchester, Mass.	1906
Bondi, Beulah	Chicago, Ill.	1892
Bordoni, Irene	Paris, France	1895
Bourneuf, Philip	Boston, Mass.	1912
Boyer, Charles	Figeac, France	1899

Brady, William A.	San Francisco, Cal.	1863
Braham, Horace	London, England	1896
Brent, Romney	Saltillo, Mex.	1902
Brice, Fannie	Brooklyn, N. Y.	1891
Bruce, Carol	Great Neck, L. I.	1919
Bruce, Nigel	San Diego, Cal.	1895
Burke, Billie	Washington, D. C.	1885
Byington, Spring	Colorado Springs, Colo.	1898
Cagney, James	New York	1904
Cagney, Jeanne	New York	1920
Cahill, Lily	Texas	1891
Calhern, Louis	New York	1895
Cantor, Eddie	New York	1894
Carlisle, Kitty	New Orleans, La.	1912
Carnovsky, Morris	St. Louis, Mo.	1898
Carradine, John	New York City	1906
Carroll, Leo G.	Weedon, England	1892
Carroll, Madeleine	West Bromwich, England	1906
Catlett, Walter	San Francisco, Cal.	1889
Caulfield, Joan	New York City	1924
Chandler, Helen	Charleston, N. C.	1906
Chatterton, Ruth	New York	1893
Christians, Mady	Vienna, Austria	1907
Claire, Helen	Union Springs, Ala.	1908
Claire, Ina	Washington, D. C.	1892
Clark, Bobby	Springfield, Ohio	1888
Clayton, Jan	Alamogordo, N. M.	1921
Clift, Montgomery	Omaha, Neb.	1921
Clive, Colin	St. Malo, France	1900
Coburn, Charles	Macon, Ga.	1877
Cohan, George M.	Providence, R. I.	1878
Colbert, Claudette	Paris	1905
Collinge, Patricia	Dublin	1894
Collins, Russell	New Orleans, La.	1901
Colt, Ethel Barrymore	Mamaroneck, N. Y.	1911
Colt, John Drew	New York	1914
Conroy, Frank	London, England	1885
Cook, Donald	Portland, Ore.	1902
Cooper, Gladys	Lewisham, England	1888
Cooper, Melville	Birmingham, England	1896
Corbett, Leonora	London, England	1908
Corey, Wendell	Dracut, Mass.	1907

456   BURNS MANTLE BEST PLAYS OF 1948-49

Cornell, Katharine	Berlin, Germany	1898
Cossart, Ernest	Cheltenham, England	1876
Coulouris, George	Manchester, England	1906
Coward, Noel	Teddington, England	1899
Cowl, Jane	Boston, Mass.	1887
Crothers, Rachel	Bloomington, Ill.	1878
Crouse, Russel	Findlay, Ohio	1893
Cummings, Constance	Seattle, Wash.	1911
Dale, Margaret	Philadelphia, Pa.	1880
Davis, Owen	Portland, Me.	1874
Derwent, Clarence	London, England	1884
Digges, Dudley	Dublin, Ireland	1880
Douglas, Susan	Prague, Czechoslovakia	1925
Dowling, Eddie	Woonsocket, R. I.	1895
Drake, Alfred	New York City	1914
Duncan, Augustin	San Francisco	1873
Dunning, Philip	Meriden, Conn.	1890
Edney, Florence	London, England	1879
Eggerth, Marta	Budapest, Hungary	1915
Eldridge, Florence	Brooklyn, N. Y.	1901
Evans, Edith	London, England	1888
Evans, Maurice	Dorchester, England	1901
Evans, Wilbur	Philadelphia, Pa.	1908
Ewell, Tom	Owensboro, Ky.	1912
Fabray, Nanette	New Orleans, La.	1921
Fay, Frank	San Francisco	1897
Ferber, Edna	Kalamazoo, Mich.	1887
Ferrer, Jose	Puerto Rico	1912
Field, Sylvia	Allston, Mass.	1902
Fitzgerald, Barry	Dublin, Ireland	1888
Fletcher, Bramwell	Bradford, Yorkshire, Eng.	1904
Fonda, Henry	Grand Island, Neb.	1905
Fontanne, Lynn	London, England	1887
Forbes, Brenda	London, England	1909
Forbes, Ralph	London, England	1905
Foy, Eddie, Jr.	New Rochelle, N. Y.	1907
Francis, Arlene	Boston, Mass.	1908
Garfield, John	New York City	1913
Garrett, Betty	St. Louis, Mo.	1919

Gaxton, William	San Francisco, Cal.	1893
Geddes, Barbara Bel	New York	1922
Geddes, Norman Bel	Adrian, Mich.	1893
Gershwin, Ira	New York	1896
Gielgud, John	London, England	1904
Gillmore, Margalo	England	1901
Gilmore, Virginia	El Monte, Cal.	1919
Gish, Dorothy	Dayton, Ohio	1898
Gish, Lillian	Springfield, Ohio	1896
Gleason, James	New York	1885
Golden, John	New York	1874
Goodner, Carol	New York City	1904
Gordon, Ruth	Wollaston, Mass.	1896
Gough, Lloyd	New York City	1906
Greaza, Walter	St. Paul, Minn.	1900
Greenstreet, Sydney	England	1880
Gwenn, Edmund	Glamorgan, Wales	1875
Hammerstein, Oscar 2d	New York City	1895
Hampden, Walter	Brooklyn, N. Y.	1879
Hannen, Nicholas	London, England	1881
Hardie, Russell	Griffin Mills, N. Y.	1906
Hardwicke, Sir Cedric	Lye, Stourbridge, England	1893
Harris, Jed	Vienna, Austria	1900
Harrison, Rex	Huyton, Lancs., Eng.	1908
Hart, Richard	Providence, R. I.	1915
Havoc, June	Seattle, Wash.	1916
Haydon, Julie	Oak Park, Ill.	1910
Hayes, Helen	Washington, D. C.	1900
Heflin, Frances	Oklahoma City, Okla.	1924
Heinemann, Eda	Japan	1891
Heming, Violet	Leeds, England	1893
Henie, Sonja	Oslo, Norway	1912
Hepburn, Katharine	Hartford, Conn.	1907
Hobbes, Halliwell	Stratford, England	1877
Holliday, Judy	New York City	1924
Hopkins, Arthur	Cleveland, Ohio	1878
Hopkins, Miriam	Bainbridge, Ga.	1904
Holmes, Taylor	Newark, N. J.	1872
Hull, Josephine	Newtonville, Mass.	1886
Hull, Henry	Louisville, Ky.	1888
Hunt, Martita	Argentine Repub.	1900

Hussey, Ruth .... Providence, R. I. 1917
Huston, Walter .... Toronto 1884

Inescort, Frieda .... Hitchin, Scotland 1905
Ives, Burl .... Hunt Township, Ill. 1909

Jagger, Dean .... Columbus Grove, Ohio 1904
Jameson, House .... Austin, Texas 1902
Jolson, Al .... Washington, D. C. 1883
Johnson, Harold J. (Chic) .. Chicago, Ill. 1891
Joy, Nicholas .... Paris, France 1892

Kane, Whitford .... Larne, Ireland 1882
Kanin, Garson .... Rochester, N. Y. 1912
Karloff, Boris .... Dulwich, England 1887
Kaufman, George S. .... Pittsburgh, Pa. 1889
Kaye, Danny .... New York City 1914
Kazan, Elia .... Constantinople 1909
Keith, Robert .... Scotland 1899
Kelly, Gene .... Pittsburgh, Pa. 1912
Kerrigan, J. M. .... Dublin, Ireland 1885
Kiepura, Jan .... Warsaw, Poland 1902
Kilbride, Percy .... San Francisco, Cal. 1880
King, Dennis .... Coventry, England 1897
Kingsford, Walter .... England 1876
Kingsley, Sidney .... New York City 1906
Kirkland, Patricia .... New York 1927
Kruger, Otto .... Toledo, Ohio 1885

Lackland, Ben .... Waco, Texas 1901
Landi, Elissa .... Venice, Italy 1904
Landis, Jessie Royce ...... Chicago, Ill. 1904
Laughton, Charles .... Scarborough, England 1899
Lawrence, Gertrude .... London 1898
Lee, Canada .... New York City 1907
Le Gallienne, Eva .... London, England 1899
Lillie, Beatrice .... Toronto, Canada 1898
Lindsay, Howard .... Waterford, N. Y. 1889
Linn, Bambi .... Brooklyn, N. Y. 1926
Loeb, Philip .... Philadelphia, Pa. 1892
Lonergan, Lenore .... Toledo, Ohio 1928
Lord, Pauline .... Hanford, Cal. 1890
Logan, Joshua .... Texarkana, Tex. 1908

Lukas, Paul	Budapest, Hungary	1895
Lunt, Alfred	Milwaukee, Wis.	1893
Lytell, Bert	New York City	1885
MacMahon, Aline	McKeesport, Pa.	1899
Mamoulian, Rouben	Tiflis, Russia	1897
March, Fredric	Racine, Wis.	1897
Margetson, Arthur	London, England	1897
Margo	Mexico	1918
Marshall, Everett	Worcester, Mass.	1902
Marshall, Herbert	London, England	1890
Mason, James	Huddersfield, England	1909
Massey, Raymond	Toronto, Canada	1896
Matteson, Ruth	San Jose, Cal.	1905
McClintic, Guthrie	Seattle, Wash.	1893
McCormick, Myron	Albany, Ind.	1907
McCracken, Joan	Philadelphia, Pa.	1923
McGrath, Paul	Chicago, Ill.	1900
McGuire, Dorothy	Omaha, Neb.	1918
Mielziner, Jo	Paris, France	1901
Menotti, Gian-Carlo	Italy	1912
Meredith, Burgess	Cleveland, Ohio	1908
Merman, Ethel	Astoria, R. I.	1909
Middleton, Ray	Chicago, Ill.	1907
Miller, Arthur	New York City	1915
Miller, Gilbert	New York	1884
Mitchell, Grant	Columbus, Ohio	1874
Mitchell, Thomas	Elizabeth, N. J.	1892
Moore, Victor	Hammondton, N. J.	1876
Morgan, Claudia	New York	1912
Morgan, Ralph	New York City	1889
Morison, Patricia	New York City	1919
Morley, Robert	Semley, Wilt., Eng.	1908
Morris, Mary	Boston	1894
Morris, McKay	San Antonio, Texas	1890
Moss, Arnold	Brooklyn, N. Y.	1910
Muni, Paul	Lemberg, Austria	1895
Myrtil, Odette	Paris, France	1898
Nagel, Conrad	Keokuk, Iowa	1897
Natwick, Mildred	Baltimore, Md.	1908
Nolan, Lloyd	San Francisco, Cal.	1903
Nugent, Elliott	Dover, Ohio	1900

O'Brien-Moore, Erin	Los Angeles, Cal.	1908
Odets, Clifford	Philadelphia	1906
Oenslager, Donald	Harrisburg, Pa.	1902
Olivier, Laurence	Dorking, Surrey, England	1907
Olsen, John Siguard (Ole)	Peru, Ind.	1892
O'Malley, Rex	London, England	1906
O'Neal, Frederick	Brookville, Miss.	1905
O'Neill, Eugene Gladstone	New York	1888
Ouspenskaya, Maria	Tula, Russia	1876
Patterson, Elizabeth	Savannah, Tenn.	1898
Pemberton, Brock	Leavenworth, Kansas	1885
Petina, Irra	Leningrad, Russia	1900
Picon, Molly	New York City	1898
Pinza, Ezio	Rome, Italy	1895
Pollock, Channing	Washington, D. C.	1880
Porter, Cole	Peru, Indiana	1892
Price, Vincent	St. Louis, Mo.	1914
Rains, Claude	London, England	1889
Raitt, John	Santa Ana, Cal.	1917
Rathbone, Basil	Johannesburg	1892
Redman, Joyce	Newcastle, Ireland	1918
Reed, Florence	Philadelphia, Pa.	1883
Rennie, James	Toronto, Canada	1890
Richardson, Ralph	Cheltenham, England	1902
Rice, Elmer	New York City	1892
Roberts, Joan	New York City	1918
Robinson, Bill	Richmond, Va.	1878
Robinson, Edward G.	Bucharest, Roumania	1893
Rodgers, Richard	New York City	1902
Ross, Anthony	New York	1906
Royle, Selena	New York	1905
Ruben, José	Belgium	1886
Sarnoff, Dorothy	Brooklyn, N. Y.	1919
Scheff, Fritzi	Vienna, Austria	1879
Scott, Martha	Jamesport, Mo.	1914
Segal, Vivienne	Philadelphia, Pa.	1897
Shannon, Effie	Cambridge, Mass.	1867
Sherman, Hiram	Boston, Mass.	1908
Sherwood, Robert Emmet	New Rochelle, N. Y.	1896
Sidney, Sylvia	New York	1910

Simms, Hilda .... Minneapolis, Minn. 1920
Skinner, Cornelia Otis .... Chicago 1902
Smith, Kent .... Smithfield, Me. 1910
Stickney, Dorothy .... Dickinson, N. D. 1903
Stoddard, Haila .... Great Falls, Mont. 1914
Stone, Carol .... New York 1917
Stone, Dorothy .... New York 1905
Stone, Ezra .... New Bedford, Mass. 1918
Stone, Fred .... Denver, Colo. 1873
Sullavan, Margaret .... Norfolk, Va. 1910

Tandy, Jessica .... London, Eng. 1909
Tetzel, Joan .... New York 1923
Thomas, John Charles .... Baltimore, Md. 1887
Tone, Franchot .... Niagara Falls, N. Y. 1907
Tozere, Frederick .... Brookline, Mass. 1901
Tracy, Spencer .... Milwaukee, Wis. 1900
Travers, Henry .... Berwick, England 1874
Truex, Ernest .... Red Hill, Mo. 1890

Van Druten, John .... London, Eng. 1902
Van Patten, Dickie .... New York 1929
Van Patten, Joyce .... New York City 1934
Varden, Evelyn .... Venita, Okla. 1893

Walker, Nancy .... Philadelphia, Pa. 1922
Walker, June .... New York 1904
Wanamaker, Sam .... Chicago, Ill. 1919
Ward, Penelope .... London, England 1914
Warfield, David .... San Francisco, Cal. 1866
Waring, Richard .... Buckinghamshire, England..1912
Waters, Ethel .... Chester, Pa. 1900
Watson, Lucile .... Quebec, Canada 1879
Watson, Minor .... Marianna, Ark. 1889
Webb, Clifton .... Indiana 1891
Webster, Margaret .... New York City 1905
Welles, Orson .... Kenosha, Wis. 1915
West, Mae .... Brooklyn, N. Y. 1892
Weston, Ruth .... Boston, Mass. 1911
Whiting, Jack .... Philadelphia, Pa. 1901
Whorf, Richard .... Winthrop, Mass. 1908
Widmark, Richard .... Sunrise, Minn. 1914
Willard, Catherine .... Dayton, Ohio 1895

Williams, Rhys .... Wales 1903
Williams, Tennessee .... Columbus, Miss. 1914
Wilson, John C. .... New York City 1899
Wiman, Dwight Deere ...... Moline, Ill. 1895
Winwood, Estelle .... England 1883
Wood, Peggy .... Brooklyn, N. Y. 1894
Wyatt, Jane .... Campgaw, N. J. 1912
Wynn, Ed .... Philadelphia, Pa. 1886
Wynn, Keenan .... New York City 1917

Yurka, Blanche .... Bohemia 1893

NECROLOGY

June 1, 1948—June 1, 1949

Benda, Wladyslaw Theodor, artist, 75. Creator of masks for many theatrical productions, notably Eugene O'Neill's "The Great God Brown." Born Poland; died New York, December 2, 1948.

Berard, Christian, 46. Painter, fashion designer (he created the "new look" in women's clothing) and scenic artist. His settings of "The Madwoman of Chaillot" were brought from Paris for the New York run of the play. Born France; died Paris, February 12, 1949.

Bradley, Oscar, musical conductor, 55. First conducted London production of "Irene"; in New York conducted "The Lady in Ermine," "The Love Song," "The Student Prince," "Rio Rita," "Whoopee," "Show Boat," "Rosalie," "Bitter Sweet" and other New York musicals; later became conductor of many radio shows. Born London; died Norwalk, Conn., Aug. 31, 1948.

Brian, Donald, actor, 73. Most famed as Prince Danilo in "The Merry Widow"; made stage debut near Boston in 1896; New York debut in 1899 in "On the Wabash"; appeared in many musicals, including "Florodora"; was leading man in musical comedy from 1907 ("The Merry Widow") to 1931, when this great hit was revived. Born Newfoundland; died Great Neck, N. Y., December 22, 1948.

Bryant, Charles, actor, 67. Was Alla Nazimova's leading man, 1912 to 1923, and for some years was married to her; last New York appearance in "Yes, My Darling Daughter"; made debut in London in 1901. Born England; died Mt. Kisco, N. Y., Aug. 7, 1948.

Bulgakov, Leo, 60. Actor and producer; member of Moscow Art Theatre, 1912 to 1923; won critics' notices on first visit of Moscow Art to New York; remained to appear in "The Miracle"; subsequently acted in many plays, including "Gods of the Lightning"; directed "One Sunday Afternoon," "Prologue to Glory," "The Night Remembers" and other plays. Born Russia; died Binghamton, N. Y., July 20, 1948.

Cain, Patrick J., 70, warehouse man. Until 1938 operated Cain's Warehouse, noted storehouse for theatrical scenery. Born New York; died New York May 13, 1949.

Carroll, Earl, producer, playwright and songwriter, 55. Began theatrical career as program seller in Pittsburgh at age of 10. Wrote lyrics and music of "So Long, Letty," "Canary Cottage" and other musicals. Produced many editions of "Earl Carroll Vanities" and several plays including "White Cargo." In 1938 opened a restaurant and night club in Hollywood. Born Pittsburgh; died in airplane crash June 17, 1948.

Carte, Rupert D'Oyly, producer, 71. Last surviving son of Richard D'Oyly Carte, founder of the Savoy Theatre, London; as boy attended rehearsals of earliest Gilbert and Sullivan operettas; became associated with his father in production in 1894; assumed management of D'Oyly Carte Company in 1913; also directed London restaurants and hotels he had inherited. Born England; died Savoy Hotel, London, September 12, 1948.

Cawthorn, Joseph, actor, 81. Made stage debut at 4; spent 47 years on musical stage, starring in "The Fortune Teller," "The Girl from Utah," "Sunny" and many others; Victor Herbert expressly wrote a role for him in "Naughty Marietta"; made film debut in 1926; for 8 years co-starred with Julia Sanderson in musicals. Born New York City; died Beverly Hills, Calif., January 21, 1949.

Chase, William B., music and drama critic, 76. Served 20 years each on the N. Y. *Sun* and the N. Y. *Times* as music or drama critic; in 1935, after retirement, organized Yale Forty-Niner Summer theatre on his New Hampshire estate. Born Syracuse, N. Y.; died Whitefield, N. H., Aug. 25, 1948.

Chauvenet, Virginia, 65. Actress. Made debut in 1908 in "The Devil"; supported such stars as Nance O'Neil, Constance Collier, Ethel Barrymore, Minnie Maddern Fiske and Lynn Fontanne. Was secretary of Overseas Theatre League in World War I; in World War II was an executive of American Theatre Wing. Born Pennsylvania; died New York, March 6, 1949.

Christie, George, 76, actor. Was with Richard Mansfield's company; also appeared with Henry Miller, Julia Marlowe, Ina Claire and George M. Cohan; last appearance was in Players' revival of "The County Chairman." Born Philadelphia; died Toms River, N. J., May 20, 1949.

Davis, Owen, Jr., 42, actor and television producer. Made debut in "The Barker" in 1927. Appeared in "Jezebel," "Mr. and Mrs. North" and many other plays, and in many films, including "All Quiet on the Western Front." Born New York; died New York, May 22, 1949.

Eaton, Mary, actress, 46. Starred in "Ziegfeld Follies" from 1923 to 1930, first as dancer, later as singer also; co-starred with Eddie Cantor in "Kid Boots"; made N. Y. debut in "Over the Top." Born Norfolk, Va.; died Hollywood, Calif., October 10, 1948.

Foster, Lillian, 63, actress. Once called "the American Duse"; her greatest success was in "Conscience"; played stock throughout the U. S. and Canada; last appearance in "Goodbye, My Fancy." Born Centralia, Ill.; died New York, May 15, 1949.

Gaige, Crosby, 66. Producer. Began as author's agent with Elisabeth Marbury, next joined Selwyn & Co., discovering such dramatists as Bayard Veiller and Eugene Walter. Plays of which he was producer or co-producer included "Within the Law," "Broadway," "Coquette," "The Butter and Egg Man," "The House Beautiful" and "The Eternal Road." Born Nelson, N. Y.; died Peekskill, N. Y., March 8, 1949.

Gallatin, Alberta, actress, 87. Appeared with Edwin Booth, Joseph Jefferson, Richard Mansfield, Johnston Forbes-Robertson, Maurice Barrymore, Otis Skinner, E. H. Sothern and others; in 1920 founded the Edgar Allan Poe Society of America. Born West Virginia; died New York Aug. 27, 1948.

Gard, Alex, artist, 48. Noted as a caricaturist of stage stars, contributing to metropolitan newspapers and national magazines; artist of several books of caricature, including "Ballet Laughs" and "Hollywood off Guard." Born Russia; died New York June 1, 1948.

Glaspell, Susan, playwright, 66. With husband, George Cram Cook, founded Provincetown (Mass.) Playhouse, introduced Eugene O'Neill's first plays there; in 1930 wrote "Alison's House," which won Pulitzer Prize; wrote other plays and several novels. Born Davenport, Ia.; died Provincetown, Mass., July 17, 1948.

Greneker, Claude P., 68, publicity man. After working as newspaperman in Augusta, Charleston and Pittsburgh. Succeeded A. Toxen Worm as publicity and advertising director for the

Shuberts in 1909. Born Newberry, S. C.; died New York April 7, 1949.

Hancock, Myrtle J. (Marty), female minstrel, 65. Noted as "end man" of Emmett Welch's minstrels. Born San Francisco; died Philadelphia, August 19, 1948.

Heggen, Thomas O., 29, novelist and dramatist. Wrote best-selling war novel, "Mister Roberts," and with Joshua Logan adapted it for stage. Born Fort Dodge, Iowa; died New York, May 19, 1949.

Hicks, Sir Edward Seymour, 78, actor and playwright. Went on English stage at age of 16; two years later toured U. S. with the Kendals. Married Ellaline Terriss and co-starred with her in many comedies. His acting and writing career occupies five columns in Who's Who in the Theatre. Born island of Jersey; died Hampshire April 6, 1949.

Howard, Willie, comedian, 62. (Real name William Levkowitz.) Son of a German cantor, was brought to New York at age of 1; made debut at 14 as boy soprano in Proctor's 125th St. vaudeville theatre; became song plugger for Witmark; in 1903 joined elder brother, Eugene, in vaudeville act; starred in Ziegfeld and George White musicals and in Gershwin's "Girl Crazy"; also was in motion pictures. Born Germany; died New York, January 12, 1949.

Husch, Richard J., 72. (Pseudonym, Richard Gerard.) Lyric writer; best known for words of "Sweet Adeline," for which Harry Armstrong wrote music. Born New York City; died New York City July 2, 1948.

Landi, Elissa, actress, playwright and novelist, 43. Child of an Austrian officer and an Italian countess; educated Canada and England; began stage and film careers in England, France and Sweden; made New York debut in 1930 in "A Farewell to Arms"; starred in many films in Hollywood; last New York appearance in "Dark Hammock," 1944. Born Italy; died Kingston, N. Y., October 21, 1948.

Lehar, Franz, composer, 78. Composed first musical work at age of 6; studied violin in childhood; when he was 20 Anton Dvorak persuaded him to try composition; when he was 35 he wrote his greatest hit—"The Merry Widow"; other operettas included "Gipsy Love," "The Count of Luxembourg" and "Frederika." Born Hungary; died Vienna, October 24, 1948.

Leventhal, Jules J., 60, producer. Operated touring and stock companies along the Eastern Seaboard and was producer of

BURNS MANTLE BEST PLAYS OF 1948-49

or silent backer of many Broadway plays. Born Minsk, Russia; died New York April 14, 1949.

Lewis, Lloyd Downs, 57, critic, historian and playwright. Drama critic Chicago *Daily News,* 1920-1930; co-author with Sinclair Lewis of Civil War drama, "Jayhawker." Born Pendleton, Ind.; died Libertyville, Ill., April 21, 1949.

Maxwell, Edwin, stage and motion picture actor, 58. Directed first talking picture, "The Jazz Singer"; played in more than 150 films; last stage role, Clarence Day, Sr., in touring company of "Life with Father." Born Ireland; died Hyannis, Mass., Aug. 13, 1948.

McNutt, Patterson, playwright, producer and writer of short stories and scenarios, 52. Made stage debut with Otis Skinner in "Mister Antonio," as a juvenile; was reporter on the *Evening Sun,* the *Globe* and the *World* in N. Y.; in 1924 collaborated with Anne Morrison on "Pigs"; in 1925 produced "The Poor Nut"; subsequently produced other plays and wrote many motion picture scripts. Born Illinois; died New York, October 22, 1948.

Pulaski, Jack, theatrical reporter and editor (real name Isme Beringer Pulaski). Noted as *Ibee* in the pages of *Variety;* began as Atlantic City correspondent of *Variety* in 1905; later wrote sports for New York *Evening Mail;* began drama reporting and criticism for *Variety* in 1918. Born Cuthbert, Ga.; died New York July 16, 1948.

Smith, Sir C. Aubrey, actor, 85. Noted for 20 years in Hollywood for portrayals of British characters; made stage debut in England in 1892; made American debut in "The Morals of Marcus," Boston, 1907; appeared in many New York productions, including "The Runaway," "The Lie," "The Constant Wife" and "The Bachelor Father"; began Hollywood film career in 1930. Born England; died Beverly Hills, Calif., December 20, 1948.

Speaks, Oley, composer, 72. Wrote more than 250 songs, including "Sylvia," "On the Road to Mandalay," "Morning," "When the Boys Come Home" and "The Bells of Youth"; former director of the American Society of Composers, Authors and Publishers; began career as baritone soloist in New York churches and on concert tours. Born Ohio; died New York, August 28, 1948.

Stebbins, Rowland, producer (under name of Laurence Rivers), 66. Engineer and financier; began stage career as "angel" for plays; first production, "Merry Andrew," in 1929; greatest success, "The Green Pastures," 1930; other productions included The Players' tour of "Uncle Tom's Cabin" and "White Horse Inn." Born New York; died New York, December 12, 1948.

Thompson, Fred, 65, librettist. Best known in the U. S. for his books of "Rio Rita" and "Lady Be Good." Born London; died London April 10, 1949.

Towne, Charles Hanson, 72. Writer and editor. In 1940 played role of clergyman in tour of "Life with Father." Born Kentucky; died New York, February 28, 1949.

Volmoeller, Karl, playwright, 69. Best known as author of "The Miracle." Born Germany; died Hollywood, Calif., October 17, 1948.

Woodbury, Clare, 69, actress. Made her first success as Lil, the pianist, in "Broadway." Played in "Little Accident," "Green Grow the Lilacs," "Missouri Legend," "Johnny Belinda" and other offerings. Born Philadelphia; died New York March 13, 1949.

Worthing, Helen Lee, actress, 43. Noted as one of the beauties of "The Ziegfeld Follies." Born New York; died Hollywood, Calif., Aug. 26, 1948.

Zacchini, Ildebrando, 79. Originated circus act of man being shot from a cannon. Born Spain; died Tampa, Fla., July 17, 1948.

THE DECADES' TOLL

(Persons of Outstanding Prominence in the Theatre
Who Have Died in Recent Years)

	Born	Died
Arliss, George	1869	1946
Baker, George Pierce	1866	1935
Barrymore, John	1882	1942
Belasco, David	1856	1931
Bernhardt, Sarah	1845	1923
Campbell, Mrs. Patrick	1865	1940
Cohan, George Michael	1878	1942
Collier, Willie	1866	1943
Digges, Dudley	1879	1947
Drew, John	1853	1927
Duse, Eleanora	1859	1924
Fields, W. C.	1880	1946
Fiske, Minnie Maddern	1865	1932
Fiske, Harrison Grey	1861	1942
Frohman, Daniel	1851	1940
Galsworthy, John	1867	1933
Gershwin, George	1898	1937
Greet, Sir Philip (Ben)	1858	1936
Herbert, Victor	1859	1924
Hooker, Brian	1881	1947
Kern, Jerome	1882	1945
Mantle (Robert) Burns	1873	1948
May, Edna	1879	1948
Perry, Antoinette	1888	1946
Pinero, Sir Arthur Wing	1855	1934
Reinhardt, Max	1873	1943
Skinner, Otis	1858	1942
Sothern, Edwin Hugh	1859	1933
Tarkington, Booth	1869	1946
Taylor, Laurette	1884	1946
Terry, Ellen	1848	1928
Thomas, Augustus	1857	1934
Thomas, A. E.	1872	1947
Tyler, George C.	1867	1946
Whitty, Dame May	1865	1948
Youmans, Vincent	1899	1946

INDEX OF AUTHORS

Abbott, George, 17, 388, 441, 442
Achard, Marcel, 42, 47
Adair, Tom, 406
Adamson, Harold, 394
Ade, George, 437
Akins, Zoe, 51, 435, 438, 446
Allardice, James B., 16, 415
Alsberg, Henry G., 441
Amsterdam, Morey, 379
Anderson, Maxwell, 5, 12, 26, 50, 88, 368, 399, 434, 435, 440, 441, 443, 444, 445, 446, 447, 448, 450, 451, 452
Andreyev, Leonid, 439
Anouilh, Jean, 49, 452
Ansky, S., 441
Anspacher, Louis Kaufman, 438
Archer, William, 438
Arlen, Michael, 441
Arnold, Stanley, 379
Atlas, Leopold, 445
Aumont, Jean Pierre, 15, 27, 411
Axelrod, George, 380

Baker, Melville, 440
Balderston, John, 443
Barker, Albert Wineman, 6, 383
Barker, Ambrose, 42
Barrie, James M., 439
Barry, Philip, 15, 27, 411, 439, 441, 442, 443, 444, 448, 451
Batson, George, 17, 29, 420
Battista, Miriam, 375
Baum, Vicki, 444
Beach, Lewis, 440
Behrman, S. N., 42, 43, 47, 118, 444, 445, 446, 448, 451
Belasco, David, 437
Benelli, Sem, 438
Bennett, Robert Russell, 405, 419
Benson, E. F., 12, 27, 401
Berg, Gertrude, 453
Bergerson, Baldwin, 380
Berlin, Irving, 372
Berns, Julie, 395
Berton, Eugene, 46

Besier, Rudolf, 444
Biggers, Earl Derr, 437
Bodeen, De Witt, 50
Bolitho, William, 44
Bolton, Guy, 438, 440
Boothe, Clare, 447, 448, 449
Bradford, Roark, 443
Brennan, Frederick Hazlitt, 381
Breuer, Bessie, 6, 21, 378
Bridgers, Ann, 442
Britten, Benjamin, 13, 404
Brown, Billings, 380
Browne, Maurice, 443
Browne, Porter Emerson, 439
Buckmaster, Henrietta, 51
Butler, Rachel Barton, 438
Byrne, Dolly, 438

Camus, Albert, 49
Capek, Josef, 376
Capek, Karel, 376, 440
Carroll, Paul Vincent, 447, 448
Casella, Alberto, 443
Chase, Mary Coyle, 23, 436, 451
Cheever, John, 6, 383
Chodorov, Edward, 451
Chodorov, Jerome, 449, 450
Clements, Colin, 450
Coffee, Lenore, 448
Cohan, George M., 437, 445
Coley, Thomas, 30, 420
Colton, John, 439
Conkle, E. P., 448
Connelly, Marc, 6, 16, 382, 435, 439, 440, 441, 443, 446
Cormack, Bartlett, 442
Coward, Noel, 7, 20, 48, 385, 445, 450
Cowen, William Joyce, 448
Craven, Frank, 438
Crothers, Rachel, 439, 440, 443, 444, 445, 448
Crouse, Russel, 8, 207, 371, 391, 436, 448, 451
Curran, Homer, 381

INDEX OF AUTHORS

Dane, Clemence, 439
Daudet, Alphonse, 44
Davis, Donald, 447
Davis, Owen, 376, 435, 439, 447, 449
Day, Clarence, 207, 391
Dayton, Katharine, 446
De Casalis, Jeanne, 447
De Hartog, Jan, 453
Dell, Floyd, 443
Deval, Jacques, 447
Dodd, Lee Wilson, 440
Drake, W. A., 444
Drinkwater, John, 438
Duncan, Ronald, 13, 404
Dunning, Philip, 441
D'Usseau, Arnaud, 450, 451

Elser, Frank B., 446
Emerson, Edward, 52
Emery, Gilbert, 439, 440
Engel, Lehman, 400
Ervine, St. John, 438, 443
Euripides, 48, 421

Fauchois, René, 445
Ferber, Edna, 10, 25, 378, 393, 441, 442, 445, 447
Ferris, Walter, 443
Field, Salisbury, 438
Fields, Joseph, 449, 450
Fitch, Clyde, 437
Flavin, Martin, 443
Forbes, James, 438
Forrest, George, 381
Frank, Pat, 17, 42, 423
Franken, Rose, 444, 449, 451

Galantiere, Lewis, 452
Gale, Zona, 435
Galsworthy, John, 439, 442
Gardner, Dorothy, 453
Gaynor, Charles, 12, 19, 26, 400
George, Grace, 439
Geraldy, Paul, 439
Gershwin, George and Ira, 435, 444
Gilbert and Sullivan, 37
Giraudoux, Jean, 5, 13, 118, 369, 403, 434
Glaspell, Susan, 435, 444
Gleason, James, 441
Glickman, Will, 30, 400, 422
Goetz, Ruth and Augustus, 48, 453
Goldsmith, Clifford, 448

Goodman, Jeles Eckert, 52
Gordon, Ruth, 8, 24, 39, 333, 389, 451, 452
Gore-Browne, R. F., 445
Gorney, Jay, 380
Goulding, Edmund, 441
Gow, James, 450, 451
Granville-Barker, H. and H., 438, 443
Green, Paul, 435, 442, 444, 447, 449
Greendale, Alexander, 44
Grundman, Clare, 400
Guitry, Sacha, 13, 404, 438

Hagan, James, 445
Haines, William Wister, 453
Hamilton, Patrick, 450
Hammerstein, Oscar 2d, 17, 23, 29, 47, 378, 409, 419, 434, 450, 453
Harris, Howard, 379
Hart, Moss, 11, 19, 24, 238, 372, 397, 435, 444, 446, 447, 448, 449, 450, 452
Harwood, H. M., 445
Hayden, John, 446
Hayes, Joseph, 27, 408
Hecht, Ben, 443
Heggen, Thomas, 453
Hellman, Lillian, 11, 434, 446, 448, 449, 451, 452
Herbert, F. Hugh, 39, 450
Heyward, Dorothy, 10, 24, 392
Heyward, Du Bose, 442
Hiken, Nat, 407
Hopkins, Arthur, 442
Housman, Laurence, 446
Howard, Joe, 42
Howard, Sidney, 15, 28, 413, 435, 440, 442, 445, 452
Hughes, Hatcher, 435, 440
Hughes, Richard, 9, 391
Hurlbut, William, 441

Ibsen, Henrik, 44, 49
Irving, Washington, 5
Irwin, Will, 452

Jamerson, Pauline, 26, 402
James, Dan, 450
Jeffers, Robinson, 20, 48, 421
Jenkins, Gordon, 406
Jerome, Helen, 447
Job, Thomas, 450

INDEX OF AUTHORS

Kandel, Aben, 52
Kandel, Judith, 51
Kanin, Fay, 10, 333, 373, 395
Kanin, Garson, 13, 30, 333, 406, 452
Katzin, Winifred, 441
Kaufman, George S., 10, 25, 88, 179, 238, 372, 393, 435, 439, 440, 441, 442, 443, 444, 445, 446, 447, 448, 449, 451
Kaye, Buddy, 379
Kelly, George, 435, 440, 441, 442, 452
Kennedy, Mary, 441
Kern, Jerome, 23, 378
Kerr, Jean, 401
Kesselring, Joseph, 449
Kingsley, Sidney, 5, 16, 147, 370, 416, 434, 435, 445, 446, 448, 450
Kirkland Jack, 17, 42, 423
Koch, Howard, 449
Krasna, Norman, 7, 42, 48, 384, 451, 452
Kummer, Clare, 438, 445

Lampl, Carl, 379
Langley, Noel, 5, 6, 179, 370, 385
Lardner, Ring W., 443
Laun, Louis, 380
Laurents, Arthur, 451
Lavery, Emmet, 452
Lee, Lester, 408
Leigh, Rowland, 390
Lerner, Alan Jay, 8, 19, 22, 386, 452
Lessner, George, 375
Levy, Benn W., 444
Lewis, Sinclair, 445
Linder, Jack, 410
Lindsay, Howard, 8, 207, 371, 391, 436, 448, 451
Livy, 405
Loesser, Frank, 388
Loewe, Frederick, 452
Logan, Joshua, 17, 29, 38, 419, 434, 453
Lonsdale, Frederick, 441
Loos, Anita, 48

MacArthur, Charles, 443
Mackaye, Percy, 45, 50
Maloney, Russell, 375
Manoff, Arnold, 52
Marquand, John P., 451
Marquis, Don, 440
Marx, Groucho, 7, 42, 48, 384

Maugham, William Somerset, 439, 442
Mayer, Edwin Justus, 440
McCarthy, Justin Huntly, 437
McCollum, Charles Ray, 415
McEnroe, Robert E., 11, 23, 266, 397
McGinley, Phyllis, 380
McGroarty, John S., 47
McGuire, William Anthony, 439
McHugh, Jimmy, 394
McLaughlin, Mignon and Robert, 30, 422
McLellan, C. M. S., 437
Meloney, Rose Franken, *see* Franken, Rose
Menander, 44
Menotti, Gian-Carlo, 399
Michener, James A., 17, 419, 434
Middleton, George, 438
Miller, Arthur, 5, 15, 53, 368, 412, 434, 435, 436, 452
Milne, Alan Alexander, 439, 443
Mitchell, Thomas, 443
Molnar, Ferenc, 409, 439, 440, 442
Moody, William Vaughn, 437
Moran, Alan, 377, 424
Morley, Robert, 5, 6, 179, 370, 385
Morris, Lloyd, 450
Murray, Gilbert, 44

Nash, N. Richard, 11, 396
Nelson, Mervyn, 17, 29, 418
Nichols, Robert, 443
North, Alex, 412
Nugent, Elliott, 449

Obey, André, 405
O'Casey, Sean, 23, 442
O'Dea, John, 52
Odets, Clifford, 16, 18, 28, 413, 446, 448
O'Neill, Eugene, 88, 435, 438, 439, 440, 441, 442, 444, 445, 452
Osborn, Paul, 447, 449, 451

Paonessa, Ralph, 42
Parker, Louis N., 437
Pascal, Milton, 407
Paton, Alan, 369
Patrick, John, 451, 452
Percy, Edward, 14, 407
Pollock, Channing, 439, 441
Porter, Cole, 13, 17, 301, 405, 434

INDEX OF AUTHORS

Powys, Stephen, 404
Priestley, J. B., 453
Pyzel, Robert, 414

Randolph, Clemence, 439
Raphaelson, Samson, 446, 449, 450
Rattigan, Terence, 48, 452, 453
Reed, Mark, 447
Reines, Bernard, 409
Reizenstein, Elmer, 438
Rice, Elmer, 435, 442, 444, 445, 449, 452
Richman, Arthur, 439
Riggs, Lynn, 444
Roberts, Allan, 408
Rodgers, Richard, 17, 29, 47, 409, 418, 434, 450, 453
Roerick, William, 30, 420
Romberg, Sigmund, 8, 24, 390
Roos, William, 394
Rotter, Fritz, 450
Royal, Ted, 375, 389, 394
Royle, Edwin Milton, 437
Ryerson, Florence, 450
Ryskind, Morrie, 435, 444

Saroyan, William, 434, 435, 449
Sartre, Jean-Paul, 11, 18, 26, 398
Selden, Albert, 380
Selver, Paul, 440
Selwyn, Edgar, 441
Shairp, Mordaunt, 446
Shakespeare, William, 13, 405, 411, 434
Shaw, George Bernard, 14, 48, 49, 423
Shaw, Irwin, 49
Sheldon, Edward, 8, 24, 390, 437, 438
Shelley, Elsa, 451
Sherman, Charles, 407
Sherriff, R. C., 443, 447
Sherwood, Robert E., 25, 435, 442, 444, 446, 447, 448, 452
Shulman, Max, 408
Sierra, G. Martinez, 442, 443
Smith, Dodie, 447
Smith, Edward Percy, 407
Smith, Harry James, 437
Snodgrass, James, 46
Spalding, Charles, 380
Spewack, Bella and Samuel, 13, 16, 301, 373, 405, 414, 434, 446

Spialek, Hans, 375, 389
Stallings, Laurence, 369, 440
Stein, Joseph, 30, 400, 422
Steinbeck, John, 434, 447, 449
Stephens, Peter John, 51
Stewart, Donald Ogden, 443
Stillman, Al, 377, 424
Strauss, Johann, 42, 47
Sturges, Preston, 443
Stutz, Richard, 407

Taradash, Daniel, 398
Tarkington, Booth, 437, 438
Telfer, Ronald, 26, 402
Thomas, A. E., 445
Thomas, Augustus, 437
Thomas, Brandon, 388
Thurber, James, 449
Tonkonogy, Gertrude, 383
Totheroh, Dan, 441
Treadwell, Sophie, 443, 450
Trivers, Barry, 380
Trumbo, Dalton, 16, 28, 416
Turney, Robert, 447

Underhill, John Garrett, 442

Valency, Maurice, 5, 13, 118, 369, 403, 434
Van Druten, John, 12, 26, 401, 441, 446, 450, 451
Vane, Sutton, 440
Varesi, Gilda, 438
Viertel, Peter, 49
Villa-Lobos, Heitor, 7, 43, 381
Vincent, Allen, 450
Vollmer, Lula, 440

Walker, Don, 390
Walter, Eugene, 437
Warren, Ruth, 441
Watkins, Maurine, 441
Watters, George Manker, 442
Weill, Kurt, 8, 19, 22, 26, 88, 369, 386
Weinberger, Jaromir, 44
Weitzenkorn, Louis, 444
West, Mae, 15, 35, 410
Wexley, John, 443, 445
Wharton, Edith, 50
White, Hugh, 42, 48
Wilder, Thornton, 405, 435, 447, 450
Wilk, Max, 380
Williams, Charles, 52

INDEX OF AUTHORS

Williams, Emlyn, 449
Williams, Jesse Lynch, 435, 438, 440
Williams, Tennessee, 7, 386, 434, 435, 436, 451, 452
Wilson, Harry Leon, 437, 440
Winter, Keith, 446
Wodehouse, P. G., 442
Wolfson, Victor, 447
Wouk, Herman, 16, 417

Wright, Richard, 449
Wright, Robert, 381

Yeats, W. B., 44
Yordan, Philip, 451

Zelinka, Sidney, 379
Zilboorg, Gregory, 439

INDEX OF PLAYS AND CASTS

Bold face page numbers refer to pages on which Cast of Characters may be found.

Abe Lincoln in Illinois, 435, 448
Abie's Irish Rose, 432
Abraham Lincoln, 438
Accent on Youth, 446
Adam and Eva, 438
Adding Machine, The, 49
Adonis, 432
Ah, Wilderness, 445
Alien Corn, 445
Alison's House, 435, 444
All for Love, 14, **408**
All My Sons, 44, 49, 368, 434, 452
All You Need Is One Good Break, 52
Allegro, 26, 34, 35, 39, 43, 46, 48, 431, 543
Along Fifth Avenue, 14, 19, 27, 34, 35, 406, **407**
Ambush, 439
American Way, The, 448
Amphitryon 38, 42, 118, 369, 448
And So to Bed, 49
Androcles and the Lion, 44
Angel in the Wings, 39, 40
Angel Street, 432, 450
Animal Kingdom, The, 444
Anna Christie, 435, 439
Anna Lucasta, 34, 49, 432, 451
Anne of the Thousand Days, 5, 12, 34, 35, 36, 88, 368, **399**
Annie Get Your Gun, 39, 43, 45, 431, 432
Another Language, 444
Another Part of the Forest, 452
Antigone, 44, 49, 51, 452
Anybody Home, 16, **414**
Anything Goes, 46, 371
April Fool, 42, 48
Arbitration, The, 44
Arms and the Man, 44
Arsenic and Old Lace, 371, 432, 449
As Husbands Go, 444
As the Girls Go, 3, 10, 19, 24, 25, **394**
As Thousands Cheer, 372

At War with the Army, 16, **19**, 28, 34, 35, **415**
Auprez de Ma Blonde, 42, **47**
Awake and Sing, 446
Away We Go, 20

Bad Man, The, 439
Ballet Ballads, 431
Barbara Frietchie, 437
Barretts of Wimpole Street, The, 444
Bat, The, 432
Beaux' Stratagem, The, 21
Beggar on Horseback, 440
Behold the Bridegroom, 442
Bell for Adano, A, 451
Berkeley Square, 443
Beyond the Horizon, 435, 438
Big Knife, The, 16, 18, 19, 20, 28, **413**
Biggest Thief in Town, The, 16, 34, 35, **416**
Bill of Divorcement, A, 439
Biography, 445
Bird in Hand, 433
Blackbirds, 433
Blackouts, 51
Blithe Spirit, 432, 450
Bloomer Girl, 432
Blossom Time, 8, 40, 433
Blue Danube, The, 42, 47
Boomerang, The, 433
Born Yesterday, 30, 34, 35, 44, 48, 51, 333, 432, 452
Both Your Houses, 435, 445
Boy Meets Girl, 373, 432, 446
Bravo, 10, **393**
Bride of the Lamb, 441
Brief Moment, 444
Brigadoon, 28, 34, 35, 39, 43, 431, 433, 452
Broadway, 432, 441
Brother Rat, 433
Build No Fence Around Me, 44
Bunner Sisters, The, 50
Burlesque, 20, 48, 442
Butter and Egg Man, The, 441

476

INDEX OF PLAYS AND CASTS

Café Crown, 49
Caligula, 48
Call It a Day, 447
Call Me Mister, 432
Camille, 51
Candida, 13
Candle in the Wind, 450
Carmen Jones, 433
Carousel, 17, 43, 46, 48, **409**, 432
Castle on the Sand, 51
Cat and the Canary, The, 34, 36
Changelings, The, 440
Charleston, 1822, 24
Charley's Aunt, 8, 388
Chauve Souris, 432
Chicago, 441
Chicken Feed, 440
Children's Hour, The, 11, 432, 446
Christopher Blake, 372, 452
Circle, The, 439
Clarence, 438
Claudia, 432, 449
Climbers, The, 437
Comedy of Good and Evil, A, 9, 391
Command Decision, 20, 23, 34, 35, 36, 38, 40, 51, **431**, 453
Constant Wife, The, 51, 442
Coquette, 442
Corn Is Green, The, 449
County Chairman, The, 437
Cradle Song, The, 442
Craig's Wife, 435, 441
Criminal Code, The, 443
Cry the Beloved Country, 88, 369
Cynara, 445

Daisy Mayme, 442
Damask Cheek, The, 450
Damon and Pythias, 51
Dancing Mothers, 441
Dark of the Moon, 51
Darling of the Gods, The, 437
Daughters of Atreus, 447
Dead End, 147, 370, 432, 446
Dear Ruth, 432, 451
Death of a Salesman, 5, 15, 17, 34, 35, 36, 47, 53, 368, **412**, 434, 435, 436
Death Takes a Holiday, 443
Deburau, 438
Decision, 451
Déclassée, 438
Deep Are the Roots, 451
Desert Song, The, 27, 34, 35, 40, 47

Design for Living, 20, 445
Desire Under the Elms, 440
Detective Story, 5, 16, 34, 35, 36, 147, 370, 371, **416**
Devil Passes, The, 444
Diamond Lil, 15, 34, 35, **410**
Dinner at Eight, 445
Disraeli, 437
Distaff Side, The, 446
Doctor in Spite of Himself, A, 49
Dodsworth, 445
Doll's House, The, 49
Don't Listen, Ladies, 13, **404**
Double Dealer, The, 44
Doughgirls, The, 432, 450
Dover Road, The, 439
Dream Girl, 51, 452
Druid Circle, The, 44
Drunkard, The, 39, 51
Dulcy, 439
Dybbuk, The, 441

Easiest Way, The, 437
East Is West, 432
Eastward in Eden, 453
Ed Wynn's Laugh Carnival, 42
Edward My Son, 3, 5, 6, 179, 370, **385**
Elizabeth the Queen, 50, 444
Emerald Staircase, The, 28
Emperor Jones, The, 439
End of Summer, 446
Enemy, The, 441
Enter Madame, 438
Escape, 442
Escape Me Never, 34
Ethan Frome, 447
Eurydice, 49
Eve of St. Mark, The, 450
Excursion, 447

Fabulous Invalid, The, 238
Face the Music, 372
Fall Guy, The, 441
Family Portrait, 448
Famous Mrs. Fair, The, 438
Fanchon the Cricket, 51
Farm of Three Echoes, 371
Farmer Takes a Wife, The, 446
Fashion, 51
Fatal Weakness, The, 452
Figure of a Girl, 27, 34, 35
Finian's Rainbow, 23, 25, 34, 35, 39, 431, 432

INDEX OF PLAYS AND CASTS

Firebrand, The, 440
First Lady, 446
First Mrs. Fraser, The, 50, 443
First Year, The, 432, 438
Five-Star Final, 444
Flight to the West, 449
Follow the Girls, 432
Fool, The, 439
Fool in Eden Garden, The, 50
Foolish Notion, 451
For Heaven's Sake, Mother, 10, 34, 35, **395**
For Love or Money, 34, 39, 40, 431
Forward the Heart, 15, **409**
Front Page, The, 443
Funzapoppin, 39, 40

Gang's All Here, The, 372
Gayden, 17, 30, **422**
Gentleman from Athens, 51
George and Margaret, 26
George Washington Slept Here, 449
George Worthing, American, 52
Ghost of Elsinore, The, 50
Ghosts, 49
Glass Menagerie, The, 7, 37, 51, 433, 434, 451
Glass Pool, The, 51
Golden Boy, 448
Goodbye, My Fancy, 10, 333, 373, **395**
Good Gracious, Annabelle, 438
Good News, 47, 433
Goose Hangs High, The, 440
Grand Hotel, 444
Grandma's Diary, 6, 22, **383**
Great Divide, The, 437
Great God Brown, The, 441
Great Waltz, The, 43, 47
Green Bay Tree, The, 446
Green Goddess, The, 438
Green Grow the Lilacs, 444
Green Hat, The, 441
Green Pastures, The, 432, 435, 443
Gypsy, 443

Hairy Ape, The, 44
Hamlet, 50
Happiest Years, The, 17, 30, **420**
Happy Birthday, 48, 433
Harriet, 450
Harvey, 23, 34, 35, 39, 40, 43, 48, 431, 432, 436, 451
Hasty Heart, The, 44, 371, 451

Hats Off to Ice, 432
He Who Gets Slapped, 439
Heartbreak House, 26
Heaven on Earth, 4, 6, 21, 22, **380**
Heiress, The, 20, 29, 34, 35, 36, 38, 40, 43, 48, 431, 453
Hell-bent fer Heaven 435, 440
Hellzapoppin, 43, 432
Her Master's Voice, 445
Here Come the Clowns, 448
Hero, The, 439
Herschel the Jester, 28
High Button Shoes, 34, 35, 39, 43, 432
High Tor, 434, 447
Hilarities, 5, **379**
Hold It, 14, 431
Holdup Man, The, 372
Holiday, 443
Home of the Brave, 451
Honeymoon, The, 51
Hope for a Harvest, 450
Hope Is the Thing with Feathers, 38, 40
House of Connelly, The, 444
How Sad, 179
Howdy, Mr. Ice, **377, 424**

I Know My Love, 42, 47, 48
I Remember Mama, 51, 432, 451
Icebound, 435, 439
Iceman Cometh, The, 452
Idiot's Delight, 435, 446
If I Were King, 437
In Abraham's Bosom, 435, 442
In Time to Come, 449
Innocent Voyage, The, 451
Insect Comedy, The, **376**
Inside U. S. A., 28, 34, 35, 37, 39, 431
Inspector Calls, An, 51, 453
Irene, 432
Is Zat So, 432
Ivy Green, The, 17, 29, 34, **418**

Jacobowsky and the Colonel, 451
Jane Clegg, 438
Janie, 432
Japhet, 26
Jason, 450
Jenny Kissed Me, 12, 26, **401**
Jest, The, 438
Joan of Lorraine, 452
John Ferguson, 438

INDEX OF PLAYS AND CASTS

John Loves Mary, 20, 40, 452
Johnny Johnson, 447
Journey's End, 443
Joy to the World, 431
June Moon, 443
Junior Miss, 432, 450
Juno and the Paycock, 23

Key Largo, 448
Kiki, 433
Kind Lady, 21, 51
King Oedipus, 44
Kingdom of God, The, 443
Kiss and Tell, 432, 450
Kiss Me Kate, 13, 16, 17, 34, 35, 36, 43, 301, 373, **405**, 434
Kiss the Boys Good-bye, 448
Knickerbocker Holiday, 26

Ladder, The, 432
Lady in the Dark, 47, 372, 449
Lady of Lyons, 50
Lady Windermere's Fan, 43
Last Mile, The, 443
Last of Mrs. Cheyney, The, 20, 441
Late Christopher Bean, The, 445
Late George Apley, The, 451
Leading Lady, The, 8, 24, 39, 40, 333, **389**
Leaf and Bough, 14, 27, 34, 35, **408**
Leah Kleshna, 437
Left Bank, The, 444
Lend an Ear, 12, 19, 26, 45, 46, **400**
Let Us Be Gay, 443
Let's Face It, 433
Letters to Lucerne, 450
Life with Father, 8, 51, 207, 432, 448
Life with Mother, 4, 8, 34, 35, 36, 207, 371, **391**
Light Up the Sky, 11, 19, 24, 34, 35, 36, 238, 372, **397**
Lightnin', 432
Liliom, **409**, 439
Little Accident, 443
Little Eyolf, 44
Little Foxes, The, 20, 448
London Assurance, 51
Look, Ma, I'm Dancin', 431
Lost Horizons, 446
Love in Upper Sandusky, 52
Love Life, 8, 19, 22, 386, **387**
Loyalties, 439
Lucia, 12
Lute Song, 452

Machinal, 443
Madwoman of Chaillot, The, 5, 13, 118, 369, **403**, 434
Magdalena, 4, 6, 7, 43, 45, **381**
Magnificent Yankee, The, 452
Magnolia Alley, 17, 29, **420**
Major Barbara, 49
Make Mine Manhattan, 27, 34, 36, 39, 431
Make Way for Lucia, 12, 26, 34, 35, **401**
Male Animal, The, 449
Mamma's Affair, 438
Man and Superman, 34, 35, 36, 39, 43, 48, **423**, 431
Man from Home, The, 437
Man Who Came to Dinner, The, 372, 432, 449
Man Who Had All the Luck, The, 368
Marble Heart, The, 51
Margin for Error, 449
Marie Antoinette in Pennsylvania, 46
Marquise, The, 20
Mary of Scotland, 445
Mary Rose, 439
Mary the 3d, 440
Me and Molly, 431, 453
Medea, 20, 29, 34, 36, 38, 40, 43, 48, **421**
Medium, The, **399**
Men in White, 147, 370, 435, 445
Merrily We Roll Along, 47, 446
Merry Widow, The, 47
Merton of the Movies, 440
Michael and Mary, 443
Mikado, The, 40
Minick, 441
Minnie and Mr. Williams, 9, 24, 25, **391**
Miss Liberty, 33
Miss Lulu Bett, 435
Miss Swan Expects, 373
Mission Play, The, 47
Mister Roberts, 4, 35, 37, 38, 40, 433, 453
Moon Is Down, The, 449
Morning's at Seven, 449
Mourning Becomes Electra, 444
Mr. Adam, 17, 38, 40, 42, **423**
Mr. and Mrs. North, 449
Mrs. Bumpstead-Leigh, 437
Mrs. Gibbons' Boys, 17, 30, **422**
Mrs. Partridge Presents, 441

INDEX OF PLAYS AND CASTS

Music in the Air, 47
Music Master, The, 433
Music Sends Me, 46
My Name Is Aquilon, 15, 411, **412**
My Romance, 8, 24, **390**
My Sister Eileen, 432, 449
Mystery of Hamlet, King of Denmark, The, 45, 50

Native Son, 449
Naughty Marietta, 43, 46, 47
Nest, The, 439
New Moon, The, 47, 433
Nice People, 439
No More Ladies, 445
No Regrets, 179
No Time for Comedy, 448
Now Is the Winter, 52

O Mistress Mine, 28, 34, 452
Of Mice and Men, 44, 434, 447
Of Thee I Sing, 435, 444
Oh, Mr. Meadowbrook, 13, 26, 34, 35, **402**
Oklahoma, 17, 20, 28, 34, 35, 40, 47, 432, 450
Ol' Man Adam an' His Chillun, 443
Old Maid, The, 435, 446
Old Soak, The, 440
Oliver Erwenter, 266
On Approval, 40
On Borrowed Time, 447
On Trial, 438
Once in a Lifetime, 238, 372, 444
One Fine Day, 42, 48
One Sunday Afternoon, 445
One Touch of Venus, 433
Oscar Wilde, 6, 179
Othello, 20, 21, 44
Our Town, 18, 435, 447
Out of Order, 46
Outrageous Fortune, 451
Outward Bound, 440
Over 21, 451
Overture, 444

Panama Hattie, 433
Paris Bound, 442
Patience, 40
Patriots, The, 147, 370, 434, 450
Payment Deferred, 26
Peg o' My Heart, 432
Perfect Fool, The, 42
Personal Appearance, 433

Peter Grimes, 13, 44
Petrified Forest, The, 44, 446
Pick-up Girl, 451
Philadelphia Story, The, 448
Pigeons and People, 445
Pilgrimage Play, 51
Pinafore, 40
Pins and Needles, 432
Pirates of Penzance, 40
Play with Fire, 14, 407
Play's the Thing, The, 34, 35, 431, 442
Plough and the Stars, The, 442
Porgy, 10, 442
Present Laughter, 34, 36, 39
Pride and Prejudice, 447
Private Lives, 3, 7, 34, 35, 43, 48, **385**
Prologue to Glory, 448

Queer Cargo, 179

Racket, The, 442
Rain, 49, 432, 439
Ramona, 51
Ramshackle Inn, 17, 29
Rape of Lucretia, The, 13, **404**
Raze the Roof, 39
Rebound, 443
Red Gloves, 11, 18, 20, 26, **398**
Red Mill, The, 433
Relapse, The, 44
Respectful Prostitute, The, 12, 38, 40, 431
Reunion in Vienna, 444
Richard III, 14, 15, 18, 19, 26, **411**
Rivals, The, 44
Road to Rome, The, 25, 51, 442
Rocket to the Moon, 448
Romance, 8, 24, 390, 437
Room Service, 433
Rosalinda, 433
Rose Marie, 433
Royal Family, The, 10, 442
Rugged Path, The, 452
R.U.R., 440

Sailor, Beware, 433
Sally, 431, 433
St. Helena, 447
Saturday's Children, 441
Scandals, 51
Searching Wind, The, 451
Separate Rooms, 49, 432

INDEX OF PLAYS AND CASTS 481

Serena Blandish, 51
Serpent in the Orchard, The, 50
Set My People Free, 24, 34, 35, **392**
Seven Keys to Baldpate, 20, 437
Seventh Heaven, 432
Shadow and Substance, 447
Shining Hour, The, 446
Shop at Sly Corner, The, 14, 27, 34, 51, **407**
Short Story, 179, 371
Show Boat, 5, 23, 39, 47, 378, **379**, 433
Show-Off, The, 433, 440
Shuffle Along, 433
Shvanda, the Bagpiper, 44
Siegfried, 118, 369
Silver Cord, The, 442
Silver Whistle, The, 11, 19, 23, 38, 40, 266, 372, **397**
Six Cylinder Love, 439
Skin Game, The, 439
Skin of Our Teeth, The, 26, 435, 450
Skipper Next to God, 453
Skylark, 449
Sleepy Hollow, 5, **375**
Small Wonder, 6, 19, 21, **380**
Smile of the World, The, 13, 34, 35, 333, **406**
Soldier's Wife, 451
Song of Norway, 432
Sons o' Fun, 432
South Pacific, 17, 19, 29, 418, **419**, 434
Springtime for Henry, 21
Squaw Man, The, 437
Stage Door, 447
Star and Garter, 432
Star-Wagon, The, 447
Stars on Ice, 432
State of the Union, 371, 432, 436, 451
Storm Operation, 451
Story for Strangers, A, 6, **382**
Story of Mary Surratt, The, 452
Strange Bedfellows, 431
Strange Interlude, 435, 442
Street Scene, 432, 435, 442
Streetcar Named Desire, A, 7, 35, 37, 38, 40, 432, 434, 435, 436, 452
Strictly Dishonorable, 433, 443
Student Prince, The, 8, 46, 432
Sultan of Sulu, The, 44
Summer and Smoke, 7, **386**
Sundown Beach, 5, 21, **378**
Sunny, 433

Sun-up, 440
Survivors, The, 49
Susan and God, 448
Swan, The, 440
Sweethearts, 43, 46

Tales of the South Pacific, 17, **419**, 434
Taming of the Shrew, The, 13, 434
Tarnish, 440
Telephone, The, **399**
Ten Million Ghosts, 147, 370
That's the Ticket, 34, 35
There Shall Be No Night, 435, 448
They Knew What They Wanted, 15, 18, 20, 28, 34, 36, **413**, 435, 440
They Shall Not Die, 445
This Young World, 51
Three Men on a Horse, 51, 432
Time for Elizabeth, 7, 42, 48, **384**
Time of Your Life, The, 434, 435, 449
Tobacco Road, 432
Tomorrow and Tomorrow, 444
Tomorrow the World, 433, 450
Tongue in Cheek, 46
Tovarich, 447
Town House, 6, 22, **383**
Traitor, The, 16, **417**
Trial by Jury, 37, 40
Trial of Mary Dugan, The, 23
Trip to Chinatown, A, 432
Two Blind Mice, 16, 34, 36, 301, 373, 414, **415**
Two Mrs. Carrolls, The, 433

Unchastened Woman, The, 438
Uncle Harry, 450
Up in Central Park, 433

Vagabond King, The, 47, 433
Valley Forge, 446
Vanities, 51
Varieties, 42
Victoria Regina, 433, 446
Voice of the Turtle, The, 432, 451

Walrus and the Carpenter, The, 371
Watch on the Rhine, 434, 449
We, the People, 445
Wedding Bells, 438
Wednesday's Child, 445
What a Life, 433, 448

INDEX OF PLAYS AND CASTS

What Price Glory, 44, 52, 88, 369, 440
When Ladies Meet, 445
Where's Charley?, 8, 34, 35, **388**
White Cargo, 432
White Steed, The, 448
Why Marry, 435, 438
Why Not, 440
Wild Birds, 441
Winged Victory, 372, 450
Wings Over Europe, 443
Winslow Boy, The, 20, 25, 38, 40, 43, 48, 51, 253
Winter Soldiers, 450
Winterset, 434, 446
Wisdom Tooth, The, 47, 441
Witching Hour, The, 437
Within the Law, 433
Woman Bites Dog, 373
Women, The, 432, 447
World We Make, The, 370, 448

Years Ago, 8, 333, 452
Yes, My Darling Daughter, 447
You and I, 439
You Can't Take It with You, 372, 432, 435, 447
You Twinkle Only Once, 52
Young and Fair, The, 11, **396**
Young Woodley, 441
Youngest, The, 441

Ziegfeld Follies, 433

INDEX OF PRODUCERS, DIRECTORS AND DESIGNERS

Abbott, George, 16, 389, 422
Actman, Irving, 375
Actors' Studio, 5, 378
Aldrich & Myers, 333, 395
Alswang, Ralph, 380, 383, 393, 402
American National Theatre Association, 50
American Theatre Group, 383
Amsterdam, Morey, 5
Anderson, John Murray, 22, 380
Armistead, Horace, 399
Aronson, Boris, 388, 416
Ashmore, Peter, 385
Ayres, Lemuel, 405

Balaban, Emanuel, 399
Balanchine, George, 389
Ballard, Lucinda, 388, 401
Ballet Society, 399
Barr, Richard, 411, 418
Barratt, Watson, 390
Bauer, George, 400
Bay, Howard, 382, 394, 414
Berard, Christian, 13, 119, 403
Berns, Julie, 395
Bloomgarden, Kermit, 412
Bogdanoff, Rose, 386, 393
Bolger, Mrs. Ray, 388
Boston Repertory Association, 18, 25
Boston Summer Theatre, 18, 20, 23
Bowles, Paul, 386
Breden-Savoy Gilbert and Sullivan Company, 40
Breisach, Paul, 405
Brodkin, Herbert, 377, 398
Bronesky, Leon J., 409
Buchanan, Jack, 404
Burke, William H., 377

Capp, Al, 20
Cardelli, Giovanni, 404
Carroll, Earl, 7, 51
Cassini, Oleg, 394
Castillo, 393, 412, 421
Castle, Nick, 380

Champion, Gower, 380, 400
Chaney, Stewart, 207, 391, 398, 412, 418
Charlton, Richard, 51
Circle Theatre, 49
Civic Repertory Theatre, 118, 369
Clurman, Harold, 396
Cochran, Charles B., 385
Cohen, Alexander H., 401
Cole, Jack, 382
Connelly, Marc, 375, 383
Cowles, Chandler, 399
Crabtree, Paul, 398
Crawford, Cheryl, 21, 23, 386
Crouse, Russel, 371, 416
Curran, Homer, 7, 381
Cutler, Lester, 420

Dalrymple, Jean, 398
Danielli, Fred, 389
Dassin, Jules, 382
Davenport, Pembroke, 405
Davey, Leon, 404
Davis, Blevins, 50
De Forest, William, 410
De Liagre, Alfred, Jr., 403
Dell'Isola, Salvatore, 419
De Mille, Agnes, 405
Derro, John, 380, 384
Dietz, David, 391
Dolin, Garry, 389
Dowling, Eddie, 21, 380, 392
Du Bois, Raoul Pene, 380, 400
Du Pont, Paul, 410

Edwards, Ben, 378, 410, 421
Eisele, Lou, 390
Ellerbe, Harry, 402
Ellis, Michael, 401
Elson, Charles, 385
Ephraim, Lee, 404
Evans, Maurice, 423
Ewing, Marjorie and Sherman, 404
Eythe, William, 12, 45, 400

INDEX OF PRODUCERS, DIRECTORS, DESIGNERS

Falk, Lee, 20
Farrell, Anthony Brady, 14, 408
Ferrer, Jose, 377
Ferrer, Mel, 49
Feuer, Cy, 388
Ffolkes, David, 375, 389, 407
Fields, William, 389
Forbes, Ralph, 414
Ford, John, 52
Fox, Frederick, 397, 413
Freedley, Vincent, 396
Freeman, Charles K., 410
Freezer, Herbert J., 410
Fretwell, Joseph, III, 417
Freitag, Dorothy, 400
Fried, Walter, 412
Friedman, Charles, 407
Frye, Peter, 409

Gaither, Gant, 407, 422
Gassner, John, 391
Gassner, Mordi, 392
Gerson, Hal, 400
Gilbert, Edward, 408, 420
Gilbert, Franklin, 400
Goberman, Max, 389
Golden, John, 15, 18, 413
Goldsmith, Eleanor, 396, 402, 417
Gordon, Max, 6, 10, 22, 25, 30, 383, 393
Greek Theatre, 46, 47

Hammerstein, Oscar, 2d, 378, 418
Hargrave, Roy, 418
Harris, Jed, 16, 398, 417
Harris, Sam H., 238
Hart, Bernard, 397
Hart, Moss, 397
Hayward, Leland, 12, 399, 418
Heidt, Charles P., 408
Helburn, Theresa, 398
Henie, Sonja, 377, 424
Holden, Phyllis, 414
Holm, Hanya, 377, 405
Howell, John Daggett, 405
Hull, Henry, 52
Hunter, Ross, 46
Huston, Grace, 424
Hyman, Joseph M., 397

Jenkins, George, 384
Johnson, Albert, 415
Jones, Margo, 7, 14, 386

Jouvet, Louis, 118
Judels, May, 377

Kanin, Garson, 389, 406
Kanin, Michael, 10, 333, 374, 395
Katzell, William R., 400
Kaufman, George S., 6, 22, 384, 393
Kay, Arthur, 382
Kay, David, 395
Kazan, Elia, 5, 21, 23, 378, 388, 412
Kelly, Fredric N., 390
Kennel, Louis, 414
Kent, Carl, 14, 408
Kent, Guy, 420
Kerz, Leo, 393, 395, 417
Kidd, Michael, 388
King, Archer, 414
Kingsley, Sidney, 416
Kirkland, Jack, 17, 423, 424
Kiviette, 397
Knighton, Willis, 17, 407, 422
Krakeur, Richard W., 396
Krasna, Norman, 384
Kuhn, Katherine, 377, 424

Lambert, Sammy, 408
Lang, Phil, 389
Langner, Lawrence, 43, 398
Lee, Ann, 51
Lee, Joshua, 393
Le Gallienne, Eva, 369
Leigh, Rowland, 390
Leontovich, Eugenie, 46, 49
Lesser, Arthur, 406
Lester, Edwin, 7, 43, 45, 382
Lester, Lorraine, 375
Levin, Herman, 411
Lewis, Robert, 27
Lewis, Russell, 48, 384
Lindsay, Howard, 371, 416
Linenthal, Michael, 25
Littau, Joseph, 388
Little, Lucille, 402, 414
Littlefield, Catherine, 377, 424
Litwack, Ned C., 380
Livingston, Billy, 377, 408, 424
Lloyd, John Robert, 422
Logan, Joshua, 418, 419
Los Angeles Civic Light Opera Association, 45, 47
Lubin, Arthur, 51
Luytens, Edith, 399

INDEX OF PRODUCERS, DIRECTORS, DESIGNERS

Macy, Gertrude, 420
Mainbocher, 389, 406
Maine, Bruno, 377, 424
Mamoulian, Rouben, 14, 408
Manulis, Martin, 385
Mapes, Jacque, 46
Martin, Ernest H., 388
Martin, Hugh, 394
May, Henry, 415
McClintic, Guthrie, 48, 391, 421
Meth, Max, 394
Mielziner, Jo, 7, 12, 88, 375, 386, 400, 412, 419
Miller, Gilbert, 41, 385
Morrison Paul, 396
Motley, 400, 419
Murray, Ken, 51

Neilson, James, 421
New York City Center of Music and Drama, 376, 378, 399, 421, 423
Nichols, George, 3d, 380

Oenslager, Donald, 384, 389, 391, 396, 406, 415
Olsen and Johnson, 39, 40, 43
O'Shaughnessy, John, 375

Pan, Hermes, 394
Pardoll, David M., 389
Pasadena Playhouse, 45
Pascal, Gabriel, 398
Perry, Margaret, 407
Perry, Robert, 413
Piper, John, 405
Playwrights' Company, 12, 88, 399, 406
Potter, H. C., 12, 400
Proser, Monte, 380

Raiguel, Phil, 424
Reveaux, Edward, 408
Rice, Allyn, 393
Richards, Lex, 422
Rickard, Gwen, 388
Ritt, Martin, 393
Robey, Ken, 379
Roche, Emeline, 377, 396, 398, 422
Rodgers, Richard, 378, 418
Root, John, 422
Rosen, Albert H., 410
Rosenfeld, Jerome E., 415
Roth, Wolfgang, 402

Russell, James, 421
Russo, James, 401, 402

Sabinson, Lee, 416
Samrock, Victor, 389
San Francisco Light Opera Association, 43
Savory, Gerald, 25
Schraps, Ernest, 393, 398
Serlin, Oscar, 9, 207, 391
Shain, Carl, 420
Shapiro, Clarence M., 401
Sharaff, 382
Shelton, Hal, 418
Sherek, Henry, 385
Shevelove, Burt, 380
Shubert, Messrs., 8, 25, 33, 390
Shumlin, Herman, 417
Sidney, Robert, 407
Sillman, Leonard, 413
Sinclair, Robert B., 412
Singer, Louis J., 378
Skulnik, Menasha, 29
Small, Paul, 42
Smith, Oliver, 407
Sokolow, Anna, 375
Sovey, Raymond, 385, 417
Spewack, Samuel, 415
Stanford Players, 44
Stoker, Willard, 404
Stone, Ezra, 16, 415
Strasberg, Lee, 414
Subber, Saint, 405
Sutherland, Millie, 383, 416
Sze, Julia, 412

Thayer, Forrest, 406
Theatre Enterprises, Inc., 409
Theatre Guild, 10, 11, 13, 15, 23, 24, 27, 35, 43, 45, 46, 48, 118, 266, 368, 369, 373, 392, 397, 401, 409, 411, 413
Thompson, Frank, 405
Todd, Michael, 10, 19, 24, 25, 394

Valentina, 412
Van Druten, John, 401
Victor, Eric, 408

Walter, Natalie Barth, 415
Wanamaker, Sam, 396
Warnick, Clay, 408
Watkins, Perry, 409

486 INDEX OF PRODUCERS, DIRECTORS, DESIGNERS

White, George, 42, 51
Whorf, Richard, 18, 19, 26, 411
Wico Company, 382
Wilson, John C., 385, 386, 405
Wiman, Dwight Deere, 382, 413
Wirtz, Arthur M., 377, 424
Woodhull, Harrison, 414

Yorke, John, 402
Young, Howard, 27, 48, 384

Zeller, Robert, 382
Ziegfeld, Florenz, 7
Zimbalist, Efrem, Jr., 399
Zucker, Stan, 379